OFFICE OF POPULATION

Classification of occupations
and coding index

London: Her Majesty's Stationery Office

© *Crown copyright 1980*
First published 1980

ISBN 0 11 690728 2*

Classification of Occupations 1980 Supplement

This supplement has been prepared to update the Alphabetical index for classifying occupations. Most of the additions and amendments have originated from queries raised during the coding of occupations on the 1981 Census forms.

Page		Code number	Page		Code number	Page		Code number
6	Insert to read		25	Insert to read		49	Insert to read	
	Agent;			Consultant;			Handler;	
	commission-			sales	013		dog	172
	raw materials	129		scheme *(community industries)*	034		freight *(warehousing)*	335
	commission agents	129	30	Insert to read		49	Insert to read	
8	Revise to read			Designer-			Helper;	
	Assembler;			*artificial flower mfr.*	056		ancilliary *(school)*	151
	clock	284		*broadcasting*	055		bakehouse	200
	watch	284	32	Insert to read		50	Insert and revise layout to read	
8	Revise to read			Driller-			Hygienist;	
	Assembler-			*asbestos composition goods mfr.*	230		dental	050
	watches and clocks	284		*asbestos goods mfr.*	230		occupational	039
11	Insert to read		35	Insert to read		50	Insert and revise layout to read	
	Assistant;			Engineer;			Illustrator-	
	trust *(Public Trustees)*	006		motor;			self-employed	055
	T.S.S.U.	156		road *(railways)*	069		*advertising*	055
11	Insert to read			mud *(oil wells)*	068		*government*	079
	Assistant-		38	Insert to read		51	Revise to read	
	tailoring	210		Executive; *see also Manager*			Inspector;	
	take-away food shop *see Assistant; shop-*			advertising	014		gaming *(gaming club)*	F165
11	Insert to read			chief *(local government)*	022	52	Insert to read	
	Associate;			editorial *(newspaper)*	M054		Inspector-	
	research-			postal *(P.O.)-*			*asbestos-cement goods mfr.*	299
	textile	080		grade A,B	099		*asbestos goods mfr.*	299
	sales *(insurance)*	134		grade C	F115		*cartridge mfr.*	299
15	Insert to read			grade D	F123		casino	F165
	Bindery worker	189	38	Insert to read		53	Insert to read	
	Bingo operative	165		Fabric worker	212		Instructor; *see also notes p.4*	
21	Insert to read			Fabricator;			training;	034
	Checker;			steel	263		physical	053
	paper *(paper mfr.)*	294		window	248	53	Insert and revise layout to read	
	photographic *(printed circuit board mfr.)*	227	38	Insert and revise layout to read			Insulator-	
24	Insert to read			Farm worker;			construction	316
	Collector-			fish	171		*electrical appliances mfr.*	230
	entertainment	115		sewage	310	53	Revise to read	
	finance company	115	44	Insert to read			Jeweller; *see also notes p.4*	
				Foreman-			watch	284
				bottling	F287	55	Insert to read	
				bus service	F324		Lancer; thermic	265
			46	Insert to read			Land girl	166
				Framer;		55	Insert to read	
				aluminium	248		Landlord-	
				bag	299		*property managing/owning*	025
							public house	103

		Code number
Page		
56	Insert and revise layout to read	

Leader-
    abrasive wheel mfr. **270**
    children's home **037**

67   Insert to read

Manager;

    airport **095**
    arcade (amusement hall) ... **106**

    branch-
        manufacturing ... **111**
        television, radio hire ... **111**

    practice *(medical and dental practices)* ... **099**
    prescription *(glass mfr.)* ... **F192**

68   Insert to read

Manager;

    shop-
        retail trade- **101**
            pharmacists ... **044**
            television, radio hire ... **111**

    yard; **097**
        boat **091**
        ship **091**

68   Insert to read

Manager-

    broadcasting **106**
    building and contracting ... **092**
    building society ... **099**
    car hire **111**
    car park **111**

    coke ovens **091**
    commission agents ... **129**

    ship broker's **129**
    shipping and freight forwarding agency **099**

    storage **097**
    television, radio hire ... **111**

69   Insert to read

Marker;

    billiard **165**
    board (bookmaker's) ... **165**

71   Insert to read

Midwife; **043**
    superintendent ... **F043**
Midwife-tutor **F043**

71   Insert to read

Mill hand- **204**

    rubber goods mfr. ... **194**
    textile mfr. **199**

71   Insert to read

Miller;

    corn **202**
    diamond (jewellery mfr.) ... **266**

72   Insert and revise layout to read

Monitor;
    industrial *(atomic energy establishment)* ... **080**
    physics; health ... **080**

73   Insert to read

Moulder-
    abrasives mfr. **230**
    asbestos-cement goods mfr. ... **230**

74   Insert and revise layout to read

Officer;

    budget and cost ... **115**
    building *(hospital service)* ... **092**

    control;
        development ... **082**
        duct *(coal mine)* ... **039**

    control-
        ambulance service ... **111**
        fire service ... **122**

    education- **035**
        museum **030**
    effluent *(water board, sewage works)* **019**

75   Delete and insert to read

Officer;

    prevention;
        accident **039**
        fire **138**
    preventive **019**
    pricing **115**
    principal-
        children's home ... **037**
        local government ... **022**
        government- ... **021**
            prison service ... **F139**
        old people's home ... **037**

75   Delete and insert to read

Officer;

    radio- **087**
        aircraft **122**
        government ... **111**
        telecommunications ... **122**

76   Insert, revise layout and code to read

Officer;

    services;
        cabin *(airline)* ... **F152**
        management ... **028**

    technical;
        telecommunications *(Civil Aviation Authority)* ... **259**

76   Insert to read

Officer-in-charge *(local government-social services dept.)* **037**
Officer's boy **152**

77   Insert and revise layout to read

Operator;

    control;
        fire *(fire service)* ... **122**
        pest **165**

78   Insert to read

Operator;

    point; transfer... ... **338**
    pot *(aluminium mfr.)* ... **231**

    printer's **207**
    process; chemical ... **184**

79   Insert to read

Operator;

    scanner *(printing)* ... **061**
    scoreboard **165**

    stretcher *(metal mfr.)* ... **276**
    submersible **316**

81   Insert to read

Perfumer **184**
Perfusionist *(hospital service)* ... **050**

82   Insert to read

Pilot;

    river **087**
    submersible **316**

		Code number
Page		
84	Revise to read	
	Presser-	
	textile mfr.-	182
	textile packing	287
	tobacco mfr.	201
	waste merchants	287
	wood pulp mfr.	203
	Presser and threader	199
85	Insert to read	
	Process worker-	
	abrasives mfr.	230
	adhesives and sealants mfr.	184
	chemical mfr.	184
	chocolate mfr.	202
	electrical engineering	276
	explosives mfr.	184
	nickel mfr.	231
	nuclear fuel production	184
	oil refining	184
	ordnance factory	184
	organic oil and fat processing	202
	paint mfr.	184
	paper mfr.	203
	paper and board products mfr.	227
	printing	227
	printing ink mfr.	184
	rubber reclamation	204
	soap and detergent mfr.	184
	soft drinks mfr.	202
	starch mfr.	202
	sugar and sugar confectionery mfr.	202
	tobacco mfr.	201
	toilet preparations mfr.	184
85	Insert to read	
	Processor;	
	poultry	187
	word	118
86	Insert to read	
	Psychometrist-	036
	entertainment	059
	Psychotherapist	036
87	Insert and revise to read	
	Receptionist;	
	vehicle (male - garage)	249
	Receptionist-	117
	male (garage)	249
	cinema, theatre	165
	television, radio hire	115
87	Insert to read	
	Refrigerator man (brewery)	197
	Refueller; aircraft	338
89	Insert to read	
	Retort worker see Retort man-	
	Retoucher;	
	photographic	227
	photolitho	227
90	Insert to read	
	Salesman;	
	van-	128
	manufacturing	133
	wholesale trade	133
91	Insert and revise layout to read	
	Seaman;	
	landing stage	338
	merchant	317
93	Insert to read	
	Setter;	
	tray (hospital sterile supplies)	156
	tube (textile mfr.)	199
95	Insert to read	
	Sorter;	
	lime	298
	linen (hospital service)	298
95	Insert to read	
	Specialist;	
	software	012
	systems	012
99	Insert to read	
	Superintendent;	
	station;	
	assistant	F137
	power	094
	rescue	F142
99	Insert to read	
	Superintendent;	
	wharf	097
	works; gas	094
	works-	091
	building and contracting	092
	electricity board	094
	gas board	094
	local government	092
	water board	094
	workshop	091
99	Insert to read	
	Superintendent-	
	garage	091
	gas board	094
99	Insert to read	
	Supervisor;	
	nursery-	F043
	horticulture	F167
100	Insert to read	
	Supervisor;	
	switchboard	F121
	technical-	
100	Delete to read	
	Surveyor;	
	fire	090
	insurance	090
100	Revise to read	
	T.T.O.-	
	Civil Aviation Authority	259
101	Insert to read	
	Technician;	
	lens; contact	192
	lighting; stage	253
104	Insert and revise layout to read	
	Treatment worker;	
	heat (metal trades)	237
	water	310
105	Insert and revise to read	
	Turner;	
	engine; rose	266
	engine-	239
	jewellery mfr.	266

CONTENTS

Classification of occupations

	Page
Introduction	v
Classification of occupations	vi
Classification of industries	vii
Classification by employment status	vii
Classification by economic position	ix
Social and socio-economic classifications	x
Summary of the OPCS 1980 occupation groups with condensed KOS headings	xiv
Occupation groups with short descriptions of contents and CODOT definitions	xxx
Appendix A Condensed KOS headings and associated KOS groups	lxxi
Appendix B Social Classes and Socio-economic groups	lxxxiii
B.1 Socio-economic Group and Social Class allocations of Occupation and Employment Status Groups	lxxxiv
B.2 Details of Socio-economic groups and Social Classes in terms of Occupation and Employment Status groups	cv
Appendix C Summary of Socio-economic Classes	cxviii
Appendix D Summary of Industry groups	cxx
Appendix E European Economic Community Status Groups and allocations of Occupation and Employment Status Groups	cxxvi

Coding Index

Notes on coding

Description of index	1
Notes on coding occupations	3
Notes on coding employment status	5
Alphabetical index for classifying occupations	6
Appendix F List of Conventional Codings	110
Appendix G Relationship between the 1980 operational codes used in the alphabetical index and the 1980 occupation groups	111

CLASSIFICATION OF OCCUPATIONS

Introduction

Types of economic activity classification

A fourfold classification of the economically active or former active population will be used in the analyses of the information collected at the Census of Population to be taken in 1981 namely, by:

(1) Occupation,
(2) Industry,
(3) Employment status,
(4) Economic position.

These four classifications are independent and relate to four separate aspects of the employment or former employment of a person.

Occupation. The occupation of a person is the kind of work which he or she performs, due regard being paid to the conditions under which it is performed; and this alone determines the particular group in an occupation classification to which the person is assigned. The nature of the factory, business, or service in which the person is employed has no bearing upon the classification of his occupation, except to the extent that it enables the nature of his duties to be more clearly defined. This perhaps will be made clearer by an example. A crane driver may be employed in a shipyard, an engineering works or in building and construction, but this has no bearing upon his occupation and all crane drivers should be classified to the same occupation group.

Industry. The industry in which an individual is engaged is determined (whatever may be his occupation) by reference to the business or economic activity in which his occupation is followed. As a single business may employ a number of individuals of widely varying occupations for the purpose of affording a particular service or creating a particular product, it will be seen that the industrial classification differs essentially from the occupational in that the latter takes account only of the nature of the work performed by the individual, while the former has regard only to the nature of the service or product to which his labour contributes. The man who is occupationally a carpenter or a carman, for instance, is classified industrially to building, if employed by a builder, but to brewing, if employed by a brewer.

Employment status. This is primarily a distinction between the 'employed' and the 'self-employed'. The 'employee' category is sub-divided to indicate relative levels within an occupation, e.g. apprentices or foremen.

Economic position. This distinguishes those economically active from the inactive and among the latter those previously active. Among the active population separate groups are provided for those in employment and various categories of those seeking employment.

Further details of the classification are given on pp. ix–x.

Application of the classification to the total enumerated populations

The fourfold classification is applicable to all persons enumerated in the Census who are working in the United Kingdom. The Classification by Industry provides a separate code to distinguish those whose employment is outside the United Kingdom.

Time reference for coding economic activity

The economic activity to which these codes will apply will be that of the main work for pay or profit during the week before Census and no lower limit to the hours worked will be specified. No questions on usual occupation will be asked. As regards those seeking work, disabled and/or retired, the reference will be to the most recent employment.

Classification of occupations

General
The OPCS Classification of Occupations 1980 is based on the Classification of Occupations and Directory of Occupational Titles (CODOT) published by the Department of Employment. The groups in the Key Occupations for Statistical Purposes (KOS), CODOT, Vol. 1, pp. 89–103 (HMSO, 1972), have been aggregated and form the basis of the OPCS classification. The relationship between KOS and the aggregated or condensed KOS is shown in Appendix A on pp. lxxi–lxxxi. The OPCS classification is summarised on pp. xiv–xxix. A definition of each group and its relationship to CODOT is shown on pp. xxx–lxx. It has been necessary to create four groups within the OPCS classification but outside the condensed KOS structure, to cover cases where there is insufficient information to allocate more satisfactorily. These four groups are:

- .1 Foremen (engineering and allied trades) ⎫ appearing between
- .2 Trainee craftsmen (engineering and allied trades) ⎬ condensed KOS groups 131 and 132

- .1 Inadequately described occupations ⎫ appearing after condensed
- .2 Occupations not stated ⎬ KOS group 161

The current classification has been designed to maintain a high degree of comparability with the OPCS Classification of Occupations 1970. A tabulation showing the relationship between the 1970 and 1980 classifications is in course of preparation and will be available free of charge from OPCS, on application.

Basis of the classification
The main purpose has been to provide groups with at least one common characteristic. The basic common factor of all groups is the kind of work done and the nature of the operation performed. But if, by reason of the material worked in, the degree of skill involved, the physical energy required, the environmental conditions, the social and economic status associated with the occupation, or any combination of these factors, unit groups based solely on kind of work done seemed too comprehensive they were further broken down on the basis of these other factors in order to identify what are substantially separate occupations.

Certain limiting conditions have also operated, e.g. that the number of individuals likely to be included in a unit is sufficiently large to be worth separate identification on a 10% sample basis, that the identification of a unit group is likely to be tolerably complete and accurate from the limited information obtained from a Census, that there is sufficient potential interest in the group to justify separate identification, and that statistics for the group could not be obtained from the cross-classification of occupation by industry.

Certain principles of the classification
Certain groups of persons in employment, in particular the self-employed and the managers give rise to difficult conceptual problems.

Self-employed. In certain cases the self-employed are treated as managers because they have independent responsibility which involves the performance of managerial functions. This can apply even though they may not have supervisors under their control. Thus owners of wholesale and retail establishments, catering and lodging establishments and farms, for example, are classified under managerial occupations. Self-employed travel agents, employment agents and ticket agents are assigned to 037.2. However, owners of small undertakings who exercise a professional or craft function, and whose management role is clearly subordinate to the application of specialist skills are classified to those skills; for example self-employed accountants, bakers and electricians are classified as accountants, bakers and electricians, and not as managers. All professional and semi-professional workers are classified to that profession. There are instances where the proprietor may not carry out the functions e.g. a nursing home proprietor or even a proprietor of a dental practice. Because of the small number involved and the impossibility of determining whether they actually perform the professional duties, these persons are included in the professions. Self-employed forestry workers and minor agricultural workers e.g. bee keepers, maggot breeders, hedgers and ditchers and gardeners are classified as workers. Self-employed manufacturers are classified with the workers, thus a proprietor of a silk weaving business is classified as a weaver. The proprietor of more general functions e.g. textile manufacturer is assigned to the appropriate not elsewhere classified (n.e.c.) group. Owners of firms providing services, such as a typewriting bureau or photographic agency with regard to whom there is no evidence that they perform the actual work associated with such services are classified in group 057.6 unless specifically mentioned elsewhere. Self-employed builders and contractors will be assigned to group 140.6.

Managers. The growing recognition of management as an occupation in itself which is to a certain extent independent of the particular field in which it is exercised, has led to managers being included in specific groups. There are however, exceptions to this. In some fields, mainly services, the title of manager is given to persons with comparatively limited responsibilities and also because in some cases the main activity is that of an occupation other than management. Managers of professional activities whose work chiefly comprises maintaining the professional or technical quality of the work done are assigned to the relevant professional or technical group. Therefore such persons as chief accountants, Borough engineers, headmasters and editors are classified within the groups for accountants, civil engineers, teachers and writers respectively.*

Supervisors/Foremen. Generally supervisors are classified in separate groups which can be related to the type of work supervised. Where a foreman controls a variety of workers or is identified only by branch of industry he is classified in the group relating to workers n.e.c. most appropriate to the branch of industry. Thus a clothing factory foreman is classified in 101.6 and a food factory foreman is classified in 090.6. Such foremen in the engineering industries are however allocated to -.1 Foremen (engineering and allied trades). Works, general and senior foremen in manufacturing and construction are considered managers and coded accordingly to groups 034.0 and 035.1 respectively.

Labourers. The groups 159.1–159.8, 160.1–160.8 assigned to labourers are strictly limited to persons performing occupations requiring little or no training or experience and for this reason certain groups of persons who have some degree of skill but are returned as labourers, e.g. fitters' labourers, are excluded.
Allocation of these groups is on a strictly industrial basis, thus departing from the general basis of classification elsewhere; the industry concerned is that of the 'establishment'† taken as a whole. This split is purely for convenience and, with the exception that foundry labourers are separated into groups 159.5 and 160.5, the resulting information could also be obtained from a cross-classification by industry.

Apprentices, articled pupils and learners are classified to the group appropriate to those whose training is completed. Graduate and student apprentices are classified to the professional occupation for which they are training.

Armed Forces. For the various economic activity and social classifications it is intended to keep distinct all uniformed members of the Services and officers are in separate groups from the men. Medical officers and chaplains are accordingly assigned to the groups for Armed Forces officers, 041.0, 042.0.

Classification of industries

The Industrial Classification for use in the Census of Population will be based on the Standard Industrial Classification.§ A list of the groups to be used in 1981 is given in Appendix D.

Classification by employment status

The classification by Employment status used in 1970 has been continued, with the exception that the family worker status is no longer separately identified but is included within 'employees n.e.c.'.

---

* For a more extended discussion see *CODOT* vol. 1 pp. 14–15, HMSO 1972
† For definition of 'establishment' see *Standard Industrial Classification* HMSO 1980 page 4 paragraph 23 (a)
§ *Standard Industrial Classification* HMSO 1980

The classification by Employment status divides the 'employee' from the 'self-employed' and further sub-divides these groups as follows:

- A. Self-employed
  - (1) Without employees
  - (2) With employees
    - (a) Large establishments
    - (b) Small establishments
- B. Employees
  - (1) Managers
    - (a) Large establishments
    - (b) Small establishments
  - (2) Foremen and Supervisors
    - (a) Manual
    - (b) Non-manual
  - (3) Apprentices, articled pupils, formal trainees
  - (4) Employees n.e.c. (not elsewhere classified).

The definitions of the Employment status codes are:

A. Self-employed

Persons not employed by any person or company and persons working in their own home for an employer (out-workers).

Note: As far as practicable all Class II insured persons are included here.

The following, for example, are included:
Proprietors of businesses (including members of partnerships).
Medical practitioners who are principals in the National Health Service and in private practice (but see below).

The following, for example, are excluded:
Directors and Managers of limited companies.
All persons in national and local government and nationalised undertakings.
Medical practitioners in private practice who are also employed as National Health Service consultants.

(1) Without employees

Persons included above who work without paid assistance.
The following are included:
Out-workers
Members of a partnership without paid employee(s).

(2) With employees

All self-employed persons not included in (1)
(a) Large establishments
Employers (except farmers) whose establishments number 25 or more persons.
(b) Small establishments
Other (including all farmers).

B. Employees

All persons not self-employed.

(1) Managers

Includes all persons classified to occupation groups 002.5, 005.3, 005.4, 007.1, 007.2, 008.0, 035.1, 036.1–4, 037.1, 039.4, 041.0, 042.0, 043.1–3; all persons not being self-employed classified to occupation groups 002.6, 002.7, 003.1, 005.1, 005.2, 009.1, 009.3, 032.3, 037.2, 038.2–4, 039.1–3, 039.5, 040.0, 044.1–4, 057.1, 057.3, 075.4, 075.5; persons occupied as managers, persons returned as managers and other persons of equivalent status whose occupation code is preceded by an 'M' in the occupation index.

Excludes professional workers classified in groups 001.0, 002.1, 004.1, 009.6, 010.1, 012.2, 012.3, 014.0, 015.1, 015.2, 017.1, 017.3, 018.2, 024.1–3, 025.0, 026.1, 026.2, 027.1, 027.2, 028.1–6, 031.1 even if returned as managers.

- (a) Large establishments

  Managers in establishments, except farms, employing 25 or more persons including all civil servants, local government officials and ships' officers coded as managers, and aircraft captains.

- (b) Small establishments

  Others including farmers, trawler skippers and foresters.

(2) Foremen and Supervisors

Persons returned as foremen or equivalent as defined in the notes on coding occupations, and other persons with supervisory functions not equivalent to management, whose occupation code number is preceded by an 'F' in the occupation index.

- (a) Manual supervisors

  Persons as above, supervising manual occupations

- (b) Non-manual supervisors

  Others

(3) Apprentices and trainees

Apprentices

Articled clerks

Articled pupils

Graduate apprentices

Management trainees

Student apprentices

Trainee craftsmen

Trainee technicians

i.e. persons undergoing training for a period fixed in advance, leading to recognition as a skilled worker or technician and/or to a recognised technical, commercial or professional qualification or management post.

(4) Employees n.e.c.

All occupied or retired persons not elsewhere classified.

Classification by economic position

The Classification by Economic Position divides the economically active from the inactive and provides further sub-division of these groups as follows:

- A. Economically active
  - (1) Persons in employment
  - (2) Persons out of employment
    - (a) Waiting to take up a job already accepted
    - (b) Seeking work
    - (c) Prevented by temporary sickness from seeking work

- B. Economically inactive
  - (1) Permanently sick or disabled
  - (2) Housewife
  - (3) Wholly retired from employment
  - (4) Full time student at an educational establishment not provided by an employer
  - (5) Other persons economically inactive

In addition the codes provide the facilities for counting the number of students who were also in employment during the week before Census.

The groups are defined as follows:

A. Economically active

(1) Persons in employment

Persons with a paid job or self-employed or working in a family business. Temporary, part-time, or casual employment is included. Persons absent from their employment due to holidays, strikes, lockouts, short time working or temporary stoppage are regarded as in employment. Persons off work sick are regarded as 'in employment' if their job is waiting for them on their return.

(2) Persons out of employment

Persons without a paid job:
- (a) Waiting to take up a job already accepted
- (b) Seeking work
- (c) Prevented by temporary sickness from seeking work

B. Economically inactive

(1) Permanently sick or disabled

Persons, whether or not previously in employment not now seeking employment because of permanent sickness or disability. Persons also included are those who have spent more than six months in a chronic sick or psychiatric hospital and are returned as out of employment.

(2) Housewives

Persons engaged entirely in unpaid domestic duties.

(3) Retired

Formerly occupied persons who have ceased working are no longer seeking further employment. Females engaged on unpaid domestic duties even though previously employed are treated as 'other economically inactive'.

(4) Students in educational establishments

Persons aged 16 and over who are or will be attending full time, during the next term, at an educational establishment not provided by an employer:
- (a) those with a paid job
- (b) those without a paid job

(5) Others economically inactive

All persons who have never been in employment and are not now seeking employment, and those who have spent more than six months in a prison and are returned as out of employment. Persons also included are those of independent means or engaged entirely on unpaid domestic duties even though they may have had paid work at some time.

In the 1981 Census the economic position will relate to the week ending 5 April 1981.

Social and socio-economic classifications

To provide a convenient summary of economic activity information for many social and medical purposes the structure of the two separate classifications, namely by 'Social Class' and by 'Socio-economic group' used in the 1971 Census are retained unchanged. In the allocation of individual occupations changes have been necessitated by the revision of the Classification of Occupations.

Social Class

Since the 1911 Census it has been customary, for certain analytical purposes, to arrange the large number of groups of the occupational classification into a small number of broad categories called Social Classes* as follows:

---

* The present Social Class grouping follows the same general lines adopted in 1921, 1931 and 1951, although the allocation of occupations to the five groups has varied from Census to Census in accordance with changes in economic conditions and with the intention of preserving the gradient rather than literal continuity. Fuller details of all earlier classifications can be found in the Registrar General's Annual Report, 1911, pp. xl, xli, Decennial Supplement, 1921, Part II, p. viii, Decennial Supplement, 1931, Part IIA, pp. 7, 8, Census 1951, Classification of Occupations, p. vii, Classification of Occupations 1970, p. x, Population Trends 8, pp. 1–7. A paper by Dr. T.H.C. Stevenson, C.B.E., M.D., then Statistical Officer at the General Register Office, and a discussion on the origins of this form of social classification will be found in the *Journal of the Royal Statistical Society*, Volume XCI. (1928), pp. 207–230.

I   **Professional, etc. occupations**
II   **Intermediate occupations**
III   **Skilled occupations**
    (N) non-manual
    (M) manual
IV   **Partly skilled occupations**
V   **Unskilled occupations**

The occupation groups included in each of these categories have been selected in such a way as to bring together, so far as is possible, people with similar levels of occupational skill. In general each occupation group is assigned as a whole to one or another social class and no account is taken of differences between individuals in the same occupation group e.g. differences of education or level of remuneration. However persons of a particular employment status within occupation groups are allocated to the appropriate Social Classes as derived by the following rules:

(a) each occupation is given a basic Social Class

(b) persons of foreman status whose basic Social Class is IV or V are allotted to Social Class III

(c) persons of manager status are allocated to Social Class II except for the following:
    Social Class I for group 007.1
    Social Class III for groups 039.4 and 057.3 and if the basic class is IV or V.

Socio-economic groups

Classification by socio-economic groups was introduced in 1951 and extensively amended in 1961. The classification aims to bring together people with jobs of similar social and economic status. The allocation of occupied persons to socio-economic groups is determined by considering their employment status and occupation (and industry, though for practical purposes no direct reference is made since it is possible in Great Britain to use classification by occupation as a means of distinguishing effectively those engaged in agriculture).

The socio-economic groups with brief definitions are:

(1) **Employers and managers in central and local government, industry, commerce, etc.—large establishments**

    1.1 Employers in industry, commerce, etc.

        Persons who employ others in non-agricultural enterprises employing 25 or more persons.

    1.2 Managers in central and local government, industry, commerce, etc.

        Persons who generally plan and supervise in non-agricultural enterprises employing 25 or more persons.

(2) **Employers and managers in industry, commerce, etc.—small establishments**

    2.1 Employers in industry, commerce, etc.—small establishments. As in 1.1 but in establishments employing fewer than 25 persons.

    2.2 Managers in industry, commerce, etc.—small establishments. As in 1.2 but in establishments employing fewer than 25 persons.

(3) **Professional workers—self-employed**

Self-employed persons engaged in work normally requiring qualifications of university degree standard.

(4) **Professional workers—employees**

Employees engaged in work normally requiring qualifications of university degree standard.

(5) **Intermediate non-manual workers**

    5.1 Ancillary workers and artists

        Employees engaged in non-manual occupations ancillary to the professions, not normally requiring qualifications of university degree standard; persons engaged in artistic work and not employing others therein. Self-employed nurses, medical auxiliaries, teachers, work study engineers and technicians are included.

5.2 Foremen and supervisors non-manual

Employees (other than managers) engaged in occupations included in group 6, who formally and immediately supervise others engaged in such occupations.

(6) **Junior non-manual workers**

Employees, not exercising general planning or supervisory powers, engaged in clerical, sales and non-manual communications occupations, excluding those who have additional and formal supervisory functions (these are included in group 5.2).

(7) **Personal service workers**

Employees engaged in service occupations caring for food, drink, clothing and other personal needs.

(8) **Foremen and supervisors—manual**

Employees (other than managers) who formally and immediately supervise others engaged in manual occupations, whether or not themselves engaged in such occupations.

(9) **Skilled manual workers**

Employees engaged in manual occupations which require considerable and specific skills.

(10) **Semi-skilled manual workers**

Employees engaged in manual occupations which require slight but specific skills.

(11) **Unskilled manual workers**

Other employees engaged in manual occupations.

(12) **Own account workers (other than professional)**

Self-employed persons engaged in any trade, personal service or manual occupation not normally requiring training of university degree standard and having no employees other than family workers.

(13) **Farmers—employers and managers**

Persons who own, rent or manage farms, market gardens or forests, employing people other than family workers in the work of the enterprise.

(14) **Farmers—own account**

Persons who own or rent farms, market gardens or forests and having no employees other than family workers.

(15) **Agricultural workers**

Persons engaged in tending crops, animals, game or forests, or operating agricultural or forestry machinery.

(16) **Members of armed forces**

(17) **Inadequately described and not stated occupations**

Classification by size of establishment

It is not practicable to include in the Census questions on the degree of responsibility exercised by employers and managers. An indirect, and necessarily rather crude distinction between greater and lesser responsibility is therefore provided by further classifying employers and managers by the size of the establishment in which they work. All civil servants, local authority officials and ships' officers coded as managers and aircraft captains are conventionally regarded as managers in large establishments. Farmers, trawler skippers, and foresters are conventionally regarded as working in small establishments.

Detailed allocation

The detailed allocation of the occupation/employment status groups to the social class and socio-economic groups and details of the socio-economic groups and social classes in terms of the occupation and employment status groups are shown in Appendix B.

Application of the socio-economic classification to the whole population
The 17 socio-economic groups detailed above may be applied to the economically active or retired population either combined or independently. For some purposes, however, it is more appropriate to treat retired persons as a separate socio-economic group and assign only the economically active population to the individual groups.

If it is desired to extend the socio-economic groups to include the remaining categories of the economically inactive, the following groups are recommended:

(1) **Inactive residents in non-private households**
(2) **Students and children under 16**
(3) **Other economically inactive persons**

Socio-economic class
The classifications by Socio-economic group and by Social Class are not interconvertible. In order to meet a need for a classification from which both Socio-economic group and Social Class can be derived some tables in the 1981 Census series will be produced for a series of groups formed from a complete cross-classification of Socio-economic group by Social Class. For convenience this classification is referred to as the 'Socio-economic class' classification and details are shown in Appendix C.

European Economic Community Socio-economic status groups
In order to increase the comparability of international statistics the EEC has devised a Socio-economic classification based on the International Standard Classification of Occupations* and employment status. This classification will be used by OPCS for the purpose of international comparison. Details of this classification and its relationship to the OPCS Classification of Occupations are given in Appendix E.

---

* International Labour Office. *International Standard Classification of Occupations, Geneva* 1968

Summary of the OPCS 1980 occupation groups with condensed KOS headings

Order 1 Professional and related supporting management; senior national and local government managers

001 Judges, barristers, advocates, solicitors
   0 Judges, barristers, advocates, solicitors

002 Accountants, valuers, finance specialists
   1 Chartered and certified accountants
   2 Cost and works accountants
   3 Estimators
   4 Valuers, claims assessors
   5 Financial managers
   6 Underwriters, brokers, investment analysts
   7 Taxation experts

003 Personnel and industrial relations managers; O and M, work study and operational research officers
   1 Personnel and industrial relations officers
   2 O and M, work study and OR officers

004 Economists, statisticians, systems analysts, computer programmers
   1 Economists, statisticians, actuaries
   2 Systems analysts, computer programmers

005 Marketing, sales, advertising, public relations and purchasing managers
   1 Marketing and sales managers and executives
   2 Advertising and PR executives
   3 Buyers (retail trade)
   4 Buyers and purchasing officers (not retail)

006 Statutory and other inspectors
   1 Environmental health officers
   2 Building inspectors
   3 Inspectors (statutory and similar)

007 General administrators—national government
   1 General administrators—national government (Assistant Secretary level and above)
   2 General administrators—national government (HEO to Senior Principal level)

008 Local government officers (administrative and executive functions)
   0 Local government officers (administrative and executive functions)

009 All other professional and related supporting management and administration
   1 Company secretaries
   2 Officials of trade associations, trade unions, professional bodies and charities
   3 Property and estate managers
   4 Librarians, information officers
   5 Legal service and related occupations
   6 Management consultants
   7 Managers' personal assistants
   8 Professional workers and related supporting management and administration n.e.c.

Note: n.e.c. = not elsewhere classified

Order 2 Professional and related in education, welfare and health

   010 Teachers in higher education
- 1 University academic staff
- 2 Teachers in establishments for further and higher education

   011 Teachers n.e.c.
- 0 Teachers n.e.c.

   012 Vocational and industrial trainers, education officers, social and behavioural scientists
- 1 Vocational and industrial trainers
- 2 Education officers, school inspectors
- 3 Social and behavioural scientists

   013 Welfare workers
- 1 Matrons, houseparents
- 2 Playgroup leaders
- 3 Welfare occupations n.e.c.

   014 Clergy, ministers of religion
- 0 Clergy, ministers of religion

   015 Medical and dental practitioners
- 1 Medical practitioners
- 2 Dental practitioners

   016 Nurse administrators, nurses
- 0 Nurse administrators, nurses

   017 Pharmacists, radiographers, therapists n.e.c.
- 1 Pharmacists
- 2 Medical radiographers
- 3 Ophthalmic and dispensing opticians
- 4 Physiotherapists
- 5 Chiropodists
- 6 Therapists n.e.c.

   018 All other professional and related in education, welfare and health
- 1 Medical technicians, dental auxiliaries
- 2 Veterinarians
- 3 Driving instructors (not HGV)
- 4 Professional and related in education, welfare and health n.e.c.

Order 3 Literary, artistic and sports

   019 Authors, writers, journalists
- 0 Authors, writers, journalists

   020 Artists, designers, window dressers
- 1 Artists, commercial artists
- 2 Industrial designers (not clothing)
- 3 Clothing designers
- 4 Window dressers

   021 Actors, musicians, entertainers, stage managers
- 1 Actors, entertainers, singers, stage managers
- 2 Musicians

   022 Photographers, cameramen, sound and vision equipment operators
- 1 Photographers, cameramen
- 2 Sound and vision equipment operators

Note: n.e.c. = not elsewhere classified

023 All other literary, artistic and sports
   1 Professional sportsmen, sports officials
   2 Literary, artistic and sports workers n.e.c.

Order 4 Professional and related in science, engineering, technology and similar fields

024 Scientists, physicists, mathematicians
   1 Biological scientists, biochemists
   2 Chemical scientists
   3 Physical and geological scientists, mathematicians

025 Civil, structural, municipal, mining and quarrying engineers
   0 Civil, structural, municipal, mining and quarrying engineers

026 Mechanical and aeronautical engineers
   1 Mechanical and aeronautical engineers
   2 Design and development engineers (mechanical)

027 Electrical and electronic engineers
   1 Electrical engineers
   2 Electronic engineers

028 Engineers and technologists n.e.c.
   1 Chemical engineers
   2 Production engineers
   3 Planning and quality control engineers
   4 Engineers n.e.c.
   5 Metallurgists
   6 Technologists n.e.c.

029 Draughtsmen
   0 Draughtsmen

030 Laboratory and engineering technicians, technician engineers
   1 Laboratory technicians
   2 Engineering technicians, technician engineers

031 Architects, town planners, quantity, building and land surveyors
   1 Architects, town planners
   2 Quantity surveyors
   3 Building, land and mining surveyors

032 Officers (ships and aircraft), air traffic planners and controllers
   1 Aircraft flight deck officers
   2 Air traffic planners and controllers
   3 Deck, engineering and radio officers and pilots, ship

033 Professional and related in science, engineering and other technologies and similar fields n.e.c.
   1 Architectural and town planning technicians
   2 Building and civil engineering technicians
   3 Technical and related workers n.e.c.

Order 5 Managerial

034 Production, works and maintenance managers, works foremen
   0 Production, works and maintenance managers, works foremen

035 Site and other managers, agents and clerks of works, general foremen (building and civil engineering)
   1 Managers in building and contracting
   2 Clerks of works

Note: n.e.c. = not elsewhere classified

036 Managers in transport, warehousing, public utilities and mining
   1 Managers in mining and public utilities
   2 Transport managers
   3 Stores controllers
   4 Managers in warehousing and materials handling n.e.c.

037 Office managers
   1 Credit controllers
   2 Office managers n.e.c.

038 Managers in wholesale and retail distribution
   1 Garage proprietors
   2 Butchers (managers and proprietors)
   3 Fishmongers (managers and proprietors)
   4 Other proprietors and managers (sales)

039 Managers of hotels, clubs, etc., and in entertainment and sport
   1 Hotel and residential club managers
   2 Publicans
   3 Restaurateurs
   4 Club stewards
   5 Entertainment and sports managers

040 Farmers, horticulturists, farm managers
   0 Farmers, horticulturists, farm managers

041 Officers, UK armed forces
   0 Officers, UK armed forces

042 Officers, foreign and Commonwealth armed forces
   0 Officers, foreign and Commonwealth armed forces

043 Senior police, prison and fire service officers
   1 Prison officers (chief officers and above)
   2 Police officers (inspectors and above)
   3 Fire service officers

044 All other managers
   1 Proprietors and managers, service flats, holiday flats, caravan sites, etc.
   2 Managers of laundry and dry cleaning receiving shops
   3 Hairdressers' and barbers' managers and proprietors
   4 Managers n.e.c.

Order 6 Clerical and related

045 Supervisors of clerks, civil service executive officers
   1 Civil service executive officers
       Supervisors of—
   2   Stores and despatch clerks
   3   Tracers, drawing office assistants
   4   Other clerks and cashiers (not retail)
   5   Retail shop cashiers, check-out and cash and wrap operators

046 Clerks
   1 Stores and despatch clerks
   2 Tracers, drawing office assistants
   3 Other clerks and cashiers (not retail)

047 Retail shop cashiers, check-out and cash and wrap operators
   0 Retail shop cashiers, check-out and cash and wrap operators

---

Note: n.e.c. = not elsewhere classified

048 Supervisors of typists, office machine operators, telephonists, etc.
    Supervisors of—
- 1 Typists, shorthand writers, secretaries
- 2 Office machine operators
- 3 Telephone operators
- 4 Radio and telegraph operators

049 Secretaries, shorthand typists, receptionists
- 1 Receptionists
- 2 Typists, shorthand writers, secretaries

050 Office machine operators
- 0 Office machine operators

051 Telephonists, radio and telegraph operators
- 1 Telephonist receptionists
- 2 Telephone operators
- 3 Radio and telegraph operators

052 Supervisors of postmen, mail sorters, messengers
    Supervisors of—
- 1 Postmen, mail sorters
- 2 Messengers

053 Postmen, mail sorters, messengers
- 1 Postmen, mail sorters
- 2 Messengers

Order 7 Selling

054 Sales supervisors
    Supervisors of—
- 1 Shop salesmen and assistants
- 2 Petrol pump, forecourt attendants
- 3 Roundsmen, van salesmen

055 Salesmen, sales assistants, shop assistants, shelf fillers, petrol pump, forecourt attendants
- 1 Shop salesmen and assistants
- 2 Shelf fillers
- 3 Petrol pump, forecourt attendants

056 Roundsmen, van salesmen
- 0 Roundsmen, van salesmen

057 Sales representatives and agents
- 1 Importers, exporters, commodity brokers
- 2 Market and street traders and assistants
- 3 Scrap dealers, general dealers, rag and bone merchants
- 4 Credit agents, collector salesmen
- 5 Sales representatives
- 6 Sales representatives (property and services), other agents

Order 8 Security and protective service

058 NCOs and other ranks, UK armed forces
- 0 NCOs and other ranks, UK armed forces

059 NCOs and other ranks, foreign and Commonwealth armed forces
- 0 NCOs and other ranks, foreign and Commonwealth armed forces

Note: n.e.c. = not elsewhere classified

060 Supervisors (police sergeants, fire fighting and related)
   1 Police sergeants
   2 Fire service supervisors
   3 Prison service principal officers
      Supervisors of—
   4   Security guards and officers, patrolmen, watchmen
   5   Traffic wardens
   6   Security and protective service workers n.e.c.

061 Policemen, firemen, prison officers
   1 Policemen (below sergeant)
   2 Firemen
   3 Prison officers (below principal officer)

062 Other security and protective service workers
   1 Security guards and officers, patrolmen, watchmen
   2 Traffic wardens
   3 Security and protective service workers n.e.c.

Order 9 Catering, cleaning, hairdressing and other personal service

063 Catering supervisors
      Supervisors of—
   1   Chefs, cooks
   2   Waiters, waitresses
   3   Barmen, barmaids
   4   Counter hands, assistants

064 Chefs, cooks
   0 Chefs, cooks

065 Waiters and bar staff
   1 Waiters, waitresses
   2 Barmen, barmaids

066 Counter hands, assistants, kitchen porters, hands
   1 Counter hands, assistants
   2 Kitchen porters, hands

067 Supervisors—housekeeping and related
   1 Housekeepers (non-domestic)
      Supervisors of—
   2   Other domestic and school helpers
   3   Travel stewards and attendants
   4   Hospital porters
   5   Hotel porters
   6   Ambulancemen
   7   Hospital, ward orderlies

068 Domestic staff and school helpers
   1 Domestic housekeepers
   2 Nursery nurses
   3 Other domestic and school helpers

069 Travel stewards and attendants, hospital and hotel porters
   1 Travel stewards and attendants
   2 Hospital porters
   3 Hotel porters

Note: n.e.c. = not elsewhere classified

070 Ambulancemen, hospital orderlies
    1 Ambulancemen
    2 Hospital, ward orderlies

071 Supervisors, foremen—caretaking, cleaning and related
    Supervisors of—
    1 Caretakers
    2 Cleaners, window cleaners, chimney sweeps, road sweepers
    3 Railway stationmen
    4 Lift and car park attendants

072 Caretakers, road sweepers and other cleaners
    1 Caretakers
    2 Cleaners, window cleaners, chimney sweeps, road sweepers

073 Hairdressing supervisors
    0 Hairdressing supervisors

074 Hairdressers, barbers
    0 Hairdressers, barbers

075 All other in catering, cleaning and other personal service
    1 Railway stationmen
    2 Lift and car park attendants
    3 Launderers, dry cleaners, pressers
    4 Undertakers
    5 Bookmakers, betting shop managers
    6 Service workers n.e.c.

Order 10 Farming, fishing and related

076 Foremen—farming, horticulture, forestry
    1 Farm foremen
    2 Horticultural foremen
    3 Foremen gardeners and groundsmen
    4 Agricultural machinery foremen
    5 Forestry foremen
    6 Other foremen in farming and related

077 Farm workers
    0 Farm workers

078 Horticultural workers, gardeners, groundsmen
    1 Horticultural workers
    2 Gardeners, groundsmen

079 Agricultural machinery drivers, operators
    0 Agricultural machinery drivers, operators

080 Forestry workers
    0 Forestry workers

081 Supervisors, mates—fishing
    0 Supervisors, mates—fishing

082 Fishermen
    0 Fishermen

083 All other in farming and related
    0 All other in farming and related

Note: n.e.c. = not elsewhere classified

Order 11 Materials processing; making and repairing (excluding metal and electrical)

  084 Foremen—tannery and leather (including leather substitutes) working
        Foremen—
    1 Tannery production workers
    2 Shoe repairers
    3 Leather cutters and sewers, footwear lasters, makers, finishers
    4 Other making and repairing, leather

  085 Tannery and leather (including leather substitutes) workers
    1 Tannery production workers
    2 Shoe repairers
    3 Leather cutters and sewers, footwear lasters, makers, finishers

  086 Foremen—textile processing
        Foremen—
    1 Preparatory fibre processors
    2 Spinners, doublers, twisters
    3 Winders, reelers
    4 Warp preparers
    5 Weavers
    6 Knitters
    7 Bleachers, dyers, finishers
    8 Menders, darners
    9 Other material processing, textiles

  087 Textile workers
    1 Preparatory fibre processors
    2 Spinners, doublers, twisters
    3 Winders, reelers
    4 Warp preparers
    5 Weavers
    6 Knitters
    7 Bleachers, dyers, finishers
    8 Menders, darners

  088 Foremen—chemical processing
    0 Foremen—chemical processing

  089 Chemical, gas and petroleum process plant operators
    0 Chemical, gas and petroleum process plant operators

  090 Foremen—food and drink processing
        Foremen—
    1 Bakers, flour confectioners
    2 Butchers, meat cutters
    3 Fishmongers, poultry dressers
    4 Brewery and vinery process workers
        Other material processing—
    5   Bakery and confectionery workers
    6   Food and drink n.e.c.

  091 Bakers, flour confectioners
    0 Bakers, flour confectioners

  092 Butchers
    1 Butchers, meat cutters
    2 Fishmongers, poultry dressers

Note: n.e.c. = not elsewhere classified

093 Foremen—paper and board making and paper products
   Foremen—
   1   Paper, paperboard and leatherboard workers
   2   Bookbinders and finishers
   3   Cutting and slitting machine operators (paper and paper products making)
   4   Other material processing, wood and paper
   5   Other making and repairing, paper goods and printing

094 Paper, board and paper product makers, bookbinders
   1   Paper, paperboard and leatherboard workers
   2   Bookbinders and finishers
   3   Cutting and slitting machine operators (paper and paper products making)

095 Foremen—glass, ceramics, rubber, plastics, etc.
   Foremen—
   1   Glass and ceramics furnacemen, kilnsetters
   2   Glass formers and shapers, finishers, decorators
   3   Casters and other pottery makers
   4   Rubber process workers, moulding machine operators, tyre builders
   5   Calendar and extruding machine operators, moulders (plastics)
   6   Man-made fibre makers
   7   Washers, screeners and crushers in mines and quarries
   Other making and repairing—
   8   Glass and ceramics
   9   Rubber
   10   Plastics

096 Glass and ceramics furnacemen and workers
   1   Glass and ceramics furnacemen, kilnsetters
   2   Glass formers and shapers, finishers, decorators
   3   Casters and other pottery makers

097 Rubber and plastics workers
   1   Rubber process workers, moulding machine operators, tyre builders
   2   Calendar and extruding machine operators, moulders (plastics)

098 All other in processing materials (other than metal)
   1   Man-made fibre makers
   2   Brewery and vinery process workers
   3   Washers, screeners and crushers in mines and quarries
   Other material processing—
   4   Textiles
   5   Bakery and confectionery workers
   6   Tobacco
   7   Food and drink n.e.c.
   8   Wood and paper
   9   All other (excluding metal) n.e.c.

099 Foremen—printing
   Foremen—
   1   Compositors
   2   Electrotypers, stereotypers, printing plate and cylinder preparers
   3   Printing machine minders and assistants
   4   Screen and block printers
   5   Printers (so described)

Note: n.e.c. = not elsewhere classified

100 Printing workers, screen and block printers
  1 Compositors
  2 Electrotypers, stereotypers, printing plate and cylinder preparers
  3 Printing machine minders and assistants
  4 Screen and block printers
  5 Printers (so described)

101 Foremen—textile materials working
     Foremen—
  1   Tailors, tailoresses, dressmakers
  2   Clothing cutters, milliners, furriers
  3   Sewers, embroiderers
  4   Coach trimmers, upholsterers, mattress makers
  5   Carpet fitters
  6   Other making and repairing, clothing and related products

102 Tailors, dressmakers and other clothing workers
  1 Tailors, tailoresses, dressmakers
  2 Clothing cutters, milliners, furriers
  3 Sewers, embroiderers

103 Coach trimmers, upholsterers, mattress makers
  0 Coach trimmers, upholsterers, mattress makers

104 Foremen—woodworking
     Foremen—
  1   Carpenters, joiners
  2   Cabinet makers
  3   Case and box makers
  4   Pattern makers (moulds)
  5   Sawyers, veneer cutters, woodworking machinists
  6   Other making and repairing, wood

105 Woodworkers, pattern makers
  1 Carpenters, joiners
  2 Cabinet makers
  3 Case and box makers
  4 Pattern makers (moulds)

106 Sawyers, veneer cutters, woodworking machinists
  0 Sawyers, veneer cutters, woodworking machinists

107 All other in making and repairing (excluding metal and electrical)
  1   Labourers and mates to woodworking craftsmen
  2   Dental technicians
  3   Carpet fitters
  4   Musical instrument makers, piano tuners
      Other making and repairing—
  5   Glass and ceramics
  6   Wood
  7   Leather
  8   Clothing and related products
  9   Paper goods and printing
  10 Rubber
  11 Plastics
  12 All other (excluding metal and electrical) n.e.c.

Note: n.e.c. = not elsewhere classified

Order 12 Processing, making, repairing and related (metal and electrical)

  108 Foremen—metal making and treating
      Foremen—
    1   Furnace operating occupations (metal)
    2   Rollermen
    3   Smiths, forgemen
    4   Metal drawers
    5   Moulders, coremakers, die casters
    6   Electroplaters
    7   Annealers, hardeners, temperers (metal)
    8   Galvanizers, tin platers, dip platers
    9   Metal making and treating workers n.e.c.

  109 Furnacemen (metal), rollermen, smiths, forgemen
    1 Furnace operating occupations (metal)
    2 Rollermen
    3 Smiths, forgemen

  110 Metal drawers, moulders, die casters, electroplaters, annealers
    1 Metal drawers
    2 Moulders, coremakers, die casters
    3 Electroplaters
    4 Annealers, hardeners, temperers (metal)

  111 Foremen—engineering machining
      Foremen—
    1   Press and machine tool setters
    2   Centre lathe turners
    3   Machine tool setter operators
    4   Machine tool operators
    5   Press, stamping and automatic machine operators
    6   Metal polishers
    7   Fettlers, dressers
    8   Shot blasters

  112 Press and machine tool setter operators and operators, turners
    1 Press and machine tool setters
    2 Centre lathe turners
    3 Machine tool setter operators
    4 Machine tool operators

  113 Machine attendants, minders, press and stamping machine operators, metal polishers, fettlers, dressers
    1 Press, stamping and automatic machine operators
    2 Metal polishers
    3 Fettlers, dressers

  114 Foremen—production fitting (metal)
      Foremen—
    1   Tool makers, tool fitters, markers-out
    2   Precision instrument makers and repairers
    3   Watch and chronometer makers and repairers
    4   Metal working production fitters and fitter/machinists
    5   Motor mechanics, auto engineers
    6   Maintenance fitters (aircraft engines)
    7   Office machinery mechanics

  115 Tool makers, tool fitters, markers-out
    0 Tool makers, tool fitters, markers-out

Note: n.e.c. = not elsewhere classified

116 Instrument and watch and clock makers and repairers
   1 Precision instrument makers and repairers
   2 Watch and chronometer makers and repairers

117 Metal working production fitters and fitter/machinists
   0 Metal working production fitters and fitter/machinists

118 Motor vehicle and aircraft mechanics
   1 Motor mechanics, auto engineers
   2 Maintenance fitters (aircraft engines)

119 Office machinery mechanics
   0 Office machinery mechanics

120 Foremen—production fitting and wiring (electrical)
    Foremen—
   1 Production fitters (electrical, electronic)
   2 Electricians, electrical maintenance fitters
   3 Plant operators and attendants n.e.c.
   4 Telephone fitters
   5 Cable jointers, linesmen
   6 Radio and TV mechanics
   7 Other electronic maintenance engineers

121 Production fitters, electricians, electricity power plant operators, switchboard attendants
   1 Production fitters (electrical, electronic)
   2 Electricians, electrical maintenance fitters
   3 Electrical engineers (so described)
   4 Plant operators and attendants n.e.c.

122 Telephone fitters, cable jointers, linesmen
   1 Telephone fitters
   2 Cable jointers, linesmen

123 Radio, TV and other electronic maintenance fitters and mechanics
   1 Radio and TV mechanics
   2 Other electronic maintenance engineers

124 Foremen—metal working, pipes, sheets, structures
    Foremen—
   1 Plumbers, heating and ventilating fitters, gas fitters
   2 Sheet metal workers
   3 Metal plate workers, shipwrights, riveters
   4 Steel erectors, benders, fixers
   5 Scaffolders, stagers
   6 Welders
   7 Riggers

125 Plumbers, heating and ventilating fitters, gas fitters
   0 Plumbers, heating and ventilating fitters, gas fitters

126 Sheet metal workers, platers, shipwrights, riveters, etc.
   1 Sheet metal workers
   2 Metal plate workers, shipwrights, riveters

127 Steel erectors, scaffolders, steel benders, fixers
   1 Steel erectors, benders, fixers
   2 Scaffolders, stagers

Note: n.e.c. = not elsewhere classified

128 Welders
   0 Welders

129 Foremen—other processing, making and repairing (metal and electrical)
      Foremen—
   1 Goldsmiths, silversmiths, precious stone workers
   2 Engravers, etchers (printing)
   3 Coach and vehicle body builders
   4 Oilers, greasers, lubricators
   5 Electronics wiremen
   6 Coil winders

130 Goldsmiths, silversmiths, etc., engravers, etchers
   1 Goldsmiths, silversmiths, precious stone workers
   2 Engravers, etchers (printing)

131 All other in processing, making and repairing (metal and electrical)
   1 Coach and vehicle body builders
   2 Galvanizers, tin platers, dip platers
   3 Metal making and treating workers n.e.c.
   4 Oilers, greasers, lubricators
   5 Riggers
   6 Electronics wiremen
   7 Coil winders
   8 Shot blasters
   9 Other metal, jewellery, electrical production workers

—
   1 Foremen (engineering and allied trades)
   2 Trainee craftsmen (engineering and allied trades)

Order 13 Painting, repetitive assembling, product inspecting, packaging and related

132 Foremen—painting and similar coating
      Foremen—
   1 Pottery decorators
   2 Coach painters (so described)
   3 Other spray painters
   4 Painters and decorators n.e.c., french polishers

133 Painters, decorators, french polishers
   1 Pottery decorators
   2 Coach painters (so described)
   3 Other spray painters
   4 Painters and decorators n.e.c., french polishers

134 Foremen—product assembling (repetitive)
      Foremen assemblers—
   1 Electrical, electronic
   2 Instruments
   3 Vehicles and other metal goods
   4 Paper production, processing and printing
   5 Plastics goods

135 Repetitive assemblers (metal and electrical goods)
   1 Assemblers (electrical, electronic)
   2 Instrument assemblers
   3 Assemblers (vehicles and other metal goods)

Note: n.e.c. = not elsewhere classified

136 Foremen—product inspection and packaging
　　Foremen inspectors, viewers, examiners—
　1　Metal, electrical goods
　2　Textiles
　3　Food
　4　Rubber goods
　5　Plastics goods
　6　Woodwork
　　Foremen—
　7　Packers, bottlers, canners, fillers
　8　Laboratory assistants
　9　Inspectors, sorters in paper production, processing and printing
　10　Weighers
　11　Graders, sorters, selectors n.e.c.

137　Inspectors, viewers, testers, packers, bottlers, etc.
　1　Inspectors, viewers (metal, electrical goods)
　2　Packers, bottlers, canners, fillers

138　All other in painting, repetitive assembling, product inspection, packaging and related
　1　Laboratory assistants
　　Inspectors, viewers, examiners—
　2　Textiles
　3　Food
　4　Rubber goods
　5　Plastics goods
　6　Woodwork
　7　Inspectors, sorters in paper production, processing and printing
　8　Assemblers in paper production, processing and printing
　9　Assemblers (plastics goods)
　10　Weighers
　11　Graders, sorters, selectors n.e.c.
　12　Painting, assembling and related occupations n.e.c.

Order 14　Construction, mining and related not identified elsewhere

139　Foremen—building and civil engineering n.e.c.
　　Foremen—
　1　Bricklayers, tile setters
　2　Masons, stone cutters
　3　Plasterers
　4　Roofers, glaziers
　5　Handymen, general building workers
　6　Railway lengthmen
　7　Road surfacers, concreters
　8　Roadmen
　9　Paviors, kerb layers
　10　Sewage plant attendants
　11　Mains and service layers, pipe jointers
　12　Construction workers n.e.c.

140　Building and construction workers
　1　Bricklayers, tile setters
　2　Masons, stone cutters
　3　Plasterers
　4　Roofers, glaziers
　5　Handymen, general building workers
　6　Builders (so described)

Note: n.e.c. = not elsewhere classified

141 Concreters, road surfacers, railway lengthmen
  1 Railway lengthmen
  2 Road surfacers, concreters
  3 Roadmen
  4 Paviors, kerb layers

142 Sewage plant attendants, sewermen (maintenance), mains and service layers, pipe jointers (gas, water, drainage, oil), inspectors (water supply), turncocks
  1 Sewage plant attendants
  2 Mains and service layers, pipe jointers

143 Civil engineering labourers, craftsmen's mates and other builders' labourers n.e.c.
  1 Craftsmen's mates
  2 Building and civil engineering labourers

144 Foremen/deputies—coalmining
  0 Foremen/deputies—coalmining

145 Face-trained coalmining workers
  0 Face-trained coalmining workers

146 All other in construction, mining, quarrying, well drilling and related n.e.c.
  1 Miners (not coal), quarrymen, well drillers
  2 Construction workers n.e.c.

Order 15 Transport operating, materials moving and storing and related

147 Foremen—ships, lighters and other vessels
  0 Foremen—ships, lighters and other vessels

148 Deck, engine-room hands, bargemen, lightermen, boatmen
  0 Deck, engine-room hands, bargemen, lightermen, boatmen

149 Foremen—rail transport operating
    Foremen—
  1 Railway guards
  2 Signalmen and crossing keepers, railway
  3 Shunters, pointsmen
  4 Other foremen rail transport

150 Rail transport operating staff
  1 Drivers, motormen, secondmen, railway engines
  2 Railway guards
  3 Signalmen and crossing keepers, railway
  4 Shunters, pointsmen

151 Foremen—road transport operating, bus inspectors
  1 Bus inspectors
    Foremen—
  2 Drivers of road goods vehicles
  3 Other foremen road transport

152 Bus, coach, lorry drivers, etc.
  1 Bus and coach drivers
  2 Drivers of road goods vehicles
  3 Other motor drivers

153 Bus conductors, drivers' mates
  1 Bus conductors
  2 Drivers' mates

Note: n.e.c. = not elsewhere classified

154 Foremen—civil engineering plant operating, materials handling equipment operating
    Foremen—
  1 Mechanical plant drivers, operators (earth moving and civil engineering)
  2 Crane drivers, operators
  3 Fork lift, mechanical truck drivers
  4 Slingers

155 Mechanical plant, fork lift, mechanical truck drivers, crane drivers, operators
  1 Mechanical plant drivers, operators (earth moving and civil engineering)
  2 Crane drivers, operators
  3 Fork lift, mechanical truck drivers

156 Foremen—materials moving and storing
    Foremen—
  1 Storekeepers, warehousemen
  2 Stevedores, dockers
  3 Goods porters
  4 Refuse collectors, dustmen

157 Storekeepers, stevedores, warehouse, market and other goods porters
  1 Storekeepers, warehousemen
  2 Stevedores, dockers
  3 Goods porters
  4 Refuse collectors, dustmen

158 All other in transport operating, materials moving and storing and related n.e.c.
  1 Slingers
  2 Workers in transport operating, materials moving and storing and related n.e.c.

Order 16 Miscellaneous

159 Foremen—miscellaneous
    Foremen—
      Labourers and unskilled workers n.e.c.—
  1   Textiles (not textile goods)
  2   Chemicals and allied trades
  3   Coke ovens and gas works
  4   Glass and ceramics
  5   Foundries in engineering and allied trades
  6   Engineering and allied trades
  7   Coal mines
  8   Other
  9 Boiler operators

160 General labourers
    Labourers and unskilled workers n.e.c.—
  1 Textiles (not textile goods)
  2 Chemicals and allied trades
  3 Coke ovens and gas works
  4 Glass and ceramics
  5 Foundries in engineering and allied trades
  6 Engineering and allied trades
  7 Coal mines
  8 Other

161 All other in miscellaneous occupations n.e.c.
  1 Boiler operators
  2 All other in miscellaneous occupations n.e.c.

Order 17 Inadequately described and not stated

—
  1 Inadequately described occupations
  2 Occupations not stated

Note: n.e.c. = not elsewhere classified

Occupation groups with short descriptions of contents and CODOT definitions

Please note that the CODOT occupations with numbers ending in .98, trainees, have been omitted from these definitions (see item Apprentices, articled pupils and learners on page vii). The CODOT equivalent of KOS group 002 (i.e. CODOT unit group 002 except 002.65) has been omitted because its individual occupations are divided between groups under condensed KOS headings 034–040 and 044 as appropriate.

001.0 Judges, barristers, advocates, solicitors
Persons qualified as barristers, solicitors or advocates (Scotland) drawing up legal documents, giving legal advice, pleading in court, presiding over judicial proceedings.
CODOT
021, 022

002.1 Chartered and certified accountants
Persons with professional qualifications performing accountancy services; auditors and assistant auditors in the Department of the Environment. Local authority treasurers and investment advisers are excluded and classified in 002.5 and 002.6 respectively.
CODOT
032.10 pt. Remainder in 002.5
032.99

002.2 Cost and works accountants
Persons with professional qualifications performing accountancy duties that assist management in the planning and control of an undertaking's income and expenditure. Qualified management accountants are included.
CODOT
032.20

002.3 Estimators
Persons calculating probable costs of projects and products, including rates and charges officers (transport).
CODOT
033.00 pt., 033.99 pt. Remainders in 002.4
033.10, 033.20, 033.30, 033.40

002.4 Valuers, claims assessors
Persons assessing values of real and other property; investigating, assessing liability and calculating monetary settlements in respect of insurance claims and marine losses. Rating and valuation surveyors, rent officers and Inland Revenue examiners are included.
CODOT
033.00 pt., 033.99 pt. Remainders in 002.3
033.50, 033.60, 033.70

002.5 Financial managers
Persons dealing with the financial aspects of a company. Local authority treasurers, trust officers and managers of merchant banks are included.
CODOT
032.00
032.10 pt. Remainder in 002.1
034.40
034.99 pt. Remainder in 002.6

002.6 Underwriters, brokers, investment analysts
Persons dealing in stocks and shares and bills of exchange, advising on investment and insurance; underwriting insurance. Advance advisers (banking), foreign exchange brokers and stockbrokers' attachés are included.
CODOT
034 pt. Excludes—034.40, 034.99 pt. included in 002.5

002.7 Taxation experts
Persons advising on tax matters. Inspectors of taxes are included.
CODOT
039.40, 039.50

003.1 Personnel and industrial relations officers
Persons administering personnel and industrial relations policies. Conciliation officers are included.
CODOT
041

003.2 O and M, work study and OR officers
Persons advising on and implementing methods to improve the efficient and economic use of manpower, materials, equipment and other resources, including organisation and methods officers and operational research officers. Safety officers, progress engineers and work study assistants are excluded and classified in 013.3, 028.3 and 046.3 respectively.
CODOT
042

004.1 Economists, statisticians, actuaries
Persons working in economic, statistical and actuarial specialist occupations.
CODOT
043

004.2 Systems analysts, computer programmers
Persons planning and controlling computer installations; developing procedures and preparing programmes for the processing of data automatically. Systems engineers are included.
CODOT
044

005.1 Marketing and sales managers and executives
Persons determining and implementing sales policy; executives in charge of headquarters' sales organisation in industry, commerce and services. Persons managing local teams of sales representatives such as field sales managers, area managers and regional managers are excluded and classified in 057.5.
CODOT
051.05, 051.10, 051.15

005.2 Advertising and PR executives
Persons planning and organising advertising campaigns and similar activities and promoting the public relations of an organisation.
CODOT
051 pt. Excludes—051.05, 051.10, 051.15

005.3 Buyers (retail trade)
Persons buying merchandise from manufacturers, importers, wholesalers and other sources for resale through retail distribution.
CODOT
061.00 pt., 061.99 pt. Remainders in 005.4
061.10

005.4 Buyers and purchasing officers (not retail)
Persons buying merchandise, materials, equipment and other items and services on behalf of an industrial, commercial or public undertaking, or for wholesale distribution.
CODOT
061 pt. Excludes—061.00 pt., 061.10, 061.99 pt. included in 005.3

006.1 Environmental health officers
Persons working as environmental health officers.
CODOT
064.05

006.2 Building inspectors
Persons inspecting plans and buildings to ensure compliance with regulations.
CODOT
064.30

006.3 Inspectors (statutory and similar)
Persons undertaking investigations authorised by Acts, orders, regulations, etc., including inspectors of factories, public utilities, trading standards; Customs and Excise officers, driving examiners, immigration officers, ships' surveyors, water bailiffs. Housing and planning inspectors, inspectors of schools and traffic wardens are excluded and classified in 009.5, 012.2 and 062.2 respectively.
CODOT
064 pt. Excludes—064.05, 064.30

007.1 General administrators—national government (Assistant Secretary level and above)
Persons of Assistant Secretary or equivalent rank and above in the Civil Service; Members of Parliament not classifiable elsewhere and foreign and Commonwealth diplomatic representatives. Inspectors of taxes are excluded and classified in 002.7.
CODOT
001 pt. Excludes—001.40 included in 008.0
002.65
069.20 pt. Remainder in 007.2

007.2 General administrators—national government (HEO to Senior Principal level)
Persons returned as senior principal, principal, senior and higher executive officers or equivalent rank in the Civil Service. Managers of government Job Centres and Social Security offices are included. Government service intelligence officers and managers of government training centres are excluded and classified in 009.4 and 012.1 respectively.
CODOT
069.20 pt. Remainder in 007.1
281.02 pt. Remainder in 008.0, 037.2 and 045.1
281.28, 281.30, 281.32

008.0 Local government officers (administrative and executive functions)
Persons of administrative or executive rank in local authority employ. Local authority treasurers, statutory inspectors, directors of education, and housing managers are excluded and classified in 002.5, 006.3, 012.2 and 013.3 respectively.
CODOT
001.40
031.20
069.30
281.02 pt. Remainder in 007.2, 037.2 and 045.1
281.34

009.1 Company secretaries
Persons having responsibility for all work connected with the meetings with the board of directors and shareholders; giving advice on company law and practise; acting as legal representatives of the company. Company registrars are excluded and classified in 009.8.
CODOT
031.10

009.2 Officials of trade associations, trade unions, professional bodies and charities
Persons working as paid officials of trade or political associations, trade unions, professional bodies and charities. Secretaries of health authorities and boards are excluded and classified in 009.8.

CODOT
031.30, 031.40, 031.50, 031.60
031.99 pt. Remainder in 009.8

009.3 Property and estate managers
Persons managing estates and buying and selling real property on behalf of clients and employers. Estate agents are included. Property negotiators are excluded and classified in 057.6.

CODOT
062

009.4 Librarians, information officers
Persons organising and controlling library services, collecting and disseminating information. Government service intelligence officers are included.

CODOT
063.10, 063.30, 063.40

009.5 Legal service and related occupations
Persons undertaking legal service and related functions not elsewhere classified. Housing and planning inspectors, legal executives and barristers' and solicitors' managing clerks are included. Qualified solicitors are excluded and classified in 001.0.

CODOT
023, 029

009.6 Management consultants
Persons advising industrial, commercial, governmental and other organisations on various management and technical matters.

CODOT
049

009.7 Managers' personal assistants
Persons assisting with tasks or functions which form part of the duties of a director or manager.

CODOT
069.10

009.8 Professional workers and related supporting management and administration n.e.c.
Persons in professional and related occupations supporting management and administration not elsewhere classified including archivists, bursars, company registrars, curators, secretaries of health authorities and boards, trade-mark agents.

CODOT
031.99 pt. Remainder in 009.2
039 pt. Excludes—039.40, 039.50 included in 002.7
063.20, 063.50, 063.99
069.40, 069.50, 069.99

010.1 University academic staff
Persons lecturing or teaching at universities or university colleges.

CODOT
091

010.2 Teachers in establishments for further and higher education
Persons lecturing or teaching at technical colleges, colleges of education and further education.

CODOT
092, 093

011.0 Teachers n.e.c.
Persons teaching at nursery, primary and secondary schools. Teachers of physical training, diversionary activities; private tutors; private dancing and music teachers are excluded and classified in 018.4. Private driving instructors and sports instructors are excluded and classified in 018.3 and 023.1 respectively.

CODOT
094, 095, 096, 097

012.1 Vocational and industrial trainers
Persons giving instruction in manual, manipulative and other vocational skills and organising, controlling and advising on instruction within industrial, commercial and similar undertakings. Persons teaching people to drive heavy goods and public service vehicles and managers of government training centres are included.

CODOT
098

012.2 Education officers, school inspectors
Persons organising educational activities within a local education authority area. Inspectors of schools employed by central government are included.

CODOT
099.00, 099.01, 099.10

012.3 Social and behavioural scientists
Persons working as social and behavioural scientists including sociologists, historians, psychologists and geographers.

CODOT
101

013.1 Matrons, houseparents
Persons managing welfare institutions such as day or residential nurseries; working as houseparents in children's homes or establishments for young offenders; matrons or wardens of old people's homes. Matrons of schools and hospitals, hostels and lodging houses are excluded and classified in 016.0, and 044.4 respectively.

CODOT
102.18, 102.20, 102.22, 102.24

013.2 Playgroup leaders
Persons supervising play and other activities for pre-school age children. Persons assisting playgroup leaders are excluded and classified in 075.6.
CODOT
102.99 pt. Remainder in 013.3

013.3 Welfare occupations n.e.c.
Persons engaged in social welfare and related services, including housing managers, probation officers, safety engineers and officers, social workers, community workers, home help organisers and youth leaders.
CODOT
102 pt. Excludes—102.18, 102.20, 102.22, 102.24
—102.99 pt. included in 013.2

014.0 Clergy, ministers of religion
Clergy, ministers of religion and members of religious communities. Persons engaged in other professional or technical occupations, e.g. teaching, are excluded.
CODOT
103

015.1 Medical practitioners
Qualified persons diagnosing, prescribing and giving medical and surgical treatment for physical and mental disorders of the human body. Medical administrators and radiotherapists are included. Bacteriologists, pathologists and physiologists are excluded and classified in 024.1.
CODOT
111

015.2 Dental practitioners
Qualified persons treating by medicine or surgery dental or oral diseases and disorders.
CODOT
112

016.0 Nurse administrators, nurses
Persons providing, or training to provide, nursing or midwifery care. Hospital sisters and matrons, and school matrons are included. Nursery nurses and assistants; ward orderlies and first-aid attendants are excluded and classified in 068.2; and 070.2 respectively.
CODOT
113

017.1 Pharmacists
Qualified persons compounding and dispensing medicines. Pharmacists owning or managing retail chemists' shops are included. Dispensers are excluded and classified in 018.1.
CODOT
114

017.2 Medical radiographers
Persons employed as medical radiographers. Radiotherapists and industrial radiographers are excluded and classified in 015.1 and 030.2 respectively.
CODOT
115

017.3 Ophthalmic and dispensing opticians
Qualified persons testing eye sight and/or dispensing spectacles. Opticians owning or managing retail establishments are included. Orthoptists are excluded and classified in 017.6.
CODOT
116

017.4 Physiotherapists
Persons working as physiotherapists.
CODOT
117.10

017.5 Chiropodists
Persons working as chiropodists.
CODOT
119.10

017.6 Therapists n.e.c.
Persons carrying out therapeutic treatments and activities, not elsewhere classified, including occupational therapists, orthoptists, osteopaths, remedial gymnasts and speech therapists.
CODOT
117 pt. Excludes—117.10

018.1 Medical technicians, dental auxiliaries
Persons undertaking a variety of medical, dental, pharmaceutical and related tasks, including artificial limb fitters; dental auxiliaries and hygienists; dispensers; prosthetists; audiology, cardiological, encephalographic and pharmacy technicians. Dietitians, laboratory technicians and dental technicians are excluded and classified in 018.4, 030.1 and 107.2 respectively.
CODOT
119 pt. Excludes—119.05
—119.10 included in 017.5

018.2 Veterinarians
Professionally qualified persons treating and preventing animal diseases; treating animal ailments and injuries.
CODOT
121

018.3 **Driving instructors (not HGV)**
Persons teaching people to drive cars and light commercial vehicles who are included in the Register of Approved Driving Instructors. Persons teaching people to drive heavy goods and public service vehicles are excluded and classified in 012.1.

CODOT
099.05 pt. Remainder in 018.4
099.80

018.4 **Professional and related in education, welfare and health n.e.c.**
Persons employed in a variety of occupations in education, welfare and health, not elsewhere classified, including teachers of physical training and diversionary activities; private tutors; private dancing and music teachers; careers officers and vocational guidance specialists; dietitians, and animal health attendants and technicians.

CODOT
099 pt. Excludes—099.00, 099.01, 099.10 included in 012.2
—099.05 pt., 099.80 included in 018.3
109
119.05
129

019.0 **Authors, writers, journalists**
Persons writing original works of fiction or non-fiction; collecting news items and presenting them in a form for publication; writing advertising copy, plays, radio, film and television scripts, song lyrics, criticisms of artistic, etc. works. Book editors, translators, interpreters, literary agents and press officers are included. Public relations officers are excluded and classified in 005.2.

CODOT
151, 159

020.1 **Artists, commercial artists**
Persons creating artistic works by painting, drawing, engraving, sculpting, etc.; drawing cartoons and illustrations for advertisements; designing interior decorations, shop window displays and stage settings; restoring paintings, etc.. Window dressers and technical illustrators are excluded and classified in 020.4 and 029.0 respectively.

CODOT
161

020.2 **Industrial designers (not clothing)**
Persons creating non-technical designs for industrial and commercial products.

CODOT
162 pt. Excludes—162.00 pt., 162.20 included in 020.3

020.3 **Clothing designers**
Persons creating designs for clothing and fashion accessories.

CODOT
162.00 pt. Remainder in 020.2
162.20

020.4 **Window dressers**
Persons displaying merchandise in shop windows.

CODOT
179.40

021.1 **Actors, entertainers, singers, stage managers**
Persons directing or producing film, radio, television or stage plays or other shows; chief cameramen (films) and lighting managers; film editors; acting; dancing; entertaining; singing; announcing radio and television programmes; creating or arranging dances. Private dancing teachers are excluded and classified in 018.4.

CODOT
171
172.30, 172.99
173 pt. Excludes—173.10, 173.20
179.10, 179.20, 179.30

021.2 **Musicians**
Persons playing a musical instrument; writing or arranging music; conducting musical performances. Private music teachers are excluded and classified in 018.4.

CODOT
172.10, 172.20
173.10, 173.20

022.1 **Photographers, cameramen**
Persons operating still, television and cine cameras. Self-employed photographers are included. Chief cameramen (films) are excluded and classified in 021.1.

CODOT
174

022.2 **Sound and vision equipment operators**
Persons operating equipment, other than cameras, to record or project sound and/or vision.

CODOT
175

023.1 **Professional sportsmen, sports officials**
Persons managing teams, participating in and controlling sporting events and training sportsmen. Teachers of physical training are excluded and classified in 018.4.

CODOT
181

023.2 **Literary, artistic and sports workers n.e.c.**
Persons not elsewhere classified in literary, artistic and sporting occupations. Florists (including retail florists) are included.
CODOT
179.50, 179.60, 179.70, 179.99

024.1 **Biological scientists, biochemists**
Persons planning, directing and undertaking research, development, technical advisory, consultancy and related work in the field of biological science and the chemistry of living organisms. Only persons performing work normally requiring training of university degree standard are included, including biologists, botanists, entomologists, geneticists, microbiologists, pathologists, pharmacologists, physiologists and zoologists.
CODOT
211
219.00 pt. Remainder in 024.2 and 024.3
219.10

024.2 **Chemical scientists**
Persons planning, directing and undertaking research, development, analysis, technical advisory, consultancy and related work in the field of chemical science or in relation to the physical aspects of chemical structure and chemical change. Only persons performing work normally requiring training of university degree standard are included.
CODOT
212
219.00 pt. Remainder in 024.1 and 024.3
219.30

024.3 **Physical and geological scientists, mathematicians**
Persons planning, directing and undertaking research, development, technical advisory, consultancy and related work in the fields of physics, mathematics, the physics of living organisms and geology. Only persons performing work normally requiring training of university degree standard are included, including meteorologists, mineralogists and physicists.
CODOT
213
214
215
219.00 pt. Remainder in 024.1 and 024.2
219.20, 219.99

025.0 **Civil, structural, municipal, mining and quarrying engineers**
Persons planning, organising and technically supervising the construction and repair of roads, bridges, sanitation systems, reservoirs, other structures, mines and quarries or acting as adviser for such projects. Only persons performing work normally requiring training of university degree standard are included. Building inspectors are excluded and classified in 006.2.
CODOT
221, 222

026.1 **Mechanical and aeronautical engineers**
Persons planning and technically supervising the production or repair and maintenance of engines, machines, vehicles and other mechanical products or acting as adviser, including marine engineers and naval architects. Only persons performing work normally requiring training of university degree standard are included. Estimators are excluded and classified in 002.3.
CODOT
223 pt. Excludes—223.00 pt., 223.31, 223.32, 223.33, 223.34, 223.35, 223.36, 223.37, 223.39, 223.99 pt. included in 026.2

026.2 **Design and development engineers (mechanical)**
Persons originating, from product ideas or requirements, engineering designs in the field of general mechanical engineering.
CODOT
223.00 pt., 223.99 pt. Remainders in 026.1
223.31, 223.32, 223.33, 223.34, 223.35, 223.36, 223.37, 223.39

027.1 **Electrical engineers**
Persons designing, planning and technically supervising the production or repair and maintenance of electrical and telephonic equipment, technically supervising the operation of power stations or acting as adviser in electrical engineering matters. Only persons performing work normally requiring training of university degree standard are included. Systems engineers are excluded and classified in 004.2.
CODOT
224.12, 224.15, 224.22, 224.25, 224.32, 224.35, 224.42, 224.45, 224.52, 224.55, 224.62, 224.65, 224.72, 224.75
All remaining occupations of unit group 224 are divided between 027.1 and 027.2

027.2 **Electronic engineers**
Persons designing, planning and technically supervising the production or repair and maintenance of electronic equipment, including radio communication, radar and industrial electronic equipment. Only persons performing work normally requiring training of university degree standard are included.
CODOT
224 pt. Excludes—224.12, 224.15, 224.22, 224.25, 224.32, 224.35, 224.42, 224.45, 224.52, 224.55, 224.62, 224.65, 224.72, 224.75
All remaining occupations of unit group 224 are divided between 027.1 and 027.2

028.1 **Chemical engineers**
Persons planning, directing, undertaking research and development and related work in respect of chemical manufacture. Only persons performing work normally requiring training of university degree standard are included.
CODOT
225

028.2 **Production engineers**
Persons overseeing the technical aspects of production programmes. Only persons performing work normally requiring training of university degree standard are included.
CODOT
226

028.3 **Planning and quality control engineers**
Persons planning production schedules and work procedures in production fields; planning procedures for the maintenance of standards. Only persons performing work normally requiring training of university degree standard are included.
CODOT
259.10, 259.40

028.4 **Engineers n.e.c.**
Engineers performing work normally requiring training of university degree standard developing, etc., all types of industrial processes not elsewhere classified. Environmental and traffic engineers are included. Ships' surveyors and naval architects are excluded and classified in 006.3 and 026.1 respectively.
CODOT
229

028.5 **Metallurgists**
Persons studying the properties of metals, developing, etc. processes for the production of metals from their ores and advising on their utilisation. Only persons performing work normally requiring training of university degree standard are included.
CODOT
231.05

028.6 **Technologists n.e.c.**
Persons planning, directing, undertaking research and development, and related work in particular materials products and processes, other than in engineering; including textile and rubber technologists, fuel technologists, brewers and technologists not elsewhere classified. Only persons performing work normally requiring training of university degree standard are included.
CODOT
231 pt. Excludes—231.05

029.0 **Draughtsmen**
Persons preparing technical drawings, plans, maps, charts and similar items, including technical illustrators. Tracers and drawing office assistants are excluded and classified in 046.2.
CODOT
253

030.1 **Laboratory technicians**
Persons carrying out technical functions requiring the application of established or prescribed procedures in physical, chemical, biological, botanical, medical and other laboratories. Laboratory assistants are excluded and classified in 138.1.
CODOT
254

030.2 **Engineering technicians, technician engineers**
Persons performing a variety of engineering technical functions, (excluding architectural, constructional and related functions); technically controlling the installation and testing of engineering systems, diagnosing and correcting complex faults. Industrial radiographers are included.
CODOT
256

031.1 **Architects, town planners**
Professionally qualified persons designing buildings; planning the layout of urban and rural areas or acting as adviser in these matters. Housing and planning inspectors, and architectural and town planning assistants are excluded and classified in 009.5, and 033.1 respectively.
CODOT
251

031.2 **Quantity surveyors**
Persons advising on financial and contractual matters relating to, and preparing bills of quantities for, construction projects; including technical assistants to quantity surveyors.
CODOT
255.10, 255.20

031.3 **Building, land and mining surveyors**
Persons conducting building, land and mining surveys. Insurance surveyors are excluded and classified in 033.3.
CODOT
252.10, 252.30, 252.40

032.1 **Aircraft flight deck officers**
Persons flying and navigating aircraft and servicing them in flight. Hovercraft pilots and navigators are excluded and classified in 033.3.
CODOT
241

032.2 **Air traffic planners and controllers**
Persons preparing flight plans, authorising flight departures and maintaining contact with aircraft to provide safe and orderly movement of air traffic. Air traffic control assistants are excluded and classified in 051.3.
CODOT
242

032.3 **Deck, engineering and radio officers and pilots, ship**
Persons commanding and navigating seagoing ships and craft operating in coastal and inland waters; organising, directing and supervising the activities of deck ratings, advising ships' masters on the navigation of ships in hazardous waters. Pilots and navigators of hovercraft and skippers of fishing vessels are excluded and classified in 033.3 and 044.4 respectively.
CODOT
243, 244

033.1 Architectural and town planning technicians
Persons assisting architects and town planners by carrying out technical functions related to the design of buildings and the planning of urban and rural areas.
CODOT
255.30, 255.40

033.2 Building and civil engineering technicians
Persons performing a variety of functions requiring the application of prescribed engineering procedures in the field of civil engineering, including structural engineering and building.
CODOT
255.50, 255.99

033.3 Technical and related workers n.e.c.
Persons carrying out a variety of technical and scientific occupations not elsewhere classified including hovercraft pilots and navigators, marine surveyors, insurance surveyors and patent agents and examiners.
CODOT
249
252.20, 252.50, 252.99
259.20, 259.30, 259.50, 259.60, 259.70, 259.99

034.0 Production, works and maintenance managers, works foremen
Persons managing the work and resources necessary for such industrial operations as production, processing and maintenance. Post Office area engineers and engineers directly responsible for production and maintenance in factories and maintenance in transport undertakings, mines, etc. and works, general and senior foremen in manufacturing are included.
CODOT
271
272
273 pt. Excludes—273.20 pt. included in 038.1

035.1 Managers in building and contracting
Managers in construction, including works, general and senior foremen and persons responsible for civil engineering work on the railways and building maintenance.
CODOT
274 pt. Excludes—274.35

035.2 Clerks of works
Persons representing clients on construction projects to ensure contractors' compliance with design specifications and standards.
CODOT
274.35

036.1 Managers in mining and public utilities
Managers in mining, quarrying, and in the production and supply of electricity, gas and water. Mining overmen are included.
CODOT
275, 276

036.2 Transport managers
Persons managing activities and resources necessary for the transportation of passengers and freight.
CODOT
277 pt. Excludes—277.32, 277.34, 277.36, 277.38, 277.40

036.3 Stores controllers
Persons managing activities and resources for maintaining stocks of material, products or commodities and for storing and issuing such items. Stores managers are included.
CODOT
277.34, 277.36

036.4 Managers in warehousing and materials handling n.e.c.
Persons organising and directing activities for the receipt, warehousing and despatch of goods, commodities, products and other items. Freight managers and wharf managers are included.
CODOT
277.32, 277.38, 277.40

037.1 Credit controllers
Persons organising offices responsible for credit control and debt collection.
CODOT
281.06

037.2 Office managers n.e.c.
Persons managing offices carrying out clerical and related functions; including computer operations managers, medical records officers, sales office managers, bank managers, building society managers. Owners and managers of travel agencies and private employment agencies are included. Insurance office managers are included but managers of local agents are excluded and classified in 057.6. Sub-postmasters are included except the self-employed who are excluded and classified in 038.4.
CODOT
281 pt. Excludes—281.02 pt. included in 007.2, 008.0 and 045.1
  —281.28, 281.30, 281.32 included in 007.2
  —281.34 included in 008.2

038.1 Garage proprietors
Persons owning garages and filling stations.
CODOT
273.20 pt. Remainder in 034.0
283.99 pt. Remainder in 038.4 and 044.2

038.2 **Butchers (managers and proprietors)**
Persons owning and managing butchers' shops.
CODOT
283.40 pt., 283.60 pt. Remainders in 038.3 and 038.4

038.3 **Fishmongers (managers and proprietors)**
Persons owning and managing fishmongers' shops.
CODOT
283.40 pt., 283.60 pt. Remainders in 038.2 and 038.4

038.4 **Other proprietors and managers (sales)**
Persons owning or managing wholesale and retail establishments. Pawnbrokers, self-employed sub-postmasters and managers of mail order establishments and trading stamp redemption offices are included. Pharmacists, opticians (ophthalmic and dispensing) and managers of laundry and dry cleaning receiving shops are excluded and classified in 017.1, 017.3 and 044.2 respectively.
CODOT
282
283 pt. Excludes—283.40 pt., 283.60 pt. included in 038.2 and 038.3
—283.99 pt. included in 038.1 and 044.2

039.1 **Hotel and residential club managers**
Persons owning or managing boarding houses, hotels and residential clubs. Pursers are included.
CODOT
284.05, 284.10, 284.15

039.2 **Publicans**
Persons owning or managing public houses. 'Innkeepers' so described are excluded and classified in 044.4.
CODOT
284.70

039.3 **Restaurateurs**
Persons owning or managing restaurants and canteens.
CODOT
284.30, 284.35, 284.40, 284.45, 284.50, 284.55, 284.60, 284.65

039.4 **Club stewards**
Persons organising the bar and catering services at non-residential clubs.
CODOT
284.80

039.5 **Entertainment and sports managers**
Persons owning or managing sporting, recreational and amenity services including cinemas and theatres, including park superintendents. Producers and directors of stage, television, radio and film productions are excluded and classified in 021.1.
CODOT
285

040.0 **Farmers, horticulturists, farm managers**
Persons owning or managing farms or market gardens including fruit farmers, poultry farmers, agricultural contractors and tenants of a croft or holding under, and in terms of, the Crofters (Scotland) Act, 1955, not elsewhere classified. Fish farmers and trainers of horses are excluded and classified in 044.4.
CODOT
286 pt. Excludes—286.40, 286.50, 286.55, 286.60, 286.99 pt. included in 044.4

041.0 **Officers, UK armed forces**
All full time commissioned officers of the armed forces of the United Kingdom.
CODOT
287.10 pt. Remainder in 042.0

042.0 **Officers, foreign and Commonwealth armed forces**
All full time commissioned officers of the armed forces of foreign and Commonwealth countries.
CODOT
287.10 pt. Remainder in 041.0

043.1 **Prison officers (chief officers and above)**
Governors and chief officers in prisons or similar institutions. Wardens of detention centres are included.
CODOT
288.40

043.2 **Police officers (inspectors and above)**
Persons organising a specific geographical or functional area of general or specialised police work.
CODOT
288.10

043.3 **Fire service officers**
Persons organising a specific physical or functional area of a statutory or private fire brigade. Salvage corps senior officers are included.
CODOT
288.20, 288.30

044.1 **Proprietors and managers, service flats, holiday flats, caravan sites, etc.**
Persons owning or managing service flats, holiday flats and chalets, holiday camps, and camping and caravan sites.
CODOT
284.99 pt. Remainder in 044.4

044.2 **Managers of laundry and dry cleaning receiving shops**
Managers of launderettes and premises used for the receipt and despatch of items for laundering and dry cleaning.
CODOT
283.99 pt. Remainder in 038.1 and 038.4

044.3 **Hairdressers' and barbers' managers and proprietors**
Persons owning and managing hairdressing, beauty treatment or similar establishments.
CODOT
289.40

044.4 **Managers n.e.c.**
Managers not elsewhere classified, including managers of gardening/grounds keeping services; tree surgeons; managers of animal establishments (other than farm livestock); head housekeepers of large hotels, hospitals, institutions or residential buildings; managers of residential hostels for students, hikers or wanderers; registrars of educational establishments; skippers of fishing vessels; fish farmers; fieldmen; ambulance station superintendents; innkeepers; administration and general service managers. Owners and managers of laundries, dry cleaning works (not receiving shops) and firms hiring or servicing machinery and equipment, undertaking cleaning and related services are included.
CODOT
279
284.20, 284.25, 284.75
284.99 pt. Remainder in 044.1
286.40, 286.50, 286.55, 286.60
286.99 pt. Remainder in 040.0
288.50, 288.99
289 pt. Excludes—289.40

045.1 **Civil Service executive officers**
Persons of the basic grade of executive officer in the Civil Service or of equivalent rank. Customs and Excise Officers, waterguards, preventive officers, immigration officers are excluded and classified in 006.3.
CODOT
281.02 pt. Remainder in 007.2, 008.0 and 037.2
310.80 pt. Remainder in 045.3 and 045.4

045.2 **Supervisors of stores and despatch clerks**
Supervisors of persons classified in 046.1.
CODOT
310.50 pt. Remainder in 045.4

045.3 **Supervisors of tracers, drawing office assistants**
Supervisors of persons classified in 046.2.
CODOT
310.80 pt. Remainder in 045.1 and 045.4

045.4 **Supervisors of other clerks and cashiers (not retail)**
Supervisors of persons classified in 046.3.
CODOT
310 pt. Excludes—310.20 pt. included in 045.5
—310.50 pt. included in 045.2
—310.80 pt. included in 045.1 and 045.3

045.5 **Supervisors of retail shop cashiers, check-out and cash and wrap operators**
Supervisors of persons classified in 047.0.
CODOT
310.20 pt. Remainder in 045.4

046.1 **Stores and despatch clerks**
Persons checking and recording details of stock movements, preparing requisitions or despatch documents for ordered goods.
CODOT
314.15, 314.20

046.2 **Tracers, drawing office assistants**
Persons employed as tracers or drawing office assistants.
CODOT
319.28

046.3 **Other clerks and cashiers (not retail)**
Persons keeping records of cash; collecting cash or issuing tickets at theatres, etc., taking readings of meters and emptying coin boxes; performing all types of office work. Proof readers, ADP tape librarians, library clerks and assistants, debt and rent collectors are included but credit agents and collector salesmen are excluded and classified in 057.4. Civil Servants and local government officers, etc., so described are included.
CODOT
311
312 pt. Excludes—312.90, 312.91 included in 047.0
313
314 pt. Excludes—314.15, 314.20
315
316
319 pt. Excludes—319.28
—319.56, 319.58, 319.60 included in 049.1

047.0 **Retail shop cashiers, check-out and cash and wrap operators**
Persons employed as cashiers, check-out and cash and wrap operators in retail shops and cafés.
CODOT
312.90, 312.91

048.1 **Supervisors of typists, shorthand writers, secretaries**
Supervisors of persons classified in 049.2.
CODOT
320

048.2 **Supervisors of office machine operators**
Supervisors of persons classified in 050.0.
CODOT
330

048.3 **Supervisors of telephone operators**
Supervisors of persons classified in 051.2.
CODOT
340.10

048.4 **Supervisors of radio and telegraph operators**
Supervisors of persons classified in 051.3.
CODOT
340.20, 340.30
340.99 pt. Remainder in 052.2

049.1 **Receptionists**
Persons receiving callers at commercial, industrial and other establishments. Hotel, dental and medical receptionists are included.
CODOT
319.56, 319.58, 319.60

049.2 **Typists, shorthand writers, secretaries**
Persons typing; taking shorthand records; acting as personal secretary. 'Secretaries' so described are included. Proprietors and managers of typewriting bureaux, if not typists, are excluded and classified in 057.6 and 044.4 respectively.
CODOT
321, 322

050.0 **Office machine operators**
Persons operating office machines, including photo and blue printers; duplicator, key punch, computer and peripheral equipment operators. Offset duplicating machine operators are excluded and classified in 107.9.
CODOT
331, 332, 333, 334, 339

051.1 **Telephonist receptionists**
Persons combining the functions of operating a telephone switchboard and receiving callers at commercial, industrial and other establishments.
CODOT
341.20 pt. Remainder in 051.2

051.2 **Telephone operators**
Persons operating telephone switchboards.
CODOT
341.10
341.20 pt. Remainder in 051.1

051.3 **Radio and telegraph operators**
Persons operating radio, telegraph and teleprinter equipment to transmit and receive signals and messages. Air traffic control assistants are included.
CODOT
342

052.1 **Supervisors of postmen, mail sorters**
Supervisors of persons classified in 053.1.
CODOT
340.40 pt. Remainder in 052.2

052.2 **Supervisors of messengers**
Supervisors of persons classified in 053.2.
CODOT
340.40 pt. Remainder in 052.1
340.99 pt. Remainder in 048.4

053.1 **Postmen, mail sorters**
Persons collecting, delivering and sorting mail.
CODOT
343.10, 343.50

053.2 **Messengers**
Persons collecting and distributing correspondence within an establishment or delivering messages, etc., elsewhere as instructed. Delivery and errand boys are included.
CODOT
343.90, 343.99

054.1 **Supervisors of shop salesmen and assistants**
Supervisors of persons included in 055.1.
CODOT
360.10 pt. Remainder in 054.2
360.99

054.2 Supervisors of petrol pump, forecourt attendants
Supervisors of persons included in 055.3.
CODOT
360.10 pt. Remainder in 054.1

054.3 Supervisors of roundsmen, van salesmen
Supervisors of persons included in 056.0.
CODOT
360.20

055.1 Shop salesmen and assistants
Persons selling goods and services to customers in shops and similar establishments. Sub-post office assistants, programme sellers and assistants in take-away food shops are included. Cash and wrap operators are excluded and classified in 047.0.
CODOT
361 pt. Excludes—361.92
369.99 pt. Remainder in 055.2

055.2 Shelf fillers
Persons replenishing stocks of goods in self service stores and, where required, marking prices on goods before displaying.
CODOT
369.99 pt. Remainder in 055.1

055.3 Petrol pump, forecourt attendants
Persons selling petrol, etc., at a petrol service station or garage.
CODOT
361.92

056.0 Roundsmen, van salesmen
Persons delivering and selling food, drink and other goods and collecting and delivering laundry. Mobile shop salesmen are included. Coal delivery drivers are excluded and classified in 152.2.
CODOT
362
363.10

057.1 Importers, exporters, commodity brokers
Persons acting as agents in the purchase, sale, import and export of commodities in bulk, including ship and air brokers, and principals and managers of import and export agencies.
CODOT
379.10, 379.20, 379.30, 379.40, 379.50
379.99 pt. Remainder in 057.6

057.2 Market and street traders and assistants
Persons selling goods, other than refreshments, from a stall or barrow in a market place or street (including self-employed traders); hawkers. Trolleymen selling refreshments are excluded and classified in 066.1.
CODOT
363.20
363.99 pt. Remainder in 057.3 and 057.4

057.3 Scrap dealers, general dealers, rag and bone merchants
Persons trading in scrap metal, rags, waste materials, etc. (including self-employed traders).
CODOT
363.99 pt. Remainder in 057.2 and 057.4

057.4 Credit agents, collector salesmen
Persons visiting private households to solicit orders and collect payments for goods and services. Debt and rent collectors are excluded and classified in 046.3.
CODOT
363.99 pt. Remainder in 057.2 and 057.3
379.90, 379.95

057.5 Sales representatives
Persons soliciting orders for machinery, equipment and materials; the wholesale provision of food, drink, clothing and other consumer goods. Manufacturers' agents are included.
CODOT
371, 372

057.6 Sales representatives (property and services), other agents
Persons selling property and soliciting orders for insurance, financial, security, cleaning and other services. Auctioneers, demonstrators, way-leave officers, telephone canvassers and property negotiators are included. Estate agents are excluded and classified in 009.3.
CODOT
369.10
373
379.99 pt. Remainder in 057.1

058.0 NCOs and other ranks, UK armed forces
All full time members of the armed forces of the United Kingdom, except commissioned officers who are excluded and classified in 041.0.
CODOT
400.10 pt., 401.10 pt. Remainders in 059.0

059.0   **NCOs and other ranks, foreign and Commonwealth armed forces**
All full time members of the armed forces of foreign and Commonwealth countries, except commissioned officers who are excluded and classified in 042.0.
CODOT
400.10 pt., 401.10 pt. Remainders in 058.0

060.1   **Police sergeants**
Sergeants employed by statutory police authorities, including railway, dock and airport police.
CODOT
410.10, 410.20

060.2   **Fire service supervisors**
Supervisors of persons included in 061.2.
CODOT
410.30

060.3   **Prison service principal officers**
Principal officers in the prison service.
CODOT
410.40
410.99 pt. Remainder in 060.4, 060.5 and 060.6

060.4   **Supervisors of security guards and officers, patrolmen, watchmen**
Supervisors of persons included in 062.1.
CODOT
410.50
410.99 pt. Remainder in 060.3, 060.5 and 060.6

060.5   **Supervisors of traffic wardens**
Supervisors of persons included in 062.2.
CODOT
410.99 pt. Remainder in 060.3, 060.4 and 060.6

060.6   **Supervisors of security and protective service workers n.e.c.**
Supervisors of persons included in 062.3.
CODOT
410.99 pt. Remainder in 060.3, 060.4 and 060.5

061.1   **Policemen (below sergeant)**
Uniformed members and detectives employed by statutory police authorities, including railway, dock and airport police.
CODOT
411

061.2   **Firemen**
Persons fighting fires, advising on fire hazards and salvaging goods during or after fires as members of public or private fire brigades. Woodland fire fighting patrols are excluded and classified in 080.0.
CODOT
412

061.3   **Prison officers (below principal officer)**
Persons, below principal officers, guarding inmates in prisons, borstals, detention centres or young offenders' institutions.
CODOT
419.20

062.1   **Security guards and officers, patrolmen, watchmen**
Persons employed in protecting persons, premises and property from injury, damage or theft. Store, hotel and private detectives, gate-keepers, park keepers and estate rangers are included.
CODOT
419 pt. Excludes—419.10, 419.30, 419.99 pt. included in 062.3
            —419.20 included in 061.3
            —419.93

062.2   **Traffic wardens**
Persons patrolling areas to detect and prevent infringements of local parking regulations. Parking meter attendants are included.
CODOT
419.93

062.3   **Security and protective service workers n.e.c.**
Persons engaged in security services not elsewhere classified. Coastguards, bailiffs, life guards, museum and art gallery attendants and road crossing attendants are included.
CODOT
419.10, 419.30
419.99 pt. Remainder in 062.1

063.1   **Supervisors of chefs, cooks**
Supervisors of persons classified in 064.0.
CODOT
430.10, 430.20, 430.30

063.2   **Supervisors of waiters, waitresses**
Supervisors of persons classified in 065.1.
CODOT
430.40, 430.50

063.3 **Supervisors of barmen, barmaids**
Supervisors of persons classified in 065.2.
CODOT
430.60

063.4 **Supervisors of counter hands, assistants**
Supervisors of persons classified in 066.1.
CODOT
430.70

064.0 **Chefs, cooks**
Persons preparing and cooking meals. Persons peeling vegetables, washing dishes, etc.; cook-housekeepers; and cooks employed in food products manufacturing are excluded and classified in 066.2; 068.1; and 098.7 respectively.
CODOT
431

065.1 **Waiters, waitresses**
Persons guiding diners to tables; serving food and refreshments at tables.
CODOT
432

065.2 **Barmen, barmaids**
Persons serving drinks at or from the licensed bars of clubs, hotels, public houses and similar establishments; including bar stewards. Club stewards and wine waiters are excluded and classified in 039.4 and 065.1 respectively.
CODOT
433

066.1 **Counter hands, assistants**
Persons serving food and other refreshments from counters of self service restaurants, buffets, cafés, canteens and similar establishments. Trolleymen selling refreshments and school meals assistants and attendants are included. School helpers, mid-day assistants and school meals supervisors are excluded and classified in 068.3.
CODOT
434

066.2 **Kitchen porters, hands**
Persons preparing vegetables, washing crockery, etc. and performing various cleaning, fetching, carrying and similar tasks in kitchens.
CODOT
435.10, 435.20, 435.30

067.1 **Housekeepers (non-domestic)**
Persons acting as housekeepers in hotels, schools and similar non-private establishments.
CODOT
440.10 pt. Remainder in 067.2

067.2 **Supervisors of other domestic and school helpers**
Supervisors of persons included in 068.3.
CODOT
440.10 pt. Remainder in 067.1
440.20

067.3 **Supervisors of travel stewards and attendants**
Supervisors of persons included in 069.1.
CODOT
440.30, 440.40
440.99 pt. Remainder in 067.4 and 067.5

067.4 **Supervisors of hospital porters**
Supervisors of persons included in 069.2.
CODOT
440.99 pt. Remainder in 067.3 and 067.5

067.5 **Supervisors of hotel porters**
Supervisors of persons included in 069.3.
CODOT
440.99 pt. Remainder in 067.3 and 067.4

067.6 **Supervisors of ambulancemen**
Supervisors of persons included in 070.1.
CODOT
440.50 pt. Remainder in 067.7

067.7 **Supervisors of hospital, ward orderlies**
Supervisors of persons included in 070.2.
CODOT
440.50 pt. Remainder in 067.6

068.1 **Domestic housekeepers**
Persons acting as housekeepers in private homes. Cook-housekeepers are included.
CODOT
441.05

068.2 Nursery nurses
Persons caring for healthy children in day or residential nurseries, children's homes, maternity hospitals or units or similar establishments, including nursery assistants. Nannies and children's nurses employed in private households are excluded and classified in 068.3.
CODOT
441.25, 441.30

068.3 Other domestic and school helpers
Persons attending to the personal needs and comforts of others, cleaning and tidying living quarters in private households, hotels, hospitals and similar establishments; assisting teachers with non-teaching activities and supervising children in playgrounds and dining rooms. Companions, domestics, nannies and children's nurses in private housholds and ward maids are included. Playgroup leaders are excluded and classified in 013.2.
CODOT
441 pt. Excludes—441.05, 441.25, 441.30
—441.35, 441.50, 441.99 included in 075.6

069.1 Travel stewards and attendants
Persons attending to the needs and comforts of travellers and conducting or assisting tourists on holiday.
CODOT
442

069.2 Hospital porters
Persons working as porters in hospitals.
CODOT
449.30

069.3 Hotel porters
Persons employed as porters in hotels or similar residential establishments including hall porters and page boys.
CODOT
449 pt. Excludes—449.30
—449.99 included in 075.6

070.1 Ambulancemen
Persons transporting sick, injured or convalescent persons by ambulance; giving first aid during journey. Ambulance station superintendents and first aid attendants are excluded and classified in 044.4 and 070.2 respectively.
CODOT
443.20

070.2 Hospital, ward orderlies
Persons working as orderlies or attendants in hospitals and similar institutions; first aid attendants; care assistants in homes for the elderly or infirm. Ward maids are excluded and classified in 068.3.
CODOT
443 pt. Excludes—443.20

071.1 Supervisors of caretakers
Supervisors of persons included in 072.1.
CODOT
450.30 pt. Remainder in 071.4

071.2 Supervisors of cleaners, window cleaners, chimney sweeps, road sweepers
Supervisors of persons included in 072.2.
CODOT
450.10, 450.99

071.3 Supervisors of railway stationmen
Supervisors of persons included in 075.1.
CODOT
450.20

071.4 Supervisors of lift and car park attendants
Supervisors of persons included in 075.2.
CODOT
450.30 pt. Remainder in 071.1

072.1 Caretakers
Persons taking care of premises and keeping them in a clean and orderly condition.
CODOT
451

072.2 Cleaners, window cleaners, chimney sweeps, road sweepers
Persons cleaning interiors of aircraft, buildings, road vehicles, ships and trains; cleaning chimneys and windows; manually cleaning streets and washing down vehicle exteriors. Mechanical road sweeper drivers and vehicle washing plant attendants are excluded and classified in 152.3 and 161.2 respectively.
CODOT
452

073.0 Hairdressing supervisors
Supervisors of persons classified in 074.0.
CODOT
470.10

074.0 Hairdressers, barbers
Persons cutting, styling and shampooing hair. Manicurists and beauticians are excluded and classified in 075.6.
CODOT
471.05, 471.10

075.1 Railway stationmen
Persons performing various duties on railway station platforms, including ticket collectors, porters, stationmen and railmen (so described).
CODOT
453

075.2 Lift and car park attendants
Persons operating passenger or goods lifts; controlling parking of vehicles in public or private parking areas.
CODOT
459.30, 459.45

075.3 Launderers, dry cleaners, pressers
Persons washing, dry cleaning, ironing and pressing clothing, household linen, carpets and similar articles; including persons directly supervising these activities. 'Dyers and cleaners' are included but job dyers are excluded and classified in 087.7.
CODOT
460, 461

075.4 Undertakers
Persons owning or managing funeral services.
CODOT
470.20

075.5 Bookmakers, betting shop managers
Persons offering odds and accepting bets on the results of sporting or other events or directly supervising these activities. Turf accountants and owners and managers of betting establishments are included.
CODOT
470.40

075.6 Service workers n.e.c.
Persons performing manual tasks in mortuaries; assisting with funerals; giving beauty treatments; attending baths and toilets; operating entertainments such as amusement arcades, bingo halls, cinemas, dance halls, fairgrounds, ice rinks and theatres; providing personal services not elsewhere classified. Playgroup assistants, pest control operators, wardrobe mistresses, commissionaires, ushers and usherettes are included.
CODOT
430.99
435.40, 435.99
439
441.35, 441.50, 441.99
449.99
459 pt. Excludes—459.30, 459.45
470.30, 470.99
471 pt. Excludes—471.05, 471.10 included in 074.0
472
479

076.1 Farm foremen
Supervisors of persons included in 077.0.
CODOT
500.10, 500.20, 500.30

076.2 Horticultural foremen
Supervisors of persons included in 078.1.
CODOT
500.50

076.3 Foremen gardeners and groundsmen
Supervisors of persons included in 078.2.
CODOT
500.60

076.4 Agricultural machinery foremen
Supervisors of persons included in 079.0.
CODOT
500.70

076.5 Forestry foremen
Supervisors of persons included in 080.0.
CODOT
500.80

076.6 Other foremen in farming and related
Supervisors of persons included in 083.0.
CODOT
500.40, 500.99

077.0 Farm workers
Persons carrying out general farm duties in the cultivation of arable crops and in tending and breeding farm animals. Agricultural workers, cowmen, pigmen, poultrymen, shepherds and farm stockmen are included. Hatchery workers and persons tending horses, dogs, mink and zoo animals are excluded and classified in 083.0.
CODOT
501
502.02, 502.04, 502.06, 502.08, 502.10, 502.50

078.1 Horticultural workers
Persons cultivating plants and crops grown in glass houses, nurseries, market gardens and orchards. Propagators and persons employed as bulb, mushroom or watercress growers are included.
CODOT
503

078.2 Gardeners, groundsmen
Persons laying out and tending public or private gardens (excluding market gardens) and sports grounds, landscape gardeners, turf layers and cutters and green keepers are included. Managers of gardening/grounds keeping services and park superintendents are excluded and classified in 044.4 and 039.5 respectively.
CODOT
504

079.0 Agricultural machinery drivers, operators
Persons driving and operating agricultural tractors, implements and machines. Agricultural contractors and managers are excluded and classified in 040.0.
CODOT
505

080.0 Forestry workers
Persons carrying out tasks related to the cultivation and harvesting of trees, guarding against fire or other damage. Forest rangers, osier growers, tree fellers, woodcutters and woodmen are included. Persons tending fruit trees and peat cutters are excluded and classified in 078.1 and 083.0 respectively.
CODOT
506
509.20

081.0 Supervisors, mates—fishing
Supervisors of persons included in 082.0.
CODOT
510

082.0 Fishermen
Persons engaged in catching fish at sea; cultivating and harvesting shellfish; breeding and rearing fish. Trawlermen, oyster bed workers, fish hatchers, harpooners (whales), seaweed and mussel gatherers are included. Fishing vessel skippers are excluded and classified in 044.4.
CODOT
511, 519

083.0 All other in farming and related
Persons performing various tasks related to farming, horticulture and forestry; tending horses, dogs, mink and zoo animals; including gamekeepers, beekeepers, hatchery workers, canine beauticians, huntsmen, inseminators, livestock classifiers, peat cutters, seasonal crop harvesters and mushroom pickers.
CODOT
502 pt. Excludes—502.02, 502.04, 502.06, 502.08, 502.10, 502.50 included in 077.0
509 pt. Excludes—509.20 included in 080.0

084.1 Foremen—Tannery production workers
Foremen of persons included in 085.1.
CODOT
530

084.2 Foremen—Shoe repairers
Foremen of persons included in 085.2.
CODOT
660.60

084.3 Foremen—Leather cutters and sewers, footwear lasters, makers, finishers
Foremen of persons included in 085.3.
CODOT
660 pt. Excludes—660.40, 660.60

084.4 Foremen—Other making and repairing, leather
Foremen of persons included in 107.7.
CODOT
660.40

085.1 Tannery production workers
Persons treating hides, skins and pelts to prepare them for making up into leather, skin and fur products.
CODOT
531

085.2 Shoe repairers
Persons repairing worn and damaged footwear.
CODOT
666

085.3 **Leather cutters and sewers, footwear lasters, makers, finishers**
Persons cutting out component parts, sewing, making up and decorating footwear (including leather substitute and rubber), and leather and leather substitute goods, other than garments; performing finishing tasks in the manufacture of footwear, including footwear examiners. Persons moulding rubber footwear, and assemblers of footwear and leather goods are excluded and classified in 097.1 and 138.12 respectively.

CODOT
661, 662, 663, 665
669.14, 669.60, 669.62, 669.64, 669.66, 669.94

086.1 **Foremen—Preparatory fibre processors**
Foremen of persons included in 087.1.

CODOT
540.05

086.2 **Foremen—Spinners, doublers, twisters**
Foremen of persons included in 087.2.

CODOT
540.10
540.15 pt. Remainder in 086.3

086.3 **Foremen—Winders, reelers**
Foremen of persons included in 087.3.

CODOT
540.15 pt. Remainder in 086.2

086.4 **Foremen—Warp preparers**
Foremen of persons included in 087.4.

CODOT
540.20

086.5 **Foremen—Weavers**
Foremen of persons included in 087.5.

CODOT
540.25
540.99 pt. Remainder in 086.9

086.6 **Foremen—Knitters**
Foremen of persons included in 087.6.

CODOT
540.30

086.7 **Foremen—Bleachers, dyers, finishers**
Foremen of persons included in 087.7.

CODOT
540.35, 540.40

086.8 **Foremen—Menders, darners**
Foremen of persons included in 087.8.

CODOT
540.45

086.9 **Foremen—Other material processing, textiles**
Foremen of persons included in 098.4.

CODOT
540.50, 540.55, 540.60
540.99 pt. Remainder in 086.5

087.1 **Preparatory fibre processors**
Persons preparing fibres for spinning into yarn and making into non-woven fabric; dressing bristles and fibres for use as brush fillings. Carders, combers, drawers, fibre openers and rag grinders are included. Carbonisers, washers, driers and fur fibre mixers; persons maintaining textile fibre preparing machinery, card grinders; and wool sorters are excluded and classified in 098.4; 131.9; and 138.11 respectively.

CODOT
541

087.2 **Spinners, doublers, twisters**
Persons operating spinning and doubling (twisting) machines in the manufacture of yarn and thread, including chenille makers and piecers. Setter fitter-mechanics of textile machinery are excluded and classified in 117.0.

CODOT
542 pt. Excludes—542.65, 542.80, 542.90, 542.92, 542.99 pt. included in 087.3

087.3 **Winders, reelers**
Persons operating machines which wind yarn and thread from one package to another, including yarn curlers and openers, twine ballers and spoolers. Setter fitter-mechanics of textile machinery are excluded and classified in 117.0.

CODOT
542.65, 542.80, 542.90, 542.92
542.99 pt. Remainder in 087.2

087.4 **Warp preparers**
Persons operating machines which wind warp yarn on to packages and beams; arranging warp threads ready for dyeing, knitting or weaving. Setter fitter-mechanics of textile machinery are excluded and classified in 117.0.

CODOT
543

087.5 **Weavers**
Persons weaving yarn of natural and man-made fibres into carpets and fabric; including lace weavers and net makers. Warp lace makers and setter fitter-mechanics of textile machinery are excluded and classified in 087.6 and 117.0 respectively.
CODOT
544

087.6 **Knitters**
Persons operating knitting machines or knitting by hand, including warp lace makers. Setter fitter-mechanics of textile machinery are excluded and classified in 117.0.
CODOT
545

087.7 **Bleachers, dyers, finishers**
Persons bleaching, dyeing and otherwise treating textile fabrics, yarn, cloth and goods including gassers, calenderers, stenterers and dyers of piece goods. Carbonisers, driers, fullers, washers; and textile printers are excluded and classified in 098.4; and 107.9 respectively.
CODOT
546 pt. Excludes—546.50, 546.85, 546.86, 546.89 included in 098.4

087.8 **Menders, darners**
Persons rectifying faults arising during the course of manufacture of textile goods; repairing worn garments and other used articles by invisible mending. Burlers are included.
CODOT
547

088.0 **Foremen—Chemical processing**
Foremen of persons included in 089.0.
CODOT
560

089.0 **Chemical, gas and petroleum process plant operators**
Persons operating plant to process chemical and related materials by heat treatment, chemical reaction, crushing, milling, mixing and mechanically separating. Persons evaporating brine, calcining and sintering metallic ores, distilling alcoholic beverages, softening water; coal gas and coke oven furnacemen are included. Man-made fibre spinners; mineral crushers at mines and quarries; millers of ceramic materials and colour mixers; and fillers of cartridges, detonators and fireworks are excluded and classified in, 098.1; 098.3; 098.9; and 107.12 respectively.
CODOT
561

090.1 **Foremen—Bakers, flour confectioners**
Foremen of persons included in 091.0.
CODOT
570.10

090.2 **Foremen—Butchers, meat cutters**
Foremen of persons included in 092.1.
CODOT
570.20

090.3 **Foremen—Fishmongers, poultry dressers**
Foremen of persons included in 092.2.
CODOT
570.30

090.4 **Foremen—Brewery and vinery process workers**
Foremen of persons included in 098.2.
CODOT
570.40 pt., 570.70 pt. Remainders in 090.5 and 090.6
570.99 pt. Remainder in 090.6

090.5 **Foremen—Other material processing—Bakery and confectionery workers**
Foremen of persons included in 098.5.
CODOT
570.40 pt., 570.70 pt. Remainders in 090.4 and 090.6
570.50 pt. Remainder in 090.6

090.6 **Foremen—Other material processing—Food and drink n.e.c.**
Foremen of persons included in 098.7.
CODOT
570.40 pt., 570.70 pt. Remainders in 090.4 and 090.5
570.50 pt. Remainder in 090.5
570.60
570.99 pt. Remainder in 090.4

091.0 **Bakers, flour confectioners**
Persons making bread and flour confectionery; finishing flour confectionery products by hand. Ovensmen, mixers, machine operators and minders and biscuit makers are excluded and classified in 098.5.
CODOT
571

092.1 **Butchers, meat cutters**
Persons slaughtering animals and preparing carcasses for processing and sales. Butchers' shop managers and proprietors are excluded and classified in 038.2.
CODOT
572.10, 572.20, 572.30
572.99 pt. Remainder in 092.2

092.2 Fishmongers, poultry dressers
Persons cleaning, cutting and preparing fish and poultry carcasses for processing and sales. Fishmongers' managers and proprietors are excluded and classified in 038.3.
CODOT
572.50, 572.60, 572.90
572.99 pt. Remainder in 092.1

093.1 Foremen—Paper, paperboard and leatherboard workers
Foremen of persons included in 094.1.
CODOT
580.20 pt., 580.40 pt. Remainders in 093.4

093.2 Foremen—Bookbinders and finishers
Foremen of persons included in 094.2.
CODOT
640.10

093.3 Foremen—Cutting and slitting machine operators (paper and paper products making)
Foremen of persons included in 094.3.
CODOT
640.20 pt. Remainder in 093.5

093.4 Foremen—Other material processing, wood and paper
Foremen of persons included in 098.8.
CODOT
580.10, 580.30, 580.99
580.20 pt., 580.40 pt. Remainders in 093.1

093.5 Foremen—Other making and repairing, paper goods and printing
Foremen of persons included in 107.9.
CODOT
630.30 pt., 630.99 pt. Remainders in 099.3
630.50
640.20 pt. Remainder in 093.3

094.1 Paper, paperboard and leatherboard workers
Persons operating machinery to beat and mix fluid pulps, to dry and to finish, to impart a glaze and to wind and rewind in the process of the production of paper, paperboard and leatherboard. Beatermen, calendermen, dryermen, reelermen, refinermen and winder operators are included. Spoolers are excluded and classified in 107.9.
CODOT
582.10, 582.50
584.05, 584.10, 584.65, 584.80

094.2 Bookbinders and finishers
Persons engaged in book binding occupations.
CODOT
641

094.3 Cutting and slitting machine operators (paper and paper products making)
Persons operating machinery to cut or slit paper or similar materials. Paper pattern cutting machine operators are excluded and classified in 107.9.
CODOT
642.54, 642.56

095.1 Foremen—Glass and ceramics furnacemen, kilnsetters
Foremen of persons included in 096.1.
CODOT
590.10 pt. Remainder in 098.9
590.99 pt. Remainder in 095.7 and 098.9

095.2 Foremen—Glass formers and shapers, finishers, decorators
Foremen of persons included in 096.2.
CODOT
610

095.3 Foremen—Casters and other pottery makers
Foremen of persons included in 096.3.
CODOT
620.10 pt. Remainder in 095.8

095.4 Foremen—Rubber process workers, moulding machine operators, tyre builders
Foremen of persons included in 097.1.
CODOT
590.20 pt. Remainder in 095.7
680.10 pt. Remainder in 095.5, 095.9 and 095.10
680.20 pt. Remainder in 095.9

095.5 Foremen—Calender and extruding machine operators, moulders (plastics)
Foremen of persons included in 097.2.
CODOT
680.10 pt. Remainder in 095.4, 095.9 and 095.10
680.30 pt. Remainder in 095.10

095.6 Foremen—Man-made fibre makers
Foremen of persons included in 098.1.
CODOT
590.40 pt. Remainder in 095.7 and 098.9

095.7 Foremen—Washers, screeners and crushers in mines and quarries
Foremen of persons included in 098.3.
CODOT
590.20 pt. Remainder in 095.4
590.30 pt. Remainder in 139.10
590.40 pt. Remainder in 095.6 and 098.9
590.99 pt. Remainder in 095.1 and 098.9

095.8 Foremen—Other making and repairing—Glass and ceramics
Foremen of persons included in 107.5.
CODOT
620.10 pt. Remainder in 095.3
620.20, 620.99

095.9 Foremen—Other making and repairing—Rubber
Foremen of persons included in 107.10.
CODOT
680.10 pt. Remainder in 095.4, 095.5 and 095.10
680.20 pt. Remainder in 095.4

095.10 Foremen—Other making and repairing—Plastics
Foremen of persons included in 107.11.
CODOT
680.10 pt. Remainder in 095.4, 095.5 and 095.9
680.30 pt. Remainder in 095.5

096.1 Glass and ceramics furnacemen, kilnsetters
Persons operating furnaces and kilns in the production of glass and ceramics, positioning articles ready for firing in kilns, including carriers-in, kiln placers and brick kiln attendants. Saggar packers are excluded and classified in 098.9.
CODOT
591.10, 591.50, 591.52, 591.54, 591.58, 591.62, 591.90
599.10, 599.50
599.99 pt. Remainder in 098.9

096.2 Glass formers and shapers, finishers, decorators
Persons forming glassware and glass products by blowing, moulding and pressing; finishing glassware by removing surplus glass; grinding and polishing; decorating glassware by cutting, acid etching and sandblasting.
CODOT
611, 612, 613, 614

096.3 Casters and other pottery makers
Persons forming ceramic ware (including porcelain, pottery, stoneware and refractory goods) by casting, extruding, moulding, pressing and shaping. Brick makers, crucible makers, furnace moulders, plaster casters and saggar makers are excluded and classified in 107.5.
CODOT
621.06, 621.08, 621.10, 621.16, 621.18, 621.26, 621.50, 621.52, 621.54, 621.58, 621.60, 621.90

097.1 Rubber process workers, moulding machine operators, tyre builders
Persons operating machines to masticate raw or reclaimed rubber; preparing rubber compound, dough or solution; building tyres. Calenderers and extruders (rubber), masticating millmen and press and vacuum moulding machinists are included.
CODOT
592.55, 592.70
594.60 pt., 594.62 pt. Remainders in 097.2
681.06
681.60 pt., 681.90 pt., 681.92 pt. Remainders in 097.2

097.2 Calender and extruding machine operators, moulders (plastics)
Persons operating calendering, extruding and moulding machines in the processing of plastics.
CODOT
594.60 pt., 594.62 pt.
681.60 pt., 681.90 pt., 681.92 pt. } Remainders in 097.1

098.1 Man-made fibre makers
Persons employed in the manufacturing process producing man-made fibres, including rayon spinners.
CODOT
594.58

098.2 Brewery and vinery process workers
Persons producing malt liquors, beers, wines and related products by crushing, mixing, malting, cooking and fermenting grains and fruits; producing yeast and vinegar.
CODOT
573.20, 573.25, 573.66, 573.68
573.50 pt., 573.80 pt.
574.50 pt., 574.58 pt. } Remainders in 098.7
575.99 pt.
576.76
579.25, 579.30, 579.50, 579.55

098.3 **Washers, screeners and crushers in mines and quarries**
Persons washing, dry cleaning, crushing or screening coal, stone or ores.
CODOT
592.50 pt., 592.60 pt., 592.90 pt. ⎫
593.35 pt., 593.99 pt. ⎭ Remainders in 098.9
593.05, 593.10, 593.15, 593.20, 593.25, 593.30, 593.40
594.99 pt. Remainder in 098.9

098.4 **Other material processing—Textiles**
Persons making braid, plait, line and rope from yarn. Persons performing various textile processing, fabricating and finishing tasks including back washers, battery fillers, braiders, carbonisers, colour matchers, creelers, doffers, driers, fullers, harness builders, lappers, line and rope makers, loom cleaners, plaiters, scourers, textile machine operators' assistants, twine spinners and twisters, tufters and washers.
CODOT
546.50, 546.85, 546.86, 546.89
548
549
592.05 pt. Remainder in 098.9

098.5 **Other material processing—Bakery and confectionery workers**
Persons employed in the processing of bread and flour confectionery including ovensmen, mixers, machine operators and minders and biscuit makers. Bakers and flour confectioners are excluded and classified in 091.0.
CODOT
573.72
574.54
576.50
576.85 pt. Remainder in 098.7

098.6 **Other material processing—Tobacco**
Persons employed in processing tobacco leaves and making cigarettes and other tobacco products by hand or machine.
CODOT
550, 551

098.7 **Other material processing—Food and drink n.e.c.**
Persons crushing, grinding, blending grains, spices, seeds; refining sugar; making glucose, sugar and chocolate confectionery; making animal feeding stuffs; curing, freezing, cooling foodstuffs; processing milk and cream; producing butter, cheese and ice cream; making sausages; making non-alcoholic beverages; making macaroni and similar products; making ice; extracting juice from fruit; shelling, cleaning, etc. nuts.
CODOT
573 pt. Excludes—573.20, 573.25, 573.50 pt., 573.66, 573.68, 573.80 pt. included in 098.2
    —573.72
574 pt. Excludes—574.50 pt., 574.58 pt. included in 098.2
    —574.54
575 pt. Excludes—575.99 pt. included in 098.2
576 pt. Excludes—576.50, 576.85 pt. included in 098.5
    —576.76
579 pt. Excludes—579.25, 579.30, 579.50, 579.55

098.8 **Other material processing—Wood and paper**
Persons in wood processing and paper, paperboard and leatherboard making not elsewhere classified; operating kilns to season wood; attending wood mills; operating filtering and straining and other separating equipment; operating machines to coat or impregnate paper and paperboard. Beatermen, calendermen, dryermen, reelermen, refinermen and winder operators are excluded and classified in 094.1.
CODOT
581
582.60, 582.90, 582.99
583
584 pt. Excludes—584.05, 584.10, 584.65, 584.80 included in 094.1
589
594.56

098.9 **Other material processing—All other (excluding metal) n.e.c.**
Paint colour matchers, concrete mixer drivers, kiln burners (cement), ceramic glaze makers, liquor men (leather tanning), mica splitters, dough preparers (artificial teeth), saggar packers; persons operating kilns to fire abrasive and carbon products, operating machines to produce slurry for making asbestos-cement goods, operating equipment to make and dry plasterboard, making pipes and sheets of asbestos-cement; persons in material processing (excluding metal) not elsewhere classified.
CODOT
590.10 pt. Remainder in 095.1
590.40 pt. Remainder in 095.6 and 095.7
590.99 pt. Remainder in 095.1 and 095.7
591 pt. Excludes—591.10, 591.50, 591.52, 591.54, 591.58, 591.62, 591.90 included in 096.1
592 pt. Excludes—592.05 pt. included in 098.4
    —592.50 pt., 592.60 pt., 592.90 pt. included in 098.3
    —592.55, 592.70 included in 097.1
593.35 pt., 593.99 pt. Remainders in 098.3
594 pt. Excludes—594.56, 594.58
    —594.60, 594.62 included in 097.1 and 097.2
    —594.99 pt. Remainder in 098.3
599 pt. Excludes—599.10, 599.50, 599.99 pt. included in 096.1

099.1 **Foremen—Compositors**
Foremen of persons included in 100.1.
CODOT
630.10 pt. Remainder in 099.5

099.2 **Foremen—Electrotypers, stereotypers, printing plate and cylinder preparers**
Foremen of persons included in 100.2.
CODOT
630.20

099.3 **Foremen—Printing machine minders and assistants**
Foremen of persons included in 100.3.
CODOT
630.30 pt., 630.99 pt. Remainders in 093.5

099.4 **Foremen—Screen and block printers**
Foremen of persons included in 100.4.
CODOT
630.40

099.5 **Foremen—Printers (so described)**
Foremen of persons included in 100.5.
CODOT
630.10 pt. Remainder in 099.1

100.1 **Compositors**
Persons setting up printing type by hand or machine. Lay-out men and make-up hands are included.
CODOT
632

100.2 **Electrotypers, stereotypers, printing plate and cylinder preparers**
Persons in printing plate and cylinder preparing occupations. Engravers of metal printing plates and rollers are excluded and classified in 130.2.
CODOT
633

100.3 **Printing machine minders and assistants**
Persons setting, operating and assisting in operating letterpress, lithographic, photogravure and web-offset printing machines. Offset duplicating machine operators are excluded and classified in 107.9.
CODOT
634.05, 634.10, 634.15, 634.20
639.50, 639.52, 639.54

100.4 **Screen and block printers**
Persons printing lettering and designs on fabric and other materials by screen and block method.
CODOT
635

100.5 **Printers (so described)**
Persons returned as 'printer', 'general printer', 'master printer', 'printer and stationer' without more specific description, including principals of printing firms.
CODOT
631

101.1 **Foremen—Tailors, tailoresses, dressmakers**
Foremen of persons included in 102.1.
CODOT
650.05
650.10 pt. Remainder in 101.6

101.2 **Foremen—Clothing cutters, milliners, furriers**
Foremen of persons included in 102.2.
CODOT
650.20, 650.25
650.30 pt. Remainder in 101.6

101.3 **Foremen—Sewers, embroiderers**
Foremen of persons included in 102.3.
CODOT
650.35, 650.40

101.4 **Foremen—Coach trimmers, upholsterers, mattress makers**
Foremen of persons included in 103.0.
CODOT
650.15 pt. Remainder in 101.6

101.5 **Foremen—Carpet fitters**
Foremen of persons included in 107.3.
CODOT
650.99 pt. Remainder in 101.6

101.6 **Foremen—Other making and repairing, clothing and related products**
Foremen of persons included in 107.8.
CODOT
650.10 pt. Remainder in 101.1
650.15 pt. Remainder in 101.4
650.30 pt. Remainder in 101.2
650.45
650.99 pt. Remainder in 101.5

102.1 Tailors, tailoresses, dressmakers
Persons making or fitting and altering tailored garments, dresses and other articles of light clothing. Persons described as tailors, tailors' assistants and tailors' fitters in manufacturing or retail trade are included. Corset makers are excluded and classified in 107.8.
CODOT
651
652.10, 652.30, 652.40

102.2 Clothing cutters, milliners, furriers
Persons cutting out, shaping and trimming material, including fur, for the manufacture of garments; making women's, girls' and children's hats throughout.
CODOT
654, 655
656.10, 656.12, 656.14, 656.16, 656.18, 656.20, 656.50, 656.52, 656.54, 656.56, 656.58

102.3 Sewers, embroiderers
Persons sewing and embroidering either by hand or machine, garments and other products made from textile fabric, fur and skin.
CODOT
657, 658

103.0 Coach trimmers, upholsterers, mattress makers
Persons upholstering vehicle and aircraft seating; fixing trimmings to the interiors of vehicles and aircraft; upholstering furniture; making mattresses, curtains and other soft furnishings.
CODOT
653 pt. Excludes—653.50, 653.99 included in 107.8

104.1 Foremen—Carpenters, joiners
Foremen of persons included in 105.1.
CODOT
670.10
670.30 pt. Remainder in 104.3 and 104.6

104.2 Foremen—Cabinet makers
Foremen of persons included in 105.2.
CODOT
670.20

104.3 Foremen—Case and box makers
Foremen of persons included in 105.3.
CODOT
670.30 pt. Remainder in 104.1 and 104.6

104.4 Foremen—Pattern makers (moulds)
Foremen of persons included in 105.4.
CODOT
670.60

104.5 Foremen—Sawyers, veneer cutters, woodworking machinists
Foremen of persons included in 106.0.
CODOT
670.40, 670.50

104.6 Foremen—Other making and repairing, wood
Foremen of persons included in 107.6.
CODOT
670.30 pt. Remainder in 104.1 and 104.3
670.99

105.1 Carpenters, joiners
Persons constructing, erecting, installing and repairing wooden structures and fittings on site and on board ship; building and repairing small wooden craft and preparing launchways; making wooden internal fittings for aircraft, scenic equipment for theatres and film studios. Scale model makers and template makers are included.
CODOT
671
673.05, 673.10, 673.15, 673.20, 673.25, 673.30

105.2 Cabinet makers
Persons performing the more highly skilled tasks in making and repairing wooden furniture and piano and cabinet cases. Assemblers of wood products are excluded and classified in 138.12.
CODOT
672

105.3 Case and box makers
Persons cutting and assembling wood to make packing cases, crates or similar articles. Coopers are included.
CODOT
673.40, 673.45

105.4 Pattern makers (moulds)
Persons making patterns of wood, metal or other materials for moulds used in metal casting.
CODOT
677

106.0 **Sawyers, veneer cutters, woodworking machinists**
Persons setting and/or operating all types of wood cutting or woodworking machinery, including wood turners.
CODOT
674, 675, 676
799.06

107.1 **Labourers and mates to woodworking craftsmen**
Persons assisting woodworking craftsmen and woodworking machine operators.
CODOT
679.90, 679.92

107.2 **Dental technicians**
Persons engaged in making and repairing dentures.
CODOT
692.20

107.3 **Carpet fitters**
Persons laying carpets on customers' premises. Carpet planners are excluded and classified in 107.8.
CODOT
659.40

107.4 **Musical instrument makers, piano tuners**
Persons making, repairing, adjusting, stringing and tuning musical instruments; fitting and regulating piano action parts and making bows for stringed instruments.
CODOT
690.10
691

107.5 **Other making and repairing—Glass and ceramics**
Brick makers, crucible makers, furnace moulders, plaster casters, saggar makers and persons performing various tasks n.e.c. in glass, clay and stone working and ceramics forming and finishing.
CODOT
619
621.02, 621.04, 621.12, 621.14, 621.20, 621.22, 621.24, 621.28, 621.56, 621.62, 621.92, 621.99
622
629

107.6 **Other making and repairing—Wood**
Persons carving and bending wood; laying hardwood strip and wood block floors; matching, joining and repairing veneers and performing various tasks not elsewhere classified. Makers of handcarts, ladders, picture frames, sports equipment, textile bobbins and shuttles, timber fences; stockers (bespoke guns) and wheelwrights are included.
CODOT
673.35, 673.50, 673.55, 673.60, 673.99
679 pt. Excludes—679.90, 679.92

107.7 **Other making and repairing—Leather**
Persons engaged in the manufacture of footwear, leather and leather substitute goods other than garments and gloves, not elsewhere classified. Harness makers and saddlers are included. Upholsterers and leather goods assemblers are excluded and classified in 103.0 and 138.12 respectively.
CODOT
664
669 pt. Excludes—669.14, 669.60, 669.62, 669.64, 669.66, 669.94 included in 085.3

107.8 **Other making and repairing—Clothing and related products**
Persons making patterns for the manufacture of garments and upholstery; marking and cutting out parts of articles other than garments; making canvas goods such as awnings, boat covers, flags, sails and tents; performing various tasks in the manufacture of fabric bags and sacks. Carpet planners, corset makers, hood and apron makers (perambulators) and persons shaping hats by hand or machine are included.
CODOT
652.20, 652.99
653.50, 653.99
656 pt. Excludes—656.10, 656.12, 656.14, 656.16, 656.18, 656.20, 656.50, 656.52, 656.54, 656.56, 656.58 included in 102.2
659 pt. Excludes—659.40

107.9 **Other making and repairing—Paper goods and printing**
Persons engaged in setting and operating die stamping and embossing machines; processing, printing and finishing still and cine film; performing various tasks in printing, photographic processing and manufacture of paper and paperboard products not elsewhere classified. Printers (textile and wallpaper), offset duplicating machine operators, paper pattern cutting machine operators, provers, spoolers and upper markers (footwear) are included. All other cutting and slitting machine operators (paper goods and printing) are excluded and classified in 094.3.
CODOT
634 pt. Excludes—634.05, 634.10, 634.15, 634.20 included in 100.3
636
639 pt. Excludes—639.50, 639.52, 639.54 included in 100.3
642 pt. Excludes—642.54, 642.56 included in 094.3

107.10 **Other making and repairing—Rubber**
Persons making and repairing articles of rubber material not elsewhere classified; sheathing cables and wires; lining and covering industrial plant, equipment and products. Tyre repairers and restorers are included but tyre builders are excluded and classified in 097.1.
CODOT
681.02, 681.04, 681.50, 681.52, 681.70, 681.72, 681.74, 681.76, 681.78, 681.80, 681.96
681.08 pt., 681.10 pt., 681.56 pt., 681.58 pt., 681.62 pt., 681.64 pt., 681.66 pt., 681.94 pt., 681.99 pt. Remainders in 107.11

107.11 Other making and repairing—Plastics
Persons making and repairing articles of plastics materials, including glass fibre reinforced plastics, not elsewhere classified; sheathing cables and wires. Artificial eye makers and spectacle frame makers are included.

CODOT
681.12, 681.14, 681.16, 681.54, 681.68
681.08 pt., 681.10 pt., 681.56 pt., 681.58 pt., 681.62 pt., 681.64 pt., 681.66 pt., 681.94 pt., 681.99 pt. Remainders in 107.10

107.12 Other making and repairing—All other (excluding metal and electrical) n.e.c.
Persons forming and finishing concrete, asbestos-cement, abrasive stone and related products; making and repairing orthopaedic and orthodontic appliances; brush makers; wicker product makers; wig makers and racket stringers. Fillers of cartridges, detonators and fireworks are included. Persons operating machines producing pipes and sheets of asbestos-cement, and dental technicians are excluded and classified in 098.9 and 107.2 respectively.

CODOT
620.30
623
690.20, 690.99
692.10, 692.30, 692.40, 692.99
699

108.1 Foremen—Furnace operating occupations (metal)
Foremen of persons included in 109.1.

CODOT
710.10

108.2 Foremen—Rollermen
Foremen of persons included in 109.2.

CODOT
710.20 pt. Remainder in 108.4 and 108.9

108.3 Foremen—Smiths, forgemen
Foremen of persons included in 109.3.

CODOT
710.40 pt. Remainder in 108.9

108.4 Foremen—Metal drawers
Foremen of persons included in 110.1.

CODOT
710.20 pt. Remainder in 108.2 and 108.9

108.5 Foremen—Moulders, core makers, die casters
Foremen of persons included in 110.2.

CODOT
710.30 pt. Remainder in 108.9

108.6 Foremen—Electroplaters
Foremen of persons included in 110.3.

CODOT
710.50 pt. Remainder in 108.8

108.7 Foremen—Annealers, hardeners, temperers (metal)
Foremen of persons included in 110.4.

CODOT
710.60

108.8 Foremen—Galvanizers, tin platers, dip platers
Foremen of persons included in 131.2.

CODOT
710.50 pt. Remainder in 108.6

108.9 Foremen—Metal making and treating workers n.e.c.
Foremen of persons included in 131.3.

CODOT
710.20 pt. Remainder in 108.2 and 108.4
710.30 pt. Remainder in 108.5
710.40 pt. Remainder in 108.3
710.99

109.1 Furnace operating occupations (metal)
Persons operating furnaces, etc. to smelt metalliferous ores, refine metal, melt metal for casting, reheat metal for further working. Persons heating metal for annealing, etc. and ladlemen are excluded and classified in 110.4 and 131.3 respectively.

CODOT
711

109.2 Rollermen
Persons operating or directing the operation of steel rolling mill to roll slabs, blooms, billets, bars, rods, strip, sheet, plates, sections or tubes. Assistant rollers are included but rolling mill assistants, third and fourth hand rollers, and bar, etc. straighteners are excluded and classified in 131.3.

CODOT
712.05, 712.10

109.3 Smiths, forgemen
Persons shaping heated metal by hand hammering on an anvil; by power hammer or forging press. Chain makers (forging) are included. Forge assistants and smiths' strikers are excluded and classified in 131.3.

CODOT
714 pt. Excludes—714.50, 714.55, 714.60, 714.65, 714.70, 714.75, 714.99 pt. included in 131.3

110.1 Metal drawers
Persons setting up and operating machines to draw wire, tubes, rods or bars.
CODOT
712.70, 712.75

110.2 Moulders, coremakers, die casters
Persons making moulds or cores either by hand or machine for use in casting molten metal; pouring metal into dies or operating die casting machinery.
CODOT
713.05, 713.10, 713.15, 713.20, 713.25, 713.50, 713.52, 713.54, 713.68, 713.70, 713.92

110.3 Electroplaters
Persons coating articles or parts electrolytically, in tanks or vats, with chromium, copper, nickel, or other non-ferrous metal. Anodisers and electroformers are excluded and classified in 131.2.
CODOT
715.05

110.4 Annealers, hardeners, temperers (metal)
Persons heat treating metal to anneal, harden or temper.
CODOT
716

111.1 Foremen—Press and machine tool setters
Foremen of persons included in 112.1.
CODOT
720.10 pt. Remainder in 111.2, 111.3 and 111.4
720.20 pt. Remainder in 111.5

111.2 Foremen—Centre lathe turners
Foremen of persons included in 112.2.
CODOT
720.10 pt. Remainder in 111.1, 111.3 and 111.4

111.3 Foremen—Machine tool setter operators
Foremen of persons included in 112.3.
CODOT
720.10 pt. Remainder in 111.1, 111.2 and 111.4

111.4 Foremen—Machine tool operators
Foremen of persons included in 112.4.
CODOT
720.10 pt. Remainder in 111.1, 111.2 and 111.3

111.5 Foremen—Press, stamping and automatic machine operators
Foremen of persons included in 113.1.
CODOT
720.20 pt. Remainder in 111.1
720.30

111.6 Foremen—Metal polishers
Foremen of persons included in 113.2.
CODOT
720.40 pt. Remainder in 111.7, 111.8 and 131.9

111.7 Foremen—Fettlers, dressers
Foremen of persons included in 113.3.
CODOT
720.40 pt. Remainder in 111.6, 111.8 and 131.9

111.8 Foremen—Shot blasters
Foremen of persons included in 131.8.
CODOT
720.40 pt. Remainder in 111.6, 111.7 and 131.9

112.1 Press and machine tool setters
Persons setting up press and machine tool and metal working machines.
CODOT
721

112.2 Centre lathe turners
Persons setting up and operating centre lathes. Roll turners and 'fitters and turners' are excluded and classified in 112.4 and 117.0 respectively.
CODOT
722.04

112.3 Machine tool setter operators
Persons setting up and operating boring, drilling, grinding and milling machines (except centre lathes). Metal spinners are included.
CODOT
722 pt. Excludes—722.04

112.4　Machine tool operators
　　Persons operating previously set up machine tools to cut, shape and otherwise machine metal workpieces. Roll turners and persons returned as 'engineer' or 'mechanical engineer', without further information, are included.
　　CODOT
　　723

113.1　Press, stamping and automatic machine operators
　　Persons operating presses and preset machines for shaping of cold metal parts. Press bending machinists are included.
　　CODOT
　　724, 725

113.2　Metal polishers
　　Persons polishing metal including jewellery polishers, die polishers and barrel polishers.
　　CODOT
　　726.20, 726.50, 726.55, 726.60

113.3　Fettlers, dressers
　　Persons removing surplus metal and rough surfaces from castings, forgings or components with hand and power tools. Shot blasters, and chippers and grinders (steel dressing) are excluded and classified in 131.8, and 131.9 respectively.
　　CODOT
　　726.90

114.1　Foreman—Tool makers, tool fitters, markers-out
　　Foremen of persons included in 115.0.
　　CODOT
　　730.10

114.2　Foremen—Precision instrument makers and repairers
　　Foremen of persons included in 116.1.
　　CODOT
　　730.20 pt., 740.40 pt. Remainders in 114.3

114.3　Foremen—Watch and chronometer makers and repairers
　　Foremen of persons included in 116.2.
　　CODOT
　　730.20 pt., 740.40 pt. Remainders in 114.2

114.4　Foremen—Metal working production fitters and fitter/machinists
　　Foremen of persons included in 117.0.
　　CODOT
　　730.30, 730.40, 730.50
　　740.10

114.5　Foremen—Motor mechanics, auto engineers
　　Foremen of persons included in 118.1.
　　CODOT
　　740.20

114.6　Foremen—Maintenance fitters (aircraft engines)
　　Foremen of persons included in 118.2.
　　CODOT
　　740.30

114.7　Foremen—Office machinery mechanics
　　Foremen of persons included in 119.0.
　　CODOT
　　740.50

115.0　Tool makers, tool fitters, markers-out
　　Persons making, maintaining and repairing press tools, dies, gauges, jigs and fixtures; marking out metal for machine tool working.
　　CODOT
　　731

116.1　Precision instrument makers and repairers
　　Persons making and repairing precision and optical instruments including calibrators. Office machinery mechanics; dental and surgical instrument makers and repairers; and instrument assemblers are excluded and classified in 119.0; 131.9; and 135.2 respectively.
　　CODOT
　　732 pt. Excludes—732.15
　　744 pt. Excludes—744.30

116.2　Watch and chronometer makers and repairers
　　Persons making, repairing, cleaning and adjusting watches, clocks and chronometers. Watch and clock assemblers are excluded and classified in 135.2.
　　CODOT
　　732.15
　　744.30

117.0 Metal working production fitters and fitter/machinists
Persons erecting, installing, repairing and servicing engineering and mechanical plant and industrial machinery, including ship machinery and related fittings, airframes, coin operated machines, locks and railway rolling stock. Engine fitters, maintenance fitters, setter fitter-mechanics and 'fitters and turners' (so described) are included. Persons maintaining and repairing aircraft engines are excluded and classified in 118.2.
CODOT
733, 734, 741
799.02, 799.04

118.1 Motor mechanics, auto engineers
Persons repairing and servicing mechanical parts of motor vehicles. Oilers and greasers of motor vehicles are included. Engine fitters are excluded and classified in 117.0.
CODOT
742
746.10

118.2 Maintenance fitters (aircraft engines)
Persons repairing and servicing aircraft engines; repairing and servicing both aircraft engines and frames. Persons repairing and servicing airframes but not engines are excluded and classified in 117.0.
CODOT
743
749.05, 749.35

119.0 Office machinery mechanics
Persons repairing and servicing mechanical office machinery, cash tills and registers. Electrical office machinery service engineers and electronic office machinery service engineers are excluded and classified in 121.2 and 123.2 respectively.
CODOT
745

120.1 Foremen—Production fitters (electrical, electronic)
Foremen of persons included in 121.1.
CODOT
750.10, 750.20

120.2 Foremen—Electricians, electrical maintenance fitters
Foremen of persons included in 121.2.
CODOT
750.30
760.10 pt., 760.20 pt., 760.30 pt. Remainders in 120.3

120.3 Foremen—Plant operators and attendants n.e.c.
Foremen of persons included in 121.4.
CODOT
760.10 pt., 760.20 pt., 760.30 pt. Remainders in 120.2
970.10 pt. Remainder in 159.9

120.4 Foremen—Telephone fitters
Foremen of persons included in 122.1.
CODOT
760.40 pt., 760.50 pt. Remainders in 120.6 and 120.7

120.5 Foremen—Cable jointers, linesmen
Foremen of persons included in 122.2.
CODOT
760.60

120.6 Foremen—Radio and TV mechanics
Foremen of persons included in 123.1.
CODOT
760.40 pt., 760.50 pt. Remainders in 120.4 and 120.7

120.7 Foremen—Other electronic maintenance engineers
Foremen of persons included in 123.2.
CODOT
760.40 pt., 760.50 pt. Remainders in 120.4 and 120.6

121.1 Production fitters (electrical, electronic)
Persons fitting and assemblng parts and sub-assemblies in the manufacture of electrical and electronic equipment. Electrical and electronic fitters not otherwise specified are included.
CODOT
751

121.2 Electricians, electrical maintenance fitters
Persons installing, maintaining and repairing electrical wiring systems, electrical plant, machinery and other equipment, including electrical wiremen. Electricity board inspectors, power switchboard operators and wirers of electronic equipment are excluded and classified in 006.3, 121.4 and 131.6 respectively.
CODOT
752
761.10 pt., 761.20 pt., 761.30 pt., 761.40 pt., 761.50 pt., 761.60 pt. Remainders in 121.3
761.70, 761.80, 761.99
762.10 pt., 762.20 pt., 762.30 pt. Remainders in 121.3
762.40, 762.99

121.3 Electrical engineers (so described)
Persons returned as 'electrical engineer' without more specific description.
CODOT
761.10 pt., 761.20 pt., 761.30 pt., 761.40 pt., 761.50 pt., 761.60 pt., 762.10 pt., 762.20 pt., 762.30 pt. Remainders in 121.2

121.4 Plant operators and attendants n.e.c.
Persons operating and attending machinery, plant and equipment such as compressors, electrical substations and switchboards, turbines, nuclear generating stations.
CODOT
971 pt. Excludes—971.15, 971.92 included in 161.1
—971.91, 971.93 included in 161.2
973
979.10

122.1 Telephone fitters
Persons installing and maintaining public and private telephone systems.
CODOT
763.10

122.2 Cable jointers, linesmen
Persons installing, maintaining and repairing overhead lines for electricity supply, electric traction and telecommunications; jointing underground, submarine and surface electric and telecommunications cables.
CODOT
764

123.1 Radio and TV mechanics
Persons repairing and maintaining domestic radios and television receivers.
CODOT
763.65, 763.70

123.2 Other electronic maintenance engineers
Persons installing, maintaining and repairing electronic equipment other than domestic radio and television receivers. Installers and fitters of computer systems are included.
CODOT
763 pt. Excludes—763.10 included in 122.1
—763.65, 763.70

124.1 Foremen—Plumbers, heating and ventilating fitters, gas fitters
Foremen of persons included in 125.0.
CODOT
770.10 pt. Remainder in 131.9

124.2 Foremen—Sheet metal workers
Foremen of persons included in 126.1.
CODOT
770.20

124.3 Foremen—Metal plate workers, shipwrights, riveters
Foremen of persons included in 126.2.
CODOT
770.30 pt. Remainder in 131.9

124.4 Foremen—Steel erectors, benders, fixers
Foremen of persons included in 127.1.
CODOT
770.40 pt. Remainder in 124.5

124.5 Foremen—Scaffolders, stagers
Foremen of persons included in 127.2.
CODOT
770.40 pt. Remainder in 124.4

124.6 Foremen—Welders
Foremen of persons included in 128.0.
CODOT
770.50

124.7 Foremen—Riggers
Foremen of persons included in 131.5.
CODOT
770.99 pt. Remainder in 131.9

125.0 Plumbers, heating and ventilating fitters, gas fitters
Persons installing, maintaining and repairing plumbing fixtures, heating and ventilating systems, pipe systems and lead, lead lined and lead covered plant.
CODOT
771 pt. Excludes—771.40, 771.99 included in 131.9

126.1 Sheet metal workers
Persons marking out, cutting, shaping and fitting sheet metal to make and repair products and components. Metal spinners, press operators, and sheet metal bending and rolling machine operators are excluded and classified in 112.3, 113.1, and 131.9 respectively.
CODOT
772

126.2 Metal plate workers, shipwrights, riveters
Persons marking off, drilling, bending, positioning and riveting metal plates and girders and sealing joints in metal plate. Shipwrights and shipyard steelworkers are included. Holders-up and shipyard frame benders are excluded and classified in 131.9.
CODOT
773 pt. Excludes—773.50, 773.99 included in 131.9

127.1 Steel erectors, benders, fixers
Persons fitting and erecting structural metal work, making up metal framework by hand to form reinforcing core for concrete structures or products. Metal shuttering erectors are excluded and classified in 131.5.
CODOT
774.20, 774.50

127.2 Scaffolders, stagers
Persons erecting and dismantling scaffolding, and temporary working platforms for use in ship construction and repair.
CODOT
774.25, 774.30

128.0 Welders
Persons joining metal parts and fabrications by welding, brazing and soldering; cutting metal to specifications and removing defects by means of gas flame and oxygen jet, electric arc or laser beam. Assemblers of vehicles and other metal goods are excluded and classified in 135.3.
CODOT
775

129.1 Foremen—Goldsmiths, silversmiths, precious stone workers
Foremen of persons included in 130.1.
CODOT
790.10

129.2 Foremen—Engravers, etchers (printing)
Foremen of persons included in 130.2.
CODOT
790.20 pt. Remainder in 131.9

129.3 Foremen—Coach and vehicle body builders
Foremen of persons included in 131.1.
CODOT
790.30

129.4 Foremen—Oilers, greasers, lubricators
Foremen of persons included in 131.4.
CODOT
740.99 pt. Remainder in 131.9

129.5 Foremen—Electronics wiremen
Foremen of persons included in 131.6.
CODOT
750.99 pt. Remainder in 129.6

129.6 Foremen—Coil winders
Foremen of persons included in 131.7.
CODOT
750.99 pt. Remainder in 129.5

130.1 Goldsmiths, silversmiths, precious stone workers
Persons making and repairing jewellery and precious metal ware; cutting, polishing and setting precious and semi-precious stones; making jewellery patterns. Precious metal spinners and jewellery engravers are excluded and classified in 112.3 and 131.9 respectively.
CODOT
791

130.2 Engravers, etchers (printing)
Persons engraving and etching metal printing cylinders, plates and rollers; engraving metal dies and punches.
CODOT
792 pt. Excludes—792.18, 792.20, 792.50, 792.99 included in 131.9

131.1 Coach and vehicle body builders
Persons constructing and repairing vehicle bodies (including railway coaches and wagons) and fixing fittings to vehicle and aircraft bodies. Vehicle body assemblers are excluded and classified in 135.3.
CODOT
793

131.2 Galvanizers, tin platers, dip platers
Persons coating articles, sheet, wire, etc. with metal, including anodisers and electroformers. Electroplaters are excluded and classified in 110.3.
CODOT
715 pt. Excludes—715.05 included in 110.3

131.3 Metal making and treating workers n.e.c.

Persons making and treating metal in operations n.e.c. including rolling mill assistants, core turners, casters (not die casters), ladlemen, smiths' strikers, forge assistants, and bar, etc. straighteners. Persons returned as labourers are excluded and classified in groups 160.1–160.8.

CODOT
712 pt. Excludes—712.05, 712.10 included in 109.2
　　　　　　　　—712.70, 712.75 included in 110.1
713 pt. Excludes—713.05, 713.10, 713.15, 713.20, 713.25, 713.50, 713.52, 713.54, 713.68, 713.70, 713.92 included in 110.2
714 pt. Excludes—714.05, 714.10, 714.15, 714.20, 714.25, 714.30, 714.35, 714.99 pt. included in 109.3
719 pt. Excludes—719.84, 719.85, 719.86, 719.87, 719.88, 719.99 pt. included in 160.5
　　　　　　　　—719.89 included in 160.6

131.4 Oilers, greasers, lubricators

Persons lubricating moving parts of stationary engines, rolling stock, other machinery and mechanical equipment. Oilers and greasers of motor vehicles are excluded and classified in 118.1.

CODOT
746 pt. Excludes—746.10 included in 118.1
　　　　　　　　—746.60

131.5 Riggers

Persons preparing, installing, repairing and splicing ropes, wires and cables, setting up lifting equipment. Metal shuttering erectors are included.

CODOT
774 pt. Excludes—774.20, 774.50 included in 127.1
　　　　　　　　—774.25, 774.30 included in 127.2

131.6 Electronics wiremen

Persons wiring up prepared parts and/or sub-assemblies in the manufacture of various types of electronic equipment. Electrical wiremen are excluded and classified in 121.2.

CODOT
759.05, 759.10, 759.15

131.7 Coil winders

Persons making coils and wiring harnesses for electrical and electronic equipment. Cable formers and neon sign assemblers are included.

CODOT
759 pt. Excludes—759.05, 759.10, 759.15

131.8 Shot blasters

Persons cleaning and/or smoothing metal surfaces by the use of vapour jet or compressed air and abrasive material.

CODOT
726.92

131.9 Other metal, jewellery, electrical production workers

Chippers and grinders (steel dressing), dental and surgical instrument makers and repairers, sheet metal bending and rolling machine operators, holders-up and shipyard frame benders, jewellery engravers, mates to metal working craftsmen, strippers and grinders (card clothing); persons engaged in metal, jewellery, engineering electrical and electronics products and parts making or repairing not elsewhere classified.

CODOT
720.40 pt. Remainder in 111.6, 111.7 and 111.8
720.99
726 pt. Excludes—726.20, 726.50, 726.55, 726.60 included in 113.2
　　　　　　　　—726.90 included in 113.3
　　　　　　　　—726.92
729
730.99
739
740.99 pt. Remainder in 129.4
746.60
749 pt. Excludes—749.05, 749.35 included in 118.2
760.99
769
770.10 pt. Remainder in 124.1
770.30 pt. Remainder in 124.3
770.99 pt. Remainder in 124.7
771.40, 771.99
773.50, 773.99
776
779
790.20 pt. Remainder in 129.2
790.99
792.18, 792.20, 792.50, 792.99
799 pt. Excludes—799.02, 799.04 included in 117.0
　　　　　　　　—799.06 included in 106.0

—.1 Foremen (engineering and allied trades)

Persons returned as foremen in engineering and allied trades (S.I.C. Division 3) and not associated with a specific occupation. Technical supervisors employed in government factories are included. Works, general and senior foremen are excluded and classified in 034.0.

CODOT
—

—.2 Trainee craftsmen (engineering and allied trades)

Persons returned as trainee craftsmen or apprentices in engineering and allied trades not associated with a specific occupation.

CODOT
—

132.1　Foremen—Pottery decorators
　　Foremen of persons included in 133.1.
　　CODOT
　　810.20 pt. Remainder in 132.4 and 138.12
　　810.30 pt. Remainder in 132.2 and 132.3
　　810.40 pt., 810.99 pt. Remainders in 138.12

132.2　Foremen—Coach painters (so described)
　　Foremen of persons included in 133.2.
　　CODOT
　　810.30 pt. Remainder in 132.1 and 132.3

132.3　Foremen—Other spray painters
　　Foremen of persons included in 133.3.
　　CODOT
　　810.30 pt. Remainder in 132.1 and 132.2

132.4　Foremen—Painters and decorators n.e.c., french polishers
　　Foremen of persons included in 133.4.
　　CODOT
　　810.10, 810.50
　　810.20 pt. Remainder in 132.1 and 138.12

133.1　Pottery decorators
　　Persons dipping and spraying ceramics with glaze, painting ceramics and applying transfers. Ground layers are included. Ceramic stencillers are excluded and classified in 138.12.
　　CODOT
　　812 pt. Excludes—812.05
　　　　　　　　　—812.10, 812.70, 812.99 included in 138.12
　　813.50, 813.90
　　814.10
　　819.10, 819.55, 819.92

133.2　Coach painters (so described)
　　Persons returned as 'coach painter' without more specific description.
　　CODOT
　　813.20 pt. Remainder in 133.3
　　819.20

133.3　Other spray painters
　　Persons applying paint, enamel or lacquer by spraying, but persons spraying ceramics are excluded and classified in 133.1.
　　CODOT
　　813 pt. Excludes—813.20 pt. included in 133.2
　　　　　　　　　—813.50, 813.90

133.4　Painters and decorators n.e.c., french polishers
　　Persons preparing surfaces and applying paint, wallpaper and other protective materials, not elsewhere classified; staining, waxing and french polishing wood surfaces. Signwriters are included.
　　CODOT
　　811
　　812.05
　　815

134.1　Foremen assemblers—Electrical, electronic
　　Foremen of persons included in 135.1.
　　CODOT
　　820.10 pt. Remainder in 134.2, 134.3, 134.5 and 138.12

134.2　Foremen assemblers—Instruments
　　Foremen of persons included in 135.2.
　　CODOT
　　820.10 pt. Remainder in 134.1, 134.3, 134.4, 134.5 and 138.12

134.3　Foremen assemblers—Vehicles and other metal goods
　　Foremen of persons included in 135.3.
　　CODOT
　　820.10 pt. Remainder in 134.1, 134.2, 134.4, 134.5 and 138.12

134.4　Foremen assemblers—Paper production, processing and printing
　　Foremen of persons included in 138.8.
　　CODOT
　　820.10 pt. Remainder in 134.1, 134.2, 134.3, 134.5 and 138.12

134.5　Foremen assemblers—Plastics goods
　　Foremen of persons included in 138.9.
　　CODOT
　　820.10 pt. Remainder in 134.1, 134.2, 134.3, 134.4 and 138.12

135.1　Assemblers (electrical, electronic)
　　Persons engaged in the semi-skilled or repetitive assembly of electrical and electronic equipment.
　　CODOT
　　821.45

135.2 Instrument assemblers
Persons engaged in the routine assembly of precision instruments such as gauges, meters, watches and clocks, etc..
CODOT
821.35 pt., 821.40 pt. Remainders in 135.3

135.3 Assemblers (vehicles and other metal goods)
Persons engaged in the routine assembly of vehicles and other metal and engineering products.
CODOT
821.35 pt., 821.40 pt. Remainders in 135.2

136.1 Foremen inspectors, viewers, examiners—Metal, electrical goods
Foremen of persons included in 137.1.
CODOT
830.10, 830.20

136.2 Foremen inspectors, viewers, examiners—Textiles
Foremen of persons included in 138.2.
CODOT
830.30 pt. Remainder in 136.3, 136.4, 136.5, 136.6 and 136.9

136.3 Foremen inspectors, viewers, examiners—Food
Foremen of persons included in 138.3.
CODOT
830.30 pt. Remainder in 136.2, 136.4, 136.5, 136.6 and 136.9

136.4 Foremen inspectors, viewers, examiners—Rubber goods
Foremen of persons included in 138.4.
CODOT
830.30 pt. Remainder in 136.2, 136.3, 136.5, 136.6 and 136.9

136.5 Foremen inspectors, viewers, examiners—Plastics goods
Foremen of persons included in 138.5.
CODOT
830.30 pt. Remainder in 136.2, 136.3, 136.4, 136.6 and 136.9

136.6 Foremen inspectors, viewers, examiners—Woodwork
Foremen of persons included in 138.6.
CODOT
830.30 pt. Remainder in 136.2, 136.3, 136.4, 136.5 and 136.9

136.7 Foremen—Packers, bottlers, canners, fillers
Foremen of persons included in 137.2.
CODOT
840.10

136.8 Foremen—Laboratory assistants
Foremen of persons included in 138.1.
CODOT
830.99 pt. Remainder in 136.10

136.9 Foremen—Inspectors, sorters in paper production, processing and printing
Foremen of persons included in 138.7.
CODOT
830.30 pt. Remainder in 136.2, 136.3, 136.4, 136.5 and 136.6

136.10 Foremen—Weighers
Foremen of persons included in 138.10.
CODOT
830.99 pt. Remainder in 136.8

136.11 Foremen—Graders, sorters, selectors n.e.c.
Foremen of persons included in 138.11.
CODOT
830.40

137.1 Inspectors, viewers (metal, electrical goods)
Persons inspecting or testing metal, engineering and electrical products or parts. Industrial radiographers are excluded and classified in 030.2.
CODOT
831, 832

137.2 Packers, bottlers, canners, fillers
Persons packing, wrapping, filling, labelling, sealing, containers by hand or machine.
CODOT
841, 842

138.1 Laboratory assistants
Persons carrying out routine procedures, not requiring professional training, in physical, chemical, biological, botanical, medical and other laboratories. Laboratory technicians are excluded and classified in 030.1.
CODOT
839.30

138.2 Inspectors, viewers, examiners—Textiles
Persons inspecting or testing textile materials or products for processing or manufacturing defects. Yarn straighteners are included.
CODOT
833.05, 833.10, 833.35
833.55 pt. Remainder in 138.12
833.99 pt. Remainder in 138.3 and 138.12

138.3 Inspectors, viewers, examiners—Food
Persons inspecting or examining food for processing defects. Egg candlers and foodstuffs samplers are included.
CODOT
833.90
833.99 pt. Remainder in 138.2 and 138.12

138.4 Inspectors, viewers, examiners—Rubber goods
Persons inspecting or examining rubber material or goods, for processing or manufacturing defects.
CODOT
833.45 pt. Remainder in 138.5

138.5 Inspectors, viewers, examiners—Plastics goods
Persons inspecting or examining plastics materials or goods, for processing or manufacturing defects.
CODOT
833.45 pt. Remainder in 138.4

138.6 Inspectors, viewers, examiners—Woodwork
Persons inspecting or examining wood or wood products, for processing or manufacturing defects.
CODOT
833.20

138.7 Inspectors, sorters in paper production, processing and printing
Persons inspecting, examining or sorting paper, paper products or printed matter, for processing or manufacturing defects.
CODOT
833.25

138.8 Assemblers in paper production, processing and printing
Persons engaged in routine assembly in paper production, processing and printing. Paper pattern folders are included.
CODOT
821.10
821.99 pt. Remainder in 138.12

138.9 Assemblers (plastics goods)
Persons engaged in routine assembly of plastics goods or components.
CODOT
821.30 pt. Remainder in 138.12

138.10 Weighers
Persons weighing and measuring materials, goods and products. Weighbridgemen and weighbridge clerks are included.
CODOT
835

138.11 Graders, sorters, selectors n.e.c.
Persons sorting and grading materials, products and other articles. Mail sorters are excluded and classified in 053.1.
CODOT
834

138.12 Painting, assembling and related occupations n.e.c.
Ceramic stencillers, wallpaper grounders, jewellery enamellers, mottlers (ceramics), glass examiners, footwear assemblers, fishing rod pluggers, fence assemblers, windscreen fitters, goods vehicle testers, cask smellers, leaf inspectors (tobacco) and persons engaged in painting, routine assembly and product inspection and related occupations not elsewhere classified.
CODOT
810.20 pt. Remainder in 132.1 and 132.4
810.40 pt., 810.99 pt. Remainders in 132.1
812.10, 812.70, 812.99
814 pt. Excludes—814.10 included in 133.1
819 pt. Excludes—819.10, 819.55, 819.92 included in 133.1
    —819.20 included in 133.2
820.10 pt. Remainder in 134.1, 134.2, 134.3, 134.4 and 134.5
821.05, 821.15, 821.20, 821.25
821.30 pt. Remainder in 138.9
821.99 pt. Remainder in 138.8
833.15, 833.30, 833.40, 833.50
833.55 pt. Remainder in 138.2
833.99 pt. Remainder in 138.2 and 138.3
839 pt. Excludes—839.30

139.1 Foremen—Bricklayers, tile setters
Foremen of persons included in 140.1.
CODOT
860.05, 860.20

139.2 Foremen—Masons, stone cutters
Foremen of persons included in 140.2.
CODOT
620.40
860.10

139.3 Foremen—Plasterers
Foremen of persons included in 140.3.
CODOT
860.15

139.4 Foremen—Roofers, glaziers
Foremen of persons included in 140.4.
CODOT
860.25, 860.30

139.5 Foremen—Handymen, general building workers
Foremen of persons included in 140.5.
CODOT
860.99 pt. Remainder in 139.7, 139.10, 139.11 and 139.12

139.6 Foremen—Railway lengthmen
Foremen of persons included in 141.1.
CODOT
860.40, 860.45, 860.50

139.7 Foremen—Road surfacers, concreters
Foremen of persons included in 141.2.
CODOT
860.35 pt. Remainder in 139.8 and 139.9
860.55
860.99 pt. Remainder in 139.5, 139.10, 139.11 and 139.12

139.8 Foremen—Roadmen
Foremen of persons included in 141.3.
CODOT
860.35 pt. Remainder in 139.7 and 139.9

139.9 Foremen—Paviors, kerb layers
Foremen of persons included in 141.4.
CODOT
860.35 pt. Remainder in 139.7 and 139.8

139.10 Foremen—Sewage plant attendants
Foremen of persons included in 142.1.
CODOT
590.30 pt. Remainder in 095.7
860.99 pt. Remainder in 139.5, 139.7, 139.11 and 139.12

139.11 Foremen—Mains and service layers, pipe jointers
Foremen of persons included in 142.2.
CODOT
860.99 pt. Remainder in 139.5, 139.7, 139.10 and 139.12

139.12 Foremen—Construction workers n.e.c.
Foremen of persons included in 146.2.
CODOT
860.99 pt. Remainder in 139.5, 139.7, 139.10 and 139.11

140.1 Bricklayers, tile setters
Persons building and repairing brick structures, setting wall and floor tiles and mosaics, laying and finishing granolithic and terrazzo mixtures, building fireplaces. Terrazzo and mosaic tile casters are excluded and classified in 107.12.
CODOT
861 pt. Excludes—861.40
863

140.2 Mason, stone cutters
Persons building and repairing stone structures; facing brick, cement or steel backing with stone; cutting, shaping and finishing, granite, marble, slate and other stone. Stone engravers and monumental masons are included.
CODOT
624
861.40

140.3 Plasterers
Persons applying plaster or cement mixtures to walls and ceilings; casting and fixing ornamental plaster work, carrying out other plastering tasks.
CODOT
862

140.4 Roofers, glaziers
Persons covering roofs with felt, slates, tiles and thatch; cutting, fitting and setting glass in windows, doors, etc..
CODOT
864, 865

140.5 Handymen, general building workers
Persons engaged in a combination of operations in the construction, alteration, maintenance and repair of buildings. Tunnellers and well sinkers are included. Handymen in residential buildings are excluded and classified in 146.2.
CODOT
869.02 pt. Remainder in 140.6
872.20
872.99 pt. Remainder in 145.0

140.6 Builders (so described)
Persons returned as 'builder', 'builder and decorator', 'building contractor', 'builder and contractor' without more specific description.
CODOT
869.02 pt. Remainder in 140.5

141.1 Railway lengthmen
Persons laying and maintaining railway tracks.
CODOT
866.20, 866.30

141.2 Road surfacers, concreters
Persons spreading, sealing and smoothing newly laid asphalt road or similar surface; pouring and levelling concrete in the construction of buildings and roads. Persons driving and operating asphalt spreading machines and concrete paving machines are excluded and classified in 155.1.
CODOT
866.60, 866.90
867
869.54

141.3 Roadmen
Persons carrying out a variety of tasks in the construction or repair of roads; road lengthmen, chippers, road markers.
CODOT
866.50, 866.92, 866.99

141.4 Paviors, kerb layers
Persons laying paving slabs and kerbstones to form pavements and street gutters.
CODOT
866.10

142.1 Sewage plant attendants
Persons attending plant in which sewage is treated; maintaining main sewerage system. Turncocks are included.
CODOT
593.45
869.20
972.60

142.2 Mains and service layers, pipe jointers
Persons laying or jointing pipes for drainage, gas, water or similar piping systems. Water supply waste inspectors are included.
CODOT
869.28, 869.30, 869.32, 869.34

143.1 Craftsmen's mates
Persons returned as labourers, assistants and mates to building craftsmen.
CODOT
868 pt. Excludes—868.50, 868.60, 860.70, 868.99 pt. included in 143.2

143.2 Building and civil engineering labourers
Labourers and unskilled workers n.e.c., in building and civil engineering. Trenchmen and street light erectors are included.
CODOT
868.50, 868.60, 868.70
868.99 pt. Remainder in 143.1

144.0 Foremen/deputies—Coalmining
Foremen, deputies and deputy overmen supervising the working of an underground district of a coal mine. Overmen are excluded and classified in 036.1.
CODOT
870.30

145.0 Face-trained coalmining workers
Coal mine face workers; including rippers, drillers, shotfirers, packers, timberers, wastemen, manhole makers, linesmen and roof bolters. Onsetters, haulage men and conveyor operators, and coal miners not otherwise specified are excluded and classified in 155.2, 158.2 and 160.7 respectively.
CODOT
871.05, 871.15
872.10
872.99 pt. Remainder in 140.5
873
879.20 pt., 879.99 pt. Remainders in 146.1
879.30

146.1 Miners (not coal), quarrymen, well drillers
Persons extracting minerals, other than coal, from underground workings and quarries; setting up and operating equipment, including wirelines to drill wells. Stone and ore crushers and washers are excluded and classified in 098.3.
CODOT
870 pt. Excludes—870.30 included in 144.0
871 pt. Excludes—871.05, 871.15 included in 145.0
879 pt. Excludes—879.20 pt., 879.30, 879.99 pt. included in 145.0

146.2 Construction workers n.e.c.
Persons performing various tasks in building and civil engineering; working under water, cleaning and restoring exteriors of buildings, laying composition floors and linoleum; steeplejacks, demolition workers, fence erectors, handymen in residential buildings, grave diggers, building insulators, other building and construction workers not elswhere classified.
CODOT
869 pt. Excludes—869.02 included in 140.5 and 140.6
—869.20 included in 142.1
—869.28, 869.30, 869.32, 869.34 included in 142.2
—869.54 included in 141.2

147.0 **Foremen—Ships, lighters and other vessels**
Foremen of persons included in 148.0.
CODOT
910 pt. Excludes—910.50, 910.99 pt. included in 158.2

148.0 **Deck, engine-room hands, bargemen, lightermen, boatmen**
Persons carrying out deck and engine-room duties on board ships and craft operating at sea and in coastal and inland waters; including ferrymen. Fishermen and dredgermen are excluded and classified to 082.0 and 155.1.
CODOT
911

149.1 **Foremen—Railway guards**
Foremen of persons included in 150.2.
CODOT
920.10 pt. Remainder in 149.4

149.2 **Foremen—Signalmen and crossing keepers, railway**
Foremen of persons included in 150.3.
CODOT
920.30

149.3 **Foremen—Shunters, pointsmen**
Foremen of persons included in 150.4.
CODOT
920.20

149.4 **Other foremen rail transport**
Foremen of workers in the operation of rail transport not elsewhere classified. Station foremen are excluded and classified in 071.3.
CODOT
920.10 pt. Remainder in 149.1
920.40, 920.99

150.1 **Drivers, motormen, secondmen, railway engines**
Persons driving railway engines, driving or acting as assistant to the driver on all types of locomotives on surface and underground railways.
CODOT
921

150.2 **Railway guards**
Persons in charge of passenger and goods trains on surface and underground railways.
CODOT
922

150.3 **Signalmen and crossing keepers, railway**
Persons operating signals to control the movements of trains; opening and closing gates at level crossings.
CODOT
923.60, 923.99

150.4 **Shunters, pointsmen**
Persons operating manual points; guiding and linking wagons and coaches to form complete trains.
CODOT
923.10, 923.50

151.1 **Bus inspectors**
Persons supervising activities of drivers and conductors of public service vehicles.
CODOT
930.10

151.2 **Foremen—Drivers of road goods vehicles**
Foremen of persons included in 152.2.
CODOT
930.20 pt., 930.99 pt. Remainders in 151.3

151.3 **Other foremen road transport**
Foremen of workers in the operation of road transport, other than vehicle maintenance workers, not elsewhere classified. Traffic foremen and yard foremen are included.
CODOT
930.20 pt., 930.99 pt. Remainders in 151.2
930.30

152.1 **Bus and coach drivers**
Persons driving road passenger carrying vehicles such as buses, coaches, mini buses, trolley buses and trams.
CODOT
931

152.2 **Drivers of road goods vehicles**
Persons driving motor vehicles to transport goods or animals by road. Coal delivery drivers are included but roundsmen are excluded and classified in 056.0.
CODOT
932
933.10

152.3 Other motor drivers
   Persons driving taxis; chauffeurs, mechanical road sweeper drivers, road patrolmen. Ambulance drivers are excluded and classified in 070.1.
   CODOT
   933 pt. Excludes—933.10

153.1 Bus conductors
   Persons collecting fares, issuing tickets and controlling passengers on buses.
   CODOT
   934

153.2 Drivers' mates
   Persons accompanying drivers of road vehicles and assisting with loading and unloading.
   CODOT
   935

154.1 Foremen—Mechanical plant drivers, operators (earth moving and civil engineering)
   Foremen of persons included in 155.1.
   CODOT
   940.10

154.2 Foremen—Crane drivers, operators
   Foremen of persons included in 155.2.
   CODOT
   940.20 pt. Remainder in 154.3, 154.4 and 158.2

154.3 Foremen—Fork lift, mechanical truck drivers
   Foremen of persons included in 155.3.
   CODOT
   940.20 pt. Remainder in 154.2, 154.4 and 158.2

154.4 Foremen—Slingers
   Foremen of persons included in 158.1.
   CODOT
   940.20 pt. Remainder in 154.2, 154.3 and 158.2

155.1 Mechanical plant drivers, operators (earth moving and civil engineering)
   Persons operating machines to excavate, level and compact earth, gravel, sand and similar materials, drive piles into the ground, lay surfaces of asphalt and concrete, dredge rivers, canals, etc.. Concrete mixer drivers and dumper drivers are excluded and classified in 098.9 and 155.3 respectively.
   CODOT
   941

155.2 Crane drivers, operators
   Persons driving and operating cranes and hoists (including winding engines at mines). Mine onsetters are included.
   CODOT
   942.05, 942.10, 942.30, 942.50, 942.52, 942.54, 942.56, 942.58, 942.60

155.3 Fork lift, mechanical truck drivers
   Persons driving and operating fork lift and similar trucks in factories, warehouses and on sites to transfer goods or materials. Coal chargers and coke carmen (coal-gas ovens, coke ovens), and dumper drivers are included.
   CODOT
   942.62, 942.64, 942.66, 942.74

156.1 Foremen—Storekeepers, warehousemen
   Foremen of persons included in 157.1.
   CODOT
   950.10
   950.99 pt. Remainder in 156.3, 156.4 and 158.2

156.2 Foremen—Stevedores, dockers
   Foremen of persons included in 157.2.
   CODOT
   950.20

156.3 Foremen—Goods porters
   Foremen of persons included in 157.3.
   CODOT
   950.99 pt. Remainder in 156.1, 156.4 and 158.2

156.4 Foremen—Refuse collectors, dustmen
   Foremen of persons included in 157.4.
   CODOT
   950.99 pt. Remainder in 156.1, 156.3 and 158.2

157.1 Storekeepers, warehousemen
   Persons storing, selecting and issuing materials, goods, etc. and maintaining stock records; including cellarmen, timber tallymen, linen keepers, lampmen (mining).
   CODOT
   951

157.2 **Stevedores, dockers**
Persons loading and discharging ships' cargoes; supplying berthed ships with water and performing related tasks.
CODOT
952

157.3 **Goods porters**
Persons loading, unloading and moving goods, materials and equipment about warehouses, stores, goods depots, shops, markets or slaughterhouses; loading and unloading goods, etc. on to and from vehicles and aircraft; moving furniture; carrying baggage at docks and air terminals.
CODOT
959.10, 959.50, 959.65, 959.70

157.4 **Refuse collectors, dustmen**
Persons collecting refuse from premises.
CODOT
959.85

158.1 **Slingers**
Persons placing wires, chains or ropes round articles to be lifted; signaling instructions to crane operators.
CODOT
942.76

158.2 **Workers in transport operating, materials moving and storing and related n.e.c.**
Conveyor operators, haulage men (coalmine), horse drawn vehicle drivers; persons handling ships in docks and aircraft on the ground, operating locks and lighthouses, carrying out transport and material handling occupations not elsewhere classified.
CODOT
910.50
910.99 pt. Remainder in 147.0
919
939
940.20 pt. Remainder in 154.2, 154.3 and 154.4
940.99
942.15, 942.20, 942.25, 942.68, 942.70, 942.72, 942.78, 942.80, 942.82, 942.99
949
950.99 pt. Remainder in 156.1, 156.3 and 156.4
959.55, 959.60, 959.75, 959.80, 959.99

Labourers and unskilled workers n.e.c.
Persons performing occupations not elsewhere classified requiring little or no training. 'Factory workers' not otherwise specified and maintenance hands n.e.c. and maintenance workers n.e.c. are included. Assignment to the various groups 159.1–159.8 and 160.1–160.8 is in accordance with the industry of the establishment in which they are employed.

159.1 **Foremen—Labourers and unskilled workers n.e.c.—Textiles (not textile goods)**
Foremen of persons included in 160.1.
CODOT
990.00 pt., 990.10 pt., 990.20 pt. Remainders in 159.2, 159.3, 159.4, 159.5, 159.6, 159.7 and 159.8

159.2 **Foremen—Labourers and unskilled workers n.e.c.—Chemicals and allied trades**
Foremen of persons included in 160.2.
CODOT
990.00 pt., 990.10 pt., 990.20 pt. Remainders in 159.1, 159.3, 159.4, 159.5, 159.6, 159.7 and 159.8

159.3 **Foremen—Labourers and unskilled workers n.e.c.—Coke ovens and gas works**
Foremen of persons included in 160.3.
CODOT
990.00 pt., 990.10 pt., 990.20 pt. Remainders in 159.1, 159.2, 159.4, 159.5, 159.6, 159.7 and 159.8

159.4 **Foremen—Labourers and unskilled workers n.e.c.—Glass and ceramics**
Foremen of persons included in 160.4.
CODOT
990.00 pt., 990.10 pt., 990.20 pt. Remainders in 159.1, 159.2, 159.3, 159.5, 159.6, 159.7 and 159.8

159.5 **Foremen—Labourers and unskilled workers n.e.c.—Foundries in engineering and allied trades**
Foremen of persons included in 160.5.
CODOT
990.00 pt., 990.10 pt., 990.20 pt. Remainders in 159.1, 159.2, 159.3, 159.4, 159.6, 159.7 and 159.8

159.6 **Foremen—Labourers and unskilled workers n.e.c.—Engineering and allied trades**
Foremen of persons included in 160.6.
CODOT
990.00 pt., 990.10 pt., 990.20 pt. Remainders in 159.1, 159.2, 159.3, 159.4, 159.5, 159.7 and 159.8

159.7 **Foremen—Labourers and unskilled workers n.e.c.—Coal mines**
Foremen of persons included in 160.7.
CODOT
990.00 pt., 990.10 pt., 990.20 pt. Remainders in 159.1, 159.2, 159.3, 159.4, 159.5, 159.6 and 159.8

159.8 **Foremen—Labourers and unskilled workers n.e.c.—Other**
Foremen of persons included in 160.8.
CODOT
990.00 pt., 990.10 pt., 990.20 pt. Remainders in 159.1, 159.2, 159.3, 159.4, 159.5, 159.6 and 159.7

159.9 **Foremen—Boiler operators**
Foremen of persons included in 161.1.
CODOT
970.10 pt. Remainder in 120.3

160.1 **Labourers and unskilled workers n.e.c.—Textiles (not textile goods)**
Labourers, etc. in establishments assigned to S.I.C. Class 43. 'Textile operatives', 'cotton operatives' and 'textile workers' so described are included.
CODOT
991.10 pt., 991.20 pt. Remainders in 160.2, 160.3, 160.4, 160.5, 160.6, 160.7 and 160.8

160.2 **Labourers and unskilled workers n.e.c.—Chemicals and allied trades**
Labourers, etc. in establishments assigned to S.I.C. Classes 14, 15, 25 and 26.
CODOT
991.10 pt., 991.20 pt. Remainders in 160.1, 160.3, 160.4, 160.5, 160.6, 160.7 and 160.8

160.3 **Labourers and unskilled workers n.e.c.—Coke ovens and gas works**
Labourers, etc. in establishments assigned to S.I.C. Class 12 and Group 162.
CODOT
991.10 pt., 991.20 pt. Remainders in 160.1, 160.2, 160.4, 160.5, 160.6, 160.7 and 160.8

160.4 **Labourers and unskilled workers n.e.c.—Glass and ceramics**
Labourers, etc. in establishments assigned to S.I.C. Groups 241, 243, 247 and 248.
CODOT
991.10 pt., 991.20 pt. Remainders in 160.1, 160.2, 160.3, 160.5, 160.6, 160.7 and 160.8

160.5 **Labourers and unskilled workers n.e.c.—Foundries in engineering and allied trades**
Labourers, etc. in foundries in the engineering and allied trades (S.I.C. Class 22 and Division 3).
CODOT
719.84, 719.85, 719.86, 719.87, 719.88
719.99 pt. Remainder in 131.3
991.10 pt., 991.20 pt. Remainders in 160.1, 160.2, 160.3, 160.4, 160.6, 160.7 and 160.8

160.6 **Labourers and unskilled workers n.e.c.—Engineering and allied trades**
Labourers, etc. in establishments assigned to S.I.C. Class 22 and Division 3. 'Steelworkers' and 'metal workers' so described are included. Unskilled workers in foundries are excluded and classified in 160.5.
CODOT
719.89
991.10 pt., 991.20 pt. Remainders in 160.1, 160.2, 160.3, 160.4, 160.5, 160.7 and 160.8

160.7 **Labourers and unskilled workers n.e.c.—Coal mines**
Labourers, etc. in coal mines assigned to S.I.C. Activity Heading 1113. 'Coal miners' not otherwise specified are included.
CODOT
991.10 pt., 991.20 pt. Remainders in 160.1, 160.2, 160.3, 160.4, 160.5, 160.6 and 160.8

160.8 **Labourers and unskilled workers n.e.c.—Other**
Labourers, etc. in industries not elsewhere classified. Building and civil engineering labourers are excluded and classified in 143.2.
CODOT
991.10 pt., 991.20 pt. Remainders in 160.1, 160.2, 160.3, 160.4, 160.5, 160.6 and 160.7

161.1 **Boiler operators**
Persons operating boilers to produce steam or hot water for central heating systems and industrial use.
CODOT
971.15, 971.92

161.2 **All other in miscellaneous occupations n.e.c.**
Person carrying out various tasks not classified elsewhere including crematorium attendants, incinerator operators, pumpmen, gas cylinder preparers, vehicle washing plant attendants, stage hands (entertainment).
CODOT
970.20, 970.30, 970.99
971.91, 971.93
972.10, 972.50, 972.99
979.50, 979.55, 979.60, 979.65, 979.99
991.30
999.99

—.1 **Inadequately described occupations**
Persons with inadequately described occupations including persons described as 'Foremen', 'Manager', 'Workman' without further information.
CODOT
—

—.2 **Occupations not stated**
Persons in employment, seeking work, permanently sick or retired with no statement of occupation.
CODOT
—

Appendix A

Condensed KOS headings and associated KOS groups

Con. KOS	KOS	
001		Judges, barristers, advocates, solicitors
	003	Judges, barristers, advocates and solicitors
002		Accountants, valuers, finance specialists
	007	Accountants
	008	Estimators, valuers and assessors
	009	Finance, investment, insurance and tax specialists
003		Personnel and industrial relations managers; O and M, work study and operational research officers
	010	Personnel and industrial relations officers and managers
	011	Organisation and Methods, work study and operational research officers
004		Economists, statisticians, systems analysts, computer programmers
	012	Economists, statisticians, actuaries
	013	Systems analysts and computer programmers
005		Marketing, sales, advertising, public relations and purchasing managers
	014	Marketing and sales managers and executives
	015	Advertising and public relations managers and executives
	016	Purchasing officers and buyers
006		Statutory and other inspectors
	019	Environmental health officers
	020	Other statutory and similar inspectors
007		General administrators—national government
	001 pt.	Top managers—national government and other non-trading organisations
	021	Civil servants (administrative and executive functions) not identified elsewhere
	094 pt.	Office managers—national government
008		Local government officers (administrative and executive functions)
	001 pt.	Top managers—national government and other non-trading organisations
	005	Town Clerks and other clerks to local authorities
	022	Local government officers (administrative and executive functions) not identified elsewhere
	095	Office managers—local government
009		All other professional and related supporting management and administration
	004	Company secretaries
	006	Secretaries of trade associations, trade unions, professional bodies and charities
	017	Property and estate managers
	018	Librarians and information officers
	023	All other professional and related supporting management and administration
010		Teachers in higher education
	024	University academic staff
	025	Teachers in establishments for further and higher education
011		Teachers n.e.c.
	026	Secondary teachers
	027	Primary teachers
	028	Pre-primary teachers
	029	Special education teachers
012		Vocational and industrial trainers, education officers, social and behavioural scientists
	030	Vocational/industrial trainers
	031	Directors of education, education officers, school inspectors
	032	Social and behavioural scientists
013		Welfare workers
	033	Welfare workers (social, medical, industrial, educational and moral)
014		Clergy, ministers of religion
	034	Clergy, ministers of religion

Con.
KOS KOS

015   Medical and dental practitioners
- 035 Medical practitioners
- 036 Dental practitioners

016   Nurse administrators, nurses
- 037 Nurse administrators and nurse executives
- 038 State registered and state enrolled nurses and state certified midwives
- 039 Nursing auxiliaries and assistants

017   Pharmacists, radiographers, therapists n.e.c.
- 040 Pharmacists
- 041 Medical radiographers
- 042 Ophthalmic and dispensing opticians
- 043 Remedial therapists
- 044 Chiropodists

018   All other professional and related in education, welfare and health
- 045 Medical technicians and dental auxiliaries
- 046 Veterinarians
- 047 All other professional and related in education, welfare and health

019   Authors, writers, journalists
- 048 Authors, writers and journalists

020   Artists, designers, window dressers
- 049 Artists, commercial artists
- 050 Industrial designers
- 054 Window dressers

021   Actors, musicians, entertainers, stage managers
- 051 Actors, musicians, entertainers, stage managers

022   Photographers, cameramen, sound and vision equipment operators
- 052 Photographers and cameramen
- 053 Sound and vision equipment operators

023   All other literary, artistic and sports
- 055 Professional sportsmen, sports officials
- 056 All other literary, artistic and sports

024   Scientists, physicists, mathematicians
- 057 Biological scientists and biochemists
- 058 Chemical scientists
- 059 Physical and geological scientists and mathematicians

025   Civil, structural, municipal, mining and quarrying engineers
- 060 Civil, structural and municipal engineers
- 061 Mining, quarrying and drilling engineers

026   Mechanical and aeronautical engineers
- 062 Mechanical engineers
- 063 Aeronautical engineers

027   Electrical and electronic engineers
- 064 Electrical engineers
- 065 Electronic engineers
- 066 Electrical/Electronic engineers

028   Engineers and technologists n.e.c.
- 067 Chemical engineers
- 068 Production engineers
- 069 Planning and quality control engineers
- 070 Heating and ventilating engineers
- 071 General and other engineers
- 072 Metallurgists
- 073 All other technologists

029   Draughtsmen
- 074 Engineering draughtsmen
- 075 Architectural and other draughtsmen

030   Laboratory and engineering technicians, technician engineers
- 076 Laboratory technicians (scientific and medical)
- 077 Engineering technicians and technician engineers

Con. KOS	KOS	
031		Architects, town planners, quantity, building and land surveyors
	078	Architects and town planners
	080	Quantity surveyors
	081	Building, land and mining surveyors
032		Officers (ships and aircraft), air traffic planners and controllers
	082	Aircraft flight deck officers
	083	Air traffic planners and controllers
	084	Ships' masters, deck officers and pilots
	085	Ships' engineer officers
	086	Ships' radio officers
033		Professional and related in science, engineering and other technologies and similar fields n.e.c.
	079	Town planning, architectural and building technicians
	087	All other professional and related in science, engineering and other technologies and similar fields
034*		Production, works and maintenance managers, works foremen
	088	Production managers, works managers, works foremen
	089	Engineering maintenance managers
035*		Site and other managers, agents and clerks of works, general foremen (building and civil engineering)
	090	Site and other managers, agents and clerks of works, general foremen (building and civil engineering)
036*		Managers in transport, warehousing, public utilities and mining
	091	Managers—underground mining and public utilities
	092	Transport managers—air, sea, rail, road, harbour
	093	Managers—warehousing and materials handling
037*		Office managers
	096	Other office managers
038*		Managers in wholesale and retail distribution
	097	Managers—wholesale distribution
	098	Managers—department store, variety chain store, supermarket and departmental managers
	099	Branch managers of shops other than above
	100	Managers of independent shops (employees)
	101	Shop keepers (employers and self-employed)
039*		Managers of hotels, clubs, etc., and in entertainment and sport
	102	Hotel and residential club managers
	103	Publicans (employers and self-employed)
	104	Publicans (employees)
	105	Catering and non-residential club managers
	106	Entertainment and sports managers
040*		Farmers, horticulturists, farm managers
	107	Farmers and horticulturists (employers and self-employed)
	108	Farm managers (employees)
041		Officers, UK armed forces
	109 pt.	Officers (Armed Forces) not identified elsewhere (i.e. service officers with no civilian occupational counterpart)
042		Officers, foreign and Commonwealth armed forces
	109 pt.	Officers (Armed Forces) not identified elsewhere (i.e. service officers with no civilian occupational counterpart)
043		Senior police, prison and fire service officers
	110	Police officers (inspectors and above)
	111	Prison officers (chief officers and above)
	112	Fire service officers
044*		All other managers
	113	All other managers
045		Supervisors of clerks, civil service executive officers
	094 pt.	Office managers—national government
	114	Supervisors of clerks
046		Clerks
	115	Clerks

---

* And KOS 002—General, central, divisional managers—trading organisations, as appropriate

Con. KOS	KOS	
047		Retail shop cashiers, check-out and cash and wrap operators
	116	Retail shop cashiers
	117	Retail shop check-out and cash and wrap operators
048		Supervisors of typists, office machine operators, telephonists, etc.
	119	Supervisors of typists, etc.
	122	Supervisors of office machine operators
	124	Supervisors of telephonists, radio and telegraph operators
049		Secretaries, shorthand typists, receptionists
	118	Receptionists
	120	Personal secretaries, shorthand writers and shorthand typists
	121	Other typists
050		Office machine operators
	123	Office machine operators
051		Telephonists, radio and telegraph operators
	125	Telephonists
	126	Radio and telegraph operators
052		Supervisors of postmen, mail sorters, messengers
	127	Supervisors of postmen, mail sorters and messengers
053		Postmen, mail sorters, messengers
	128	Postmen, mail sorters and messengers
054		Sales supervisors
	129	Sales supervisors
055		Salesmen, sales assistants, shop assistants, shelf fillers, petrol pump, forecourt attendants
	130	Salesmen, sales assistants, shop assistants and shelf fillers
	131	Petrol pump/forecourt attendants
056		Roundsmen, van salesmen
	132	Roundsmen and van salesmen
057		Sales representatives and agents
	133	Technical sales representatives
	134	Sales representatives (wholesale goods)
	135	Other sales representatives and agents
058		NCOs and other ranks, UK armed forces
	136 pt.	Non-commissioned Officers and Other Ranks (Armed Forces) not identified elsewhere (i.e. with no civilian occupational counterpart)
059		NCOs and other ranks, foreign and Commonwealth armed forces
	136 pt.	Non-commissioned Officers and Other Ranks (Armed Forces) not identified elsewhere (i.e. with no civilian occupational counterpart)
060		Supervisors (police sergeants, fire fighting and related)
	137	Supervisors (police sergeants, fire fighting and related)
061		Policemen, firemen, prison officers
	138	Policemen (below sergeant)
	139	Firemen
	140	Prison officers below principal officer
062		Other security and protective service workers
	141	Security officers and detectives
	142	Security guards, patrolmen
	143	Traffic wardens
	144	All other in security and protective service
063		Catering supervisors
	145	Catering supervisors
064		Chefs, cooks
	146	Chefs, cooks
065		Waiters and bar staff
	147	Waiters, waitresses
	148	Barmen, barmaids

Con. KOS	KOS	
066		Counter hands, assistants, kitchen porters, hands
	149	Counter hands/assistants
	150	Kitchen porters/hands
067		Supervisors—housekeeping and related
	151	Supervisors—housekeeping and related
068		Domestic staff and school helpers
	152	Domestic housekeepers
	153	Home and domestic helpers, maids
	154	School helpers and school supervisory assistants
069		Travel stewards and attendants, hospital and hotel porters
	155	Travel stewards and attendants
	158	Hospital porters
	159	Hotel porters
070		Ambulancemen, hospital orderlies
	156	Ambulancemen
	157	Hospital/ward orderlies
071		Supervisors, foremen—caretaking, cleaning and related
	160	Supervisors/foremen—caretaking, cleaning and related
072		Caretakers, road sweepers and other cleaners
	161	Caretakers
	162	Road sweepers (manual)
	163	Other cleaners
073		Hairdressing supervisors
	167	Hairdressing supervisors
074		Hairdressers, barbers
	168	Hairdressers (men), barbers
	169	Hairdressers (ladies)
075		All other in catering, cleaning and other personal service
	164	Railway stationmen
	165	Lift and car park attendants
	166	Garment pressers
	170	All other in catering, cleaning, hairdressing and other personal service
076		Foremen—farming, horticulture, forestry
	171	Foremen—farming, horticulture, forestry
077		Farm workers
	172	General farm workers
	173	Dairy cowmen
	174	Pig and poultry men
	175	Other stockmen
078		Horticultural workers, gardeners, groundsmen
	176	Horticultural workers
	177	Domestic gardeners (private gardens)
	178	Non-domestic gardeners and groundsmen
079		Agricultural machinery drivers, operators
	179	Agricultural machinery drivers/operators
080		Forestry workers
	180	Forestry workers
081		Supervisors, mates—fishing
	181	Supervisors/mates—fishing
082		Fishermen
	182	Fishermen
083		All other in farming and related
	183	All other in farming and related

Con. KOS	KOS	
084		Foremen—tannery and leather (including leather substitutes) working
	184	Foremen—tannery production workers
	244	Foremen—leather and leather substitutes working
085		Tannery and leather (including leather substitutes) working
	185	Tannery production workers
	245	Boot and shoe makers (bespoke) and repairers
	246	Leather and leather substitutes—cutters
	247	Footwear lasters
	248	Leather and leather substitutes—sewers
	249	Footwear finishers
086		Foremen—textile processing
	186	Foremen—textile processing
087		Textile workers
	187	Preparatory fibre processors
	188	Spinners, doublers/twisters
	189	Winders, reelers
	190	Warp preparers
	191	Weavers
	192	Knitters
	193	Bleachers, dyers, finishers
	194	Burlers, menders, darners
088		Foremen—chemical processing
	195	Foremen—chemical processing
089		Chemical, gas and petroleum process plant operators
	196	Chemical, gas and petroleum process plant operators
090		Foremen—food and drink processing
	197	Foremen—food and drink processing
091		Bakers, flour confectioners
	198	Bread bakers (hand)
	199	Flour confectioners
092		Butchers
	200	Butchers, meat cutters
093		Foremen—paper and board making and paper products
	201	Foremen—paper and board making
	228	Foremen—bookbinding
	229	Foremen—paper products making
094		Paper, board and paper product makers, bookbinders
	202	Beatermen, refinerman (paper and board making)
	203	Machinemen, dryermen, calendermen, reelermen (paper and board making)
	230	Bookbinders and finishers
	231	Cutting and slitting machine operators (paper and paper products making)
095		Foremen—glass, ceramics, rubber, plastics, etc.
	204	Foremen—processing—glass, ceramics, rubber, plastics, etc.
	213	Foremen—glass working
	216	Foremen—clay and stone working
	261	Foremen—rubber and plastics working
096		Glass and ceramics furnacemen and workers
	205	Glass and ceramic furnacemen and kilnmen
	206	Kiln setters
	214	Glass formers and shapers
	215	Glass finishers and decorators
	217	Casters and other pottery makers
097		Rubber and plastics workers
	207	Masticating millmen (rubber and plastics)
	208	Rubber mixers and compounders
	209	Calender and extruding machine operators (rubber and plastics)
	262	Tyre builders
	263	Moulding machine operators/attendants (rubber and plastics)
098		All other in processing materials (other than metal)
	210	Man-made fibre makers
	212	All other in processing materials (other than metal)

Con. KOS	KOS	
099		Foremen—printing
	219	Foremen—printing
100		Printing workers, screen and block printers
	220	Compositors
	221	Electrotypers, stereotypers
	222	Other printing plate and cylinder preparers
	223	Printing machine minders (letterpress)
	224	Printing machine minders (lithography)
	225	Printing machine minders (photogravure)
	226	Printing machine assistants (letterpress, lithography, photogravure)
	227	Screen and block printers
101		Foremen—textile materials working
	232	Foremen—textile materials working
102		Tailors, dressmakers and other clothing workers
	233	Bespoke tailors and tailoresses
	234	Dressmakers
	237	Milliners
	238	Furriers
	239	Clothing cutters and markers (measure)
	240	Other clothing cutters and markers
	241	Hand sewers and embroiderers
	242	Linkers
	243	Sewing machinists (textile materials)
103		Coach trimmers, upholsterers, mattress makers
	235	Coach trimmers
	236	Upholsterers, mattress makers
104		Foremen—woodworking
	250	Foremen—woodworking
105		Woodworkers, pattern makers
	251	Carpenters and joiners (construction sites and maintenance)
	252	Carpenters and joiners (ship and stage)
	253	Carpenters and joiners (others)
	254	Cabinet makers
	255	Case and box makers
	259	Patternmakers (moulds)
106		Sawyers, veneer cutters, woodworking machinists
	256	Wood sawyers and veneer cutters
	257	Woodworking machinists (setters and setter operators)
	258	Other woodworking machinists (operators and minders)
	332	Setter operators of woodworking *and* metal working machines
107		All other in making and repairing (excluding metal and electrical)
	260	Labourers and mates to woodworking craftsmen
	264	Dental mechanics
	265	All other in making and repairing (excluding metal and electrical)
108		Foremen—metal making and treating
	266	Foremen—metal making and treating
109		Furnacemen (metal), rollermen, smiths, forgemen
	267	Blast furnacemen
	268	Furnacemen (steel smelting)
	269	Other furnacemen (metal)
	270	Rollermen (steel)
	275	Smiths, forgemen
110		Metal drawers, moulders, die casters, electroplaters, annealers
	271	Metal drawers
	272	Moulders and moulder/coremakers
	273	Machine moulders, shell moulders and machine coremakers
	274	Die casters
	276	Electroplaters
	277	Annealers, hardeners, temperers (metal)
111		Foremen—engineering machining
	278	Foremen—engineering machining

lxxvii

Con.
KOS KOS

112		Press and machine tool setter operators and operators, turners
	279	Press and machine tool setters
	280	Roll turners, roll grinders
	281	Other centre lathe turners
	282	Machine tool setter operators
	283	Machine tool operators (not setting-up)
113		Machine attendants, minders, press and stamping machine operators, metal polishers, fettlers, dressers
	284	Press and stamping machine operators
	285	Automatic machine attendants/minders
	286	Metal polishers
	287	Fettlers/dressers
114		Foremen—production fitting (metal)
	288	Foremen—production fitting (metal)
	294	Foremen—installation and maintenance—machines and instruments
115		Tool makers, tool fitters, markers-out
	289	Toolmakers, tool fitters, markers-out
116		Instrument and watch and clock makers and repairers
	290	Precision instrument makers
	301	Watch and clock repairers
	302	Instrument mechanics
117		Metal working production fitters and fitter/machinists
	291	Metal working production fitters (fine limits)
	292	Metal working production fitter-machinists (fine limits)
	293	Other metal working production fitters (not to fine limits)
	295	Machinery erectors and installers
	296	Maintenance fitters (non-electrical) plant and industrial machinery
	297	Knitting machine mechanics (industrial)
	331	Maintenance and installation fitters (mechanical *and* electrical)
118		Motor vehicle and aircraft mechanics
	298	Motor vehicle mechanics (skilled)
	299	Other motor vehicle mechanics
	300	Maintenance and service fitters (aircraft engines)
119		Office machinery mechanics
	303	Office machinery mechanics
120		Foremen—production fitting and wiring (electrical)
	304	Foremen—production fitting and wiring (electrical/electronic)
	307	Foremen—installation and maintenance (electrical/electronic)
121		Production fitters, electricians, electricity power plant operators, switchboard attendants
	305	Production fitters (electrical/electronic)
	306	Production electricians
	308	Electricians (installation and maintenance) plant and machinery
	309	Electricians (installation and maintenance) premises and ships
	400	Electricity power plant operators and switchboard attendants
122		Telephone fitters, cable jointers, linesmen
	310	Telephone fitters
	312	Cable jointers and linesmen
123		Radio, TV and other electronic maintenance fitters and mechanics
	311	Radio, TV and other electronic maintenance fitters and mechanics
124		Foremen—metal working, pipes, sheets, structures
	313	Foremen/supervisors—metal working—pipes, sheets, structures
125		Plumbers, heating and ventilating fitters, gas fitters
	314	Plumbers, pipe fitters
	315	Heating and ventilating engineering fitters
	316	Gas fitters
126		Sheet metal workers, platers, shipwrights, riveters, etc.
	317	Sheet metal workers
	318	Platers and metal shipwrights
	319	Caulker burners, riveters and drillers (constructional metal)
	<u>320</u>	General steelworkers (shipbuilding and repair)

Con. KOS	KOS	
127		Steel erectors, scaffolders, steel benders, fixers
	321	Steel erectors
	322	Scaffolders/stagers
	323	Steel benders, bar benders and fixers
128		Welders
	324	Welders (skilled)
	325	Other welders
129		Foremen—other processing, making and repairing (metal and electrical)
	326	Foremen—other processing, making and repairing (metal and electrical)
130		Goldsmiths, silversmiths, etc., engravers, etchers
	327	Goldsmiths, silversmiths and precious stone workers
	328	Engravers and etchers (printing)
131		All other in processing, making and repairing (metal and electrical)
	329	Coach and vehicle body builders/makers
	330	Aircraft finishers
	333	All other skilled in processing, making and repairing (metal and electrical)
	334	All other non-skilled in processing, making and repairing (metal and electrical)
132		Foremen—painting and similar coating
	335	Foremen—painting and similar coating
133		Painters, decorators, french polishers
	336	Painters and decorators
	337	Pottery decorators
	338	Coach painters
	339	Other spray painters
	340	French polishers
134		Foremen—product assembling (repetitive)
	341	Foremen—product assembling (repetitive)
135		Repetitive assemblers (metal and electrical goods)
	342	Repetitive assemblers (metal and electrical goods)
136		Foremen—product inspection and packaging
	343	Foremen—product inspection
	346	Foremen—packaging
137		Inspectors, viewers, testers, packers, bottlers, etc.
	344	Inspectors and testers (skilled) (metal and electrical engineering)
	345	Viewers (metal and electrical engineering)
	347	Packers, bottlers, canners, fillers
138		All other in painting, repetitive assembling, product inspection, packaging and related
	348	All other in painting, repetitive assembling, product inspection, packaging and related
139		Foremen—building and civil engineering n.e.c.
	349	Foremen—building and civil engineering not identified elsewhere
140		Building and construction workers
	218	Cutters, shapers and polishers (stone)
	350	Bricklayers
	351	Fixers/walling masons
	352	Plasterers
	353	Floor and wall tilers, terrazzo workers
	354	Roofers and slaters
	355	Glaziers
	361	General builders
	369	Tunnellers
141		Concreters, road surfacers, railway lengthmen
	356	Railway lengthmen
	357	Asphalt and bitumen road surfacers
	358	Other roadmen
	359	Concrete erectors/assemblers
	360	Concrete levellers/screeders

Con.
KOS KOS

142 Sewage plant attendants, sewermen (maintenance), mains and service layers, pipe jointers (gas, water, drainage, oil), inspectors (water supply), turncocks
- 211 Sewage plant attendants
- 362 Sewermen (maintenance)
- 363 Mains and service layers and pipe jointers (gas, water, drainage, oil)
- 364 Waste inspectors (water supply)
- 401 Turncocks (water supply)

143 Civil engineering labourers, craftsmen's mates and other builders' labourers n.e.c.
- 365 Craftsmen's mates and other builders' labourers not identified elsewhere
- 366 Civil engineering labourers

144 Foremen/deputies—coalmining
- 367 Foremen/deputies—coalmining

145 Face-trained coalmining workers
- 368 Face-trained coalmining workers

146 All other in construction, mining, quarrying, well drilling and related n.e.c.
- 370 All other in construction, mining, quarrying, well drilling and related, not identified elsewhere

147 Foremen—ships, lighters and other vessels
- 371 Foremen—ships, lighters and other vessels

148 Deck, engine-room hands, bargemen, lightermen, boatmen
- 372 Deck and engine-room hands (sea-going)
- 373 Bargemen, lightermen, boatmen, tugmen

149 Foremen—rail transport operating
- 374 Foremen—rail transport operating

150 Rail transport operating staff
- 375 Railway engine drivers, motormen
- 376 Secondmen (railways)
- 377 Railway guards
- 378 Railway signalmen and shunters

151 Foremen—road transport operating, bus inspectors
- 379 Foremen—road transport operating
- 380 Bus inspectors

152 Bus, coach, lorry drivers, etc.
- 381 Bus and coach drivers
- 382 Heavy goods drivers (over 3 tons unladen weight)
- 383 Other goods drivers
- 384 Other motor drivers

153 Bus conductors, drivers' mates
- 385 Bus conductors
- 386 Drivers' mates

154 Foremen—civil engineering plant operating, materials handling equipment operating
- 387 Foremen—civil engineering plant operating
- 389 Foremen—materials handling equipment operating

155 Mechanical plant, fork lift, mechanical truck drivers, crane drivers, operators
- 388 Mechanical plant drivers/operators (earth moving and civil engineering)
- 390 Crane drivers/operators
- 391 Fork lift and other mechanical truck drivers/operators

156 Foremen—materials moving and storing
- 392 Foremen—materials moving and storing

157 Storekeepers, stevedores, warehouse, market and other goods porters
- 393 Storekeepers, warehousemen
- 394 Stevedores and dockers
- 395 Furniture removers
- 396 Warehouse, market and other goods porters
- 397 Refuse collectors/dustmen

158 All other in transport operating, materials moving and storing and related n.e.c.
- 398 All other in transport operating, materials moving and storing and related not identified elsewhere

Con.
KOS KOS

159 Foremen—miscellaneous
    399   Foremen—miscellaneous

160 General labourers
    402   General labourers (engineering and shipbuilding)
    403   Other general labourers

161 All other in miscellaneous occupations n.e.c.
    404   All other in miscellaneous occupations not identified elsewhere

Appendix B

Social Classes and Socio-economic groups

The following appendices show the allocation of the groups arising from the cross-classification of Occupation and Employment status to the Social Classes and Socio-economic groups (details of which are given on pages x–xii).

Persons with Employment status 'Apprentices, articled pupils, etc.' are included with Employees not elsewhere classified (n.e.c.) except management trainees who are included with Managers.

Appendix B.1 is intended primarily as a key to the allocation of persons to Social Class or Socio-economic group when their occupation code and employment status group have been determined.

Appendix B.2 provides details of the composition of the Social Classes and Socio-economic groups in terms of the individual occupation and employment status groups.

Where no distinction is made in these appendices between Socio-economic groups 1.1 and 2.1 or 1.2 and 2.2 allocation is determined by the size of the establishment which the person owns or manages. For details see pages xi–xii.

Appendix B.1

Socio-economic Group and Social Class allocations of Occupation and Employment Status Groups

Occupation	Manual / Non-manual	Self-employed with employees S.E.G.	Self-employed with employees Social Class	Self-employed without employees S.E.G.	Self-employed without employees Social Class	Managers S.E.G.	Managers Social Class	Foremen S.E.G.	Foremen Social Class	Apprentices, etc., Employees n.e.c. S.E.G.	Apprentices, etc., Employees n.e.c. Social Class
001 Judges, barristers, advocates, solicitors											
0 Judges, barristers, advocates, solicitors	NM	3	I	3	I	—	—	—	—	4	I
002 Accountants, valuers, finance specialists											
1 Chartered and certified accountants	NM	3	I	3	I	1.2, 2.2	I	—	—	4	I
2 Cost and works accountants	NM	5.1	II	5.1	II	1.2, 2.2	II	—	—	5.1	II
3 Estimators	NM	5.1	II	5.1	II	1.2, 2.2	II	—	—	5.1	II
4 Valuers, claims assessors	NM	5.1	II	5.1	II	1.2, 2.2	II	—	—	5.1	II
5 Financial managers	NM	1.1, 2.1	II	—	—	1.2, 2.2	II	—	—	—	—
6 Underwriters, brokers, investment analysts	NM	5.1	II	5.1	II	1.2, 2.2	II	—	—	—	—
7 Taxation experts	NM	—	—	5.1	II	1.2, 2.2	II	—	—	—	—
003 Personnel and industrial relations managers; O and M, work study and operational research officers											
1 Personnel and industrial relations officers	NM	5.1	II	5.1	II	1.2, 2.2	II	—	—	5.1	II
2 O and M, work study and OR officers	NM	5.1	II	5.1	II	1.2, 2.2	II	—	—	—	—
004 Economists, statisticians, systems analysts, computer programmers											
1 Economists, statisticians, actuaries	NM	3	I	3	I	—	—	—	—	4	I
2 Systems analysts, computer programmers	NM	5.1	II	5.1	II	1.2, 2.2	II	—	—	5.1	II
005 Marketing, sales, advertising, public relations and purchasing managers											
1 Marketing and sales managers and executives	NM	1.1, 2.1	II	5.1	II	1.2, 2.2	II	—	—	—	—
2 Advertising and PR executives	NM	1.1, 2.1	II	5.1	II	1.2, 2.2	II	—	—	—	—
3 Buyers (retail trade)	NM	—	—	—	—	1.2, 2.2	II	—	—	—	—
4 Buyers and purchasing officers (not retail)	NM	—	—	—	—	1.2, 2.2	II	—	—	—	—
006 Statutory and other inspectors											
1 Environmental health officers	NM	—	—	—	—	—	—	—	—	5.1	II
2 Building inspectors	NM	—	—	—	—	—	—	—	—	5.1	II
3 Inspectors (statutory and similar)	NM	—	—	—	—	—	—	—	—	5.1	II
007 General administrators—national government											
1 General administrators—national government (Assistant Secretary level and above)	NM	—	—	—	—	1.2	I	—	—	—	—
2 General administrators—national government (HEO to Senior Principal level)	NM	—	—	—	—	1.2	II	—	—	—	—
008 Local government officers (administrative and executive functions)											
0 Local government officers (administrative and executive functions)	NM	—	—	—	—	1.2	II	—	—	—	—

009	All other professional and related supporting management and administration										
1	Company secretaries	NM	5.1	II	5.1	II	1.2, 2.2	II	—	—	—	—
2	Officials of trade associations, trade unions, professional bodies and charities	NM	—	II	—	II	1.2, 2.2	II	—	—	5.1	II
3	Property and estate managers	NM	5.1	II	5.1	II	1.2, 2.2	II	—	—	5.1	—
4	Librarians, information officers	NM	—	—	—	—	1.2, 2.2	II	—	—	5.1	II
5	Legal service and related occupations	NM	5.1	II	5.1	II	1.2, 2.2	II	—	—	5.1	II
6	Management consultants	NM	3	—	3	—	—	—	—	—	4	—
7	Managers' personal assistants	NM	—	—	—	—	—	—	—	—	6	—
8	Professional workers and related supporting management and administration n.e.c.	NM	—	—	—	—	—	—	—	—	—	III N
010	Teachers in higher education											
1	University academic staff	NM	—	—	—	—	—	—	—	—	4	—
2	Teachers in establishments for further and higher education	NM	5.1	II	5.1	II	1.2, 2.2	II	—	—	5.1	II
011	Teachers n.e.c.											
0	Teachers n.e.c.	NM	5.1	II	5.1	II	1.2, 2.2	II	—	—	5.1	II
012	Vocational and industrial trainers, education officers, social and behavioural scientists											
1	Vocational and industrial trainers	NM	5.1	II	5.1	II	1.2, 2.2	II	—	—	5.1	II
2	Education officers, school inspectors	NM	—	—	—	—	—	—	—	—	4	—
3	Social and behavioural scientists	NM	3	—	3	—	—	—	—	—	4	—
013	Welfare workers											
1	Matrons, houseparents	NM	1.1, 2.1	II	12	II	1.2, 2.2	II	—	—	7	II
2	Playgroup leaders	NM	2.1	III N	12	III N	—	—	—	—	6	III N
3	Welfare occupations n.e.c.	NM	—	—	—	—	1.2, 2.2	II	—	—	5.1	II
014	Clergy, ministers of religion											
0	Clergy, ministers of religion	NM	3	—	3	—	—	—	—	—	4	—
015	Medical and dental practitioners											
1	Medical practitioners	NM	3	—	3	—	—	—	—	—	4	—
2	Dental practitioners	NM	3	—	3	—	—	—	—	—	4	—
016	Nurse administrators, nurses											
0	Nurse administrators, nurses	NM	5.1	II	5.1	II	1.2, 2.2	II	5.1	II	5.1	II
017	Pharmacists, radiographers, therapists n.e.c.											
1	Pharmacists	NM	3	—	3	—	—	II	—	II	4	II
2	Medical radiographers	NM	5.1	II	5.1	II	1.2, 2.2	II	5.1	—	5.1	II
3	Ophthalmic and dispensing opticians	NM	3	—	3	—	—	—	—	II	4	—
4	Physiotherapists	NM	5.1	II	5.1	II	1.2, 2.2	II	5.1	II	5.1	II
5	Chiropodists	NM	5.1	II	5.1	II	1.2, 2.2	II	—	—	5.1	II
6	Therapists n.e.c.	NM	5.1	II	5.1	II	1.2, 2.2	II	5.1	II	5.1	II

Occupation	Manual Non-manual	Self-employed with employees		Self-employed without employees		Managers		Foremen		Apprentices, etc., Employees n.e.c.	
		S.E.G.	Social Class	S.E.G.	Social Class	S.E.G.	Social Class	S.E.G.	Social Class	S.E.G.	Social Class
018 All other professional and related in education, welfare and health											
1 Medical technicians, dental auxiliaries	NM	5.1	II	5.1	II	1.2, 2.2	II	5.1	II	5.1	II
2 Veterinarians	NM	3	I	3	I	—	II	—	—	4	I
3 Driving instructors (not HGV)	NM	2.1	III N	12	III N	2.2	II	—	—	6	III N
4 Professional and related in education, welfare and health n.e.c.	NM	5.1	II	5.1	II	1.2, 2.2	II	—	—	5.1	II
019 Authors, writers, journalists											
0 Authors, writers, journalists	NM	1.1, 2.1	II	5.1	II	1.2, 2.2	II	5.1	II	5.1	II
020 Artists, designers, window dressers											
1 Artists, commercial artists	NM	1.1, 2.1	II	5.1	II	1.2, 2.2	II	—	—	5.1	II
2 Industrial designers (not clothing)	NM	1.1, 2.1	II	5.1	II	1.2, 2.2	II	—	—	5.1	II
3 Clothing designers	NM	1.1, 2.1	II	5.1	II	1.2, 2.2	II	—	—	5.1	II
4 Window dressers	NM	1.1, 2.1	II	5.1	II	1.2, 2.2	II	—	—	5.1	II
021 Actors, musicians, entertainers, stage managers											
1 Actors, entertainers, singers, stage managers	NM	1.1, 2.1	II	5.1	II	1.2, 2.2	II	—	—	5.1	II
2 Musicians	NM	1.1, 2.1	II	5.1	II	1.2, 2.2	II	—	—	5.1	II
022 Photographers, cameramen, sound and vision equipment operators											
1 Photographers, cameramen	NM	1.1, 2.1	III N	12	III N	1.2, 2.2	II	5.2	III N	6	III N
2 Sound and vision equipment operators	NM	1.1, 2.1	III N	12	III N	1.2, 2.2	II	5.2	III N	6	III N
023 All other literary, artistic and sports											
1 Professional sportsmen, sports officials	NM	1.1, 2.1	III N	12	III N	1.2, 2.2	II	—	—	6	III N
2 Literary, artistic and sports workers n.e.c.	NM	1.1, 2.1	III N	12	III N	1.2, 2.2	II	—	—	6	III N
024 Scientists, physicists, mathematicians											
1 Biological scientists, biochemists	NM	3	I	3	I	—	—	—	—	4	I
2 Chemical scientists	NM	3	I	3	I	—	—	—	—	4	I
3 Physical and geological scientists, mathematicians	NM	3	I	3	I	—	—	—	—	4	I
025 Civil, structural, municipal, mining and quarrying engineers											
0 Civil, structural, municipal, mining and quarrying engineers	NM	3	I	3	I	—	—	—	—	4	I
026 Mechanical and aeronautical engineers											
1 Mechanical and aeronautical engineers	NM	3	I	3	I	—	—	—	—	4	I
2 Design and development engineers (mechanical)	NM	3	I	3	I	—	—	—	—	4	I
027 Electrical and electronic engineers											
1 Electrical engineers	NM	3	I	3	I	—	—	—	—	4	I
2 Electronic engineers	NM	3	I	3	I	—	—	—	—	4	I

Code	Occupation										
028	Engineers and technologists n.e.c.										
1	Chemical engineers	NM	3	—	3	—	—	—	4	I
2	Production engineers	NM	3	—	3	—	—	—	4	I
3	Planning and quality control engineers	NM	3	—	3	—	—	—	4	I
4	Engineers n.e.c.	NM	3	—	3	—	—	—	4	I
5	Metallurgists	NM	3	—	3	—	—	—	4	I
6	Technologists n.e.c.	NM	3	—	3	—	—	—	4	I
029	Draughtsmen										
0	Draughtsmen	NM	1.1, 2.1	III N	12	III N	1.2, 2.2	II	5.2	III N	6	III N
030	Laboratory and engineering technicians, technician engineers										
1	Laboratory technicians	NM	5.1	II	5.1	II	2.2	II	5.1	II	5.1	II
2	Engineering technicians, technician engineers	NM	5.1	II	5.1	II	1.2, 2.2	II	5.1	II	5.1	II
031	Architects, town planners, quantity, building and land surveyors										
1	Architects, town planners	NM	3	I	3	I	—	—	—	—	4	I
2	Quantity surveyors	NM	5.1	II	5.1	II	—	—	—	—	5.1	II
3	Building, land and mining surveyors	NM	3	I	3	I	—	—	—	—	4	I
032	Officers (ships and aircraft), air traffic planners and controllers										
1	Aircraft flight deck officers	NM	1.1	II	12	II	1.2	II	—	—	5.1	II
2	Air traffic planners and controllers	NM	—	—	—	—	—	—	—	—	5.1	II
3	Deck, engineering and radio officers and pilots, ship	NM	1.1	II	12	II	1.2	II	5.1	II	—	—
033	Professional and related in science, engineering and other technologies and similar fields n.e.c.										
1	Architectural and town planning technicians	NM	—	—	5.1	II	—	—	—	—	5.1	II
2	Building and civil engineering technicians	NM	—	—	—	—	1.2, 2.2	—	—	—	5.1	II
3	Technical and related workers n.e.c.	NM	5.1	II	5.1	II	1.2, 2.2	II	5.1	II	5.1	II
034	Production, works and maintenance managers, works foremen										
0	Production, works and maintenance managers, works foremen	NM	—	—	—	—	1.2, 2.2	II	5.2	III N	—	—
035	Site and other managers, agents and clerks of works, general foremen (building and civil engineering)										
1	Managers in building and contracting	NM	—	—	—	—	1.2, 2.2	II	—	—	—	—
2	Clerks of works	NM	—	—	—	—	—	—	—	—	6	III N
036	Managers in transport, warehousing, public utilities and mining										
1	Managers in mining and public utilities	NM	—	—	—	—	1.2, 2.2	II	—	—	—	—
2	Transport managers	NM	—	—	—	—	1.2, 2.2	II	—	—	—	—
3	Stores controllers	NM	—	—	—	—	1.2, 2.2	II	—	—	—	—
4	Managers in warehousing and materials handling n.e.c.	NM	—	—	—	—	1.2, 2.2	II	—	—	—	—
037	Office managers										
1	Credit controllers	NM	—	—	—	—	1.2, 2.2	II	—	—	—	—
2	Office managers n.e.c.	NM	1.1, 2.1	II	12	II	1.2, 2.2	II	—	—	—	—

Occupation	Manual Non-manual	Self-employed with employees		Self-employed without employees		Managers		Foremen		Apprentices, etc., Employees n.e.c.	
		S.E.G.	Social Class	S.E.G.	Social Class	S.E.G.	Social Class	S.E.G.	Social Class	S.E.G.	Social Class
038 Managers in wholesale and retail distribution											
1 Garage proprietors	NM	1.1, 2.1	II	12	II	—	—	—	—	—	—
2 Butchers (managers and proprietors)	NM	1.1, 2.1	III N	12	III N	2.2	II	—	—	—	—
3 Fishmongers (managers and proprietors)	NM	1.1, 2.1	III N	12	III N	2.2	II	—	—	—	—
4 Other proprietors and managers (sales)	NM	1.1, 2.1	II	12	II	1.2, 2.2	II	—	—	—	—
039 Managers of hotels, clubs, etc., and in entertainment and sport											
1 Hotel and residential club managers	NM	1.1, 2.1	II	12	II	1.2, 2.2	II	—	—	—	—
2 Publicans	NM	1.1, 2.1	II	12	II	1.2, 2.2	II	—	—	—	—
3 Restaurateurs	NM	1.1, 2.1	III N	12	III N	1.2, 2.2	III N	—	—	—	—
4 Club stewards	NM	—	—	—	—	2.2	II	—	—	—	—
5 Entertainment and sports managers	NM	1.1, 2.1	III N	12	III N	1.2, 2.2	II	—	—	—	—
040 Farmers, horticulturists, farm managers											
0 Farmers, horticulturists, farm managers	NM	13	II	14	II	13	II	—	—	—	—
041 Officers, UK armed forces											
0 Officers, UK armed forces	—	—	—	—	—	16	—	—	—	—	—
042 Officers, foreign and Commonwealth armed forces											
0 Officers, foreign and Commonwealth armed forces	—	—	—	—	—	16	—	—	—	—	—
043 Senior police, prison and fire service officers											
1 Prison officers (chief officers and above)	NM	—	—	—	—	1.2	II	—	—	—	—
2 Police officers (inspectors and above)	NM	—	—	—	—	1.2	II	—	—	—	—
3 Fire service officers	NM	—	—	—	—	1.2	II	—	—	—	—
044 All other managers											
1 Proprietors and managers, service flats, holiday flats, caravan sites, etc.	NM	1.1, 2.1	III N	12	III N	1.2, 2.2	II	—	—	—	—
2 Managers of laundry and dry cleaning receiving shops	NM	2.1	IV	12	IV	2.2	III N	—	—	—	—
3 Hairdressers' and barbers' managers and proprietors	NM	1.1, 2.1	III N	12	III N	1.2, 2.2	II	—	—	—	—
4 Managers n.e.c.	NM	1.1, 2.1	II	12	II	1.2, 2.2	II	—	—	—	—
045 Supervisors of clerks, civil service executive officers											
1 Civil service executive officers	NM	—	—	—	—	—	—	5.1	II	—	—
2 Supervisors of—											
2 Stores and despatch clerks	NM	—	—	—	—	—	—	5.2	III N	—	—
3 Tracers, drawing office assistants	NM	—	—	—	—	—	—	5.2	III N	—	—
4 Other clerks and cashiers (not retail)	NM	—	—	—	—	—	—	5.2	III N	—	—
5 Retail shop cashiers, check-out and cash and wrap operators	NM	—	—	—	—	—	—	5.2	III N	—	—

Code		Occupation									
046		Clerks	NM	—	—	—	—	—	—	—	—
	1	Stores and despatch clerks	NM	—	—	12	—	—	—	—	6	III N
	2	Tracers, drawing office assistants	NM	1.1, 2.1	III N	12	III N	—	—	—	6	III N
	3	Other clerks and cashiers (not retail)	NM	—	III N	12	III N	—	—	—	6	III N
047	0	Retail shop cashiers, check-out and cash and wrap operators	NM	—	—	—	—	—	—	—	6	III N
048		Supervisors of typists, office machine operators, telephonists, etc.										
		Supervisors of—										
	1	Typists, shorthand writers, secretaries	NM	—	—	—	—	—	—	5.2	III N	—	—
	2	Office machine operators	NM	—	—	—	—	—	—	5.2	III N	—	—
	3	Telephone operators	NM	—	—	—	—	—	—	5.2	III N	—	—
	4	Radio and telegraph operators	NM	—	—	—	—	—	—	5.2	III N	—	—
049		Secretaries, shorthand typists, receptionists										
	1	Receptionists	NM	1.1, 2.1	—	12	—	—	—	—	6	III N
	2	Typists, shorthand writers, secretaries	NM	1.1, 2.1	III N	12	III N	—	—	—	6	III N
050	0	Office machine operators	NM	1.1, 2.1	III N	12	III N	—	—	—	6	III N
051		Telephonists, radio and telegraph operators										
	1	Telephonist receptionists	NM	—	—	—	—	—	—	—	6	III N
	2	Telephone operators	NM	—	—	—	—	—	—	—	6	IV
	3	Radio and telegraph operators	NM	—	—	—	—	—	—	—	6	III N
052		Supervisors of postmen, mail sorters, messengers										
		Supervisors of—										
	1	Postmen, mail sorters	M	—	—	—	—	—	—	8	III M	—	—
	2	Messengers	M	—	—	—	—	—	—	8	III M	—	—
053		Postmen, mail sorters, messengers										
	1	Postmen, mail sorters	M	—	—	12	V	—	—	—	10	IV
	2	Messengers	M	—	—	—	—	—	—	—	11	V
054		Sales supervisors										
		Supervisors of—										
	1	Shop salesmen and assistants	NM	—	—	—	—	—	—	5.2	III N	—	—
	2	Petrol pump, forecourt attendants	NM	—	—	—	—	—	—	5.2	III N	—	—
	3	Roundsmen, van salesmen	NM	—	—	—	—	—	—	5.2	III N	—	—
055		Salesmen, sales assistants, shop assistants, shelf fillers, petrol pump, forecourt attendants										
	1	Shop salesmen and assistants	NM	—	—	—	—	—	—	—	6	III N
	2	Shelf fillers	NM	—	—	—	—	—	—	—	6	IV
	3	Petrol pump, forecourt attendants	NM	—	—	—	—	—	—	—	6	III N
056	0	Roundsmen, van salesmen	M	1.1, 2.1	III M	12	III M	II	1.2, 2.2	—	9	III M

Occupation	Manual Non-manual	Self-employed with employees		Self-employed without employees		Managers		Foremen		Apprentices, etc., Employees n.e.c.	
		S.E.G.	Social Class	S.E.G.	Social Class	S.E.G.	Social Class	S.E.G.	Social Class	S.E.G.	Social Class
057 Sales representatives and agents											
1 Importers, exporters, commodity brokers	NM	1.1, 2.1	II	12	II	1.2, 2.2	II	—	—	—	—
2 Market and street traders and assistants	NM	1.1, 2.1	IV	12	IV	2.2	III N	—	—	6	IV
3 Scrap dealers, general dealers, rag and bone merchants	NM	1.1, 2.1	III N	12	III N	1.2, 2.2	III N	—	—	—	—
4 Credit agents, collector salesmen	NM	1.1, 2.1	IV	12	IV	2.2	III N	—	—	6	IV
5 Sales representatives	NM	1.1, 2.1	III N	12	III N	2.2	II	—	—	6	III N
6 Sales representatives (property and services), other agents	NM	1.1, 2.1	III N	12	III N	1.2, 2.2	II	—	—	6	III N
058 NCOs and other ranks, UK armed forces											
0 NCOs and other ranks, UK armed forces	—	—	—	—	—	—	—	—	—	16	—
059 NCOs and other ranks, foreign and Commonwealth armed forces											
0 NCOs and other ranks, foreign and Commonwealth armed forces	—	—	—	—	—	—	—	—	—	16	—
060 Supervisors (police sergeants, fire fighting and related)											
1 Police sergeants	NM	—	—	—	—	—	—	5.2	III N	—	—
2 Fire service supervisors	NM	—	—	—	—	—	—	5.2	III N	—	—
3 Prison service principal officers	NM	—	—	—	—	—	—	5.2	III N	—	—
Supervisors of—											
4 Security guards and officers, patrolmen, watchmen	NM	—	—	—	—	—	—	5.2	III N	—	—
5 Traffic wardens	NM	—	—	—	—	—	—	5.2	III N	—	—
6 Security and protective service workers n.e.c.	NM	—	—	—	—	—	—	5.2	III N	—	—
061 Policemen, firemen, prison officers											
1 Policemen (below sergeant)	NM	—	—	—	—	—	—	—	—	6	III N
2 Firemen	NM	—	—	—	—	—	—	—	—	6	III N
3 Prison officers (below principal officer)	NM	—	—	—	—	—	—	—	—	6	IV
062 Other security and protective service workers											
1 Security guards and officers, patrolmen, watchmen	M	1.1, 2.1	IV	12	IV	—	—	—	—	10	IV
2 Traffic wardens	M	—	—	—	—	—	—	—	—	10	IV
3 Security and protective service workers n.e.c.	M	1.1, 2.1	IV	12	IV	—	—	—	—	10	IV
063 Catering supervisors											
Supervisors of—											
1 Chefs, cooks	M	—	—	—	—	—	—	7	III M	—	—
2 Waiters, waitresses	M	—	—	—	—	—	—	7	III M	—	—
3 Barmen, barmaids	M	—	—	—	—	—	—	7	III M	—	—
4 Counter hands, assistants	M	—	—	—	—	—	—	7	III M	—	—
064 Chefs, cooks											
0 Chefs, cooks	M	1.1, 2.1	III M	12	III M	1.2, 2.2	II	—	—	7	III M

Code		Occupation											
065		Waiters and bar staff	M	—	—	—	—	—	—	—	—	7	IV
	1	Waiters, waitresses	M	—	—	—	IV	—	—	—	—	7	IV
	2	Barmen, barmaids	M	—	—	—	IV	—	—	—	—	7	IV
066		Counter hands, assistants, kitchen porters, hands	M	—	—	—	—	—	—	—	—	—	—
	1	Counter hands, assistants	M	—	—	—	—	—	—	8	III M	7	IV
	2	Kitchen porters, hands	M	—	—	—	—	—	—	—	—	11	V
067		Supervisors—housekeeping and related	M	—	—	—	—	—	—	—	—	—	—
	1	Housekeepers (non-domestic)	M	—	—	—	—	—	—	7	III M	—	—
		Supervisors of—											
	2	Other domestic and school helpers	M	—	—	—	—	—	—	7	III M	—	—
	3	Travel stewards and attendants	M	—	—	—	—	—	—	7	III M	—	—
	4	Hospital porters	M	—	—	—	—	—	—	8	III M	—	—
	5	Hotel porters	M	—	—	—	—	—	—	8	III M	—	—
	6	Ambulancemen	M	—	—	—	—	—	—	8	III M	—	—
	7	Hospital, ward orderlies	M	—	—	—	—	—	—	8	III M	—	—
068		Domestic staff and school helpers	M	—	—	—	—	—	—	—	—	—	—
	1	Domestic housekeepers	M	1.1, 2.1	III M	12	III M	—	—	—	—	7	III M
	2	Nursery nurses	M	—	—	12	IV	—	—	—	—	7	III M
	3	Other domestic and school helpers	M	—	—	—	—	—	—	—	—	7	IV
069		Travel stewards and attendants, hospital and hotel porters	M	—	—	—	—	—	—	—	—	—	—
	1	Travel stewards and attendants	M	—	—	12	III M	—	—	—	—	7	III M
	2	Hospital porters	M	—	—	—	—	—	—	—	—	10	IV
	3	Hotel porters	M	—	—	—	—	—	—	—	—	10	IV
070		Ambulancemen, hospital orderlies	M	—	—	—	—	—	—	—	—	—	—
	1	Ambulancemen	M	—	—	—	—	—	—	—	—	9	III M
	2	Hospital, ward orderlies	M	—	—	—	—	—	—	—	—	10	IV
071		Supervisors, foremen—caretaking, cleaning and related	M	—	—	—	—	—	—	—	—	—	—
		Supervisors of—											
	1	Caretakers	M	—	—	—	—	—	—	8	III M	—	—
	2	Cleaners, window cleaners, chimney sweeps, road sweepers	M	—	—	—	—	—	—	8	III M	—	—
	3	Railway stationmen	M	—	—	—	—	—	—	8	III M	—	—
	4	Lift and car park attendants	M	—	—	—	—	—	—	8	III M	—	—
072		Caretakers, road sweepers and other cleaners	M	—	—	—	—	—	—	—	—	—	—
	1	Caretakers	M	1.1, 2.1	V	12	V	2.2	III M	—	—	10	IV
	2	Cleaners, window cleaners, chimney sweeps, road sweepers	M	—	—	—	—	—	—	—	—	11	V
073		Hairdressing supervisors	M	—	—	—	—	—	—	7	III M	—	—
	0	Hairdressing supervisors	M	—	—	—	—	—	—	—	—	—	—
074		Hairdressers, barbers	M	—	—	—	—	—	—	—	—	7	III M
	0	Hairdressers, barbers	M	—	—	—	—	—	—	—	—	—	—

Occupation	Manual Non-manual	Self-employed with employees		Self-employed without employees		Managers		Foremen		Apprentices, etc., Employees n.e.c.	
		S.E.G.	Social Class	S.E.G.	Social Class	S.E.G.	Social Class	S.E.G.	Social Class	S.E.G.	Social Class
075 All other in catering, cleaning and other personal service											
1 Railway stationmen	M	—	—	—	—	—	—	—	—	11	V
2 Lift and car park attendants	M	—	—	—	—	—	—	—	—	11	V
3 Launderers, dry cleaners, pressers	M	1.1, 2.1	III M	12	—	1.2, 2.2	III M	8	III M	10	IV
4 Undertakers	M	1.1, 2.1	III M	12	III M	1.2, 2.2	II	—	—	—	—
5 Bookmakers, betting shop managers	M	1.1, 2.1	III M	12	III M	1.2, 2.2	II	—	—	—	—
6 Service workers n.e.c.	M	1.1, 2.1	IV	12	IV	1.2, 2.2	III M	8	III M	10	IV
076 Foremen—farming, horticulture, forestry											
1 Farm foremen	M	—	—	—	—	—	—	15	III M	—	—
2 Horticultural foremen	M	—	—	—	—	—	—	15	III M	—	—
3 Foremen gardeners and groundsmen	M	—	—	—	—	—	—	8	III M	—	—
4 Agricultural machinery foremen	M	—	—	—	—	—	—	15	III M	—	—
5 Forestry foremen	M	—	—	—	—	—	—	15	III M	—	—
6 Other foremen in farming and related	M	—	—	—	—	—	—	15	III M	—	—
077 Farm workers											
0 Farm workers	M	15	IV	15	IV	—	—	—	—	15	IV
078 Horticultural workers, gardeners, groundsmen											
1 Horticultural workers	M	15	IV	15	IV	—	—	—	—	15	IV
2 Gardeners, groundsmen	M	1.1, 2.1	IV	12	IV	1.2, 2.2	III M	—	—	10	IV
079 Agricultural machinery drivers, operators											
0 Agricultural machinery drivers, operators	M	15	IV	15	IV	—	—	—	—	15	IV
080 Forestry workers											
0 Forestry workers	M	15	IV	15	IV	—	—	—	—	15	IV
081 Supervisors, mates—fishing											
0 Supervisors, mates—fishing	M	—	—	—	—	—	—	8	III M	—	—
082 Fishermen											
0 Fishermen	M	2.1	IV	12	IV	2.2	III M	—	—	10	IV
083 All other in farming and related											
0 All other in farming and related	M	15	IV	15	IV	—	—	—	—	15	IV

084	Foremen—tannery and leather (including leather substitutes) working											
	Foremen—											
1	Tannery production workers	M	—	—	—	—	—	—	III M	8	III M	—	—
2	Shoe repairers	M	—	—	—	—	—	—	III M	8	III M	—	—
3	Leather cutters and sewers, footwear lasters, makers, finishers	M	—	—	—	—	—	—	III M	8	III M	—	—
4	Other making and repairing, leather	M	—	—	—	—	—	—	—	—	—	—	—
085	Tannery and leather (including leather substitutes) workers											
1	Tannery production workers	M	1.1, 2.1	III M	12	III M	2.2	II	—	—	III M	9	III M
2	Shoe repairers	M	1.1, 2.1	III M	12	III M	2.2	II	—	—	III M	9	III M
3	Leather cutters and sewers, footwear lasters, makers, finishers	M	1.1, 2.1	III M	12	III M	2.2	II	—	—	III M	9	III M
086	Foremen—textile processing											
	Foremen—											
1	Preparatory fibre processors	M	—	—	—	—	—	—	III M	8	III M	—	—
2	Spinners, doublers, twisters	M	—	—	—	—	—	—	III M	8	III M	—	—
3	Winders, reelers	M	—	—	—	—	—	—	III M	8	III M	—	—
4	Warp preparers	M	—	—	—	—	—	—	III M	8	III M	—	—
5	Weavers	M	—	—	—	—	—	—	III M	8	III M	—	—
6	Knitters	M	—	—	—	—	—	—	III M	8	III M	—	—
7	Bleachers, dyers, finishers	M	—	—	—	—	—	—	III M	8	III M	—	—
8	Menders, darners	M	—	—	—	—	—	—	III M	8	III M	—	—
9	Other material processing, textiles	M	—	—	—	—	—	—	III M	8	III M	—	—
087	Textile workers											
1	Preparatory fibre processors	M	1.1, 2.1	IV	12	IV	2.2	III M	—	—	IV	10	IV
2	Spinners, doublers, twisters	M	1.1, 2.1	IV	12	IV	2.2	III M	—	—	IV	10	IV
3	Winders, reelers	M	1.1, 2.1	IV	12	IV	2.2	III M	—	—	IV	10	IV
4	Warp preparers	M	1.1, 2.1	III M	12	III M	2.2	II	—	—	III M	9	III M
5	Weavers	M	1.1, 2.1	III M	12	III M	2.2	II	—	—	III M	9	III M
6	Knitters	M	1.1, 2.1	III M	12	III M	2.2	II	—	—	III M	9	III M
7	Bleachers, dyers, finishers	M	1.1, 2.1	III M	12	III M	2.2	II	—	—	III M	9	III M
8	Menders, darners	M	1.1, 2.1	III M	12	III M	2.2	II	—	—	III M	9	III M
088	Foremen—chemical processing											
0	Foremen—chemical processing	M	—	—	—	—	—	—	III M	8	III M	—	—
089	Chemical, gas and petroleum process plant operators											
0	Chemical, gas and petroleum process plant operators	M	1.1, 2.1	IV	12	IV	2.2	III M	—	—	—	10	IV
090	Foremen—food and drink processing											
	Foremen—											
1	Bakers, flour confectioners	M	—	—	—	—	—	—	III M	8	III M	—	—
2	Butchers, meat cutters	M	—	—	—	—	—	—	III M	8	III M	—	—
3	Fishmongers, poultry dressers	M	—	—	—	—	—	—	III M	8	III M	—	—
4	Brewery and vinery process workers	M	—	—	—	—	—	—	III M	8	III M	—	—
	Other material processing—											
5	Bakery and confectionery workers	M	—	—	—	—	—	—	III M	8	III M	—	—
6	Food and drink n.e.c.	M	—	—	—	—	—	—	III M	8	III M	—	—

Occupation	Manual / Non-manual	Self-employed with employees		Self-employed without employees		Managers		Foremen		Apprentices, etc., Employees n.e.c.	
		S.E.G.	Social Class	S.E.G.	Social Class	S.E.G.	Social Class	S.E.G.	Social Class	S.E.G.	Social Class
091 Bakers, flour confectioners											
0 Bakers, flour confectioners	M	1.1, 2.1	III M	12	III M	2.2	II	—	—	9	III M
092 Butchers											
1 Butchers, meat cutters	M	—	—	—	—	—	—	—	—	9	III M
2 Fishmongers, poultry dressers	M	—	—	—	—	—	—	—	—	9	III M
093 Foremen—paper and board making and paper products											
Foremen—											
1 Paper, paperboard and leatherboard workers	M	—	—	—	—	—	—	8	III M	—	—
2 Bookbinders and finishers	M	—	—	—	—	—	—	8	III M	—	—
3 Cutting and slitting machine operators (paper and paper products making)	M	—	—	—	—	—	—	8	III M	—	—
4 Other material processing, wood and paper	M	—	—	—	—	—	—	8	III M	—	—
5 Other making and repairing, paper goods and printing	M	—	—	—	—	—	—	8	III M	—	—
094 Paper, board and paper product makers, bookbinders											
1 Paper, paperboard and leatherboard workers	M	1.1, 2.1	III M	12	III M	2.2	II	—	—	9	III M
2 Bookbinders and finishers	M	1.1, 2.1	III M	12	III M	—	—	—	—	9	III M
3 Cutting and slitting machine operators (paper and paper products making)	M	—	—	—	—	—	—	—	—	9	III M
095 Foremen—glass, ceramics, rubber, plastics, etc.											
Foremen—											
1 Glass and ceramics furnacemen, kilnsetters	M	—	—	—	—	—	—	8	III M	—	—
2 Glass formers and shapers, finishers, decorators	M	—	—	—	—	—	—	8	III M	—	—
3 Casters and other pottery makers	M	—	—	—	—	—	—	8	III M	—	—
4 Rubber process workers, moulding machine operators, tyre builders	M	—	—	—	—	—	—	8	III M	—	—
5 Calender and extruding machine operators, moulders (plastics)	M	—	—	—	—	—	—	8	III M	—	—
6 Man-made fibre makers	M	—	—	—	—	—	—	8	III M	—	—
7 Washers, screeners and crushers in mines and quarries	M	—	—	—	—	—	—	8	III M	—	—
Other making and repairing—											
8 Glass and ceramics	M	—	—	—	—	—	—	8	III M	—	—
9 Rubber	M	—	—	—	—	—	—	8	III M	—	—
10 Plastics	M	—	—	—	—	—	—	8	III M	—	—
096 Glass and ceramics furnacemen and workers											
1 Glass and ceramics furnacemen, kilnsetters	M	1.1, 2.1	III M	12	III M	2.2	II	—	—	9	III M
2 Glass formers and shapers, finishers, decorators	M	1.1, 2.1	III M	12	III M	2.2	II	—	—	9	III M
3 Casters and other pottery makers	M	—	—	—	—	—	—	—	—	9	III M

097	Rubber and plastics workers										
1	Rubber process workers, moulding machine operators, tyre builders	M	1.1, 2.1	III M	12	III M	2.2	II	—	—	9	III M
2	Calender and extruding machine operators, moulders (plastics)	M	1.1, 2.1	IV	12	IV	2.2	III M	—	—	10	IV
098	All other in processing materials (other than metal)										
1	Man-made fibre makers	M	—	—	—	—	—	—	—	—	10	IV
2	Brewery and vinery process workers	M	1.1, 2.1	III M	12	III M	2.2	II	—	—	9	III M
3	Washers, screeners and crushers in mines and quarries	M	—	—	—	—	—	—	—	—	10	IV
	Other material processing—										
4	Textiles	M	1.1, 2.1	IV	12	IV	—	—	—	—	10	IV
5	Bakery and confectionery workers	M	1.1, 2.1	III M	12	III M	—	—	—	—	9	III M
6	Tobacco	M	—	—	—	—	—	—	8	—	10	IV
7	Food and drink n.e.c.	M	1.1, 2.1	IV	12	IV	2.2	—	—	—	10	IV
8	Wood and paper	M	1.1, 2.1	III M	12	III M	—	—	—	III M	9	III M
9	All other (excluding metal) n.e.c.	M	1.1, 2.1	IV	12	IV	—	—	8	III M	10	IV
099	Foremen—printing										
	Foremen—										
1	Compositors	M	—	—	—	—	—	—	8	III M	—	—
2	Electrotypers, stereotypers, printing plate and cylinder preparers	M	—	—	—	—	—	—	8	III M	—	—
3	Printing machine minders and assistants	M	—	—	—	—	—	—	8	III M	—	—
4	Screen and block printers	M	—	—	—	—	—	—	8	III M	—	—
5	Printers (so described)	M	—	—	—	—	—	—	—	III M	—	—
100	Printing workers, screen and block printers										
1	Compositors	M	1.1, 2.1	III M	12	III M	2.2	II	8	—	9	III M
2	Electrotypers, stereotypers, printing plate and cylinder preparers	M	1.1, 2.1	III M	12	III M	2.2	II	8	—	9	III M
3	Printing machine minders and assistants	M	1.1, 2.1	III M	12	III M	—	—	8	—	9	III M
4	Screen and block printers	M	1.1, 2.1	III M	12	III M	2.2	II	8	—	9	III M
5	Printers (so described)	M	1.1, 2.1	III M	12	III M	2.2	II	8	—	9	III M
101	Foremen—textile materials working										
	Foremen—										
1	Tailors, tailoresses, dressmakers	M	—	—	—	—	—	—	—	III M	—	—
2	Clothing cutters, milliners, furriers	M	—	—	—	—	—	—	—	III M	—	—
3	Sewers, embroiderers	M	—	—	—	—	—	—	—	III M	—	—
4	Coach trimmers, upholsterers, mattress makers	M	—	—	—	—	—	—	—	III M	—	—
5	Carpet fitters	M	—	—	—	—	—	—	—	III M	—	—
6	Other making and repairing, clothing and related products	M	—	—	—	—	—	—	—	III M	—	—
102	Tailors, dressmakers and other clothing workers										
1	Tailors, tailoresses, dressmakers	M	1.1, 2.1	III M	12	III M	2.2	II	—	—	9	III M
2	Clothing cutters, milliners, furriers	M	1.1, 2.1	III M	12	III M	2.2	II	—	—	9	III M
3	Sewers, embroiderers	M	1.1, 2.1	IV	12	IV	—	—	—	—	10	IV
103	Coach trimmers, upholsterers, mattress makers										
0	Coach trimmers, upholsterers, mattress makers	M	1.1, 2.1	III M	12	III M	2.2	II	—	—	9	III M

Occupation	Manual Non-manual	Self-employed with employees		Self-employed without employees		Managers		Foremen		Apprentices, etc., Employees n.e.c.	
		S.E.G.	Social Class	S.E.G.	Social Class	S.E.G.	Social Class	S.E.G.	Social Class	S.E.G.	Social Class
104 Foremen—woodworking											
Foremen—											
1 Carpenters, joiners	M	—	—	—	—	—	—	8	III M	—	—
2 Cabinet makers	M	—	—	—	—	—	—	8	III M	—	—
3 Case and box makers	M	—	—	—	—	—	—	8	III M	—	—
4 Pattern makers (moulds)	M	—	—	—	—	—	—	8	III M	—	—
5 Sawyers, veneer cutters, woodworking machinists	M	—	—	—	—	—	—	8	III M	—	—
6 Other making and repairing, wood	M	—	—	—	—	—	—	8	III M	—	—
105 Woodworkers, pattern makers											
1 Carpenters, joiners	M	1.1, 2.1	III M	12	III M	2.2	II	—	—	9	III M
2 Cabinet makers	M	1.1, 2.1	III M	12	III M	2.2	II	—	—	9	III M
3 Case and box makers	M	1.1, 2.1	III M	12	III M	2.2	II	—	—	9	III M
4 Pattern makers (moulds)	M	1.1, 2.1	III M	12	III M	2.2	II	—	—	9	III M
106 0 Sawyers, veneer cutters, woodworking machinists											
Sawyers, veneer cutters, woodworking machinists	M	1.1, 2.1	III M	12	III M	2.2	II	—	—	9	III M
107 All other in making and repairing (excluding metal and electrical)											
1 Labourers and mates to woodworking craftsmen	M	—	—	—	—	—	—	—	—	9	III M
2 Dental technicians	M	1.1, 2.1	III M	12	III M	2.2	II	8	III M	9	III M
3 Carpet fitters	M	1.1, 2.1	III M	12	III M	—	—	—	—	9	III M
4 Musical instrument makers, piano tuners	M	1.1, 2.1	III M	12	III M	2.2	II	8	III M	9	III M
Other making and repairing—											
5 Glass and ceramics	M	1.1, 2.1	III M	12	III M	2.2	II	—	—	9	III M
6 Wood	M	1.1, 2.1	III M	12	III M	2.2	II	—	—	9	III M
7 Leather	M	1.1, 2.1	III M	12	III M	2.2	II	—	—	9	III M
8 Clothing and related products	M	1.1, 2.1	III M	12	III M	2.2	II	—	—	9	III M
9 Paper goods and printing	M	1.1, 2.1	III M	12	III M	2.2	II	—	—	9	III M
10 Rubber	M	1.1, 2.1	III M	12	III M	2.2	III M	—	—	10	IV
11 Plastics	M	1.1, 2.1	IV	12	IV	2.2	III M	—	—	10	IV
12 All other (excluding metal and electrical) n.e.c.	M	1.1, 2.1	IV	12	IV	2.2	II	8	III M	—	—
108 Foremen—metal making and treating											
Foremen—											
1 Furnace operating occupations (metal)	M	—	—	—	—	—	—	8	III M	—	—
2 Rollermen	M	—	—	—	—	—	—	8	III M	—	—
3 Smiths, forgemen	M	—	—	—	—	—	—	8	III M	—	—
4 Metal drawers	M	—	—	—	—	—	—	8	III M	—	—
5 Moulders, coremakers, die casters	M	—	—	—	—	—	—	8	III M	—	—
6 Electroplaters	M	—	—	—	—	—	—	8	III M	—	—
7 Annealers, hardeners, temperers (metal)	M	—	—	—	—	—	—	8	III M	—	—
8 Galvanizers, tin platers, dip platers	M	—	—	—	—	—	—	8	III M	—	—
9 Metal making and treating workers n.e.c.	M	—	—	—	—	—	—	8	III M	—	—

109		Furnacemen (metal), rollermen, smiths, forgemen										
	1	Furnace operating occupations (metal)	M	1.1, 2.1	III M	12	III M	—	—	—	9	III M
	2	Rollermen	M	1.1, 2.1	III M	12	III M	II	—	—	9	III M
	3	Smiths, forgemen	M	1.1, 2.1	III M	12	III M	II	—	—	9	III M
110		Metal drawers, moulders, die casters, electroplaters, annealers										
	1	Metal drawers	M	1.1, 2.1	III M	12	III M	—	—	—	9	III M
	2	Moulders, coremakers, die casters	M	1.1, 2.1	III M	12	III M	—	—	—	9	III M
	3	Electroplaters	M	1.1, 2.1	III M	12	III M	2.2	—	—	9	III M
	4	Annealers, hardeners, temperers (metal)	M	1.1, 2.1	IV	12	IV	—	—	—	10	IV
111		Foremen—engineering machining										
		Foremen—										
	1	Press and machine tool setters	M	—	—	—	—	—	8	III M	—	—
	2	Centre lathe turners	M	—	—	—	—	—	8	III M	—	—
	3	Machine tool setter operators	M	—	—	—	—	—	8	III M	—	—
	4	Machine tool operators	M	—	—	—	—	—	8	III M	—	—
	5	Press, stamping and automatic machine operators	M	—	—	—	—	—	8	III M	—	—
	6	Metal polishers	M	—	—	—	—	—	8	III M	—	—
	7	Fettlers, dressers	M	—	—	—	—	—	8	III M	—	—
	8	Shot blasters	M	—	—	—	—	—	—	—	—	—
112		Press and machine tool setter operators and operators, turners										
	1	Press and machine tool setters	M	1.1, 2.1	III M	12	III M	II	—	—	9	III M
	2	Centre lathe turners	M	1.1, 2.1	III M	12	III M	II	—	—	9	III M
	3	Machine tool setter operators	M	1.1, 2.1	III M	12	III M	II	—	—	9	III M
	4	Machine tool operators	M	1.1, 2.1	IV	12	IV	—	—	—	10	IV
113		Machine attendants, minders, press and stamping machine operators, metal polishers, fettlers, dressers										
	1	Press, stamping and automatic machine operators	M	1.1, 2.1	IV	12	IV	2.2	—	—	10	IV
	2	Metal polishers	M	1.1, 2.1	III M	12	III M	2.2	—	—	9	III M
	3	Fettlers, dressers	M	1.1, 2.1	IV	12	IV	—	—	—	10	IV
114		Foremen—production fitting (metal)										
		Foremen—										
	1	Tool makers, tool fitters, markers-out	M	—	—	—	—	III M	8	III M	—	—
	2	Precision instrument makers and repairers	M	—	—	—	—	II	8	III M	—	—
	3	Watch and chronometer makers and repairers	M	—	—	—	—	—	8	III M	—	—
	4	Metal working production fitters and fitter/machinists	M	—	—	—	—	—	8	III M	—	—
	5	Motor mechanics, auto engineers	M	—	—	—	—	—	8	III M	—	—
	6	Maintenance fitters (aircraft engines)	M	—	—	—	—	—	8	III M	—	—
	7	Office machinery mechanics	M	—	—	—	—	—	8	—	—	—
115		Tool makers, tool fitters, markers-out										
	0	Tool makers, tool fitters, markers-out	M	1.1, 2.1	III M	12	III M	II	—	—	9	III M
116		Instrument and watch and clock makers and repairers										
	1	Precision instrument makers and repairers	M	1.1, 2.1	III M	12	III M	II	—	—	9	III M
	2	Watch and chronometer makers and repairers	M	1.1, 2.1	III M	12	III M	II	—	—	9	III M

Occupation	Manual Non-manual	Self-employed with employees		Self-employed without employees		Managers		Foremen		Apprentices, etc., Employees n.e.c.	
		S.E.G.	Social Class	S.E.G.	Social Class	S.E.G.	Social Class	S.E.G.	Social Class	S.E.G.	Social Class
117 Metal working production fitters and fitter/machinists											
Metal working production fitters and fitter/machinists	M	1.1, 2.1	III M	12	III M	2.2	II	—	—	9	III M
118 Motor vehicle and aircraft mechanics											
1 Motor mechanics, auto engineers	M	1.1, 2.1	III M	12	III M	2.2	II	—	—	9	III M
2 Maintenance fitters (aircraft engines)	M	—	—	12	III M	—	—	—	—	9	III M
119 Office machinery mechanics											
0 Office machinery mechanics	M	1.1, 2.1	III M	12	III M	2.2	II	—	—	9	III M
120 Foremen—production fitting and wiring (electrical)											
Foremen—											
1 Production fitters (electrical, electronic)	M	—	—	—	—	—	—	8	III M	—	—
2 Electricians, electrical maintenance fitters	M	—	—	—	—	—	—	8	III M	—	—
3 Plant operators and attendants n.e.c.	M	—	—	—	—	—	—	8	III M	—	—
4 Telephone fitters	M	—	—	—	—	—	—	8	III M	—	—
5 Cable jointers, linesmen	M	—	—	—	—	—	—	8	III M	—	—
6 Radio and TV mechanics	M	—	—	—	—	—	—	8	III M	—	—
7 Other electronic maintenance engineers	M	—	—	—	—	—	—	8	III M	—	—
121 Production fitters, electricians, electricity power plant operators, switchboard attendants											
1 Production fitters (electrical, electronic)	M	1.1, 2.1	III M	12	III M	2.2	II	—	—	9	III M
2 Electricians, electrical maintenance fitters	M	1.1, 2.1	III M	12	III M	2.2	II	—	—	9	III M
3 Electrical engineers (so described)	M	1.1, 2.1	III M	12	III M	2.2	II	—	—	9	III M
4 Plant operators and attendants n.e.c.	M	—	—	—	—	—	—	—	—	9	III M
122 Telephone fitters, cable jointers, linesmen											
1 Telephone fitters	M	—	—	12	III M	—	—	—	—	9	III M
2 Cable jointers, linesmen	M	—	—	12	III M	—	—	—	—	9	III M
123 Radio, TV and other electronic maintenance fitters and mechanics											
1 Radio and TV mechanics	M	1.1, 2.1	III M	12	III M	2.2	II	—	—	9	III M
2 Other electronic maintenance engineers	M	1.1, 2.1	III M	12	III M	2.2	II	—	—	9	III M
124 Foremen—metal working, pipes, sheets, structures											
Foremen—											
1 Plumbers, heating and ventilating fitters, gas fitters	M	—	—	—	—	—	—	8	III M	—	—
2 Sheet metal workers	M	—	—	—	—	—	—	8	III M	—	—
3 Metal plate workers, shipwrights, riveters	M	—	—	—	—	—	—	8	III M	—	—
4 Steel erectors, benders, fixers	M	—	—	—	—	—	—	8	III M	—	—
5 Scaffolders, stagers	M	—	—	—	—	—	—	8	III M	—	—
6 Welders	M	—	—	—	—	—	—	8	III M	—	—
7 Riggers	M	—	—	—	—	—	—	8	III M	—	—

125	Plumbers, heating and ventilating fitters, gas fitters									
	0 Plumbers, heating and ventilating fitters, gas fitters	M	1.1, 2.1	III M	12	III M	2.2	II	—	—	9	III M
126	Sheet metal workers, platers, shipwrights, riveters, etc.									
	1 Sheet metal workers	M	1.1, 2.1	III M	12	III M	2.2	II	—	—	9	III M
	2 Metal plate workers, shipwrights, riveters	M	1.1, 2.1	III M	12	III M	2.2	II	—	—	9	III M
127	Steel erectors, scaffolders, steel benders, fixers									
	1 Steel erectors, benders, fixers	M	1.1, 2.1	III M	12	III M	2.2	II	—	—	9	III M
	2 Scaffolders, stagers	M	1.1, 2.1	IV	12	IV	—	—	—	—	10	IV
128	Welders									
	0 Welders	M	1.1, 2.1	III M	12	III M	2.2	II	—	—	9	III M
129	Foremen—other processing, making and repairing (metal and electrical)									
	Foremen—									
	1 Goldsmiths, silversmiths, precious stone workers	M	—	—	—	—	—	—	8	III M	—	—
	2 Engravers, etchers (printing)	M	—	—	—	—	—	—	8	III M	—	—
	3 Coach and vehicle body builders	M	—	—	—	—	—	—	8	III M	—	—
	4 Oilers, greasers, lubricators	M	—	—	—	—	—	—	8	III M	—	—
	5 Electronics wiremen	M	—	—	—	—	—	—	8	III M	—	—
	6 Coil winders	M	—	—	—	—	—	—	8	III M	—	—
130	Goldsmiths, silversmiths, etc., engravers, etchers									
	1 Goldsmiths, silversmiths, precious stone workers	M	1.1, 2.1	III M	12	III M	2.2	II	—	—	9	III M
	2 Engravers, etchers (printing)	M	1.1, 2.1	III M	12	III M	—	—	—	—	9	III M
131	All other in processing, making and repairing (metal and electrical)									
	1 Coach and vehicle body builders	M	1.1, 2.1	III M	12	III M	2.2	II	—	—	9	III M
	2 Galvanizers, tin platers, dip platers	M	1.1, 2.1	III M	12	III M	—	—	—	—	9	III M
	3 Metal making and treating workers n.e.c.	M	1.1, 2.1	III M	12	III M	—	—	—	—	9	III M
	4 Oilers, greasers, lubricators	M	—	—	—	—	—	—	—	—	9	III M
	5 Riggers	M	1.1, 2.1	III M	12	III M	2.2	II	—	—	9	III M
	6 Electronics wiremen	M	—	—	—	—	—	—	—	—	9	III M
	7 Coil winders	M	1.1, 2.1	III M	12	III M	2.2	II	—	—	9	III M
	8 Shot blasters	M	—	—	—	—	—	—	—	—	10	IV
	9 Other metal, jewellery, electrical production workers	M	1.1, 2.1	IV	12	IV	2.2	III M	8	III M	10	IV
	1 Foremen (engineering and allied trades)	M	—	—	—	—	—	—	8	III M	—	—
	2 Trainee craftsmen (engineering and allied trades)	M	—	—	—	—	—	—	—	—	9	III M
132	Foremen—painting and similar coating									
	Foremen—									
	1 Pottery decorators	M	—	—	—	—	—	—	8	III M	—	—
	2 Coach painters (so described)	M	—	—	—	—	—	—	8	III M	—	—
	3 Other spray painters	M	—	—	—	—	—	—	8	III M	—	—
	4 Painters and decorators n.e.c., french polishers	M	—	—	—	—	—	—	8	III M	—	—

Occupation	Manual Non-manual	Self-employed with employees		Self-employed without employees		Managers		Foremen		Apprentices, etc., Employees n.e.c.	
		S.E.G.	Social Class	S.E.G.	Social Class	S.E.G.	Social Class	S.E.G.	Social Class	S.E.G.	Social Class
133 Painters, decorators, french polishers											
1 Pottery decorators	M	1.1, 2.1	III M	12	III M	—	—	—	—	9	III M
2 Coach painters (so described)	M	1.1, 2.1	III M	12	III M	2.2	II	—	—	9	III M
3 Other spray painters	M	1.1, 2.1	IV	12	IV	2.2	III M	—	—	10	IV
4 Painters and decorators n.e.c., french polishers	M	1.1, 2.1	III M	12	III M	2.2	II	—	—	9	III M
134 Foremen—product assembling (repetitive)											
1 Electrical, electronic	M	—	—	—	—	—	—	8	III M	—	—
2 Instruments	M	—	—	—	—	—	—	8	III M	—	—
3 Vehicles and other metal goods	M	—	—	—	—	—	—	8	III M	—	—
4 Paper production, processing and printing	M	—	—	—	—	—	—	8	III M	—	—
5 Plastics goods	M	—	—	—	—	—	—	8	III M	—	—
135 Repetitive assemblers (metal and electrical goods)											
1 Assemblers (electrical, electronic)	M	1.1, 2.1	IV	12	IV	—	—	—	—	10	IV
2 Instrument assemblers	M	—	—	12	III M	—	—	—	—	9	III M
3 Assemblers (vehicles and other metal goods)	M	—	—	12	IV	—	—	—	—	10	IV
136 Foremen—product inspection and packaging Foremen inspectors, viewers, examiners—											
1 Metal, electrical goods	M	—	—	—	—	—	—	8	III M	—	—
2 Textiles	M	—	—	—	—	—	—	8	III M	—	—
3 Food	M	—	—	—	—	—	—	8	III M	—	—
4 Rubber goods	M	—	—	—	—	—	—	8	III M	—	—
5 Plastics goods	M	—	—	—	—	—	—	8	III M	—	—
6 Woodwork	M	—	—	—	—	—	—	8	III M	—	—
Foremen—											
7 Packers, bottlers, canners, fillers	M	—	—	—	—	—	—	8	III M	—	—
8 Laboratory assistants	M	—	—	—	—	—	—	8	III M	—	—
9 Inspectors, sorters in paper production, processing and printing	M	—	—	—	—	—	—	8	III M	—	—
10 Weighers	M	—	—	—	—	—	—	8	III M	—	—
11 Graders, sorters, selectors n.e.c.	M	—	—	—	—	—	—	8	III M	—	—
137 1 Inspectors, viewers, testers, packers, bottlers, etc. Inspectors, viewers (metal, electrical goods)	M	—	—	12	IV	—	—	—	—	10	IV
2 Packers, bottlers, canners, fillers	M	1.1, 2.1	IV	12	IV	—	—	—	—	10	IV

Code		Occupation									
138		All other in painting, repetitive assembling, product inspection, packaging and related										
	1	Laboratory assistants	M	—	—	—	—	—	—	—	9	III M
		Inspectors, viewers, examiners—										
	2	Textiles	M	—	—	—	—	—	—	—	9	III M
	3	Food	M	—	—	—	—	—	—	—	10	IV
	4	Rubber goods	M	—	—	—	—	—	—	—	10	IV
	5	Plastics goods	M	—	—	—	—	—	—	—	10	IV
	6	Woodwork	M	—	—	—	—	—	—	—	9	III M
	7	Inspectors, sorters in paper production, processing and printing	M	—	—	12	III M	—	—	—	9	III M
	8	Assemblers in paper production, processing and printing	M	—	—	—	—	—	—	—	9	IV
	9	Assemblers (plastics goods)	M	—	—	—	—	—	—	—	10	IV
	10	Weighers	M	—	—	—	—	—	—	—	10	IV
	11	Graders, sorters, selectors n.e.c.	M	—	—	—	—	—	—	—	10	IV
	12	Painting, assembling and related occupations n.e.c.	M	1.1, 2.1	IV	12	IV	2.2	III M	8	III M	10	IV
139		Foremen—building and civil engineering n.e.c.										
		Foremen—										
	1	Bricklayers, tile setters	M	—	—	—	—	—	—	8	III M	—	—
	2	Masons, stone cutters	M	—	—	—	—	—	—	8	III M	—	—
	3	Plasterers	M	—	—	—	—	—	—	8	III M	—	—
	4	Roofers, glaziers	M	—	—	—	—	—	—	8	III M	—	—
	5	Handymen, general building workers	M	—	—	—	—	—	—	8	III M	—	—
	6	Railway lengthmen	M	—	—	—	—	—	—	8	III M	—	—
	7	Road surfacers, concreters	M	—	—	—	—	—	—	8	III M	—	—
	8	Roadmen	M	—	—	—	—	—	—	8	III M	—	—
	9	Paviors, kerb layers	M	—	—	—	—	—	—	8	III M	—	—
	10	Sewage plant attendants	M	—	—	—	—	—	—	8	III M	—	—
	11	Mains and service layers, pipe jointers	M	—	—	—	—	—	—	8	III M	—	—
	12	Construction workers n.e.c.	M	—	—	—	—	—	—	8	III M	—	—
140		Building and construction workers										
	1	Bricklayers, tile setters	M	1.1, 2.1	III M	12	III M	2.2	II	—	—	9	III M
	2	Masons, stone cutters	M	1.1, 2.1	III M	12	III M	2.2	II	—	—	9	III M
	3	Plasterers	M	1.1, 2.1	III M	12	III M	2.2	II	—	—	10	III M
	4	Roofers, glaziers	M	1.1, 2.1	IV	12	IV	2.2	III M	—	—	10	IV
	5	Handymen, general building workers	M	1.1, 2.1	IV	12	IV	2.2	III M	—	—	10	IV
	6	Builders (so described)	M	1.1, 2.1	III M	12	III M	2.2	II	—	—	9	III M
141		Concreters, road surfacers, railway lengthmen										
	1	Railway lengthmen	M	—	—	—	—	—	—	—	—	10	IV
	2	Road surfacers, concreters	M	2.1	V	12	IV	—	—	—	—	10	IV
	3	Roadmen	M	1.1, 2.1	IV	12	V	—	—	—	—	11	V
	4	Paviors, kerb layers	M	—	IV	12	IV	—	—	—	—	10	IV
142		Sewage plant attendants, sewermen (maintenance), mains and service layers, pipe jointers (gas, water, drainage, oil), inspectors (water supply), turncocks										
	1	Sewage plant attendants	M	—	—	—	—	—	—	—	—	11	V
	2	Mains and service layers, pipe jointers	M	1.1, 2.1	IV	12	IV	—	—	—	—	10	IV

Occupation	Manual Non-manual	Self-employed with employees		Self-employed without employees		Managers		Foremen		Apprentices, etc., Employees n.e.c.	
		S.E.G.	Social Class	S.E.G.	Social Class	S.E.G	Social Class	S.E.G.	Social Class	S.E.G.	Social Class
143 Civil engineering labourers, craftsmen's mates and other builders' labourers n.e.c.											
1 Craftsmen's mates	M	2.1	IV	12	IV	—	—	8	III M	10	IV
2 Building and civil engineering labourers	M	2.1	V	12	V	—	—	8	III M	11	V
144 Foremen/deputies—coalmining											
0 Foremen/deputies—coalmining	M	—	—	—	—	—	—	8	III M	—	—
145 Face-trained coalmining workers											
0 Face-trained coalmining workers	M	1.1, 2.1	III M	12	III M	—	—	—	—	9	III M
146 All other in construction, mining, quarrying, well drilling and related n.e.c.											
1 Miners (not coal), quarrymen, well drillers	M	1.1, 2.1	IV	12	IV	2.2	III M	8	III M	10	IV
2 Construction workers n.e.c.	M	1.1, 2.1	IV	12	IV	2.2	III M	—	—	10	IV
147 Foremen—ships, lighters and others vessels											
0 Foremen—ships, lighters and other vessels	M	—	—	—	—	—	—	8	III M	—	—
148 Deck, engine-room hands, bargemen, lightermen, boatmen											
0 Deck, engine-room hands, bargemen, lightermen, boatmen	M	1.1, 2.1	IV	12	IV	—	—	—	—	10	IV
149 Foremen—rail transport operating											
Foremen—											
1 Railway guards	M	—	—	—	—	—	—	8	III M	—	—
2 Signalmen and crossing keepers, railway	M	—	—	—	—	—	—	8	III M	—	—
3 Shunters, pointsmen	M	—	—	—	—	—	—	8	III M	—	—
4 Other foremen rail transport	M	—	—	—	—	—	—	8	III M	—	—
150 Rail transport operating staff											
1 Drivers, motormen, secondmen, railway engines	M	—	—	—	—	—	—	—	—	9	III M
2 Railway guards	M	—	—	—	—	—	—	—	—	9	III M
3 Signalmen and crossing keepers, railway	M	—	—	—	—	—	—	—	—	9	III M
4 Shunters, pointsmen	M	—	—	—	—	—	—	—	—	9	III M
151 Foremen—road transport operating, bus inspectors											
1 Bus inspectors	M	—	—	—	—	—	—	8	III M	—	—
Foremen—											
2 Drivers of road goods vehicles	M	—	—	—	—	—	—	8	III M	—	—
3 Other foremen road transport	M	—	—	—	—	—	—	8	III M	—	—

152	Bus, coach, lorry drivers, etc.											
1	Bus and coach drivers	M	1.1, 2.1	III M	12	III M	2.2	II	—	—	9	III M
2	Drivers of road goods vehicles	M	1.1, 2.1	III M	12	III M	2.2	II	—	—	9	III M
3	Other motor drivers	M	1.1, 2.1	III M	12	III M	2.2	II	—	—	9	III M
153	Bus conductors, drivers' mates											
1	Bus conductors	M	—	—	12	IV	—	—	—	—	10	IV
2	Drivers' mates	M	—	—	—	—	—	—	—	—	11	V
154	Foremen—civil engineering plant operating, materials handling equipment operating											
	Foremen—											
1	Mechanical plant drivers, operators (earth moving and civil engineering)	M	—	—	—	—	—	—	8	III M	—	—
2	Crane drivers, operators	M	—	—	—	—	—	—	8	III M	—	—
3	Fork lift, mechanical truck drivers	M	—	—	—	—	—	—	8	III M	—	—
4	Slingers	M	—	—	—	—	—	—	8	III M	—	—
155	Mechanical plant, fork lift, mechanical truck drivers, crane drivers, operators											
1	Mechanical plant drivers, operators (earth moving and civil engineering)	M	1.1, 2.1	III M	12	III M	2.2	II	—	—	9	III M
2	Crane drivers, operators	M	—	—	—	—	—	—	—	—	9	III M
3	Fork lift, mechanical truck drivers	M	—	—	12	III M	—	—	—	—	9	III M
156	Foremen—materials moving and storing											
	Foremen—											
1	Storekeepers, warehousemen	M	—	—	—	—	—	—	8	III M	—	—
2	Stevedores, dockers	M	—	—	—	—	—	—	8	III M	—	—
3	Goods porters	M	—	—	—	—	—	—	8	III M	—	—
4	Refuse collectors, dustmen	M	—	—	—	—	—	—	8	III M	—	—
157	Storekeepers, stevedores, warehouse, market and other goods porters											
1	Storekeepers, warehousemen	M	1.1, 2.1	IV	12	IV	2.2	III M	—	—	10	IV
2	Stevedores, dockers	M	1.1, 2.1	V	12	V	—	—	—	—	11	V
3	Goods porters	M	1.1, 2.1	V	12	V	2.2	III M	—	—	11	V
4	Refuse collectors, dustmen	M	—	—	—	—	—	—	—	—	11	V
158	All other in transport operating, materials moving and storing and related n.e.c.											
1	Slingers	M	—	—	—	—	—	—	—	—	9	III M
2	Workers in transport operating, materials moving and storing and related n.e.c.	M	1.1, 2.1	III M	12	III M	—	—	8	III M	9	III M

Occupation	Manual Non-manual	Self-employed with employees		Self-employed without employees		Managers		Foremen		Apprentices, etc., Employees n.e.c.	
		S.E.G.	Social Class	S.E.G.	Social Class	S.E.G.	Social Class	S.E.G.	Social Class	S.E.G.	Social Class
159 Foremen—miscellaneous											
Foremen—											
1 Textiles (not textile goods)	M	—	—	—	—	—	—	8	III M	—	—
2 Chemicals and allied trades	M	—	—	—	—	—	—	8	III M	—	—
3 Coke ovens and gas works	M	—	—	—	—	—	—	8	III M	—	—
4 Glass and ceramics	M	—	—	—	—	—	—	8	III M	—	—
5 Foundries in engineering and allied trades	M	—	—	—	—	—	—	8	III M	—	—
6 Engineering and allied trades	M	—	—	—	—	—	—	8	III M	—	—
7 Coal mines	M	—	—	—	—	—	—	8	III M	—	—
8 Other	M	—	—	—	—	—	—	8	III M	—	—
9 Boiler operators	M	—	—	—	—	—	—	8	III M	—	—
160 General labourers											
Labourers and unskilled workers n.e.c.—											
1 Textiles (not textile goods)	M	—	—	—	—	—	—	—	—	11	V
2 Chemicals and allied trades	M	—	—	—	—	—	—	—	—	11	V
3 Coke ovens and gas works	M	—	—	—	—	—	—	—	—	11	V
4 Glass and ceramics	M	—	—	—	—	—	—	—	—	11	V
5 Foundries in engineering and allied trades	M	—	—	—	—	—	—	—	—	11	V
6 Engineering and allied trades	M	—	—	—	—	—	—	—	—	11	V
7 Coal mines	M	2.1	V	12	V	—	—	—	—	10	IV
8 Other	M	—	—	—	—	—	—	—	—	11	V
161 All other in miscellaneous occupations n.e.c.											
1 Boiler operators	M	1.1, 2.1	III M	12	III M	—	—	8	III M	10	IV
2 All other in miscellaneous occupations n.e.c.	M	—	—	—	—	—	—	—	—	9	III M
— 1 Inadequately described occupations	—	17	—	17	—	17	—	17	—	17	—
2 Occupations not stated	—	—	—	—	—	—	—	—	—	17	—

Appendix B. 2

Details of Socio-economic groups and Social Classes in terms of Occupation and Employment Status groups

S.E.G. 1.1 Employers in industry, commerce, etc.—large establishments

(a) Social Class II Intermediate occupations

Employment status—*Self-employed with employees*

002.6	Underwriters, brokers, investment analysts	021.2	Musicians
005.1	Marketing and sales managers and executives	032.1	Aircraft flight deck officers
005.2	Advertising and PR executives	032.3	Deck, engineering and radio officers and pilots, ship
013.1	Matrons, houseparents	037.2	Office managers n.e.c.
019.0	Authors, writers, journalists	038.1	Garage proprietors
020.1	Artists, commercial artists	038.4	Other proprietors and managers (sales)
020.2	Industrial designers (not clothing)	039.1	Hotel and residential club managers
020.3	Clothing designers	039.2	Publicans
020.4	Window dressers	044.4	Managers n.e.c.
021.1	Actors, entertainers, singers, stage managers	057.1	Importers, exporters, commodity brokers

(b) Social Class III (N) Skilled occupations—Non-manual

Employment status—*Self-employed with employees*

022.1	Photographers, cameramen	044.1	Proprietors and managers, service flats, holiday flats, caravan sites, etc.
022.2	Sound and vision equipment operators	044.3	Hairdressers' and barbers' managers and proprietors
023.1	Professional sportsmen, sports officials	046.3	Other clerks and cashiers (not retail)
023.2	Literary, artistic and sports workers n.e.c.	049.2	Typists, shorthand writers, secretaries
029.0	Draughtsmen	050.0	Office machine operators
038.2	Butchers (managers and proprietors)	057.3	Scrap dealers, general dealers, rag and bone merchants
038.3	Fishmongers (managers and proprietors)	057.5	Sales representatives
039.3	Restaurateurs	057.6	Sales representatives (property and services), other agents
039.5	Entertainment and sports managers		

(c) Social Class III (M) Skilled occupations—Manual

Employment status—*Self-employed with employees*

056.0	Roundsmen, van salesmen	106.0	Sawyers, veneer cutters, woodworking machinists
064.0	Chefs, cooks	107.2	Dental technicians
068.2	Nursery nurses	107.3	Carpet fitters
075.4	Undertakers	107.4	Musical instrument makers, piano tuners
075.5	Bookmakers, betting shop managers		Other making and repairing—
085.1	Tannery production workers	107.5	Glass and ceramics
085.2	Shoe repairers	107.6	Wood
085.3	Leather cutters and sewers, footwear lasters, makers, finishers	107.7	Leather
087.4	Warp preparers	107.8	Clothing and related products
087.5	Weavers	107.9	Paper goods and printing
087.6	Knitters	107.10	Rubber
087.7	Bleachers, dyers, finishers	109.1	Furnace operating occupations (metal)
087.8	Menders, darners	109.2	Rollermen
091.0	Bakers, flour confectioners	109.3	Smiths, forgemen
094.1	Paper, paperboard and leatherboard workers	110.1	Metal drawers
094.2	Bookbinders and finishers	110.2	Moulders, coremakers, die casters
096.2	Glass formers and shapers, finishers, decorators	110.3	Electroplaters
096.3	Casters and other pottery makers	112.1	Press and machine tool setters
097.1	Rubber process workers, moulding machine operators, tyre builders	112.2	Centre lathe turners
		112.3	Machine tool setter operators
098.2	Brewery and vinery process workers	113.2	Metal polishers
	Other material processing—	115.0	Tool makers, tool fitters, markers-out
098.5	Bakery and confectionery workers	116.1	Precision instrument makers and repairers
098.8	Wood and paper	116.2	Watch and chronometer makers and repairers
100.1	Compositors	117.0	Metal working production fitters and fitter/machinists
100.2	Electrotypers, stereotypers, printing plate and cylinder preparers	118.1	Motor mechanics, auto engineers
		119.0	Office machinery mechanics
100.3	Printing machine minders and assistants	121.1	Production fitters (electrical, electronic)
100.4	Screen and block printers	121.2	Electricians, electrical maintenance fitters
100.5	Printers (so described)	121.3	Electrical engineers (so described)
102.1	Tailors, tailoresses, dressmakers	123.1	Radio and TV mechanics
102.2	Clothing cutters, milliners, furriers	123.2	Other electronic maintenance engineers
103.0	Coach trimmers, upholsterers, mattress makers	125.0	Plumbers, heating and ventilating fitters, gas fitters
105.1	Carpenters, joiners	126.1	Sheet metal workers
105.2	Cabinet makers	126.2	Metal plate workers, shipwrights, riveters
105.3	Case and box makers	127.1	Steel erectors, benders, fixers
105.4	Pattern makers (moulds)	128.0	Welders
		130.1	Goldsmiths, silversmiths, precious stone workers

130.2	Engravers, etchers (printing)	140.3	Plasterers
131.1	Coach and vehicle body builders	140.6	Builders (so described)
131.2	Galvanizers, tin platers, dip platers	145.0	Face-trained coalmining workers
131.3	Metal making and treating workers n.e.c.	152.1	Bus and coach drivers
131.5	Riggers	152.2	Drivers of road goods vehicles
131.7	Coil winders	152.3	Other motor drivers
133.1	Pottery decorators	155.1	Mechanical plant drivers, operators (earth moving and civil engineering)
133.2	Coach painters (so described)		
133.4	Painters and decorators n.e.c., french polishers	158.2	Workers in transport operating, materials moving and storing and related n.e.c.
140.1	Bricklayers, tile setters		
140.2	Masons, stone cutters	161.2	All other in miscellaneous occupations n.e.c.

(c) Social Class IV Partly skilled occupations

Employment status—*Self-employed with employees*

057.2	Market and street traders and assistants	110.4	Annealers, hardeners, temperers (metal)
057.4	Credit agents, collector salesmen	112.4	Machine tool operators
062.1	Security guards and officers, patrolmen, watchmen	113.1	Press, stamping and automatic machine operators
062.3	Security and protective service workers n.e.c.	113.3	Fettlers, dressers
075.6	Service workers n.e.c.	127.2	Scaffolders, stagers
078.2	Gardeners, groundsmen	131.9	Other metal, jewellery, electrical production workers
087.1	Preparatory fibre processors	133.3	Other spray painters
087.2	Spinners, doublers, twisters	135.1	Assemblers, (electrical, electronic)
087.3	Winders, reelers	137.2	Packers, bottlers, canners, fillers
089.0	Chemical, gas and petroleum process plant operators	138.12	Painting, assembling and related occupations n.e.c.
097.2	Calender and extruding machine operators, moulders (plastics)	140.4	Roofers, glaziers
		140.5	Handymen, general building workers
	Other material processing—	141.4	Paviors, kerb layers
098.4	Textiles	142.2	Mains and service layers, pipe jointers
098.7	Food and drink n.e.c.	146.1	Miners (not coal), quarrymen, well drillers
098.9	All other (excluding metal) n.e.c.	146.2	Construction workers n.e.c.
102.3	Sewers, embroiderers	148.0	Deck, engine-room hands, bargemen, lightermen, boatmen
	Other making and repairing—	157.1	Storekeepers, warehousemen
107.11	Plastics		
107.12	All other (excluding metal and electrical) n.e.c.		

(c) Social Class V Unskilled occupations—Manual

Employment status—*Self-employed with employees*

072.2	Cleaners, window cleaners, chimney sweeps, road sweepers	157.3	Goods porters
157.2	Stevedores, dockers		

S.E.G. 1.2 Managers in central and local government, industry, commerce, etc.—large establishments

(d) Social Class I Professional, etc. occupations

Employment status—*Managers*

007.1	General administrators—national government (Assistant Secretary level and above)

(e) Social Class II Intermediate occupations

Employment status—*Managers*

002.3	Estimators	009.8	Professional workers and related supporting management and administration n.e.c.
002.4	Valuers, claims assessors		
002.5	Financial managers	010.2	Teachers in establishments for further and higher education
002.6	Underwriters, brokers, investment analysts		
002.7	Taxation experts	011.0	Teachers n.e.c.
003.1	Personnel and industrial relations officers	012.1	Vocational and industrial trainers
003.2	O and M, work study and OR officers	013.1	Matrons, houseparents
004.2	Systems analysts, computer programmers	013.3	Welfare occupations n.e.c.
005.1	Marketing and sales managers and executives	016.0	Nurse administrators, nurses
005.2	Advertising and PR executives	017.2	Medical radiographers
005.3	Buyers (retail trade)	017.4	Physiotherapists
005.4	Buyers and purchasing officers (not retail)	017.5	Chiropodists
007.2	General administrators—national government (HEO to Senior Principal level)	017.6	Therapists n.e.c.
		018.1	Medical technicians, dental auxiliaries
008.0	Local government officers (administrative and executive functions)	018.4	Professional and related in education, welfare and health n.e.c.
009.1	Company secretaries	019.0	Authors, writers, journalists
009.2	Officials of trade associations, trade unions, professional bodies and charities	020.1	Artists, commercial artists
		020.2	Industrial designers (not clothing)
009.3	Property and estate managers	020.3	Clothing designers
009.4	Librarians, information officers	020.4	Window dressers
009.5	Legal service and related occupations	021.1	Actors, entertainers, singers, stage managers

021.2	Musicians		038.4	Other proprietors and managers (sales)
022.1	Photographers, cameramen		039.1	Hotel and residential club managers
022.2	Sound and vision equipment operators		039.2	Publicans
023.1	Professional sportsmen, sports officials		039.3	Restaurateurs
023.2	Literary, artistic and sports workers n.e.c.		039.5	Entertainment and sports managers
029.0	Draughtsmen		043.1	Prison officers (chief officers and above)
030.2	Engineering technicians, technician engineers		043.2	Police officers (inspectors and above)
032.1	Aircraft flight deck officers		043.3	Fire service officers
032.3	Deck, engineering and radio officers and pilots, ship		044.1	Proprietors and managers, service flats, holiday flats, caravan sites, etc.
033.3	Technical and related workers n.e.c.		044.3	Hairdressers' and barbers' managers and proprietors
034.0	Production, works and maintenance managers, works foremen		044.4	Managers n.e.c.
035.1	Managers in building and contracting		056.0	Roundsmen, van salesmen
036.1	Managers in mining and public utilities		057.1	Importers, exporters, commodity brokers
036.2	Transport managers		057.6	Sales representatives (property and services), other agents
036.3	Stores controllers		064.0	Chefs, cooks
036.4	Managers in warehousing and materials handling n.e.c.		075.4	Undertakers
037.1	Credit controllers		075.5	Bookmakers, betting shop managers
037.2	Office managers n.e.c.			

(f) Social Class III (N) Skilled occupations—Non-manual

Employment status—*Managers*

057.3	Scrap dealers, general dealers, rag and bone merchants

(g) Social Class III (M) Skilled occupations—Manual

Employment status—*Managers*

075.3	Launderers, dry cleaners, pressers		078.2	Gardeners, groundsmen
075.6	Service workers n.e.c.			

S.E.G. 2.1 Employers in industry, commerce, etc.—small establishments

(h) Social Class II Intermediate occupations

Employment status—*Self-employed with employees*

002.6	Underwriters, brokers, investment analysts		021.1	Actors, entertainers, singers, stage managers
005.1	Marketing and sales managers and executives		021.2	Musicians
005.2	Advertising and PR executives		037.2	Office managers n.e.c.
013.1	Matrons, houseparents		038.1	Garage proprietors
019.0	Authors, writers, journalists		038.4	Other proprietors and managers (sales)
020.1	Artists, commercial artists		039.1	Hotel and residential club managers
020.2	Industrial designers (not clothing)		039.2	Publicans
020.3	Clothing designers		044.4	Managers n.e.c.
020.4	Window dressers		057.1	Importers, exporters, commodity brokers

(j) Social Class III (N) Skilled occupations—Non-manual

Employment status—*Self-employed with employees*

013.2	Playgroup leaders		039.5	Entertainment and sports managers
018.3	Driving instructors (not HGV)		044.1	Proprietors and managers, service flats, holiday flats, caravan sites, etc.
022.1	Photographers, cameramen		044.3	Hairdressers' and barbers' managers and proprietors
022.2	Sound and vision equipment operators		046.3	Other clerks and cashiers (not retail)
023.1	Professional sportsmen, sports officials		049.2	Typists, shorthand writers, secretaries
023.2	Literary, artistic and sports workers n.e.c.		050.0	Office machine operators
029.0	Draughtsmen		057.3	Scrap dealers, general dealers, rag and bone merchants
038.2	Butchers (managers and proprietors)		057.5	Sales representatives
038.3	Fishmongers (managers and proprietors)		057.6	Sales representatives (property and services), other agents
039.3	Restaurateurs			

(k) Social Class III (M) Skilled occupations—Manual

Employment status—*Self-employed with employees*

056.0	Roundsmen, van salesmen	109.1	Furnace operating occupations (metal)
064.0	Chefs, cooks	109.2	Rollermen
068.2	Nursery nurses	109.3	Smiths, forgemen
075.4	Undertakers	110.1	Metal drawers
075.5	Bookmakers, betting shop managers	110.2	Moulders, coremakers, die casters
085.1	Tannery production workers	110.3	Electroplaters
085.2	Shoe repairers	112.1	Press and machine tool setters
085.3	Leather cutters and sewers, footwear lasters, makers, finishers	112.2	Centre lathe turners
087.4	Warp preparers	112.3	Machine tool setter operators
087.5	Weavers	113.2	Metal polishers
087.6	Knitters	115.0	Tool makers, tool fitters, markers-out
087.7	Bleachers, dyers, finishers	116.1	Precision instrument makers and repairers
087.8	Menders, darners	116.2	Watch and chronometer makers and repairers
091.0	Bakers, flour confectioners	117.0	Metal working production fitters and fitter/machinists
094.1	Paper, paperboard and leatherboard workers	118.1	Motor mechanics, auto engineers
094.2	Bookbinders and finishers	119.0	Office machinery mechanics
096.2	Glass formers and shapers, finishers, decorators	121.1	Production fitters (electrical, electronic)
096.3	Casters and other pottery makers	121.2	Electricians, electrical maintenance fitters
097.1	Rubber process workers, moulding machine operators, tyre builders	121.3	Electrical engineers (so described)
098.2	Brewery and vinery process workers	123.1	Radio and TV mechanics
	Other material processing—	123.2	Other electronic maintenance engineers
098.5	Bakery and confectionery workers	125.0	Plumbers, heating and ventilating fitters, gas fitters
098.8	Wood and paper	126.1	Sheet metal workers
100.1	Compositors	126.2	Metal plate workers, shipwrights, riveters
100.2	Electrotypers, stereotypers, printing plate and cylinder preparers	127.1	Steel erectors, benders, fixers
100.3	Printing machine minders and assistants	128.0	Welders
100.4	Screen and block printers	130.1	Goldsmiths, silversmiths, precious stone workers
100.5	Printers (so described)	130.2	Engravers, etchers (printing)
102.1	Tailors, tailoresses, dressmakers	131.1	Coach and vehicle body builders
102.2	Clothing cutters, milliners, furriers	131.2	Galvanizers, tin platers, dip platers
103.0	Coach trimmers, upholsterers, mattress makers	131.3	Metal making and treating workers n.e.c.
105.1	Carpenters, joiners	131.5	Riggers
105.2	Cabinet makers	131.7	Coil winders
105.3	Case and box makers	133.1	Pottery decorators
105.4	Pattern makers (moulds)	133.2	Coach painters (so described)
106.0	Sawyers, veneer cutters, woodworking machinists	133.4	Painters and decorators n.e.c., french polishers
107.2	Dental technicians	140.1	Bricklayers, tile setters
107.3	Carpet fitters	140.2	Masons, stone cutters
107.4	Musical instrument makers, piano tuners	140.3	Plasterers
	Other making and repairing—	140.6	Builders (so described)
107.5	Glass and ceramics	145.0	Face-trained coalmining workers
107.6	Wood	152.1	Bus and coach drivers
107.7	Leather	152.2	Drivers of road goods vehicles
107.8	Clothing and related products	152.3	Other motor drivers
107.9	Paper goods and printing	155.1	Mechanical plant drivers, operators (earth moving and civil engineering)
107.10	Rubber	158.2	Workers in transport operating, materials moving and storing and related n.e.c.
		161.2	All other in miscellaneous occupations n.e.c.

(l) Social Class IV Partly skilled occupations

Employment status—*Self-employed with employees*

044.2	Managers of laundry and dry cleaning receiving shops	110.4	Annealers, hardeners, temperers (metal)
057.2	Market and street traders and assistants	112.4	Machine tool operators
057.4	Credit agents, collector salesmen	113.1	Press, stamping and automatic machine operators
062.1	Security guards and officers, patrolmen, watchmen	113.3	Fettlers, dressers
062.3	Security and protective service workers n.e.c.	127.2	Scaffolders, stagers
075.6	Service workers n.e.c.	131.9	Other metal, jewellery, electrical production workers
078.2	Gardeners, groundsmen	133.3	Other spray painters
082.0	Fishermen	135.1	Assemblers (electrical, electronic)
087.1	Preparatory fibre processors	137.2	Packers, bottlers, canners, fillers
087.2	Spinners, doublers, twisters	138.12	Painting, assembling and related occupations n.e.c.
087.3	Winders, reelers	140.4	Roofers, glaziers
089.0	Chemical, gas and petroleum process plant operators	140.5	Handymen, general building workers
097.2	Calender and extruding machine operators, moulders (plastics)	141.4	Paviors, kerb layers
		142.2	Mains and service layers, pipe jointers
	Other material processing—	143.1	Craftsmen's mates
098.4	Textiles	146.1	Miners (not coal), quarrymen, well drillers
098.7	Food and drink n.e.c.	146.2	Construction workers n.e.c.
098.9	All other (excluding metal) n.e.c.	148.0	Deck, engine-room hands, bargemen, lightermen, boatmen
102.3	Sewers, embroiderers	157.1	Storekeepers, warehousemen
	Other making and repairing—		
107.11	Plastics		
107.12	All other (excluding metal and electrical) n.e.c.		

(m) Social Class V Unskilled occupations

Employment status—*Self-employed with employees*

072.2	Cleaners, window cleaners, chimney sweeps, road sweepers	157.3	Goods porters
141.3	Roadmen		Labourers and unskilled workers n.e.c.—
143.2	Building and civil engineering labourers	160.8	Other
157.2	Stevedores, dockers		

S.E.G. 2.2 Managers in industry, commerce, etc.—small establishments

(n) Social Class II Intermediate occupations

Employment status—*Managers*

002.3	Estimators	075.5	Bookmakers, betting shop managers
002.4	Valuers, claims assessors	085.1	Tannery production workers
002.5	Financial managers	085.2	Shoe repairers
002.6	Underwriters, brokers, investment analysts	085.3	Leather cutters and sewers, footwear lasters, makers, finishers
002.7	Taxation experts	087.4	Warp preparers
003.1	Personnel and industrial relations officers	087.5	Weavers
003.2	O and M, work study and OR officers	087.6	Knitters
004.2	Systems analysts, computer programmers	087.7	Bleachers, dyers, finishers
005.1	Marketing and sales managers and executives	087.8	Menders, darners
005.2	Advertising and PR executives	091.0	Bakers, flour confectioners
005.3	Buyers (retail trade)	094.2	Bookbinders and finishers
005.4	Buyers and purchasing officers (not retail)	096.2	Glass formers and shapers, finishers, decorators
009.1	Company secretaries	096.3	Casters and other pottery makers
009.2	Officials of trade associations, trade unions, professional bodies and charities	097.1	Rubber process workers, moulding machine operators, tyre builders
009.3	Property and estate managers	098.2	Brewery and vinery process workers
009.4	Librarians, information officers	100.1	Compositors
009.5	Legal service and related occupations	100.2	Electrotypers, stereotypers, printing plate and cylinder preparers
009.8	Professional workers and related supporting management and administration n.e.c.	100.4	Screen and block printers
010.2	Teachers in establishments for further and higher education	100.5	Printers (so described)
011.0	Teachers n.e.c.	102.1	Tailors, tailoresses, dressmakers
012.1	Vocational and industrial trainers	102.2	Clothing cutters, milliners, furriers
013.1	Matrons, houseparents	103.0	Coach trimmers, upholsterers, mattress makers
013.3	Welfare occupations n.e.c.	105.1	Carpenters, joiners
016.0	Nurse administrators, nurses	105.2	Cabinet makers
017.2	Medical radiographers	105.3	Case and box makers
017.4	Physiotherapists	105.4	Pattern makers (moulds)
017.5	Chiropodists	106.0	Sawyers, veneer cutters, woodworking machinists
017.6	Therapists n.e.c.	107.2	Dental technicians
018.1	Medical technicians, dental auxiliaries	107.4	Musical instrument makers, piano tuners
018.3	Driving instructors (not HGV)		Other making and repairing—
018.4	Professional and related in education, welfare and health n.e.c.	107.6	Wood
019.0	Authors, writers, journalists	107.7	Leather
020.1	Artists, commercial artists	107.8	Clothing and related products
020.2	Industrial designers (not clothing)	107.9	Paper goods and printing
020.3	Clothing designers	107.10	Rubber
020.4	Window dressers	109.2	Rollermen
021.1	Actors, entertainers, singers, stage managers	109.3	Smiths, forgemen
021.2	Musicians	110.3	Electroplaters
022.1	Photographers, cameramen	112.1	Press and machine tool setters
022.2	Sound and vision equipment operators	112.2	Centre lathe turners
023.1	Professional sportsmen, sports officials	112.3	Machine tool setter operators
023.2	Literary, artistic and sports workers n.e.c.	113.2	Metal polishers
029.0	Draughtsmen	115.0	Tool makers, tool fitters, markers-out
030.1	Laboratory technicians	116.1	Precision instrument makers and repairers
030.2	Engineering technicians, technician engineers	116.2	Watch and chronometer makers and repairers
033.3	Technical and related workers n.e.c.	117.0	Metal working production fitters and fitter/machinists
034.0	Production, works and maintenance managers, works foremen	118.1	Motor mechanics, auto engineers
035.1	Managers in building and contracting	119.0	Office machinery mechanics
036.1	Managers in mining and public utilities	121.1	Production fitters (electrical, electronic)
036.2	Transport managers	121.2	Electricians, electrical maintenance fitters
036.3	Stores controllers	121.3	Electrical engineers (so described)
036.4	Managers in warehousing and materials handling n.e.c.	123.1	Radio and TV mechanics
037.1	Credit controllers	123.2	Other electronic maintenance engineers
037.2	Office managers n.e.c.	125.0	Plumbers, heating and ventilating fitters, gas fitters
038.2	Butchers (managers and proprietors)	126.1	Sheet metal workers
038.3	Fishmongers (managers and proprietors)	126.2	Metal plate workers, shipwrights, riveters
038.4	Other proprietors and managers (sales)	127.1	Steel erectors, benders, fixers
039.1	Hotel and residential club managers	128.0	Welders
039.2	Publicans	130.1	Goldsmiths, silversmiths, precious stone workers
039.3	Restaurateurs	131.1	Coach and vehicle body builders
039.5	Entertainment and sports managers	131.5	Riggers
044.1	Proprietors and managers, service flats, holiday flats, caravan sites, etc.	131.7	Coil winders
044.3	Hairdressers' and barbers' managers and proprietors	133.2	Coach painters (so described)
044.4	Managers n.e.c.	133.4	Painters and decorators n.e.c., french polishers
056.0	Roundsmen, van salesmen	140.1	Bricklayers, tile setters
057.1	Importers, exporters, commodity brokers	140.2	Masons, stone cutters
057.5	Sales representatives	140.3	Plasterers
057.6	Sales representatives (property and services), other agents	140.6	Builders (so described)
064.0	Chefs, cooks	152.1	Bus and coach drivers
075.4	Undertakers	152.2	Drivers of road goods vehicles
		152.3	Other motor drivers
		155.1	Mechanical plant drivers, operators (earth moving and civil engineering)

(o) Social Class III (N) Skilled occupations—Non-manual

Employment status—*Managers*

039.4	Club stewards	057.3	Scrap dealers, general dealers, rag and bone merchants
044.2	Managers of laundry and dry cleaning receiving shops	057.4	Credit agents, collector salesmen
057.2	Market and street traders and assistants		

(p) Social Class III (M)   Skilled occupations—Manual

Employment status—*Managers*

072.2	Cleaners, window cleaners, chimney sweeps, road sweepers		Other making and repairing—
075.3	Launderers, dry cleaners, pressers	107.11	Plastics
075.6	Service workers n.e.c.	107.12	All other (excluding metal and electrical) n.e.c.
078.2	Gardeners, groundsmen	113.1	Press, stamping and automatic machine operators
082.0	Fishermen	131.9	Other metal, jewellery, electrical production workers
087.1	Preparatory fibre processors	133.3	Other spray painters
087.2	Spinners, doublers, twisters	138.12	Painting, assembling and related occupations n.e.c.
087.3	Winders, reelers	140.4	Roofers, glaziers
089.0	Chemical, gas and petroleum process plant operators	140.5	Handymen, general building workers
097.2	Calender and extruding machine operators, moulders (plastics)	146.1	Miners (not coal), quarrymen, well drillers
		146.2	Construction workers n.e.c.
	Other material processing—	157.1	Storekeepers, warehousemen
098.7	Food and drink n.e.c.	157.3	Goods porters

S.E.G. 3   Professional workers—self-employed

(q) Social Class I   Professional, etc. occupations

Employment status—*Self-employed with and without employees*

001.0	Judges, barristers, advocates, solicitors	025.0	Civil, structural, municipal, mining and quarrying engineers
002.1	Chartered and certified accountants	026.1	Mechanical and aeronautical engineers
004.1	Economists, statisticians, actuaries	026.2	Design and development engineers (mechanical)
009.6	Management consultants	027.1	Electrical engineers
012.3	Social and behavioural scientists	027.2	Electronic engineers
014.0	Clergy, ministers of religion	028.1	Chemical engineers
015.1	Medical practitioners	028.2	Production engineers
015.2	Dental practitioners	028.3	Planning and quality control engineers
017.1	Pharmacists	028.4	Engineers n.e.c.
017.3	Ophthalmic and dispensing opticians	028.5	Metallurgists
018.2	Veterinarians	028.6	Technologists n.e.c.
024.1	Biological scientists, biochemists	031.1	Architects, town planners
024.2	Chemical scientists	031.3	Building, land and mining surveyors
024.3	Physical and geological scientists, mathematicians		

S.E.G. 4   Professional workers—employees

(r) Social Class I   Professional, etc. occupations

Employment status—*Apprentices, etc., Employees n.e.c.*

001.0	Judges, barristers, advocates, solicitors	024.3	Physical and geological scientists, mathematicians
002.1	Chartered and certified accountants	025.0	Civil, structural, municipal, mining and quarrying engineers
004.1	Economists, statisticians, actuaries	026.1	Mechanical and aeronautical engineers
009.6	Management consultants	026.2	Design and development engineers (mechanical)
010.1	University academic staff	027.1	Electrical engineers
012.2	Education officers, school inspectors	027.2	Electronic engineers
012.3	Social and behavioural scientists	028.1	Chemical engineers
014.0	Clergy, ministers of religion	028.2	Production engineers
015.1	Medical practitioners	028.3	Planning and quality control engineers
015.2	Dental practitioners	028.4	Engineers n.e.c.
017.1	Pharmacists	028.5	Metallurgists
017.3	Ophthalmic and dispensing opticians	028.6	Technologists n.e.c.
018.2	Veterinarians	031.1	Architects, town planners
024.1	Biological scientists, biochemists	031.3	Building, land and mining surveyors
024.2	Chemical scientists		

S.E.G. 5.1   Ancillary workers and artists

(s) Social Class II   Intermediate occupations

Employment status—*Foreman and Supervisors*

016.0	Nurse administrators, nurses	020.1	Artists, commercial artists
017.2	Medical radiographers	030.1	Laboratory technicians
017.4	Physiotherapists	030.2	Engineering technicians, technician engineers
017.6	Therapists n.e.c.	033.3	Technical and related workers n.e.c.
018.1	Medical technicians, dental auxiliaries	045.1	Civil service executive officers

Employment status—*Apprentices, etc., Employees n.e.c.*

002.2	Cost and works accountants	017.5	Chiropodists
002.3	Estimators	017.6	Therapists n.e.c.
002.4	Valuers, claims assessors	018.1	Medical technicians, dental auxiliaries
003.2	O and M, work study and OR officers	018.4	Professional and related in education, welfare and health n.e.c.
004.2	Systems analysts, computer programmers		
006.1	Environmental health officers	019.0	Authors, writers, journalists
006.2	Building inspectors	020.1	Artists, commercial artists
006.3	Inspectors (statutory and similar)	020.2	Industrial designers (not clothing)
009.2	Officials of trade associations, trade unions, professional bodies and charities	020.3	Clothing designers
		020.4	Window dressers
009.4	Librarians, information officers	021.1	Actors, entertainers, singers, stage managers
009.5	Legal service and related occupations	021.2	Musicians
009.8	Professional workers and related supporting management and administration n.e.c.	030.1	Laboratory technicians
		030.2	Engineering technicians, technician engineers
010.2	Teachers in establishments for further and higher education	031.2	Quantity surveyors
		032.1	Aircraft flight deck officers
011.0	Teachers n.e.c.	032.2	Air traffic planners and controllers
012.1	Vocational and industrial trainers	033.1	Architectural and town planning technicians
013.3	Welfare occupations n.e.c.	033.2	Building and civil engineering technicians
016.0	Nurse administrators, nurses	033.3	Technical and related workers n.e.c.
017.2	Medical radiographers		
017.4	Physiotherapists		

Employment status—*Self-employed with employees*

002.2	Cost and works accountants	012.1	Vocational and industrial trainers
002.3	Estimators	016.0	Nurse administrators, nurses
002.4	Valuers, claims assessors	017.2	Medical radiographers
002.7	Taxation experts	017.4	Physiotherapists
003.1	Personnel and industrial relations officers	017.5	Chiropodists
003.2	O and M, work study and OR officers	017.6	Therapists n.e.c.
004.2	Systems analysts, computer programmers	018.1	Medical technicians, dental auxiliaries
009.1	Company secretaries	018.4	Professional and related in education, welfare and health n.e.c.
009.3	Property and estate managers		
009.5	Legal service and related occupations	030.1	Laboratory technicians
009.8	Professional workers and related supporting management and administration n.e.c.	030.2	Engineering technicians, technician engineers
		031.2	Quantity surveyors
010.2	Teachers in establishments for further and higher education	033.3	Technical and related workers n.e.c.
011.0	Teachers n.e.c.		

Employment status—*Self-employed without employees*

002.2	Cost and works accountants	017.2	Medical radiographers
002.3	Estimators	017.4	Physiotherapists
002.4	Valuers, claims assessors	017.5	Chiropodists
002.6	Underwriters, brokers, investment analysts	017.6	Therapists n.e.c.
002.7	Taxation experts	018.1	Medical technicians, dental auxiliaries
003.1	Personnel and industrial relations officers	018.4	Professional and related in education, welfare and health n.e.c.
003.2	O and M, work study and OR officers		
004.2	Systems analysts, computer programmers	019.0	Authors, writers, journalists
005.1	Marketing and sales managers and executives	020.1	Artists, commercial artists
005.2	Advertising and PR executives	020.2	Industrial designers (not clothing)
009.1	Company secretaries	020.3	Clothing designers
009.3	Property and estate managers	020.4	Window dressers
009.5	Legal service and related occupations	021.1	Actors, entertainers, singers, stage managers
009.8	Professional workers and related supporting management and administration n.e.c.	021.2	Musicians
		030.1	Laboratory technicians
010.2	Teachers in establishments for further and higher education	030.2	Engineering technicians, technician engineers
		031.2	Quantity surveyors
011.0	Teachers n.e.c.	033.1	Architectural and town planning technicians
012.1	Vocational and industrial trainers	033.3	Technical and related workers n.e.c.
016.0	Nurse administrators, nurses		

S.E.G. 5.2 Foreman and supervisors—Non-manual

(t) Social Class III (N) Skilled occupations—Non-manual

Employment status—*Foremen and Supervisors*

022.1	Photographers, cameramen		Supervisors of—
022.2	Sound and vision equipment operators	048.3	Telephone operators
029.0	Draughtsmen	048.4	Radio and telegraph operators
034.0	Production, works and maintenance managers, works foremen	054.1	Shop salesmen and assistants
		054.2	Petrol pump, forecourt attendants
	Supervisors of—	054.3	Roundsmen, van salesmen
045.2	Stores and despatch clerks	060.1	Police sergeants
045.3	Tracers, drawing office assistants	060.2	Fire service supervisors
045.4	Other clerks and cashiers (not retail)	060.3	Prison service principal officers
045.5	Retail shop cashiers, check-out and cash and wrap operators		Supervisors of—
		060.4	Security guards and officers, patrolmen, watchmen
048.1	Typists, shorthand writers, secretaries	060.5	Traffic wardens
048.2	Office machine operators	060.6	Security and protective service workers n.e.c.

S.E.G. 6 Junior non-manual workers

(u) Social Class III (N) Skilled occupations—Non-manual
Employment status—Apprentices, etc., Employees n.e.c.

009.7	Managers' personal assistants	047.0	Retail shop cashiers, check-out and cash and wrap operators
013.2	Playgroup leaders	049.1	Receptionists
018.3	Driving instructors (not HGV)	049.2	Typists, shorthand writers, secretaries
022.1	Photographers, cameramen	050.0	Office machine operators
022.2	Sound and vision equipment operators	051.1	Telephonist receptionists
023.1	Professional sportsmen, sports officials	051.3	Radio and telegraph operators
023.2	Literary, artistic and sports workers n.e.c.	055.1	Shop salesmen and assistants
029.0	Draughtsmen	055.3	Petrol pump, forecourt attendants
035.2	Clerks of works	057.5	Sales representatives
046.1	Stores and despatch clerks	057.6	Sales representatives (property and services), other agents
046.2	Tracers, drawing office assistants	061.1	Policemen (below sergeant)
046.3	Other clerks and cashiers (not retail)	061.2	Firemen

(v) Social Class IV Partly skilled occupations
Employment status—Employees n.e.c.

051.2	Telephone operators	057.4	Credit agents, collector salesmen
055.2	Shelf fillers	061.3	Prison officers (below principal officer)
057.2	Market and street traders and assistants		

S.E.G. 7 Personal service workers

(w) Social Class II Intermediate occupations
Employment status—Employees n.e.c.

013.1	Matrons, houseparents

(x) Social Class III (M) Skilled occupations—Manual
Employment status—Foremen and Supervisors

	Supervisors of—	067.1	Housekeepers (non-domestic)
063.1	Chefs, cooks		Supervisors of—
063.2	Waiters, waitresses	067.2	Other domestic and school helpers
063.3	Barmen, barmaids	067.3	Travel stewards and attendants
063.4	Counter hands, assistants	073.0	Hairdressing supervisors

Employment status—Apprentices, etc., Employees n.e.c.

064.0	Chefs, cooks	069.1	Travel stewards and attendants
068.1	Domestic housekeepers	074.0	Hairdressers, barbers
068.2	Nursery nurses		

(y) Social Class IV Partly skilled occupations
Employment status—Employees n.e.c.

065.1	Waiters, waitresses	066.1	Counter hands, assistants
065.2	Barmen, barmaids	068.3	Other domestic and school helpers

S.E.G. 8 Foremen and supervisors—Manual

(z) Social Class III (M) Skilled occupations—Manual

Employment status—*Foremen and Supervisors*

Supervisors of—
- 052.1 Postmen, mail sorters
- 052.2 Messengers
- 066.2 Kitchen porters, hands

Supervisors of—
- 067.4 Hospital porters
- 067.5 Hotel porters
- 067.6 Ambulancemen
- 067.7 Hospital, ward orderlies
- 071.1 Caretakers
- 071.2 Cleaners, window cleaners, chimney sweeps, road sweepers
- 071.3 Railway stationmen
- 071.4 Lift and car park attendants
- 075.3 Launderers, dry cleaners, pressers
- 075.6 Service workers n.e.c.
- 076.3 Foremen gardeners and groundsmen
- 081.0 Supervisors, mates—fishing

Foremen—
- 084.1 Tannery production workers
- 084.2 Shoe repairers
- 084.3 Leather cutters and sewers, footwear lasters, makers, finishers
- 084.4 Other making and repairing, leather
- 086.1 Preparatory fibre processors
- 086.2 Spinners, doublers, twisters
- 086.3 Winders, reelers
- 086.4 Warp preparers
- 086.5 Weavers
- 086.6 Knitters
- 086.7 Bleachers, dyers, finishers
- 086.8 Menders, darners
- 086.9 Other material processing, textiles
- 088.0 Chemical processing
- 090.1 Bakers, flour confectioners
- 090.2 Butchers, meat cutters
- 090.3 Fishmongers, poultry dressers
- 090.4 Brewery and vinery process workers

Other material processing—
- 090.5 Bakery and confectionery workers
- 090.6 Food and drink n.e.c.
- 093.1 Paper, paperboard and leatherboard workers
- 093.2 Bookbinders and finishers
- 093.3 Cutting and slitting machine operators (paper and paper products making)
- 093.4 Other material processing, wood and paper
- 093.5 Other making and repairing, paper goods and printing
- 095.1 Glass and ceramics furnacemen, kilnsetters
- 095.2 Glass formers and shapers, finishers, decorators
- 095.3 Casters and other pottery makers
- 095.4 Rubber process workers, moulding machine operators, tyre builders
- 095.5 Calender and extruding machine operators, moulders (plastics)
- 095.6 Man-made fibre makers
- 095.7 Washers, screeners and crushers in mines and quarries

Other making and repairing—
- 095.8 Glass and ceramics
- 095.9 Rubber
- 095.10 Plastics

Other material processing—
- 098.6 Tobacco
- 098.9 All other (excluding metal) n.e.c.

Foremen—
- 099.1 Compositors
- 099.2 Electrotypers, stereotypers, printing plate and cylinder preparers
- 099.3 Printing machine minders and assistants
- 099.4 Screen and block printers
- 099.5 Printers (so described)
- 101.1 Tailors, tailoresses, dressmakers
- 101.2 Clothing cutters, milliners, furriers
- 101.3 Sewers, embroiderers
- 101.4 Coach trimmers, upholsterers, mattress makers
- 101.5 Carpet fitters
- 101.6 Other making and repairing, clothing and related products
- 104.1 Carpenters, joiners
- 104.2 Cabinet makers
- 104.3 Case and box makers
- 104.4 Pattern makers (moulds)
- 104.5 Sawyers, veneer cutters, woodworking machinists
- 104.6 Other making and repairing, wood
- 107.2 Dental technicians
- 107.4 Musical instrument makers, piano tuners

Other making and repairing—
- 107.12 All other (excluding metal and electrical) n.e.c.

Foremen—
- 108.1 Furnace operating occupations (metal)
- 108.2 Rollermen
- 108.3 Smiths, forgemen
- 108.4 Metal drawers
- 108.5 Moulders, coremakers, die casters
- 108.6 Electroplaters

Foremen—(contd)
- 108.7 Annealers, hardeners, temperers (metal)
- 108.8 Galvanizers, tin platers, dip platers
- 108.9 Metal making and treating workers n.e.c.
- 111.1 Press and machine tool setters
- 111.2 Centre lathe turners
- 111.3 Machine tool setter operators
- 111.4 Machine tool operators
- 111.5 Press, stamping and automatic machine operators
- 111.6 Metal polishers
- 111.7 Fettlers, dressers
- 111.8 Shot blasters
- 114.1 Tool makers, tool fitters, markers-out
- 114.2 Precision instrument makers and repairers
- 114.3 Watch and chronometer makers and repairers
- 114.4 Metal working production fitters and fitter/machinists
- 114.5 Motor mechanics, auto engineers
- 114.6 Maintenance fitters (aircraft engines)
- 114.7 Office machinery mechanics
- 120.1 Production fitters (electrical, electronic)
- 120.2 Electricians, electrical maintenance fitters
- 120.3 Plant operators and attendants n.e.c.
- 120.4 Telephone fitters
- 120.5 Cable jointers, linesmen
- 120.6 Radio and TV mechanics
- 120.7 Other electronic maintenance engineers
- 124.1 Plumbers, heating and ventilating fitters, gas fitters
- 124.2 Sheet metal workers
- 124.3 Metal plate workers, shipwrights, riveters
- 124.4 Steel erectors, benders, fixers
- 124.5 Scaffolders, stagers
- 124.6 Welders
- 124.7 Riggers
- 129.1 Goldsmiths, silversmiths, precious stone workers
- 129.2 Engravers, etchers (printing)
- 129.3 Coach and vehicle body builders
- 129.4 Oilers, greasers, lubricators
- 129.5 Electronics wiremen
- 129.6 Coil winders
- 131.9 Other metal, jewellery, electrical production workers
- —.1 Foremen (engineering and allied trades)

Foremen—
- 132.1 Pottery decorators
- 132.2 Coach painters (so described)
- 132.3 Other spray painters
- 132.4 Painters and decorators n.e.c., french polishers

Foremen assemblers—
- 134.1 Electrical, electronic
- 134.2 Instruments
- 134.3 Vehicles and other metal goods
- 134.4 Paper production, processing and printing
- 134.5 Plastics goods

Foremen inspectors, viewers, examiners—
- 136.1 Metal, electrical goods
- 136.2 Textiles
- 136.3 Food
- 136.4 Rubber goods
- 136.5 Plastics goods
- 136.6 Woodwork

Foremen—
- 136.7 Packers, bottlers, canners, fillers
- 136.8 Laboratory assistants
- 136.9 Inspectors, sorters in paper production, processing and printing
- 136.10 Weighers
- 136.11 Graders, sorters, selectors n.e.c.
- 138.12 Painting, assembling and related occupations n.e.c.

Foremen—
- 139.1 Bricklayers, tile setters
- 139.2 Masons, stone cutters
- 139.3 Plasterers
- 139.4 Roofers, glaziers
- 139.5 Handymen, general building workers
- 139.6 Railway lengthmen
- 139.7 Road surfacers, concreters
- 139.8 Roadmen
- 139.9 Paviors, kerb layers
- 139.10 Sewage plant attendants
- 139.11 Mains and service layers, pipe jointers
- 139.12 Construction workers n.e.c.
- 143.1 Craftsmen's mates
- 143.2 Building and civil engineering labourers
- 144.0 Foremen/deputies—coalmining
- 146.1 Miners (not coal), quarrymen, well drillers
- 147.0 Foremen—ships, lighters and other vessels

Foremen—
- 149.1 Railway guards
- 149.2 Signalmen and crossing keepers, railway
- 149.3 Shunters, pointsmen
- 149.4 Other foremen rail transport
- 151.1 Bus inspectors

Foremen—
- 151.2 Drivers of road goods vehicles
- 151.3 Other foremen road transport

	Foremen—			Foremen—
154.1	Mechanical plant drivers, operators (earth moving and civil engineering)			Labourers and unskilled workers n.e.c.—
			159.1	Textiles (not textile goods)
154.2	Crane drivers, operators		159.2	Chemicals and allied trades
154.3	Fork lift, mechanical truck drivers		159.3	Coke ovens and gas works
154.4	Slingers		159.4	Glass and ceramics
156.1	Storekeepers, warehousemen		159.5	Foundries in engineering and allied trades
156.2	Stevedores, dockers		159.6	Engineering and allied trades
156.3	Goods porters		159.7	Coal mines
156.4	Refuse collectors, dustmen		159.8	Other
158.2	Workers in transport operating, materials moving and storing and related n.e.c.		159.9	Boiler operators
			161.2	All other in miscellaneous occupations n.e.c.

S.E.G. 9 Skilled manual workers

(aa) Social Class III (M) Skilled occupations—Manual

Employment status—*Apprentices, etc., Employees n.e.c.*

056.0	Roundsmen, van salesmen		115.0	Tool makers, tool fitters, markers-out
070.1	Ambulancemen		116.1	Precision instrument makers and repairers
085.1	Tannery production workers		116.2	Watch and chronometer makers and repairers
085.2	Shoe repairers		117.0	Metal working production fitters and fitter/machinists
085.3	Leather cutters and sewers, footwear lasters, makers, finishers		118.1	Motor mechanics, auto engineers
			118.2	Maintenance fitters (aircraft engines)
087.4	Warp preparers		119.0	Office machinery mechanics
087.5	Weavers		121.1	Production fitters (electrical, electronic)
087.6	Knitters		121.2	Electricians, electrical maintenance fitters
087.7	Bleachers, dyers, finishers		121.3	Electrical engineers (so described)
087.8	Menders, darners		121.4	Plant operators and attendants n.e.c.
091.0	Bakers, flour confectioners		122.1	Telephone fitters
092.1	Butchers, meat cutters		122.2	Cable jointers, linesmen
092.2	Fishmongers, poultry dressers		123.1	Radio and TV mechanics
094.1	Paper, paperboard and leatherboard workers		123.2	Other electronic maintenance engineers
094.2	Bookbinders and finishers		125.0	Plumbers, heating and ventilating fitters, gas fitters
094.3	Cutting and slitting machine operators (paper and paper products making)		126.1	Sheet metal workers
			126.2	Metal plate workers, shipwrights, riveters
096.1	Glass and ceramics furnacemen, kilnsetters		127.1	Steel erectors, benders, fixers
096.2	Glass formers and shapers, finishers, decorators		128.0	Welders
096.3	Casters and other pottery makers		130.1	Goldsmiths, silversmiths, precious stone workers
097.1	Rubber process workers, moulding machine operators, tyre builders		130.2	Engravers, etchers (printing)
			131.1	Coach and vehicle body builders
098.2	Brewery and vinery process workers		131.2	Galvanizers, tin platers, dip platers
	Other material processing—		131.3	Metal making and treating workers n.e.c.
098.5	Bakery and confectionery workers		131.4	Oilers, greasers, lubricators
098.8	Wood and paper		131.5	Riggers
100.1	Compositors		131.6	Electronics wiremen
100.2	Electrotypers, stereotypers, printing plate and cylinder preparers		131.7	Coil winders
			—.2	Trainee craftsmen (engineering and allied trades)
100.3	Printing machine minders and assistants		133.1	Pottery decorators
100.4	Screen and block printers		133.2	Coach painters (so described)
100.5	Printers (so described)		133.4	Painters and decorators n.e.c., french polishers
102.1	Tailors, tailoresses, dressmakers		135.2	Instrument assemblers
102.2	Clothing cutters, milliners, furriers		138.1	Laboratory assistants
103.0	Coach trimmers, upholsterers, mattress makers			Inspectors, viewers, examiners—
105.1	Carpenters, joiners		138.2	Textiles
105.2	Cabinet makers		138.4	Rubber goods
105.3	Case and box makers		138.6	Woodwork
105.4	Pattern makers (moulds)		138.7	Inspectors, sorters in paper production, processing and printing
106.0	Sawyers, veneer cutters, woodworking machinists			
107.1	Labourers and mates to woodworking craftsmen		138.8	Assemblers in paper production, processing and printing
107.2	Dental technicians		140.1	Bricklayers, tile setters
107.3	Carpet fitters		140.2	Masons, stone cutters
107.4	Musical instrument makers, piano tuners		140.3	Plasterers
	Other making and repairing—		140.6	Builders (so described)
107.5	Glass and ceramics		145.0	Face-trained coalmining workers
107.6	Wood		150.1	Drivers, motormen, secondmen, railway engines
107.7	Leather		150.2	Railway guards
107.8	Clothing and related products		150.3	Signalmen and crossing keepers, railway
107.9	Paper goods and printing		150.4	Shunters, pointsmen
107.10	Rubber		152.1	Bus and coach drivers
109.1	Furnace operating occupations (metal)		152.2	Drivers of road goods vehicles
109.2	Rollermen		152.3	Other motor drivers
109.3	Smiths, forgemen		155.1	Mechanical plant drivers, operators (earth moving and civil engineering)
110.1	Metal drawers			
110.2	Moulders, coremakers, die casters		155.2	Crane drivers, operators
110.3	Electroplaters		155.3	Fork lift, mechanical truck drivers
112.1	Press and machine tool setters		158.1	Slingers
112.2	Centre lathe turners		158.2	Workers in transport operating, materials moving and storing and related n.e.c.
112.3	Machine tool setter operators			
113.2	Metal polishers		161.2	All other in miscellaneous occupations n.e.c.

S.E.G. 10 Semi-skilled manual workers

(ab) Social Class IV Partly skilled occupations

Employment status—*Apprentices, etc., Employees n.e.c.*

053.1	Postmen, mail sorters	113.3	Fettlers, dressers
062.1	Security guards and officers, patrolmen, watchmen	127.2	Scaffolders, stagers
062.2	Traffic wardens	131.8	Shot blasters
062.3	Security and protective service workers n.e.c.	131.9	Other metal, jewellery, electrical production workers
069.2	Hospital porters	133.3	Other spray painters
069.3	Hotel porters	135.1	Assemblers (electrical, electronic)
070.2	Hospital, ward orderlies	135.3	Assemblers (vehicles and other metal goods)
072.1	Caretakers	137.1	Inspectors, viewers (metal, electrical goods)
075.3	Launderers, dry cleaners, pressers	137.2	Packers, bottlers, canners, fillers
075.6	Service workers n.e.c.		Inspectors, viewers, examiners—
078.2	Gardeners, groundsmen	138.3	Food
082.0	Fishermen	138.5	Plastics goods
087.1	Preparatory fibre processors	138.9	Assemblers (plastics goods)
087.2	Spinners, doublers, twisters	138.10	Weighers
087.3	Winders, reelers	138.11	Graders, sorters, selectors n.e.c.
089.0	Chemical, gas and petroleum process plant operators	138.12	Painting, assembling and related occupations n.e.c.
097.2	Calender and extruding machine operators, moulders (plastics)	140.4	Roofers, glaziers
098.1	Man-made fibre makers	140.5	Handymen, general building workers
098.3	Washers, screeners and crushers in mines and quarries	141.1	Railway lengthmen
	Other material processing—	141.2	Road surfacers, concreters
098.4	Textiles	141.4	Paviors, kerb layers
098.6	Tobacco	142.2	Mains and service layers, pipe jointers
098.7	Food and drink n.e.c.	143.1	Craftsmen's mates
098.9	All other (excluding metal) n.e.c.	146.1	Miners (not coal), quarrymen, well drillers
102.3	Sewers, embroiderers	146.2	Construction workers n.e.c.
	Other making and repairing—	148.0	Deck, engine-room hands, bargemen, lightermen, boatmen
107.11	Plastics	153.1	Bus conductors
107.12	All other (excluding metal and electrical) n.e.c.	157.1	Storekeepers, warehousemen
110.4	Annealers, hardeners, temperers (metal)		Labourers and unskilled workers n.e.c.—
112.4	Machine tool operators	160.7	Coal mines
113.1	Press, stamping and automatic machine operators	161.1	Boiler operators

---

S.E.G. 11 Unskilled manual workers

(ac) Social Class V Unskilled occupations

Employment status—*Employees n.e.c.*

053.2	Messengers	157.3	Goods porters
066.2	Kitchen porters, hands	157.4	Refuse collectors, dustmen
072.2	Cleaners, window cleaners, chimney sweeps, road sweepers		Labourers and unskilled workers n.e.c.—
075.1	Railway stationmen	160.1	Textiles (not textile goods)
075.2	Lift and car park attendants	160.2	Chemicals and allied trades
141.3	Roadmen	160.3	Coke ovens and gas works
142.1	Sewage plant attendants	160.4	Glass and ceramics
143.2	Building and civil engineering labourers	160.5	Foundries in engineering and allied trades
153.2	Drivers' mates	160.6	Engineering and allied trades
157.2	Stevedores, dockers	160.8	Other

S.E.G. 12 Own account workers (other than professional)

(ad) Social Class II Intermediate occupations

Employment status—*Self-employed without employees*

013.1	Matrons, houseparents	038.4	Other proprietors and managers (sales)
032.1	Aircraft flight deck officers	039.1	Hotel and residential club managers
032.3	Deck, engineering and radio officers and pilots, ships	039.2	Publicans
037.2	Office managers n.e.c.	044.4	Managers n.e.c.
038.1	Garage proprietors	057.1	Importers, exporters, commodity brokers

---

(ae) Social Class III (N) Skilled occupations—Non-manual

Employment status—*Self-employed without employees*

013.2	Playgroup leaders	044.1	Proprietors and managers, service flats, holiday flats, caravan sites, etc.
018.3	Driving instructors (not HGV)	044.3	Hairdressers' and barbers' managers and proprietors
022.1	Photographers, cameramen	046.2	Tracers, drawing office assistants
022.2	Sound and vision equipment operators	046.3	Other clerks and cashiers (not retail)
023.1	Professional sportsmen, sports officials	049.2	Typists, shorthand writers, secretaries
023.2	Literary, artistic and sports workers n.e.c.	050.0	Office machine operators
029.0	Draughtsmen	057.3	Scrap dealers, general dealers, rag and bone merchants
038.2	Butchers (managers and proprietors)	057.5	Sales representatives
038.3	Fishmongers (managers and proprietors)	057.6	Sales representatives (property and services), other agents
039.3	Restaurateurs		
039.5	Entertainment and sports managers		

(af) Social Class III (M) Skilled occupations—Manual

Employment status—*Self-employed without employees*

056.0	Roundsmen, van salesmen	110.1	Metal drawers
064.0	Chefs, cooks	110.2	Moulders, coremakers, die casters
068.2	Nursery nurses	110.3	Electroplaters
069.1	Travel stewards and attendants	112.1	Press and machine tool setters
075.4	Undertakers	112.2	Centre lathe turners
075.5	Bookmakers, betting shop managers	112.3	Machine tool setter operators
085.1	Tannery production workers	113.2	Metal polishers
085.2	Shoe repairers	115.0	Tool makers, tool fitters, markers-out
085.3	Leather cutters and sewers, footwear lasters, makers, finishers	116.1	Precision instrument makers and repairers
		116.2	Watch and chronometer makers and repairers
087.4	Warp preparers	117.0	Metal working production fitters and fitter/machinists
087.5	Weavers	118.1	Motor mechanics, auto engineers
087.6	Knitters	118.2	Maintenance fitters (aircraft engines)
087.7	Bleachers, dyers, finishers	119.0	Office machinery mechanics
087.8	Menders, darners	121.1	Production fitters (electrical, electronic)
091.0	Bakers, flour confectioners	121.2	Electricians, electrical maintenance fitters
094.1	Paper, paperboard and leatherboard workers	121.3	Electrical engineers (so described)
094.2	Bookbinders and finishers	122.1	Telephone fitters
096.2	Glass formers and shapers, finishers, decorators	122.2	Cable jointers, linesmen
096.3	Casters and other pottery makers	123.1	Radio and TV mechanics
097.1	Rubber process workers, moulding machine operators, tyre builders	123.2	Other electronic maintenance engineers
		125.0	Plumbers, heating and ventilating fitters, gas fitters
098.2	Brewery and vinery process workers	126.1	Sheet metal workers
	Other material processing—	126.2	Metal plate workers, shipwrights, riveters
098.5	Bakery and confectionery workers	127.1	Steel erectors, benders, fixers
098.8	Wood and paper	128.0	Welders
100.1	Compositors	130.1	Goldsmiths, silversmiths, precious stone workers
100.2	Electrotypers, stereotypers, printing plate and cylinder preparers	130.2	Engravers, etchers (printing)
		131.1	Coach and vehicle body builders
100.3	Printing machine minders and assistants	131.2	Galvanizers, tin platers, dip platers
100.4	Screen and block printers	131.3	Metal making and treating workers n.e.c.
100.5	Printers (so described)	131.5	Riggers
102.1	Tailors, tailoresses, dressmakers	131.6	Electronics wiremen
102.2	Clothing cutters, milliners, furriers	131.7	Coil winders
103.0	Coach trimmers, upholsterers, mattress makers	133.1	Pottery decorators
105.1	Carpenters, joiners	133.2	Coach painters (so described)
105.2	Cabinet makers	133.4	Painters and decorators n.e.c., french polishers
105.3	Case and box makers	135.2	Instrument assemblers
105.4	Pattern makers (moulds)	138.8	Assemblers in paper production, processing and printing
106.0	Sawyers, veneer cutters, woodworking machinists	140.1	Bricklayers, tile setters
107.2	Dental technicians	140.2	Masons, stone cutters
107.3	Carpet fitters	140.3	Plasterers
107.4	Musical instrument makers, piano tuners	140.6	Builders (so described)
	Other making and repairing—	145.0	Face-trained coalmining workers
107.5	Glass and ceramics	152.1	Bus and coach drivers
107.6	Wood	152.2	Drivers of road goods vehicles
107.7	Leather	152.3	Other motor drivers
107.8	Clothing and related products	155.1	Mechanical plant drivers, operators (earth moving and civil engineering)
107.9	Paper goods and printing		
107.10	Rubber	155.3	Fork lift, mechanical truck drivers
109.1	Furnace operating occupations (metal)	158.2	Workers in transport operating, materials moving and storing and related n.e.c.
109.2	Rollermen		
109.3	Smiths, forgemen	161.2	All other in miscellaneous occupations n.e.c.

(ag) Social Class IV Partly skilled occupations

Employment status—*Self-employed without employees*

044.2	Managers of laundry and dry cleaning receiving shops	110.4	Annealers, hardeners, temperers (metal)
057.2	Market and street traders and assistants	112.4	Machine tool operators
057.4	Credit agents, collector salesmen	113.1	Press, stamping and automatic machine operators
062.1	Security guards and officers, patrolmen, watchmen	113.3	Fettlers, dressers
062.3	Security and protective service workers n.e.c.	127.2	Scaffolders, stagers
065.1	Waiters, waitresses	131.9	Other metal, jewellery, electrical production workers
065.2	Barmen, barmaids	133.3	Other spray painters
068.3	Other domestic and school helpers	135.1	Assemblers (electrical, electronic)
075.6	Service workers n.e.c.	135.3	Assemblers (vehicles and other metal goods)
078.2	Gardeners, groundsmen	137.1	Inspectors, viewers (metal, electrical goods)
082.0	Fishermen	137.2	Packers, bottlers, canners, fillers
087.1	Preparatory fibre processors	138.12	Painting, assembling and related occupations n.e.c.
087.2	Spinners, doublers, twisters	140.4	Roofers, glaziers
087.3	Winders, reelers	140.5	Handymen, general building workers
089.0	Chemical, gas and petroleum process plant operators	141.2	Road surfacers, concreters
097.2	Calender and extruding machine operators, moulders (plastics)	141.4	Paviors, kerb layers
		142.2	Mains and service layers, pipe jointers
	Other material processing—	143.1	Craftsmen's mates
098.4	Textiles	146.1	Miners (not coal), quarrymen, well drillers
098.7	Food and drink n.e.c.	146.2	Construction workers n.e.c.
098.9	All other (excluding metal) n.e.c.	148.0	Deck, engine-room hands, bargemen, lightermen, boatmen
102.3	Sewers, embroiderers	153.1	Bus conductors
	Other making and repairing—	157.1	Storekeepers, warehousemen
107.11	Plastics		
107.12	All other (excluding metal and electrical) n.e.c.		

(ah) Social Class V Unskilled occupations

Employment status—*Self-employed without employees*

053.2	Messengers	157.2	Stevedores, dockers
072.2	Cleaners, window cleaners, chimney sweeps, road sweepers	157.3	Goods porters
141.3	Roadmen		Labourers and unskilled workers n.e.c.—
143.2	Building and civil engineering labourers	160.8	Other

S.E.G. 13 Farmers—employers and managers

(aj) Social Class II Intermediate occupations

Employment status—*Managers, Self-employed with employees*

040.0 Farmers, horticulturists, farm managers

S.E.G. 14 Farmers—own account

(ak) Social Class II Intermediate occupations

Employment status—*Self-employed without employees*

040.0 Farmers, horticulturists, farm managers

S.E.G. 15 Agricultural workers

(al) Social Class III (M) Skilled occupations—Manual

Employment status—*Foremen and Supervisors*

076.1	Farm foremen	076.5	Forestry foremen
076.2	Horticultural foremen	076.6	Other foremen in farming and related
076.4	Agricultural machinery foremen		

(am) Social Class IV Partly skilled occupations

Employment status—*Employees n.e.c.*

077.0	Farm workers	080.0	Forestry workers
078.1	Horticultural workers	083.0	All other in farming and related
079.0	Agricultural machinery drivers, operators		

Employment status—*Self-employed with and without employees*

077.0	Farm workers	080.0	Forestry workers
078.1	Horticultural workers	083.0	All other in farming and related
079.0	Agricultural machinery drivers, operators		

S.E.G. 16 Members of armed forces

Employment status—*Managers*

041.0	Officers, UK armed forces	042.0	Officers, foreign and Commonwealth armed forces

Employment status—*Employees n.e.c.*

058.0	NCOs and other ranks, UK armed forces	059.0	NCOs and other ranks, foreign and Commonwealth armed forces

S.E.G. 17 Inadequately described and not stated occupations

Employment status—*Managers, Foremen and Supervisors, Self-employed with and without employees*

—.1 Inadequately described occupations

Employment status—*Apprentices, etc., Employees n.e.c.*

—.1	Inadequately described occupations	—.2	Occupations not stated

Appendix C

Summary of Socio-economic Classes

S.E.G. 1.1 Employers in industry, commerce, etc.—large establishments

    (a)   Social Class II   Intermediate occupations
    (b)   Social Class III(N)   Skilled occupations—Non-manual
    (c)   Social Class III(M)   Skilled occupations—Manual*

S.E.G. 1.2 Managers in central and local government, industry, commerce, etc.—large establishments

    (d)   Social Class I   Professional, etc. occupations
    (e)   Social Class II   Intermediate occupations
    (f)   Social Class III(N)   Skilled occupations—Non-manual
    (g)   Social Class III(M)   Skilled occupations—Manual

S.E.G. 2.1 Employers in industry, commerce, etc.—small establishments

    (h)   Social Class II   Intermediate occupations
    (j)   Social Class III(N)   Skilled occupations—Non-manual
    (k)   Social Class III(M)   Skilled occupations—Manual
    (l)   Social Class IV   Partly skilled occupations
    (m)   Social Class V   Unskilled occupations

S.E.G. 2.2 Managers in industry, commerce, etc.—small establishments

    (n)   Social Class II   Intermediate occupations
    (o)   Social Class III(N)   Skilled occupations—Non-manual
    (p)   Social Class III(M)   Skilled occupations—Manual

S.E.G. 3 Professional workers—self-employed

    (q)   Social Class I   Professional, etc. occupations

S.E.G. 4 Professional workers—employees

    (r)   Social Class I   Professional, etc. occupations

S.E.G. 5.1 Ancillary workers and artists

    (s)   Social Class II   Intermediate occupations

S.E.G. 5.2 Foremen and supervisors—Non-manual

    (t)   Social Class III(N)   Skilled occupations—Non-manual

S.E.G. 6 Junior non-manual workers

    (u)   Social Class III(N)   Skilled occupations—Non-manual
    (v)   Social Class IV   Partly skilled occupations

S.E.G. 7 Personal service workers

    (w)   Social Class II   Intermediate occupations
    (x)   Social Class III(M)   Skilled occupations—Manual
    (y)   Social Class IV   Partly skilled occupations

---

* Including very small numbers of persons in Social Classes IV and V

S.E.G. 8	Foremen and supervisors—Manual		
	(z)	Social Class III(M)	Skilled occupations—Manual

S.E.G. 9	Skilled manual workers		
	(aa)	Social Class III(M)	Skilled occupations—Manual

S.E.G. 10	Semi-skilled manual workers		
	(ab)	Social Class IV	Partly skilled occupations

S.E.G. 11	Unskilled manual workers		
	(ac)	Social Class V	Unskilled Occupations

S.E.G. 12	Own account workers (other than professional)		
	(ad)	Social Class II	Intermediate occupations
	(ae)	Social Class III(N)	Skilled occupations—Non-manual
	(af)	Social Class III(M)	Skilled occupations—Manual
	(ag)	Social Class IV	Partly skilled occupations
	(ah)	Social Class V	Unskilled occupations

S.E.G. 13	Farmers—employers and managers		
	(aj)	Social Class II	Intermediate occupations

S.E.G. 14	Farmers—own account		
	(ak)	Social Class II	Intermediate occupations

S.E.G. 15	Agricultural workers		
	(al)	Social Class III(M)	Skilled occupations—Manual
	(am)	Social Class IV	Partly skilled occupations

S.E.G. 16   **Members of armed forces**

S.E.G. 17   **Inadequately described and not stated occupations**

Appendix D

Industrial Classification for the 1981 Census
Summary of Classes, Activity Headings and Subdivisions where applicable

Class	Activity	
		DIVISION 0 AGRICULTURE, FORESTRY AND FISHING
01		Agriculture and horticulture
02		Forestry
03		Fishing
		DIVISION 1 ENERGY AND WATER SUPPLY INDUSTRIES
11		Coal extraction and manufacture of solid fuels
	1113	Deep coal mines
	1114	Opencast coal working
	1115	Manufacture of solid fuels
12		Coke ovens
13		Extraction of mineral oil and natural gas
14		Mineral oil processing
	1401	Mineral oil refining
	1402	Other treatment of petroleum products (excluding petrochemicals manufacture)
15		Nuclear fuel production
16		Production and distribution of electricity, gas and other forms of energy
	1610	Production and distribution of electricity
	1620	Public gas supply
	1630	Production and distribution of other forms of energy
17		Water supply industry
		DIVISION 2 EXTRACTION OF MINERALS AND ORES OTHER THAN FUELS; MANUFACTURE OF METALS, MINERAL PRODUCTS AND CHEMICALS
21		Extraction and preparation of metalliferous ores
22		Metal manufacturing
	2210	Iron and steel industry (as defined in the European Coal and Steel Community Treaty of Paris 1951)
	2220	Steel tubes
	2234	Drawing and manufacture of steel wire and steel wire products
	2235	Other drawing, cold rolling and cold forming of steel
	2245	Aluminium and aluminium alloys
	2246	Copper, brass and other copper alloys
	2247	Other non-ferrous metals and their alloys
23		Extraction of minerals not elsewhere specified
	2310	Extraction of stone, clay, sand and gravel
	2330	Salt extraction and refining
	2396	Extraction of other minerals not elsewhere specified
24		Manufacture of non-metallic mineral products
	2410	Structural clay products
	2420	Cement, lime and plaster
	2436	Ready mixed concrete
	2437	Other building products of concrete, cement or plaster
	2440	Asbestos goods
	2450	Working of stone and other non-metallic minerals not elsewhere specified
	2460	Abrasive products
	2471	Flat glass
	2478	Glass containers
	2479	Other glass products
	2481	Refractory goods
	2489	Ceramic goods

Class	Activity	
		DIVISION 2 *(continued)*
25		Chemical industry
	2511	Inorganic chemicals except industrial gases
	2512	Basic organic chemicals except specialised pharmaceutical chemicals
	2513	Fertilisers
	2514	Synthetic resins and plastics materials
	2515	Synthetic rubber
	2516	Dyestuffs and pigments
	2551	Paints, varnishes and painters' fillings
	2552	Printing ink
	2562	Formulated adhesives and sealants
	2563	Chemical treatment of oils and fats
	2564	Essential oils and flavouring materials
	2565	Explosives
	2567	Miscellaneous chemical products for industrial use
	2568	Formulated pesticides
	2569	Adhesive film, cloth and foil
	2570	Pharmaceutical products
	2581	Soap and synthetic detergents
	2582	Perfumes, cosmetics and toilet preparations
	2591	Photographic materials and chemicals
	2599	Chemical products not elsewhere specified
26		Production of man-made fibres
		DIVISION 3 METAL GOODS, ENGINEERING AND VEHICLES INDUSTRIES
31		Manufacture of metal goods not elsewhere specified
	3111	Ferrous metal foundries
	3112	Non-ferrous metal foundries
	3120	Forging, pressing and stamping
	3137	Bolts, nuts, washers, rivets, springs and non-precision chains
	3138	Heat and surface treatment of metals, including sintering
	3142	Metal doors, windows, etc.
	3161	Hand tools and implements
	3162	Cutlery, spoons, forks and similar tableware; razors
	3163	Metal storage vessels (mainly non-industrial)
	3164	Packaging products of metal
	3165	Domestic heating and cooking appliances (non-electrical)
	3166	Metal furniture and safes
	3167	Domestic and similar utensils of metal
	3169	Finished metal products not elsewhere specified
32		Mechanical engineering
	3204	Fabricated constructional steelwork
	3205	Boilers and process plant fabrications
	3211	Agricultural machinery
	3212	Wheeled tractors
	3221	Metal-working machine tools
	3222	Engineers' small tools
	3230	Textile machinery
	3244	Food, drink and tobacco processing machinery; packaging and bottling machinery
	3245	Chemical industry machinery; furnaces and kilns; gas, water and waste treatment plant
	3246	Process engineering contractors
	3251	Mining machinery
	3254	Construction and earth moving equipment
	3255	Mechanical lifting and handling equipment
	3261	Precision chains and other mechanical power transmission equipment
	3262	Ball, needle and roller bearings
	3275	Machinery for working wood, rubber, plastics, leather and making paper, glass, bricks and similar materials; laundry and dry cleaning machinery
	3276	Printing, bookbinding and paper goods machinery
	3281	Internal combustion engines (except for road vehicles, wheeled tractors primarily for agricultural purposes and aircraft) and other prime movers
	3283	Compressors and fluid power equipment
	3284	Refrigerating machinery, space heating, ventilating and air conditioning equipment
	3285	Scales, weighing machinery and portable power tools
	3286	Other industrial and commercial machinery
	3287	Pumps
	3288	Industrial valves
	3289	Mechanical, marine and precision engineering not elsewhere specified
	3290	Ordnance, small arms and ammunition

Class	Activity	
		DIVISION 3 *(continued)*
33		Manufacture of office machinery and data processing equipment
	3301	Office machinery
	3302	Electronic data processing equipment
34		Electrical and electronic engineering
	3410	Insulated wires and cables
	3420	Basic electrical equipment
	3432	Batteries and accumulators
	3433	Alarms and signalling equipment
	3434	Electrical equipment for motor vehicles, cycles and aircraft
	3435	Electrical equipment for industrial use not elsewhere specified
	3441	Telegraph and telephone apparatus and equipment
	3442	Electrical instruments and control systems
	3443	Radio and electronic capital goods
	3444	Components other than active components, mainly for electronic equipment
	3452	Gramophone records and pre-recorded tapes
	3453	Active components and electronic sub-assemblies
	3454	Electronic consumer goods and other electronic equipment not elsewhere specified
	3460	Domestic-type electric appliances
	3470	Electric lamps and other electric lighting equipment
	3480	Electrical equipment installation
35		Manufacture of motor vehicles and parts thereof
	3510	Motor vehicles and their engines
	3521	Motor vehicle bodies
	3522	Trailers and semi-trailers
	3523	Caravans
	3530	Motor vehicle parts
36		Manufacture of other transport equipment
	3610	Shipbuilding and repairing
	3620	Railway and tramway vehicles
	3633	Motor cycles and parts
	3634	Pedal cycles and parts
	3640	Aerospace equipment manufacturing and repairing
	3650	Other vehicles
37		Instrument engineering
	3710	Measuring, checking and precision instruments and apparatus
	3720	Medical and surgical equipment and orthopaedic appliances
	3731	Spectacles and unmounted lenses
	3732	Optical precision instruments
	3733	Photographic and cinematographic equipment
	3740	Clocks, watches and other timing devices
		DIVISION 4 OTHER MANUFACTURING INDUSTRIES
41/42		Food, drink and tobacco manufacturing industries
	4115	Margarine and compound cooking fats
	4116	Processing organic oils and fats (other than crude animal fat production)
	4121	Slaughterhouses
	4122	Bacon curing and meat processing
	4123	Poultry slaughter and processing
	4126	Animal by-product processing
	4130	Preparation of milk and milk products
	4147	Processing of fruit and vegetables
	4150	Fish processing
	4160	Grain milling
	4180	Starch
	4196	Bread and flour confectionery
	4197	Biscuits and crispbread
	4200	Sugar and sugar by-products
	4213	Ice cream
	4214	Cocoa, chocolate and sugar confectionery
	4221	Compound animal feeds
	4222	Pet foods and non-compound animal feeds
	4239	Miscellaneous foods
	4240	Spirit distilling and compounding
	4261	Wines, cider and perry
	4270	Brewing and malting
	4283	Soft drinks
	4290	Tobacco industry

Class	Activity	
		DIVISION 4 *(continued)*
43		Textile industry
	4310	Woollen and worsted industry
	4321	Spinning and doubling on the cotton system
	4322	Weaving of cotton, silk and man-made fibres
	4336	Throwing, texturing, etc. of continuous filament yarn
	4340	Spinning and weaving of flax, hemp and ramie
	4350	Jute and polypropylene yarns and fabrics
	4363	Hosiery and other weft knitted goods and fabrics
	4364	Warp knitted fabrics
	4370	Textile finishing
	4384	Pile carpets, carpeting and rugs
	4385	Other carpets, carpeting, rugs and matting
	4395	Lace
	4396	Rope, twine and net
	4398	Narrow fabrics
	4399	Other miscellaneous textiles
44		Manufacture of leather and leather goods
	4410	Leather (tanning and dressing) and fellmongery
	4420	Leather goods
45		Footwear and clothing industries
	4510	Footwear
	4531	Weatherproof outerwear
	4532	Men's and boys' tailored outerwear
	4533	Women's and girls' tailored outerwear
	4534	Work clothing and men's and boys' jeans
	4535	Men's and boys' shirts, underwear and nightwear
	4536	Women's and girls' light outerwear, lingerie and infants' wear
	4537	Hats, caps and millinery
	4538	Gloves
	4539	Other dress industries
	4555	Soft furnishings
	4556	Canvas goods, sacks and other made-up textiles
	4557	Household textiles
	4560	Fur goods
46		Timber and wooden furniture industries
	4610	Sawmilling, planing, etc. of wood
	4620	Manufacture of semi-finished wood products and further processing and treatment of wood
	4630	Builders' carpentry and joinery
	4640	Wooden containers
	4650	Other wooden articles (except furniture)
	4663	Brushes and brooms
	4664	Articles of cork and basketware, wickerwork and other plaiting materials
	4671	Wooden and upholstered furniture
	4672	Shop and office fitting
47		Manufacture of paper and paper products; printing and publishing
	4710	Pulp, paper and board
	4721	Wall coverings
	4722	Household and personal hygiene products of paper
	4723	Stationery
	4724	Packaging products of paper and pulp
	4725	Packaging products of board
	4728	Other paper and board products
	4751	Printing and publishing of newspapers
	4752	Printing and publishing of periodicals
	4753	Printing and publishing of books
	4754	Other printing and publishing
48		Processing of rubber and plastics
	4811	Rubber tyres and inner tubes
	4812	Other rubber products
	4820	Retreading and specialist repairing of rubber tyres
	4831	Plastic coated textile fabric
	4832	Plastics semi-manufacturers
	4833	Plastics floorcoverings
	4834	Plastics building products
	4835	Plastics packaging products
	4836	Plastics products not elsewhere specified

Class	Activity	
		DIVISION 4 *(continued)*
49		Other manufacturing industries
	4910	Jewellery and coins
	4920	Musical instruments
	4930	Photographic and cinematographic processing laboratories
	4941	Toys and games
	4942	Sports goods
	4954	Miscellaneous stationers' goods
	4959	Other manufacturers not elsewhere specified

DIVISION 5 CONSTRUCTION

Class	Activity	
50		Construction

DIVISION 6 DISTRIBUTION, HOTELS AND CATERING; REPAIRS

Class	Activity	
61		Wholesale distribution (except dealing in scrap and waste materials)
	6148	Wholesale distribution of motor vehicles and parts and accessories
61 rem.		Remainder of Wholesale distribution (except dealing in scrap and waste materials)
62		Dealing in scrap and waste materials
63		Commission agents
64/65		Retail distribution
	6510	Retail distribution of motor vehicles and parts
	6520	Filling stations (motor fuel and lubricants)
64/65 rem.		Remainder of Retail distribution
66		Hotels and catering
	6611	Eating places supplying food for consumption on the premises
	6612	Take-away food shops
	6620	Public houses and bars
	6630	Night clubs and licensed clubs
	6640	Canteens and messes
	6650	Hotel trade
	6670	Other tourist or short-stay accommodation
67		Repair of consumer goods and vehicles
	6710	Repair and servicing of motor vehicles
	6720	Repair of footwear and leather goods
	6730	Repair of other consumer goods

DIVISION 7 TRANSPORT AND COMMUNICATION

Class	Activity	
71		Railways
72		Other inland transport
	7210	Scheduled road passenger transport and urban railways
	7220	Other road passenger transport
	7230	Road haulage
	7260	Transport not elsewhere specified
74		Sea transport
75		Air transport
76		Supporting services to transport
	7610	Supporting services to inland transport
	7630	Supporting services to sea transport
	7640	Supporting services to air transport
77		Miscellaneous transport services and storage not elsewhere specified
79		Postal services and telecommunications
	7901	Postal services
	7902	Telecommunications

DIVISION 8 BANKING, FINANCE, INSURANCE, BUSINESS SERVICES AND LEASING

Class	Activity	
81		Banking and finance
	8140	Banking and bill-discounting
	8150	Other financial institutions
82		Insurance, except for compulsory social security

Class	Activity	
		DIVISION 8 *(continued)*
83		Business services
	8310	Activities auxiliary to banking and finance
	8320	Activities auxiliary to insurance
	8340	House and estate agents
	8350	Legal services
	8360	Accountants, auditors, tax experts
	8370	Professional and technical services not elsewhere specified
	8380	Advertising
	8394	Computer services
	8395	Business services not elsewhere specified
	8396	Central offices not allocable elsewhere
84		Renting of movables
	8410	Hiring out agricultural and horticultural equipment
	8420	Hiring out construction machinery and equipment
	8430	Hiring out office machinery and furniture
	8460	Hiring out consumer goods
	8480	Hiring out transport equipment
	8490	Hiring out other movables
85		Owning and dealing in real estate

Class	Activity	
		DIVISION 9 OTHER SERVICES
91		Public administration, national defence and compulsory social security
	9111	National government service not elsewhere specified
	9112	Local government service not elsewhere specified
	9120	Justice
	9130	Police
	9140	Fire services
	9150	National defence
	9190	Social security
92		Sanitary services
	9211	Refuse disposal, street cleaning, fumigation, etc.
	9212	Sewage disposal
	9230	Cleaning services
93		Education
	9310	Higher education
	9320 pt.	School education (nursery, primary and secondary)—maintained
	9320 pt.	School education (nursery, primary and secondary)—non-maintained
	9330	Education not elsewhere specified and vocational training
	9360	Driving and flying schools
94		Research and development
95		Medical and other health services: veterinary services
	9510	Hospitals, nursing homes, etc.
	9520	Other medical care institutions
	9530	Medical practices
	9540	Dental practices
	9550	Agency and private midwives, nurses, etc.
	9560	Veterinary practices and animal hospitals
96		Other services provided to the general public
	9611	Social welfare, charitable and community services
	9631	Trade unions, business and professional associations
	9660	Religious organisations and similar associations
	9690	Tourist offices and other community services
97		Recreational services and other cultural services
	9711	Film production, distribution and exhibition
	9741	Radio and television services, theatres, etc.
	9760	Authors, music composers and other own account artists not elsewhere specified
	9770	Libraries, museums, art galleries, etc.
	9791	Sport and other recreational services
98		Personal services
	9811	Laundries
	9812	Dry cleaning and allied services
	9820	Hairdressing and beauty parlours
	9890	Personal services not elsewhere specified
99		Domestic services
00		Diplomatic representation, international organisations, allied armed forces

Appendix E

European Economic Community Status Groups

1. Farmers
2. Other agricultural workers
3. Employers in industry, construction, trade, transport and services
4. Own-account workers in industry, construction, trade, transport and services
5. Employers and own-account workers in liberal and related professions
6. Managers, legislative officials and government administrators
7. Employees with liberal and related professions
8. Foremen and supervisors of manual workers (employees)
9. Skilled and semi-skilled manual workers (employees)
10. Labourers (employees)
11. Supervisors of clerical workers, sales workers and service staff; government executive officials
12. Clerical, sales and service workers
13. Armed forces (regular members and persons on compulsory military service)
14. Economically active persons not elsewhere classified

European Economic Community Socio-economic Status Group allocations of Occupation and Employment Status Groups

Occupation	Self-employed with employees	Self-employed without employees	Managers	Foremen	Apprentices, etc., Employees n.e.c.
001 Judges, barristers, advocates, solicitors					
0 Judges, barristers, advocates, solicitors	5	5	—	—	7
002 Accountants, valuers, finance specialists					
1 Chartered and certified accountants	5	5	—	—	7
2 Cost and works accountants	5	5	—	—	7
3 Estimators	5	5	7	—	7
4 Valuers, claims assessors	3	4	12	—	12
5 Financial managers	—	—	6	—	—
6 Underwriters, brokers, investment analysts	3	4	12	—	—
7 Taxation experts	5	5	7	—	—
003 Personnel and industrial relations managers; O and M, work study and operational research officers					
1 Personnel and industrial relations officers	3	4	6	—	—
2 O and M, work study and OR officers	5	5	7	—	7
004 Economists, statisticians, systems analysts, computer programmers					
1 Economists, statisticians, actuaries	5	5	—	—	7
2 Systems analysts, computer programmers	5	5	7	—	7
005 Marketing, sales, advertising, public relations and purchasing managers					
1 Marketing and sales managers and executives	3	4	6	—	—
2 Advertising and PR executives	3	4	6	—	—
3 Buyers (retail trade)	—	—	11	—	—
4 Buyers and purchasing officers (not retail)	—	—	11	—	—
006 Statutory and other inspectors					
1 Environmental health officers	—	—	—	—	11
2 Building inspectors	—	—	—	—	11
3 Inspectors (statutory and similar)	—	—	—	—	11
007 General administrators—national government					
1 General administrators—national government (Assistant Secretary level and above)	—	—	6	—	—
2 General administrators—national government (HEO to Senior Principal level)	—	—	6	—	—
008 Local government officers (administrative and executive functions)					
0 Local government officers (administrative and executive functions)	—	—	6	—	—

Occupation	Self-employed with employees	Self-employed without employees	Managers	Foremen	Apprentices, etc., Employees n.e.c.
009 All other professional and related supporting management and administration					
1 Company secretaries	3	4	6	—	—
2 Officials of trade associations, trade unions, professional bodies and charities	—	—	6	—	6
3 Property and estate managers	3	4	12	—	—
4 Librarians, information officers	—	—	7	—	7
5 Legal service and related occupations	5	5	7	—	7
6 Management consultants	5	5	—	—	7
7 Managers' personal assistants	—	—	—	—	12
8 Professional workers and related supporting management and administration n.e.c.	3	4	6	—	6
010 Teachers in higher education					
1 University academic staff	—	—	—	—	7
2 Teachers in establishments for further and higher education	5	5	7	—	7
011 Teachers n.e.c.					
0 Teachers n.e.c.	5	5	7	—	7
012 Vocational and industrial trainers, education officers, social and behavioural scientists					
1 Vocational and industrial trainers	5	5	7	—	7
2 Education officers, school inspectors	—	—	—	—	6
3 Social and behavioural scientists	5	5	—	—	7
013 Welfare workers					
1 Matrons, houseparents	5	5	7	—	7
2 Playgroup leaders	5	5	—	—	7
3 Welfare occupations n.e.c.	—	—	7	—	7
014 Clergy, ministers of religion					
0 Clergy, ministers of religion	5	5	—	—	7
015 Medical and dental practitioners					
1 Medical practitioners	5	5	—	—	7
2 Dental practitioners	5	5	—	—	7
016 Nurse administrators, nurses					
0 Nurse administrators, nurses	5	5	7	7	7
017 Pharmacists, radiographers, therapists n.e.c.					
1 Pharmacists	5	5	—	—	7
2 Medical radiographers	5	5	7	7	7
3 Ophthalmic and dispensing opticians	5	5	—	—	7
4 Physiotherapists	5	5	7	7	7
5 Chiropodists	5	5	7	—	7
6 Therapists n.e.c.	5	5	7	7	7
018 All other professional and related in education, welfare and health					
1 Medical technicians, dental auxiliaries	5	5	7	7	7
2 Veterinarians	5	5	—	—	7
3 Driving instructors (not HGV)	3	4	9	—	9
4 Professional and related in education, welfare and health n.e.c.	5	5	7	—	7
019 Authors, writers, journalists					
0 Authors, writers, journalists	5	5	7	—	7
020 Artists, designers, window dressers					
1 Artists, commercial artists	5	5	7	7	7
2 Industrial designers (not clothing)	5	5	7	—	7
3 Clothing designers	5	5	7	—	7
4 Window dressers	5	5	7	—	7
021 Actors, musicians, entertainers, stage managers					
1 Actors, entertainers, singers, stage managers	3	4	11	—	11
2 Musicians	3	4	11	—	11
022 Photographers, cameramen, sound and vision equipment operators					
1 Photographers, cameramen	5	5	7	7	7
2 Sound and vision equipment operators	3	4	9	9	9
023 All other literary, artistic and sports					
1 Professional sportsmen, sports officials	3	4	11	—	11
2 Literary, artistic and sports workers n.e.c.	5	5	7	—	7
024 Scientists, physicists, mathematicians					
1 Biological scientists, biochemists	5	5	—	—	7
2 Chemical scientists	5	5	—	—	7
3 Physical and geological scientists, mathematicians	5	5	—	—	7
025 Civil, structural, municipal, mining and quarrying engineers					
0 Civil, structural, municipal, mining and quarrying engineers	5	5	—	—	7
026 Mechanical and aeronautical engineers					
1 Mechanical and aeronautical engineers	5	5	—	—	7
2 Design and development engineers (mechanical)	5	5	—	—	7
027 Electrical and electronic engineers					
1 Electrical engineers	5	5	—	—	7
2 Electronic engineers	5	5	—	—	7

Occupation	Self-employed with employees	Self-employed without employees	Managers	Foremen	Apprentices, etc., Employees n.e.c.
028 Engineers and technologists n.e.c.					
1 Chemical engineers	5	5	—	—	7
2 Production engineers	5	5	—	—	7
3 Planning and quality control engineers	5	5	—	—	7
4 Engineers n.e.c.	5	5	—	—	7
5 Metallurgists	5	5	—	—	7
6 Technologists n.e.c.	5	5	—	—	7
029 Draughtsmen					
0 Draughtsmen	5	5	7	7	7
030 Laboratory and engineering technicians, technician engineers					
1 Laboratory technicians	5	5	7	7	7
2 Engineering technicians, technician engineers	5	5	7	7	7
031 Architects, town planners, quantity, building and land surveyors					
1 Architects, town planners	5	5	—	—	7
2 Quantity surveyors	5	5	—	—	7
3 Building, land and mining surveyors	5	5	—	—	7
032 Officers (ships and aircraft), air traffic planners and controllers					
1 Aircraft flight deck officers	5	5	7	—	7
2 Air traffic planners and controllers	—	—	—	—	11
3 Deck, engineering and radio officers and pilots, ship	5	5	7	—	—
033 Professional and related in science, engineering and other technologies and similar fields n.e.c.					
1 Architectural and town planning technicians	—	5	—	—	7
2 Building and civil engineering technicians	—	—	—	—	7
3 Technical and related workers n.e.c.	5	5	7	7	7
034 Production, works and maintenance managers, works foremen					
0 Production, works and maintenance managers, works foremen	—	—	6	8	—
035 Site and other managers, agents and clerks of works, general foremen (building and civil engineering)					
1 Managers in building and contracting	—	—	6	—	—
2 Clerks of works	—	—	—	—	6
036 Managers in transport, warehousing, public utilities and mining					
1 Managers in mining and public utilities	—	—	6	—	—
2 Transport managers	—	—	6	—	—
3 Stores controllers	—	—	6	—	—
4 Managers in warehousing and materials handling n.e.c.	—	—	6	—	—
037 Office managers					
1 Credit controllers	—	—	6	—	—
2 Office managers n.e.c.	3	4	6	—	—
038 Managers in wholesale and retail distribution					
1 Garage proprietors	3	4	—	—	—
2 Butchers (managers and proprietors)	3	4	6	—	—
3 Fishmongers (managers and proprietors)	3	4	6	—	—
4 Other proprietors and managers (sales)	3	4	6	—	—
039 Managers of hotels, clubs, etc., and in entertainment and sport					
1 Hotel and residential club managers	3	4	6	—	—
2 Publicans	3	4	6	—	—
3 Restaurateurs	3	4	6	—	—
4 Club stewards	—	—	6	—	—
5 Entertainment and sports managers	3	4	6	—	—
040 Farmers, horticulturists, farm managers					
0 Farmers, horticulturists, farm managers	1	1	2	—	—
041 Officers, UK armed forces					
0 Officers, UK armed forces	—	—	13	—	—
042 Officers, foreign and Commonwealth armed forces					
0 Officers, foreign and Commonwealth armed forces	—	—	13	—	—
043 Senior police, prison and fire service officers					
1 Prison officers (chief officers and above)	—	—	6	—	—
2 Police officers (inspectors and above)	—	—	6	—	—
3 Fire service officers	—	—	6	—	—
044 All other managers					
1 Proprietors and managers, service flats, holiday flats, caravan sites, etc.	3	4	6	—	—
2 Managers of laundry and dry cleaning receiving shops	3	4	6	—	—
3 Hairdressers' and barbers' managers and proprietors	3	4	12	—	—
4 Managers n.e.c.	3	4	6	—	—
045 Supervisors of clerks, civil service executive officers					
1 Civil service executive officers	—	—	—	11	—
Supervisors of—					
2 Stores and despatch clerks	—	—	—	11	—
3 Tracers, drawing office assistants	—	—	—	11	—
4 Other clerks and cashiers (not retail)	—	—	—	11	—
5 Retail shop cashiers, check-out and cash and wrap operators	—	—	—	11	—

Occupation	Self-employed		Managers	Foremen	Apprentices, etc., Employees n.e.c.
	with employees	without employees			
046 Clerks					
1 Stores and despatch clerks	—	—	—	—	12
2 Tracers, drawing office assistants	—	4	—	—	12
3 Other clerks and cashiers (not retail)	3	4	—	—	12
047 Retail shop cashiers, check-out and cash and wrap operators					
0 Retail shop cashiers, check-out and cash and wrap operators	—	—	—	—	12
048 Supervisors of typists, office machine operators, telephonists, etc.					
Supervisors of—					
1 Typists, shorthand writers, secretaries	—	—	—	11	—
2 Office machine operators	—	—	—	11	—
3 Telephone operators	—	—	—	11	—
4 Radio and telegraph operators	—	—	—	11	—
049 Secretaries, shorthand typists, receptionists					
1 Receptionists	—	—	—	—	12
2 Typists, shorthand writers, secretaries	3	4	—	—	12
050 Office machine operators					
0 Office machine operators	3	4	—	—	12
051 Telephonists, radio and telegraph operators					
1 Telephonist receptionists	—	—	—	—	12
2 Telephone operators	—	—	—	—	12
3 Radio and telegraph operators	—	—	—	—	12
052 Supervisors of postmen, mail sorters, messengers					
Supervisors of—					
1 Postmen, mail sorters	—	—	—	11	—
2 Messengers	—	—	—	11	—
053 Postmen, mail sorters, messengers					
1 Postmen, mail sorters	—	—	—	—	12
2 Messengers	—	4	—	—	12
054 Sales supervisors					
Supervisors of—					
1 Shop salesmen and assistants	—	—	—	11	—
2 Petrol pump, forecourt attendants	—	—	—	11	—
3 Roundsmen, van salesmen	—	—	—	11	—
055 Salesmen, sales assistants, shop assistants, shelf fillers, petrol pump, forecourt attendants					
1 Shop salesmen and assistants	—	—	—	—	12
2 Shelf fillers	—	—	—	—	12
3 Petrol pump, forecourt attendants	—	—	—	—	12
056 Roundsmen, van salesmen					
0 Roundsmen, van salesmen	3	4	12	—	12
057 Sales representatives and agents					
1 Importers, exporters, commodity brokers	3	4	6	—	—
2 Market and street traders and assistants	3	4	12	—	12
3 Scrap dealers, general dealers, rag and bone merchants	3	4	6	—	—
4 Credit agents, collector salesmen	3	4	12	—	12
5 Sales representatives	3	4	12	—	12
6 Sales representatives (property and services), other agents	3	4	12	—	12
058 NCOs and other ranks, UK armed forces					
0 NCOs and other ranks, UK armed forces	—	—	—	—	13
059 NCOs and other ranks, foreign and Commonwealth armed forces					
0 NCOs and other ranks, foreign and Commonwealth armed forces	—	—	—	—	13
060 Supervisors (police sergeants, fire fighting and related)					
1 Police sergeants	—	—	—	12	—
2 Fire service supervisors	—	—	—	12	—
3 Prison service principal officers	—	—	—	12	—
Supervisors of—					
4 Security guards and officers, patrolmen, watchmen	—	—	—	12	—
5 Traffic wardens	—	—	—	12	—
6 Security and protective service workers n.e.c.	—	—	—	12	—
061 Policemen, firemen, prison officers					
1 Policemen (below sergeant)	—	—	—	—	12
2 Firemen	—	—	—	—	12
3 Prison officers (below principal officer)	—	—	—	—	12
062 Other security and protective service workers					
1 Security guards and officers, patrolmen, watchmen	3	4	—	—	12
2 Traffic wardens	—	—	—	—	12
3 Security and protective service workers n.e.c.	3	4	—	—	12
063 Catering supervisors					
Supervisors of—					
1 Chefs, cooks	—	—	—	12	—
2 Waiters, waitresses	—	—	—	12	—
3 Barmen, barmaids	—	—	—	12	—
4 Counter hands, assistants	—	—	—	12	—

Occupation	Self-employed		Managers	Foremen	Apprentices, etc., Employees n.e.c.
	with employees	without employees			
064 Chefs, cooks					
0 Chefs, cooks	3	4	12	—	12
065 Waiters and bar staff					
1 Waiters, waitresses	—	4	—	—	12
2 Barmen, barmaids	—	4	—	—	12
066 Counter hands, assistants, kitchen porters, hands					
1 Counter hands, assistants	—	—	—	—	12
2 Kitchen porters, hands	—	—	—	10	10
067 Supervisors—housekeeping and related					
1 Housekeepers (non-domestic)	—	—	—	11	—
Supervisors of—					
2 Other domestic and school helpers	—	—	—	12	—
3 Travel stewards and attendants	—	—	—	11	—
4 Hospital porters	—	—	—	10	—
5 Hotel porters	—	—	—	12	—
6 Ambulancemen	—	—	—	12	—
7 Hospital, ward orderlies	—	—	—	12	—
068 Domestic staff and school helpers					
1 Domestic housekeepers	—	—	—	—	11
2 Nursery nurses	3	4	—	—	12
3 Other domestic and school helpers	—	4	—	—	12
069 Travel stewards and attendants, hospital and hotel porters					
1 Travel stewards and attendants	—	4	—	—	12
2 Hospital porters	—	—	—	—	10
3 Hotel porters	—	—	—	—	12
070 Ambulancemen, hospital orderlies					
1 Ambulancemen	—	—	—	—	12
2 Hospital, ward orderlies	—	—	—	—	12
071 Supervisors, foremen—caretaking, cleaning and related					
Supervisors of—					
1 Caretakers	—	—	—	12	—
2 Cleaners, window cleaners, chimney sweeps, road sweepers	—	—	—	12	—
3 Railway stationmen	—	—	—	9	—
4 Lift and car park attendants	—	—	—	12	—
072 Caretakers, road sweepers and other cleaners					
1 Caretakers	—	—	—	—	12
2 Cleaners, window cleaners, chimney sweeps, road sweepers	3	4	12	—	12
073 Hairdressing supervisors					
0 Hairdressing supervisors	—	—	—	12	—
074 Hairdressers, barbers					
0 Hairdressers, barbers	—	—	—	—	12
075 All other in catering, cleaning and other personal service					
1 Railway stationmen	—	—	—	—	9
2 Lift and car park attendants	—	—	—	—	12
3 Launderers, dry cleaners, pressers	—	—	12	12	12
4 Undertakers	3	4	12	—	—
5 Bookmakers, betting shop managers	3	4	12	—	—
6 Service workers n.e.c.	3	4	12	12	12
076 Foremen—farming, horticulture, forestry					
1 Farm foremen	—	—	—	2	—
2 Horticultural foremen	—	—	—	2	—
3 Foremen gardeners and groundsmen	—	—	—	2	—
4 Agricultural machinery foremen	—	—	—	2	—
5 Forestry foremen	—	—	—	2	—
6 Other foremen in farming and related	—	—	—	2	—
077 Farm workers					
0 Farm workers	1	1	—	—	2
078 Horticultural workers, gardeners, groundsmen					
1 Horticultural workers	1	1	—	—	2
2 Gardeners, groundsmen	1	1	2	—	2
079 Agricultural machinery drivers, operators					
0 Agricultural machinery drivers, operators	1	1	—	—	2
080 Forestry workers					
0 Forestry workers	1	1	—	—	2
081 Supervisors, mates—fishing					
0 Supervisors, mates—fishing	—	—	—	2	—
082 Fishermen					
0 Fishermen	1	1	2	—	2
083 All other in farming and related					
0 All other in farming and related	1	1	—	—	2

	Occupation	Self-employed		Managers	Foremen	Apprentices, etc., Employees n.e.c.
		with employees	without employees			
084	Foremen—tannery and leather (including leather substitutes) working					
	Foremen—					
1	Tannery production workers	—	—	—	9	—
2	Shoe repairers	—	—	—	9	—
3	Leather cutters and sewers, footwear lasters, makers, finishers	—	—	—	9	—
4	Other making and repairing, leather	—	—	—	9	—
085	Tannery and leather (including leather substitutes) workers					
1	Tannery production workers	3	4	9	—	9
2	Shoe repairers	3	4	9	—	9
3	Leather cutters and sewers, footwear lasters, makers, finishers	3	4	9	—	9
086	Foremen—textile processing					
	Foremen—					
1	Preparatory fibre processors	—	—	—	9	—
2	Spinners, doublers, twisters	—	—	—	9	—
3	Winders, reelers	—	—	—	9	—
4	Warp preparers	—	—	—	9	—
5	Weavers	—	—	—	9	—
6	Knitters	—	—	—	9	—
7	Bleachers, dyers, finishers	—	—	—	9	—
8	Menders, darners	—	—	—	9	—
9	Other material processing, textiles	—	—	—	9	—
087	Textile workers					
1	Preparatory fibre processors	3	4	9	—	9
2	Spinners, doublers, twisters	3	4	9	—	9
3	Winders, reelers	3	4	9	—	9
4	Warp preparers	3	4	9	—	9
5	Weavers	3	4	9	—	9
6	Knitters	3	4	9	—	9
7	Bleachers, dyers, finishers	3	4	9	—	9
8	Menders, darners	3	4	9	—	9
088	Foremen—chemical processing					
0	Foremen—chemical processing	—	—	—	9	—
089	Chemical, gas and petroleum process plant operators					
0	Chemical, gas and petroleum process plant operators	3	4	9	—	9
090	Foremen—food and drink processing					
	Foremen—					
1	Bakers, flour confectioners	—	—	—	9	—
2	Butchers, meat cutters	—	—	—	9	—
3	Fishmongers, poultry dressers	—	—	—	9	—
4	Brewery and vinery process workers	—	—	—	9	—
	Other material processing—					
5	Bakery and confectionery workers	—	—	—	9	—
6	Food and drink n.e.c.	—	—	—	9	—
091	Bakers, flour confectioners					
0	Bakers, flour confectioners	3	4	9	—	9
092	Butchers					
1	Butchers, meat cutters	—	—	—	—	9
2	Fishmongers, poultry dressers	⊥	—	—	—	9
093	Foremen—paper and board making and paper products					
	Foremen—					
1	Paper, paperboard and leatherboard workers	—	—	—	9	—
2	Bookbinders and finishers	—	—	—	9	—
3	Cutting and slitting machine operators (paper and paper products making)	—	—	—	9	—
4	Other material processing, wood and paper	—	—	—	9	—
5	Other making and repairing, paper goods and printing	—	—	—	9	—
094	Paper, board and paper product makers, bookbinders					
1	Paper, paperboard and leatherboard workers	3	4	—	—	9
2	Bookbinders and finishers	3	4	9	—	9
3	Cutting and slitting machine operators (paper and paper products making)	—	—	—	—	9
095	Foremen—glass, ceramics, rubber, plastics, etc.					
	Foremen—					
1	Glass and ceramics furnacemen, kilnsetters	—	—	—	9	—
2	Glass formers and shapers, finishers, decorators	—	—	—	9	—
3	Casters and other pottery makers	—	—	—	9	—
4	Rubber process workers, moulding machine operators, tyre builders	—	—	—	9	—
5	Calender and extruding machine operators, moulders (plastics)	—	—	—	9	—
6	Man-made fibre makers	—	—	—	9	—
7	Washers, screeners and crushers in mines and quarries	—	—	—	9	—
	Other making and repairing—					
8	Glass and ceramics	—	—	—	9	—
9	Rubber	—	—	—	9	—
10	Plastics	—	—	—	9	—
096	Glass and ceramics furnacemen and workers					
1	Glass and ceramics furnacemen, kilnsetters	—	—	—	—	9
2	Glass formers and shapers, finishers, decorators	3	4	9	—	9
3	Casters and other pottery makers	3	4	9	—	9

Occupation	Self-employed with employees	Self-employed without employees	Managers	Foremen	Apprentices, etc., Employees n.e.c.
097 Rubber and plastics workers					
1 Rubber process workers, moulding machine operators, tyre builders	3	4	9	—	9
2 Calender and extruding machine operators, moulders (plastics)	3	4	9	—	9
098 All other in processing materials (other than metal)					
1 Man-made fibre makers	—	—	—	—	9
2 Brewery and vinery process workers	3	4	9	—	9
3 Washers, screeners and crushers in mines and quarries	—	—	—	—	9
Other material processing—					
4 Textiles	3	4	—	—	9
5 Bakery and confectionery workers	3	4	—	—	9
6 Tobacco	—	—	—	9	9
7 Food and drink n.e.c.	3	4	9	—	9
8 Wood and paper	3	4	—	—	9
9 All other (excluding metal) n.e.c.	3	4	—	9	9
099 Foremen—printing					
Foremen—					
1 Compositors	—	—	—	9	—
2 Electrotypers, stereotypers, printing plate and cylinder preparers	—	—	—	9	—
3 Printing machine minders and assistants	—	—	—	9	—
4 Screen and block printers	—	—	—	9	—
5 Printers (so described)	—	—	—	9	—
100 Printing workers, screen and block printers					
1 Compositors	3	4	9	—	9
2 Electrotypers, stereotypers, printing plate and cylinder preparers	3	4	9	—	9
3 Printing machine minders and assistants	3	4	—	—	9
4 Screen and block printers	3	4	9	—	9
5 Printers (so described)	3	4	9	—	9
101 Foremen—textile materials working					
Foremen—					
1 Tailors, tailoresses, dressmakers	—	—	—	9	—
2 Clothing cutters, milliners, furriers	—	—	—	9	—
3 Sewers, embroiderers	—	—	—	9	—
4 Coach trimmers, upholsterers, mattress makers	—	—	—	9	—
5 Carpet fitters	—	—	—	9	—
6 Other making and repairing, clothing and related products	—	—	—	9	—
102 Tailors, dressmakers and other clothing workers					
1 Tailors, tailoresses, dressmakers	3	4	9	—	9
2 Clothing cutters, milliners, furriers	3	4	9	—	9
3 Sewers, embroiderers	3	4	—	—	9
103 Coach trimmers, upholsterers, mattress makers					
0 Coach trimmers, upholsterers, mattress makers	3	4	9	—	9
104 Foremen—woodworking					
Foremen—					
1 Carpenters, joiners	—	—	—	9	—
2 Cabinet makers	—	—	—	9	—
3 Case and box makers	—	—	—	9	—
4 Pattern makers (moulds)	—	—	—	9	—
5 Sawyers, veneer cutters, woodworking machinists	—	—	—	9	—
6 Other making and repairing, wood	—	—	—	9	—
105 Woodworkers, pattern makers					
1 Carpenters, joiners	3	4	9	—	9
2 Cabinet makers	3	4	9	—	9
3 Case and box makers	3	4	9	—	9
4 Pattern makers (moulds)	3	4	9	—	9
106 Sawyers, veneer cutters, woodworking machinists					
0 Sawyers, veneer cutters, woodworking machinists	3	4	9	—	9
107 All other in making and repairing (excluding metal and electrical)					
1 Labourers and mates to woodworking craftsmen	—	—	—	—	10
2 Dental technicians	3	4	9	9	9
3 Carpet fitters	3	4	—	—	9
4 Musical instrument makers, piano tuners	3	4	9	9	9
Other making and repairing—					
5 Glass and ceramics	3	4	—	—	9
6 Wood	3	4	9	—	9
7 Leather	3	4	9	—	9
8 Clothing and related products	3	4	9	—	9
9 Paper goods and printing	3	4	9	—	9
10 Rubber	3	4	9	—	9
11 Plastics	3	4	9	—	9
12 All other (excluding metal and electrical) n.e.c.	3	4	9	9	9
108 Foremen—metal making and treating					
Foremen—					
1 Furnace operating occupations (metal)	—	—	—	9	—
2 Rollermen	—	—	—	9	—
3 Smiths, forgemen	—	—	—	9	—
4 Metal drawers	—	—	—	9	—
5 Moulders, coremakers, die casters	—	—	—	9	—
6 Electroplaters	—	—	—	9	—
7 Annealers, hardeners, temperers (metal)	—	—	—	9	—
8 Galvanizers, tin platers, dip platers	—	—	—	9	—
9 Metal making and treating workers n.e.c.	—	—	—	9	—

	Occupation	Self-employed with employees	Self-employed without employees	Managers	Foremen	Apprentices, etc., Employees n.e.c.
109	Furnacemen (metal), rollermen, smiths, forgemen					
1	Furnace operating occupations (metal)	3	4	—	—	9
2	Rollermen	3	4	9	—	9
3	Smiths, forgemen	3	4	9	—	9
110	Metal drawers, moulders, die casters, electroplaters, annealers					
1	Metal drawers	3	4	—	—	9
2	Moulders, coremakers, die casters	3	4	—	—	9
3	Electroplaters	3	4	9	—	9
4	Annealers, hardeners, temperers (metal)	3	4	—	—	9
111	Foremen—engineering machining Foremen—					
1	Press and machine tool setters	—	—	—	9	—
2	Centre lathe turners	—	—	—	9	—
3	Machine tool setter operators	—	—	—	9	—
4	Machine tool operators	—	—	—	9	—
5	Press, stamping and automatic machine operators	—	—	—	9	—
6	Metal polishers	—	—	—	9	—
7	Fettlers, dressers	—	—	—	9	—
8	Shot blasters	—	—	—	9	—
112	Press and machine tool setter operators and operators, turners					
1	Press and machine tool setters	3	4	9	—	9
2	Centre lathe turners	3	4	9	—	9
3	Machine tool setter operators	3	4	9	—	9
4	Machine tool operators	3	4	—	—	9
113	Machine attendants, minders, press and stamping machine operators, metal polishers, fettlers, dressers					
1	Press, stamping and automatic machine operators	3	4	9	—	9
2	Metal polishers	3	4	9	—	9
3	Fettlers, dressers	3	4	—	—	9
114	Foremen—production fitting (metal) Foremen—					
1	Tool makers, tool fitters, markers-out	—	—	—	9	—
2	Precision instrument makers and repairers	—	—	—	9	—
3	Watch and chronometer makers and repairers	—	—	—	9	—
4	Metal working production fitters and fitter/machinists	—	—	—	9	—
5	Motor mechanics, auto engineers	—	—	—	9	—
6	Maintenance fitters (aircraft engines)	—	—	—	9	—
7	Office machinery mechanics	—	—	—	9	—
115	Tool makers, tool fitters, markers-out					
0	Tool makers, tool fitters, markers-out	3	4	9	—	9
116	Instrument and watch and clock makers and repairers					
1	Precision instrument makers and repairers	3	4	9	—	9
2	Watch and chronometer makers and repairers	3	4	9	—	9
117	Metal working production fitters and fitter/machinists					
0	Metal working production fitters and fitter/machinists	3	4	9	—	9
118	Motor vehicle and aircraft mechanics					
1	Motor mechanics, auto engineers	3	4	9	—	9
2	Maintenance fitters (aircraft engines)	—	4	—	—	9
119	Office machinery mechanics					
0	Office machinery mechanics	3	4	9	—	9
120	Foremen—production fitting and wiring (electrical) Foremen—					
1	Production fitters (electrical, electronic)	—	—	—	9	—
2	Electricians, electrical maintenance fitters	—	—	—	9	—
3	Plant operators and attendants n.e.c.	—	—	—	9	—
4	Telephone fitters	—	—	—	9	—
5	Cable jointers, linesmen	—	—	—	9	—
6	Radio and TV mechanics	—	—	—	9	—
7	Other electronic maintenance engineers	—	—	—	9	—
121	Production fitters, electricians, electricity power plant operators, switchboard attendants					
1	Production fitters (electrical, electronic)	3	4	9	—	9
2	Electricians, electrical maintenance fitters	3	4	9	—	9
3	Electrical engineers (so described)	3	4	9	—	9
4	Plant operators and attendants n.e.c.	—	—	—	—	9
122	Telephone fitters, cable jointers, linesmen					
1	Telephone fitters	—	4	—	—	9
2	Cable jointers, linesmen	—	4	—	—	9
123	Radio, TV and other electronic maintenance fitters and mechanics					
1	Radio and TV mechanics	3	4	9	—	9
2	Other electronic maintenance engineers	3	4	9	—	9
124	Foremen—metal working, pipes, sheets, structures Foremen—					
1	Plumbers, heating and ventilating fitters, gas fitters	—	—	—	9	—
2	Sheet metal workers	—	—	—	9	—
3	Metal plate workers, shipwrights, riveters	—	—	—	9	—
4	Steel erectors, benders, fixers	—	—	—	9	—
5	Scaffolders, stagers	—	—	—	9	—
6	Welders	—	—	—	9	—
7	Riggers	—	—	—	9	—

	Occupation	Self-employed with employees	Self-employed without employees	Managers	Foremen	Apprentices, etc., Employees n.e.c.
125	Plumbers, heating and ventilating fitters, gas fitters					
0	Plumbers, heating and ventilating fitters, gas fitters...	3	4	9	—	9
126	Sheet metal workers, platers, shipwrights, riveters, etc.					
1	Sheet metal workers ...	3	4	9	—	9
2	Metal plate workers, shipwrights, riveters ...	3	4	9	—	9
127	Steel erectors, scaffolders, steel benders, fixers					
1	Steel erectors, benders, fixers ...	3	4	9	—	9
2	Scaffolders, stagers ...	3	4	—	—	9
128	Welders					
0	Welders ...	3	4	9	—	9
129	Foremen—other processing, making and repairing (metal and electrical)					
	Foremen—					
1	Goldsmiths, silversmiths, precious stone workers...	—	—	—	9	—
2	Engravers, etchers (printing) ...	—	—	—	9	—
3	Coach and vehicle body builders ...	—	—	—	9	—
4	Oilers, greasers, lubricators ...	—	—	—	9	—
5	Electronics wiremen ...	—	—	—	9	—
6	Coil winders ...	—	—	—	9	—
130	Goldsmiths, silversmiths, etc., engravers, etchers					
1	Goldsmiths, silversmiths, precious stone workers ...	3	4	9	—	9
2	Engravers, etchers (printing) ...	3	4	—	—	9
131	All other in processing, making and repairing (metal and electrical)					
1	Coach and vehicle body builders ...	3	4	9	—	9
2	Galvanizers, tin platers, dip platers ...	3	4	—	—	9
3	Metal making and treating workers n.e.c. ...	3	4	—	—	9
4	Oilers, greasers, lubricators ...	—	—	—	—	9
5	Riggers ...	3	4	9	—	9
6	Electronics wiremen ...	—	4	—	—	9
7	Coil winders ...	3	4	9	—	9
8	Shot blasters ...	—	—	—	—	9
9	Other metal, jewellery, electrical production workers	3	4	9	9	9
1	Foremen (engineering and allied trades) ...	—	—	—	9	—
2	Trainee craftsmen (engineering and allied trades) ...	—	—	—	—	9
132	Foremen—painting and similar coating					
	Foremen—					
1	Pottery decorators ...	—	—	—	9	—
2	Coach painters (so described) ...	—	—	—	9	—
3	Other spray painters ...	—	—	—	9	—
4	Painters and decorators n.e.c., french polishers ...	—	—	—	9	—
133	Painters, decorators, french polishers					
1	Pottery decorators ...	3	4	—	—	9
2	Coach painters (so described) ...	3	4	9	—	9
3	Other spray painters ...	3	4	9	—	9
4	Painters and decorators n.e.c., french polishers ...	3	4	9	—	9
134	Foremen—product assembling (repetitive)					
	Foremen assemblers—					
1	Electrical, electronic...	—	—	—	9	—
2	Instruments ...	—	—	—	9	—
3	Vehicles and other metal goods ...	—	—	—	9	—
4	Paper production, processing and printing ...	—	—	—	9	—
5	Plastics goods ...	—	—	—	9	—
135	Repetitive assemblers (metal and electrical goods)					
1	Assemblers (electrical, electronic) ...	3	4	—	—	9
2	Instrument assemblers ...	—	4	—	—	9
3	Assemblers (vehicle and other metal goods) ...	—	4	—	—	9
136	Foremen—product inspection and packaging					
	Foremen inspectors, viewers, examiners—					
1	Metal, electrical goods ...	—	—	—	9	—
2	Textiles ...	—	—	—	9	—
3	Food ...	—	—	—	9	—
4	Rubber goods ...	—	—	—	9	—
5	Plastics goods ...	—	—	—	9	—
6	Woodwork ...	—	—	—	9	—
	Foremen—					
7	Packers, bottlers, canners, fillers ...	—	—	—	9	—
8	Laboratory assistants ...	—	—	—	9	—
9	Inspectors, sorters in paper production, processing and printing ...	—	—	—	9	—
10	Weighers ...	—	—	—	9	—
11	Graders, sorters, selectors n.e.c. ...	—	—	—	9	—
137	Inspectors, viewers, testers, packers, bottlers, etc.					
1	Inspectors, viewers (metal, electrical goods) ...	—	4	—	—	9
2	Packers, bottlers, canners, fillers ...	3	4	—	—	9

Occupation	Self-employed with employees	Self-employed without employees	Managers	Foremen	Apprentices, etc., Employees n.e.c.
138 All other in painting, repetitive assembling, product inspection, packaging and related					
1 Laboratory assistants	—	—	—	—	9
Inspectors, viewers, examiners—					
2 Textiles	—	—	—	—	9
3 Food	—	—	—	—	9
4 Rubber goods	—	—	—	—	9
5 Plastics goods	—	—	—	—	9
6 Woodwork	—	—	—	—	9
7 Inspectors, sorters in paper production, processing and printing	—	—	—	—	9
8 Assemblers in paper production, processing and printing	—	4	—	—	9
9 Assemblers (plastics goods)	—	—	—	—	9
10 Weighers	—	—	—	—	9
11 Graders, sorters, selectors n.e.c.	—	—	—	—	9
12 Painting, assembling and related occupations n.e.c.	3	4	9	9	9
139 Foremen—building and civil engineering n.e.c.					
Foremen—					
1 Bricklayers, tile setters	—	—	—	9	—
2 Masons, stone cutters	—	—	—	9	—
3 Plasterers	—	—	—	9	—
4 Roofers, glaziers	—	—	—	9	—
5 Handymen, general building workers	—	—	—	9	—
6 Railway lengthmen	—	—	—	9	—
7 Road surfacers, concreters	—	—	—	9	—
8 Roadmen	—	—	—	9	—
9 Paviors, kerb layers	—	—	—	9	—
10 Sewage plant attendants	—	—	—	9	—
11 Mains and service layers, pipe jointers	—	—	—	9	—
12 Construction workers n.e.c.	—	—	—	9	—
140 Building and construction workers					
1 Bricklayers, tile setters	3	4	9	—	9
2 Masons, stone cutters	3	4	9	—	9
3 Plasterers	3	4	9	—	9
4 Roofers, glaziers	3	4	9	—	9
5 Handymen, general building workers	3	4	9	—	9
6 Builders (so described)	3	4	9	—	9
141 Concreters, road surfacers, railway lengthmen					
1 Railway lengthmen	—	—	—	—	10
2 Road surfacers, concreters	—	4	—	—	9
3 Roadmen	3	4	—	—	9
4 Paviors, kerb layers	3	4	—	—	9
142 Sewage plant attendants, sewermen (maintenance), mains and service layers, pipe jointers (gas, water, drainage, oil), inspectors (water supply), turncocks					
1 Sewage plant attendants	—	—	—	—	9
2 Mains and service layers, pipe jointers	3	4	—	—	9
143 Civil engineering labourers, craftsmen's mates and other builders' labourers n.e.c.					
1 Craftsmen's mates	3	4	—	9	9
2 Building and civil engineering labourers	3	4	—	10	10
144 Foremen/deputies—coalmining					
0 Foremen/deputies—coalmining	—	—	—	9	—
145 Face-trained coalmining workers					
0 Face-trained coalmining workers	3	4	—	—	9
146 All other in construction, mining, quarrying, well drilling and related n.e.c.					
1 Miners (not coal), quarrymen, well drillers	3	4	9	9	9
2 Construction workers n.e.c.	3	4	9	—	9
147 Foremen—ships, lighters and other vessels					
0 Foremen—ships, lighters and other vessels	—	—	—	11	—
148 Deck, engine-room hands, bargemen, lightermen, boatmen					
0 Deck, engine-room hands, bargemen, lightermen, boatmen	3	4	—	—	9
149 Foremen—rail transport operating					
Foremen—					
1 Railway guards	—	—	—	11	—
2 Signalmen and crossing keepers, railway	—	—	—	11	—
3 Shunters, pointsmen	—	—	—	11	—
4 Other foremen rail transport	—	—	—	11	—
150 Rail transport operating staff					
1 Drivers, motormen, secondmen, railway engines	—	—	—	—	9
2 Railway guards	—	—	—	—	12
3 Signalmen and crossing keepers, railway	—	—	—	—	9
4 Shunters, pointsmen	—	—	—	—	9
151 Foremen—road transport operating, bus inspectors					
1 Bus inspectors	—	—	—	11	—
Foremen—					
2 Drivers of road goods vehicles	—	—	—	11	—
3 Other foremen road transport	—	—	—	11	—
152 Bus, coach, lorry drivers, etc.					
1 Bus and coach drivers	3	4	9	—	9
2 Drivers of road goods vehicles	3	4	9	—	9
3 Other motor drivers	3	4	9	—	9

Occupation	Self-employed with employees	Self-employed without employees	Managers	Foremen	Apprentices, etc., Employees n.e.c.
153 Bus conductors, drivers' mates					
1 Bus conductors	—	4	—	—	12
2 Drivers' mates	—	—	—	—	10
154 Foremen—civil engineering plant operating, materials handling equipment operating					
Foremen—					
1 Mechanical plant drivers, operators (earth moving and civil engineering)	—	—	—	9	—
2 Crane drivers, operators	—	—	—	9	—
3 Fork lift, mechanical truck drivers	—	—	—	9	—
4 Slingers	—	—	—	9	—
155 Mechanical plant, fork lift, mechanical truck drivers, crane drivers, operators					
1 Mechanical plant drivers, operators (earth moving and civil engineering)	3	4	9	—	9
2 Crane divers, operators	—	4	—	—	9
3 Fork lift, mechanical truck drivers	—	4	—	—	9
156 Foremen—materials moving and storing					
Foremen—					
1 Storekeepers, warehousemen	—	—	—	11	—
2 Stevedores, dockers	—	—	—	9	—
3 Goods porters	—	—	—	9	—
4 Refuse collectors, dustmen	—	—	—	10	—
157 Storekeepers, stevedores, warehouse, market and other goods porters					
1 Storekeepers, warehousemen	3	4	12	—	12
2 Stevedores, dockers	3	4	—	—	9
3 Goods porters	3	4	9	—	9
4 Refuse collectors, dustmen	—	—	—	—	10
158 All other in transport operating, materials moving and storing and related n.e.c.					
1 Slingers	—	—	—	—	9
2 Workers in transport operating, materials moving and storing and related n.e.c.	3	4	—	9	9
159 Foremen—miscellaneous					
Foremen—					
Labourers and unskilled workers n.e.c.—					
1 Textiles (not textile goods)	—	—	—	10	—
2 Chemicals and allied trades	—	—	—	10	—
3 Coke ovens and gas works	—	—	—	10	—
4 Glass and ceramics	—	—	—	10	—
5 Foundries in engineering and allied trades	—	—	—	10	—
6 Engineering and allied trades	—	—	—	10	—
7 Coal mines	—	—	—	10	—
8 Other	—	—	—	10	—
9 Boiler operators	—	—	—	9	—
160 General labourers					
Labourers and unskilled workers n.e.c.—					
1 Textiles (not textile goods)	—	—	—	—	10
2 Chemicals and allied trades	—	—	—	—	10
3 Coke ovens and gas works	—	—	—	—	10
4 Glass and ceramics	—	—	—	—	10
5 Foundries in engineering and allied trades	—	—	—	—	10
6 Engineering and allied trades	—	—	—	—	10
7 Coal mines	—	—	—	—	10
8 Other	3	4	—	—	10
161 All other in miscellaneous occupations n.e.c.					
1 Boiler operators	—	—	—	—	9
2 All other in miscellaneous occupations n.e.c.	3	4	—	9	9
1 Inadequately described occupations	14	14	14	14	14
2 Occupations not stated	—	—	—	—	14

CODING INDEX

Notes on coding

The three digit codes used in the alphabetical index are an operational series of numbers only and must be used in combination with employment status to achieve allocation to the occupation groups. Four employment statuses, self-employed, manager, foremen and others are necessary. The derivation of the occupation group from the index number and employment status is shown in Appendix G.

Description of the index

General. Occupation titles are arranged in this index under the word most nearly describing the operation performed,

> e.g. 'glass blower' is indexed under 'Blower'
>
> 'x-ray operator' is indexed under 'Operator'

For this purpose words such as 'assistant' and 'officer' are regarded as indexing words but the following terms are not:

Boy	Girl	Hand	Lad	Man
Operative	Woman	Workman	Worker	

> e.g. 'errand boy' is indexed under 'Errand' but
> 'clerical officer' is indexed under 'Officer'

The index is arranged in alphabetical order of complete words. Words joined by a hyphen are treated as single words. Words joined by 'and' are indexed immediately following the single words. Occupational titles ending in any of the terms listed above are regarded for indexing purposes as two words, e.g. 'bagman' is indexed as though it were 'bag man' and therefore appears before 'bagger' in the index.

Compound words, such as 'postmaster', the final word of which may be used as an occupation title, are indexed under the final word, e.g. Master; post, Keeper; book. Some very common terms have also been indexed in their natural order.

The feminine form of an occupation title is not indexed unless it is very common or its coding differs from that of the masculine equivalent thus 'abbot' is indexed but not 'abbess'.

Three letters appear in the index against code numbers, of these 'M' and 'F' relate to employment status coding, see page 5. The letter 'L' indicates that the person is a labourer and that any of the codes 339–346 can be applied to this occupation depending on the industry of the establishment in which it is carried out. The quoted code should be used when the industry cannot be determined.

> e.g. *Index entry*   Ash man L346
>
> *Occupation statement*   Ash man (cotton spinning mill)   code 339
>
> *Occupation statement*   Ash man (paint manufacturers)   code 340
>
> *Occupation statement*   Ash man ... ...code 346

Qualifying terms

(*a*) The word used for indexing purposes is very rarely sufficient in itself to enable the occupation title to be correctly coded.

Frequently a term is made specific by the addition of a qualifying term, e.g. 'turner' may be specified by 'brass' and then becomes codable. These qualifying terms are entered in the index after the index word and separated from it by a semi-colon. The qualified terms may be used to code not only the specific term shown but also that term further qualified (unless the further qualification is itself indexed). Thus the index entry 'Controller; depot' could be used to code 'freight depot controller'.

An occupational title may be qualified by a clause following the word used for indexing purposes as, for example, 'Clerk in Holy Orders'. These terms are indexed at the end of the list of specifically qualified terms. As these terms are usually very specific, special care is necessary in coding any such term not actually in the index.

(b) An occupational title may depend for its coding on the branch of industry in which the person is employed. The industrial qualifications (which relate to the activity actually engaged in and not that of the establishment as a whole) appear in the index in italics. The term so qualified is followed by a dash, or alternatively, a single qualification may appear in brackets. These entries may be used to code occupational titles where the industry is part of the title, or may be inferred from it, unless an index entry as described in (a) or (c) is relevant, e.g. the index entry 'Furnacemen—*metal trades*' can be used to code 'furnaceman'—industry 'steelworks', 'blast furnace furnaceman' or 'steel furnaceman'.

(c) In a small number of cases the qualification for coding purposes is more easily stated in terms of materials worked on or dealt in, or the machinery used, or process involved and this enables a number of specific terms to be summarised by stating the specific qualification in a more general form. This type of qualification appears immediately preceding the industrial qualifications e.g. 'Turner—metal' (which would apply to titles 'aluminium turner' or 'lead turner', or in a limited number of cases indented below an industrial qualification e.g. 'Machinist—*hosiery mfr.*—sewing'.

(d) Where a code number appears against an index word that code applies to all occupation titles which include the index word unless they are listed specifically, generally or industrially as exceptions. Thus, referring to 'Smith' on page 95 of the index, all 'Smiths', e.g. blacksmith, hammersmith, are coded 233 except for those different codes in the list starting with boilersmith.

(e) Occupation titles qualified by terms such as 'assistant', 'head', 'deputy', 'apprentice' are normally coded as though the qualification did not exist. If, however, the coding is altered by the qualification the complete title is indexed but these entries only apply in the industry shown. If no industry is given in the index this means either that the particular term is only used in one industry or that this title is to be so coded in all industries.

(f) The letters n.o.s. stand for 'not otherwise specified'. When used in the index they mean that the particular index entry relates to that precise occupational term without further qualification.

Industrial qualifications. It must be noted, that it is the activity in which the person is actually engaged and not that of the establishment as a whole which is the determining factor. Thus a person in the cardboard box making department of a food factory must be referred in the index to 'cardboard box manufacture' and not 'food products manufacture'. N.B. This does not apply to persons coded as labourers to codes 339–346 for which see page 1.

The abbreviation 'mfr.' is used to cover manufacture, manufacturing, making, building and repairing.

The following Industrial terms are used in a special sense:

Term	**SIC Activity Heading**
Manufacturing	2210–2247, 2410–4959
Metal trades	2210–2247, 3111–3740
Clothing mfr.	4531–4536, 4539
Ceramic mfr.	2410, 2481, 2489
Paper goods mfr.	4721–4728
Engineering	3204–3740
Food products mfr.	4115, 4121–4180, 4213, 4221–4239
Glass mfr.	2471–2479 and the grinding of lenses and prisms from 3731–3733
Flour confectionery mfr.	4196, 4197
Sugar confectionery mfr.	4214
Mine, not coal	1300, 2100, 2310–2396

Shipping means service afloat other than in barges, small boats, fishing vessels, launches and dredgers.

Fishing means service afloat in a vessel actually engaged in fishing, not a factory ship or tender.

Boat, barge means service afloat in a boat, barge, launch, dredger or hopper and excludes service in a fishing vessel.

Notes on coding occupations
A. General

Use of the index. Occupational titles, unless consisting of an indexing word only, are coded by first referring to the list of specific terms and then using the generalised or industrially qualified entries in the sense indicated in sub-paragraphs (*b*) and (*c*) on page 2.

Armed forces. The more usual terms for forces personnel have been included because it is necessary to make a distinction between officers and other ranks. Officers will be given the employment status of manager. There are two codes to separate UK armed forces (135) from those of foreign and Commonwealth countries (136).

Diplomatic personnel. Members of foreign or Commonwealth diplomatic staffs are coded 020.

Persons looking for work. Persons looking for work without stated occupation are coded 350.

Coal miners. The correct coding of many occupational titles in the coal mining industry is dependent on whether the person is a face-trained coal miner. If sufficient information is given the occupation is coded according to the index; if the occupation title is vague but there is a statement indicating working at the coal face the occupation is coded to 314. Where this cannot be determined code 345 is used.

Foreman

(*a*) The following terms with certain listed exceptions may be regarded as synonymous with 'Foreman':

Boss	Gaffer	Overlooker
Charge hand	Ganger	Overseer
Charge man	Headman	Supervisor

and also assistant foreman, assistant supervisor, etc.

(*b*) No index entries have been made for foreman over particular groups of workers, e.g. 'foreman of labourers', or for foremen whose title included a specific occupation, e.g. 'foreman carpenter', as these are coded to the group appropriate to the people supervised or the occupation stated, i.e. as labourer and carpenter respectively.

(*c*) If the entry to be coded is not for a foreman, supervisor, etc. over a particular occupation the index is first referred to under the particular term, e.g. supervisor, and if not found there, is referred to 'Foreman' in the index.

(*d*) Works foremen, general foremen and senior foremen in manufacturing although allocated to group 091 keep the employment status of foremen.

Conventional codings. Many terms frequently used for describing occupations cannot be coded without further information either as to materials worked with or the industry in which the occupation is followed. It is necessary, therefore, to assign arbitrary codes for these occupational statements on the basis of the most probable occupation. The most common cases and the codes assigned are listed separately. In any case not listed the most probable code is assigned so long as there is a reasonable chance of correct coding (a knowledge of local industries may be of assistance in this respect). Where no such chance of correct coding exists, as for example, with statements such as 'Foreman' or 'Manager', without industry information, or 'Workman', code 349 is used; but where no statement of occupation is given code 350 is used.

B. Treatment of terms referred from the index

(1) **Apprentice**
 Articled clerk
 Articled pupil
 Graduate apprentice
 Management trainee
 Student apprentice
 Learner
 Trainee
 Trainee craftsman
 Trainee technician

All persons in training for an occupation or profession are coded to the occupation or profession for which they are training.
Where it is not possible to determine the precise occupation for which they are in training the following conventions are applied:

unspecified apprentices or trainee craftsmen (so described) } generally coded 230 but in Industry 'metal trades' coded 278

student apprentices ... ... ⎫
graduate apprentices ... ... ⎬ coded 076
management trainees ... ... coded 111

Students in educational establishments are coded to Economic position 'Student' and excluded from the classification by occupation. An apprenticeship training school is not regarded as an educational establishment for this purpose.

Improver. The term 'improver' is sometimes used as a synonym for apprentice, e.g. 'fitter's improver', for 'apprentice fitter', and is coded accordingly.

(2) **Chairman.** Apart from the industry of glass blowing a chairman is regarded as a 'company chairman' and coded as a 'Company Director' (see note (5)).

(3) **Checker.** A large number of checkers are listed in the index. Checkers not included in the index are coded as follows: if they appear to be checking articles they are coded to the 'not elsewhere classified' group, or, if metal goods, to code 286. Thus a checker of textiles is coded 289 and a checker of rubber goods 291. Unspecified checkers are coded as above in manufacturing industries and to code 299 otherwise.

(4) **Clerk.** It is not practicable to list all the various chief clerks such as 'chief accounts clerk', 'chief claims clerk'. Except as shown in the index, clerks coded 115 retain this code when qualified by 'chief' but take Employment status code 'Foreman' unless employed in central and local government, in which case codes 021 or 022 respectively apply.

(5) **Director/Company Director.** Directors with specific titles, e.g. sales director, are coded as shown in the index. Unspecified directors, company directors and company chairmen are coded as follows:

(a) If another occupation is stated or professional qualifications are shown they are coded to the appropriate occupation or profession. If not then:

(b) (i) If a single company is shown they are coded as a 'manager' in the appropriate industry.

(ii) If no company or more than one company is shown they are coded to group 111.

(6) **Engineer.** The term engineer presents difficulty because it is commonly used in such a variety of circumstances. The index provides for the coding of various specific engineers but even with these terms doubt often exists as to whether the person is of professional status. If the specific title is prefixed by the terms professional, chartered, administrative, advisory, chief, commissioning, consultant, consulting, design, designing, development, research, senior, superintending, or if membership of a professional institution is stated, e.g. AMIEE, it is assumed that the person is a professional engineer. In cases of doubt the person is regarded as non-professional.

Persons returned simply as 'engineers' or 'mechanical engineers' without any indication of professional status (see preceding paragraph) are coded to group 241. There are, however, a few industries in which these terms are commonly used in a specific sense and these exceptions are listed in the index under 'Engineer; n.o.s.'. Similarly code 254 covers all electrical engineers with the exceptions listed in the index under 'Engineer; electrical; n.o.s.'.

(7) **Instructor/Lecturer/Teacher/Tutor.**

(a) In educational establishments—are coded 031, 032, 033 depending on whether the establishment is a university, further education establishment, or primary or secondary school. The term further education establishment encompasses colleges of education, technical colleges and colleges of technology.

(b) Elsewhere—are coded 033 unless considered vocational and industrial trainers, teaching occupational skills—who are coded 034.
Driving instructors giving tuition for driving private motor vehicles are coded 052.

(c) Teachers of physical training and teachers of recreational subjects, at evening institutes and other similar establishments, also private tutors, including private music teachers and dancing teachers are coded 053.

(8) **Jeweller.** An attempt is made to distinguish between jewellers engaged in manufacture or repair, proper to code 266, and those wholesaling or retailing only, proper to code 101. If the distinction cannot be made code 101 is used.

(9) **Journeyman.** The term 'journeyman' is ignored in coding occupations except that, where doubt exists as to whether an occupation is in manufacture or distribution, as, for example, 'Confectioner', the term journeyman may be taken as implying manufacture. If no other occupation is stated persons so returned are coded 349.

(10) **Leading hand.** If another occupation is stated code to that occupation e.g. 'Plater; chrome' is used to code 'leading hand, chrome plater'. Where no other occupation is stated refer to index entries 'Leading hand—'.

(11) **Manager.** The general principles involved in coding managers are given on page vii. Persons managing a professional activity, such as the manager of a firm of consulting engineers or of the research department of a firm, are coded to their appropriate professions.

All managers are coded in accordance with the industry appropriate to the branch of the establishment in which they are employed and not necessarily the industry of the establishment as a whole. Thus all 'office managers' are coded to occupation group 099, 'sales managers' to group 013 and 'transport managers' to group 095 irrespective of the main activity of the establishment.

The following terms may be regarded as synonymous with 'Manager':

Assistant Manager	Mill Manager
Under Manager	Works Manager
Departmental Manager	Factory Superintendent
Factory Manager	Works Superintendent
General Manager	Managing Director
Chairman	
Director	But see note (5)
Company Director	

(12) **Quality controller.** Persons described as quality controller who hold professional qualifications are coded 075, otherwise they are coded to the groups 289–294, 299 as appropriate or, if metal or electrical goods, to code 286.

(13) **Farmer's wife.** Persons described as 'Farmer's wife' are coded 166 and are allocated the employment status of employees n.e.c. (which includes family workers) irrespective of any statement of employment status.

Notes on coding employment status

(a) The status categories are listed on page vii. The division between the 'employed' and 'self-employed' and the recognition of apprentices depend on the information available. 'Self-employed' takes precedence over 'manager' and 'foreman'; 'apprentice' takes precedence over 'manager', (but see (13) above). With this exception the managerial and foremen codes are applied as follows:

(b) The managerial code is applied to

(i) All persons coded to occupation groups 006, 015, 016, 020–022, 092, 094–098, 105, 108.

(ii) All persons, not being self-employed, coded to occupation groups 007–009, 013, 014, 023, 025, 087, 099, 101–104, 106, 107, 109–111, 129, 131, 163, 164.

(iii) All persons, not being self-employed, whose occupation code is preceded by an 'M' in the occupation index.

(iv) All persons returned as directors of companies, except those coded to occupation groups 001, 002, 011, 028, 031, 035, 036, 040–042, 044, 046, 051, 065–078, 082.

(v) All persons coded 091 unless preceded by an 'F' in the occupation index.

(c) The foreman code is applied to

(i) All persons coded to occupation groups 112, 148, 277, 318, 323, 324.

(ii) All persons returned as foremen or with one of the synonyms listed on page 3 but excluding assistant foreman, assistant supervisor, etc.

(iii) All persons whose occupation code number is preceded by an 'F' in the occupation index.

(Ab—Ag)

Alphabetical index for classifying occupations

Please note that the codes appearing in this index are intended for coding purposes only. For the relationship between these codes and the occupation groups see Appendix G.

A

	Code number
A.B.-	
armed forces-	
foreign and Commonwealth	136
U.K.	135
shipping	317
A.C.A.	002
A.C.I.S.	023
A.C.W.A.	003
A.P.A. (*power station*)	255
A.P.(T) (*local government*)-	
grade 1, 2, 3	115
grade 4, 5	022
A.R.C.O.	060
A.S.A.A.	002
Abbot	040
Above ground worker-	
coal mine	345
mine, not coal	L346
Abstractor; technical	030
Abstractor (press cuttings)	115
Abstractor-translator	054
Accompanist	060
Accountant;	
barrack(s)	115
borough	002
certified	002
chartered	002
cost-	115
qualified	003
cost and management	003
district	002
financial (*N.C.B.*)	115
group	115
incorporated	002
management (qualified)	003
principal	002
stores	113
turf	164
works-	115
qualified	003
Accountant-	115
qualified-	002
cost and works accountancy	003
cost and management accountancy	003
government	002
Accountant and auditor	115
Accountant of Court (Scotland)	001
Accountant-secretary (*N.C.B.*)	002
Acetoner	348
Acid man-	184
dyestuffs mfr.	333
sugar refining	202
Acid worker-	184
ceramic mfr.	223
Acidifier	184
Acrobat	059
Actor	059
Actor-manager	M059
Actuary	011
Acupuncturist-	050
medically qualified	041
Addresser	115
Addressograper	119
Adjudicator (national insurance regulations)	027
Adjuster;	
average	005
brake	248
claims	005
compass	246
dial (*telephone mfr.*)	286
envelope	227
lift	276

	Code number
Adjuster; *continued*	
loss	005
machine-	
paper products mfr.	227
textile mfr.	248
relay	259
spring; set	248
unit-	
electricity board	249
L.T.E.	249
weight	276
Adjuster-	
gramophones	276
instruments	246
motor vehicles	249
record changers	276
scales	248
watches and clocks	247
weighing machines	248
Adjutant-	
armed forces-	
foreign and Commonwealth	M136
U.K.	M135
Adjutant-General-	
armed forces-	
foreign and Commonwealth	M136
U.K.	M135
Administrator; *see also Manager*	
hospital	111
trust (*banking*)	006
university	111
Admiral-	
armed forces-	
foreign and Commonwealth	M136
U.K.	M135
Admiral of the Fleet-	
armed forces-	
foreign and Commonwealth	M136
U.K.	M135
Advertisement hand	165
Adviser;	
advance (*banking*)	007
agricultural	065
art	055
beauty	165
bottling	078
business	010
careers	053
catering	104
cellar (*catering*)	333
commercial	013
county planning	082
development; sales	013
economic	011
education	035
employment (*Dept. of Emp. Job Centre*)	F112
fashion	057
financial	002
heating-	260
professional	076
home service (*gas board*)	134
horticultural	065
housecraft (*electricity board*)	134
housing	039
insurance	007
investment	007
legal	001
literary	054
management	028
marine	030
market	013
medical	041
packaging	078
pension	011

	Code number
Adviser; *continued*	
personnel	009
poultry	065
prevention; fire	138
production	074
promotion; sales	013
relations; industrial	009
safety	039
security	140
service-	134
garage	249
stewardship; Christian	040
systems	012
taxation	008
technical-	081
accountancy	002
textile	078
traffic	030
training	034
transport	030
welfare	039
Adviser-	
agriculture	065
education	035
law	001
marketing	013
railways	115
Advisor *see* Adviser	
Advocate	001
Aerialist	059
Aero-dynamicist	067
Aerograph worker	281
Aerographer-	281
ceramic mfr.	279
Agent;	
advertisement	014
advertising	014
agricultural	134
area (*civil engineering*)	092
assurance	134
au pair	099
bank	134
bloodstock	101
brewer's	134
brewery	134
builder's	092
business	134
buying	016
cargo (*airport*)	115
cattle	101
chemical	101
clerical	134
club	132
coaling	101
collecting	115
colliery	094
commercial	101
commission-	
farm produce	101
manufactured goods	133
raw materials	129
insurance	134
manufacturing	133
turf accountant's	164
wholesale, retail trade	101
company's; tug	134
concert	059
contractor's	092
corn	101
credit	132
dairy	101
depot; coal	101
depot (*railways*)	095
district (*insurance*)	134
draper's;	101
credit	132

(Ag—Ar)

	Code number
Agent; *continued*	
dry cleaner's	125
dyer's	125
east indian	129
election	024
emigration	134
employment	099
engineering; civil	092
engineer's	133
enquiry	140
esparto	129
estate	025
estate and insurance	025
excursion	099
export	129
farm	107
film	059
financial	007
forage	101
foreign	134
forwarding	134
fruit	101
general	134
goods	095
hiring; film	134
horticultural	101
house	025
house and estate	025
insurance	134
land	025
land and estate	025
laundry	125
law	001
literary	054
Lloyd's	134
manchester	134
manufacturer's	133
mercantile	134
metal	129
mine	094
miner's	024
money	007
mortgage	007
mutuality	115
naturalisation	134
news	101
newspaper	101
parcels-	097
railways	095
parliamentary	001
partnership	134
passenger	095
passenger and parcels	095
passport	134
patent	090
political	024
pools; football	115
posting; bill	134
potato	101
press	054
press cutting	F115
property	025
protection; trade	140
provision	101
publicity	014
publisher's	133
purchase; house	025
purchasing	016
railway	134
receiving; laundry	125
reference	140
repossession	142
river and canal	134
sales	133
seed	101
ship's (*shipping company*)	095
shipping (self-employed)	134
site	092
spirit	101
surface	094
tea	101
textile	101
theatrical	059
ticket	099

	Code number
Agent; *continued*	
tourist	099
trademark	030
trading; check	115
traffic-	095
canal	134
transfer; business	025
travel	099
trimming	101
underwriter's	134
variety	059
yeast	101
Agent-	
advertising	014
agricultural estate	025
assurance	134
football pools	115
insurance	134
manufacturer's	133
travel	099
building and contracting	092
mail order house	132
manufacturing	133
mining	094
wholesale, retail trade-	101
credit trade	132
door to door sales	132
party plan sales	132
Agent and collector (*insurance*)	134
Agent and valuer; land	025
Agent-collector	115
Ager-	
electrical lamps	182
	286
Ager man	182
Agricultural worker-	
self-employed	166
agricultural contracting	107
	169
Agriculturist	107
Agronomist	065
Agrostologist	065
Aid;	
family	039
laboratory	288
nurse's	156
Aide-de-Camp-	
armed forces-	
Commonwealth	M136
U.K.	M135
Airman; hot	231
Airman-	
armed forces-	
foreign and Commonwealth	136
U.K.	135
Aircraft hand (*airport*)	338
Aircraftman-	
armed forces-	
foreign and Commonwealth	136
U.K.	135
Aircraftwoman-	
armed forces-	
foreign and Commonwealth	136
U.K.	135
Aircraft worker	L344
Aircrew; master-	
armed forces-	
foreign and Commonwealth	136
U.K.	135
Airport hand	338
Airwayman (*mine, not coal*)	315
Aligner-	
radio and television	283
typewriters	248
Alley girl	299
Allocator;	
meat	115
traffic	322
Allocator (*metal trades*)	115
Allowance man (*brewery*)	146
Alloyman (*copper*)	231
All-rounder	175
Almoner	039
Alteration hand-	
footwear	210
	225

	Code number
Alterer;	
loom	199
pattern (*carpet mfr.*)	199
Alterer (*textile mfr.*)	199
Ambassador of commerce	133
Ambulance corps worker	155
Ambulance man	155
Ammunition worker	L340
Anaesthetist	041
Analyser	080
Analyst;	
chief	066
computer	012
cost	115
county	066
critical path	010
financial	007
investment	007
market	013
methods	010
network	010
objectives; management by	010
occupational	010
parts (*vehicle mfr.*)	115
procedure	010
public	066
purchase	115
research;	
market	013
operational	010
schedules (*transport*)	095
statistical	011
stress	079
study; work	010
system(s);	012
clerical	010
tool	079
value	010
Analyst-	080
market research	013
programming	012
work study	010
Analyst-programmer	012
Anatomist	065
Anchorer	270
Animator (cartoon films)	055
Annealer; pot	191
Annealer-	237
ceramics	191
chemicals	184
glass	191
Annealing man	237
Announcer-	
entertainment	059
transport	122
Anodiser	269
Anthropologist	036
Antiquary	036
Apiarist	172
Applicator; mastic	316
Applicator (work study)	010
Appraiser	030
Appraiser and valuer	005
Apprentice; see also notes pp.3–4	
commercial	115
Arbitragist	007
Arbitrator (*valuing*)	005
Arboriculturist	170
Archman-	
brick	300
glass	192
Archaeologist	036
Archbishop	040
Archdeacon	040
Archer; brick	300
Architect;	082
garden	168
landscape	082
naval	069
Archivist	030
Armourer;	248
cable	230
hose	230
Army worker; Church	040

7

(Ar—As)

	Code number
Arranger;	
floral	064
flower	064
music	060
Artex worker	282
Artexer	282
Artificer;	248
instrument	246
Artist;	
aerograph	281
boot and shoe	056
commercial	055
costume	055
display	055
fashion	055
film	059
floral	064
graphic	055
hairdressing	159
lay-out; studio	206
lettering	055
litho	115
lithographic	115
make-up (films)	165
medical (*hospital services*)	055
paste-up	206
photographic	061
pottery	279
press	055
scenic	055
shoe	056
technical	055
Artist-	055
ceramic decorating	279
entertainment	059
glass decorating	192
mask mfr.	282
Artist and designer; fashion	055
Artiste	059
Asbestos worker	L346
Ash and muck man	L346
Ash boy	338
Ash lad	338
Ash man	L346
Asphalter	307
Assayer	077
Assayist	077
Assembler;	
accumulator	283
action;	248
piano	222
aerial	283
aircraft	248
ammeter	284
apparatus (*electricity board*)	283
armature	283
bakelite	283
battery	283
bedstead	248
belt	283
bench (*engineering*)	248
bias	226
bi-focal	299
binocular	284
blind	230
body (vehicle)	285
box	299
brake	285
brass	285
brush	299
cabinet	299
cable	283
camera	284
carbon block	299
carbon brush	299
card (*printing*)	295
case (*gramophone mfr.*)	299
cell (*chemical mfr.*)	184
clock	285
clothing	299
coil	283
commutator	283
component-	
electrical	283

	Code number
Assembler; *continued*	
component- *continued*	
mechanical	285
computer	283
concrete	307
conveyor	248
cooker;	
gas	285
electric	283
core-	
electrical engineering	283
foundry	235
corset	212
cosmetics	299
cutlery	248
cycle	285
detonator	285
doll	299
dynamo	283
electric fire	283
engine	285
fencing	299
filament	283
film	227
filter (*machinery mfr.*)	285
final (*cabinet making*)	215
firework	299
flask; vacuum	299
footwear	299
frame;	
bed	285
spectacle	299
frame (*engineering*)	248
furniture	299
gramophone	283
grocer's	333
gun-	285
hand	248
harness; jacquard	199
hood; perambulator	299
instrument;	284
electrical	283
optical	284
telephone	283
jewellery	285
lamp;	285
electric	283
ligature; surgical	299
load	333
magnet	283
mattress	213
meter	284
motor-	
electric	252
gramophone	283
engineering	285
mould (monotype)	205
negative (films)	227
neon sign	274
optical	284
order	333
pad; stamp	299
pen	299
pianoforte	222
plastics	296
player	222
ply material	299
poppy	295
pottery	299
printed circuit	283
quartz crystal	283
radar	283
radio	283
record change	283
rectifier	283
refrigerator	285
relay	283
rifle	285
seat; spring	285
sheet (*plastics goods mfr.*)	296
spectacle frame	299
spring	285
stator	283
stove-	285

	Code number
Assembler; *continued*	
stove- *continued*	
electric	283
switchboard-	283
electrical power	252
switchgear	283
telephone	283
television	283
temple	248
toy	299
transformer	283
treble hook	276
trim	213
tub	285
tube (*plastics goods mfr.*)	296
umbrella	212
valve-	283
engineer's valves	285
vehicle; motor	285
venetian blind	230
warehouse	333
watch	285
woodwork	299
yarn	178
Assembler-	
accumulators	283
binoculars	284
calculating machines	283
cameras	284
cloth hats	212
clothing	299
coach trimming	213
concrete	307
corsets	212
cutlery	248
cycles	285
domestic apparatus	283
electrical goods	283
electronic equipment	283
footwear	299
furniture	299
gramophone	283
grocer's	333
guns	285
instruments	284
jewellery	285
metal goods	285
motor vehicles	285
optical instruments	284
paper goods	295
photo-lithographic plates	206
plastics goods	296
pottery	299
radio and television	283
refrigerators	285
rubber goods	299
silver goods	266
surgical ligatures	299
telephones	283
textile goods	299
toys	299
watches and clocks	285
wholesale and retail trades	333
yarn	178
Assembler-fitter	248
Assembly hand *see Assembler*	
Assembly man (textile piece goods)	298
Assembly worker *see Assembler*	
Assessor;	005
bonus	115
claims	005
insurance	005
study; work	010
technical	081
Assistant;	
accountancy	115
accountant's	115
accounts	115
actuarial	011
adjusters; average	115
administrative-	115
educational establishment	111
hospital service	099

(As)

	Code number
Assistant; *continued*	
administrative- *continued*	
local government-	022
town planning	088
petroleum	099
advertising	134
agent's;	
coal	125
commission	115
estate	134
patent	090
alteration	210
analyst's	288
anatomical	288
ancillary (*education*)	151
architect's	088
architectural	088
armouring	230
assay	077
assayer's	077
auctioneer's	335
audit	115
bakehouse	200
baker's	185
bakery	200
bank	115
banksman's (*coal mine*)	338
bar; snack	146
bar-	145
non-alcoholic	146
barker's	L346
barrow	130
beaterman's	204
beater's	204
binder's	189
bindery	189
bingo	165
blender's (*margarine*)	202
blower's; glass	223
boiler's, sugar	202
board; medical	115
bookbinder's	189
bookseller's	125
bookstall	125
borer's (*coal mine*)	314
bottling	287
brewer's-	078
non-alcoholic	202
bricklayer's	312
broker's	115
budget	115
building	089
bundler's (metal)	298
bureau	115
burner's	276
bursar's	115
butcher's	186
buttery	146
buyer's	115
C.S.S.D.	156
cafe(teria)	146
calender-	
paper mfr.	203
textile mfr.	182
calenderman's (*paper mfr.*)	203
cameraman's	061
canteen	146
canvassing (*insurance*)	134
care;	156
child	165
caretaker's	157
carpenter's	219
cartographic	079
cash and wrap	116
cashier's	115
caterer's	146
catering	146
centre;	
play	165
service	125
chairside	165
char house (*sugar*)	202
checker's (*metal trades*)	299
cheesemonger's	125

	Code number
Assistant; *continued*	
chemical	288
chemist's-	288
retail trade	125
chief-	
library	115
local government	022
churner's	202
circulation	115
civil	115
claims	115
class; nursery	151
clerical	115
clerk's;	115
justices	115
clinic;	156
animal	151
clinical	156
clothier's	125
collection	115
collector's; rate	115
collier('s)	314
commercial	115
computer	119
confectioner and tobacconist's	125
confectioner's-	125
flour confectionery	185
sugar confectionery mfr.	202
conference	115
consular	115
contracts	115
control;	
air traffic	122
load (aircraft)	115
passenger (*air transport*)	152
production	115
quality	115
sensitometric	227
control (*L.T.E.*)	095
controller (*banking*)	115
conveyancing	115
cookery	147
cook's	147
correspondence	115
cost	115
costing	115
counter-	125
bookmaker's, turf accountant's	115
catering	146
library	115
P.O.	115
take-away food shop	125
craft (*railways*)	276
crematorium	348
curator's	115
cutter's; paper	227
cutter's-	
clothing mfr.	211
paper mfr.	227
paper pattern mfr.	227
dairy (*retail trade*)	125
dairyman's-	
milk processing	202
retail trade	125
dealer's	125
dental	156
department; operating	156
depot; chart	333
depot-	
L.T.E.-	
rail	F318
road	F324
design	079
designer's (*textile mfr.*)	115
despatch	333
dip; hot	269
dipper's (*ceramic mfr.*)	299
director's; funeral	165
dispensary	050
dispenser's	050
dispensing	050

	Code number
Assistant; *continued*	
display-	
retail trade-	055
shelf filling	126
distribution (*water board*)	310
diver's; sea	316
divisional (*insurance*)	115
domestic	151
draper's	125
draughtsman's	114
drayman's	329
driver's;	
crane	337
dumper	338
engine	255
lorry	329
motor wagon	329
turbine	255
van	329
driver's (*road transport*)	329
dryerman's (*paper*)	188
dyer's (*textile mfr.*)	199
editorial	054
editor's; newspaper	115
electrician's	276
electronics	081
electroplating	270
embosser's	223
employment	115
engineering;	081
civil	089
engineer's-	081
maintenance	276
establishment	115
estates	115
estimating	115
estimator's	115
etcher's	223
ethical	115
executive-	111
insurance	099
L.T.E.	111
experimental;	090
senior	090
export	115
extrusion-	
plastics	229
rubber	228
factory	L346
farm;	166
mink	172
fashion (*printing*)	115
fashion artist and designer's	115
fatstock	115
film	062
financial	115
fingerprint	115
fireman's	138
first (millinery)	211
fishmonger's	187
fitter's	276
flanger's	L344
floor (*retail trade*)	125
florist's	125
foreman's	115
forge	270
frier's; fish	146
fruiterer's	125
funeral	165
furnace (*metal trades*)	231
furnisher's;	
funeral	165
house	125
furrier's	125
gallery; art	142
galvanizer's	L344
garage	249
gardener's-	168
market gardening	167
nursery	167
gas regulator's	L341
general-	115
catering	146
home for the disabled	156

(As)

	Code number			Code number			Code number
Assistant; *continued*			Assistant; *continued*			Assistant; *continued*	
general- *continued*			maker's; *continued*			plasterer's ...	312
hotel ...	151		crucible ...	223		plater's ...	276
old people's home ...	156		dress ...	226		plating (*electroplating*)	270
retail trade ...	125		rope ...	199		play leader's ...	165
school meals ...	146		shoe ...	175		playgroup ...	165
gilder's (electro-gilding)	270		taper ...	230		plumber's ...	276
glazer's ...	276		tool ...	L344		point; check ...	116
glazier's ...	312		management; housing	115		polisher's; glass	223
grade I, II (*electricity board*)	115		manager's ...	115		post-mortem ...	165
grinder's- ...	L344		market ...	130		postal (*P.O.*) ...	115
plate glass ...	223		marketing ...	115		post office-	115
grocer's- ...	125		mason's ...	312		sub-post office	125
mobile ...	128		master's; harbour	115		potter's ...	223
group officer's (*ordnance factory*)	115		matcher's; colour	199		poulterer's ...	125
			mathematical ...	067		poultry ...	166
haberdashery ...	125		matron's ...	151		prescription (*optician's*)	192
hairdresser's ...	159		meals; school ...	146		presentation (*printing*)	227
hammer ...	270		measurement; work ...	010		press; electric cable ...	230
hammerman's ...	270		mechanical ...	081		press (*printing*) ...	207
hardener's ...	L344		mechanic's ...	276		principal-	
hatchery ...	166		media ...	115		building society ...	099
heater's (*metal trades*)	231		medical (*hospital*)	156		local government ...	022
horticultural ...	167		melting pot (electric cable)	204		public utilities ...	094
hotel ...	115		mercantile ...	115		printer's ...	207
house;			mercer's ...	125		printing ...	207
boarding ...	151		merchant's coal	113		process (*printing*) ...	227
cook ...	147		merchant's ...	125		producer's (*entertainment*)	059
dye ...	199		metallurgical ...	090		production- ...	115
green- ...	167		meteorological ...	067		broadcasting ...	059
ceramic *mfr.*	299		meter ...	276		professional (*local government-surveyor's dept.*)	084
test (*steelworks*) ...	288		methods ...	010		programme (*broadcasting*)	059
household ...	151		mid-day (*school*) ...	151		progress ...	115
housing ...	115		mill; ...	L346		provision ...	125
hydropulper ...	203		offal (*tobacco mfr.*)	201		publicity ...	014
income ...	115		rolling ...	270		publisher's ...	333
information ...	115		miller's (food) ...	202		purchasing ...	115
inspector's-			milliner's ...	211		rate fixing ...	115
banking- ...	115		millwright's ...	276		rating ...	115
local government ...	115		minder's; machine (*printing*)	207		reader's ...	115
metal trades ...	299		minder's (*cotton mfr.*) ...	199		records ...	115
insurance ...	115		mixer's; colour ...	204		reelerman's (*paper mfr.*)	203
iron checker's ...	L344		moulder's (*abrasive mfr.*)	223		refectory ...	146
jeweller's ...	125		museum ...	030		refiner's ...	184
joiner's ...	219		N.A.A.F.I. ...	125		registrar's ...	115
jointer's ...	276		news (*broadcasting*) ...	115		relations;	
keeper('s);			newsagent's ...	125		customer ...	115
hall (*local government*)	157		non-teaching (*schools*)	151		employee ...	115
school ...	157		nursery- ...	150		public ...	115
store ...	333		agriculture ...	167		remover's; furniture ...	335
kiln ...	204		nursing ...	043		repairer's; wagon ...	276
kitchen ...	147		off-licence ...	125		repairer's (*coal mine*)	345
laboratory ...	288		office; ...	115		reprographic ...	119
ladler's (glass) ...	223		drawing ...	114		research; marketing ...	115
laminating (*paper mfr.*)	203		receiving ...	125		research- ...	080
land(s) ...	115		officer's; group ...	115		broadcasting ...	030
language ...	053		onsetter's ...	338		journalism ...	030
launderette ...	162		operating; railway ...	095		printing and publishing	030
laundry ...	162		operation; programme ...	059		university ...	031
legal ...	027		operator's; cinematograph ...	062		reservations ...	115
letterpress ...	207		optician's ...	230		reshearer's ...	276
library ...	115		organisation and methods	115		roller's ...	270
licensee's ...	145		outfitter's ...	125		room;	
lifter's ...	276		output (*L.T.E.*) ...	115		blowing ...	176
lighting; street ...	165		oven (*bakery*) ...	200		control-	
linesman's ...	276		painter's ...	299		L.T.E. ...	255
linotype ...	L346		passenger (*railways*) ...	095		fire service ...	115
lithographer's ...	299		pastry ...	185		cutting (*clothing mfr.*)	211
lithographic ...	206		pawnbroker's ...	125		dark ...	227
litigation ...	115		perfumer's ...	125		dining ...	146
loader's ...	L341		personal; manager's ...	029		engine ...	255
machine *see Machinist*			personal- ...	118		grey ...	333
machine man's (*paper mfr.*)	203		managerial ...	029		linen ...	333
machinery; outdoor (*British Rail*)	091		personnel ...	009		pattern (*textile mfr.*)	333
magisterial ...	115		pharmacy ...	125		print (*engineering*)	119
mains (*water company*)	L346		photographer's ...	061		publishing ...	115
maintenance- ...	276		photographic ...	061		receiving (*tailoring*)	338
machinery, plant ...	271		physiotherapy ...	047		retort (*food products mfr.*)	202
maker's;			pickler's (galvanized sheet) ...	270		sale-	
boiler ...	276		planning; town ...	088		auctioneer's ...	335
book ...	165		planning- ...	090		retail, wholesale trade ...	125
cheese ...	202		local government ...	088		sample ...	333
coach ...	276		plans (*land registry*) ...	115		show ...	125
			plant; pilot ...	276			

(As—At)

	Code number
Assistant; *continued*	
room; *continued*	
smoke	145
still	146
stock	333
test (electrical)	299
rotary (*printing*)	207
safety	039
salaries	115
sales *see* Assistant; shop-	
sample-	
textiles	115
choc. confectionery mfr.	202
sawyer's (*railways*)	219
schedule (*L.T.E.*)	115
school; nursery	151
scientific	080
sculptor's	055
secretarial	118
secretary's	115
seedsman's	125
senior-	F115
retail trade	F125
servery (*dairy*)	125
service;	
customer	115
passenger	152
shipping	115
shipwright's	276
shop;	
machine	L344
paint	299
spreading (cables)	276
work (*education establishments*)	165
shop-	125
take-away food shop	125
shotfirer's (*coal mine*)	314
showman's	059
silverer's	269
sinker's	315
slitter's (film)	190
smith's;	270
boiler	276
copper	276
gold	266
silver	266
sorting (*P.O.*)	123
sound	062
spinner's-	
textile mfr.	199
tobacco mfr.	201
spreader's; colour	L346
staff-	115
railways	009
stall;	130
book	125
stamper's (*drop forging*)	270
station-	
air transport	115
electricity board	255
stationer's-	125
printing warehouse	227
statistical	011
stenter	199
stenterer's	199
stereotyper's	206
stevedore	334
steward's	152
stock	333
stoker's	347
stores-	333
retail trade	125
stretcher	199
studio	062
study; work	115
sub-post office	125
sub-station	255
supervisory (school meals)	151
supplies	333
surgery; dental	156
surgery-	156
general medical service	117
hospital	156

	Code number
Assistant; *continued*	
survey; hydrographic	338
survey-	
government	316
local government	115
surveying	316
surveyor's;	316
quantity	083
tailor's	210
taster's; tea	298
taxation	115
teacher's	151
teaser	L342
technical-	090
quantity surveyor's	083
veterinarian's	053
civil engineering	089
temperer's	L344
tender's; machine; pasteboard	203
terminals (*transport*)	338
test	090
tester's; meter	299
theatre; operating	156
therapy; occupational	049
thrower's	223
timberman('s) (*coal mine*)	314
time study	115
timekeeper's	115
tool grinder's	L344
trade(s) (*shipbuilding*)	276
trader's;	
market	130
street	130
tradesman's (*metal trades*)	276
traffic; passenger (*air transport*)	152
traffic (*P.O.*)	121
traveller's	327
treasurer's	115
trimmer's (*upholstering*)	226
trust (*Public Trustees*)	006
undertaker's	165
upholsterer's	212
underwriter's	115
valuation	115
valveman's	348
veterinary surgeon's	053
victualler's; licensed	145
ward	156
wardrobe	165
warehouse;	333
printing	227
warehouseman's	333
wayleave	115
weaver's	199
weights and measures	115
welder's	265
welfare;	039
school	151
wind tunnel test	080
wireman's	276
work; social	039
workers; butter	L346
works (*railways*)	089
work study (*railways*)	115
x-ray	045
yard	L346
Assistant-	
catering	146
dressmaking	226
dry cleaners	162
investigation branch (*P.O.*)	140
library	115
retail trade see Assistant; shop-	
tailoring	210
Associate;	
research-	067
agricultural	065
biology	065
chemistry	066
economic	011
fuel	080
medical	080

	Code number
Associate; *continued*	
research- *continued*	
mining	068
photographic	080
plastics	080
scientific	067
textile	080
Assorter-	
galvanized sheet	286
tinplate	286
Astronomer	067
Athlete	063
Attache-	030
stockbroking	007
Attacher	299
Attendant;	
aerial (*mine, above ground*)	338
aerodrome	338
aid;	
filter	184
first	156
alternator	255
ambulance	155
amenity	165
amusement	165
animal	172
anode	269
aquarium	172
arcade	165
ash	338
auto(matic)	242
backwash	199
bar-	145
non-alcoholic	146
basin; outflow	202
bath(s);	165
copper (*glass mfr.*)	269
salt	237
battery-	276
mine, not coal	L346
bay;	
lubrication	249
sick	156
wash	348
beach	140
bed;	
bacteria	L346
filter (*water works*)	184
belt;	338
casting	223
bingo	165
block; amenity	165
board;	
control	255
spread	176
switch-	255
telephones	121
boat	317
boiler;	347
temper (margarine)	202
vacuum (margarine)	202
booster	255
bosh	338
box;	
dod	193
drawing	176
gill	176
bridge;	338
railway	321
sluice	338
swing	338
weigh	297
buffet	146
bunker-	338
coal mine	338
burner (coalite)	204
bus; school	152
cab	165
cabin;	
lamp (*coal mine*)	333
weigh	297
cage	331
calender-	
linoleum	204

11

(At)

Attendant; *continued*
  calender- *continued*
paper	188
rubber	194
textiles	182
camp	165
canteen	146
car;	
dining	144
mine	338
restaurant	144
sleeping	152
car-	
airport	161
steel mfr.	338
card (*textile mfr.*)	176
care	156
carriage (*railways*)	152
caster; monotype	205
cemetery	L346
centrifugal-	
chemical mfr.	184
food products mfr.	202
textile mfr.	199
chair	165
charge	156
children's	151
chlorination	184
cinema	165
class	151
cleaning	158
cleansing	158
clinic	156
club	165
coach	165
coal	338
cock; wash-off	202
composition (matches)	184
compression; air	255
compressor	255
condenser-	
blast furnace	348
power station	255
conditioner-	
paper mfr.	188
tobacco mfr.	201
converter; tow-to-top	176
conveyor	338
cooler	202
crane	337
creche	150
creel; sisal	188
creeper (*coal mine*)	338
crematorium	348
crossing-	
railway	321
road	142
crusher; coal	198
crusher	198
cupola	231
customs	333
cylinder	201
dental	156
depot (*coal mine*)	345
diffuser	202
dipper's	299
diver's	316
donor; blood	156
door	165
dormitory (*college*)	151
dryer-	
macadam	204
plasterboard	204
dynamo	255
earth; fuller's (*margarine*)	202
electric (*shipping*)	317
electrolytic	269
elevator;	333
wet char	L346
engine; winding	331
engine-	255
shipping	317
engineer's (*D.O.E.*)	L346

Attendant; *continued*
  equipment; automatic
(*food products mfr.*)	202
evaporator; steepwater	202
evaporator-	184
food products mfr.	202
exchange (*P.O.*)	121
exhaust(er)	348
expeller; oil (maize)	202
explosive(s) (*coal mine*)	333
fair; fun	165
fan	348
felt (*paper mfr.*)	203
field; playing	165
filter-	
starch mfr.	202
water works	184
filtration	184
forecourt (*garage*)	127
frame; twist	177
frame-	
mine, not coal	198
textile mfr.	176
furnace;	
blast	231
crematorium	348
furnace-	
chemical mfr.	184
glass mfr.	191
metal trades-	
annealing	237
games	165
garage	249
gas (*steelworks*)	255
gate;	140
flood	338
toll	115
gear, extractor (*gas works*)	184
gear (*coal mine*)	255
gearhead	338
generator	255
governor (*gas works*)	348
grainer (*paper mfr.*)	203
granary	333
green; bowling	165
grinder (cement)	204
ground;	168
fair	165
play	151
gun	L344
gymnasium	165
hall;	
billiard	165
bingo	165
dance	165
dining	146
town	157
hammer	270
health; animal	053
health (*local government*)	115
heat(s)	184
heating	347
hoist	331
holder; gas	271
hopper-	
coal mine	345
mine, not coal	L346
refuse destruction	L346
hospital	156
hostel	165
hotel	165
house;	
bath	165
benzol	184
blower	348
boiler	347
boiling	184
booster	255
compressor	255
engine	348
exhaust	348
filter-	204
mine, not coal	198
waterworks	184

Attendant; *continued*
  house; *continued*
meter (*gas works*)	115
powder	333
power	255
press	310
pump	348
retort	184
screen	L346
shift	165
slip	204
wash	162
humidifier	188
hydro (*laundry*)	162
hydrotherapy	165
incinerator (*hospital services*)	348
instrument-	
chemical mfr.	184
steelworks	231
invalid	156
inversion	202
jigger (*asbestos opening*)	176
journey (*coal mine*)	338
kennel	172
kiln-	
brick mfr.	191
cement mfr.	204
ceramic mfr.	191
glaze and colour mfr.	204
kiosk	125
kitchen	147
knife; machine	211
laboratory	L346
lamp-	165
coal mine	333
railways	L346
landing (*coal mine*)	338
landsale	338
larder	143
lathe;	241
rubber	228
launderette	162
laundry	162
lavatory	165
lehr	191
library	115
lid; carbonising	248
lift	161
light(ing)	165
light and bell	253
light and power	253
loader (*coal mine*)	338
loading; barge	334
lobby	165
locomotive	L344
lodge	140
loom	179
lorry	329
lubrication-	271
motor vehicles	249
luggage; left	165
machine *see* Machinist	
machinery;	255
lift	271
magazine;	333
plasterboard	204
mail; paddy (*coal mine*)	320
main; hydraulic	L341
male-	156
cinema	165
hospital service	156
marine	317
market	L346
mayor's	142
meals; school	146
medical	156
mess	146
meter; parking	141
midday (school meals)	151
mill;	
mortar	204
rod	248
saw	218
wash	184

(At)

Attendant; continued	Code number
mill; continued	
wood	203
mill-	
cement mfr.	204
metal goods mfr.	248
rolling mill	248
mixer; concrete	204
mixer-	
ceramic mfr.	204
food products mfr.	202
molasses	202
montejuice	202
mortuary	165
motor;	255
road	329
mouth; drift (*coal mine*)	331
multiplex (margarine)	202
museum	142
neutraliser	202
night-	
home for the disabled	156
hospital service	156
old people's home	156
nursery	150
nursing	156
office;	115
call	121
outfall works	L346
oven;	
coke	184
core	270
drying; cylinder	184
gas	184
oven-	
bakery	200
ceramic mfr.	191
chemical mfr.	184
coke ovens	184
food products mfr.	202
overall	165
paddy (*coal mine*)	338
pan (*food products mfr.*)	202
panzer (*coal mine*)	314
paraffin	184
park;	140
amusement	165
car	161
petrol	127
picker; waste	176
pier-	338
entertainment	165
pig	166
plan	333
plant;	
acid	184
ammonia	184
ash	348
auxiliary	255
benzol (*gas works*)	184
boiler	347
breeze	204
chlorination	184
cleaning; air	348
coal	198
coke	338
conditioning; air	348
cooling; dry	184
crushing; ore	198
drainage (*mining*)	348
electric	255
extraction; benzole	184
fume (*lead mfr.*)	276
gas	184
grading; coke	204
lime	198
purifying; water	184
recovery; benzole	184
refrigerating	348
retort	184
sewage	310
shot blast	242
softening; water	184
sulphate	184

Attendant; continued	Code number
plant; continued	
tar	184
tar and liquor	184
treatment; water	184
washing; vehicles	348
water	184
welding	265
plant-	255
chemical mfr.	184
gas works	184
quarry	198
plodder (margarine)	202
point;	322
transfer; conveyor	338
polisher's; glass	192
pool; swimming	165
potter's	223
poultry	166
press-	
ceramic mfr.	193
chemical mfr.	184
sugar refining	202
producer; gas	184
property; lost	165
pump;	
air-	255
sugar refining	202
petrol	127
pump-	348
garage	127
sewage works	310
pumping	348
punch	242
purifier	184
pyrometer (*metal mfr.*)	231
quencher; coke	L341
refrigerator	348
reservoir	316
retort (*coal gas, coke ovens*)	184
ring (*entertainment*)	165
river	316
roll;	
cold	270
milling (asbestos)	204
roller; edge	192
room;	
ambulance	155
ball	165
bath	165
battery	348
blowing	176
boiler	347
changing	165
cloak	165
cold (*brewery*)	197
compressor	255
cooling (*baths*)	165
dining	146
dressing	165
engine-	348
shipping	317
first aid	156
grey	333
ice	202
ladies'	165
lamp	333
linen	333
locker	165
luggage	165
medical	156
mess	146
plan	333
power	255
print	207
pump	348
refreshment	146
rest	165
sample (*food products mfr.*)	290
show	125
sick	156
still	146
stock	333
tool	333

Attendant; continued	Code number
room; continued	
waiting	165
ward	144
wash	165
rope (*coal mine*)	338
rotary (asbestos)	176
safety (*chemical works*)	039
saloon	145
sanitary	158
scale;	297
green	L340
smith's	270
school	165
scraper (*coal mine*)	314
screen-	
ceramic mfr.	204
coal mine	198
gas works	204
mine, not coal	198
scrubber (*coke ovens*)	348
scutcher	176
seat	165
sewage	310
sewerage	310
shed; cycle	165
shed (*transport*)	L346
shunter	322
sieve; rotary	201
silo	333
sluice	338
softener; water	184
softening and filtering	184
sprinkler	310
stall;	
coffee	146
market	130
stall (*amusements*)	165
stand (*L.T.E.*)	L346
station;	
ambulance	155
filling	127
petrol	127
power	255
pumping	348
service	127
sub (*electricity board*)	255
station (*gas works*)	348
statutory	329
sterilizer-	
distillery	197
medical services	156
still	184
storage; liquor	184
store;	333
liquor	197
stores-	333
retail trade	125
stove;	204
core	270
starch	202
studio	165
sub-station	255
surgery	156
switch (*coal mine*)	322
synagogue	157
syphon	348
tank-	
cable mfr.	230
local government	L346
sugar refining	202
tar and liquor	184
teaser	176
telephone	121
theatre-	165
hospital	156
thickener;	203
dorr	184
thrower's	223
tip	L346
tipper (*coal mine*)-	314
above ground	338
tippler (*coal mine*)	338
toilet	165

13

(At—Ba)

Occupation	Code number
Attendant; *continued*	
traffic (*coal mine*)	321
train-	152
coal mine	320
transfer (*coal mine*)	314
transformer	255
travel	152
treatment; water	184
tumbler	162
turbine	255
turnstile	115
unit; cracker	198
valve	348
van	329
vat (*textile dyeing*)	182
ventilation	348
wagon	338
ward	156
washer;	184
beet	202
washer's	202
washery (*coal mine*)	198
water	348
welfare	039
wharf; oil	334
winch	331
Attendant-	
agricultural machinery	169
public conveniences	165
road goods vehicles	329
ambulance service	155
art gallery	142
baths	165
catering	146
domestic service	151
entertainment	165
gas works	184
government	124
home for the disabled	156
hospital service	156
local government	165
museum	142
old people's home	156
racing stables	172
sewage farm	310
water works	310
Attender (*tinplate mfr.*)	270
Attorney	001
Au pair	151
Auctioneer	134
Audiologist	050
Audiometrician	050
Auditor;	
chief (*N.C.B.*)	002
internal	115
Auditor-	115
qualified	002
government	002
insurance	115
local government	002
Auditor of Court (Scotland)	001
Aurist-	041
not registered	050
Author-	054
technical	054
Autoclave worker (*aluminium refining*)	184
Autolysis man	202
Auto-setter (*metal trades*)	238
Auto-weigher	297
Auxiliary;	
dental	050
nursing;	043
animal	053
Aviator	085
Axeman	170
Axle worker (*perambulator mfr.*)	233

B

Occupation	Code number
B.Ch.	041
Babbitter	270
Back end man (*textile mfr.*)	182
Back girl	226
Back hand (*leather cloth mfr.*)	199
Back man (*textile mfr.*)	182
Back room man (*distillery*)	197
Back-bye man	315
Back-edger (corset)	212
Back-end man (*cement mfr.*)	204
Backer;	
mirror	269
professional	165
saw	276
spindle (*rolling mill*)	270
stencil paper	203
Backer-	
bookbinding	189
clothing mfr.	212
fustian mfr.	182
linoleum mfr.	204
paper mfr.	203
rolling mill	270
Backer-up-	
printing	206
sawmilling	219
steelworks	270
Backwasher	199
Bacon hand	125
Bacteriologist	065
Badge worker	212
Badger	192
Bag hand-	226
paper products mfr.	227
Bagman (*cement mfr.*)	287
Bag woman	226
Baggage man	235
Bagger;	
cake	287
coal	287
fibre (*asbestos mfr.*)	287
Bagger-	287
clothing mfr.	212
footwear mfr.	175
textile finishing	212
Bagger-off (*starch mfr.*)	287
Bagger-out	212
Bagger-up	287
Bagging-off man	287
Bailer see Baler	
Bailiff;	
broker's	142
estate	107
farm	107
land	107
landlord's	142
rent	142
reservoir	316
river	019
water	019
Bailiff-	
certificated	142
county, high courts	142
level, sewer commissioners	F316
local government	142
property owning	142
Baister-see Baster	
Baker; hand oven	200
Baker-	
bakery	185
flour confectionery mfr.	185
food products mfr.	202
retail trade-	101
employee	185
shipping	185
textile mfr.	182
Baker and confectioner-	
bakery	185
retail trade-	101
employee	185
Bakery hand	200
Bakery worker	200

Occupation	Code number
Baking powder operative	202
Balancer;	
armature	252
crank	286
crank shaft	286
dynamic(s)	286
flyer	248
sound	062
wheel-	
abrasive mfr.	230
railway workshops	286
Balancer-	
abrasive mfr.	230
engineering	286
Balcony man	192
Baler;	
hay	169
paper	287
salle	287
scrap	276
Baler-	287
oil wells	348
Ballast man	334
Baller;	
cross	178
wool	178
Baller-	
twine	178
yarn	178
ceramic mfr.	204
iron works	231
wool combing	176
Ballistician	067
Band master	060
Bander;	
armature	283
cigar	287
clay	299
coil	287
glass	299
wash	279
Bander-	
boot polish mfr.	287
cardboard box mfr.	227
ceramic mfr.	279
iron and steelworks	287
rubber tyre mfr.	228
textile mfr.-	271
textile bleaching, dyeing	182
Bandyman (*provender milling*)	202
Bank hand-	
coal mine	331
rope mfr.	199
Bankman; rail	338
Bankman (*rolling mill*)	L344
Banker-	
stone working	301
finance-	099
self-employed	007
merchant banking	006
mine, not coal	331
totalisator	115
yarn warping	177
Banker hand	301
Banksman;	
crane	337
staple pit	331
Banksman-	
blast furnace	L344
canal contractors	316
civil engineers	337
coal mine	331
manufacturing	337
mine, not coal	331
opencast coal mining	297
salt works	331
Barber	159
Bargain man-	
coal mine	314
mine, not coal-	
above ground	L346
below ground	315
Barge boy	317
Barge hand	317

(Ba—Bl)

Occupation	Code number
Bargeman	317
Bargee	317
Bark worker	218
Barker (*rope mfr.*)	182
Barmaid	145
Barman;	
coffee	146
head	F145
tea	146
Barman—	
catering, hotels, public houses, etc.	145
railway shed	248
Barrelman (*rice starch*)	202
Barreller	243
Barrer (*footwear mfr.*)	175
Barrister	001
Barrow boy—	338
retail trade	130
Barrow man—	338
retail trade	130
Basket man (*retail trade*)	L346
Basket worker	230
Bassoonist	060
Baster	210
Baster-in	210
Baster-on	210
Baster-out	210
Baster-under	210
Batman (*civilian*)	151
Batcher; concrete	204
Batcher (*textile finishing*)	176
Batchman (*glass mfr.*)	204
Bater	173
Bathman—	
bacon curing	202
baths	165
Batter; felt	199
Batter (*pottery mfr.*)	223
Batterman	223
Batterer	242
Batter-out	223
Battery man—	
coke ovens	338
food products mfr.	202
iron and steelworks	276
mine, not coal	L346
Battery worker	L346
Bayman; service	249
Bayman (*steelworks*)	L344
Beader—	
coach building	268
embroidering	212
footwear mfr.	225
tin box mfr.	242
Beadle	157
Beamer;	
brush (yarn)	179
chain	179
dry (canvas)	179
lace	179
scotch	179
warp	179
Beamer—	
shipbuilding	262
textile mfr.	179
textile finishing	199
wire weaving	276
Bearer; mace	165
Bearer (*funeral direction*)	165
Beater;	
carpet	162
feather	199
fire	347
gold	266
leaf	270
panel	261
seat (*footwear mfr.*)	225
silver	266
welt (*footwear mfr.*)	225
Beater—	
feather dressing	199
metal trades	261
paper mill	188

Occupation	Code number
Beater- *continued*	
textile finishing	182
Beaterman; spare	188
Beaterman—	
asbestos-cement mfr.	204
celluloid mfr.	184
paper mfr.	188
Beater-up	201
Beatster	183
Beautician;	165
canine	172
Bedman—	
asphalt mfr.	204
blast furnace	231
Bed worker; blue	184
Bedder—	
ceramic mfr.	204
college	151
Beekeeper	172
Beetler	182
Beetster	183
Behinder	270
Bell boy (*shipping*)	152
Bell man—	
blast furnace	231
mining	253
Bellows man (*shipbuilding*)	L344
Bellyman; piano	224
Belt hand	338
Belt lad	338
Belt worker;	338
conveyor	338
Beltman; machine	225
Beltman—	
coal mine—	338
above ground	198
engineering	225
patent fuel mfr.	L346
Belter (forks and spades)	243
Bench boy	338
Bench hand; saw	276
Bench hand—	
cabinet making	215
cardboard box mfr.	295
chemical mfr.	184
coach trimming	213
footwear mfr.—	225
bespoke	175
joinery mfr.	214
leather goods mfr.	225
metal trades—	276
brass foundry	270
electrical engineering	252
instrument mfr.	246
plastics goods mfr.	229
printing—	L346
newspaper printing	287
rubber flooring mfr.	228
stationers	287
sugar confectionery mfr.	202
Bench man; laboratory	288
Bench man—	
cabinet making	215
chemical mfr.	184
coke ovens	L341
footwear mfr.—	225
bespoke	175
joinery mfr.	214
rolling mill	L344
Bench worker—	
cabinet making	215
engineering	276
footwear mfr.	225
glass mfr.	192
instrument mfr.	246
laminated plastics mfr.	229
leather goods mfr.	225
newspaper printing	287
Bender;	
arch	270
bar;	276
handle	270
copper (generators)	274
element	283

Occupation	Code number
Bender; *continued*	
fish hook	276
frame (shipyard)	276
glass	192
iron	233
knife	276
pipe	276
plate	262
spoke (*cycle mfr.*)	270
spring (*spring mfr.*)	233
steel	263
timber	224
tube—	276
glass	192
wire	276
Bender—	
cardboard box mfr.	227
glass mfr.	192
rolling mill	270
stick making	224
wood products mfr.	224
Bender and fixer; bar	263
Bender and slotter (cardboard)	227
Berthing man	338
Beveller; card	227
Beveller—	
footwear mfr.	175
glass mfr.	192
printing	227
Bhandary	143
Bibliographer	054
Billet man	L344
Billeter (*rolling mill*)	270
Bin man; tempering	202
Binman—	
local government—	L346
cleansing dept.	336
Binder;	
armature	283
blanket	212
book	189
carpet	212
chair	226
cord (telephone)	230
cylinder (*slipper mfr.*)	225
iron	L344
leather;	189
hat	212
mat(ting)	212
printer's	189
publisher's	189
slipper	225
stationer's	189
straw	169
umbrella	226
vellum	189
Binder—	
blanket mfr.	212
bookbinding	189
brush mfr.	230
canvas goods mfr.	212
cardboard box mfr.	227
fabric glove mfr.	212
footwear mfr.—	225
rubber footwear	299
hat mfr.	212
hosiery mfr.	212
printing	189
Bindery worker	189
Biochemist	065
Biographer	054
Biologist	065
Biometrician	011
Biophysicist	067
Bishop	040
Bitter (*cardboard box mfr.*)	227
Bitumen worker	184
Blacker—	299
ceramic mfr.	223
Blacker-in (enamelled slate)	299
Blacksmith	233
Blacksmith-engineer	233
Blader (turbines)	248
Blancher (fruit, vegetables)	202

15

(Bl—Bo)

	Code number
Blaster;	
hot	175
sand-	275
briar pipe mfr.	224
ceramic mfr.	223
shot	275
vapour	275
Blaster-	
furnace	231
mine, not coal	315
Bleach hand (textile mfr.)	182
Bleach worker (textile mfr.)	182
Bleacher; yarn	182
Bleacher-	
feather	182
flour	202
oil	184
paper	188
textiles	182
wood pulp	188
Bleacher and dyer	182
Blender;	
batch	184
butter	202
coal-	
coke ovens	184
steel mfr.	204
cocoa	202
coffee	202
colour-	
chemical mfr.	184
textile spinning	176
flour	202
grease (mineral oil)	184
in-line	184
liquor	204
oil	184
pigment (chemicals)	184
rag	176
shade (wool)	176
spice	202
tea	202
varnish	184
whisky	197
Blender-	184
margarine	202
spirits	197
wines	197
wool	F176
arc welding electrode mfr.	184
asbestos composition goods mfr.	176
candle mfr.	204
cast stone products mfr.	204
chemical mfr.	184
explosives mfr.	184
food products mfr.	202
fur fibre mfr.	199
linoleum mfr.	204
man-made fibre mfr.	204
mineral oil refining	184
mineral water mfr.	202
oilskin mfr.	199
petroleum storage and distribution	184
plastics goods mfr.	204
tobacco mfr.	201
wool blending	F176
Blockman-	
butchers	186
fishmongers	187
metal trades	L344
mine, not coal	301
Block worker; concrete	230
Blocker;	
fur	211
gold	227
hat	226
lens	223
pan (hat mfr.)	226
prism	223
sole	225
Blocker-	
bookbinding	189

	Code number
Blocker- continued	
brick mfr.	223
footwear mfr.	225
hat mfr.	226
laundry	162
leather goods mfr.	225
lens mfr.	223
lifting tackle mfr.	248
textile mfr.	199
wood heel mfr.	218
Blouse hand	210
Blower;	
bottle	192
bulb (lamp, valve)	192
core	235
dry	182
fur	199
glass	192
glaze	279
sand	275
shot	275
soot (power station)	255
steam	195
thermometer	192
tube (glass mfr.)	192
Blower-	
ceramic mfr.	279
chemical mfr.	255
cotton mfr.	182
glass mfr.	192
plastics goods mfr.	195
slag wool mfr.	204
steelworks	231
textile finishing	182
Blower-up (textile mfr.)	176
Blowing room hand	176
Blowing room operative	176
Blowlamp worker (shipbuilding)	262
Blowpipe worker (quartz glass)	192
Blowroom operative	176
Blue coat (holiday camp)	165
Blue-button	115
Bluer; china	279
Bluer-	
metal goods	237
laundry	162
textile mfr.	182
Board boy (bookmakers)	124
Boardman-	
bakery	185
bookmakers	165
Boarder (hosiery mfr.)	182
Boat boy	317
Boat hand	317
Boatman;	317
foy	317
Boatswain-	F317
fishing	F171
Boatswain's boy	317
Boatwright	262
Bobber;	
emery	243
fish	334
Bobber-	
metal goods	243
wood products	224
arc welding electrode mfr.	243
embroidery mfr.	L346
fish dock	334
Bobber and polisher; spur	243
Bobbin and carriage hand	248
Bobbin boy	338
Bobbin worker; bottle	178
Bobbiner	178
Bodier (ceramic mfr.)	279
Bodyer (organ, piano mfr.)	282
Bodyguard	140
Boiler;	
acid	204
biscuit	200
fat	204
fruit	202
glue	184
grease	184

	Code number
Boiler; continued	
gum-	
sugar confectionery mfr.	202
textile dyeing	182
jelly	202
liquorice	202
oil-	184
oilskin mfr.	199
pan (sugar refinery)	202
rag	203
salt	184
sauce	202
size	184
sizing	184
soap	184
starch	184
steam	347
sugar	202
tar-	
building and contracting	316
gas works	184
woodpulp	203
Boiler-	
chemicals	184
flax	182
food products	202
sugar confectionery	202
paper mfr.	203
textile finishing	182
Boilerman-	347
food products mfr.	202
gelatine, glue, size mfr.	184
paper mfr.	203
textile waste merchants	199
Boiling hand; soap	184
Boiling man; tar (cable mfr.)	204
Boiling-off man	182
Bolter; roof (coal mine)	314
Bolter-	
metal trades	262
textile dyeing	287
Bolter-down (metal trades)	270
Bolter-up (metal trades)	285
Bombadier-	
armed forces-	
foreign and Commonwealth	136
U.K.	135
Bonder; garment; rainproof	226
Bonder (electrical)	283
Bonderiser	269
Boner-	
corsets	299
fish	187
meat	186
Book hand (printing)	205
Bookbinder	189
Booker	115
Bookman (timber yard)	115
Bookstall boy	125
Booster; gas (steelworks)	255
Boot and shoe operative	175
Boot and shoe worker	175
Boots (hotel)	165
Borer;	
artesian	315
brush	230
cylinder	241
fine; barrel	241
gas emission (coal mine)	314
hole (shipbuilding)	262
horizontal	241
iron	241
ironstone	315
jig	241
methane (coal mine)	314
scissors	241
shot	315
spill (barrel, small arms)	241
tong (tubes)	241
tool room	240
tunnel	304
tyre	241
universal	241
vertical	241

(Bo—Br)

	Code number
Borer; *continued*	
well	315
wheel	241
wide (tobacco pipes) ...	224
wood	218
Borer-	
brush mfr.	230
coal mine-	
above ground ...	314
above ground ...	316
fancy comb, slide mfr. ...	230
metal trades	241
mine, not coal	315
shipbuilding	262
wood wind instruments mfr.	218
Borer and cutter; cross ...	218
Borer hand; brush	230
Boss; *see also* Foreman	
mine	094
shift	F315
Bo'sun-	F317
fishing	F171
Botanist	065
Botcher	216
Bottle hand	192
Bottler	287
Bottom hand (*coal mine*) ...	331
Bottom man (*coke ovens*) ...	338
Bottomer-	
cardboard box mfr. ...	227
metal goods mfr. ...	242
surgical footwear mfr. ...	175
Bouker	182
Boule de table	165
Bowker	182
Bowler; tyre	L344
Bowler-	
entertainment	063
steelworks	L344
Bowyer	224
Box hand-	
printing	205
sugar refining	338
Box worker;	
cardboard	227
metal	242
Boxman (*steel mfr.*)	231
Boxer-	287
carpet mfr.	227
entertainment	063
Boxer-in	247
Boxer-off	287
Boxer-up (*ceramic mfr.*) ...	287
Boy (*shipping*)	317
Braider;	
asbestos	199
net	199
twine (*fishing net mfr.*) ...	199
whip	230
wire	230
Braider-	
basket mfr.	230
cable mfr.	230
clothing mfr.	212
cordage mfr.	199
fishing net mfr.	199
flexible tubing mfr. ...	230
rubber hose mfr. ...	228
telephone mfr.	230
textile smallwares mfr. ...	199
vehicle building ...	226
Brake hand (*printing*) ...	207
Brakeman *see* Brakesman	
Braker; wagon	338
Braker-	
mine, not coal	338
Brakesman;	
assistant (*biscuit mfr.*) ...	200
engine	338
Brakesman-	
biscuit mfr.	200
blast furnace	338
coal mine	338
mine, not coal	338
printing	207

	Code number
Brakesman-*continued*	
transport-	
... ...	326
railways	320
Brakeman and steersman ...	326
Brancher (*coal mine*)	314
Brander	227
Brass worker	276
Brazer	265
Brazier	265
Breaker;	
bear	270
billet	276
boiler	276
cake	202
can	176
car	276
coal	198
cotton	176
egg	202
engine	276
horse	172
house	316
iron	L343
limestone (*blast furnace*)	L344
ore (*blast furnace*) ...	204
rail	276
rock-	198
construction	313
scrap	276
ship	276
skull	270
slag	204
stone-	204
mine, not coal ...	198
wagon	338
waste	176
woodpulp	203
Breaker-	
blast or puddling furnace	L344
mine, not coal	198
paper mfr.	203
rolling mill	270
scrap merchant	276
textile finishing ...	199
textile spinning	176
Breaker and filler	198
Breakerman; rag	203
Breakerman-	
foundry	L343
paper mfr.	203
Breaker-down (*rolling mill*) ...	270
Braker-off-	
foundry	244
glass mfr.	223
type foundry	276
Breaker-up-	L344
textile mfr.	176
Breaking off boy (*type foundry*)	276
Breaksman *see* Brakesman	
Breaster; heel-	175
wood	218
Breaster (*clothing mfr.*) ...	212
Breeches hand	210
Breeder; plant (*research estab.*)	065
Breeder-	
dog	111
fish	171
horse	111
maggot	172
mealworm	172
stock	107
fishing net mfr. ...	199
Breeze man	338
Brewer;	
assistant	078
ginger beer	202
head	078
herb beer	202
technical	078
under	078
vinegar	078
working	078
Brewer-	
brewery	078

	Code number
Brewer- *continued*	
distillery	078
mineral water mfr. ...	202
vinegar mfr.	078
Brewery worker	197
Brick hand	223
Brick worker	223
Brickel lad	L342
Bricker;	
ladles (*iron works*) ...	300
mould	300
Bricklayer	300
Bricky	300
Brickyard boy	L342
Bridge boy	317
Bridgeman;	338
sluice	338
weigh	297
Bridgemaster	338
Brigademan; rescue (*coal mine*)	142
Brigadier-	
armed forces-	
foreign and Commonwealth	M136
U.K.	M135
Bright worker (*fish hook mfr.*)	287
Brightener;	243
oil	184
Brineman	202
Brineller	286
Briner	202
Broacher	241
Broadcaster	059
Broilerman	166
Broker;	
air	129
bill	007
bullion	129
commodity	129
diamond	129
discount	007
exchange	007
financial	007
foreign exchange	007
insurance	007
investment	007
jewel	129
licensed	007
marine	129
mortgage	007
pawn	101
printer's	134
produce	129
scrap	131
share	007
ship	129
stock	007
stock and share	007
tea	129
yacht	129
Broker-	
finance	007
insurance	007
transport	129
wholesale, retail trade ...	129
Bronze worker;	
architectural	276
ornamental	276
Bronzer;	
lithographer's	227
metal	269
printer's	227
Bronzer-	269
printing	227
Brother	040
Brow hand (*mining*)	338
Browner	269
Bruiser-	
enamel sign mfr. ...	261
leather dressing ...	173
Brush hand; paint	230
Brush hand-	282
brush mfr.	230
coach painting	299
Brush worker	230

17

(Br—Bu)

Brusher;
- cloth (*textile finishing*) ... 182
- dry ... 223
- enamel ... 299
- flannelette ... 182
- flour ... 202
- glaze ... 279
- glove ... 173
- paint ... 299
- pigment ... 188
- roller ... 182
- sanitary ... 279
- scratch ... 243
- tube (*railways*) ... 276
- ware (*ceramic mfr.*) ... 223
- wire ... 243

Brusher-
- carpet mfr. ... 182
- ceramic mfr. ... 223
- clothing mfr. ... L346
- coal mine ... 314
- dyeing and cleaning ... 162
- file mfr. ... L344
- footwear mfr. ... 175
- foundry ... 244
- hosiery mfr. ... 182
- leather finishing ... 173
- needle mfr. ... 276
- paper mfr. ... 188
- scissors mfr. ... 243
- textile mfr. ... 182
- wallpaper mfr. ... 188
- wool spinning ... 182

Brusher-in; scratch ... 243

Brusher-off-
- clothing mfr. ... L346
- metal trades ... 299

Brusher-up- ... 223
- footwear mfr. ... 175

Buckler ... 299

Budder; rose ... 167

Buddler ... 198

Buffer;
- band ... 228
- blacksmith's ... 243
- blade ... 243
- bottom ... 175
- brass ... 243
- comb- ... 229
  - metal ... 243
- cutlery ... 243
- hollow-ware ... 243
- lime ... 243
- sand ... 243
- spoon and fork ... 243
- wheel; emery ... 173

Buffer-
- bone, etc. ... 230
- flax processing ... 176
- footwear mfr. ... 175
- furniture mfr. ... 299
- glass mfr. ... 192
- leather dressing ... 173
- metal trades ... 243
- rubber goods mfr. ... 228

Buffer and polisher ... 243

Builder;
- ambulance ... 268
- arch; brick ... 300
- armature ... 252
- barge ... 262
- barrow ... 224
- bead (tyre) ... 228
- belt (*rubber goods mfr.*) ... 228
- boat ... 214
- body (vehicle) ... 268
- box (*P.O.*) ... 300
- caravan ... 268
- carriage ... 268
- cart ... 224
- chassis ... 265
- chimney ... 300
- coach ... 268
- commutator ... 252

Builder; *continued*
- condenser ... 283
- conveyor ... 248
- core ... 283
- cupola ... 300
- cycle ... 248
- drum (cables) ... 216
- fireplace ... 300
- float ... 224
- fork (cycles) ... 248
- frame-
  - cycle mfr. ... 248
  - vehicle mfr. ... 268
- furnace ... 300
- garage ... 304
- harness (*textile mfr.*) ... 199
- heel ... 299
- hoarding ... 214
- horticultural ... 214
- hose ... 228
- house ... 305
- jobbing ... 304
- kiln; brick ... 300
- lathe ... 248
- loom ... 248
- machine ... 248
- maintenance ... 304
- manhole ... 300
- master ... 305
- micanite ... 204
- millstone ... 301
- mop (*steelworks*) ... 270
- motor ... 248
- organ ... 222
- oven ... 300
- plate (mica, micanite) ... 204
- pole ... 214
- radiator; car ... 261
- retort ... 300
- roller ... 228
- rolley ... 224
- rubber ... 228
- sewer ... 300
- shed ... 214
- ship ... 262
- staircase ... 214
- stove ... 300
- table (sewing machine) ... 248
- tank (rubber lining) ... 228
- tool; machine ... 248
- transformer ... 252
- tyre ... 194
- vat ... 216
- vehicle ... 268
- wagon ... 268
- wheel-
  - perambulators ... 285
  - rubber ... 228
  - vehicles ... 285
  - wood ... 224
- wheelbarrow ... 224

Builder-
- building and contracting ... 305
- plastics goods mfr. ... 229
- printing ... 206

Builder and contractor ... 305
Builder and decorator ... 305
Builder and repairer; boat ... 214
Builder-up; last ... 225
Building operative ... 304
Building worker ... 304

Bulb worker-
- glassware mfr. ... 192
- horticulture ... 167

Bulker (*tobacco mfr.*) ... 201
Bummaree ... 335

Bumper-
- ceramic mfr. ... 223
- coal mine ... 338
- hat mfr. ... 199
- textile mfr. ... 199
- tin box mfr. ... 242

Buncher;
- hank ... 199

Buncher; *continued*
- watercress ... 287

Buncher-
- cigar mfr. ... 201
- textile mfr. ... 199

Bundler;
- bag ... 287
- flax ... 199
- press ... 287
- scrap ... 298
- sheet (metal) ... 298
- waste (*textile mfr.*) ... 287

Bundler- ... 287
- brush mfr. ... 298
- clothing mfr. ... 299
- metal trades ... 298

Bundler and wrapper (cigarettes) ... 287

Bunker-
- coal mine ... 338
- docks ... 334
- footwear mfr. ... 175

Bunkerman; kiln-
- chemical mfr. ... 184
- lime burning ... 184

Bunkerman-
- blast furnace ... 338
- chemical mfr. ... 184
- coal gas, coke ovens ... 338
- coal mine ... 338
- power station ... L346

Burden man ... 182
Burler ... 183
Burler and mender ... 183

Burner;
- acetylene ... 265
- brick ... 191
- chalk ... 184
- gas-
  - building and contracting ... 265
  - coal gas, coke ovens ... 184
- gypsum ... 184
- head (*ceramic mfr.*) ... 191
- kiln-
  - carbon goods mfr. ... 204
  - cement mfr. ... 204
  - ceramic mfr. ... 191
  - glass mfr. ... 191
- lead ... 265
- lime ... 204
- mould (*rubber tyre mfr.*) ... 204
- oxy-acetylene ... 265
- profile ... 265
- rotary furnace (*aluminium refining*) ... 184
- sand ... 191
- scrap (*steelworks*) ... 265
- tile ... 191

Burner-
- scrap metal ... 265
- cement mfr. ... 204
- ceramic mfr. ... 191
- charcoal mfr. ... 204
- chemical mfr. ... 184
- coal mine ... 265
- demolition ... 265
- glass mfr. ... 191
- lime burning ... 204
- metal trades ... 265
  - sinter plant ... 270
- railways ... 265

Burnerman; acid ... 184
Burnerman ... 184

Burner-off-
- incandescent mantles ... 204
- glass mfr. ... 192

Burnisher;
- gold (*ceramic mfr.*) ... 223
- heel ... 175

Burnisher-
- ceramic mfr. ... 223
- footwear mfr. ... 175
- metal trades ... 243

Burr man ... 199
Burrer ... 173

(Bu—Ca)

Term	Code number
Bursar; ...	...M030
domestic ...	... 111
Burster ...	... 314
Busman ...	... 325
Busher; lead ...	... 270
Busher (*piano mfr.*) ...	... 222
Busker (corsets) ...	... 212
Butcher- ...	... 186
fish, poultry ...	... 187
Butcher-driver ...	... 186
Butcher's boy ...	... 124
Butler; ...	... F151
wine ...	... 144
Buttman (*coal mine*) ...	... 314
Butterman ...	... L346
Butter worker ...	... 202
Butter and tacker; welt ...	... 175
Button man;	
colliery ...	... 338
haulage ...	... 338
Button worker ...	... 230
Buttoner-	
clothing mfr. ...	... 226
footwear mfr. ...	... 225
rolling mill ...	... 270
Buttoner-up (bolts and nuts) ...	... 276
Buttonhole hand ...	... 212
Buttonhole worker ...	... 212
Butty (*mine, not coal*) ...	... 158
Buyer;	
advertising ...	... 016
job ...	... 134
print ...	... 016
space ...	... 016
Buyer- ...	... 016
retail trade ...	... 015
wholesale trade ...	... 016
Byeworker (*coal mine*) ...	... 345
By-product worker ...	... 184
Byreman ...	... 166

C

Term	Code number
Cabman ...	... 338
Cabin boy; dobby ...	... 199
Cabin boy-	
mine, not coal ...	... 158
shipping ...	... 152
Cabin man (*mine, not coal*) ...	... 158
Cabinet worker; ...	... 215
sugar (*jam mfr.*) ...	... 202
Cable hand-	... 276
L.T.E. ...	... 257
tramways ...	... 257
Cable man ...	... 276
Cable tank man ...	... 230
Cable worker (*cable mfr.*) ...	... 276
Caddie ...	... 165
Cadet; officer-	
armed forces-	
foreign and Commonwealth	M136
U.K. ...	...M135
Cadet-	
nursing ...	... 043
police ...	... 137
shipping ...	... 087
Café worker ...	... 146
Cafeteria hand ...	... 146
Cage hand (*coal mine*) ...	... 331
Cageman (*mine, not coal*) ...	... 331
Cager ...	... 173
Caisson man ...	... 338
Cake man; linseed ...	... 202
Caker (liquorice) ...	... 202
Calciner; dextrin ...	... 202
Calciner ...	... 184
Calciner-	
mine, not coal ...	... 204
Calculator;	
colour ...	... 199
sensitometric ...	... 227
Calculator and checker (totalisator) ...	... 115
Calender hand; fabric ...	... 182
Calender hand-	
laundry ...	... 162
leathercloth mfr. ...	... 182
linoleum mfr. ...	... 204
plastics goods mfr. ...	... 195
rubber mfr. ...	... 194
Calenderman;	
friction glazed ...	... 188
super ...	... 188
Calenderman-	
asbestos-cement goods mfr.	204
linoleum mfr. ...	... 204
paper mfr. ...	... 188
rubber mfr. ...	... 194
textile mfr. ...	... 182
Calenderer;	
asbestos ...	... 204
rubber ...	... 194
Calenderer-	
canvas hosepipe mfr. ...	... 182
laundry ...	... 162
paper mfr. ...	... 188
rubber mfr. ...	... 194
textile mfr. ...	... 182
Calibrator (instruments) ...	... 246
Call boy-	
entertainment ...	... 165
railways ...	... 160
Caller; bingo ...	... 165
Caller-off (*railways*) ...	... 115
Caller-over (*glass mfr.*) ...	... 333
Caller-up (*railways*) ...	... 160
Calligrapher ...	... 055
Cameraman; ...	... 061
chief (*films*) ...	...M059
Campanologist ...	... 060
Can lad ...	... 338
Canchman (*coal mine*) ...	... 314
Candler; egg ...	... 290
Cane worker ...	... 230
Caner- ...	... 230
corset mfr. ...	... 299
Canner ...	... 287
Cannery worker ...	... 287
Canon ...	... 040
Canroyer ...	... 182
Canteen hand ...	... 147
Canteen worker ...	... 147
Canvasser;	
advertisement ...	... 134
advertising ...	... 134
book ...	... 132
directory ...	... 132
freight ...	... 134
insurance ...	... 134
mutuality club ...	... 132
political ...	... 024
telephone ...	... 134
traffic ...	... 134
Canvasser-	
advertising ...	... 134
clothing mfr. ...	... 212
insurance ...	... 134
transport ...	... 134
Canvasser and collector ...	... 132
Capper;	
bobbin ...	... 285
bottle ...	... 287
paper ...	... 287
toe ...	... 225
Capper- ...	... 283
cartridge mfr. ...	... 230
lamp, valve mfr. ...	... 283
polish mfr. ...	... 287
Capper and sealer; end ...	... 276
Capstan hand; brass ...	... 241
Capstan hand (*railways*) ...	... 331
Capstan man ...	... 331
Capsuler ...	... 287
Captain;	
barge ...	... 087
Captain; *continued*	
dredger ...	... 087
ferry ...	... 087
fire ...	...M138
float ...	... 087
keel ...	... 087
launch ...	... 087
lighter ...	... 087
port ...	... 095
shore ...	... 097
underground ...	... F315
Captain-	
hovercraft ...	...M090
aircraft ...	...M085
armed forces-	
foreign and Commonwealth	M136
U.K. ...	...M135
boat, barge ...	... 087
Church Army ...	... 040
fishing ...	... 111
mine, not coal ...	... F315
Salvation Army ...	... 040
shipping ...	... 087
Captain-superintendent ...	... 091
Car worker ...	... 285
Carbide worker ...	... 184
Carbon worker ...	... 230
Carbonatation hand (sugar) ...	... 202
Carbonating hand ...	... 202
Carbonating man ...	... 202
Carbonation man (sugar) ...	... 202
Carbonator man ...	... 184
Carbonator (*brewery*) ...	... 197
Carboniser;	
cloth ...	... 199
nickel (*valve mfr.*) ...	... 223
piece ...	... 199
rag ...	... 199
wool ...	... 199
Carboniser-	
ball bearing mfr. ...	... 237
gas works ...	... 184
textile mfr. ...	... 199
Carburizer ...	... 237
Card and drawing hand (jute) ...	176
Card boy ...	... 176
Card hand (flax, hemp) ...	... 176
Card room hand ...	... 176
,, ,, man ...	... 176
,, ,, operative ...	... 176
,, ,, worker ...	... 176
Carder;	
asbestos ...	... 176
comb ...	... 287
cotton ...	... 176
fibre ...	... 176
hair ...	... 176
head ...	...F176
speed ...	... 176
under ...	...F176
velour ...	... 226
Carder-	
button mfr. ...	... 287
hook mfr. ...	... 287
pencil mfr. ...	... 287
textile mfr.- ...	... 176
lace finishing ...	... 182
Carding operative (textile) ...	... 176
Carding room man ...	... 176
Cardiographer ...	... 050
Cardiologist ...	... 041
Caretaker- ...	... 157
reservoir ...	... 316
woodlands ...	... 170
Caretaker-operator ...	... 121
Cargo worker ...	... 334
Carman- ...	... 326
blast furnace ...	... 338
coal merchants ...	... 326
coke ovens ...	... 332
Carpenter ...	... 214
Carpenter and joiner ...	... 214
Carpenter-diver ...	... 316
Carpet worker ...	... 180

19

(Ca—Ch)

	Code number
Carrier;	
bag-	338
docks	335
bar	270
barley	338
batch (rubber)	338
beam (carpets)	338
board	338
bobbin	338
brick	338
clay	338
cloth	338
coal	326
colour (*textile printing*)	338
cop	338
cotton; hosiery	338
deal-	338
docks	334
dust	338
fillet; card	338
fish box	334
general	326
glass (*glass mfr.*)	338
hod	312
lap	338
liquor	338
metal	338
piece	338
pitwood	334
pole (linoleum)	338
prop	334
rag	338
railway	326
rivet	276
roller	L346
rover	338
roving	338
sack (cement)	338
sample	338
sanitary pipe	338
set	333
sheet (paper)	338
skip	338
sliver (flax, hemp)	338
timber-	338
docks	334
tool	338
top (*textile printing*)	338
tow	338
ware	338
weft	338
wool	338
yarn	338
Carrier-	338
docks	334
mine, not coal-	326
below ground	338
n.o.s.	326
transport	326
Carrier-away	338
Carrier-in (*glass mfr.*)	191
Carrier-off	338
Carrotter	173
Cart boy; top (*rope mfr.*)	199
Cart boy (*textile mfr.*)	338
Cartman	338
Carter; coal	326
Carter-	
farming	172
mine, not coal	338
transport	338
Carter's boy-	
farming	172
transport	329
Cartographer	079
Cartographer-draughtsman	079
Cartoner	287
Cartoonist	055
Cartridger	230
Carver;	
architectural	301
frame	224
gold	276
ivory	230

	Code number
Carver; *continued*	
letter-	
brass	276
wood	224
monumental	301
stock (gun)	224
stone	301
wood	224
Carver-	
food	165
furniture	224
wood	224
Case hand (*printing*)	205
Case worker; family	039
Case worker-	
piano organ mfr.	215
welfare services	039
Casein worker-	
chemical mfr.	184
food products mfr.	202
Caser;	
bone	212
die	276
Caser-	
metal	237
packing	287
corset mfr.	212
Cashier;	
chief-	F115
government	F112
Cashier-	115
café	116
canteen	116
restaurant	116
garage	116
local government	115
retail trade	116
Cast off; fishing boat	171
Caster;	
brass	270
china	193
cold (rubber)	228
concrete	230
die	235
furnace; blast	270
hollow-ware (ceramic mfr.)	193
ingot	270
iron	270
lead (*battery mfr.*)	270
metal	270
monotype	205
needle	270
parchester	303
roller (printer's)	228
sanitary	193
shot	270
slab	230
statue	223
stone	230
strip	270
tile	230
type	270
at machine	235
Caster-	
cast stone products mfr.	230
ceramic mfr.	193
footwear mfr.	228
glassware mfr.	223
metal trades	270
printing	206
Caster-off; fishing boat	171
Casting man (*blast furnace*)	270
Castrator-	172
farm livestock	166
Cataloguer	115
Catalyst man	184
Catcher;	
bar	270
bird	172
chicken	172
cigarette	299
eel	171
finishing	270
machine	299

	Code number
Catcher; *continued*	
mole	165
pole (linoleum)	204
rabbit	172
rat	165
rivet	276
roll; cold	270
sheet (paper)	203
sheet mill	270
Catcher-	
laundry	162
paper mfr.	203
steelworks	270
Catcher and sticker (wire)	270
Caterer;	104
amusement	106
Catering boy (*shipping*)	152
Catering worker	147
Catsmeat man	130
Cattleman	166
Caulker	262
Caulker-burner	262
Causticizer	184
Caver (*coal mine*)	314
Cellar boy *see* Cellarman	
Cellarer	197
Cellarman;	
bar	333
oil	333
Cellarman-	
bacon, meat curing	L346
brewery	197
catering	333
hotel	333
rubber mfr.	204
steelworks	231
textile mfr.	333
wine mfr.	333
wine merchants	333
Cellarman-waiter	144
Cellist	060
Cellophaner	287
Cellroom man	184
Cement worker	204
Cementer;	
envelope	295
outsole	299
paper	203
rubber	299
ship	316
upper	299
waterproof (*clothing mfr.*)	226
Cementer-	
ceramic mfr.-	223
electrical insulator mfr.	283
footwear mfr.	299
lens mfr.	299
metal capsule mfr.	285
plastics goods mfr.	296
rubber goods mfr.	299
Cemetery worker	L346
Centerer (*lens mfr.*)	223
Centerer and edger (*lens mfr.*)	192
Centrer *see* Centerer	
Ceramist	078
Certifier; money order	294
Chain boy	316
Chainman-	316
docks	333
mine, not coal	338
Chairman- *see also notes p.4*	
appeals tribunal, inquiry, etc.	M027
glass mfr.	192
Chalkman	182
Chamberman; cotton	176
Chamberman-	
acids	184
chemical mfr.	184
cold storage	333
Chamberlain	157
Chambermaid	151
Chambermaster	091
Chamferer	242
Chandler	101

(Ch)

	Code number
Changer;	
card	199
chart	115
drill	315
frame (carpets)	199
gold	236
money	115
mould (*rubber mfr.*)	228
pattern	217
roll	270
roller	227
rope (*coal mine*)	338
Changer-	
flax mfr.	176
textile printing	227
Channeller-	
footwear mfr.	175
metal trades	242
mine, not coal	315
Chaperone	165
Chaplain-	040
armed forces-	
foreign and Commonwealth	M136
U.K.	M135
Char house man	184
Char kiln man	184
Charman; wet	L346
Charman (*sugar refining*)	L346
Charwoman	158
Chargehand *see* Foreman	
Chargeman;	
battery	276
track (*railways*)	F306
Chargeman- *see also* Foreman	
coal mine	314
copper, zinc refining	332
Charger;	
accumulator	276
battery	276
blunger	204
cartridge	230
coal	332
cordite	230
cupola	338
drill	315
flux dust	338
furnace (*metal mfr.*)	338
kiln	184
ore	332
oven	332
retort (*gas works*)	332
spare (*blast furnace*)	338
spiegel	338
tube (*brass tube mfr.*)	L344
wool (*surgical appliance mfr.*)	226
Charger-	
coke ovens	332
firework mfr.	230
gas works	332
linoleum mfr.	204
metal mfr.-	338
tinplate mfr.	270
mine, not coal	332
slag wool mfr.	204
Chargerman	332
Charging hand; battery	276
Charlady	158
Chartist	115
Chaser;	
engineer's	115
film	115
gold	266
platework	266
progress	115
purchase	115
silver	266
stock	115
Chaser-	
metal-	276
precious metal	266
manufacturing-	115
jewellery, plate mfr.	266
Chauffeur	327
Chauffeur-gardener	327

	Code number
Chauffeur-handyman	327
Chauffeur-mechanic	327
Chauffeur-valet	327
Checker;	
bank-note	294
cable (*coal mine*)	115
coal	115
coupon (competitions)	115
delivery	113
depot	115
despatch	113
dipper	297
dock	115
drawing	079
field	115
gate	140
gauge	286
goods	115
hop	F166
ingot (*steelworks*)	286
invoice	115
iron	286
linen (*hotel, etc.*)	333
machine (*engineering*)	286
map	079
meter	115
mica	299
milk	290
moulding	293
paper (*paper mfr.*)	294
piecework	115
policy (insurance)	115
price	115
progress	115
quantity	115
railway	115
steel (*coal mine*)	333
stock	113
stores	113
supports	333
ticket-	115
entertainment	165
railways	160
timber	333
time	115
traffic	115
train (*L.T.E.*)	115
waybill	115
Checker- *see also notes* p.4	
drawing office	079
electrical/electronic equipment	286
bakery	290
Bank of England	294
bingo hall	165
brewery	290
building and contracting	115
ceramic mfr.	299
chemical mfr.	288
clothing mfr.	289
coal mine	333
dairy	F128
docks	115
drug mfr.	299
electrical/electronic engineering	286
food products mfr.	290
laundry	115
metal trades	286
oil refining	115
opencast coal works	115
paint mfr.	299
petroleum distribution	115
piano mfr.	222
printing	294
rubber goods mfr.	291
textile products mfr.	289
transport	115
warehousing	333
wholesale, retail trade	115
wood products mfr.	293
Checker and deliverer	115
Checker and packer	287
Checker and weigher	333
Checker-loader	115
Checker-out	116

	Code number
Checker-up	115
Checkweighman	297
Checkweigher	297
Cheese worker	202
Cheesemonger	101
Cheeser-	178
biscuit mfr.	200
Chef;	
head	F143
pastry	F143
Chef-	143
food products mfr.	202
Chef de cuisine	F143
Chemical worker	184
Chemicker	182
Chemist;	
agricultural	065
analytical	066
assistant research	066
biological	065
chief	066
consulting	066
development	066
dispensing	050
electroplating	066
government	066
homoeopathic	044
industrial	066
inorganic	066
laboratory	066
managing	066
manufacturing	066
metallurgical	066
organic	066
pharmaceutical	044
photographic	044
physical	066
research	066
research and development	066
shift	066
soil	065
superintending	066
technical	066
textile	066
wholesale	101
works	066
Chemist-	066
pharmaceutical	044
n.o.s.	044
retail trade	044
steelworks	066
Chemist and druggist (*retail trade*)	044
Chemist's boy (*cement mfr.*)	L346
Chequerer	223
Chick-sexer	172
Chief of staff (*cinema*)	F157
Child care worker	037
Chiller man (*brewery*)	197
Chimney hand (*building and contracting*)	304
Chipper;	
pneumatic	276
steel (*steelworks*)	276
tyre	244
Chipper-	
ceramic mfr.	223
chipboard mfr.	203
metal trades-	276
fish hook mfr.	242
shipbuilding	262
road surfacing	308
painting	299
Chipper and painter	282
Chipper and scaler	L344
Chipper and scraper	262
Chipper-in (*rolling mill*)	270
Chiropodist	048
Chiropractor	049
Chlorate of soda man	184
Chlorinator (*water works*)	184
Chlorine worker; electrolytic	184
Chocker (*coal mine*)	314
Chocolate hand	202

21

(Ch—Cl)

	Code number
Chocolate man	202
Chocolate worker	202
Chocolatier	202
Chopper;	
firewood	L346
sugar	202
wood (*sawmilling*)	218
Chopper (*clothing mfr.*)	211
Chopperman (*paper mfr.*)	176
Choreographer	059
Chorister	059
Chorus girl	059
Chromer-	182
metal trades	236
Chummer-in (*ceramic mfr.*)	223
Church Army worker	040
Church worker	040
Cider worker	197
Cinema worker	165
Cinematographer	062
Circuit man; electric light	253
Circular hand	181
Circus hand	L346
Civil servant (n.o.s.)	115
Clammer (*roller engraving*)	267
Clampman (*fire brick mfr.*)	204
Clamper-	
pencil mfr.	299
roller engraving	267
textile finishing	182
Clapper boy	062
Clapper-loader	061
Clarifier man	202
Clarinettist	060
Classer	298
Classifier;	298
livestock	172
Clatter (*celluloid*)	229
Clay boy (*metal mfr.*)	L344
Clay man-	
ceramic mfr.	204
clay pit	315
Clay worker-	
ceramic mfr.	223
clay pit	315
Cleaner;	
aircraft	158
bag	348
bank	158
bar (*catering*)	158
barrel	348
bedding	162
belt (*coal mine*)	338
berth	158
blende	198
boat	158
bobbin	199
bogie	L346
boiler	276
bone	204
book	L346
boot	175
bottle	348
box (*textile printing*)	L339
brass	L346
bristle	176
buddle	L346
building	316
bus	158
button	229
cab	158
cabinet; office; call	158
canteen	158
car	158
card	276
cardroom	199
carpet	162
carriage	158
casings; sausage	202
cask	348
casting	244
chimney	158
church	158
clock	247

	Code number
Cleaner; *continued*	
closet	158
cloth	182
clothes	162
coal	198
core	270
crane	271
cycle	L344
decomposer (*nickel mfr.*)	L344
domestic	158
drain	158
drum	L340
dry	162
dye vat (straw plait)	L346
economiser; boiler	276
engine; carding	276
engine-	
coal mine	271
railways	271
shipping	317
waterworks	271
equipment	L346
factory	158
feather	199
fish	187
floor	158
flue	158
frame (cycles, motors)	L344
french	162
fruit	202
fur	162
garment	162
general	158
glass (dry plates)	227
glove	162
gulley	L346
gut	204
hat	226
heald	276
heddle	276
hide	173
hospital	158
house;	158
boiler	276
power	158
hydraulic	271
hygiene	165
iron	244
jet	L346
kernel	202
key (locks)	276
kiosk; telephone	158
kitchen	158
laboratory	158
lace	199
lamp-	L346
coal mine	345
lens	L342
library	158
line	338
loco	271
locomotive	271
loom	199
machine-	L346
textile mfr.	199
maintenance	L346
meat	186
metal	244
meter	246
motor (*garage*)	158
mould	L346
night	158
office	158
omnibus	158
picture	055
piece	182
pipe	276
pirn	199
pit (*railways*)	L346
plant	L346
plaster	223
plate-	
catering	147
printing	227

	Code number
Cleaner; *continued*	
potato	165
press (*rolling mill*)	270
printer's	338
rag	176
ramie	182
rice	202
ring	244
river	316
road-	158
mine, not coal	L346
road and yard (*railways*)	158
roller	199
room;	
mess	158
show	158
sack	348
school	158
scrap-	L344
tobacco mfr.	201
seed	202
sheet (*plastics mfr.*)	L340
ship's	158
shop	158
silver-	276
catering, hotels, etc.	147
domestic service	147
skin; sausage	202
spillage	345
sponge	204
station (*railways*)	158
steam (*building and contracting*)	316
steel (*foundry*)	244
still	L340
stone-	316
iron	198
street	158
table (*textile mfr.*)	199
tank	L346
tape; magnetic	348
telephone	158
tin-	
bakery	L346
food canning	L346
mine, not coal	198
toilet	165
tongue	186
tramcar	158
tray (*bakery*)	L346
tripe	202
tube; boiler	276
tube-	
blast furnace	L344
lamp, valve mfr.	348
railways	276
upholstery	158
upper (*footwear mfr.*)	175
vacuum	162
vat	L346
wagon (*coal mine*)	345
ware	299
warehouse	158
warp (*textile mfr.*)	199
waste	176
watch	247
wet	162
window	158
wire (*wire mfr.*)	270
wood	203
works	158
workshop	158
yard	158
Cleaner-	158
educational establishments	158
food products	202
institutional premises	158
machinery-	L346
textile machinery	199
metal goods	276
office premises	158
residential premises	158
vehicles	158
asbestos-cement mfr.	230

(Cl—Co)

	Code number
Cleaner- *continued*	
cartridge mfr.	270
catering, hotels, etc.	158
ceramic mfr.	223
clothing mfr.	226
coal mine	345
domestic service	158
dyeing and cleaning	162
electroplating	270
enamelling	270
entertainment	158
fellmongery	173
footwear mfr.	175
foundry	244
fur goods mfr.	162
galvanized sheet mfr.	269
government	158
lamp, valve mfr.	255
local government	158
musical instruments (brass mfr.)	276
needle mfr.	276
optical instrument mfr.	L342
P.O.	158
piano mfr.	299
printing	L346
railways	158
retail trade	158
silk throwing	178
textile finishing	199
tripe dressing	202
Cleaner and balancer (weighing machine)	248
Cleaner and greaser	271
Cleaner and steam raiser (*railways*)	271
Cleaner-doorman	158
Cleaner-engineer	271
Cleaner-stoker	158
Cleanser-	
local government	336
soap mfr.	184
Clearer;	
credit	115
oven (*bakery*)	200
table	165
tuyere bottom	L344
warp	179
Clearer-	
cotton doubling	177
embroidering	226
textile finishing	182
Cleaver;	
diamond	266
lath	224
wood	224
Cleaver-	
precious stones	266
cricket bat mfr.	224
Clergyman	040
Clerical worker	115
Clerk; *see also notes* p.4	115
actuarial	115
allocator	115
articled-	
accountancy	002
legal services	001
audit-	115
qualified	002
authorised	007
barrister's	027
booking;	
stores	113
warehouse	113
booking (travel agency)	115
bookstall	125
chief-	F115
banking	F115
building society	F115
courts of justice	001
government	021
insurance	F115
local government	022
P.O.	F115

	Code number
Clerk; *continued*	
cloakroom	165
committee	030
confidential	118
control;	
air traffic	122
material	113
stock	113
conveyancing	115
coursing	106
deputy (*local government*)	022
despatch	113
head	F115
higher grade	115
judge's	027
law-	115
articled	001
left luggage	165
litigation	115
machine; weigh (*coal mine*)	297
managing-	M027
qualified solicitor	001
accountancy	M030
principal-	
government	021
local government	022
P.L.A.	095
property	115
quarter sessions	001
rating	115
receiving	113
receiving office	125
records;	115
stock	113
stores	113
secretarial	115
security	115
sheriff (Scotland)	001
sorting (*P.O.*)	123
staff-	115
government	021
local government	022
stock	113
stockroom	113
storekeeper's	113
stores	113
supervising	F115
tally;	115
timber	333
technical	115
town	022
valuation;	115
higher grade (*Inland Revenue*)	F112
warehouse	113
weigh	297
weighbridge	297
weighing	297
in holy orders	040
of arraigns	001
of the company	023
of the council	022
of the actuarie	106
of the court	001
of the executive council	M030
of the peace	001
of the scales	297
of works	093
to the assessments committee	M030
to the board (*local government*)	022
to the burial board	022
to the commissioners (*Inland Revenue*)	020
to the council	022
to the county council	022
to the district council	022
to the executive council	M030
to the justices	001
to the parish council	022
to the port sanitary authority	022
to the rural district council	022
to the urban district council	022
Clerk and steward	106

	Code number
Clerk and telegraphist; sorting	123
Clerk-in-charge	F115
Clerk-buyer	115
Clerk-messenger	115
Clerk-packer	115
Clerk-storekeeper	113
Clerk-storeman	113
Clerk-telephonist	115
Clerk-typist	115
Clerk-warehouseman	113
Clicker;	
machine	175
press	175
Clicker-	
footwear mfr.	175
leather goods mfr.	175
printing	F205
Climber (*constructional engineers*)	263
Clinker man	L340
Clipper;	
card top	276
cloth	182
horse	172
knot	182
poodle	172
press (*press cutting agency*)	115
veneer	218
Clipper-	
coal mine	338
hosiery mfr.	299
metal trades	270
rope mfr.	182
tannery	173
textile finishing	182
Clock hand (*ball bearing mfr.*)	286
Clocker	212
Clogger	225
Closer;	
channel	299
hand	175
repairs	175
toe	175
Closer-	
clothing mfr.	212
footwear mfr.	175
foundry	270
toy mfr.	175
wire rope mfr.	276
Closer-up	212
Cloth man (*clothing mfr.*)	289
Cloth worker (*textile finishing*)	182
Clothier;	
boiler	316
card	276
Clothier (*retail trade*)	101
Clothier and outfitter	101
Clown	059
Coach (sports)	063
Coach boy	338
Coachman	338
Coal man	L346
coal merchants	326
Coaler	L346
Coastguard	142
Coat and skirt hand	210
Coat hand	210
Coater;	
baryta	203
cathode	276
celluloid (*film mfr.*)	204
ceramics	279
chocolate	202
dry plate	204
emulsion	204
filament	276
hand (*oilskin mfr.*)	199
paper-	203
photographic	204
prime	282
sugar-	
confectionery mfr.	202
pharmaceutical mfr.	184
tablet	184

(Co)

	Code number			Code number			Code number
Coater; *continued*			Collector; *continued*			Commandant- *continued*	
tar (*coal gas, coke ovens*)	204		seaweed	171		armed forces-	
Coater-			senior-			foreign and Commonwealth	M136
linoleum mfr.	204		*gas board*	F115		U.K.	M135
photographic film mfr.	204		*government*	021		fire service	M138
stencil paper mfr.	203		*local government*	115		Commander-	
tinplate mfr.	269		soil; night	158		hovercraft	M090
wire mfr.	269		subscription	115		armed forces-	
Coating man (*roofing felt mfr.*)	199		superintendent (*local government*)	022		foreign and Commonwealth	M136
Cobberer	202		tax; assistant	115		U.K.	M135
Cobbleman	317		ticket-	165		shipping	087
Cobbler	174		*L.T.E.*	160		Commentator	054
Coder-	115		*railways*	160		Commissionaire	165
manufacturing	287		toll	115		Commissioner;	
Cogger (*rolling mill*)	232		tow (flax)	176		land	084
Coiffeur	159		waste (works)	338		of oaths	001
Coiler;			of Customs and Excise	021		Commissioner-	
copper	270		of parts	333		government	020
rope	199		of taxes;	F112		legal service	001
tape	199		assistant	115		police	M137
Coiler-			Collector-			Commodore-	
cable mfr.	276		*credit trade*	115		armed forces-	
electrical goods mfr.	274		*Customs and Excise*	021		foreign and Commonwealth	M136
rope mfr.	199		*electricity board*	115		U.K.	M135
rubber tubing mfr.	228		*entertainment*	115		shipping	087
spring mfr.	276		*gas board*	115		Community worker	039
steel mfr.	270		*Inland Revenue*	F112		Commutator hand	252
wire mfr.	270		*insurance*	134		Companion	151
wire rod mfr.	270		*local authority*	115		Companion-help	151
wire rope mfr.	276		*photographic films mfr.*	338		Companion-housekeeper	149
Coiner	242		*retail trade*	115		Companion-nurse	043
Coke man (*coke ovens*)	L341		*textile mfr.*	338		Companyman (*coal mine*)	314
Coke worker (*coke ovens*)	184		Collector and salesman	132		Competition hand	115
Coker; wood	184		Collector-agent-	115		Compiler;	
Coker (*coal gas, coke ovens*)	184		*insurance*	134		catalogue	115
Collar hand-			Collector-driver (*local government*)	115		crossword	054
clothing mfr.	212		refuse	326		directory	115
laundry	162		Collector-salesman	132		index	115
Collator (*printing*)	189		Collector's boy	124		order	333
Collector;			Collier-			technical	054
ash	338		*barge*	334		route	115
ash pit	338		*coal mine*	314		schedule	115
assistant (*Inland Revenue*)	115		Colliery worker	345		Completer (*toy mfr.*)	230
auto	115		Colonel-			Compo man	276
blood	186		armed forces-			Compoer	230
brewery	115		foreign and Commonwealth	M136		Composer (*music*)	060
car	327		U.K.	M135		Composite worker	314
chief (*Inland Revenue*)	021		Colonel-Commandant-			Compositor	205
cloth	338		armed forces-			Compounder-	204
club	115		foreign and Commonwealth	M136		*chemical mfr.*	184
coin	115		U.K.	M135		*food products mfr.*	202
cop	338		Colourman; artist	101		*mineral water mfr.*	202
debt	115		Colourman	204		*plastics goods mfr.*	204
dust (*local government*)	336		Colour worker-			*rubber mfr.*	194
egg-	326		*paint mfr.*	204		Compressor;	
poultry farm	166		*printing*	227		engineer's	255
excess	160		Colourer;			gas	255
excess luggage	160		hand (picture postcard)	227		heel	225
fat	326		map	115		tablet	184
fat and bone	131		print	227		Compressor hand	255
fern	172		Colourer-			Compressor man	255
glass (dry plates)	338		artificial flowers	299		Comptometrist	119
higher grade (*Inland Revenue*)	021		carpets	199		Comptroller; financial	006
insurance	134		metal	237		Computer	067
kelp	171		steel pens	237		Concaver (*footwear mfr.*)	218
meter	115		*wallpaper printing*	227		Concentrator	184
milk	326		Colourist;			Concentratorman (*paper mfr.*)	203
moss	172		map	115		Conche man	202
mutuality	115		photographic	227		Concher	202
pools	115		postcard	227		Conchologist	065
rag and waste	131		Colourist	199		Concrete worker; pre-cast	230
rate;	115		Colporteur	130		Concrete worker-	307
chief	022		Comber-			*concrete products mfr.*	230
reed	172		*fur dressing*	173		Concreter;	307
refuse	336		*textile mfr.*	176		granolithic	300
regional	021		Combiner-			Condenser-	
rent	115		*canvas goods mfr.*	199		*milk processing*	202
sack	326		*paper mfr.*	203		*textile mfr.*	176
salvage-	338		Combing operative (*textile mfr.*)	176		Condenser hand	283
local government-			Comedian	059		Condenser man-	184
cleansing dept.	336		Commandant-			*blast furnace*	231
scaleboard	338		airport	095		Conditioner;	
scrap-	338					air	348
self-employed	131					leaf	201

(Co)

	Code number
Conditioner; *continued*	
paper	188
yarn	182
Conditioner-	
food products mfr.	202
paper mfr.	188
tannery	173
textile mfr.	182
Conductor;	
bus	328
car;	
dining	144
pullman	144
floating bridge	338
music	060
musical	060
omnibus	328
paddy	338
tramcar	328
trolleybus	328
Conductor-	
entertainment	060
railways	320
road transport	328
Coner; wood (silk)	199
Coner-	
felt hood mfr.	226
textile mfr.	199
Confectionery; flour	185
Confectioner-	
employee-	185
sugar confectionery mfr.	202
Confectionery and tobacconist	101
Confectionery hand	200
Confectionery worker (*sugar confectionery mfr.*)	202
Conjurer	059
Connector;	
armature	283
cable	257
coupling	260
Connector (rubber boots and shoes)	299
Conservator; forest	111
Constable;	
chief	M137
market	140
police *see* Constable-	
private	140
Constable-	
non-statutory	140
airport	137
docks	137
government	137
Kew gardens	140
Min. of Defence	137
police service	137
railways	137
Royal parks	137
Construction worker	316
Constructionist (textiles)	080
Constructor;	
map	079
naval	069
permanent way	306
road	308
roof (*building*)	214
roofing	303
steel	263
switchboard	252
Constructor (*M.O.D.*)	069
Consul	021
Consultant;	
advertising	014
agricultural	065
aid; hearing	050
architectural	082
beauty-	165
retail trade-	125
door to door sales	132
business	010
catering	104
ceramic	078
chemical	066

	Code number
Consultant; *continued*	
colour (*paint mfr.*)	078
computer	072
corsetry	226
cosmetics	125
cost	003
costing	003
design (*engineering*)	070
economic	011
editorial	054
educational	053
engineering;	069
chemical	073
civil	068
fashion	057
financial	007
forestry	065
heating-	260
professional	076
industrial	075
insurance	134
investment	007
legal	001
machinery	069
management	028
marketing	013
medical	041
office routine	010
organisation and methods	010
patent	090
pension	011
perfumery	125
personnel	009
production	074
property	025
relations; public	014
research; operational	010
sales	013
scientific	078
security	140
shipping	134
staff (*employment agency*)	115
study; works	010
systems	012
tax	008
technical *see* Engineer-prof.-	
training	034
travel	115
wig	165
Contact man (*advertising*)	014
Contract worker (*coal mine*)	314
Contractor;	
advertisement	014
advertising	014
agricultural	107
bill posting	134
bricklaying	300
builder's	305
building	305
butcher's	101
cartage	326
catering	104
civil engineer's	316
cleaning (self-employed)	158
clothing	101
coal	101
decorating	282
demolition	316
drainage	316
electrical	253
fencing	316
flooring	316
forestry	170
gardening	168
general	316
haulage	326
hire; plant	134
landscape	168
milk	101
office cleaning	134
painting	282
penning	316
plastering	302
ploughing	107

	Code number
Contractor; *continued*	
plumbing	260
public works	316
refreshment room	104
removal	335
road	316
stone (*coal mine*)	314
timber	101
transport (road)	326
Contractor-	
bricklaying	300
agricultural contracting	107
building and contracting	316
coal mine	316
mine, not coal	315
painting, decorating	282
pipe lagging	311
plastering	302
transport	326
Contractor's man (*coal mine*)	314
Controlman; bunker	338
Controlman-	184
blast furnace	231
margarine mfr.	202
Controller;	
account	115
ambulance	111
apron	338
area-	
market research	013
retail trade	101
budget	115
cash	115
catering	104
charge (*metal mfr.*)	338
chief (*railways*);	095
deputy	F318
coal (*metal mfr.*)	338
computer	099
contract	115
converter	F231
conveyer (*coal mine*)	338
cost	115
credit	098
data; computer	119
depot	097
despatch	097
display	055
divisional	111
economics	011
electrical-	253
railways	F255
export-	013
export agency	129
financial	006
freight (*railways*)	097
furnace-	
metal goods mfr.	231
metal mfr.	F231
sherardizing	231
gas (*steelworks*)	081
goods (*railways*)	097
hotel	102
humidity	182
inventory	096
ledger	115
loan; embodiment	115
locomotive	321
maintenance;	
planned-	248
coal mine	091
plant	248
marketing	013
materials	096
merchandise	013
mortgage	115
office	099
operations (*transport*)	095
order	113
oxygen	090
pest	165
plant	248
postal	111
power (*railways*)	F255

25

(Co)

	Code number
Controller; *continued*	
price	115
production-	091
building and contracting	092
progress	115
project (*metal trades*)	091
proof; newspaper	115
purchasing	016
quality *see notes* p.5	
radar; area	086
radio	122
regional (*government*)	021
reservation (*airline*)	115
sales	013
schedule	115
school meals	104
section (*railways*)	321
shift; despatch	097
shift	091
shipping	095
shop-	111
metal trades	091
signals	095
sound	062
spares	333
staff	009
statistical	011
stock	096
stores	096
sub-contracts-	013
production	091
building and contracting	092
supplies	096
technical *see Manager*	
telecommunications	099
temperature (*tobacco mfr.*)	201
traffic;	095
air	086
train	321
trainsman's relief	321
transport	095
treatment; water	184
wages	099
waste	115
works	091
of factories (*P.O.*)	091
of sales	013
of supplies	096
of typists	F118
Controller-	
banking	006
government	021
insurance	007
P.O.	111
railways	321
Controller hand (*printing*)	207
Convenor; works	024
Converter;	
appliance; gas	260
gas	260
merchant	101
paper-	203
paper products mfr.	227
polythene	184
steel	231
textile	101
timber	218
Converter-	
gas board	260
metal mfr.	231
textile wholesaling	101
Converter man-	
chemical mfr.	184
glucose mfr.	202
metal mfr.	231
Conveyancer	027
Conveyor	338
Conveyor hand	338
Conveyor man	338
Cook;	
chief	F143
head	F143
mastic (*asphalt mfr.*)	204

	Code number
Cook; *continued*	
pastry-	143
bakery	185
Cook-	143
bakery	200
food products mfr.	202
tripe dressing	202
Cook in charge	F143
Cook-cleaner	143
Cook-companion	143
Cook-general	143
Cook-housekeeper	149
Cook-manager	104
Cook-steward	143
Cook-supervisor	F143
Cooker; potato crisp	202
Cooker (*food products mfr.*)	202
Cookerman (*cereal food mfr.*)	202
Cooler-	
brewery	197
chemical mfr.	184
food products mfr.	202
Cooler hand (*sugar refining*)	202
Cooler man *see Cooler*	
Cooper;	
box	216
chest; tea	216
tea	216
wine	287
Cooper-	216
tobacco mfr.	216
Co-ordinator;	
computer	012
marketing	013
production	090
sales	013
training	034
Coper; horse	101
Copier;	
design	115
pattern; paper	227
Copper	178
Copperman (*textile mfr.*)	178
Copperworker; electro (*textile printing*)	227
Copper worker (*refining*)	L344
Copperas heap man	L340
Copperer (carbon brushes)	270
Copperhead worker	197
Coppersidesman	197
Coppice worker	170
Copyholder	115
Copyist;	
braille	227
design	115
designer's	115
milliner's	211
millinery; first	211
music	060
photo	119
Copyist-	
millinery mfr.	211
textile printing	115
Copytaster	054
Corder;	
cake	201
roll	201
Corder-	
footwear mfr.	175
printing	295
tobacco mfr.	201
upholstering	226
Cordite worker	184
Cordwinder	175
Core boy	270
Corer; hard	230
Corer (*foundry*)	235
Corker; segment	316
Corker-	287
fishing rod mfr.	299
Cornetist	060
Coroner	027
Corporal; underground	F331

	Code number
Corporal-	
armed forces-	
foreign and Commonwealth	136
U.K.	135
Corporation employee	L346
Corporation worker	L346
Corrector;	
chart (*Trinity House*)	079
die	245
press	115
proof; newspaper	115
spring (*vehicle mfr.*)	248
Corrector (*hosiery mfr.*)	199
Correspondent;	
banking	115
claims	115
foreign	054
newspaper	054
sales	115
school	115
technical	054
turf	054
Corrugator-	
asbestos-cement products mfr.	204
galvanized sheet mfr.	242
Corrugator lad	242
Corsetiere	226
Cosmetician	165
Coster	130
Costermonger	130
Costume hand	210
Costumier	210
Cotton operative	L339
Cotton room man	333
,, ,, worker	333
Cotton worker	L339
Coucher	203
Council employee	L346
Council worker	L346
Counsel; Queen's	001
Counsellor;	
investment	007
school	053
student	053
Counsellor (*government*)	021
Counter;	
bank-note	297
bobbin	333
paper	294
piece	113
Counter-	
bolt mfr.	287
mine, not coal	297
paper mfr.	294
printing	333
shipbuilding	115
textile mfr.	333
Counterhand *see Counterman*	
Counterman-	
chemicals	333
drugs	333
catering	146
hosiery mfr.	287
retail trade	125
take-away food shop	125
turf accountants	115
wool warehouse	333
Counter-off	333
Coupler (*hose pipe mfr.*)	299
Courier-	152
travel agency	152
Couturier	057
Coverer;	
bar; metal	276
biscuit	200
boiler	316
box (wooden fixture boxes)	299
buckle	299
bust	230
button	299
cabinet (*furniture mfr.*)	299
case	299
chocolate	202
elastic (*textile mfr.*)	199

(Co—Cu)

	Code number
Coverer; *continued*	
fireworks	295
hat	299
heel	299
helmet	299
hood (cars, perambulators)	212
lead	270
pipe	316
pipe and boiler	316
rexine	213
roller-	
printing	228
textile mfr.	225
roof	303
rubber-	
cable mfr.	228
surgical bandage mfr.	199
textile mfr.	228
tennis ball	299
umbrella	212
wheel (rubber)	228
wire (*insulated wire mfr.*)	228
Coverer-	
bookbinding	189
cardboard box mfr.	295
coat hanger mfr.	226
corset mfr.	285
insulated wire, cable mfr.	230
leather goods mfr.	299
piano mfr.	299
rubber goods mfr.	228
Coverer and liner; case	299
Cowman	166
Coxswain	087
Crabber;	
french	182
yorkshire	182
Crabber-	
fishing	171
textile mfr.	182
Cracker; egg	202
Cracker hand (*paper goods mfr.*)	295
Cracker-off	192
Craftsman;	
assistant-	
L.T.E.	276
metal trades	276
engineering	248
general (*building*)	304
leaded light	303
metal; art	276
museum	215
research and development	230
underground (*N.C.B.*)	248
Craftsman-	
government	230
instrument mfr.	246
L.T.E.	248
Cramper (nails, needles)	242
Crane boy	338
Crane man	331
Cranker (*ceramic mfr.*)	204
Cranker-up (*ceramic mfr.*)	204
Crate boy	338
Crater-	
manufacturing-	287
printing	207
Cream hand (liquorice)	202
Creamer (*biscuit mfr.*)	200
Creamery hand	202
,, worker	202
Creaser; vamp	225
Creaser-	
footwear mfr.	225
textile mfr.	199
Creaser and lapper	199
Creeler	199
Creosoter; timber	203
Creper;	182
silk	177
Crewman	334
Cricketer	063
Criminologist	036

	Code number
Crimper;	
detonator	285
edge	177
fibre	177
vamp	225
Crimper-	
cable mfr.	276
flax mfr.	177
footwear mfr.	225
textile mfr.-	182
textile spinning	177
Critic	054
Crochet worker	181
Croft boy	182
,, hand	182
,, lad	182
Crofter-	
farming	107
textile mfr.	182
Cropper; bulb	167
Cropper-	
agriculture	166
metal trades	276
textile mfr.	182
Crossing man; level	321
Croupier	165
Crowder	191
Crowner	175
Crozier	199
Crucible man (metal)	231
Crucible worker	223
Crusher;	
bone	204
burr	182
calamine	184
coal-	204
coal mine	198
malt	197
seed	202
slag	198
Crusher-	
abrasives	198
chemicals	184
minerals-	204
mines and quarries	198
rock (mine, not coal)	198
ceramic mfr.	204
seed crushing	202
Crusherman-	
rock (mine, not coal)	198
Crutter (*coal mine*)	314
Crystal worker; quartz	266
Crystalliser (*sugar confectionery mfr.*)	202
Crystallographer	067
Cuber (*seed crushing*)	202
Cultivator;	
shellfish	171
watercress-	
employee	167
Cupel man	231
Cupola hand (*metal mfr.*)	231
Cupola man	231
Cupper; shell	242
Curate	040
Curator;	
instruments (hospital)	050
picture	030
Curator-	030
art gallery	030
D.O.E.	030
museum	030
Cureman	204
Curer-	
food products	202
rubber	204
skins	173
Curler;	
feather	199
soft	178
yarn	178
Curler (*hat mfr.*)	226
Currier	173
Custodian; castle	157

	Code number
Custodian-	142
security services	140
Cutler;	276
cloth	199
silver	266
Cutlery worker	276
Cut-off man-	
corrugated paper mfr.	203
glass mfr.	192
Cutter;	
acetylene	265
alteration	211
asbestos (*mattress mfr.*)	226
bacon	186
bag-	175
canvas	226
band; rubber	228
bar	276
bass	176
belt-	175
abrasives mfr.	190
bias	226
billet (*steelworks*)	276
biscuit	200
blank (*spoon, fork mfr.*)	242
block-	
linoleum mfr.	276
wallpaper mfr.	276
blouse	211
bobbin	199
boot	175
bottom	315
box (cardboard)	190
box maker's	218
brace	175
bread (*bakery*)	200
brick	223
bridle	175
brilliant (*glass mfr.*)	192
buhl	224
butcher	186
button;	229
pearl	230
cable	276
cap	211
card-	
paper products mfr.	190
textile mfr.	199
carpet	226
chaff	169
cheese	125
circle	242
clay	315
cloth-	
bookbinding	189
clothing mfr.	211
made-up textiles mfr.	211
textile mfr.	182
clothier's	211
clothing	211
coal (*coal mine*)	314
collar-	211
rubber	228
copse	170
cork	230
corset	226
costume	211
cotton	230
design-	
clothing mfr.	226
printing	276
designer	226
diamond-	
glass mfr.	223
die-	
engraving	267
footwear mfr.	175
disc-	
cork goods mfr.	230
rubber mfr.	228
dress (fibre)	176
eastman	211
felt (*textile mfr.*)	226
fibre	176

(Cu)

Cutter; *continued*

	Code number
file	276
film-	
cine film processing	227
photographic film mfr.	190
fittings	175
flag	226
flame	265
flyer	241
frock	211
fur	211
fustian	182
gas	265
gear	241
gimson (*brake lining mfr.*)	204
glass;	223
optical	192
glass lustre	192
glove;	211
boxing	175
gold	276
grass	168
guillotine-	
asbestos-cement goods mfr.	230
metal trades	276
paper goods mfr.	190
wood products mfr.	218
hand (*clothing mfr.*)	211
hat	211
hay (*farming*)	172
heath	172
hedge	172
hemp	176
hosiery	211
insole	175
insulation	230
key	241
knife;	
band	211
hand	211
machine-	211
metal trades	276
knife (*leather glove mfr.*)	211
laces	226
leaf-	
precious metals	266
tobacco	201
leather-	175
bookbinding	189
clothing mfr.	211
tannery	173
lemon	202
lens	192
letter;	
glass	192
wood	224
letter-	
die sinking	267
monumental masons	301
linen (*button mfr.*)	211
lingerie	211
lining-	
clothing mfr.	211
footwear mfr.	175
litho (*ceramic mfr.*)	299
logwood	218
lozenge	202
machine; punching (*metal trades*)	242
machine-	
coal mine	314
clothing mfr.	211
leather goods mfr.	175
mine, not coal	315
manilla	176
mantle	211
material	211
measure	211
meat	186
metal;	276
scrap	265
mica	204
mould	245
mushroom	172

Cutter; *continued*

	Code number
negative	227
nut	270
oxy-acetylene	265
panel-	
metal	276
wood	218
paper	190
pattern;	
iron (*footwear mfr.*)	225
metal	245
paper	227
pattern-	
clothing mfr.	211
footwear mfr.	225
fur goods mfr.	226
jacquard card cutting	199
leather goods mfr.	225
textile mfr.	115
peat	172
peel	202
pile	182
pin;	276
vice	241
plastics	229
plate-	
engraving	276
photographic film mfr.	223
press-	
footwear mfr.	175
leather goods mfr.	175
made-up textiles mfr.	211
paper goods mfr.	190
textile mfr.	226
print	227
profile-	241
footwear mfr.	175
puff	175
punch	267
puzzle; wood	224
rag	176
rail	276
rasp	276
reed	172
rib (*hosiery mfr.*)	226
ribbon-	
typewriter ribbons	230
roll	226
roller	267
rotary-	
metal trades	276
paper products mfr.	190
rubber	228
sack	226
saddle	175
sample-	115
footwear mfr.	175
scallop	182
scrap	265
screw	241
seal	267
sett	301
sheet; asbestos	204
shell; pearl	230
shirt	211
shoe	175
shopman (*butcher's*)	186
silver	276
skin; rabbit	173
skin-	
clothing mfr.	211
tannery	173
slate	301
slipper	175
soap	204
sock (*footwear mfr.*)	175
sole-	175
clog	218
special	211
sponge	204
steel	265
stencil-	
ceramic mfr.	115
metal trades	261

Cutter; *continued*

	Code number
stencil- *continued*	
printing	227
stiffening	175
stilt	223
stock	211
stone	301
strap (*leather goods mfr.*)	175
straw (*farming*)	172
sugar	202
sweet	202
table (*glove mfr.*)	211
tailor's	211
test (*rolling mill*)	276
thread	226
thrum	176
tie	211
timber	218
tip (cemented carbide goods mfr.)	276
tobacco	201
tool (*metal trades*)	245
top	315
transferrer's	299
tread	228
trimming	211
tube-	
glass	192
metal	276
paper	190
turf	168
type; wood	224
tyre	228
under	211
underclothing	211
upholstery	226
velvet	182
veneer	218
wafer	200
waste (*textile mfr.*)	199
watercress	172
willow	170
wiper	176
wire	276
wood (*forestry*)	170
worm	241

Cutter-

	Code number
bone, etc.	230
clothing	211
precious stones	266
abrasive paper, cloth mfr.	190
artificial flower mfr.	226
bakery	200
bookbinding	189
butcher's shop	186
candle mfr.	230
canvas goods mfr.	226
ceramic mfr.	223
clothing mfr.	211
coach trimming	226
coal mine	314
embroidering	211
fancy goods mfr.	230
flour confectionery mfr.	200
food products mfr.	202
footwear mfr.	175
furniture mfr.	218
glass mfr.	223
glove mfr.	211
glue mfr.	204
haberdashery mfr.	211
hat mfr.	211
hosiery and knitwear mfr.	211
leather goods mfr.	175
lens mfr.	192
linoleum mfr.	204
metal trades-	276
boiler mfr.	265
cable mfr.	276
cutlery mfr.	242
nail mfr.	242
perambulator mfr.	242
shipbuilding	265
steel pen mfr.	242

(Cu—De)

	Code number
Cutter- *continued*	
mine, not coal	315
packing case (wood) mfr.	218
paper mfr.	190
paper pattern mfr.	227
paper products mfr.	190
plastics goods mfr.	229
powder puff mfr.	175
printing	190
rubber goods mfr.	228
soft toy mfr.	226
sugar confectionery mfr.	202
tannery	173
textile mfr.-	199
textile finishing	182
woollen, worsted mfr.	182
tobacco mfr.	201
upholstering	226
woodworking	218
work basket lining	226
Cutter and alterer (bricks)	223
Cutter and booker	266
Cutter and caulker (*shipbuilding*)	262
Cutter and engraver; stencil	276
Cutter and fitter	211
Cutter and grinder; tool	240
Cutter boy (paper)	227
Cutterman; coal	314
Cutterman-	
coal mine	314
paper mfr.	190
Cutter down (*rolling mill*)	270
Cutter-grinder (*metal trades*)	241
Cutter-off-	
metal trades-	276
iron pipe mfr.	244
Cutter-out (*cutlery mfr.*)	270
Cutter-through (*steelworks*)	269
Cutter-up; scrap	276
Cycle hand	285
,, worker	285
Cyclist	063
Cylinderman (*paper mfr.*)	188
Cytologist	065
Cytotaxonomist	065

D

	Code number
D.C.O.	115
Daily girl	151
Dairy hand-	
farming	166
milk processing	202
Dairyman-	
farming	166
margarine mfr.	202
milk processing	202
retail trade-	125
delivery round	128
Dairy worker *see* Dairyman	
Damper; cop	182
Damper-	
laundry	162
textile mfr.	182
Damperman (*paper mfr.*)	188
Dancer	059
Danseuse	059
Darner-	
hotel, etc.	226
textile mfr.-	183
sack repairing	226
Darner and mender (*textile mfr.*)	183
Datal hand-	
coal mine	345
mine, not coal	L346
Datal man *see* Datal hand	
Datal worker *see* Datal hand	
Dataller *see* Datal hand	
Dateler *see* Datal hand	

	Code number
Dateller *see* Datal hand	
Dauber; ladle (*iron and steelworks*)	L344
Dauber (*coal gas, coke ovens*)	L341
Dayman-	
mining see Datal hand	
theatre	L346
Day wage man *see* Datal hand	
Day worker *see* Datal hand	
Deacon	040
Dealer;	
accessories; motor	101
antiques	101
car	101
catsmeat	186
cattle	101
chipped potato	104
egg	101
estate	134
exchange; foreign (*banking*)	007
firewood	130
fish	187
fish and chip	104
game	101
general	131
investment	007
log; fire	130
money	007
paper; waste	131
pig	101
poultry	101
property	134
rag	131
rag and bone	131
scrap	131
share	007
stock and share	007
store; marine	101
travelling	130
tripe	101
tyre	101
Dealer-	
finance	007
wholesale, retail trade-	101
market trading	130
party plan sales	132
Dean-	040
university	031
Deburrer	244
Decatiser	182
Deck boy	317
Deck hand-	
fishing	171
milk processing	202
shipping	317
Deckie (*fishing*)	171
Declarator	115
Decorator;	
aerograph	281
aerographing (*ceramic mfr.*)	279
art	299
cake	185
card (greeting, etc., cards)	295
display	055
floral	064
glass-	192
painting	299
house	282
interior-	055
building and contracting	282
slip	279
tin plate	207
Decorator-	282
ceramics	279
flour confectionery	185
leather cloth	182
sugar confectionery	202
building and contracting	282
metal trades	282
wallpaper mfr.	227
Decoy man	172
Degger	182
Degreaser-	
metal trades	270

	Code number
Degreaser- *continued*	
tannery	173
Dehairer; pig	186
Dehydrator man; tar	184
Delegate; union; trade	024
Delicatessen	101
Delimer	173
Delinter	198
Deliverer;	
allowance	123
book	124
car	327
coal	326
milk	128
newspaper	124
parcel	124
Deliverer (*textile mfr.*)	338
Delivery boy-	124
bakery	128
dairy	128
Deliveryman;	
baker's	128
coal	326
parcels (*railways*)	326
Deliveryman-	326
laundry	128
newsagents	124
retail milk trade	128
textile mfr.	338
Delver (*mine, not coal*)	315
Demographer	011
Demolisher	316
Demolition worker	316
Demonstrator;	
machine tool	134
mechanisation (*coal mine*)	081
technical	134
Demonstrator-	134
educational establishments-	033
primary and secondary schools	033
university	031
Demonstrator-consultant	134
Demonstrator-salesman	134
Denierer (*man-made fibre mfr.*)	196
Dentist	042
Depalleter; concrete tile	230
Depositor-	
electroplating	269
welding	270
Depository hand (*sugar confectionery mfr.*)	202
Depot hand	335
Depotman-	335
blast furnace	338
Depot worker	335
Deputy-	
coal mine	F314
lodging house	F151
mine, not coal	F315
Dermatologist	041
Derrick floor man (*oil wells*)	315
Derrickman-	331
oil wells	315
De-ruster	270
Descaler (*steelworks*)	270
Deseamer (*steelworks*)	265
Designer;	
aircraft	069
architectural	082
art	055
bank-note	056
body (*vehicle mfr.*)	056
book	056
card (*printing*)	056
carton	056
chief	F079
circuit (*telecommunications*)	071
cloth	056
clothing	057
commercial	056
computer	072
concrete; reinforced	082
die	079

29

(De—Di)

Designer; *continued*
- display ... 055
- dress ... 057
- electric ... 071
- electrical (control systems) ... 071
- electronics ... 072
- embroidery ... 056
- exhibition ... 055
- formwork ... 082
- furniture ... 056
- garden ... 168
- gem ... 056
- graphic ... 079
- handbag ... 056
- industrial ... 056
- interior ... 055
- jewellery ... 056
- lace ... 056
- lithographic ... 056
- machinery; electrical ... 071
- mechanical ... 079
- nautical ... 069
- naval ... 069
- packaging ... 056
- pattern (*textile printing*) ... 056
- pottery ... 056
- printer's ... 056
- project *see* Engineer-prof.-
- roll (*steelworks*) ... 079
- set ... 055
- shopfitting ... 056
- stage ... 055
- stamp ... 056
- structural ... 082
- systems (*railway signalling*) ... 071
- textile ... 056
- textile print ... 056
- tool ... 079
- toy ... 056
- trade mark ... 055
- typographical ... 205

Designer-
- ceramics ... 056
- clothing ... 057
- footwear ... 056
- glassware ... 056
- leather goods ... 056
- plastics goods ... 056
- scenery ... 055
- wallpaper ... 056
- wood products ... 056
- *advertising* ... 055
- *artificial flower mfr.* ... 056
- *flour confectionery mfr.* ... 185
- *fur goods mfr.* ... 057
- *metal trades* ... 056
- *millinery mfr.* ... 057
- *rubber goods mfr.* ... 056
- *soft toy mfr.* ... 056
- *textile mfr.* ... 056

Designer and transferer (*linoleum mfr.*) ... 115

Designer-cutter-
- *clothing mfr.* ... 226
- *paper products mfr.* ... 227

Designer-detailer ... 079
Designer-draughtsman ... 079
Desilveriser ... 231
Desizer ... 199
Despatch hand ... 333
  ,, man ... 333
  ,, worker ... 333
Despatcher;
- flight ... 086
- goods ... 333
- radio ... 122
- traffic (*aircraft*) ... 115
- train ... 297
Destroyer (pest) ... 165
Destructor man; refuse ... 348
Detective;
- hotel ... 140
- private ... 140
- store ... 140

Detective-
- airport ... 137
- docks ... 137
- government ... 137
- *police service* ... 137
- *private detective agency* ... 140
- *railways* ... 137
- *retail trade* ... 140
Detector; crack (*metal mfr.*) ... 286
Detonator worker (*chemical mfr.*) ... 230
Developer;
- estate ... 134
- film ... 227
- property ... 134
Developer-
- *coal mine* ... 314
- *photographic processing* ... 227
- *textile mfr.* ... 182
Development worker (*coal mine*) 314
Devil (*printing*) ... L346
Devilman (*paper mfr.*) ... 176
Deviller ... 176
Devulcaniser man (*rubber reclamation*) ... 204
Dewer ... 182
Diagnostician-
H.M. Dockyard-
- electrical ... 259
- mechanical ... 248
Diarist ... 054
Die man (*plastics goods mfr.*) ... 195
Dietician ... 053
Digester ... 184
  ,, man ... 184
  ,, worker ... 184
Digger;
- bait ... 171
- coal (*coal mine*) ... 314
- grave ... 316
- peat ... 172
- trench ... 313
- turf ... 168
Digger (*mine, not coal*) ... 315
Digger man ... 330
Dingman ... 261
Dinker (*coal mine*) ... 314
Diplomat ... 020
Dipper;
- acid ... 270
- automatic (*ceramic mfr.*) ... 279
- brass ... 270
- cellulose ... 299
- chocolate ... 202
- core ... 270
- enamel ... 299
- fondant ... 202
- galvanizing ... 269
- glove ... 228
- hand (*sugar confectionery mfr.*) ... 202
- machine (*ceramic mfr.*) ... 279
- metal ... 269
- paint ... 299
- rubber ... 228
- tank (*petroleum distribution*) 297
- toffee ... 202
- wire ... 269
Dipper-
- *ceramic mfr.* ... 279
- *leather dressing* ... 173
- *match mfr.* ... 230
- *metal trades* ... 299
  - *arc welding electrode mfr.* 269
  - *galvanizing* ... 269
  - *precious metal, plate mfr.* 236
- *oil refining* ... 297
- *paper mfr.* ... 203
- *rubber mfr.* ... 228
- *sugar confectionery mfr.* ... 202
- *textile mfr.* ... 182
Dipper and stripper ... 270
Director; *see also notes* p.4
- art ... 055

Director; *continued*
- casting (*entertainment*) ... M059
- commercial ... 013
- divisional (*Red Cross*) ... M039
- film ... M059
- financial ... 006
- funeral ... 163
- housing ... M039
- managing *see* Manager
- media ... 014
- museum ... 030
- musical ... 060
- regional-
  - government ... 021
  - P.O. ... 099
- sales ... 013
- sales and export ... 013
- stage ... M059
- technical ... 078
- of contracts (*government*) ... 016
- of education ... 035
- of music (*entertainment*) ... M060
- of photography ... M059
- of production (*entertainment*) M059
- of programmes ... M059
- of research-
  - biological science ... 065
  - chemistry ... 066
  - physical science ... 067
- of social services ... M039
Director (*W.R.N.S.*) ... M135
Director and Secretary ... 023
Dis hand ... 227
Disc man ... 192
Discharger-
- *coal gas, coke ovens* ... 338
- *docks* ... 334
Disinfector;
- fitter ... 276 ... 165
Disintegrator-
- *asbestos composition goods mfr.* ... 176
- *food products mfr.* ... 202
Dismantler;
- engine; aircraft ... 250
- furnace ... 312
- machinery ... 276
- ship ... 276
Dismantler-
- *building and contracting* ... 316
- *coal mine* ... 314
- *scrap merchant, breakers* ... 276
Dispatch hand ... 333
Dispatch man-
- *bakery* ... 333
- *catering* ... 146
Dispense hand (*catering*) ... 146
Dispenser; drink ... 145
Dispenser-
- food and beverages ... 146
- *bakery* ... 297
- *licensed trade* ... 145
Display hand-
- *firework mfr.* ... 064
- *retail trade-* ... 055
- shelf filling ... 126
Displayman; window ... 058
Displayman-
- *printing* ... 205
- *retail trade-* ... 055
- shelf filling ... 126
Dissector (*clothing mfr.*) ... 211
Distiller- ... 184
- *lead, zinc refining* ... 231
Distributor;
- bill ... 124
- circular ... 124
- coal ... 101
- film ... 134
- food ... 101
- freight (*railways*) ... 097
- leaflet ... 124
- paste (*aluminium*) ... 270
- tract ... 124

30

(Di—Dr)

	Code number
Distributor; *continued*	
weft	338
work	338
Distributor-	
manufacturing	338
wholesale, retail trade	101
Ditcher;	316
stone	301
Diver	316
Divider;	
hand-	246
bakery	200
mathematical instrument	246
thermometer	246
Divider-	
clothing mfr.	299
type foundry	298
Divider hand (*bakery*)	200
Divider man (*bakery*)	200
Diviner; water	165
Dock crew	334
Dock man-	334
ship repairing	L344
Dock worker-	334
dry dock	L344
Docker; cork	230
Docker (*docks*)	334
Dockside worker	334
Dockyard worker	L344
Doctor;	041
saw	276
Dodger; can	176
Dodger (*textile finishing*)	176
Doffer;	199
ring	177
Doffer and setter	199
Dogger	270
Dogger-on	270
Dogger-up (tubes)	270
Dollier-	
silversmiths	243
textile mfr.	179
Dolly hand	182
Dollyer	179
Dolomite man (*iron, steelworks*)	204
Domestic	151
Domestic worker	151
Donkeyman-	331
shipping	F317
Door boy-	
catering, hotels, etc.	165
iron, steelworks	L344
Doorman; furnace	270
Doorman-	165
coke ovens	L341
forging	270
Doper-	
aircraft mfr.	299
leather dressing	173
Doubler;	
asbestos	177
cloth	199
derby	177
ring	177
warp	199
Doubler-	
metal rolling	270
textile mfr.-	177
textile bleaching	199
textile dyeing	199
Dough man	200
Draffman (whisky)	197
Drafter;	
fibre	176
policy (*insurance*)	115
slipper	176
stone	301
Drafter (*brush mfr.*)	176
Draftsman; parliamentary	001
Dragger;	
bar	231
pipe (*brickworks*)	338
set	338
skip	338

	Code number
Dragger-down	270
Drainman	L346
Drainage worker	316
Drainer-	316
brewery	L346
Dramatist	054
Draper;	101
armhole	162
credit	132
market	130
travelling	130
Draughter *see* Drafter	
Draughtsman;	079
cartographical	079
chief	F079
embroidery	115
geographical	079
lace	115
lithographic	205
photographic (chart)	079
printer's	205
Draughtsman-engineer	079
Draughtsman-surveyor	079
Drawer;	
bar	234
brick	338
brush	230
card	176
chock (*coal mine*)	314
cloth-	289
textile finishing	182
coke (*coke ovens*)	338
cotton	176
fine-	
clothes repairing	183
textile mfr.	183
fork	270
french	183
gear	179
hair	176
kiln-	
ceramic mfr.	338
chemical mfr.	184
lime-	
lime burning	204
mine, not coal	338
oven (*ceramic mfr.*)	338
pick	233
plate (wire)	270
prop-	315
coal mine	314
rod-	
glass	192
metal	234
salvage (*coal mine*)	314
steel-	234
coal mine	314
strip (metal)	234
tape (metal)	234
timber-	
coal mine	314
mine, not coal	315
tube-	
glass	192
metal	234
waste (*coal mine*)	314
wire	234
wool	176
worsted	176
yarn	176
Drawer-	
glass	192
metal	234
brush mfr.	230
ceramic mfr.	338
coal mine	338
glass mfr.	192
metal trades-	234
forging	233
puddling	231
zinc refining	231
mine, not coal	338
paper mfr.	338

	Code number
Drawer- *continued*	
textile mfr.-	176
jute mfr.	179
lace mfr.	289
textile finishing	182
textile weaving	179
Drawer and marker (*assay office*)	270
Drawer and setter (*brick mfr.*)	191
Drawer-in (*textile mfr.*)	179
Drawer-off-	
coal mine	338
textile mfr.	199
Drawing hand-	
brush, broom mfr.	230
textile mfr.	176
Drawtwist operative; nylon	177
Dray boy	329
Drayman	326
Dredgeman-	330
shell fish	171
Dredger-	330
shell fish	171
Dredgerman	330
Dredgermaster	F330
Dreep man (*by-products mfr.*)	184
Drencher	173
Dresser;	
bag	182
bass	176
bow	276
box;	287
axle	244
brick (*brick mfr.*)	223
bristle	176
card	276
casings; sausage	202
casting	244
cloth	182
coloured	179
concrete	230
core	244
cork	230
diamond	266
doll	230
fibre	176
flour	202
fly	230
fowl	187
frame (rolling mill)	265
fur	173
game	187
gypsum	204
hair; horse	176
hair-	
broom, brush mfr.	176
hairdressing	159
heald	276
iron	244
kerb	301
leather	173
lime	204
meat	186
metal	244
pipe	244
plate	244
potato	172
poultry	187
sack	182
scissors	276
seed	202
sett	301
shirt (*shirt mfr.*)	162
silk	176
skin-	173
sausage mfr.	202
slate	301
steel	244
stick	224
stone-	301
concrete products mfr.	230
tin	198

31

(Dr)

	Code number
Dresser; *continued*	
tripe	202
tube	244
wallstone	301
warp	179
weld	276
wheel	244
wig	165
window	058
wire	270
wood	224
woollen	182
yarn	179
Dresser-	
entertainment	165
footwear mfr.	175
fur dressing	173
leather dressing	173
metal trades-	244
bolt, nut mfr.	270
typefounding	276
mine, not coal	301
stone dressing	301
textile mfr.-	176
felt mfr.	182
rope, cord, twine mfr.	182
textile finishing	182
textile weaving	179
Dressmaker	210
Drier see **Dryer**	
Driftman (*coal mine*)	314
Drifter-	
coal mine	314
mine, not coal	315
Drill man (*mine, not coal*)	315
Driller;	
air	241
asbestos	230
axle box	241
barrel	241
brush	230
button	229
casement (metal)	241
ceramic	223
circle (*textile machinery mfr.*)	241
die; diamond	266
faller	241
frame	241
gas burner	241
gas ring	241
glass	192
hackle	241
hand	262
hydraulic	262
machine-	
metal trades	241
mine, not coal	315
mica	230
micanite	230
pin	241
plate	262
porcelain	223
portable	262
pottery	223
radial	241
radial arm	241
rail	241
rim	241
sample-	
mine, not coal	315
steelworks	262
shipwright's	262
test (steel)	262
tip	241
tool room	240
vertical	241
well-	315
offshore	F315
wheel	241
wire; diamond	266
wood	218
Driller-	
asbestos composition goods mfr.	230

	Code number
Driller- *continued*	
civil engineering contracting	315
coal mine-	314
workshops	241
metal trades-	241
boiler mfr.	262
constructional engineering	262
shipbuilding	262
mine, not coal	315
plastics goods mfr.	229
well sinking	315
Driver;	
ambulance	155
angle dozer	330
articulator	326
assistant-	
iron and steelworks	231
textile spinning	177
belt	338
boat	317
bogie	332
bowser	326
bridge;	338
swing	338
bulldozer	330
bus	325
cab	327
calender (*insulated wire, cable mfr.*)	230
car;	
auto	319
blast furnace	338
charger	332
coke (*gas ovens*)	332
electric (*steelworks*)	338
larry	332
motor	327
rail	319
ross	338
scale	332
shuttle	319
tram	325
carriage	327
carrier; straddle	331
cart	338
caster	270
charge	332
charger-	
coal gas, coke ovens	332
steelworks	338
chase side	330
climax	338
closer (*wire rope mfr.*)	276
coach	325
compo (*chemical mfr.*)	184
compressor	255
control (*steelworks*)	231
controller (*steelworks*)	338
conveyor	338
crane	331
crawler-	330
agricultural contracting	169
crusher (*mine, not coal*)	198
delivery-	326
car delivery service	327
derrick	331
diesel-	
coal mine	319
railways	319
digger	330
drag-line	330
dredger	330
drill (*mine, not coal*)	315
drott	330
drum (*steelworks*)	331
dumper	332
elevator	331
engine;	
cable	331
diesel (*coal mine*)	319
haulage	331
locomotive	319
shunting	319
traction	326

	Code number
Driver; *continued*	
engine; *continued*	
winding	331
engine-	255
agriculture	169
mining	255
railways	319
shipping	317
euclid	332
excavator	330
exhauster (*gas works*)	348
extruding	195
fan	348
faucet	315
ferry	327
gantry	331
gear (*rolling mill*)	232
gearhead (*coal mine*)	332
gig	182
goods	326
grab	331
grader	330
greenbatt	338
guide; coke	338
hammer	270
haulage; motor	326
haulage-	
mining	331
road transport	326
hauler (*coal mine*)	331
heading; hard	314
hearse	327
hoist	331
horse	338
house; power	255
hyster	332
incline	331
internal	332
J.C.B.	330
launch	317
library; mobile	326
lift;	331
fork	332
line; drag	330
lister	338
loader-	326
airport	335
building and contracting	330
loco	319
locomotive	319
lorry	326
machine;	
armouring	230
cable	276
cabling	276
insulating	230
lapping	230
layer-up	230
spreading (asphalt, concrete)	330
stoking	332
tubing	230
machine-	
agriculture	169
asbestos-cement goods mfr.	204
civil engineering	330
gas works	332
magnet (*steelworks*)	331
mail;	
motor	326
paddy (*coal mine*)	331
manipulator (*steelworks*)	338
mixer; concrete	204
motor;	
dumpy	332
electric	338
railway	326
telpher	331
motor-	326
coal mine	255
funeral direction	327
mower; motor	168
navvy	330
omnibus	325
paddy (*coal mine*)	331

(Dr—Dy)

	Code number
Driver; *continued*	
pile	330
plant; intake	333
plant (*building and contracting*)	330
police; civilian	327
press	270
printer's	207
pump	348
racing	063
rack (*rolling mill*)	270
ram	338
ransom	338
refuse	326
rest (*rolling mill*)	270
roll	232
roller-	330
oil wells	315
steelworks	232
rolley	326
rolly	326
saw (*metal trades*)	276
scammell	326
scoop	330
scraper	330
sentinel	330
shear(s) (*metal trades*)	276
shearer (*coal mine*)	314
shovel	330
shunter	319
skid (*rolling mill*)	270
skip (*blast furnace*)	331
spray; water (*rolling mill*)	270
stacker	332
stenter	182
surface (*coal mine*)	319
sweeper	327
table (*rolling mill*)	270
tandem (*coal mine*)	331
tank; oil	326
tanker	326
taxi	327
telpher	331
test (*motor vehicle mfr.*)	248
tilter	231
tip	331
tipper	326
tool; mechanical	330
tractor-	
agriculture	169
building and contracting	326
forestry	170
local government	326
manufacturing	326
mining	326
opencast mining	326
road transport	326
train	319
tram	325
tranport-	326
internal transport	332
traverser	338
trepanner	314
trolley	332
trolleybus	325
truck;	
bogy	332
clamp	332
electric	332
fork lift	332
lister	338
power	332
ransom	332
stacker	332
works	332
truck-	332
road transport	326
tudal	230
tug	317
turbine	255
turbo-blower	255
van	326
vehicle;	
articulated	326

	Code number
Driver; *continued*	
vehicle; *continued*	
motor	326
wagon	326
whim	338
winch	331
Driver-	
agricultural machinery	169
vehicles-	
goods transport	326
passenger transport- bus, coach	327
bus, coach	325
works trucks	332
coal mine-	
above ground	319
below ground-	
pony	338
train	319
L.T.E.	325
mine, not coal-	
above ground	332
below ground	315
railways	319
shipping	317
Driver and collector-	115
car delivery service	327
coal mine	327
laundry	128
Driver-attendant; ambulance	155
Driver-conductor	325
Driver-fitter-	326
public service vehicle	325
Driver-handyman	327
Driver-instructor-	052
public transport	034
Driver-loader (*airport*)	335
Driver-mechanic-	326
agricultural machinery	169
bus, coach	325
passenger transport vehicles	327
Driver-postman	123
Driver-salesman	128
Driver-storeman	333
Driver-warehouseman	333
Drop man (*blast furnace*)	231
Dropper; fire (*railways*)	L346
Dropper-	
bacon and meat curing	202
oil refining	184
sugar confectionery mfr.	202
sugar refining	202
textile mfr.	180
Dropperman	203
Drosser	231
Drossman	231
Drover	172
Drowner	316
Drug room man	333
Druggist-	044
wholesale trade	101
Drum and cagehand (*tannery*)	173
Drumhand	173
Drum lad (*steelworks*)	270
Drum man (*tannery*)	173
Drummer; glycerine	287
Drummer-	
entertainment	060
tannery	173
Dry dock worker	L344
Dry man-	
china clay	204
mine, not coal	158
Dry worker (*paper mfr.*)	188
Dryer;	
bacon	202
can (*textile mfr.*)	199
clay	204
clip (*textile mfr.*)	199
cloth	199
colour (*dyestuff mfr.*)	184
core (*foundry*)	270
cylinder (*textile mfr.*)	199
dyed (*textile mfr.*)	199
felt	199

	Code number
Dryer; *continued*	
gelatine	184
glue	184
grain (*malting*)	197
hair	199
kiln (*wood*)	203
machine (*textile mfr.*)	199
ore	204
pearl	204
plate (*photographic*)	227
pulp	202
rag	199
salt	204
sand	204
tobacco	201
veneer	203
warp	199
wool	199
yarn	199
Dryer-	
abrasive paper mfr.	203
cereal foods mfr.	202
chemical mfr.	184
laundry	162
metal trades	204
paper mfr.	188
photographic film mfr.	227
photographic film processing	227
refractory goods mfr.	191
soap mfr.	184
tannery	173
textile mfr.	199
vulcanised fibre mfr.	203
Dryerman *see* Dryer	
Drying man *see* Dryer	
Drysalter	101
Dubber (*textile mfr.*)	199
Duffer	338
Duler (*wool*)	176
Dumper-	
coal mine	338
mine, not coal	332
textile mfr.	182
Duplicator-	119
tape recordings	348
Dustman	336
Duster; colour	279
Duster-	
ceramic mfr.	279
coal mine	299
printing	227
Dye house operative (*textile mfr.*)	182
Dye house worker (*textile mfr.*)	182
Dye worker; natural	184
Dyer;	
beam	182
black (*textile mfr.*)	182
brush (*leather dressing*)	173
calico	182
carpet	182
chrome (*leather*)	173
clothes	182
colour	182
cop	182
cord	182
drum (*leather*)	173
fibre	182
fur	173
fustian	182
garment	182
glove	173
hair-	182
hairdressing	159
hank	182
hat	182
head	F182
jig	182
job	182
master	F182
operative	182
piece	182
skein	182
skin	173
technical	078

(Dy—En)

	Code number
Dyer; *continued*	
vat-	182
leather	173
vessel	182
warp	182
winch	182
yarn	182
Dyer-	
grass, straw, etc.	182
leather	173
plastics	204
textiles	182
artificial flowers mfr.	182
button mfr.	299
cable mfr.	182
dyeing and cleaning	182
fancy goods mfr.	182
hairdressing	159
leather goods mfr.	173
tannery	173
textile mfr.	182
Dyer and cleaner	162
Dyer's operative	182

E

	Code number
E.A. (*Dept. of Emp. Job Centre*)	F112
E.D.H.	317
E.T.G.II	081
Ebonite worker	228
Ecclesiastic	040
Ecologist	065
Economist	011
Edgeman	203
Edger;	
gilt	189
gold (*ceramic mfr.*)	279
Edger-	
ceramic mfr.	279
lens mfr.	192
Editor;	M054
computer	115
dubbing	062
film	059
map	079
sales	M054
sound	062
sub	054
technical	M054
Egger and washer	173
Elasticator	212
Electrician;	253
auto	253
chief-	F253
shipping	F317
radio	258
Electroformer	269
Electrologist	165
Electrolysist	165
Electrotyper	206
Electro-brasser (screws)	269
Electro-chemist	066
Electro-encephalographer	050
Electro-plater	236
Electro-therapeutist	047
Electro-therapist	047
Elevator man	333
Embalmer	165
Embellisher of wood	224
Embosser;	
cloth	182
glass	192
hilt (sword)	266
leather (*bookbinding*)	189
Embosser-	
glass mfr.	192
hat mfr.	227
jewellery, plate mfr.	266
leathercloth mfr.	182
leather dressing	173

	Code number
Embosser- *continued*	
metal trades	242
paper goods mfr.	227
plastics goods mfr.	195
printing	227
textile mfr.	182
wood products mfr.	224
Embroiderer	212
Embryologist	065
Employee;	L346
bank	115
Emptier;	
biscuit	338
press; electrical	193
press (*ceramic mfr.*)	193
rubbish (*steelworks*)	338
wagon (*coal mine*)	338
ware	338
wheel	L339
Emptier-	L346
ceramic mfr.	338
charcoal mfr.	204
Enamel man (*stove mfr.*)	299
Enamel worker	299
Enameller-	299
ceramic mfr.	279
Encloser	115
End boy; back	226
Ender-	
textile mfr.-	199
flax mfr.	176
Endocrinologist	065
Engineman;	
donkey-	
coal mine	331
shipping	317
haulage	331
hydraulic	255
malt	197
winding	331
Engineman-	255
railways	319
shipping	317
Engine room man (*shipping*)	317
Engine worker	255
Engineer; *see also notes* p.4	
acoustical	259
administrative *see Engineer-prof.-*	
advisory *see Engineer-prof.-*	
aerial	283
aero	248
aeronautical	069
agricultural-	248
professional	076
aircraft-	248
maintenance	250
alarm; burglar	259
applications- *see Engineer-prof.-*	
industrial *see Engineer-prof.-*	
area-	248
technical	071
P.O.	091
armament	248
assembly (*vehicle mfr.*)	248
assessing (*insurance*)	005
assistant-	
mechanical	248
unit (*coal mine*)	248
broadcasting	081
coal mine-	091
N.C.B.; H.Q. *see Engineer-prof.-*	
electricity board	071
gas board	081
government	081
local government	068
manufacturing-	081
professional *see Engineer-prof.-*	
P.O.	F256
shipping	087

	Code number
Engineer; *continued*	
automobile-	249
professional	069
bakery	248
bank	092
barge	248
battery	276
boiler	347
boilerhouse	347
boring-	315
professional	068
borough	068
branch (*electricity board*)	071
brewer's	248
building	068
cable	259
cable and wireless	259
cables (*N.C.B.*)	091
calibration	246
capstan	240
carbonisation	073
carding	248
carriage and wagon	091
catering	248
ceramic	078
charge-	
coal mine	F253
electricity board	094
chartered *see Engineer-prof.-*	
chemical	073
chief; area (*N.C.B.*)	069
chief-*see also Engineer-prof.-*	
maintenance	091
boat, barge	317
electricity board	094
fishing	317
gas board	091
shipping	087
cinema	253
cinematograph	246
circuit-	071
cinema	253
city	068
civil	068
colliery	091
combustion	078
commercial	133
commissioning-	081
professional	
see also Engineer-prof.-	
communication;	071
radio	072
computer-	259
design	072
conditioning; air-	260
professional	076
constructional-	263
professional	068
consultant *see Engineer-prof.-*	
consulting *see Engineer-prof.-*	
consumers (*electricity board*)	133
contract(s)-	081
professional	
see also Engineer-prof.-	
contractor's	068
control;	
production	074
quality	075
strata	068
vision	062
weight (*aircraft mfr.*)	079
control (*electricity board*)	094
co-ordinating *see Engineer-prof.-*	
corrosion	076
county	068
crane	248
customer (*office machinery mfr.*)	251
cycle	248
dairy	248
dental	220
depot (*transport*)	091

34

(En)

	Code number
Engineer; *continued*	
design-*see also* Engineer-*prof.*-	
mechanical ...	070
designing *see* Engineer-*prof.*-	
development-*see also* Engineer-*prof.*-	
mechanical ...	070
diesel- ...	248
professional	069
vehicle-	249
vehicle mfr.	248
distribution- ...	081
electricity board	094
district-	248
electricity board	094
railways	092
divisional-	
gas board	091
transport	091
dock(s)	068
dockboard	068
dockyard	248
domestic	260
drainage	068
dredger	317
drilling (*mining*)	068
electrical;	
area (*N.C.B.*)	071
assistant	253
auto	253
charge; assistant (*electricity board*)	094
chartered *see* Engineer-*prof.*-	
chief	071
colliery; assistant	F253
group (*N.C.B.*)	071
head	071
maintenance	253
n.o.s.-	254
professional	071
coal mine	253
gas board	091
P.O.; cable ship	087
shipping	087
senior	071
unit	253
works	071
electrical and mechanical-	253
professional	071
electro-mechanical	253
electronic-	072
maintenance	259
elevators; grain	248
environmental	076
equipment	071
erection	248
estate	248
estimating	004
excavator	248
executive (*P.O.*)	081
expediting	074
experimental	076
explosive (*N.C.B.*)	073
explosives (*demolition*)	316
extrusion (*plastics goods mfr.*)	195
fabrication	248
factory; chief (*P.O.*)	091
field-	248
computer servicing	259
radio, television servicing	258
office machinery mfr.	251
film	253
filter	248
fire	138
first-	087
fishing	317
fleet (vehicle)	249
flight	085
foundry	248
fourth	087
freezing	087
fuel	078

	Code number
Engineer; *continued*	
furnace	248
garage	249
garrison	092
gas	078
gas and water	260
generating (*electricity board*)	071
geophysical	067
glass	078
grade I, II, III (*government*) *see* Engineer-*prof.*-	
grade A, B (*broadcasting*)	072
ground	250
group *see* Engineer-*prof.*-	
handling; materials *see* Engineer-*prof.*-	
heating-	260
professional	076
heat and domestic	260
heating and lighting	260
heating and plumbing	260
heating and ventilating-	260
professional	076
heavy-	248
professional	069
helicopter	248
highway(s)	068
horological	247
horticultural	076
hosiery	248
hospital	091
house;	248
assistant	248
hovercraft	248
hydraulic-	248
professional	069
shipping	087
illuminating-	253
professional	071
industrial	075
injection; fuel	248
inspecting *see* Engineer-*prof.*-	
inspection-	286
professional	069
insurance	090
inspector	286
installation-	248
computer	259
heating and ventilating	260
radio, television	258
telephones	256
electrical contracting	253
electricity board	081
P.O.	256
instrument;	246
chief *see* Engineer-*prof.*-	
insulating	316
insulation	316
insurance	005
investigating; technical	090
investigation; defect	248
irrigation	068
laboratory;	080
radio	072
lathe	239
launch	317
laundry	248
layout; plant	074
liaison *see* Engineer-*prof.*-	
lift-	248
L.T.E.	091
light	248
lighting	071
line-	
oil refining	248
P.O.	257
locomotive-	248
professional	069
lubrication	076
machine-	248
domestic electrical appliances	253
office machines	251
machinery	248

	Code number
Engineer; *continued*	
mains; electrical	257
mains-	
electricity board	257
gas board	260
maintenance;	
aircraft	250
chief	091
electrical	253
planned (*N.C.B.*)	091
plant	248
tyre	291
maintenance-	248
aircraft	250
electronics	259
heating and ventilating	260
instruments	246
office machines	251
professional	091
radio, television	258
vehicles	249
electricity board	091
P.O.	256
making; tool	245
manufacturing	276
marine;	
chief-	069
shipping	087
senior	069
superintendent	091
marine-	248
professional	069
boat, barge	317
shipping	087
materials *see* Engineer-*prof.*-	
mechanical;	
area (*N.C.B.*)	069
chief	069
colliery-	091
assistant	F248
group (*N.C.B.*)	069
n.o.s.-	241
professional	069
gas board	091
unit (*coal mine*)	091
mechanical and electrical-	248
professional-	069
electricity board	071
mechanisation	069
meter	246
methods	010
microwave	072
mill-	248
professional	069
milling	240
mining	068
model	248
monotype	248
motor;	249
road (*railways*)	069
municipal	068
n.o.s.-	241
professional *see also* Engineer-*prof.*-	
aircraft	085
boat, barge	317
broadcasting	259
coal mine (below ground)	248
fishing	317
P.O.	256
shipping	087
nuclear	076
oil	068
operations (*electricity board*)	069
optical	192
P.O.	256
packaging	078
paper	248
patent	090
performance *see* Engineer-*prof.*-	
petroleum	068
photographic	246
pipe	260

35

(En)

Engineer; continued	Code number	Engineer; continued	Code number	Engineer; continued	Code number
planer; steel	240	service- continued		tool; machine-	248
planing	240	heating and ventilating	260	professional	069
planning	075	office machinery-	259	tool room	245
plant-	248	electrical	253	traction; electric	071
professional	091	mechanical	251	traffic	076
plastics	073	radio, television	258	transmission; power-	071
plumbing	260	telephone	256	television	072
plumbing and heating	260	*cinema*	253	transmitter; radio	259
pneumatic	248	*electrical engineering*	253	transport	249
post office	256	*electricity board*	253	trawler	317
potter's	248	*engineering*	248	treatment; heat	237
power	071	*heating engineers*	260	Trinity House	248
power and efficiency	071	*oil company*	248	tug	317
powerhouse	253	servicing *see* Engineer; service		turbine	255
precision	246	shafting	248	turner	239
pre-cost	076	shift-	248	turner; lathe	239
preparation; coal	068	*electricity board*	094	typewriter	251
press; rotary	248	*metal trades*	091	value	010
prevention;		ship's-	087	valve (radio)	072
crime	259	*fishing*	317	ventilating	260
fire	081	shop; machine	248	ventilation-	260
pricing *see* Engineer-prof.-		signal (*railways*)	091	*coal mine*	F260
printer's	248	signal and telegraph	091	water;	068
process	074	site	092	hot	260
production	074	sound	259	weight(s) (*aircraft mfr.*)	079
production and planning	074	spares	333	welding-	265
programme *see* Engineer-prof.-		staff-		professional	069
progress	075	insurance	005	winding (*coal mine*)	331
project	076	P.O.	071	wireless	258
prototype	248	standards	010	wiring	253
public health	068	station;		work measurement	010
pump	248	power (*electricity board*)	071	works;	
quarrying	068	pumping	248	n.o.s.	091
quality	075	station-	094	public	068
radar-	259	Min. of Defence	092	sewage	248
research	072	oil refining	248	technical	076
radio-	258	steam	347	water	248
professional	072	stress	079	workshop-	248
radio and television	258	structural	068	radio, television servicing	258
railway	248	study;		x-ray	259
rate fixing	010	method	010	Engineer-	
reception (*garage*)	249	time	010	professional-	069
recording	062	work	010	aeronautical	069
refrigerating-	248	subsidence	068	agricultural	076
shipping	087	sub-area (*electricity board*)	094	automobile	069
refrigeration-	248	sub-sea *see* Engineer-prof.-		broadcasting	072
professional	076	sub-station (*electricity board*)	071	carbonisation	073
shipping	087	superintendent	091	ceramic	078
regional (*P.O.*)	071	superintending *see* Engineer-prof.-		chemical	073
relay	253	supervising-	F277	civil	068
repair; motor	249	government	076	combustion	078
research *see* Engineer-prof.-		supply (*electricity board*) *see* Engineer-prof.-		conditioning; air	076
resident-	092	switchboard	252	constructional	068
electricity board	094	switchgear-	252	corrosion	076
retort	248	professional	071	design (mechanical)	070
rig; test	081	systems	012	development (mechanical)	070
road	068	technical-	076	electrical	071
rolling stock	248	P.O.	256	electronic	072
roofing	303	technician	081	environmental	076
safety	039	telecommunications-	259	fuel	078
sales	133	professional	071	gas	078
salvage; marine	069	radio; professional	072	glass	078
sanitary-	260	P.O.	256	heating and ventilating	076
professional	068	telegraph	259	highway(s)	068
scientific	076	telephone-	256	hydraulic	069
scribbling	248	professional	071	illuminating	071
sea-going	087	television	258	locomotive	069
second-	087	test-	286	lubrication	076
boat, barge	317	technician	081	marine	069
fishing	317	testing; cable;	071	mechanical	069
textile mfr.	248	assistant	081	mining	068
section (*L.T.E.*)	091	textile-	248	municipal	068
semi-skilled	276	professional	069	plastics	073
senior *see* Engineer-prof.-		thermal-	260	production	074
service;		professional	076	public health	068
chief	091	thermal and acoustic-	260	quarrying	068
lift	248	professional	076	radio	072
sales	133	third-	087	refrigeration	076
service-	248	*fishing*	317	sanitary	068
aircraft	250	time and study	010	structural	068
domestic electrical appliances	253	tool	245	textile	069
				water	068
				Engineer and architect	068

36

(En—Ex)

	Code number
Engineer and surveyor *see* Engineer-prof.-	
Engineer-designer *see* Engineer-prof.-	
Engineer-attendant	248
Engineer-draughtsman	079
Engineer-driller	240
Engineer-estimator	004
Engineer-examiner	286
Engineer-fitter	248
Engineer-in-charge (*electricity board*)	094
Engineering worker	L344
Engineer-inspector	286
Engineer-machinist	241
Engineer-surveyor- *see also* Engineer-prof.-	
insurance	090
Engineer-tool maker	245
Enginewright;	248
assistant	248
Engraver;	
bank-note	267
block; process	206
brass	276
chemical	267
copper	267
die	267
glass	192
gold	276
hand-	276
textile mfr.	267
heraldic	267
instrument	276
letter	301
line	267
machine-	267
instrument mfr.	276
jewellery, plate mfr.	276
map	267
mark; stamp	267
marquetry	224
metal	276
micrometer	276
monumental	301
music	267
pantograph (*roller engraving*)	267
parquetry	224
pattern; pottery	223
photo	206
photographic	206
photogravure	267
plate; copper	267
plate (precious metal)	276
portrait	055
potter's	267
pottery	223
process	206
punch	267
relief	267
roller	267
schreiner	267
seal	267
silver	276
stone	301
transfer	267
Engraver-	
ceramic mfr.	223
glass mfr.	192
jewellery mfr.	276
metal trades	276
monumental masons	301
Ordnance Survey	267
printing	267
textile printing	267
Engraver-etcher	276
Enlarger (films)	227
Enrober (*sugar confectionery mfr.*)	202
Enroller (*insurance*)	134
Enterer (*textile mfr.*)	179
Entertainer	059
Entomologist	065
Enumerator; census	115

	Code number
Erector;	
aerial; television	276
battery	283
beam (*shipbuilding*)	262
beam and frame	262
boiler	262
building; portable	316
ceiling	316
cell (*chemical mfr.*)	283
chassis	248
chimney; metal	263
concrete	307
conveyor-	248
coal mine	276
duct (work)	276
engine	248
engineer's	248
exhibition	214
fence	316
fencing	316
frame-	
shipbuilding	262
vehicle mfr.	248
furnace	263
garage	316
girder	263
greenhouse	316
hoarding	214
ironwork	263
lamp; gas	260
lift	248
light; street	313
locomotive	248
loom	248
machine	248
mains; gas	260
marquee	165
partitioning; office	214
pelmet	224
pipe	260
plant	248
plate; steel	263
prefab	316
pump	248
roof	303
roofing; galvanized	303
scaffolding	264
sheeter	303
shuttering;	214
metal	272
sign	316
stage (*ship repairing*)	264
staircase; iron	263
steel	263
steelwork	263
structural	263
switchgear	253
tent	165
tower	263
transformer	253
wicket (*ceramic mfr.*)	L342
Erector-	
machinery-	248
electrical	253
coal mine-	248
above ground	263
engineering-	248
structural engineering	263
Erector-fitter	248
Errand boy	124
Escort; bus; school	152
Essence hand	202
Estate worker	L346
Estimator;	004
chief	004
cost	004
print(ing)	004
technical	004
works study	010
Estimator and buyer (*retail trade*)	015
Estimator and surveyor	084
Estimator-draughtsman	079
Estimator-engineer	004

	Code number
Etcher;	
black and white	055
block; process	267
colour	267
copper (*printing*)	267
cutlery	276
deep	267
fine	267
half tone	267
hand (glass)	192
line	267
machine	192
photogravure	267
roller	267
rough	267
Etcher-	
integrated, printed circuits	276
aircraft mfr.	276
ceramic mfr.	223
cutlery mfr.	276
glass mfr.	192
jewellery, plate mfr.	276
printing	267
saw mfr.	276
Ethnologist	036
Etymologist	036
Evaluator; job	010
Evangelist	040
Evaporator man; multiple (*glucose mfr.*)	202
Evaporator man- *chemical mfr.*	184
food products mfr.	202
Eviscerator	187
Examiner;	
ammunition	299
armaments	286
assistant (*government*)	F112
audit (*D.O.E.*)	002
bag	289
bank-note	294
bankruptcy (*government*)	002
book (*printing*)	294
bottle (*brewery*)	298
boundary (*Ordnance Survey*)	079
brake (*railways*)	248
bridge (*railways*)	316
brush	299
bulb (*lamp mfr.*)	286
bullet	286
burr (*dental instrument mfr.*)	286
bus	286
car (*L.T.E.*)	286
carriage (*railways*)	248
carriage and wagon	248
chain	286
cheque	294
cigar	299
cigarette machine	299
cloth;	289
leather	299
coach (*railways*)	248
cycle	286
decorator's (*ceramic mfr.*)	299
driving (*Dept. of Transport*)	019
edge tool	286
engineering	286
file	286
film	299
final (*clothing mfr.*)	289
fruit	290
fuse; safety	183
gas (*Dept. of Energy*)	067
glass (*glass mfr.*)	299
gramophone	286
heald	183
hosiery	289
impression (*Ordnance Survey*)	294
initial (*railways*)	286
label	289
lamp (*coal mine*)	333
map (*Ordnance Survey*)	079
mechanical	286
meter (*Dept. of Industry*)	286

37

(Ex—Fe)

	Code number
Examiner; *continued*	
motor	286
pen	286
piece	289
plan (*Ordnance Survey*)	294
policy (*insurance*)	115
principal (*Patent Office*)	090
print(er's)	294
roller (*printing*)	294
scrap (*steelworks*)	298
semi-fuse	183
shaft (*coal mine*)	276
shell	299
shoe	175
soundbox; gramophone	286
spring	286
stamp	115
steel (*steelworks*)	286
stem	299
stencil	294
thread	289
ticket-	
entertainment	165
railways	160
road transport	F323
timber	293
track	306
traffic (*Dept. of Transport*)	019
traffic and driving (*Dept. of Transport*)	019
trench	316
vehicle-	286
Dept. of Transport	299
wagon	248
wheel	286
wire	286
yarn	289
Examiner-	
asbestos composition goods mfr.	299
Board of Trade	019
bookbinding	294
ceramic mfr.	299
chemical mfr.	299
clothing mfr.	289
coal mine	F314
dyeing and cleaning	299
fancy goods mfr.	299
food products mfr.	290
footwear mfr.	175
glass mfr.	299
incandescent mantle mfr.	299
Inland Revenue	005
laundry	299
leathercloth mfr.	299
leather dressing	298
legal services	115
match mfr.	299
metal trades	286
mica goods mfr.	299
Ministry of Defence	286
ordnance factory	286
paper pattern mfr.	294
Patent Office	090
pencil, crayon mfr.	299
photographic film mfr.	299
plastics goods mfr.	292
printing	294
railways	286
Royal Mint	286
rubber goods mfr.	291
tannery	298
textile mfr.	289
textile goods mfr.	289
tobacco mfr.	299
toy mfr.	299
wallpaper mfr.	294
wood products mfr.	293
Examiner and finisher (net)	183
Examiner and mender (hosiery)	183
Excavator-	
building and contracting	330
mine, not coal	315
steelworks	330

	Code number
Executive; *see also* Manager	
accounts (*advertising*)	014
advertising	014
legal	M027
marketing	013
media	014
merchandising	064
postal (*P.O.*)-	
grade A, B	099
grade C	F115
relations; public	014
sales	013
Exhauster (*lamp, valve mfr.*)	230
Exhauster man (*coal gas, coke ovens*)	348
Expander;	
boiler pipe	262
tube;	276
boiler	262
Expander-	
boiler mfr.	262
tube mfr.	276
Expeditor (*manufacturing*)	115
Expeller (*oil seed crushing*)	202
Expellerman (*oil seed crushing*)	202
Experimental worker	090
Experimentalist	080
Expert;	
art	005
business efficiency	010
marine salvage	069
systems	012
time and motion study	010
time study	010
Explosive hand	184
Explosive worker	184
Explosives man (*mining*)	333
Exporter	129
Extender;	
belt (*coal mine*)	276
conveyor (*coal mine*)	276
Exterminator (pest)	165
Extra (*entertainment*)	059
Extract worker (*tannery*)	173
Extractor;	
hydro	199
oil	202
steel (*coal mine*)	314
Extractor-	
chemical mfr.	184
coal mine	314
textile mfr.	199
Extractor man; fat	204
Extractor man-	
chemical mfr.	184
textile mfr.	199
tube mfr.	270
Extruder;	
machine (arc welding electrode mfr.)	230
metal	270
Extruder-	
ceramics	193
metal	270
plastics	195
rubber	194
Eyeletter-	
clothing mfr.	226
footwear mfr.	175
leather goods mfr.	175
Eyer (needles)	242

F

	Code number
F.C.A.	002
F.C.I.S.	023
F.C.W.A.	003
F.R.C.O.	060
F.R.C.O.G.	041
F.R.C.P.	041

	Code number
F.R.C.S.	041
F.S.A.A.	002
Fabric worker	212
Fabricator-	
cast stone products mfr.	230
plastics mfr.	229
tube mfr.	270
Face worker (*coal mine*)	314
Facer;	
plug (electroceramics)	193
steel	206
wood	218
Facer-	
coach painting	299
metal trades-	239
nut, bolt mfr.	242
stone dressing	301
Factor; *see also* Dealer	
estate (Scotland)	025
housing (Scotland)-	025
local government	M039
Factory girl; brick	223
Factory hand *see* Factory worker	
Factory operative *see* Factory worker	
Factory worker-	L346
packing	287
clothing mfr.	226
electrical goods mfr. (assembling, soldering)	283
food products mfr.	202
footwear mfr.	225
tobacco mfr.	201
Faience worker	300
Faller; timber	170
Fan man; store; cold	348
Fan man-	
coal mine	348
lead mfr.	231
Fanner (*corset mfr.*)	212
Farm hand	166
Farm lad	166
Farm worker; sewage	310
Farm worker-	166
self-employed	107
Farmer;	107
fish	111
Farmer's wife *see also notes* p.5	166
Farrier	233
Fasher	276
Fashioner; brush	230
Father; house	037
Father Christmas	125
Faultman (electricity board)	253
Faultsman (*P.O.*)	256
Feather worker	199
Feeder;	
auto *see* Feeder-	
bar	276
belt	L346
bin	L346
biscuit	200
boiler	347
bowl	176
can	287
card	176
carder	176
chicken	166
clay	204
conveyor (*metal trades*)	276
cotton	176
crusher (*mine, not coal*)	198
drum (agricultural machinery)	169
engine (*textile mfr.*)	176
furnace	231
hopper-	
ceramic mfr.	204
cigarette mfr.	201
horse	172
letterpress	207
line (*metal trades*)	L344
machine *see* Machinist	
mill	204
pallet	230

(Fe—Fi)

	Code number
Feeder; *continued*	
pan	204
pass; skin (*steelworks*)	270
platen	207
poultry	166
printer's	207
roll(s) (*metal mfr.*)	270
scutcher	176
stenter	182
stock	333
tack	242
wool	176
woollen	176
Feeder-	
card and paste board mfr.	203
cement mfr.	L346
felt hat mfr.	199
laundry	162
metal trades-	
bolt, nut, rivet mfr.	242
foundry	270
rolling mill	270
sheet metal working	242
tube mfr.	270
mine, not coal	198
printing	207
textile mfr.-	176
textile finishing	182
textile printing	182
Feeder-in (*textile mfr.*)	199
Feeder-up (*tobacco mfr.*)	201
Feller;	
double	212
timber	170
tree	170
wood	170
Feller-	
clothing mfr.	212
forestry	170
Feller hand	212
Felling hand	212
Fellmonger	173
Fellow (*university*)-	031
dentistry	042
medicine	041
surgery	041
Feltman-	
paper mfr.	203
roofing felt mfr.	199
textile mfr.	199
Felt worker	199
Felter; boiler	316
Felter-	
printing rollers	230
building and contracting	303
plastics mfr.	229
shipbuilding	L344
textile mfr.	199
Fencer	316
Fenter	199
Fermenter-	197
non-alcoholic drink	202
Fermenting man (*distillery*)	197
Ferrier	315
Ferryman-	317
railways	319
Festooner-	
linoleum mfr.	204
oilskin mfr.	204
Fetcher (*textile mfr.*)	338
Fettler;	
brass	244
card	276
castings	244
core	244
cupola	300
iron	244
machine	276
pipe; sanitary	223
shop; machine	244
tool	245
woollen	276
Fettler-	
cast concrete products mfr.	230

	Code number
Fettler- *continued*	
ceramic mfr.	223
metal trades-	244
puddling	270
textile mfr.	276
Fibre man (*asbestos-cement goods mfr.*)	176
Fibre worker-	
paper mfr.	203
rubber goods mfr.	228
Field worker;	166
brick	223
Fielder (*textile mfr.*)	338
Field(s)man-	107
professionally qualified	065
Fighter; iron	263
Filer;	
core	235
foundry	244
pattern	244
plastics	229
spoon and fork	244
tool	276
Filer-	
metal trades	244
plastics mfr.	229
tobacco pipe mfr.	224
Filler;	
ampoule	287
back	182
bag	287
bank (*textile mfr.*)	179
bar (*hosiery mfr.*)	181
barrel	287
barrow	L344
battery-	
accumulator mfr.	230
textile mfr.	199
bobbin	199
bottle	287
bottom (*boot mfr.*)	225
box-	287
blast furnace	L344
textile mfr.	199
braid (*silk*)	178
brush	230
can-	
paint mfr.	287
petroleum distribution	287
cap (*lamp, valve mfr.*)	283
card	176
cartridge	230
chocolate	202
coal	338
coke	338
conveyor-	
coal mine-	
below ground	314
cushion	226
cylinder	287
detonator	230
dresser's	176
drum (*oil refining*)	287
envelope	115
fixture (*retail trade*)	126
furnace (*blast furnace*)	338
hand-	
silk weaving	199
upholstery mfr.	226
hopper (*textile mfr.*)	199
jam	287
kiln	191
machine-	
brush mfr.	230
textile mfr.	199
magazine (*loom*)	199
medical (*oxygen works*)	287
mine (*blast furnace*)	L344
oil	287
order	333
ore (*blast furnace*)	L344
oven (*ceramic mfr.*)	191
oxygen	287
paint	287

	Code number
Filler: *continued*	
pan (*steelworks*)	231
pickle	287
pie	202
plug	231
polish	287
pot (*steelworks*)	L344
rag	176
rocket	230
salt	L340
sausage	202
scribble	176
shelf (*retail trade*)	126
shuttle	199
silk	199
spare	L344
stock	333
stone (*blast furnace*)	L344
timber	224
tin (*textile mfr.*)	199
tray	L340
truck (*coal mine*)	338
tub (*coal mine*)	338
varnish	287
wagon	338
weaver's	199
wire	234
wood	299
Filler-	
blast furnace	L344
brewery	287
cast concrete products mfr.	230
cement mfr.	287
ceramic mfr.	223
coal mine	338
coke ovens	332
docks	334
explosive mfr.	230
firework mfr.	230
food products mfr.	287
match mfr.	287
mattress, etc. mfr.	213
mine, not coal	338
oil refining	287
ordnance factory	230
paint mfr.	287
pencil mfr.	299
petroleum distribution	338
textile mfr.	199
tobacco mfr.	201
Filler-in; polisher's	299
Filler-in-	
ceramics mfr.	191
furniture mfr.	299
paper mfr.	203
pencil mfr.	299
Filler-loader (*petroleum distribution*)	338
Filler-up (*card clothing mfr.*)	276
Filleter (*fish*)	187
Film worker; colour	227
Filmer; micro	119
Filter man-	
alcoholic drink mfr.	197
chemical mfr.	184
metal trades	204
sewage farm	310
vinegar mfr.	197
Filterer-	
alcoholic drink mfr.	197
chemical mfr.	184
food products mfr.	202
water works	184
Filtration hand-	
alcoholic drink mfr.	197
chemical mfr.	184
Filtration worker; red (*aluminium refining*)	184
Financier	007
Finder;	
fault	286
land	134
tool	333
worsted (*carpet mfr.*)	199

39

(Fi)

	Code number
Finer;	
beer	197
super (*buckle mfr.*)	276
Finer (*jewellery mfr.*)	276
Finingsman	197
Finisher;	
action	222
armature	252
belt (*textile mfr.*)	182
blade	276
blanket	182
bleach (*textile mfr.*)	182
bobbin; brass	241
body (*vehicle mfr.*)	268
book (*printing*)	189
bottom	175
brass	248
brush;	299
wire	285
bush; axle	239
butcher's	186
camera	246
can (*worsted mfr.*)	176
cap	212
car	268
card-	
card clothing mfr.	276
printing	295
carpet	182
case (jewel, etc. cases)	299
caustic	184
cellulose	299
chassis	248
chromium	236
cloth	182
coach	268
coat	212
coffin	224
coil	274
collar	212
combing	176
concrete	230
cord (telephone)	230
crucible (plumbago)	223
curtain	212
cycle	248
disc; wheel	239
dress	212
dyers	182
ebonite	228
fabric	182
faller	276
felt (*hat mfr.*)	226
fork; weft	276
fork	276
frame (*cycle mfr.*)	276
fur	173
furniture	299
fuse; safety	182
glass	192
glove	212
gold	189
gown	212
hand-	
clothing mfr.	212
felt hat mfr.	226
knitted goods mfr.	212
hat	226
helmet	226
hook; spring	276
hosiery	182
jam	287
key	276
kilt	212
lace	182
leather	173
lens	192
levant	173
mantle	212
metal	261
needle (*needle mfr.*)	276
paint	299
paper	188
part (*piano mfr.*)	215

	Code number
Finisher; *continued*	
peg; shuttle	224
pencil	299
photographic	227
piece	182
pipe-	
cast concrete products mfr.	230
ceramic mfr.	223
clay tobacco pipe mfr.	223
plastics	229
plate (*paper mfr.*)	203
plush	182
post (concrete)	230
printer's	227
propeller (ships' propeller mfr.)	241
quilt	213
racquet	230
reed	230
rod; fishing	230
rug;	182
skin	212
rule	224
sanitary	223
satin (*metal trades*)	243
shirt	212
shoe	175
shop; machine	276
shuttle	218
silk	182
silver	266
smith's	244
spade	299
spoon and fork	266
spray (*furniture mfr.*)	281
spring;	237
coach	248
motor car	248
stone (cast concrete products mfr.)	230
stove	182
surface (*aircraft mfr.*)	299
tailor's	212
taper's	179
tent	226
tool; edge	276
trouser	212
tube (*steelworks*)	270
tyre	228
umbrella	212
velvet	182
wheel (*hat mfr.*)	226
whip	225
wood	218
woollen	182
wrench	276
Finisher-	
artificial teeth mfr.	230
asbestos-cement goods mfr.	230
bookbinding	189
briar pipe mfr.	282
broom, brush mfr.	299
canvas goods mfr.	226
cast concrete products mfr.	230
ceramic mfr.	223
christmas card, etc. mfr.	295
cigar mfr.	201
clothing mfr.	212
dyeing and cleaning	162
embroidery mfr.	212
firework mfr.	299
fishing rod mfr.	230
flour confectionery mfr.	200
footwear mfr.	175
fur goods mfr.	212
glass mfr.	192
hat mfr.	226
hosiery garment mfr.	212
incandescent mantle mfr.	230
knitwear mfr.	212
leather dressing	173
leather goods mfr.	225
metal trades-	276
aircraft mfr.	268

	Code number
Finisher- *continued*	
metal trades- continued	
brass foundry	248
coach building	268
coach trimming	213
cock founding	248
foundry	244
precious plate, metal mfr.	266
railway workshops	268
rolling mill	270
screw mfr.	243
spring mfr.	237
tube mfr.	270
vehicle mfr.	268
watch, clock mfr.	285
musical instrument mfr.	222
paper mfr.	188
paper products mfr.	295
pharmaceutical products mfr.	287
photographic film mfr.	204
piano mfr.	222
piano key mfr.	222
plastics goods mfr.	229
printing	227
process engraving	267
railway workshops	268
refractory goods mfr.	223
rubber goods mfr.	228
soft furnishings mfr.	212
soft toy mfr.	212
stencil paper mfr.	203
stick mfr.	224
sugar confectionery mfr.	202
textile mfr.-	182
flax, hemp mfr.	176
textile doubling	177
textile drawing	176
textile printing	182
toilet preparation mfr.	287
tooth brush mfr.	230
umbrella, parasol mfr.	212
Finisher and liner (*fur garment mfr.*)	212
Finner	242
Fire boy (*metal mfr.*)	231
Fire brigade man	138
Fireman;	
biscuit	191
boiler	347
engine-	347
locomotive	319
furnace-	
metal trades-	231
annealing	237
gas	184
industrial	138
kiln; colour	191
kiln-	
ceramic mfr.	191
food products mfr.	202
loco	319
locomotive	319
marine	317
night (*malting*)	197
oven; annealing	237
oven (*ceramic mfr.*)	191
passed	319
pot	184
private	138
retort-	184
charcoal	203
zinc	231
security	138
shed	319
soaker	231
stove	231
surface	347
works; n.o.s.	138
Fireman-	
boiler-	347
locomotive	319
abrasive mfr.	204
airport	138
bakery	200

(Fi)

	Code number
Fireman- *continued*	
ceramic mfr.	191
cinema	138
coal gas, coke ovens ...	184
coal mine	
above ground ...	347
below ground ...	F314
composition die mfr. ...	184
electricity supply ...	347
fire service	138
fishing	317
food products mfr. ...	202
L.T.E.	138
malting	197
metal trades- ...	231
annealing	237
mine, not coal ...	F315
oil refining	184
P.O.	138
pencil mfr.	204
railways	319
refuse disposal ...	348
salt mfr.	184
shipbuilding	231
shipping	317
theatre	138
Fireman and trimmer ...	317
Fireman-greaser (*shipping*)	317
Fire prevention man ...	138
Firemaster	M138
Firer;	
boiler	347
foundry (*glass mfr.*) ...	191
kiln	204
shot-	
civil engineering ...	316
coal mine	314
mine, not coal ...	315
stove-	
blast furnace ...	231
ceramic mfr. ...	191
Firer-	
ceramic mfr.	191
chemical mfr.	184
malting	197
metal mfr.	231
Firer-out (*food processing*)	202
First aid man	156
First hand-	
bakery	F185
clothing mfr.	210
retail trade- ...	125
butchers	186
steelworks	232
First sales (*drapery*) ...	125
Fish house worker ...	187
Fish worker-	
docks	334
food processing ...	187
Fisher (copper)	231
Fisher boy	171
Fisherman	171
Fisherman-crofter ...	111
Fishmonger	187
Fitter;	
aerial; television ...	276
agricultural	248
aircraft-	248
maintenance ...	250
airframe	248
alteration	210
alternator	252
anchor	248
appliance;	
domestic	253
surgical	050
armament	248
asbestos	303
assembly	248
automobile	249
axle	248
bag;	
air	299
curing	299

	Code number
Fitter; *continued*	
balustrade	276
bank	214
bar; handle	285
bar (*hotel, etc. fitting*)	214
basket; work	299
battery	230
bead; tyre	194
beam	248
bearing; brass ...	248
bedstead	248
belt (*coal mine*) ...	225
belting	225
below ground (*coal mine*)	248
bench;	248
electrical	252
billiard	230
blade (turbines) ...	248
blind	316
board; reed	222
body (vehicle) ...	268
boiler	248
bonnet (vehicle) ...	285
box;	
axle	248
cam	248
gear	248
iron	248
work	299
box-	
artists' colours mfr.	287
foundry	276
brake;	
vacuum	248
Westinghouse ...	248
brake-	248
cycle mfr.	285
brass	248
break-off	248
builder's	316
burner (*gas works*) ...	260
cabinet;	215
iron	248
cable	257
camera	246
car-	249
vehicle mfr.	248
card (*textile mfr.*) ...	176
carpet	221
carriage	248
carriage and wagon ...	248
case;	
cabinet	215
piano	215
casement (metal) ...	248
chain	248
chassis	248
chock (*coal mine*) ...	314
clock	247
clothing (*retail trade*)	210
coach	248
coat	210
cock	248
colliery	248
component; cycle ...	248
constructional ...	248
controller	252
conveyor	248
cork	287
corset; surgical ...	226
corsetry	226
crane	248
curtain	213
cycle	248
dental	220
depositor's	266
detail	248
development	248
die	245
diesel-	248
vehicle-	249
vehicle mfr. ...	248
district (*gas board*) ...	260

	Code number
Fitter; *continued*	
door;	
car	248
steel	248
door (*gas stove works*)	248
dress	210
dressmaker's	210
dynamo	252
electrical-	252
maintenance ...	253
electronic	252
engine;	248
aero-	248
maintenance ...	250
aircraft (maintenance)	250
diesel	248
engineering; ...	248
electrical	252
engineer's;	248
electrical	252
heating	260
sanitary	260
erection	248
excavator	248
exhibition	214
experimental	248
fabrication	248
fan	252
fire; gas	260
fireplace	300
fittings and furniture ...	224
frame;	
air	248
bag	299
door; metal ...	248
ring	248
frame-	
cycle mfr.	248
loco and rolling stock mfr.	248
picture frame mfr. ...	224
textile machinery mfr.	248
furnace	248
furnishing (soft) ...	213
furniture-	215
metal	248
garage	249
gas	260
gasholder	262
gate (iron)	233
gate and railings (iron)	233
gauge	246
gear	248
general	248
geyser	260
glass-	303
vehicle mfr.	299
watch mfr.	299
governor (*gas board*)	248
grate	248
grindstone	248
grip (tools)	285
gun	248
gymnastics	224
heating	260
heel	299
house;	213
light	248
power	248
hydraulic	248
industrial	248
injection; fuel ...	248
inspector	248
installation-	248
P.O.	256
instrument;	246
aircraft	259
musical	222
telephone	256
instrument (aircraft) ...	259
insulating	316
interlocking	259
ironmonger's	248
ironmongery	248
ironwork	248

(Fi)

Fitter; continued

	Code number
jig and tool	245
keg	248
knife	248
laboratory	248
lamp; arc	252
last; bespoke	175
lift	248
light (electric)	253
limb	050
lining; brake	249
lino-	316
linotype machine	248
linoleum	316
linotype	248
locking (signals)	248
locomotive	248
loom	248
machine-	248
electrical machines	252
mains-	
electricity board	253
water board	311
maintenance;	
computer	259
electrical	253
maintenance-	248
aircraft engines	250
office machinery servicing	251
radio, television servicing	258
vehicle servicing	249
gas board-	260
gas works	248
P.O.	256
marine	248
mattress (wire)	248
mechanical-	248
vehicle-	249
vehicle mfr.	248
metal	248
meter	246
mirror (*furniture mfr.*)	224
motor; gramophone	285
motor-	249
electric	252
vehicle mfr.	248
mould;	270
bottle	248
mount; boiler	248
mouthpiece (pipes)	299
mule	248
net	199
nicker and turner's	248
n.o.s.	248
office	214
optical	246
ordnance	248
organ	222
oven	248
overmantel	215
palisade	233
paragon (umbrellas)	285
paste	299
pattern (*engineering*)	245
pen; fountain	299
piano	222
pillar	253
pipe;	260
boiler	248
briar	299
drain	311
plant	248
plate;	262
boot	299
potter's	248
precision-	248
instrument mfr.	246
printing	248
pump	248
radar	259
radio	258
rail (bedstead)	248
range	248
rectification	248

Fitter; continued

	Code number
repair; engine	248
research	248
retort	248
rheostat	252
room; tool	245
rope and belt	272
ropery; wire	272
rough	248
saddle (cycles)	285
safe	248
sanitary	260
scale	246
scissors	248
screen-	
coal mine	248
vehicle mfr.	299
scythe	276
semi-skilled	285
service-	248
aircraft	250
instruments	246
office machines	251
ship	248
shoe (*retail trade*)	125
shop; machine	248
shop-	214
metal trades	248
shop and office	214
sign-	316
electric signs	253
signal; railway	259
skilled	248
skip (*coal mine*)	248
soundbox	285
speed	248
speedometer	246
spring;	248
elastic	175
hat; opera	212
spring (*forging*)	233
sprinkler	260
stand-	
exhibition stand	214
sewing machine stand	248
starter; motor	252
steam	260
steam and hot water	260
steel	248
steelyard	248
stock-	
bedstead mfr.	248
footwear mfr.	298
stove-	
building and contracting	260
stove mfr.	285
structural	248
sun-blind	316
superintendent	F248
surface	248
switch	252
switchboard	252
switchgear	252
table; billiard	230
tailor's	210
tank	248
taximeter	246
telegraph;	259
ship's	246
telephone	256
television	258
tender	248
textile	248
tool;	245
edge	245
machine	248
press	245
torpedo	248
tractor	248
transformer	252
transport	249
tread; tyre	194
trolleybus	248
truck (electric)	252

Fitter; continued

	Code number
try-out	248
tube-	260
boiler mfr.	262
locomotive mfr.	262
turbine	248
turning	248
tyre	276
umbrella	299
upholsterer's	213
valve-	
engineering	248
tyre mfr.	299
vehicles-	249
vehicle mfr.	248
ventilation	260
wagon (*railway workshops*)	248
water	260
weighbridge	248
wheel	248
window (metal)	248
windscreen	299
work; smith's	248

Fitter-

	Code number
machinery-	248
electrical machines	252
vehicles-	249
vehicle mfr.	248
bag frame mfr.	285
cabinet making	215
cardboard container mfr.	295
clothing mfr.	210
electricity board	253
fishing rod mfr.	230
footwear mfr.	175
garage	249
gas board-	260
gas works	248
heating contracting	260
leather goods mfr.	225
loose leaf book mfr.	285
metal trades-	248
instrument mfr.	246
jewellery, plate mfr.	266
mining	248
musical instrument mfr.	222
net mfr.	199
railways	248
shipbuilding	248
shop blind mfr.	316
tobacco pipe mfr.	299

Fitter and assembler ... 248
Fitter and erector- ... 248
    public lighting ... 312
    constructional engineering ... 263
Fitter and examiner ... 248
Fitter and marker-off ... 245
Fitter and tester ... 248
Fitter and trimmer ... 210
Fitter and turner ... 248
Fitter-assembler ... 248
Fitter-driver ... 248
Fitter-engineer ... 248
Fitter-erector ... 248
Fitter-in-charge ... F248
Fitter-inspector ... 248
Fitter-machinist ... 248
Fitter-mechanic- ... 248
    garage ... 249
Fitter-on ... 210
Fitter-operator;
    capstan ... 248
    machine tool ... 248
Fitter-tester ... 248
Fitter-turner ... 248
Fitter-up;
    frame; picture ... 299
    table; billiard ... 230
Fitter-up-
    clothing mfr. ... 211
    footwear mfr. ... 299
    foundry ... 248
    musical instrument mfr.- ... 222
    piano case mfr. ... 215

(Fi—Fo)

	Code number
Fitter-welder; pipe	260
Fitter-welder-	265
heating and ventilating	260
Fixer;	
advertisement	165
appliances (*gas board*)	260
asbestos	303
beam; concrete	307
blind	316
board; plaster	316
boiler	300
cap (lamp and valves)	283
carpet	221
ceiling	316
faience and mosaic	300
felt; roofing	303
fibrous	302
fireplace	300
frame; metal	316
girder (*coal mine*)	314
glazing; patent	303
grate	300
insulation	316
lath; metal	312
lens	230
light; lead	303
marble	301
mason's; stone	301
meter-	
electricity	276
gas	260
water	260
mosaic	300
motor-	248
electric	252
net	199
pad	212
panel (vehicle)	285
pattern (lace machine)	199
price	010
range	300
rate	010
reinforcement (*building and contracting*)	263
roof (*building and contracting*)	214
roofing	303
scaffolding	264
second	214
ship door and collar	262
sign-	316
electric	253
steel (*building and contracting*)	263
tape (*paper pattern mfr.*)	227
tent	165
terra-cotta	300
tile	300
transfer (japanning)	299
trimmer	211
ventilator	260
vitrolite	303
window-	316
vehicles	299
Fixer-	
carpentry and joinery	214
clothing mfr.	211
incandescent mantle mfr.	182
net mfr.	199
railways	248
Fixer and bender; steel	263
Fixer-mason	301
Flagman	321
Flagger-	309
fibre preparation	176
Flaker-on (electric cable)	270
Flanger; beam	248
Flanger-	
hat mfr.	226
sheet metal working	242
tin box mfr.	242
Flasher	192
Flasher hand (*plastics mfr.*)	229
Flatman	317

	Code number
Flattener;	
patent (galvanized sheet)	270
sheet (metal)	270
Flattener-	
glass mfr.	192
metal trades-	242
wire mfr.	276
Flattener and straightener (glass)	192
Flatter;	
cellulose	299
gold	266
paint	299
silver	266
Flatter-	
glass mfr.	192
vehicle mfr.	299
Flatter and polisher	299
Flautist	060
Flavouring man (cereals)	202
Flayer	186
Flesher	173
Flight-Lieutenant-	
armed forces-	
foreign and Commonwealth	M136
U.K.	M135
Flipper; bead	228
Flitter (*coal mine*)	276
Floater; tube	244
Floater-	
metal trades-	244
blast furnace	L344
Floor and kiln man (*malting*)	197
Floor hand (*printing*)	207
Floor man	L346
asphalt mfr.	204
malting	197
oil wells	315
race course	115
slaughterhouse	186
Florist; artificial	064
Florist	064
Flower girl	130
Flowerer (*ceramic mfr.*)	193
Fluffer	173
Flusher; starch	202
Flusher (tobacco pipe)	218
Flusher and cleanser; sewer	310
Fluter;	
drill	241
pot; tea	266
Fluter-	
ivory, bone, etc.	230
metal	241
silver, plate	266
Fly hand	207
Flyman	348
Foiler-	287
plasterboard mfr.	204
Folder;	
book	189
box-	
cardboard box mfr.	295
tin box mfr.	242
circular	115
cloth	199
curtain	287
envelope	227
handkerchief	287
map	227
net	287
paper	227
pattern; paper	299
towel (*textile mfr.*)	199
Folder-	
bookbinding	189
clothing	287
drum, keg mfr.	242
footwear mfr.	225
laundry	287
printing	189
rag book mfr.	189
textile mfr.-	199
hosiery finishing	287
silk doubling	177

	Code number
Folder-in (*glove mfr.*)	299
Folder-up (textiles)	199
Follower; crane	337
Food worker	202
Footman (*domestic service*)	165
Footballer	063
Footer (*hosiery mfr.*)	181
Forcer;	
rhubarb	167
rubber	194
Forcer-	
plastics goods mfr.	195
rubber goods mfr.	194
Forecaster; economic	011
Forecaster (meteorological)	067
Forehand-	231
rope, twine mfr.	199
Foreman; *see also notes pages 3 and 5*	
abattoir	F186
airport and stores	F333
assistant *see notes pages 3 and 5*	
bakery	F185
bank (*transport*)	F324
batch	F192
baths	F165
battery (*coke ovens*)	F184
belt (*mine, not coal*)	F338
blowing	F176
boiler	F347
bottling	F287
brewer	F197
bridge	F316
builder's	F316
building;	F316
coach	F268
cabin; lamp	F333
cable	F257
calender (*paper mfr.*)	F188
capstan	F318
carbonising (coal gas, coke ovens)	F184
card	F176
carding	F176
cartage	F338
checking (*engineering*)	F286
chemical	F184
civilian (*government*)	F316
coal	F338
colour (*carpet mfr.*)	F182
comber	F176
combing	F176
concrete	F307
contractor's	F316
corporation *see Foreman-local government*	
craftsmen	F277
cupola	F231
dairy-	F202
retail trade	F128
day *see Foreman-*	
delivery	F338
demolition	F316
departmental *see Foreman-*	
depot-	F333
coal merchants	F338
transport	F324
despatch	F333
destructor; dust	FL346
distribution (*gas board*)	F311
district-	F316
retail trade	F125
sanitary services	F336
dock	F334
doubler	F177
drainage	F311
drawing (*textile mfr.*)	F176
dredging	F330
drill (*mine, not coal*)	F315
electrical	F253
electronics	F259
electroplating	F236
engineering;	F277

(Fo)

Foreman; *continued*
  engineering; *continued*

	Code number
constructional	F263
estate(s)	F316
explosives (*mine, not coal*)	F315
export	F338
extrusion; metal	F270
factory- *see also* Foreman-P.O.	F253
farm	F166
field	F166
fittings (*gas board*)	F260
flat (*card clothing mfr.*)	F344
forecourt	F127
forging	F233
foundry	F235
frame (carding)	F176
fruit	F167
furnace; blast	F231
furnace-	
glass mfr.	F191
metal trades	F231
garage	F249
general- *see also notes* p.3	F091
building and contracting	092
goods (*railways*)	F318
hatch	F334
haulage (*coal mine*)	F331
hearth; soak	F173
heat (*gas works*)	F184
highways	F308
house;	
boiler	F347
gas	F184
glass-	F167
glass mfr.	F192
power	F255
retort	F184
wash	F162
inspection-	F286
glass mfr.	F299
installation; electrical	F253
installation (*oil refining*)	F338
instrument	F246
jetty	F334
kiln-	
carbon goods mfr.	F184
ceramic mfr.	F191
laboratory	F288
labour (*agriculture*)	F166
landscape	F168
laundry	F162
length (*river board*)	F316
lighting	F165
lime-	F173
foundry	F235
line (*metal trades*)	F285
lines; overhead	F257
lock	F338
locomotive	F318
loom	F180
maintenance;	
electrical	F253
loco	F248
maintenance-	F316
electricity board	F253
gas board	F248
manufacturing	F248
P.O.	F256
transport	F249
mechanical	F277
milk (*dairy*)	F202
mill;	
blue	F184
rolling	F232
mill (*food products mfr.*)	F202
mule	F177
night *see* Foreman-outside (*mine, not coal*)	F315
oven	F184
overhauling; vehicle	F249
painting	F282
parcel(s) (*railways*)	F318
permanent way	F306

Foreman; *continued*

	Code number
physics; health	F080
piercing	F242
piling (*civil engineering*)	F330
pipe; main	F311
pit; clay	F315
plant;	
carbonisation	F184
coal (*electricity board*)	F255
crushing	F184
dry cleaning (*coal mine*)	F198
gas	F184
mixing (*asphalt mfr.*)	F204
reforming	F184
plant-	
bakery	F185
building and contracting	F330
platform (*railways*)	F160
polish	F184
press (*metal trades*)	F242
printing	F207
process-	F184
food products mfr.	F202
production *see* Foreman-progress	F115
purification (*gas board*)	F184
purifier; gas	F184
quality (*engineering*)	F286
quay	F334
receiving	F333
refining; metal	F231
retort (*gas works*)	F184
ring	F177
road	F308
rock (*mine, not coal*)	F315
room;	
blowing	F176
card	F176
grey (*textile mfr.*)	F333
lamp (*coal mine*)	F333
machine-	
clothing mfr.	F212
printing	F207
mill (*fur dressing*)	F173
packing	F287
pattern (*textile mfr.*)	F333
sewing	F212
tool	F245
rounds	F128
running (*railways*)	F318
salle	F294
salvage	FL346
screen(s)-	F198
gas works, coke ovens	F204
scribbling	F176
section *see* Foreman-senior *see also notes* p.3	F091
sewer	F310
shed;	
press (*brick mfr.*)	F193
weaving	F180
shed-	
tannery	F173
transport-	
rail	F318
road	F324
shift *see* Foreman-shipping	F333
shop;	
auto	F241
casting	F235
cutting (*glass mfr.*)	F192
enamelling	F299
erecting (*engineering*)	F248
machine	F241
melting	F231
paint	F299
panel	F261
pattern	F217
press-	
metal trades	F242
plastics goods mfr.	F195
steel	F232
trim	F213

Foreman; *continued*

	Code number
shop-	
ceramic mfr.	F193
coal mine	F238
engineering	F241
paper mfr.	F188
retail trade	F125
site	F316
spell	F202
spinning;	F177
nylon	F196
rayon	F196
stable	F172
stage (*gas works*)	F184
staithes	F334
stamping	F242
station; pumping	F348
station (*railways*)	F160
stock	F333
store(s)	F333
surface-	
coal mine	F316
mine, not coal	F315
tank (*glass mfr.*)	F191
technical *see* Foreman-test; motor	F286
textile	F199
timber-	F218
docks	F334
tool; press	F245
traffic-	F324
coal mine (below ground)	F338
train	F318
transport; internal	F338
transport-	
rail	F318
road	F324
transporting	F338
treatment; heat	F237
turbine	F255
twisting	F177
warehouse	F333
weaving	F180
welding	F265
wharf	F334
winding	F178
woodwork	F214
wool	F176
working- *see also* Foreman-coal mine	F345
works *see also notes* p.3	F091
workshop *see* Foreman-yard;	
brick	F193
coal	F338
scrap	F338
ship	F262
steel	F333
stock-	
coal mine	F333
tan	F173
timber	F333
yard-	FL346
auctioneering	F335
builders merchants	F338
building and contracting	F338
canal	F338
coal mine	F316
local government	F338
mine, not coal	F315
railways	F318
road transport	F324
in lodge	F192
of factory (*government*)	F230
of trades (*government*)	F277
of works	F316
Foreman-	
bottling	F287
abrasive paper, etc. mfr.	F203
agricultural contracting	F169
agriculture	F166
asbestos mfr.	F199
asbestos-cement goods mfr.	F230
asphalt mfr.	F204

(Fo)

	Code number
Foreman- *continued*	
auctioneering	F335
bakery	F185
baths	F165
bedding mfr.	F213
blue and starch mfr. ...	F184
bookcloth mfr.	F180
brake linings mfr. ...	F230
brewery	F197
brush mfr.	F230
building and contracting ...	F316
calico printers	F227
canvas goods mfr. ...	F226
cardboard box mfr. ...	F227
cast concrete products mfr.	F230
catering	F146
cattle food mfr.	F202
cement mfr.	F204
cemetery	F165
ceramic mfr.	F193
chemical mfr.	F184
chocolate mfr.	F202
cigarette mfr.	F201
cinema	F165
civil engineering	F316
clothing mfr.	F226
coal merchants	F324
coke ovens	F184
construction	F316
cork mfr.	F230
cotton waste merchants ...	F176
D.O.E.	F316
dairy-	F202
retail trade	F128
denture mfr.	F220
docks	F334
dry cleaning	F162
dyeing and cleaning ...	F162
dyeworks	F182
electrical contracting ...	F253
electricity board	F253
enamelling	F299
entertainment	F165
fancy goods mfr.	F230
flooring contracting ...	F316
flour confectionery mfr. ...	F185
food canning	F287
food products mfr. ...	F202
footwear mfr.	F175
forestry	F170
furniture mfr.	F215
garage	F249
gas board-	F260
by-product plant ...	F184
gas works	F184
gelatine mfr.	F184
glass mfr.	F192
grain milling	F202
grinding wheel mfr. ...	F230
heating engineering ...	F260
horticulture	F167
joinery mfr.	F214
lairage	F172
laundry	F162
leather cloth mfr. ...	F199
leather dressing	F173
leather goods mfr. ...	F225
linoleum mfr.	F204
local government-	F316
baths dept.	F165
cleansing dept. ...	F336
council depot	F338
engineer's dept. ...	F316
highways dept. ...	F308
housing dept.	F316
parks dept.	F168
public works	F316
refuse tip	FL346
sanitary dept.	F336
sewage works	F310
surveyor's dept. ...	F316
transport dept. ...	F324
treasurer's dept. ...	F115
match mfr.	F230

	Code number
Foreman- *continued*	
metal trades-	F277
annealing	F237
assembling	F285
blast furnace	F231
cable mfr.	F276
coach building	F268
constructional engineering	F263
electronic equipment mfr.	F252
electroplating	F236
forging	F233
foundry	F235
heat treatment ...	F237
instrument mfr. ...	F246
jewellery mfr. ...	F266
lamp, valve mfr. ...	F238
machine shop	F241
metal extrusion ...	F270
metal pressing ...	F242
metal refining ...	F231
metal tube mfr. ...	F270
press tool mfr. ...	F245
radio, television mfr. ...	F252
rolling mill	F232
sheet metal working ...	F261
shipbuilding	F262
stamping and piercing	F242
tinplate mfr.	F232
tool room	F245
welding	F265
wire mfr.	F234
mine, not coal	F315
mineral water mfr. ...	F202
nursery	F167
oil refining	F184
oil seed crushing	F202
opencast coal mining ...	F315
ordnance depot	F333
ordnance factory-	
explosive mfr. ...	F184
shell filling	F230
P.L.A.	F334
P.O.-	F256
post office railway ...	F123
packing	F287
paint mfr.	F184
paper mfr.	F188
paper goods mfr. ...	F227
patent fuel mfr. ...	F184
pen mfr.	F230
pencil, crayon mfr. ...	F230
petrol station	F127
petroleum distribution ...	F338
plasterboard mfr. ...	F204
plastics goods mfr.- ...	F229
calendering	F195
extruding	F195
moulding	F195
power station	F255
printing	F207
provision merchants ...	F125
publishing	F207
railways-	F318
carriage and wagon dept.	F277
district engineer's dept.	F306
locomotive shop ...	F248
motive power dept. ...	F248
signal and telegraph dept.	F259
removal contracting ...	F335
repository	F333
retail trade	F125
river board	F316
road transport	F324
rubber goods mfr.- ...	F228
calendering	F194
extruding	F194
moulding	F194
sawmilling	F218
scrap merchants	F338
security services	F140
sewage disposal	F310
slag wool mfr.	F184
soap mfr.	F184
spirit distilling	F184

	Code number
Foreman- *continued*	
sports goods mfr. ...	F230
sugar confectionery mfr. ...	F202
sugar refining	F202
surgical dressing mfr. ...	F199
tailoring	F210
tannery	F173
textile mfr.-	F199
combing dept. ...	F176
doubling, twisting dept.	F177
dyeing dept.	F182
finishing dept. ...	F182
hosiery mfr.	F181
man-made fibre mfr. ...	F196
opening, carding dept.	F176
printing dept.	F227
spinning dept. ...	F177
weaving dept. ...	F180
winding dept. ...	F178
timber merchants ...	F333
tobacco mfr.	F201
tobacco pipe mfr. ...	F224
toilet preparation mfr. ...	F184
toy mfr.	F230
typewriter ribbon mfr. ...	F199
upholstering	F213
wallpaper mfr.	FL346
warehousing	F333
water works	F310
waterways	F316
woodware mfr.	F214
wreck raising	FL346
zoo	F172
Foreman-ganger-see also Foreman-	
maintenance	F316
agriculture	F166
building and contracting ...	F316
cable laying	F311
docks	F334
electricity board	F311
gas board	F311
local government	F316
P.O.	F257
railways	F306
water works	F311
Forewoman; factory (P.O.) ...	F283
Forewoman- see also Foreman-	
government	F158
P.O.	F227
Forest workman	170
Forest worker	170
Forester	F170
Forestry worker	170
Forge hand	270
Forgeman	270
Forge worker	270
Forger	233
Forker-	338
glass mfr.	204
wrought iron mfr. ...	231
Former;	
accumulator	276
battery	276
cable	274
cell (battery)	276
coil	274
copper (generators) ...	274
filament	276
glass	192
hat	199
lap	176
loom	274
plate; tungsten ...	276
rope	199
strand	199
toe; veldtschoen ...	175
tube	270
wire (spring mfr.) ...	276
Former-	
felt hat mfr.	199
plastics mfr.	229
tube mfr.	270
Fortune teller	165

(Fo—Ga)

	Code number
Forwarder	189
Founder; type	270
Founder-	
glass mfr.	191
metal trades-	270
blast furnace	231
copper refining	231
type foundry	270
Foundry hand	L343
Foundry man	270
Foundry worker	L343
Fourth hand (rolling mill)	270
Fractionator (chemical mfr.)	184
Fraiser	244
Frame hand; mustard	202
Frame hand-	
hosiery mfr.	181
sugar confectionery mfr.	202
Frame man (rope mfr.)	199
Frame worker;	
hand	181
knitting	181
Frame worker (rope mfr.)	199
Framer;	
bag	299
binocular	246
calico	226
curtain (laundry)	162
picture	224
ring	177
rule	218
seat	215
Framer-	
chair mfr.	215
laundry	162
leather goods mfr.	299
shipbuilding	262
textile mfr.-	176
hosiery mfr.	182
wool spinning	177
Frazer-	
metal trades	244
tobacco pipe mfr.	218
Freeman (River Thames)	317
Freezer	202
Friar	040
Fridgeman (ice cream mfr.)	202
Frier see Fryer	
Friller	212
Fringer	181
Fritter	204
Frogman	316
Front boy (clothing mfr.)	226
,, girl (clothing mfr.)	226
,, hand (clothing mfr.)	226
Frontsman (retail trade)	125
Froster-	
electric lamp mfr.	192
glass mfr.	192
Fruitman;	167
head	F167
Fruiterer-	101
market trading	130
Fryer; fish-	143
self-employed	104
Fryer-	
catering	143
food products mfr.	202
Fuelman (ship)	317
Fuller	199
Fumigator	165
Furnace hand; blast	231
Furnace hand-	
charcoal mfr.	204
metal mfr.	231
mine, not coal	204
Furnaceman;	
annealing	237
barium	184
blast	231
boiler	347
brass	231
calcining-	184
flint	204

	Code number
Furnaceman; continued	
chrome	231
cupola	231
electric	231
graphitising	204
hardening; case	237
hearth; open	231
spring; coach	237
treatment; heat	237
Furnaceman-	
ceramic mfr.	191
chemical mfr.	184
crematorium	348
electric bulb mfr.	191
gas works	184
glass mfr.	191
lead pencil mfr.	204
metal trades-	231
annealing	237
oil refining	184
red lead mfr.	184
Furnace worker;	
blast	231
talbot	270
Furnace worker (metal trades)	231
Furnisher;	
ball	104
coffin	224
house	101
funeral	163
Furnisher (retail trade)	101
Furrier-	
fur products mfr.	211
retail trade	101
Fuser; enamel	204
Fuser-	
glass mfr.	204
metal trades	204
textile products mfr.	299
Fuseroom worker (chemical mfr.)	184
Fusilier-	
armed forces-	
foreign and Commonwealth	136
U.K.	135

G

	Code number
G.I. (armed forces-foreign)	136
Gabler and corder (net)	199
Gaffer-see also Foreman-	
glass mfr.	192
Gaiter;	
beam	179
harness	248
loom	F180
warp	179
Gaiter-	
textile spinning	178
textile weaving	248
Galenical worker	184
Galley boy	147
Galley hand	147
Galvanizer	269
Gambler; professional	165
Gang man; shore (shipbuilding)	L344
Gang man (agriculture)	166
Ganger;	
electrification	F306
filtration (water works)	F184
highways	F308
mains	F311
navvy	F308
Ganger- see also Foreman-	
canal	F316
coal mine	338
docks	F334
electricity board	F311
gas board	F311
local government	F316

	Code number
Ganger- continued	
railways	F306
water works	F311
Gangwayman	334
Gantry man; forge (steelworks)	331
Gantry man	331
Garage hand	249
Garage worker (P.O.)	L346
Garde-manger	F143
Gardener;	
fruit-	107
employee	167
landscape	168
market-	107
employee	167
nursery-	107
employee	167
Gardener-	168
fruit growing-	107
employee	167
market gardening-	107
employee	167
nursery-	107
employee	167
Gardener-caretaker	168
Gardener-chauffeur	327
Gardener-groundsman	168
Gardener-handyman	168
Gardener's boy	168
Garnet worker	176
Garnetter	176
Garterer	299
Garthman	166
Gas man; assistant (iron and steelworks)	255
Gasman-	
coal gas	184
water gas	184
blast furnace	348
cider mfr.	197
gas works	184
railways	338
Gas worker;	
chlorine	184
maintenance	260
Gas worker-	L341
industrial gas	184
Gasser	182
Gateman;	
bridge	338
dock	338
flood	338
lock	338
Gateman-	140
coal mine	321
docks	338
entertaiment	165
railways	321
waterways	338
Gatekeeper-	140
coal mine	321
Gatekeeper and pointsman	321
Gatherer;	
coal; sea	L346
mussel	171
quill	338
rag-	131
woollen mfr.	338
seaweed	171
watercress	172
Gatherer-	
agricultural products	172
bookbinding	189
ceramic mfr.	338
glass mfr.	223
Gauger;	
bullet	286
cement	297
furnace	231
gut	204
mica	204
tank-	
oil refining	297
petroleum distribution	297

(Ga—Gr)

	Code number
Gauger; *continued*	
valuer's	115
Gauger-	
cast stone products mfr.	230
glass mfr.	192
metal trades-	286
lamp, valve mfr.	297
oil refining	297
valuing	115
Gaulter	315
Gear man (*docks*)	333
Gelatine man (*explosives*)	184
Gelatine worker	202
Gelder	172
Gemmologist	067
Genealogist	036
General-	
armed forces-	
foreign and Commonwealth	M136
U.K.	M135
General hand-	L346
bacon curing	202
bakery	200
bookbinding	189
dressmaking	210
hairdressing	159
hotel	158
General operative (*textile mfr.*)	L339
General worker-	L346
coal mine	345
farming	166
Generator; acetylene	184
Generator man	184
Geneticist	065
Geographer	036
Geologist	067
Geomorphologist	067
Geophysicist	067
Geotechnologist	067
Geriatrician	041
Getter;	
clay	315
coal	314
Getter-	
coal mine	314
mine, not coal	315
Ghillie	165
Gigger (*textile finishing*)	182
Gilder; edge	227
composition	299
Gilder-	
bookbinding	189
ceramic mfr.	279
furniture mfr.	299
leather dressing	173
painting and decorating	282
printing	227
wallpaper mfr.	227
Gilder and plater	236
Giller-	
motor radiator mfr.	285
textile mfr.	176
Gillie	165
Gimper	199
Giver-out	333
Glacier	143
Glassman	147
Glass worker;	
decorative	303
fibre	223
Glass worker-	
agriculture	167
glass mfr.	223
lamp, valve mfr.	192
Glazer;	
assistant (*metal trades*)	276
button	279
cutlery	243
friction	188
lens	192
optical	192
patent	303
postcard	188

	Code number
Glazer; *continued*	
pottery	279
Glazer-	
ceramic mfr.	279
glass mfr.	192
leather dressing	173
metal trades	243
paper mfr.	188
sugar confectionery mfr.	202
textile mfr.	182
wallpaper mfr.	188
Glazier;	303
lens	192
optical	192
Glazier and decorator	304
Glosser; silk	182
Glosser; (*footwear mfr.*)	175
Glove hand (knitted gloves)	181
Glove worker	211
Glover (*glove mfr.*)	212
Gluer-	
furniture mfr.	299
paper products mfr.	295
sports goods mfr.	299
Gluer-up (woodwork)	299
Glycerine worker	184
Gold worker	279
Goldsmith	266
Golf ball worker	228
Golf course man	168
Golfer	063
Goods worker;	
leather	225
railways	160
rubber	228
Gouger	262
Governess;	053
nursery	150
Governor-	
government	020
prison service	108
Governor man (*gas works*)	348
Gown hand	210
Grade I, II Technical Class (*government*)	090
Grade 5, 6, 7-	
Foreign and Commonwealth Office	021
Grade 9-	
Foreign and Commonwealth Office	F112
Grade 10-	
Foreign and Commonwealth Office	115
Grader;	
coke	204
egg	298
fat	298
fruit	298
hosiery	298
leather	298
meat	298
pattern-	
clothing mfr.	226
footwear mfr.	227
pelt (*fellmongery*)	298
pig	172
poultry (*retail trade*)	298
rag	298
sack	298
skin	298
sole	298
stock; live	172
wool	298
Grader-	
abrasive paper, etc. mfr.	227
chemical mfr.	184
coal mine	198
food products mfr.	298
glass mfr.	299
metal trades	298
paper pattern mfr.	226
photographic processing	227
plasterboard mfr.	299

	Code number
Grader- *continued*	
textile mfr.	298
tobacco pipe mfr.	298
wholesale fish trade	298
Graduator; thermometer	246
Grafter (*agriculture*)	167
Grailer (*celluloid goods mfr.*)	229
Grainer; plate	276
Grainer-	
brewery	L346
leather dressing	173
painting and decorating	282
printing	276
Grainer and marbler	282
Granary hand	L346
Granary man	333
Granulator; aluminium	270
Granulator (*chemical mfr.*)	184
Granulator man (sugar)	202
Graphologist	165
Grater (*steelworks*)	L344
Gravel worker (*gravel extraction*)	315
Grease man	184
Greaser;	
cold roll	271
donkey (*shipping*)	317
electric (*shipping*)	317
fan (*shipping*)	317
kiln	271
refrigerating (*shipping*)	317
sheave	271
tin (*bakery*)	200
Greaser-	271
motor vehicles	249
bakery	200
fishing	317
shipping	317
tin box mfr.	L344
Greengrocer-	101
market trading	130
mobile shop	128
Greensman	168
Grey man	333
Grey room hand	333
Grey room man	333
Griddler (*catering*)	143
Grieve	107
Grill hand	143
Grill man	184
Grinder;	
anvil	276
asbestos	176
assistant (*metal trades*)	276
axle	241
ball (ball bearing)	242
billet (*steelworks*)	276
bit (*coal mine*)	276
bits; drill	241
blade	276
bolster	241
bone	204
bow	276
burr	276
cam-bowl	241
carbide	184
carbon (*crucible mfr.*)	204
card	276
card clothing	276
cardroom	276
castings	244
centreless	241
clay (*ceramic mfr.*)	204
coffee	202
colour	204
comb	276
compo (*metal mfr.*)	204
composition-	
ceramic mfr.	204
metal mfr.	204
corn	202
crankshaft	241
cutlery	241

(Gr—Ha)

Grinder; *continued*
- cutter-
  - *cemented carbide goods mfr.* ... 230
  - *metal trades* ... 241
- cylinder-
  - *metal trades* ... 241
  - *textile mfr.* ... 176
- cylindrical ... 241
- disc-
  - *abrasive wheel mfr.* ... 230
  - *metal trades* ... 241
- drill ... 241
- dry (metal) ... 276
- dust ... 204
- ebonite ... 228
- edge-
  - *abrasive wheel mfr.* ... 230
  - *gramophone record mfr.* ... 229
- emery (*steelworks*) ... 244
- enamel ... 204
- face ... 241
- file ... 241
- flat- ... 176
  - glass ... 192
  - textiles ... 176
- flint (*ceramic mfr.*) ... 204
- flock ... 176
- ganister ... 198
- gear ... 241
- gelatine ... 184
- glass ... 192
- glaze (*ceramic mfr.*) ... 204
- hob ... 241
- ink ... 184
- instrument ... 241
- internal ... 241
- jig ... 241
- jobbing ... 276
- jute ... 176
- knife ... 241
- lens ... 192
- logwood ... 203
- machine (*metal trades*) ... 241
- mower; lawn ... 241
- needle ... 276
- optical ... 192
- organ ... 060
- paint ... 204
- paper ... 188
- precision ... 241
- profile; optical ... 241
- race ... 241
- rag ... 176
- razor ... 241
- resin ... 184
- roll ... 241
- roller ... 241
- rough cast ... 244
- rubber ... 204
- sand ... 204
- saw ... 241
- scissors ... 276
- segmental ... 241
- shaft ... 241
- shears ... 241
- shoddy ... 176
- silica ... 204
- slab; optical ... 192
- slag ... 204
- snuff ... 201
- soap; dry ... 184
- spindle ... 241
- spline ... 241
- spring ... 241
- steel ... 276
- stone; ... 301
  - lime (*quarry*) ... 198
  - lithographic ... 301
  - wet ... 276
- stopper; glass ... 192
- straight ... 276
- sugar ... 202

Grinder; *continued*
- surface- ... 241
  - *carbon goods mfr.* ... 230
  - *glass mfr.* ... 192
- sweep ... L344
- swing ... 276
- tool; ... 241
  - universal ... 240
- tool and cutter ... 240
- tool room ... 240
- universal ... 241
- valve ... 241
- wet- ... 276
  - chemicals ... 184
- wheel; emery- ... 276
  - *glass mfr.* ... 192

Grinder-
- *abrasive paper, etc. mfr.* ... 230
- *brake lining mfr.* ... 230
- *carbon goods mfr.* ... 230
- *cast concrete products mfr.* ... 230
- *ceramic mfr.* ... 223
- *chemical mfr.* ... 184
- *food products mfr.* ... 202
- *glass mfr.* ... 192
- *metal trades-* ... 241
  - *foundry* ... 244
  - *precious metal, plate mfr.* ... 244
- *mine, not coal* ... 198
- *paper mfr.* ... 203
- *patent fuel mfr.* ... 204
- *plastics goods mfr.* ... 229
- *printing* ... 227
- *textile mfr.-* ... 176
  - *textile finishing* ... 182

Grinder and finisher; spring ... 241
Grinder and polisher-
- *metal trades* ... 276
- *optical goods mfr.* ... 192

Grinderman-
- *grain milling* ... 202
- *paper mfr.* ... 203

Grinder-setter (*metal trades*) ... 238
Gristman (*brewery*) ... 197
Griswold hand ... 181
Grocer- ... 101
- travelling ... 128
Grommeter ... 299
Groom ... 172
Groom-gardener ... 172
Groomsman ... 172
Groover; pencil ... 218
Groover (*metal trades*) ... 241
Grosser (*textile making-up*) ... 287
Groundman; hard ... 314
Groundman (*water works*) ... 316
Ground worker (*building and contracting*) ... 313
Grounder; fur ... 299
Grounder (*wallpaper printing*) 299
Groundsman; excavator ... 330
Groundsman- ... 168
- market ... L346
Grouter; mould (*steelworks*) ... 270
Grower- ... 107
- bulb- ... 107
  - employee ... 167
- crystal ... 080
- fruit- ... 107
  - employee ... 167
- mushroom- ... 107
  - employee ... 167
- osier ... 170
- rose- ... 107
  - employee ... 167
- tomato- ... 107
  - employee ... 167
- watercress- ... 107
  - employee ... 167
- willow ... 170
- withy ... 170
- wood ... 170

Guard;
- ballast ... 320

Guard; *continued*
- bank ... 140
- body ... 140
- bus ... 328
- coast ... 142
- custody ... 140
- fire ... 138
- forest ... 170
- goods ... 320
- life ... 142
- loco ... 320
- motor ... 140
- night ... 140
- passenger ... 320
- security ... 140
- train- ... 320
  - ropes ... 338
- van ... 140
- water (*Customs and Excise*) 019
- works ... 140

Guard-
- *L.T.E.* ... 320
- *manufacturing* ... 140
- *railways* ... 320
- *road goods transport* ... 140
- *road passenger transport* ... 328

Guarder (*net mfr.*) ... 199
Guardsman; coast ... 142
Guardsman (*armed forces-U.K.*) 135
Guide; ... 152
- store ... 165
Guide man; coke ... 338
Guider-
- *textile printing* ... 227
- *tube mfr.* ... 270
Guider-in ... 199
Guillotine hand-
- *asbestos-cement products mfr.* 230
- *metal trades* ... 276
- *paper products mfr.* ... 190
Guillotine man *see* Guillotine hand
Guillotine worker *see* Guillotine hand
Guitarist ... 060
Gulley man ... L346
Gummer-
- *coal mine* ... 314
- *paper products mfr.* ... 295
Gunner;
- civilian (*Min. of Defence*) 348
Gunner-
- *armed forces-*
  - *foreign and Commonwealth* 136
  - *U.K.* ... 135
- *steelworks* ... 276
Gunsmith ... 248
Gutman ... 186
Gutta percha worker ... 228
Gutter; fish ... 187
Gymnast; ... 063
- remedial ... 049
Gynaecologist ... 041

H

H.M.F.I. ... 019
H.M.I.S. ... 035
Haberdasher- ... 101
- *market trading* ... 130
Hackler ... 176
Haematologist ... 080
Hafter ... 276
Hair hand (*brush, etc. mfr.*) ... 298
Hair worker ... 176
Hairdresser ... 159
Hall boy (*hotel*) ... 154
Hall man (*hotel*) ... 154
Halsher (wool) ... 178
Hammer lad ... 270
Hammer worker; power ... 270

(Ha—He)

	Code number
Hammerman-	233
jute mfr.	L339
L.T.E.	248
leather dressing	173
pile driving	330
precious metal, plate mfr.	266
tobacco mfr.	276
Hammerer; saw	276
Hammerer (*precious metal, plate mfr.*)	266
Hander; machine *see Machinist*	
Handicapper	063
Handler;	
aircraft	338
animal	172
bag; paper	227
baggage (*air transport*)	335
body (*vehicle mfr.*)	338
coal	338
dog	172
material	338
red press mud	184
sheet (metal)	338
spade and shovel	299
stock (asbestos-cement goods mfr.)	338
stone (*brush, etc. mfr.*)	176
tool (*edge tool mfr.*)	299
traffic	115
Handler-	
brush, etc. mfr.	299
ceramic mfr.	299
edge tool mfr.	299
photographic mfr.	227
tannery	173
Handyman;	
bar	165
builder's	304
carpenter's	219
electrician's	276
engineer's	276
estate	304
farm	166
fitter's-	276
pipe	276
garage	249
gardener's	168
general	304
maintenance	304
n.o.s.-	304
residential buildings	316
coal mine	345
gas works	276
grist milling	202
water works	276
office	L346
Handyman-driver	327
Handyman-gardener	168
Handyman-labourer	L346
Hanger;	
bell (church bells)	272
door (coach body)	285
linoleum (*linoleum mfr.*)	204
paper	282
poster	165
Hanger (*leather cloth mfr.*)	199
Hanger-on-	337
coal mine	338
Hanker-	
textile mfr.	199
textile packing	287
Hard ground man	314
Hardener;	
blade	237
case	237
die and mill	237
drill	237
felt	199
file	237
ring	237
saw	237
section	237
tool	237
wool (hats)	199

	Code number
Hardener-	
hats	199
metal	237
Harpist	060
Harpooner	171
Harvester; crop	172
Hatchman	334
Hatcher; fish	171
Hatchery worker-	
agriculture	172
fishing	171
Hatchwayman	334
Hatter-	
hat mfr.	226
retail trade	101
Hat worker	211
Haulage hand-	
coal mine	338
haulage contractor	326
mine, not coal	338
Haulage man; face	338
Haulage man (*coal mine*)	338
Haulage worker (*coal mine*)	338
Hauler;	
coal (*retail trade*)	326
timber	326
Haulerman	338
Haulier;	
butt	173
general	326
shop (*tube mfr.*)	270
timber	326
Haulier-	326
coal mine	338
Hawker	130
Head;	
departmental *see Manager*	
section-	
clerical	F115
chemical mfr.	066
of department-	
educational establishments-	
further education establishment	032
primary and secondary education	033
of section *see Manager*	
Head lad (*racing stable*)	172
Headman; gear (*coal mine*)	314
Headman- *see also Foreman*	
meat curing	186
racing stable	F172
Header;	
bolt	276
cold (rivets)	276
fish	187
stone (*coal mine*)	314
Header-	
bolts, etc., mfr.	276
coal mine	314
Header-up-	
bolts, etc., mfr.	276
cask mfr.	216
Heading man; hard	314
Heading worker; hard	314
Heald man	179
Healder	179
Hearthman (*brewery*)	197
Heatman (*linoleum mfr.*)	204
Heat treatment worker (metal)	237
Heater;	
coke oven	184
ingot	231
iron (*foundry*)	231
mill (*rolling mill*)	231
pit; soaking	231
retort (*chemical mfr.*)	184
rivet	276
rubber (*tyre mfr.*)	194
smith's	231
steel tube	231
Heater-	
coal gas, coke ovens	184
metal trades-	231

	Code number
Heater- *continued*	
metal trades- *continued*	
annealing	237
cycle mfr.	237
file mfr.	237
Heaterman (*patent fuel mfr.*)	184
Heaver; coal	334
Hedger;	172
stone	301
Hedger and ditcher	172
Heeler (footwear)	175
Helminthologist	065
Helmsman	317
Help;	
baker's	200
bar	145
canteen	146
daily	151
domestic	151
electrician's	276
farm	166
general (*bakery*)	200
home	151
kitchen	147
meals; school	146
mother's	151
moulder's	L343
part-time (*retail trade*)	125
plater's	276
printer's	207
room; dining	146
teacher's (school meals)	151
ward	156
Help (*domestic service*)	151
Helper;	
bakehouse	200
bar	145
bender's; frame	276
blacksmith's	270
bricklayer's	312
canteen	146
carpenter's	219
caster's	270
club; youth	165
collier('s)	314
cutter's	276
domestic	151
electrician's	276
erector's; steel	276
examiner's (*net mfr.*)	199
first-	
blast furnace	231
rolling mill	270
tinplate mfr.	270
fitter's	276
follower's; crane	338
forge	270
frame	276
furnace	231
furnaceman's	231
infant	151
keeper's	231
ladle	337
maker's; boiler	276
mason's	312
meals; school	146
miner's (*mine, not coal*)	315
nursery	150
operator's; wireline	315
part-time (*retail trade*)	125
people's; old	156
pickler's (*metal trades*)	270
pit	270
pitman's	270
plater's	276
playgroup	165
playschool	165
potman's (nickel)	231
press	270
repairer's (*coal mine*)	276
roller's	270
room; dining	146
school	151
second (*blast furnace*)	231

(He—In)

	Code number
Helper; *continued*	
shearer's (*metal trades*)	276
smith's;	270
boiler	276
stable	172
stamper's	270
straightener's-	276
rolling mill	270
weaver's	199
worker's; process	184
Helper-	
catering	147
metal trades-	276
blast furnace	231
copper refining	270
forging	270
rolling mill	270
tube mfr.	270
paper mfr.	203
salt mfr.	184
textile mfr.-	L339
textile weaving	199
Helper-up	338
Helver (tools)	299
Hemmer	212
Hemstitcher	212
Herbalist	050
Herdsman	166
Herring worker	187
Hewer (*coal mine*)	314
Highwayman	308
Hind	166
Hinger; last	224
Hirer;	
boat	317
site; caravan	109
Histologist	065
Histopathologist	065
Historian	036
Hitcher (*coal mine*)	338
Hobbler; to dock pilots	317
Hoistman	331
Hoister; crane	331
Holder;	
copy	115
double (*rolling mill*)	270
small-	107
forestry	170
stall-	130
entertainment	165
coal mine	314
store	333
at drill (*rolling mill*)	L344
Holder-on (riveter's)	276
Holder-up;	
boilermaker's	276
riveter's	276
Holder-up (*shipbuilding*)	276
Holdsman	334
Holer;	
button-	212
button mfr.	230
footwear mfr.	175
eyelet	175
flyer	241
Holer (*mine, not coal*)	315
Hollanderman	204
Homeopath-	050
medically qualified	041
Homicker	204
Homixer	204
Homogeniser	202
Honer	241
Hookman	L342
Hooker-	
mine, not coal	338
rolling mill	270
textile mfr.	182
Hooper; wheel	233
Hopper lad	L341
Hopperman; dredge	338
Hopperman-	
bakery	200
cement mfr.	204

	Code number
Hopperman- *continued*	
dredging contractors	338
iron and steel mfr.	338
Horologist	247
Horse boy-	172
canal	338
mine, not coal	338
Horseman-	172
timber haulage	338
canal	338
tannery	L346
Horticultural worker	167
Horticulturist-	065
local government	107
market gardening, etc.	107
Hoseman	315
Hosier;	101
elastic	181
surgical	181
Hosier and haberdasher	101
Hosiery hand	181
,, operative	181
,, worker	181
Hospital worker	156
Hostess; air	152
Hostess (*aircraft*)	152
Hostler	172
Hot plate hand (*catering*)	146
Hotel worker	151
Hotelier	102
House boy; glass	204
Houseman;	
boiler	347
cylinder	184
domestic	151
press (*coal mine*)	276
sand	203
school	151
slip	204
tun (*brewery*)	197
wash	162
Houseman-	
domestic service	151
institution	151
museum	142
Houseworker;	
power	255
retort (*coal gas, coke ovens*)	184
slaughter	186
slip	204
House worker (*domestic service*)	151
Housemaid	151
Hugger-off	L342
Humper;	
coal	L346
meat (*slaughterhouse*)	335
Humper-	
meat market	335
slaughterhouse	335
Hunter	172
Huntsman	172
Husband; ship's	095
Husbandman	166
Hwsmyn	107
Hydraulicman (*docks*)	348
Hydrapulper	203
Hydrator; lime	204
Hydro hand	162
Hydro man-	
laundry	162
textile mfr.	199
Hydrobiologist	065
Hydro-blaster	275
Hydro-extractor	199
Hydrographer	090
Hydrologist	067
Hygienist; dental	050
Hypo boy	227
Hyster	332

I

	Code number
Ice cream jack	128
Icer	202
Ichthyologist	065
Icing room worker	200
Illuminator	055
Illuminiser	269
Illusionist	059
Illustrator;	
book	055
chief	M079
leading	F079
senior	F079
technical	079
Illustrator (*government*)	079
Immunologist	065
Importer	129
Imposition hand	205
Impregnator; armature	204
Impregnator-	
asbestos composition goods mfr.	204
cable mfr.	230
Impresario	059
Impressioner (engraver's)	227
Improver; *see also notes p.4*	
cutter	211
green	168
millinery	211
Improver (*wool spinning*)	177
Incorporator	184
Incubationist (*agriculture*)	172
Incumbent	040
Indexer-	115
bookbinding	189
Inflator;	
bed; air	291
cushion; air	291
Infuser; water (*coal mine*)	314
Infusion man; water	314
Ingiver	179
Ingot man-	
non-ferrous metal mfr.	231
rolling mill	333
Injector;	
mould (*plastics goods mfr.*)	195
wax	270
Inker;	
edge	299
typewriter ribbon	199
Inker (*footwear mfr.*)	299
Inseminator; artificial	172
Inserter; coil	283
Inserter; ferrule (*water works*)	260
Inserter-	
clothing mfr.	299
lamp, valve mfr.	283
Inspector;	
A.I.D. (*Board of Trade*)	286
accounts	115
advertisement	F165
advertising	F165
aeronautical	286
aircraft	286
alkali	019
ammunition	019
apparatus; photographic	286
area-	
automatic machines	248
wholesale and retail trade	101
armaments	286
assembly	286
assistant-	
government	F112
P.O.	F123
ballast	F306
bank	M030
bank-note	294
bar (*rolling mill*)	286
beach	F140
belt (*coal mine*)	338
bench	286

(In)

	Code number
Inspector; *continued*	
bill (*advertising*)	F165
billet (*steelworks*)	286
boiler-	286
insurance	090
box (*electricity board*)	253
bridge	F316
building	018
bus	F323
business; new (*insurance*)	134
cabinet	293
cable-	257
cable mfr.	286
canal	F316
car-	286
dining car	F146
cargo	115
carpet	289
carriage (*railways*)	248
carriage and wagon	248
cartage (*railways*)	F318
cell (*chemical mfr.*)	299
cellar	197
chair; deck	F165
chemical	019
chicken (*food processing*)	290
chief-	
banking	M030
engineering-	F286
professional-	069
electrical engineering	071
electronic engineering	072
quality control	075
government	021
insurance	134
local government-	019
transport dept.	095
P.O.	111
police service	M137
railways	095
water board	F310
claims-	
insurance	005
railways	115
cleansing	F336
cloth	289
clothing-	289
Ministry of Defence	021
coal (*opencast coal mining*)	019
coil	286
coke (*coke ovens*)	F184
component(s) (*metal trades*)	286
contract	115
control;	
pest	165
quality-	
bakery	290
coal mine	248
glass mfr.	299
metal trades	286
paper mfr.	294
river, water authority	019
sugar confectionery mfr.	290
core	286
crane	019
credit	115
cylinder	286
dairy (*retail trade*)	101
depot; chief (*transport*)	095
depot-	F333
transport	F324
despatch	F333
detail	286
detective	M137
diesel (*railways*)	F248
district-	F256
gas board	019
government-	021
Min. of A.F.F.	019
Min. of Defence	076
insurance	134
retail trade	101
transport-	
rail	F318

	Code number
Inspector; *continued*	
district- *continued*	
transport- *continued*	
road	F323
water board	F310
divisional-	
government-	021
Min. of Defence	076
local government	019
police service	M137
transport	095
drain(age)	F311
drug	019
effluent	019
electrical-	286
coal mine	019
government	019
electrical and mechanical	
(*coal mine*)	019
electronics (*components mfr.*)	286
employment;	022
railway	009
enamel	286
engine	286
engineering; chief	069
engineering-	286
D.H.S.S.	069
D.O.E.	068
Dept. of Energy	081
P.O.	F256
excavating (*electricity board*)	F311
explosives	019
factory-	
clothing mfr.	289
metal trades	286
field (*P.O.*)	F257
film	299
fire-	019
fire service	M138
fishery (*Min. of A.F.F.*)	019
fitting(s)-	
gas board	019
water board	019
flight-	248
radio (*airport*)	259
floor (*engineering*)	286
food-	017
food products mfr.	290
fuel (*local government*)	019
furnace-	231
furnace mfr.	286
gaming (*club*)	165
garage	F324
garment	289
gauge	286
gas	019
glass	299
goods (*railways*)	F318
government (small arms)	286
graphite	299
guards (*railways*)	F320
health; public	017
higher grade	021
highways	F308
hosiery	289
hotel	030
houses; public	134
housing	027
housing and planning	027
industrial (*gas board*)	019
infestation	165
installation; electrical	019
installation-	
electricity board	019
gas board	019
P.O.	F256
instrument	286
insulation	286
insurance;	134
boiler	090
national	019
inwards; goods	333
jig and tool	286
laboratory (*glass mfr.*)	080

	Code number
Inspector; *continued*	
lamp	286
layout	286
leaf	299
lens	299
life (*insurance*)	134
lift-	248
D.O.E.	090
lighting; public	165
line; pipe	F311
line-	
railways	306
vehicle mfr.	286
lining (*brake lining mfr.*)	299
livestock; area	019
loading (*transport*)	F324
locomotive (*railways*)	F248
machine-	286
office machines	251
weighing machines-	248
coal mine	F248
docks	019
railways	019
machinery	248
mains	F311
maintenance-	
electricity board	F253
gas board	019
local government (housing dept.)	F316
market(s) (*local government*)	019
material(s)	090
meat	017
mechanical	286
medical	041
metal	286
meter	286
metrology	081
micrometer	286
mineral (*railways*)	F318
mines	019
mirror	299
motor	286
mould (*glass mfr.*)	299
N.A.A.F.I.	125
navigation (*river board*)	316
nylon	289
office;	
head (*railways*)	F318
n.o.s.	115
operating (*railways*)	F318
operations; flight	019
optical	299
ore	298
paint (*engineering*)	286
parcels (*railways*)	F318
park	140
patrol-	F140
metal trades	286
paving and extension	F309
plant;	
gas	248
mechanical	286
preparation (*N.C.B.*)	248
process-	248
construction	286
oil refining	248
plastics	292
plate (*steelworks*)	286
platform (*railways*)	F160
plumbing	019
police;	M137
works	111
pollution; air	017
pollution (*river, water authority*)	019
postal	F123
potato crisp	290
practice; standard	010
pre-payment	115
principal (*government*)	021
process	286
production	286
progress (*railways*)	115

(In)

	Code number
Inspector; *continued*	
quality-	
coal mine	F298
engineering	286
Queen's	F043
radio	286
rail	286
railway	F318
reader; meter	F115
receiving; goods	333
records; musical	299
reinstatement (*gas board*)	019
relay	286
rent	115
revenue (*water board*)	115
ring (*engineering*)	286
river-	316
river authority/board	019
roads; chief (*L.T.E.*)	095
road(s)-	308
L.T.E.	F323
transport	F323
rodent	F165
roller (*metal trades*)	286
room; standards	010
rope	299
rota	F128
round(s) (*wholesale and retail trades*)	F128
rubber	291
safety-	
coal mine	019
engineering	039
sales (*retail trade*)	101
sanitary-	017
ceramic mfr.	299
railways	F316
section (*waterways*)	316
security	111
senior (*Customs and Excise*)	019
service (*gas board*)	019
sewer	F310
shell	299
shipping (*telephone mfr.*)	286
shop;	
fitting	286
machine	286
shop (*retail trade*)	101
shops (*local government*)	017
shunting	F322
signal (*railways*)	F259
signal and telegraph (*railways*)	F259
signalman's	F321
site (*advertising*)	F165
smoke (*local government*)	017
staff (*government*)	021
station (*railways*)	F160
steel (*coal mine*)	276
stock; rolling	F248
stores;	F333
chief	096
street (*electricity board*)	165
sub-station (*electricity board*)	255
system	286
technical	090
telecommunications	111
telegraph (*railways*)	F259
telephones	F256
test	286
textile	289
ticket; chair	165
ticket-	
public transport	F323
railways	F160
timber	293
timing (*L.T.E.*)	F323
tool	286
tool and gauge	286
tool room	286
town planning	027
traffic; chief (*P.O.*)	095
traffic-	
rail	F318

	Code number
Inspector; *continued*	
traffic- *continued*	
road	F323
train	F318
tramways	F323
transport-	
road-	F324
public transport	F323
trench	F311
trimming; coach	299
tube	286
tunnel	F316
tyre	291
upholstery	289
V.A.T. (*Customs and Excise*)	019
veneer	293
veterinary	051
wages	019
wagon	248
waste (*water board*)	311
water;	311
chief	F311
hot (*gas board*)	019
waterways	316
way; permanent	F306
welding	286
works;	
district (*railways*)	F306
new (*railways*)	F306
public (*local government*)	F316
works-	
civil engineering	092
railways	F306
vehicle mfr.	286
workshops (*N.C.B.*)	248
yard	F318
yarn	289
of accidents (*Board of Trade*)	019
of ancient monuments	030
of armaments (*government*)	286
of audits (*D.O.E.*)	002
of doorkeepers (*P.O.*)	F140
of electrical fitters	F252
of electricians	F253
of factories (*government*)	019
of fighting vehicles	069
of fitters	F248
of mechanics	F248
of mines (*Dept. of Industry*)	019
of naval ordnance	286
of park keepers	F140
of postmen	F123
of postal services	111
of rates and rentals	022
of schools	035
of shipping	095
of shipwrights	F262
of special subjects	019
of storehousemen	F333
of stores and clothing (*Min. of Defence*)	075
of taxes	008
of weights and measures	019
of wireless telegraphy	111
of works	092
Inspector-	
abrasive paper, etc. mfr.	294
asbestos-cement goods mfr.	299
banking	M030
brewery	019
brush mfr.	299
canvas goods mfr.	289
carbon goods mfr.	299
cardboard mfr.	294
carpet and rug mfr.	289
cartridge mfr.	299
catering	F146
ceramic mfr.	299
civil engineering	092
clothing mfr.	289
dyeing and cleaning	299
electrical goods mfr.	286
electricity board	019
fancy goods mfr.	299

	Code number
Inspector- *continued*	
food products mfr.	290
footwear mfr.	299
furniture mfr.	293
gas board	019
glass mfr.	299
government-	021
Board of Trade (accident investigation branch)	019
Home Office-	021
children's dept.	M039
probation division	M039
D.O.E.-	090
inspectorate of alkali, etc. works	019
inspectorate of housing and planning	027
Dept. of Industry	019
Dept. of Transport-	
coastguard service	019
railway inspectorate	019
survey branch	084
instrument mfr.	286
insurance	134
leather cloth mfr.	299
leather dressing	298
local government-	019
cleansing dept.	F336
education dept.	035
highways dept.	F308
surveyor's dept.	084
works dept.	F316
man-made fibre mfr.	289
match mfr.	299
metal trades	286
mica goods mfr.	299
mine, not coal	019
motoring organisation	F324
N.H.B.R.C.	018
N.S.P.C.C.	039
office cleaning services	F158
opencast coal mining	019
P.O.-	F123
engineering dept.	F256
telephone dept.	F256
paper mfr.	294
paper products mfr.	294
plasterboard mfr.	299
plastics goods mfr.	292
police service	M137
printing	294
R.S.P.C.A.	019
retail trade	101
rubber goods mfr.	291
stone dressing	299
surgical goods mfr.	299
telegraph service	F257
textile mfr.-	289
wool sorting	F298
transport-	
rail	F318
road	F323
water board	311
window dressing	058
wood products mfr.	293
Inspector and packer (yarn)	289
Installation hand (*oil refinery*)	184
Installation worker (*oil refinery*)	184
Installer;	
circuit (*L.T.E.*)	257
heating	260
permanent way	306
signal (*railways*)	259
signal and telecommunications (*railways*)	259
systems; computer	259
telecommunications	259
telegraph	259
telephone	256
television	258
wireless apparatus	259
Installer-	
electrical contracting	253
railways	257

(In—Ju)

	Code number
Installer- *continued*	
telephone service	256
Instructor; *see also notes* p.4	
apprentice	034
civil defence	142
civilian (*government*)	034
craftsman; apprentice (*coal mine*)	034
dance	053
driving-	052
goods transport vehicles	034
public service vehicles	034
flying	085
handicraft(s)	053
manual	034
riding	063
simulation; flight	085
station; rescue	034
supervising	034
technical	034
trainee	034
training	034
woodwork-	
educational establishments- further education establishment	033
further education establishment	032
primary and secondary schools	033
Instructor-	
physical training-	
educational establishments	053
sports	063
apprentice school	034
coal mine	034
driving school	052
educational establishments- further education establishment	033
further education establishment	032
training centre	034
university	031
Instrumentalist	060
Insulation hand	316
Insulator;	
bitumen	230
building	316
cable	230
coil	230
electrical	276
heat and frost	316
pipe	316
refrigerator	316
thermal-	316
electrical appliances mfr.	276
Insulator (*electrical appliances mfr.*)	230
Intake man	333
Interlacer; shoe	225
Interlacer (hair and fibre)	199
Interleaver (paper)	203
Interpreter	054
Interviewer;	
commercial	115
employment agency	115
press	054
television	054
Interviewer (*market, etc. research*)	115
Inventor	030
Investigator;	
accident	039
accounts	115
claims	005
credit	140
hire purchase	140
o & m	010
private	140
research; market	115
security	140
study; work	010
Investigator-	
D.H.S.S.	115
Historical Monuments Commission	030
Invigilator	115

	Code number
Invoicer	115
Iron and steelworker	L344
Ironman (*coal mine*)	314
Iron worker;	
art	276
ornamental	233
sheet	261
wrought	233
Iron worker-	
constructional engineering	263
iron and steelworks	L344
Ironer;	
boot	299
glove	162
Ironer-	
clothing mfr.	162
footwear mfr.	299
hosiery mfr.	162
laundry	162
leather dressing	173
Ironer and finisher	162
Ironer and presser	162
Ironer-up (piano hammers)	222
Ironmonger	101
Ironstone worker	315
Irrigator	172
Issuer;	333
basket (*retail trade*)	L346
fuel (*road transport*)	333
stores	333
work (*engineering*)	FL344
Ivory worker	230

J

	Code number
Jack;	
lumber	170
smoke	158
steeple	316
Jackman	L341
Janitor	157
Japanner-	
leather dressing	173
Jennier	287
Jet man	348
Jet worker	266
Jetty hand	334
Jettyman	334
Jetty operative	334
Jeweller; *see also notes* p.4	
fancy	266
imitation	266
jobbing	266
manufacturing	266
masonic	266
watch	285
Jeweller and watch repairer	247
Jeweller and watchmaker	247
Jigman-	
constructional engineering	338
mine, not coal	198
Jigger; spindle	286
Jigger-	
ceramic mfr.	193
leather dressing	173
metal trades	270
textile dyeing	182
Jiggerman	182
Jiggerer (*ceramic mfr.*)	193
Jobber;	
agent's; estate	304
back	248
builder's	304
card	F176
carding	F176
comb	248
combing	248
doubling; ring	248

	Code number
Jobber; *continued*	
loom	248
printer's	207
property	304
ring	248
stock	007
stock and share	007
twisting	248
Jobber-	
building and contracting	304
jewellery mfr.	266
leather dressing	173
textile mfr.-	248
textile dyeing	182
Jobber lad	L339
Jobbing hand (*rope, twine mfr.*)	199
Jobbing man	266
Jockey;	063
car	161
disc	059
Jogger (*paper mfr.*)	203
Joggler	276
Joiner;	
aircraft	214
builder's	214
bulb (*valve mfr.*)	283
coach	268
film	227
fitter's; shop	214
glass	223
machine	218
pipe	311
rubber (cycle tubes)	194
ship's	214
textile	177
Joiner-	214
cabinet making	215
lamp, valve mfr.	283
rubber footwear mfr.	299
textile mfr.-	177
hosiery mfr.	181
Joiner-machinist	218
Jointer;	
cable	257
chain	265
conduit; electric	257
edge; veneer	224
electric	257
pipe; sprinkler	260
pipe-	311
stoneware pipe mfr.	223
stanford	223
tapeless	224
wire	257
Jointer-	
cable laying	257
ceramic mfr.	223
civil engineering	311
cutlery mfr.	276
electricity board	257
gas board	311
P.O.	257
soft toy mfr.	299
stoneware pipe mfr.	223
water board	311
Jointer-plumber	257
Jollier	193
Journalist	054
Journeyman *see notes* p.5	
Judge-	
entertainment	063
legal service	001
Juggler	059
Juiceman	202
Jumper; show	063
Jumper (fibre)	176
Jumper-baster	212
Junction man	338

(Ke—La)

K

	Code number
Keeker	F198
Keeper;	
alley; bowling	106
animal	172
bar-	
coffee bar	104
hotel, etc.	145
milk bar	104
shipping	145
bee	172
boat	317
book;	115
chief	F115
bridge;	338
toll	115
weigh	297
cemetery	157
chapel	157
church	157
common	140
company	L346
court	157
cow	166
crossing;	321
level	321
die	333
door-	140
synagogue	157
floor (*Bank of England*)	142
forest	170
furnace-	
glass mfr.	191
metal mfr.	231
game	172
gate;	
crossing (*railways*)	321
lock	338
pier	115
gate-	140
coal mine	331
railways	321
granary	333
grass	168
green	168
ground;	168
burial	157
hall	157
head-	
park	F140
zoological gardens	F172
heath	140
horse;	172
head	F172
hotel	102
house;	
beer	103
boarding	102
boat	157
bridge	338
daily	149
gate	140
head-	
hospital	111
hotel	111
institution	111
light	338
resident (*offices*)	157
ware	F333
house-	149
offices	157
hotel	F148
institution	F148
property management	157
school	F148
inn	111
institute	157
kennel	172
laundry	111
ledger	115
light	338
lighthouse	338

Keeper; *continued*	Code number
linen	333
lobby	157
lock	338
lodge	140
machine; weighing	297
magazine	333
menagerie	172
mortuary	157
museum	030
office;	157
box	115
paper	115
park;	140
head	F140
pattern	333
pig	107
plan (*railways*)	333
poultry	107
record	115
repository;	
fancy	101
furniture	333
horse	111
reservoir	316
restaurant	104
river	172
room(s) (*catering*)	104
school	157
ship	140
shop *see* Shopkeeper	
sluice	338
square	168
stable;	172
livery	111
stall;	130
book	101
coffee	104
stanch	338
stationery	333
stock-	333
agriculture	166
store;	333
chief	096
drug	101
general	101
head	F333
room; engine	F317
store and vault; bonded	333
swingbridge	338
switch	322
tavern	103
time	115
tool	333
vault	333
wardrobe	165
warehouse	F333
water	172
weir	338
wharf; canal	316
of the signet	001
Keeper-	
blast furnace	231
museum	030
Public Record Office	030
Trinity House	338
zoological gardens	172
Keeper and pointsman; gate	321
Keeper-clerk; store	333
Keeper-companion; house	149
Kenchman (*coal mine*)	314
Kennelman	172
Kerner (*typefounding*)	276
Kettleman	231
Keysmith	276
Kibbler (*food products mfr.*)	202
Kicker (*metal stamping*)	242
Kier man (*textile mfr.*)	182
Killer	186
Killer and plucker	187
Kiln hand (*ceramic mfr.*)	191
Kiln man;	
carbon	204
dry	204

Kiln man; *continued*	Code number
enamel	191
frit	191
glost	191
gypsum	204
lime	204
Kiln man-	
abrasive wheel mfr.	204
asbestos composition goods mfr.	204
cement mfr.	204
ceramic mfr.	191
chemical mfr.-	184
colour mfr.	204
composition die mfr.	184
distillery	197
glass mfr.	191
Kiln worker-	
ceramic mfr.	191
furniture mfr.	203
lime burning	204
Kipperer	202
Kitchen boy	147
Kitchen girl	147
Kitchen hand-	147
food products mfr.	202
Kitchen man	147
Kitchen staff	147
Kitchen worker	147
Kitter; milk	128
Knacker	186
Kneader (*bakery*)	200
Knife hand (*metal trades*)	276
Knife man (*clothing mfr.*)	211
Knitter	181
Knocker;	
catch; staple pit	338
catch (*coal mine*)	338
Knocker (*ceramic mfr.*)	223
Knocker-off-	
foundry	L343
glass mfr.	223
Knocker-out-	
chocolate mfr.	202
foundry	L343
glass mfr.	223
Knocker-up-	165
printing	190
Knock-out man	L344
Knotter;	
reel	199
warp	179
Knotter-	
textile mfr.-	199
examining dept.	183
wig mfr.	230
Kollerganger	203

L

	Code number
L.A.H.	041
L.R.C.P.	041
L.S.A.	044
Label boy	287
Labeller; colour (glass ware)	299
Labeller	287
Laboratory boy	L346
Laboratory man	288
Laboratory worker	288
Labourer;	
agricultural	166
bricklayer's	312
bricksetter's	312
builder's;	313
boat	219
bulking-floor	338
carpenter's	219
cooper's	219
Crown	170

(La)

	Code number
Labourer; *continued*	
dock;	334
dry	L344
dyer's	199
electric track	313
electrician's	276
engineering; civil	313
erector's	276
estate	166
farm	166
feller's; timber	170
fish	334
fitter's;	276
shop	L346
fixer's;	
felt	312
sheet	312
steel	276
forest	170
foundry	L343
gang; sailor	276
garden-	168
local authority	L346
market gardening	167
garden and parks	L346
gardener's-	168
market gardening	167
grab	338
jetty	334
joiner's	219
layer's;	
granolithic	312
terrazzo	312
maker's; cabinet	219
mason's;	
fixer	312
stone	223
mechanic's	276
millhouse (*textile mfr.*)	L339
millwright's	276
miner's; tunnel	315
moulder's	L343
parks	L346
pitwood	334
plasterer's	312
platelayer's	313
plater's	276
plumber's	276
policy (Scotland)	168
pontoon	334
production	L346
quay	334
quayside	334
rigger's	276
riverside	334
riveter's	276
sailor	276
ship	334
shipwright's	276
stevedore's	334
storekeeper's	335
stores	335
tea (*docks*)	334
warehouse	335
waterside	334
wharf	334
willow garth	170
wood	170
Labourer-	L346
agriculture	166
building and contracting	313
coal mine	345
docks	334
forestry	170
warehousing	335
Lace hand	180
Lace man	180
Lace worker	180
Lacer;	
card	199
corset	299
guard; dress (cycles)	299
jacquard	199
shade; lamp	299

	Code number
Lacer; *continued*	
wheel	285
Lacer-	
corset mfr.	299
footwear mfr.	225
textile weaving	199
Lacer and driller; wheel (*cycle mfr.*)	285
Lacquerer;	299
spray	281
Ladies hand (*hairdressing*)	159
Ladle man; direct	270
Ladle man (*metal mfr.*)	270
Ladler-	
copper lead refining	231
glass mfr.	223
Lady superior	040
Lagger;	316
asbestos	316
axle	224
boiler	316
drum	L346
pipe	316
Lairman	177
Laminator;	
fibreglass	229
plastic	229
wood	203
Laminator-	
paper mfr.	203
plastics mfr.	229
safety glass mfr.	223
textile mfr.	199
Lampman; signal	L346
Lampman-	
coal mine	333
mine, not coal	333
railways	L346
Lamp worker (*glass mfr.*)	192
Lance-Bombardier-	
armed forces-	
foreign and Commonwealth	136
U.K.	135
Lance-Sergeant-	
armed forces-	
foreign and Commonwealth	136
U.K.	135
Land girl	166
Land worker	166
Lander;	
clay	338
fish	334
Lander (*mine, not coal*)-	
above ground	338
below ground	331
Landholder	107
Landlord-	
boarding, lodging house	102
inn	111
public house	103
Landsaler (*N.C.B.*)	338
Landworker	166
Lapman	199
Lapidary	266
Lapper;	
barrel (gun)	241
block (*glass mfr.*)	223
cotton	199
gear	241
jeweller's	243
paper	230
tape	199
Lapper-	
cable mfr.	230
metal trades-	241
precious metal, plate mfr.	243
tin box mfr.	242
tube mfr.	270
textile mfr.	199
Laryngologist	041
Lascar	317
Lasher;	182
car	334
Laster	175

	Code number
Latchman *see* Latcher	
Latcher;	
crane (*steelworks*)	337
locomotive	322
wagon (*steelworks*)	322
Latcher-	
coal mine	338
needle mfr.	242
railways	322
steelworks	337
Latexer	228
Lathe hand	241
Lathe man-	241
textile machinery roller covering	225
Lathe worker-	241
glass mfr.	192
Lather; metal	312
Lather (*ceramic mfr.*)	223
Lather boy	165
Launch boy	317
Launch hand	317
Launch man	317
Launderer	162
Laundress	162
Laundry hand	162
Laundry maid	162
Laundry man	162
Laundry worker	162
Lawyer	001
Layman; mussel	171
Layman (*paper mfr.*)	203
Lay worker	039
Layer;	
asphalt	307
bobbin	199
block-	
blast furnace	300
mine	306
brick	300
cable	311
carpet	221
concrete	307
core	270
court; grass	168
covering; floor	316
drain	311
drum	178
duct	311
felt-	
flooring	316
roofing	303
floor;	
block	224
composition	316
concrete	307
decorative	300
granolithic	300
jointless	316
mosaic	300
n.o.s.	316
parquet	224
patent	316
plastic	316
rubber	316
stone	301
terrazzo	300
tile	300
wood	224
glass; plate	L346
green; bowling	168
ground	279
hedge	172
kerb	309
lino	316
linoleum	316
macadam; tar	307
main(s)	311
mosaic	300
parquet	224
pipe-	311
coal mine	260
plate-	306
micanite mfr.	204

(La—Li)

	Code number
Layer; *continued*	
plate- *continued*	
printing	205
printer's (*textile printing*)	227
rail	306
road	306
screen	208
service	311
sole	299
stone	309
surface (*gas board*)	307
tar	307
terrazzo	300
tile	300
track-	306
pipe	311
tramway	308
tray	L340
turf	168
veneer	203
way (*coal mine*)	306
Layer-	
paper mfr.	203
rope mfr.	199
textile spinning	177
wire rope mfr.	276
Layer and fixer; patent flooring and roofing	316
Layer-down (*textile finishing*)	226
Layer-on; machine	207
Layer-on-	
cardboard box mfr.	227
file mfr.	L344
textile mfr.	199
Layer-out;	
tobacco	201
yarn	199
Layer-out-	
glove mfr.	226
textile mfr.	338
Layer-up-	
cable mfr.	276
clothing mfr.	211
tannery	173
Lay-out man-	
advertising	055
printing	205
Lead worker;	
tea	270
Lead worker-	
stained glass	303
accumulator mfr.	230
Leader;	
band	060
club	039
coal	326
girder (*coal mine*)	338
group research *see* Engineer-prof.-	
keep-fit	053
orchestra	060
play	038
playgroup	038
red	282
section-	
clerical office	F115
drawing office	F079
production control	075
progress	115
senior	F115
ambulance service	F155
fire service	F138
retail trade	F125
shift; computer	F119
shift (*ambulance service*)	F155
squadron-	
armed forces-	
foreign and Commonwealth	M136
U.K.	M135
stallion	172
timber-	338
coal mine	314
water	338

	Code number
Leader; *continued*	
window	303
youth	039
Leader (*abrasive wheel mfr.*)	270
Leading hand-*see also notes* p.5	349
building and contracting	304
food products mfr.	202
laundry	162
metal trades-	276
blast furnace	270
foundry	270
rubber goods mfr.	228
textile mfr.	199
warehousing	333
Leading man (*building and contracting*)	316
Leadsman	338
Learner *see notes* pp.3–4	
Leaser; machine spinning	201
Leaser (*textile mfr.*)	179
Leather worker;	
fancy	225
hydraulic and mechanical	225
orthopaedic	225
Leather worker-	
artificial limb mfr.	225
leather dressing	173
leather goods mfr.	225
railways	213
vehicle mfr.	213
Lector	053
Lecturer;	
guide	053
political	030
temperance	040
university	031
Lecturer-*see also notes* p.4	
dentistry	042
medicine	041
surgery	041
educational establishments-	033
college of education	032
further education establishment	032
teacher training establishment	032
university	031
Legger; flyer	233
Legger (*hosiery finishing*)	182
Lehr man	191
Lender;	
barrow	134
money	134
Lengthener	182
Lengthman; road	308
Lengthman-	
canal	316
highway authority	308
local government	308
railways	306
Lengthsman *see* Lengthman	
Lens worker	192
Lepidopterist	065
Letter; barrow	134
Letterer (*signwriting*)	282
Levelhand	231
Leveller;	
concrete	307
plate	270
roller (*steelworks*)	270
Leveller-	
asphalt spreading machine	330
coke ovens	338
footwear mfr.	225
lithography	207
Leverman (*iron and steelworks*)	270
Lexicographer	054
Librarian;	026
tape; computer	115
Licensee;	103
off-licence	101
Lidder-	
boot polish mfr.	287
cardboard box mfr.	295

	Code number
Lieutenant-	
armed forces-	
foreign and Commonwealth	M136
U.K.	M135
Lieutenant-Colonel-	
armed forces-	
foreign and Commonwealth	M136
U.K.	M135
Lieutenant-Commander-	
armed forces-	
foreign and Commonwealth	M136
U.K.	M135
Lieutenant-General-	
armed forces-	
foreign and Commonwealth	M136
U.K.	M135
Lifeboatman	317
Lift boy	161
Liftman;	
gantry	331
service	161
steam	331
Liftman-	161
iron and steelworks	331
Lift worker	161
Lifter;	
beam	199
bin	L346
box	L343
butt	173
carriage	248
coke	338
fork	332
freight	335
heavy	272
wagon	248
Lifter-	
railway workshops	248
steelworks	331
textile mfr.	199
warehouse	335
Lifter-up-	
foundry	L343
rolling mill	270
Ligger	199
Ligger-on (wool)	199
Lighter;	
fire	L346
gas	165
lamp-	165
ships (*Trinity House*)	317
shot (*coal mine*)	314
Lighter boy	317
Lighterman	317
Lighthouse man	338
Lightsman (*lightship*)	317
Lightship man	317
Lime man-	173
steelworks	270
Lime worker	173
Limer-	
blast furnace	L344
fellmongering	173
Limes man (*entertainment*)	062
Limnologist	065
Lineman;	
life; diver's	316
power	257
pump	260
signal; power	257
traction	257
Lineman	257
Liner;	
basket	299
board	295
box; work	299
brake-	299
asbestos mfr.	299
cabinet (*upholstery mfr.*)	299
case	299
cycle	299
dry	316
furnace	300
glove	299

(Li—Ma)

	Code number
Liner; *continued*	
gold-	
ceramic *mfr.*	279
cycle *mfr.*	299
ladle	300
machine	299
picture	299
pipe-	
rubber lining	228
building and contracting	316
plant (rubber lining)	228
pouch; leather	299
roof	303
table	299
tank-	
glass fibre	229
rubber lining	228
tin (*bakery*)	200
tube	299
Liner-	
cardboard box *mfr.*	295
ceramic *mfr.*	279
clothing *mfr.*	212
fur garment *mfr.*	212
hat *mfr.*	212
metal trades-	299
safe *mfr.*	245
Liner and finisher (*vehicle mfr.*)	299
Liner-off (*engineering*)	245
Liner-out (*engineering*)	245
Liner-up (*engineering*)	245
Linesman;	
diver's	316
electrical	257
gas	260
instrument (*railways*)	257
overhead	257
power	257
progress	115
pump	260
railway	257
signal	257
survey (*coal mine*)	314
surveyor's	316
telegraph	257
telephone	257
tramways	257
Linesman-	257
brewery	287
coal mine-	314
above ground	257
electrical engineering	257
electricity board	257
P.O.	257
radio relay service	257
railways	257
water works	316
Linesman-erector	257
Lineworker (*vehicle mfr.*)	285
Linger	199
Lingerie hand	210
Linguist	054
Lining hand (hats)	212
Linisher	243
Linker;	
chain	266
sausage	202
Linker-	
textile *mfr.*-	199
hosiery and knitwear *mfr.*	212
Linkman (*entertainment*)	165
Linoleum worker	230
Lipper; glass	192
Lipper (*coal mine*)	314
Liquefier; butter	202
Liquidator; company	002
Liquor man-	
leather tanning	204
sugar refining	202
Liquorer	201
Liquorice hand	202
Lithographer; photo	206
Lithographer-	
ceramic *mfr.*	279

	Code number
Lithographer- *continued*	
printing	207
Loader;	
aircraft	335
bar (*hosiery mfr.*)	181
barge	334
boat	334
bulk (*petroleum distribution*)	338
cartridge	230
cassette; cartridge	227
central	165
coal	338
coke	338
conveyor-	L346
coal mine	338
dockside	334
film	227
fish	334
furnace (*metal trades*)	338
kiln	191
lehr	191
lorry	335
machine	L346
mechanical (*mine, not coal*)	338
milk (*dairy*)	338
mould (asbestos composition goods *mfr.*)	230
paper	L346
power (*coal mine*)	314
refuse (*local government-cleansing dept.*)	336
stone (*mine, not coal*)	338
timber-	
coal mine	338
docks	334
forestry	L346
sawmilling	338
wagon	338
warehouse	335
Loader-	335
ammunition *mfr.*	230
ceramic *mfr.*	191
charcoal *mfr.*	204
coal mine	338
coke ovens	338
docks	334
lithography	207
mine, not coal	338
Loader and unloader;	335
drying chamber	202
Loaderman;	
power (*coal mine*)	314
ship	334
Loader-checker	335
Loader-driver (*airports*)	335
Lobber (card and paste board *mfr.*)	338
Lobby boy	154
,, man	154
Lock man	338
Locker; flat	212
Locker (*hat mfr.*)	287
Lockerer (hosiery)	212
Locksmith	248
Locomotive man (*coal mine*)	319
Lodge man	140
Lofter (salt)	184
Loftsman; assistant	214
Loftsman-	
engineering	079
shipbuilding	214
Loftsman and scriever	214
Logger; well	080
Loggist	115
Lollipop man	142
Longshoreman	334
Looker;	
cloth	289
cut	289
marsh	166
piece	289
yarn	289
to ware (*ceramic mfr.*)	338
Looker-out; book	115

	Code number
Looker-out-	
ophthalmic lenses	333
pen nib *mfr.*	286
Looker-over;	
decorator's	299
piece	289
Looker-over-	
ceramic *mfr.*	299
footwear *mfr.*	175
textile finishing	289
Looker-to-ware; thrower's	299
Looker-up (footwear)	333
Look-out and A.B.	317
Look-out man (*railways*)	L346
Loom hand; warp	181
Loom hand (*loom furniture mfr.*)	230
Loom worker; hand	180
Loomer	179
Loomer and twister	179
Looper-	
hosiery *mfr.*	212
wool spinning	177
Lopper; tree	170
Lorry boy	329
Lowerer; wagon	338
Lubricator-	271
gun *mfr.*	L344
Lugger (*mine, not coal*)	198
Lumberjack	170
Lump man (*salt mfr.*)	184
Lumper; fish	334
Lumper (*docks*)	334
Lurer	226
Lurrier	227
Lustrer	279
Luter (*coke ovens*)	L341

M

	Code number
M.B.	041
M.D.	041
M.P.S.	044
M.R.C.P.	041
M.R.C.S.	041
M.R.C.V.S.	051
M.S.	041
Macer	142
Machine boy-	
paper *mfr.*	203
printing	207
Machine hand *see* Machinist	
Machine man-*see also* Machinist-	
asbestos composition goods *mfr.*	204
coal mine	314
paper *mfr.*	188
Machine operative *see* Machinist	
Machine worker *see* Machinist	
Machiner *see* Machinist	
Machinery man; grain	202
Machinist;	
accounting	119
action	241
adding	119
ageing	182
agricultural	169
anocut	241
armouring	230
assembling and cooking (electric battery *mfr.*)	283
automatic-	242
sewing	212
bolt, nut, screw, etc. *mfr.*	242
back	212
backer (footwear)	299
bag;	
carrier	227
paper; cement	227

(Ma)

	Code number
Machinist; *continued*	
bag-	
leather goods mfr. ...	175
plastics goods mfr.	296
sack mfr. ...	212
bagging ...	175
ball ...	176
balling; punching ...	176
balling-	
textile mfr.-	178
wool combing ...	176
banding ...	201
barking ...	218
barring (*clothing mfr.*) ...	212
bartack ...	212
basil ...	212
basting ...	212
battery ...	230
beading ...	225
beaming (*textile weaving*) ...	199
bearing; ball ...	242
bedding ...	212
belt; conveyor ...	212
bending; press ...	242
bending-	
iron works ...	270
sheet metal working ...	276
bias (*rubber tyre mfr.*) ...	228
binding;	212
perfect ...	189
biscuit ...	200
blake ...	175
blanket ...	212
blasting; vapour ...	275
blocking ...	226
blouse ...	212
blowing ...	176
bluffing ...	212
boarding (*leather dressing*) ...	173
boarding-in (*leather dressing*)	173
bobbin ...	178
bolt ...	276
book-keeping ...	119
boot ...	175
boring-	
metal ...	241
wood ...	218
coal mine ...	314
bottle ...	192
bottling ...	287
box;	
axle ...	241
outside (match boxes) ...	230
box (*paper goods mfr.*) ...	227
box and slide (*cardboard box mfr.*)	227
braid ...	199
braiding-	
asbestos rope mfr. ...	199
cable mfr. ...	230
brass ...	241
breadthening ...	182
brick ...	223
broaching ...	241
bronzing ...	227
brush ...	175
brushing; cross ...	182
brushing-	
leather dressing ...	173
paper mfr. ...	188
textile mfr. ...	182
buffing-	
leather cloth mfr. ...	182
leather dressing ...	173
metal trades ...	243
plastics goods mfr. ...	229
builder's ...	218
building; micanite ...	204
bullet ...	276
bullion ...	199
bumping ...	199
burnishing ...	188
butcher's ...	186

	Code number
Machinist; *continued*	
button-	230
clothing mfr.	212
buttonhole ...	212
buttoning (*clothing mfr.*) ...	212
cabinet ...	218
cable ...	230
cabling-	230
rope, twine mfr. ...	199
cajar ...	184
calculating ...	119
calender (*plastics goods mfr.*)	195
canvas ...	212
cap;	212
bottle ...	242
capping;	
bottle ...	287
lamp ...	283
capstan ...	241
capsule (metal) ...	242
carbon ...	230
carding-	176
fur dressing ...	173
carpet ...	212
casting;	
centrifugal (steel) ...	270
die ...	235
film ...	204
monotype ...	205
pig ...	270
casting (*transparent cellulose wrappings mfr.*)	204
centering ...	241
centrifugal (sugar) ...	202
chipping ...	330
chopping (meat) ...	186
cigar ...	201
cigarette ...	201
cleaning (*seed merchants*) ...	204
closing-	
canned foods mfr. ...	287
footwear mfr. ...	175
rope mfr. ...	199
wire rope mfr. ...	276
cloth; press ...	212
clothing ...	212
coat ...	212
coating; paper ...	203
coating-	
carbon paper ...	203
photographic films ...	204
plastics goods mfr. ...	229
coiling (*metal tube mfr.*) ...	270
collar-	
clothing mfr. ...	212
laundry ...	162
collotype ...	227
combining-	
paper mfr. ...	203
textile printing ...	227
textile spinning ...	176
compressing (tablets, pills) ...	184
condenser (*textile mfr.*) ...	176
constructional ...	262
cooper's ...	218
copying ...	241
cording (*paper goods mfr.*) ...	227
cork ...	230
cornel(l)y ...	212
corrugating ...	203
corset ...	212
covering;	
bullion cord ...	199
rubber ...	228
curing (rubber) ...	204
crate maker's ...	218
cropping ...	182
cutting;	
core ...	276
emery cloth ...	190
gear ...	241
glass ...	192
paper ...	190
plastics ...	229

	Code number
Machinist; *continued*	
cutting; *continued*	
plate (*shipbuilding*) ...	276
rotary (metal) ...	276
rubber ...	228
tube (cardboard) ...	190
wood ...	218
cutting-	
asbestos ...	204
cork ...	230
metal ...	276
paper ...	190
plastics ...	229
rubber ...	228
tobacco ...	201
clothing mfr. ...	211
coal mine ...	314
metal trades ...	276
paper mfr. ...	190
paper goods mfr.-	190
paper pattern mfr.	227
soap mfr. ...	204
sugar confectionery mfr. ...	202
textile mfr. ...	199
tobacco mfr. ...	201
tyre mfr. ...	228
cutting and wrapping (*bakery*)	200
cuttling ...	199
cycle ...	241
cylinder (*printing*) ...	207
dairy; wholesale ...	202
damping (*textile mfr.*) ...	182
darning (textile goods) ...	183
developing; film ...	227
dicing (meat) ...	186
dipping ...	299
doubling ...	177
dough ...	200
drawing; wire ...	234
drawing-	
textile mfr.-	176
textile warping ...	179
dress ...	212
dressing;	
fibre ...	176
pelt ...	173
surgical ...	212
dressmaker's ...	212
drilling-	
metal trades ...	241
mine, not coal ...	315
wood products mfr. ...	218
drying;	
cloth ...	199
cylinder ...	199
drying-	
food products mfr. ...	202
textile mfr. ...	199
tobacco mfr. ...	201
duplicating; ...	119
offset ...	227
dyeline ...	119
edge; roll (mattress) ...	212
edge and closing; tape (mattress) ...	212
elasticator ...	212
electrochemical ...	241
embossing- ...	227
floor and leather cloth mfr.	204
leather dressing ...	173
wood products mfr. ...	218
embroidery ...	212
engineer's ...	241
engraver's ...	276
enrobing ...	202
envelope ...	227
extruding-	
metal tube mfr. ...	270
plastics goods mfr. ...	195
rubber goods mfr. ...	194
eyelet ...	230
eyelet-hole ...	226
fabric; circular ...	181

(Ma)

	Code number
Machinist; *continued*	
facing	239
fancy	212
feather	212
felling	212
felt; needleloom	199
fibre; vulcanised	203
filling; skin (*sausage*)	202
filling-	
cosmetic mfr.	287
food canning	287
filling and capping	287
film; cellulose	204
filter (*celluloid*)	204
finisher (*textile mfr.*)	176
flag	212
flanging	242
flat; hand	181
flat-	
clothing mfr.	212
footwear mfr.	225
fleshing	173
flock	176
foam	229
folding-	
printing	189
textile mfr.	199
fondant	202
foot	212
forcing	194
forge	270
forging	270
forming (*twine mfr.*)	199
frizing (*tannery*)	173
front	212
frosting (*glass mfr.*)	192
fur	212
garnet	176
gilling	176
gimping (*pattern cards*)	199
glazing works; patent	223
glove-	
leather	212
woollen	181
gluing and winding; tube (*cardboard*)	227
gold	236
golf (*hosiery*)	181
goods	212
gown	212
grading-	
garment pattern	276
sugar	202
graphite	204
gravure (*printing*)	207
grinding; shaft	241
grinding-	
cement mfr.	204
glass mfr.	192
metal trades	241
paint mfr.	204
paper mfr.	203
guillotine-	
metal trades	276
paper goods mfr.	190
plastics goods mfr.	229
rubber goods mfr.	228
textile goods mfr.	226
gully	L346
gumming-	
gum paper, etc.	203
paper goods mfr.	295
hair; horse	176
hand-	
clothing mfr.	212
metal trades	242
handle	218
hanking	199
hardening	199
heading (*bolt, etc. mfr.*)	276
healding	179
heel; top piece	299
hemming	212
hemstitch	212

	Code number
Machinist; *continued*	
hide (*leather merchants*)	173
hobbing	241
honing	241
hood and apron (*coach trimming*)	212
hook; two needle	212
hopper	176
hosiery;	181
surgical	212
house (*twine mfr.*)	199
ice cream	202
impregnating-	
paper mfr.	203
plastics goods mfr.	204
insulating; paper	203
jacket	212
jacquard	181
jigger	193
jigging	182
joggling	276
joiner('s)	218
jolley	193
knicker	212
knife; post	175
knitting	181
knotting; warp	179
knotting (*textile mfr.*)	199
labelling	287
lace-	
lace mfr.	180
textile goods mfr.	212
lap	176
lapping-	
metal trades	241
textile mfr.	199
lashing	212
lasting	175
laundry	162
leather	175
levelling;	225
rail	330
linen	212
lining-	
clothing mfr.	212
footwear mfr.	299
hat mfr.	212
paper mfr.	203
linotype	205
lithographic	207
loading; power	314
lock; flat	212
lockstitch	212
looming	179
maintenance	241
making;	
bottle	192
box-	218
cardboard	227
brick	223
canvas	212
chain (*cycle, etc., chains*)	242
cigarette	201
sausage	202
screw	276
making-	
abrasive paper, etc. mfr.	203
plasterboard mfr.	204
mantle	212
measuring (*piece goods*)	297
mecco moore	314
medicating (*surgical dressings*)	182
metal;	241
shipyard	262
mica	204
milk; dried	202
mill;	
boring	241
moulding	218
saw	218
millinery	212

	Code number
Machinist; *continued*	
milling-	
cemented carbide goods *mfr.*	230
food products mfr.	202
metal trades	241
mincing (*meat*)	186
mixing-	
abrasive paper, etc. mfr.	203
bakery	200
food products mfr.	202
rubber mfr.	194
moser	182
moulding-	
lead refining	270
plastics goods mfr.	195
rubber goods mfr.	194
wood products mfr.	218
nail	276
nailing	299
national	119
NATSOPA	207
needle	212
net;	180
tuck	212
nosing	241
office	119
oilskin	212
opening (*asbestos opening*)	176
outer-wear	212
overhead	212
overlock	212
overlocking	212
packing	287
padding-	
clothing mfr.	212
wallpaper printing	227
paint (*paint mfr.*)	204
painting; slip	279
paper;	
carbon	203
crinkled	203
paper (*paper goods mfr.*)	227
pasteboard	203
pasting (*pasteboard*)	203
paving; concrete	330
perforating-	
footwear mfr.	175
paper goods mfr.	227
perpetual	182
photogravure	207
pickering (*textile mfr.*)	176
picking; knot (*brush mfr.*)	230
pie	200
pin	276
pipe; sanitary	223
piping (*textile smallwares mfr.*)	199
plain (*shirts*)	212
plaiting (*rope mfr.*)	199
planer; plate	276
planing; plate	276
planing-	
metal trades	241
wood products mfr.	218
plastic (*cable mfr.*)	229
plastics	229
plate-backing (*photographic plate mfr.*)	206
platen	207
plating; wire	269
plating (*metal trades*)	269
pleating;	212
paper	203
plonking	212
plug assembly	201
polishing (*velvet mfr.*)	182
post-	
clothing mfr.	212
footwear mfr.	175
powder; soap	184
power	212
powers samas	119
preparing	176

(Ma)

Machinist; *continued*

Entry	Code number
press; letter	207
press-	
metal trades	242
plastics goods mfr.	195
printing	207
rubber goods mfr.	194
pressing; transfer	299
pressing (*textile mfr.*)	182
pressure	225
print; blue	119
printer's	207
printing;	207
film	227
production (*vehicle mfr.*)	285
profiling	241
pulling; rag	176
punching-	
metal trades	242
paper goods mfr.	190
quilting	212
ragging (cotton rag)	176
raising	182
randing	199
ratchet	315
reamering	241
repairer hand	226
ribbon; typewriter	199
ring	177
rivet	276
riveting-	
leather goods mfr.	299
metal trades	285
plastics goods mfr.	296
roll; toilet	227
roller-	
plastics goods mfr.	229
textile mfr.	182
rolling-	
metal trades-	232
sheet metal working	276
textile mfr.	199
rope-	
textile	199
wire	276
rotary-	207
textile bleaching	182
router (*metal trades*)	241
rubbing (*food products mfr.*)	202
rug and blanket; horse	212
ruling	227
running-down	176
sack	212
sample	212
sanding-	
metal	275
micanite	227
wood	218
sandpapering	218
sawing (*metal trades*)	276
scouring (*textile mfr.*)	199
screen; silk	208
screw; automatic	242
screwer	241
screwing	241
scutcher	176
sealing; automatic metal	242
seaming-	
canned foods mfr.	287
metal trades	242
seamless	181
second (paperboard)	203
sensimatic	119
setting (*leather dressing*)	173
sewing; bandage	212
sewing-	
bookbinding	189
clothing mfr.	212
footwear mfr.	175
hospital service	226
institution	226
laundry	226
leather goods mfr.	175
textile mfr.	212

Machinist; *continued*

Entry	Code number
shaking	204
shaper	241
shaping-	
metal trades	241
wood products mfr.	218
shearing-	
metal trades	276
textile mfr.	182
shirt-	212
laundry	162
shirt and collar	162
shoe; canvas	175
shrinking;	182
felt hood	199
silk (*clothing mfr.*)	212
singeing	182
sinking; die	241
sizing (*textile mfr.*)	182
skiver	175
skiving (*footwear mfr.*)	175
sleeving	212
slicing; bread	200
slicing (celluloid)	229
slipper	175
slitting-	
adhesive tape mfr.	190
fabric mfr.	226
paper mfr.	190
paper products mfr.	190
slitting and cutting (photographic film)	190
slitting and winding-	226
textile mfr.	199
slotter	241
slotting	241
slugger	299
socket	276
soldering	265
souring	182
spanishing (*leather cloth mfr.*)	182
spare (paper)	203
special (*clothing mfr.*)	212
spewing	194
spindle	218
spinning (textiles)	177
splitting (*tannery*)	173
spooling (yarn)	178
spreader	176
spring;	276
coach	233
staking	173
stamping-	
metal trades	242
plastics goods mfr.	229
stapling-	
footwear mfr.	175
mattress mfr.	285
starch	202
stationary	255
steffan	202
stemming	201
stentering	182
stiffening	182
stitch	212
stitching; wire	226
stitching (*footwear mfr.*)	175
stocking (*hosiery mfr.*)	181
stone	301
stoving-	
metal goods	204
tobacco	201
stranding-	276
rope, twine mfr.	199
stretching	182
swedging	299
tableting (tablet, pill)	184
tailor's	212
tamping	330
tape (*hat mfr.*)	212
taping-	
cable mfr.	230
footwear mfr.	225

Machinist; *continued*

Entry	Code number
tapping-	241
ceramic mfr.	223
tempering (chocolate)	202
tent	212
tenterer	182
testing (*metal trades*)	286
textile-	199
clothing mfr.	212
textile machinery mfr.	241
thicknessing	218
threshing;	169
tobacco	201
ticket (*totalisator*)	115
tie	212
tile	223
timber	218
tinplate	207
tobacco	201
toffee	202
tool	241
top	212
tote	115
towel	212
toy; soft	212
tracklaying	330
trim (*motor vehicle mfr.*)	276
trimming (brushes)	230
trouser	212
tube; paper	227
tube (*silk mfr.*)	178
tucking	212
tufting-	
carpet mfr.	199
mattress mfr.	226
turning; wood	218
twisting-	
textile mfr.-	177
textile warping	179
twine mfr.	199
tying; warp	179
upholsterer's	212
upholstery	212
upsetting	270
up-taking	203
varnishing-	
lithography	203
metal trades	299
velvet	182
veneer	218
vest	212
warping	179
washing; back (worsted)	199
washing-	
bottle	L348
food products mfr.	202
laundry	162
textile mfr.	199
transport	348
washing and mixing (*abrasive mfr.*)	204
waxing	203
weaving; wire	242
weighing	297
welding; plastics	296
welt-	175
clothing mfr.	212
welting (hosiery)	212
wharfedale	207
wheel	181
winding-	
oilskin mfr.	204
textile mfr.-	199
yarn winding	178
window; metal	241
wire	234
wiring (*rubber tyre mfr.*)	194
wood-	218
paper mfr.	203
woodcutting	218
woodworking	218
wrapping	287
zigzag-	212
footwear mfr.	175

(Ma)

	Code number
Machinist-	
office machinery	119
adhesive tape mfr.	203
animal food mfr.	202
asbestos-cement goods mfr.	230
atomic energy plant	241
bakery	200
banking	119
basket mfr.	230
bedding mfr.	212
bookbinding	189
brake lining mfr.	230
brewery	197
brush mfr.	230
building and contracting	330
button mfr.	230
canvas goods mfr.	212
carbon goods mfr.	230
cast concrete products mfr.	230
ceramic mfr.	223
chemical mfr.	184
clothing mfr.	212
coal gas, coke ovens	338
coal mine-	314
above ground	241
cold storage	348
cork stopper mfr.	230
dairy	202
distillery	197
dyeing and cleaning	162
electric blanket mfr.	212
fishing rod mfr.	230
flour confectionery mfr.	200
food products mfr.	202
footwear mfr.	175
furniture mfr.	218
garage	241
glass mfr.	192
grain milling	202
hat mfr.	212
hatters' fur mfr.	199
laundry	162
lead pencil mfr.	218
leather cloth mfr.	199
leather dressing	173
leather goods mfr.	175
linoleum mfr.	204
malting	197
match mfr.	224
metal trades-	241
battery, accumulator mfr.	276
cable mfr.	230
card clothing mfr.	276
lamp, valve mfr.	276
metal smallwares mfr.	276
metal stamping	242
nail, rivet, etc. mfr.	276
nut, bolt, etc. mfr.	276
reed mfr.	230
shipbuilding	262
steel pen mfr.	242
tin box mfr.	242
wire goods mfr.	276
wire rope mfr.	276
mine, not coal	315
musical instrument mfr.	222
opencast coal mining	330
optical goods mfr.	192
P.L.A.	338
paper mfr.	203
paper dress pattern mfr.	227
paper goods mfr.	227
photographic film mfr.	204
photographic film processing	227
piano action, hammer mfr.	218
plastics goods mfr.-	229
calendering	195
extruding	195
moulding	195
printing	207
railways-	
civil engineer's dept.	330
railway workshops	241
relief stamping	227

	Code number
Machinist- continued	
rope mfr.	199
Royal Mint	242
rubber goods mfr.-	228
calendering	194
extruding	194
moulding	194
salt mfr.	184
sanitary towel mfr.	226
sewage disposal	310
soap mfr.	184
soft furnishings mfr.	212
sugar confectionery mfr.	202
sugar refining	202
surgical dressing mfr.	212
surgical goods mfr.	230
textile mfr.-	199
carpets, rugs mfr.	212
hosiery mfr.-	181
overlocking	212
sewing	212
man-made fibre mfr.	196
textile bleaching	182
textile combing	176
textile dyeing	182
textile finishing	182
textile opening	176
textile printing	227
textile weaving	180
textile goods mfr.	212
tobacco mfr.	201
toy mfr.	230
upholstering	212
wallpaper mfr.-	203
wallpaper printing	227
wood products mfr.	218
Magazine worker (explosives)	184
Magician	059
Magistrate (stipendiary)	001
Magneter	198
Maid;	151
bar	145
basement	147
buffet	146
canteen (school)	146
chamber	151
coffee	146
dispense	145
farm; dairy	166
hall; dining	146
house	151
kennel	172
kitchen	147
laundry	162
linen	333
nurse	151
pantry	147
parlour	151
room;	
coffee	146
dining	146
mess	146
still	146
sandwich	144
scullery	147
sewing	212
table	146
tea	144
ward	151
Maidservant	151
Maintainer; signal light (railways)	259
Maintenance hand;	
electrical	276
estate	304
machine-	271
textile mfr.	248
typewriter	251
Maintenance hand-	L346
aircraft	250
boilers	347
machinery	271
vehicles	249
building and contracting	304

	Code number
Maintenance hand- continued	
canals	316
coal mine	276
electricity board	253
mine, not coal	276
P.O.	256
transport-	249
railways	306
Maintenance man;	
battery	230
conveyor (coal mine)	248
electrical	253
mechanical appliances (coal mine)	248
track (railways)	306
Maintenance man-	304
aircraft	250
belt	225
boilers	347
machinery	248
office machines	251
scientific instruments	246
vehicles	249
weighing machines	248
coal mine	276
electricity board	253
gas board	248
transport-	249
railways	306
water works	316
Maintenance worker see Maintenance hand	
Maintenance and repair man;	
permanent way	306
Maitre d'hotel	F144
Major;	
blow	F176
blower	F176
room; blow	F176
Major-	
armed forces-	
foreign and Commonwealth	M136
U.K.	M135
Salvation Army	040
Major-General-	
armed forces-	
foreign and Commonwealth	M136
U.K.	M135
Maker;	
accoutrements	212
acetate	184
acid	184
action (piano mfr.)	222
album	189
ammonium chloride	184
ammunition	184
apparatus; photographic	246
appliance;	
orthopaedic	230
sanitary	193
surgical	230
apron (perambulator mfr.)	226
asphalt	204
bag;	
air	228
gun	212
hand	225
jute	226
lady's	225
nail	226
paper	227
polythene	296
rod; fishing	212
sand	212
sleeping	228
travelling	225
bag-	
canvas goods mfr.	212
leather goods mfr.	225
paper goods mfr.	227
bait	230
bakelite	204
balance (scales mfr.)	246

61

(Ma)

Maker; *continued*

	Code number
ball;	
billiard	229
cricket	225
foot	225
golf	228
ball-	
rubber goods mfr.	228
celluloid goods mfr.	229
glass mfr.	223
band (*textile smallwares mfr.*)	180
bandage	226
bar; steel (*textile machinery mfr.*)	241
barb (barbed wire)	276
barometer	246
barrel-	
gun mfr.	248
paper goods mfr.	227
barrel and cask	216
barrow	224
base (*custard powder mfr.*)	202
basin	193
basket;	
chip	299
fancy	230
ornamental (ceramic)	193
wicker	230
wire	276
basket-	230
wire goods mfr.	276
bat; cricket	224
bat (clay)	223
battery (electric)	230
bed; air	228
bed-	
bedding mfr.	213
furniture mfr.	215
school, university	151
bedstead	248
bell-	
cycle bells	285
bellows (pipe organ)	225
belly (piano)	222
belt;	
balata	228
conveyor-	
plastics goods mfr.	229
rubber goods mfr.	228
life	230
surgical	230
vee	228
belt-	212
leather	225
rubber	228
abrasive paper, etc. mfr.	299
belting-	
leather	225
rubber	228
besom	230
bicycle	285
biscuit; dog	202
blade; razor	242
blanket	212
blind	230
block;	
asphalt	204
brake	228
breeze	230
building	230
carbon	230
cement	230
clog	224
concrete	230
cork	203
cylinder	270
engraver's	224
fuel (patent fuel)	204
hat	224
radiator	270
block-	
ceramic mfr.	223
printing	206

Maker; *continued*

	Code number
block- *continued*	
rubber goods mfr.	228
wood products mfr.	224
blouse	210
board; printed circuit	273
board (*paper mfr.*)	203
boat	214
bobbin-	
cardboard	227
metal	276
wood	224
electric battery mfr.	230
body;	
carriage	268
coach	268
motor	268
wicker cart	230
body-	
vehicles	268
hat mfr.	226
motor vehicle mfr.	268
railways	268
safe mfr.	248
boiler	262
bolster (cutlery)	233
bolt-	276
forged	233
clock mfr.	242
bon-bon (*sugar confectionery mfr.*)	202
book;	
pattern	189
pocket	189
book-	
betting	164
bookbinding	189
boot;	
jobbing	175
surgical	175
boot-	175
bespoke	175
rubber	299
retail trade	101
boot and shoe	175
bottle-	192
rubber	194
stoneware	193
bow-	
clothing mfr.	212
musical instrument mfr.	222
sports goods mfr.	224
bowl-	
ceramic mfr.	193
sports goods mfr.	224
textile machinery mfr.	224
box;	
card	227
cardboard	227
cigar	299
core	217
match	230
ointment	227
paper	227
paperboard	227
tin	261
wooden	216
box-	
cardboard	227
metal	261
n.o.s.-	
female	227
male	216
wood	216
match mfr.	230
brace; elastic	212
bracelet	266
braces	225
brake; car	285
brayle	199
breeches	210
brick	223
bridge;	242
weigh	248

Maker; *continued*

	Code number
bridle	225
brine (*preserves mfr.*)	202
briquette	204
brooch	266
broom	230
brush; twisted-in	276
brush-	230
carbon, electric	230
bucket-	
metal	261
plastics	195
buffer	225
bulb (*electric lamp mfr.*)	283
bullet	276
bunch	201
bush	248
butter	202
button	230
cabinet-	215
metal	248
cable;	
chain	233
rope	199
wire	276
cable-	
electric cable mfr.	230
spring mfr.	276
cake;	
fish	202
pontefract	202
cake-	
flour confectionery mfr.	185
sugar confectionery mfr.	202
camera	246
can; fibre	227
can (metal)	242
candle	230
candlewick	177
canister	261
canopy	212
cap; butt (fishing rods)	242
cap-	
clothing mfr.	211
electric lamp mfr.	242
capsule (*drug mfr.*)	184
caramel (*sugar refining*)	202
carbon (*carbon goods mfr.*)	204
carbon dioxide	184
carbon tissue	230
card;	
pattern	227
shade	295
show	227
card (*paper mfr.*)	188
carmine	184
carriage;	
invalid	285
lace	248
cart	224
carton	227
cartridge	230
case;	
attache	225
battery	229
book	215
brush	225
cabinet	215
cardboard	227
cigarette (precious metal)	266
clock-	239
wood	215
cutlery	215
division	215
dressing	225
hat	225
instrument	215
jewel	215
jewel and plate	215
leather-	225
bookbinding	189
mattress	213
meter	261

(Ma)

Maker; *continued*	Code number
case; *continued*	
packing;	216
zinc	261
pattern	295
sausage	202
show	215
small	225
spectacle	230
spring (small arms)	242
suit	225
television	215
tin	261
watch	239
wireless	215
case-	216
accumulator mfr.	229
firework mfr.	295
mattress mfr.	213
musical instrument mfr.	215
packing case mfr.	216
paper goods mfr.	227
safe mfr.	248
tyre mfr.	194
watch, clock mfr.	239
casement-	
metal	248
wood	214
casing; sausage	202
cast; plaster	223
catheter (rubber)	228
cell (*accumulator, battery mfr.*)	230
cellulose	204
cement	204
chain-	
metal-	
precious metal	266
metal trades-	276
forging	233
textile mfr.	199
chair-	215
cane	230
foundry	235
metal furniture mfr.	285
cheese	202
chemical(s); fine	184
chenille	177
chloroform	184
chocolate	202
chronometer	247
churn	216
cider	197
cigar	201
cigarette	201
clay	204
clip; wire	242
clock	247
clog	225
cloth;	
brattice	182
glass	203
club; golf	224
coach	268
coat-	210
knitted coats	181
coffin	215
coffin and casket	215
cog (*clock mfr.*)	247
coil (electric)	274
coin	242
collar; hose	225
collar (*clothing mfr.*)	212
colour-	204
flag mfr.	226
comb-	229
textile machinery mfr.	248
compass	246
components (*telephone mfr.*)	252
composition-	184
boiler covering	316
concrete	230
condenser (electric)	283
cone (*loudspeaker mfr.*)	227

Maker; *continued*	Code number
confectionery-	
flour confectionery	185
sugar confectionery	202
cord	199
core;	
cable	230
glass	192
core-	
coal mine	235
metal trades	235
rope mfr.	199
corset	226
corticine	184
cosmetic	184
costume	210
coupling	233
cover;	
loose	212
mattress	213
wagon	212
waterproof	228
cover (*ceramic mfr.*)	193
cracker (*paper goods mfr.*)	295
crank	193
crate;	216
steel	276
crayon	230
cream-	202
cosmetic mfr.	184
crucible	223
crystal	184
cue; billiard	224
cup	193
cream (*paper products mfr.*)	227
curb (*cast concrete products mfr.*)	230
curtain	212
cushion;	213
air	228
table; billiard	228
cycle	285
desk	215
detonator	230
dial	247
die	245
dish	193
doctor	276
doll	299
dolly (*toy mfr.*)	299
door;	
fireproof	230
steel	248
door-	214
safe, strong room mfr.	248
dough (*flour confectionery mfr.*)	200
drawer (safes)	261
drawers	215
dress	210
dressing; surgical	212
drum; cable	216
drum-	
metal	261
wood	216
musical instrument mfr.	222
drum and keg	261
dust (*ceramic mfr.*)	204
dye	184
eiderdown	213
electrode (carbon)	230
element	276
embroidery	212
emulsion	184
enamel	184
envelope (*paper products mfr.*)	227
essence (food)	202
eye;	
artificial-	
glass	223
plastics	229
dolls (glass)	223
fabric; glove	181
fan (*electrical goods mfr.*)	283

Maker; *continued*	Code number
fastening	212
feather	182
feed (*fountain pen mfr.*)	230
felt-	199
piano mfr.	222
fence; timber	224
fender; ship's	199
ferrule-	242
boiler ferrules	239
fertilizer	184
fibre; man-made	196
fichu	212
figure;	193
wax	230
filament;	283
continuous	196
file;	233
box	227
finings	197
fire; electric	283
fireplace (tiled)	300
firework(s)	230
fittings; tube	270
fittings (*safe mfr.*)	248
flag-	
cast concrete products mfr.	230
paper products mfr.	295
flake	201
flange (*electric lamp mfr.*)	192
flat (*ceramic mfr.*)	193
float (*sports goods mfr.*)	224
flow (*ceramic mfr.*)	204
flower;	
artificial-	230
plastics	296
flower (*ceramic mfr.*)	193
fly-	
sports goods mfr.	230
textile machinery mfr.	248
foot	192
football	225
footwear	175
form-	224
cable mfr.	274
ceramic mfr.	223
forme (*paper box mfr.*)	245
frame;	
bed	214
chair	215
cork	299
handbag	276
hood	276
mirror	224
optical	229
oxon	224
photo-	224
leather	225
picture	224
racquet	224
show-wood	215
spectacle	229
stuff-over	215
umbrella	285
window-	
metal	248
wood	214
wire	276
frame-	
box spring mattress mfr.	214
concrete mfr.	224
cycle mfr.	248
furniture mfr.	215
watch mfr.	247
fringe; metallic	180
furniture;	215
bamboo	230
brass; mediaeval	276
cane	230
garden	224
metal	248
wicker	230
fuse	283
galvanometer	246

(Ma)

Maker; *continued*

	Code number
garment	210
gas	184
gasket	230
gate	224
gauge;	
pressure	246
steam	246
gauge (*metal trades*)	245
gear; sighting; gun	248
gig	248
gimp	199
glass;	192
field	246
opera	246
glaze (*ceramic mfr.*)	204
glockenspiel	222
glove-	212
boxing	225
cricket	225
india rubber	228
surgical	228
glucose	202
glue	184
gong (clock)	247
goods;	
abrasive	230
canvas	212
fancy	230
leather	225
small	202
gown	210
grate; tile	300
gravestone	301
grease	184
grid (*wood products mfr.*)	224
grom(m)et-	199
wire rope mfr.	272
guard; fork	242
guard (*wire goods mfr.*)	276
gun	248
halter (rope)	199
hammer (*piano mfr.*)	222
handle-	
wood	218
ceramic mfr.	223
leather goods mfr.	225
precious metal mfr.	266
hanger; coat	218
harness;	225
electrical	274
harp	222
hassock	213
hat;	226
paper	295
heald;	276
yarn	181
heel-	299
rubber	194
wood	224
helmet	226
helve	218
hinge	285
hip and valley	223
hole; button	212
hollow-ware-	261
ceramic mfr.	193
precious metal mfr.	266
hone	230
hood (*perambulator mfr.*)	226
hood and apron (*perambulator mfr.*)	226
hose;	228
leather	225
hosiery	181
hurdle	224
hydrometer	246
ink	184
instrument-	246
dental	276
musical instruments-	222
brass	248
precision	246
surgical	276

Maker; *continued*

	Code number
insulator (ceramic)	223
jacquard	248
jam	202
jar (ceramic)	193
jelly	202
jewellery	266
jig	245
jig and gauge	245
joint; asbestos	230
keg-	
metal	261
wood	216
kerb	301
kerbstone (*cast concrete products mfr.*)	230
kettle	261
key-	241
clock mfr.	242
musical instrument mfr.	222
key and action (barrel organs)	222
kilt	210
knapsack	212
knife	233
label;	227
wood	218
lace;	180
boot-	
leather goods mfr.	225
textile smallwares mfr.	180
warp	181
lacquer	184
ladder	224
lamp;	
electric	283
glow	283
oil	261
lanyard	199
lard	202
last-	224
iron	270
lead;	
printer's	231
red	184
white	184
lead oxide	184
leather;	
comb	276
fancy	225
lens	192
letter (wood)	224
level; spirit	246
ligament	225
light;	
lead	303
leaded	303
lighter; fire	230
limb; artificial	230
lime	184
line;	199
clothes	199
furnished	230
lingo	276
lining-	
clothing mfr.	212
footwear mfr.	175
linoleum	204
lock	248
locket (precious metal)	266
loom	248
lozenge	202
machine; weighing	248
machine (office machinery)	248
machinery; textile	248
magneto	252
malt	197
manhole	314
mantle;	210
fur	211
gas	230
incandescent	230
mantlet (rope)	199
map;	207
dissected	295

Maker; *continued*

	Code number
margarine	202
mark	267
marker-	226
footwear mfr.	276
marquee	212
marzipan	202
mash (*leather cloth mfr.*)	204
mask-	230
beautician	165
mast (*shipbuilding*)	262
mat;	180
rubber	228
sheepskin	173
sinnet	230
wool	212
match	230
matrix (*typefounding*)	276
mattress;	213
asbestos	230
interior; spring	213
link	285
rubber	228
spring	276
wire	276
meat; potted	202
medal	267
meter;	246
gas	284
micanite	204
micrometer	246
microscope	246
mirror	192
model;	
architectural	214
display	230
exhibition	214
jewellery	266
plaster	223
ship's	214
wood	214
model-	
ceramic mfr.	223
engineering	217
toy mfr.	214
mop	230
mould; plaster (*plumbago crucible mfr.*)	223
mould-	
asbestos-cement goods mfr.	230
cast concrete products mfr.	224
ceramic mfr.	223
foundry	235
glass mfr.	248
plastics goods mfr.	245
sugar confectionery mfr.	202
mount; wig	226
movement-	247
barometer mfr.	246
nail;	242
cut	276
forged	270
frost	270
wrought	270
needle	276
net	180
nib; pen	276
nut	242
oar	224
odd-stuff	193
oil	184
ointment	184
packing; rubber	228
pad;	
sanitary	226
stamping	230
pad-	
basket mfr.	230
upholstery mfr.	213
pail-	261
wood	224
paint	184
pallet	216

(Ma)

	Code number
Maker; *continued*	
panel-	261
plaster	204
wood	218
pantile	223
paper;	188
abrasive	203
carbon	203
emery	203
fly	203
glass	203
laced	227
photographic	203
sand	203
parachute	212
parian	223
part; commutator	252
part (*piano mfr.*)	215
paste-	
chemical mfr.	184
flour confectionery mfr. ...	200
food products mfr. ...	202
paper goods mfr. ...	184
pat (*cement mfr.*)	184
pattern;	
engineer's	217
moulds	217
wood	217
pattern-	
artificial flower mfr. ...	226
cast concrete products mfr.	224
ceramic mfr.	223
clothing mfr.	211
coal mine	217
footwear mfr.	225
jacquard card cutting ...	199
metal trades—	
jewellery mfr. ...	266
plastics goods mfr. ...	214
textile mfr.	115
pedometer	246
peg	224
pen	230
pencil;	230
slate	301
pepper	202
perambulator	285
perfumery	184
petroleum	184
piano	222
picker	225
pickle	202
pie	200
pill	184
pin (*ceramic mfr.*)	193
pinch	283
pipe;	
asbestos	204
clay	193
drain	193
flexible	228
lead	270
organ	261
sanitary	193
pipe-	
cast concrete goods mfr. ...	230
ceramic mfr.	193
foundry	235
rubber goods mfr. ...	228
tobacco pipe mfr. ...	224
zinc refining	223
plaque	223
plate;	
accumulator	270
lithographic	206
stencil	261
plate-	206
ceramic mfr.	193
precious metal mfr. ...	266
pleat	210
plug; sparking	283
plug (*tobacco mfr.*)	201
plywood	203
pocket (*tyre mfr.*)	228

	Code number
Maker; *continued*	
pole	218
polish	184
poppy	230
portmanteau	225
post (concrete)	230
postcard	295
pot-	193
metal	261
glass mfr.	223
pottery	193
pouffe	225
powder-	
chemical	184
food	202
prism	192
pudding	200
puff;	
powder	226
toe	299
pulp (*paper mfr.*)	203
pump	248
punch	270
punnet	224
purse (leather)	225
putty	204
pyjama	212
quarry	193
quilt (*cricket ball mfr.*) ...	230
racquet	224
radiant; fire; gas	193
reed-	
musical instrument mfr. ...	222
textile machinery mfr. ...	230
reel; fishing	230
reel-	218
cable mfr.	216
refrigerator	248
resin	184
rib; umbrella	276
ribbon; typewriter ...	199
ridge	223
rifle	248
ring;	
asbestos	228
jump	266
wax	230
ring (*precious metal mfr.*) ...	266
rivet	276
road	307
robe	210
rocket	230
rod; fishing	224
roll; dandy	276
roller;	
printer's	228
printer's composition ...	228
rubber	228
roller-	
pianoforte mfr.	222
textile machinery mfr. ...	241
rope-	199
metal	276
rosette (leather)	225
rotor	252
rubber	228
rubber tread	194
rug	180
rule; mathematical ...	246
rule (*instrument mfr.*) ...	246
runner	231
sack and bag	212
saddle-	225
ceramic mfr.	223
saddletree (wood)	224
safe;	248
meat	224
wood	224
saggar	223
sagger	223
sail	226
saline	184
salt	184

	Code number
Maker; *continued*	
sample-	
paper products mfr. ...	227
textile mfr.	115
sandwich	165
sauce	202
saucer	193
sausage	202
saw	276
scabbard	225
scale;	248
wood (piano)	217
scale and balance	248
screen;	
malt	242
silk	227
wind	223
screen-	
wood	224
textile printing	227
screw;	276
balance	247
frost	270
watch	276
wooden	218
scull	224
scythe	233
seat;	215
cane	230
garden	224
spring	276
segment	301
sett	301
shade;	
lamp	230
shank; halter	199
shape; hosiery	224
sheet-	
vulcanised fibre	203
railways	212
shirt	210
shoe;	175
horse	233
shovel-	
steel	233
wood	224
shroud	212
shutter (wood)	214
shuttle	224
shuttlecock	230
sieve (*wire goods mfr.*) ...	276
sign-	
electric	274
metal	261
neon	274
perspex	229
wood	214
sink-	
ceramic	193
metal	242
plastics	195
sinker	242
size	184
skep	230
skewer (wood)	224
skin; sausage	202
skip	230
skirt	210
slab-	
cast concrete products mfr.	230
ceramic mfr.	223
mine, not coal	301
slate	301
sleeve (*clothing mfr.*) ...	212
sley	224
slip-	
ceramic mfr.	204
pencil, crayon mfr. ...	204
slipper	175
devonshire	225
rubber	299
snuff	201
soap;	184
chief	091

(Ma)

Maker; *continued*
- sock-
  - boots and shoes ... 299
  - *hosiery mfr.* ... 181
- solution-
  - celluloid ... 184
  - rubber ... 194
- soup ... 202
- spade ... 233
- spar-
  - metal ... 262
  - wood ... 224
- spectacle ... 229
- speedometer ... 246
- spindle-
  - *textile machinery mfr.* ... 248
- spindle and flyer ... 248
- spirit ... 184
- spring;
  - balance ... 248
  - carriage ... 242
  - coil ... 276
  - flat ... 242
  - hair ... 276
  - laminated ... 233
  - leaf ... 233
  - lock ... 242
  - railway ... 233
  - spiral ... 276
  - volute ... 276
- spring-
  - *carriage, wagon mfr.* ... 233
  - *railway locomotive mfr.* ... 233
- staging (*shipbuilding*) ... 224
- stamp;
  - bleacher's-
    - metal ... 242
    - wood ... 224
  - endorsing-
    - metal ... 299
    - rubber ... 194
  - rubber ... 299
- starch- ... 202
  - *textile mfr.* ... 204
- stave ... 224
- steelyard ... 248
- step ... 214
- stick;
  - hockey ... 224
  - walking ... 224
- stilt ... 223
- stock (*gun mfr.*) ... 224
- stone;
  - artificial ... 230
  - composition ... 230
  - concrete (precast) ... 230
  - grave ... 301
  - kerb-
    - *cast concrete products mfr.* ... 230
    - *mine, not coal* ... 301
  - oil ... 301
  - patent ... 230
  - pulp ... 301
  - rubbing ... 230
- stopper; glass ... 192
- stopper-
  - *glass mfr.* ... 192
  - *steelworks* ... 223
- stove ... 248
- strap;
  - fork ... 270
- string- ... 199
  - metal ... 230
  - *gut mfr.* ... 230
- sugar ... 202
- sulphate ... 184
- surplice ... 212
- suspender ... 212
- sweetmeat ... 202
- sweetstuff ... 202
- switch ... 283
- switchboard ... 252
- syrup ... 202

Maker; *continued*
- table; billiard ... 230
- table (*furniture mfr.*) ... 215
- tablet (*pharmaceutical mfr.*) ... 184
- tack ... 276
- tallow ... 204
- tank; ... 262
  - slate ... 301
- tape (*adhesive tape mfr.*) ... 203
- taper ... 230
- tarpaulin ... 212
- tassel ... 181
- taximeter ... 246
- tea ... 146
- teapot ... 193
- telescope ... 246
- template; wooden ... 214
- template-
  - wood ... 214
- temple ... 248
- tent ... 226
- terminal ... 193
- thermometer ... 192
- thimble-
  - *ceramic mfr.* ... 193
  - *precious metal mfr.* ... 266
  - *shipbuilding* ... 233
- thread ... 177
- ticket; ... 227
  - reel ... 207
- tie; ... 212
  - cow ... 199
- tile- ... 223
  - asbestos-cement ... 230
  - concrete ... 230
  - glass ... 192
  - plastics ... 195
  - rubber ... 194
- tinsel ... 177
- tool; ... 245
  - chasing ... 233
  - diamond ... 266
  - edge ... 233
  - engineer's ... 245
  - fine (brushes) ... 230
  - hand ... 233
  - machine ... 248
  - press ... 245
  - sash ... 230
  - small ... 245
- top (*textile mfr.*) ... 176
- towel ... 226
- toy ... 230
- transfer ... 227
- transformer ... 252
- tray-
  - metal ... 261
  - paper ... 227
  - plastics ... 195
  - wicker ... 230
  - wood ... 224
- tree; boot ... 224
- trimming(s)-
  - *clothing mfr.* ... 212
  - *slipper mfr.* ... 175
  - *tinsel mfr.* ... 177
- trouser ... 210
- truck (*hand truck mfr.*) ... 224
- trumpet (*steelworks*) ... 300
- trunk-
  - leather ... 225
  - metal ... 261
  - wood ... 216
- truss-
  - *joinery mfr.* ... 214
  - *surgical goods mfr.* ... 230
- tube;
  - flexible ... 194
  - metal ... 270
  - television ... 283
- tube-
  - glass ... 192
  - metal ... 270
  - paper ... 227

Maker; *continued*
- tube- *continued*
  - plastics ... 195
  - rubber ... 194
  - *musical instrument mfr.* ... 234
- tubing-
  - glass ... 192
  - rubber ... 194
- twine ... 199
- typewriter ... 248
- tyre ... 194
- umbrella ... 226
- underclothing ... 210
- valve (*radio valve mfr.*) ... 283
- varnish; ... 184
  - head ... F184
- vat ... 216
- vessel ... 193
- vestment ... 210
- wadding ... 199
- wafer ... 200
- wagon;
  - timber ... 224
- waistcoat ... 210
- wardrobe ... 215
- washer-
  - leather ... 225
  - micanite ... 230
  - rubber ... 228
- watch ... 247
- watch and clock ... 247
- water;
  - mineral ... 202
  - soda ... 202
- waterproof ... 226
- wattle ... 224
- wax vesta ... 230
- wedge ... 233
- weight ... 241
- welt ... 175
- whatnot ... 215
- wheel-
  - *abrasive paper, etc. mfr.* ... 227
  - *clock mfr.* ... 247
  - *cycle mfr.* ... 285
- whip ... 225
- white (*wallpaper mfr.*) ... 184
- wick ... 230
- wig ... 230
- window;
  - lead ... 303
  - stained glass ... 303
- window (*metal window mfr.*) 248
- wing (*motor car*) ... 261
- wool; wood ... 203
- wreath; artificial ... 064
- Maker-
  - *cast concrete products mfr.* 230
  - *flour confectionery mfr.* ... 185
  - *musical instrument mfr.* ... 222
  - *sports goods mfr.* ... 230
- Maker and repairer;
  - body ... 268
  - shoe ... 175
- Maker-up;
  - cloth ... 287
  - hosiery ... 212
  - jeweller's ... 266
  - piece ... 287
  - smallware ... 287
  - spool ... 287
  - yarn ... 287
- Maker-up;
  - *art needlework mfr.* ... 226
  - *handkerchief mfr.* ... 287
  - *knitwear mfr.* ... 212
  - *leather goods mfr.* ... 225
  - *metal trades-* ... 248
    - *silver and plate mfr.* ... 266
    - *small chain mfr.* ... 276
  - *paper mfr.* ... 294
  - *printing* ... 205
  - *textile mfr.* ... 199
  - *umbrella mfr.* ... 212

(Ma)

	Code number
Make-up hand	205
Malt man	197
Malt room man	197
Malter	182
Maltster;	078
floorman	197
kilnman	197
Manager;	
accounts	099
administration; sales	099
advertisement	014
advertising	014
airport	095
area; telephone	099
area-	
pools promoters	M134
sales force	M133
public houses	103
retail trade	101
transport	095
assurance; quality	075
audit	099
bank	099
banqueting	104
bar;	F145
snack	104
barber's	M159
baths	106
bingo	106
booking	099
bookmaker's	164
boxer's	059
branch-	
assurance company	099
banking	099
building society	099
electricity board	101
government	021
insurance	099
manufacturing	111
trade association	M024
transport	095
wholesale, retail trade-	101
butchers	M186
fishmongers	M187
building	092
business *see Manager-*	
butcher's	M186
camp; holiday	109
canteen	104
casino	106
catering	104
cellar-	
brewery	097
wine merchants	097
cinema	106
circuit-	
entertainment	106
petroleum distribution	097
circulation	101
claims	M005
cleansing	111
club;	
clothing	101
refreshment	104
residential	102
social	106
club-	106
catering	104
football club	M063
collection(s)	099
colliery	094
commercial	013
company; insurance	099
computer	099
contracts-	013
building and contracting	092
manufacturing	091
control;	
credit	098
loss	111
pest	111
quality	075
stock	096

	Code number
Manager; *continued*	
conveyancing	M027
copyright	099
cost(ing)	099
credit	098
dairy-	101
food products mfr.	091
department(al)- *see also Manager*	
building society	099
insurance	099
depot-	097
transport	095
wholesale, retail trade	101
despatch	097
dispatch	097
display	M058
distribution	097
district-	
assurance company	M134
catering	104
electricity board	099
friendly society	099
gas board	099
insurance	M134
manufacturing	111
retail trade	101
transport	095
wholesale trade	101
divisional-	
insurance	099
manufacturing	091
petroleum distribution	097
transport	095
docks	095
drawing (*textile mfr.*)	F176
employment	009
entertainment	106
estate	025
estimating	M004
exchange;	
employment	021
labour	021
exhibition	106
export-	013
export agency	129
factory	091
farm	107
field	M133
financial	006
fishmonger's	M187
flats;	
holiday	109
service	109
flight	095
floor (*entertainment*)	M059
forecourt (*filling station*)	101
foundry	091
freight	097
fund; pension	007
furnishing	111
garage	091
gas	094
general *see Manager-*	
hairdresser's	M159
hall;	
bingo	106
dance	106
hire; plant	111
hotel	102
house;	
acceptance	007
boarding	102
counting	099
lodging	111
public	103
slaughter	091
ware	097
wash	111
house-	
entertainment	106
housing-	111
housing association	M039
local government	M039

	Code number
Manager; *continued*	
import-	099
import agency	129
investment	007
invoice	099
kennel	111
laboratory	066
labour	009
landsale (*coal mine*)	101
launderette	110
laundry	111
lighting (*television*)	M059
machine;	
collotype	227
letterpress	207
lithographic	207
printing	207
machine-	
paper goods mfr.	227
printing	207
maintenance	091
market	111
marketing	013
media	014
merchandise	013
mill	091
office;	099
betting	164
box	099
drawing	M079
insurance;	099
D.H.S.S.	021
loan	098
post	099
printing (*P.O.*)	091
operating (*L.T.E.*)	095
operations; computer	099
outdoor (brewers)	111
packaging	097
parts; spare	096
personal (*entertainment*)	059
personnel	009
pharmacist's	044
planning (*manufacturing*)	075
plant-	091
building and contracting	092
prescription (*glass mfr.*)	F192
prevention; loss	111
processing; data	M012
produce (*retail trade*)	101
product	013
production-	091
advertising	014
building and contracting	092
film production	M059
progress	091
projects-	091
advertising	014
building and contracting	092
promotion; sales	013
property	025
publications; technical	091
publicity	014
publisher's	101
purchase; hire	098
purchasing	016
quality	075
quarry	094
regional (sales force)	M133
relations; industrial	009
research; market	013
research-	067
biology	065
chemistry	066
reservations	099
room;	
ball	106
composing	091
pattern	F333
print	091
stock	096
safety	M039
sales;	
area	M133

(Ma)

	Code number
Manager; *continued*	
sales; *continued*	
district	...M133
field	...M133
regional	...M133
sales-	013
retail trade	101
sales and advertising	013
sales and commercial	013
sales and service	013
section *see* Manager-	
security	111
service;	091
rental	111
shed (*textile mfr.*)	091
shift	091
shipping	099
shop;	
betting	164
butcher's	...M186
fishmonger's	...M187
mobile	...M128
shop-	
dyeing and cleaning ...	110
hairdressing	...M159
laundry receiving shop	110
metal trades	091
retail trade-	101
butchers	...M186
fishmongers ...	...M187
mobile shop ...	...M128
pharmacists ...	044
showroom	101
site;	092
caravan	109
society;	
bible	101
building	099
friendly	099
solicitor's	...M027
spares	096
sports	106
stable	111
staff	009
stage (*entertainment*) ...	...M059
stall	101
stall (*retail trade*)	...M130
stand (*entertainment*) ...	106
station;	
airline	095
petrol	101
stock	096
stores; ship's	096
store(s)-	096
retail trade	101
studio-	...M055
entertainment	...M059
study; works	...M010
systems	...M012
tailor's	101
taxation (*accountancy*) ...	008
team (sports)	...M063
technical-	078
lighting	...M059
telephone	099
terminal (*oil distribution*) ...	097
theatre	106
touring (*entertainment*) ...	...M059
trade	101
traffic	095
training	...M034
transport	095
travel	099
underground (*mine, not coal*)	094
valuation	...M005
wages	099
warehouse	097
wharf	097
works; sewage	111
works-	091
building and contracting ...	092
workshop(s)	091
yard;	097
ship	091

	Code number
Manager; *continued*	
of field trials (*N.I.A.B.*) ...	065
Manager-	
catering	104
accountancy	099
advertising	014
agricultural contracting ...	107
agriculture	107
auctioneering	...M134
average adjusting ...	...M008
banking and finance- ...	099
merchant banking ...	006
betting and gambling- ...	164
casino, gaming club	106
building and contracting ...	092
building society	099
car hire	111
caravan site	109
cinema	106
circulating library	101
coal mine-	094
open cast	092
coke ovens	091
credit company	098
education-	111
driving school	...M052
training centre	...M034
employment agency (*private*)	099
estate agency	025
export agency	129
fishing company	111
football club	...M063
forestry	111
funeral direction	163
gardening/grounds keeping	
services	111
hairdressing	...M159
holiday camp	109
horticulture	107
hostel	111
hotel, etc.	102
import agency	129
insurance	099
insurance brokers	007
Job Centre (*Dept. of Emp.*)	021
laundry, dry cleaners-	
launderette	110
receiving office, shop ...	110
manufacturing-	091
mine (*not coal*), quarry ...	094
market gardening ...	107
market research	013
mineral oil processing ...	091
money lending	098
N.A.A.F.I.-	
canteen	104
shop	101
night club	106
nuclear fuel production ...	091
nursing home	...M043
off-licence	101
park	106
pawn brokers	101
photographic studios ...	111
plant hire	111
postal, telecommunications	
services	099
property investment company	025
public baths	106
public house	103
public utilities	094
quarry	094
refuse disposal, sanitation,	
etc.	111
religious organisation ...	111
repairing-	
motor vehicles	091
consumer goods ...	111
residential club	102
retail trade-	101
butchers	...M186
fishmongers	...M187
market stall	...M130
mobile shop	...M128

	Code number
Manager- *continued*	
retail trade- *continued*	
opticians	046
party plan sales ...	...M132
pharmacists	044
safe deposit	111
ship broker's	129
Social Security Office ...	021
solid fuel mfr.	091
sports activities	106
stock jobbers	007
storage	097
theatre	106
trade association	...M024
trade union	...M024
trading stamp redemption	
office	101
transport-	095
loading, unloading ...	097
travel agency	099
typewriting agency ...	111
warehousing	097
welfare services	...M039
well drilling	094
wholesale trade-	101
butchers	...M186
fishmongers	...M187
Manciple	016
Mangle hand *see* Mangler	
Mangle man *see* Mangler	
Mangler; plate	270
Mangler-	
steelworks	270
textile mfr.	182
Manicurist	165
Manipulator;	
glass	192
tub (*coal mine*)	338
tube-	
metal	276
rubber	228
Manipulator-	
metal mfr.	270
plastics goods mfr. ...	229
Mannequin	064
Manual worker	L346
Manufacturer-	
badges	212
bags	225
basketry	230
bedding	213
brushes, brooms ...	230
buttons	230
canvas goods	226
cast concrete goods ...	230
ceramics	223
chemicals	184
clothing	226
fancy goods	230
firelighters	299
fireplaces	300
food products-	202
flour confectionery ...	185
sugar confectionery ...	202
footwear	175
furniture-	215
cane furniture	230
metal furniture	276
gas	184
glass	192
gloves	212
hats	226
instruments	246
jewellery, plate	266
joinery	214
leather	173
leather goods	225
machinery	248
metal goods-	276
sheet metal goods ...	261
metals	231
models	214
musical instruments ...	222
packing cases	216

(Ma)

	Code number
Manufacturer- *continued*	
paper	203
paper goods	227
plastics goods	229
rope, twine	199
rubber goods	228
shop and office fittings ...	214
soft drinks	202
sports goods	230
surgical appliances	230
textile machinery accessories	230
textiles	199
tobacco	201
toys	230
umbrellas	226
vehicles	248
watches, clocks	247
wood products	224
Marble worker	301
Marbler; paper	189
Marbler-	
bookbinding	189
leather dressing	173
Margarine worker	202
Marine-	
armed forces-	
foreign and Commonwealth	136
U.K.	135
Mariner;	
master-	087
fishing	111
Mariner-	317
fishing	171
Marker;	
bale	227
billet-	
jute mfr.	115
steelworks	270
billiard	165
box	227
button	226
buttonhole	226
cask	197
dial	299
hall (*Assay Office*)	270
ingot (*metal mfr.*)	270
lining	226
part	245
pattern (down quilt, etc.) ...	226
piece (*textile mfr.*)	226
plate (*rolling mill*)	270
plater's	276
road	308
size	227
stitch (*footwear mfr.*) ...	225
strip	175
sub-assembly line (*radio mfr.*)	283
timber	227
trade	227
upper (*footwear mfr.*) ...	227
valve	227
Marker-	
brewery	227
clothing mfr.	211
embroidery mfr.	226
footwear mfr.	225
hosiery mfr.	226
laundry	227
metal trades-	
boiler mfr.	262
clog iron mfr.	276
cutlery mfr.	242
engineering	245
file mfr.	276
fish hook mfr.	242
galvanized sheet mfr. ...	297
needle mfr.	242
pen nib mfr.	276
rolling mill	299
scales mfr.	248
sheet metal working ...	261
shipbuilding	262
steel sheet/strip mfr. ...	299
tinplate mfr.	299

	Code number
Marker- *continued*	
sugar confectionery mfr. ...	202
textile mfr.	226
Marker-off; piano	224
Marker-off-	
boiler mfr.	262
engineering	245
foundry	270
shipbuilding	262
textile mfr.	226
tube mfr.	297
wood products mfr. ...	224
Marker-out-	
engineering	245
fustian mfr.	297
glass mfr.	192
wood products mfr. ...	224
Marker-up; lens	223
Marker-up (*clothing mfr.*) ...	211
Market man-	130
coal mine	314
Marsh man	316
Marshal; air-	
armed forces-	
foreign and Commonwealth	M136
U.K.	M135
Marshal; field-	
armed forces-	
foreign and Commonwealth	M136
U.K.	M135
Marshal of the Royal Air Force	M135
Marshall(er) (*transport*) ...	338
Marshaller; aircraft	338
Marshaller (*vehicle mfr.*) ...	115
Marzipan worker	202
Mashman	197
Mash room man	197
Masher; tea	146
Masker; paint	299
Masker (files)	275
Mason;	
banker	301
fireclay	223
fixer	301
monumental	301
quarry	301
stone-	301
coal mine	300
street	309
walling	301
ware; sanitary	193
Mason-	301
coal mine	300
Mason hand	301
Masseur	049
Master;	
baggage	333
ballet	053
band	060
berthing	095
bridge	338
caddy	165
card	F176
chamber	091
choir	059
club	106
depot; railway	095
derrick	F317
dock	095
dredger	F330
dredging	F330
fire	M138
gang-	F166
drainage board ...	F311
harbour	095
head-	
educational establishments-	M033
further education	
establishment ...	M032
hopper	F338
house-	
educational establishments-	033
further education	
establishment ...	032

	Code number
Master; *continued*	
labour	009
lock	338
pay	115
pier	095
port	095
post;	099
sub-	099
self-employed ...	101
property	165
quarry	094
quarter-	333
shipping	317
quay	095
riding	063
school-	
educational establishments-	033
further education	
establishment ...	032
shed	095
ship	087
spinning	F177
staithes	097
station	095
sub-post-	099
self-employed ...	101
swingbridge	338
toast	064
tug	087
wardrobe	165
winding	F178
yacht	087
yard	095
at Arms-	
armed forces-	
foreign and Common-	
wealth	136
U.K.	135
shipping	F317
of ceremonies (*entertainment*)	064
of lightship	087
Master-	
educational establishments-	033
further education	
establishment	032
university	031
fishing	111
high courts	001
institution	M037
metal mine	F315
shipping	087
Trinity House	087
Master of works	093
Matcher;	
colour-	
leather cloth mfr. ...	199
linoleum mfr. ...	204
paint mfr.	204
plastics goods mfr. ...	204
printing	204
textile mfr.	199
hair	230
veneer	224
Matcher-	
clothing mfr.	226
hat mfr.	226
Matcher-in (clothing) ...	226
Matcher-up (clothing) ...	226
Mate;	
archer's; brick	312
asphalter's	312
bender's (metal)	276
blacksmith's	270
boat; fishing	F171
boatswain's	F317
builder's	312
burner's	276
carpenter's	219
carpenter's and joiner's ...	219
chief	087
cook's	147
coverer's; boiler	312
craftsman's-	312
wood products mfr.	219

(Ma—Me)

Mate; *continued*

	Code number
driller's (*shipbuilding*)	276
driver's;	329
crane	337
dredger	338
excavator	338
lorry	329
motor	329
scammel	329
electrician's	276
emptier's; gulley	L346
engineman's; shed	319
engineer's	276
erector's	276
examiner's; cable (*railways*)	L346
first	087
fitter's;	276
pipe	276
fixer's	312
flagger's	312
forger's; drop	270
fourth	087
fuser's	204
glazier's	312
grinder's (metal)	L344
joiner's	219
jointer's;	
cable	276
pipe	312
lagger's	312
layer's;	
brick	312
granolithic	312
main	312
plate	313
service	312
terrazzo	312
linesman's	276
liquorman's (sugar)	202
machinist's; wood	219
maker's; boiler	276
maker's (*ceramic mfr.*)	223
mason's	312
mechanic's	276
miller's (cement)	204
millwright's	276
painter's	299
pavior's	312
plasterer's	312
plater's	276
plumber's	276
plumber and jointer's	276
polisher's; french	299
printer's	207
rigger's	276
riveter's	276
roofer's	312
sawyer's	219
scaffolder's	312
second	087
sheeter's	312
shipwright's	276
slater's	312
smack; fishing	F171
smith's-	270
boiler	276
copper	276
splicer's; rope	199
stamper's	242
steeplejack's	312
stoker's	347
tester's (motor cars)	L344
third	087
tiler's	312
timberman's	312
trawler	F171
tug	087
weaver's	199
welder's	276
wheelwright's	219
wireman's	276
on barge	F317

Mate-

barge, boat	F317

Mate- *continued*

	Code number
dockyard	317
fishing	F171
shipping	087
Mate-in-charge	F317
Material man	333
Mathematician	067
Matron;	
hostel	111
laundry	F162
lodging house	111
school	M043
sewing	226
Matron-	
baths	106
institution	M037
medical services	M043
nursery	M037
prison service	142
Mattock man	316
Measurer;	
braid	297
cloth (*textile mfr.*)	297
land	084
piece	297
skin (*food products mfr.*)	297
steel	286
timber	297
wood	297
Measurer-	
cable mfr.	297
carpet mfr.	297
chemical mfr.	297
clothing mfr.	210
coal mine	115
docks	115
leather dressing	297
paper pattern mfr.	227
rolling mill	286
tape mfr.	297
Mechanic;	
agricultural	248
battery	230
builder's	316
camera	246
clock	247
colliery	248
compass	246
dental	220
dentist's	220
dictaphone	251
electrical	253
electro;	253
chief	F253
district	F253
electronic	259
experimental	248
farm	248
hosiery	248
instrument;	246
electronic	259
optical	246
junior (*P.O.*)	253
laboratory	248
loom	248
machine;	
adding	251
calculating	251
hosiery	248
knitting	248
sewing	248
weighing	248
machine-	248
office machinery	251
maintenance *see* Mechanic-	
meter (*electricity board*)	246
motor	249
mower	248
optical	223
orthopaedic	230
pen	230
piano	222
plant	248
player	222

Mechanic; *continued*

	Code number
radar	259
radio	258
refrigeration	248
research and experimental	248
semi-skilled	249
senior-	
P.O.	249
shipping	317
service-	248
garage	249
instruments	246
office machinery	251
radio and television	258
surgical	276
technical	248
telecommunications	259
telephone; assistant (*P.O.*)	253
telephone-	256
P.O. factory	253
teleprinter	259
television	258
time recorder	247
totalisator	251
typewriter	251
umbrella	276
wireless	258
Mechanic-	248
aircraft	250
auto-engines	249
instruments	246
office machinery	251
radio, television	258
telephone, telegraph apparatus	256
vehicles	249
Mechanic and driver; motor	249
Mechanical hand (*rubber goods mfr.*)	228
Mechanic of the mine	248
Mechanic-examiner	248
Mechanic-fitter; motor	249
Mechanician- *see* Mechanic	
Mechanic-in-charge	F248
Medallist	242
Medium	040
Melanger	227
Melter;	
bullion	231
electric	231
emulsion (photographic)	204
fat	204
first hand	231
gold	231
grease	184
lead	231
platinum	231
second hand	231
silver	231
steel	231
sugar	202
third hand	231
Melter-	
glass mfr.	192
Royal Mint	231
steelworks	231
sugar refining	202
zinc smelting	231
Melter man (*food products mfr.*)	202
Member;	
of the Corps of Constructors	069
of the Inner Temple	001
of Lloyds	007
of Parliament	020
of the Stock Exchange	007
of Religious Community	040
Member (appeals tribunal, inquiry, etc.)	027
Mender;	
bag	212
belt	225
box; wooden	216
carpet	183

(Me—Mi)

	Code number
Mender; *continued*	
cloth (*textile mfr.*)	183
comb	248
crate	216
curtain; lace	183
dress (hosiery)	183
dressed (lace)	183
embroidery	226
finish (hosiery)	183
finished	183
hosiery	183
invisible	183
lace	183
net	183
piece	183
road	308
rough (hosiery)	183
sack	212
sheet (wool bales)	212
shoe	174
stocking	183
strap	225
tank	261
trawl	183
tub (*coal mine*)	276
Mender-	
embroidery mfr.	226
hotel, catering, etc.	226
institution	226
laundry	226
textile mfr.	183
Mercer	101
Merceriser	182
Merchandiser	064
Merchant; *see also Agent*	
agricultural	101
builders'	101
coal	101
firewood	130
fish-	187
wholesale	101
log	130
paper; waste	131
rag and bone	131
scrap	131
wine	101
Mess boy	146
Messman	146
Messenger;	184
chief	F124
head	F124
Queen's	124
Messenger at arms	142
Messenger-clerk	115
Messroom boy	146
Metal man (*coal mine*)	314
Metal worker;	
architectural	276
art	276
ornamental	276
precious	266
sheet	261
white	266
Metal worker-	L344
hospital service	248
linoleum mfr.	276
Metaler (*glass*)	191
Metaller;	270
bronzing	227
Metalliser; spray	269
Metalliser (*lamp, valve mfr.*)	269
Metallographer	077
Metallurgist	077
Meteorologist	067
Meter; sworn	297
Meter hand	246
Meterman; coal	115
Methylator	184
Metrologist	080
Mica man (*mine, not coal*)	315
Mica worker	204
Micanite worker	204
Microbiologist	065
Microscopist; electron	080

	Code number
Middleman (*slaughterhouse*)	186
Middler (*rolling mill*)	270
Midshipman-	
armed forces-	
foreign and Commonwealth	M136
U.K.	M135
shipping	087
Midwife;	043
superintendent	F043
Milk boy (*farming*)	172
Milkman-	
farming	172
milk retailing	128
Milker	172
Milkmaid	172
Mill hand;	
finishing	184
flour	202
grain	202
grinding	184
ink	184
nitrate	L340
provender	202
roller (gramophone records)	195
rolling	270
rubber	194
saw	218
tints	184
wash (cement)	204
Mill hand-	204
cattle food mfr.	202
chemical mfr.	184
food processing	202
galvanized sheet mfr.	270
hair, fibre dressing	176
mine, not coal	198
rubber goods mfr.	194
tinplate mfr.	270
Mill man;	
lead	204
malt	197
paint	204
potter's	204
pug	204
rubber	194
Mill man-	
carbon goods mfr.	204
ceramic mfr.	204
chemical mfr.	184
leather dressing	173
metal mfr.	270
mine, not coal	198
plastics goods mfr.	204
rubber goods mfr.	194
salt mfr.	202
textile finishing	182
whiting mfr.	204
Mill operative	L346
Mill worker;	
asbestos	176
corn	L346
cotton	L339
flour	L346
grog	204
paper	203
rolling	270
rubber	194
saw	218
sheet	270
slate	301
woollen	L339
Mill worker-	L346
animal foods mfr.	202
metal mfr.	270
Miller;	
bayonet	241
blanket	182
broaching	241
cement	204
cloth	182
coal (*cement mfr.*)	204
concave (needles)	241
corn	202
die	241

	Code number
Miller; *continued*	
dry (*textile mfr.*)	182
dust (*ceramic mfr.*)	204
dyewood	204
engineer's	241
felt	182
flint (*ceramic mfr.*)	204
flour;	202
wood	203
glaze (*ceramic mfr.*)	204
grain	202
grist	202
gypsum	204
horizontal	241
lime	204
logwood	203
machine;	241
knife	241
madder	204
malt	197
metal	241
mustard	202
oil	202
optical	192
paint	204
profile	241
provender	202
rice	202
rubber	194
saw	218
soap	184
solvent	182
space band	241
spice	202
stone (*mine, not coal*)	198
tool	240
tool room	240
universal	241
vertical	241
wash (*cement mfr.*)	204
wet (*cement mfr.*)	204
woollen	182
Miller-	
animal foods mfr.	202
brewery	197
cement mfr.	204
ceramic mfr.	204
chemical mfr.	184
grain milling	202
hair, fibre dressing	176
metal trades	241
mine, not coal	198
paper mfr.	203
plastics goods mfr.	195
sugar refining	202
textile mfr.	182
whisky distilling	197
Milliner; hosiery	181
Milliner-	211
retail trade	101
Milling hand (*soap mfr.*)	184
Millwright	248
Milner (*textile finishing*)	182
Mincer; sausage meat	186
Minder:	
back (*textile mfr.*)	199
backwash	199
backwasher	199
belt (*coal mine*)-	338
above ground	338
block (*wire mfr.*)	L344
boiler	347
bowl;	
scouring	199
wash (*textile mfr.*)	199
bowl (*worsted mfr.*)	199
box (*textile mfr.*)	176
can	176
card	176
carding	176
cart	329
cell	269
chain	338
child	151

(Mi—Mo)

	Code number
Minder; *continued*	
comb	176
condenser	176
copper (straw plait)	199
crossing; railway	321
crusher (*mine, not coal*)	198
engine	255
finisher (blowing room)	176
frame;	176
cheesing	178
copping	178
lap (silk)	176
roving (jute)	176
slubbing	176
front	176
hatch	334
head;	177
balling	176
jack	176
joiner	177
machine *see Machinist*	
motion	199
mule	177
oven (*bakery*)	200
platen (*printing*)	207
pump	348
punch	176
reducer (*wool drawing*)	176
retort (*food canning*)	202
rover	176
roving	176
scribbling	176
scutcher	176
side;	177
low	182
stenter	182
stove	231
swift (wire)	L344
tool	333
turn (*coal mine*)	338
twister (*wool*)	177
Mine worker-	
coal mine- see also notes p.3	345
face working	314
mine, not coal	315
Miner;	
clay	315
coal- *see also notes* p.3	345
face working	314
tunnel	304
wall	301
Miner-	
coal mine-see also notes p.3	345
face working	314
mine, not coal	315
Mineralogist	067
Minister-	
government	020
religion	040
Missionary	040
Missioner-	040
political party	030
Mistress;	
doffing	F199
head-	
educational establishments-	M033
further education establishment	M032
needle	212
room; work	212
school-	
educational establishments-	033
further education establishment	032
sewing	F212
shifting	F199
wardrobe	165
weaving	F180
Mistress-	
educational establishments-	033
further education establishment	032
Mixer;	
acid	184

	Code number
Mixer; *continued*	
adhesive (*abrasive paper mfr.*)	203
asphalt-	204
building and contracting	313
banbury	194
batch-	202
chemical mfr.	184
glass mfr.	204
bleach (paper)	184
bristle	176
cake	200
carbide; tungsten	204
carbon	184
cement (*building and contracting*)	204
chemical(s) (*textile mfr.*)	182
chocolate	202
clay-	
ceramic mfr.	204
paper mfr.	184
colour-	204
custard powder mfr.	202
plastics goods mfr.	204
compound-	184
animal foods mfr.	202
concrete	204
cosmetic	184
cotton	176
cream; ice	202
depolariser	184
dope	184
dough-	
flour confectionery mfr.	200
plastics goods mfr.	204
rubber mfr.	194
dry-	
plastics goods mfr.	204
rubber goods mfr.	194
dubbing	062
dust (*ceramic mfr.*)	204
dye	184
electrolyte (*electric battery mfr.*)	184
emulsion	204
enamel	204
explosives	184
fibre; fur	199
flour	202
fluid (*engineering*)	204
food	202
glass	204
glaze (*ceramic mfr.*)	204
glue	184
grog (*ceramic mfr.*)	204
ink	184
lacquer	204
latex	194
linoleum	204
macadam	204
marl	204
metal	231
oil	184
paint	204
paste; lead	204
paste (*paper goods mfr.*)	184
plastic(s)	204
polish; furniture	204
powder; fluorescent	184
putty	204
recipe (*food products mfr.*)	202
resin	184
rubber	194
sand (*metal mfr.*)	270
size-	
paper mfr.	184
textile mfr.	182
slurry (*cement mfr.*)	204
soap;	184
textile bleaching	182
solution	184
sound	062
spice	202
sponge (*bakery*)	200
starch	182

	Code number
Mixer; *continued*	
sugar (*condensed milk mfr.*)	202
syrup (*mineral water mfr.*)	202
tar-	
building and contracting	316
slag macadam mfr.	204
vision (*television*)	062
wool	176
Mixer-	
abrasive paper mfr.	203
accumulator, battery mfr.	184
animal foods mfr.	202
artificial teeth mfr.	204
asbestos composition goods mfr.	176
cast concrete products mfr.	204
cement mfr.	204
cemented carbide goods mfr.	204
ceramic mfr.	204
chemical mfr.	184
composition die mfr.	204
felt hood mfr.	176
film production	062
flour confectionery mfr.	200
food products mfr.	202
glass mfr.	204
paper mfr.	188
pencil, crayon mfr.	204
plastics goods mfr.	204
rubber mfr.	194
soft drink mfr.	202
steelworks	231
tar macadam mfr.	204
textile mfr.-	176
textile proofing	182
Mixer man;	
asphalt-	204
building and contracting	316
slag; tar	184
Mixer man-	
animal foods mfr.	202
building and contracting	204
slag wool mfr.	204
steel mfr.	231
textile mfr.	182
Model	064
Modeller;	
architectural	214
artistic	055
clay	223
glass	192
pattern; paper	226
plaster	223
styling (motor vehicles)	230
wax	230
Modeller-	226
art metal work mfr.	276
ceramic mfr.	223
Moderator (Presbyterian Church)	040
Modiste	210
Monitor; industrial (*atomic energy establishment*)	080
Monitor-	
atomic energy establishment	080
broadcasting	054
Monk	040
Mooring man	338
Mopper (*metal trades*)	243
Mortician	165
Mosaic worker	300
Moss man	316
Mother;	
foster	037
house	037
Mother superior	040
Motor man;	
belt	338
haulage	331
screen	331
Motor man-	255
L.T.E.	319
railways	319
shipping	317

72

(Mo—No)

	Code number
Motor man- *continued*	
tramways	325
Mottler (*ceramic mfr.*)	299
Mould man-	
cast concrete products mfr.	230
paper mfr.	203
steelworks	235
Moulder;	
abrasive	230
aloe (plastics)	195
aluminium	235
bakelite	195
battery	270
bench	235
bottle	192
brass	235
brick	223
carbon	230
carborundum	230
chocolate	202
cigar	201
clay	193
compo.	204
compression (*plastics goods mfr.*)	195
concrete	230
connection	235
copper	235
core	235
cylinder	235
ebonite	194
faience	193
fibreglass	229
fireclay	193
floor	235
fork (digging, hay, etc.)	270
furnace	223
grate; stove	235
gutter	235
hand-	
asbestos goods mfr.	230
ceramic mfr.	193
metal trades	235
plumbago crucible mfr.	193
injection (*plastics goods mfr.*)	195
insole	225
iron	235
lead (*battery mfr.*)	270
leather	225
lens	192
loam	235
machine-	
chocolate	202
marzipan	202
metal; gun	235
mica	204
micanite	204
pattern	235
pipe;	
clay	193
iron	235
pipe-	
asbestos-cement	204
cast concrete	230
metal	235
pipe founder's	235
plaster	223
plastic	195
plate-	
glass	192
metal	235
ploughshare	235
press-	
plastics	195
rubber	194
roll	235
rubber (moulds)	228
sand	235
shell	235
sole	225
spindle-	
plastics	195
wood	218
spray	235

	Code number
Moulder; *continued*	
stamp	228
steel	235
stiffener	225
stone; patent	230
stove	235
tile; hand (ceramic)	223
tooth	230
tube;	195
rubber	194
tyre	228
wax	206
wheel; abrasive	230
wheel-	
abrasive wheel mfr.	230
metal trades	235
wood	218
Moulder-	
asbestos-cement goods mfr.	230
bakery	200
bottle cap mfr.	194
brake lining mfr.	230
candle mfr.	230
cast concrete products mfr.	230
ceramic mfr.	193
chemical mfr.	235
coal mine	235
cork goods mfr.	230
glass mfr.	192
lead pencil, chalk, crayon mfr.	230
metal trades	235
plastics goods mfr.	195
printing	206
rubber goods mfr.	194
sugar confectionery mfr.	202
tobacco mfr.	201
Moulder and coremaker (*foundry*)	235
Moulds man (*metal mfr.*)	270
Mounter;	
barometer	246
body	285
boiler	248
card;	295
pattern	199
show	295
diamond	266
drawing	295
engine	248
feather	299
filament	283
gold	266
hair	230
handle; umbrella	299
lens	299
map	295
metal	266
net (fishing nets)	199
photographer's	227
picture	230
print (lithographer's)	295
process	227
silver	266
stick; walking	299
thermometer	246
wheel	247
wheel and axle	248
wing (coach body)	285
Mounter-	
instrument mfr.	246
jewellery mfr.	266
net mfr.	199
precious metal, plate mfr.	266
printing	227
textile weaving	180
vehicle building	285
Mover; conveyor (*coal mine*)	276
Mower; lawn	168
Muffle man-	
annealing	237
foundry	231
glass mfr.	192
steel mfr.	231

	Code number
Muffle worker; foundry	231
Muffle worker (*annealing*)	237
Mule man	177
Muller	173
Multigrapher	119
Municipal worker	L346
Munitions worker	L344
Musician	060
Musseler	171
Mycologist	065

N

	Code number
Nagman	172
Nailer;	
card	276
Nailer-	
box mfr.	299
footwear mfr.	299
fur goods mfr.	211
tannery	173
Nannie	151
Nanny	151
Naturalist	065
Naturopath	050
Naumkeager	175
Navigator-	
hovercraft	090
aircraft	085
shipping	087
Navvy; slurry pond-	
cement mfr.	316
Navvy-	
mine, not coal	313
Navvy man	L346
Necker;	330
fly	276
flyer	233
Needle hand;	233
latch	212
Needle woman-	181
hospital service	212
institution	226
laundry	226
Needle worker	226
Needler (*textile making-up*)	212
Needlework hand	199
Negotiator;	212
property	
sales (building and contracting)	134
Negotiator-	134
auctioneering	134
estate agency	134
insurance	134
Nematologist	065
Net hand; braiding	199
Netter (*net mfr.*)	199
Neurologist	041
Neutraliser-	
chemical mfr.	184
textile mfr.	199
Newsboy-	
bookstall	124
News hand	125
Newsagent	207
Newspaper boy	101
Nibber (*cocoa mfr.*)	124
Nickel worker (*electroplating*)	202
Nipper (*paper mfr.*)	236
Nitrider	188
Nobber; fish	237
Normaliser	187
Norseller (net)	237
Nosseller (net)	199
Notary	199
Notcher-	027
glassware	223
tin box mfr.	242

Nu—Of)

	Code number
Numberer;	
bank-note	227
cheque	227
parts	227
piece	333
Numberer-	
bookbinding	189
printing	227
Numismatist	101
Nun	040
Nurse;	043
canine	053
charge	F043
chief male	F043
children's-	150
domestic service	151
nursery	150
orderly	156
Nurse-companion	043
Nursemaid	151
Nurse-receptionist; dental	043
Nurse-tutor	F043
Nursery hand	167
Nurseryman-	107
employee	167
Nursery worker	167
Nut room worker	202
Nutritionist;	
agricultural	065
animal	065
research	065
Nutter man	202
Nutter-up	285
Nylon worker (*nylon mfr.*)	196

O

	Code number
O.S. (*shipping*)	317
Oboist	060
Observer;	
laboratory	080
metallurgical	077
radar (marine)	122
study; works	010
teeming	F235
test; flight	081
tunnel; wind	081
Obstretrician	041
Oceanographer	067
Octagon man	184
Odd job man-	L346
agriculture	166
coal mine	345
Oddman;	
bank	L342
biscuit	191
glost	191
kiln	191
oven	191
Oddman (*ceramic mfr.*)	L342
Odd worker-	
coal mine	345
engineering	276
Offal worker (*slaughterhouse*)	186
Office boy	115
,, girl	115
,, man (*railways*)	115
Office worker;	115
post	123
Officer;	
accounting	099
accounts-	115
government	006
administration; staff	009
administrative-	111
government	021
local government	022
admission (*hospital*)	115
advisory;	
careers	053
district	065

	Code number
Officer; *continued*	
advisory-	
poultry	065
Min. of A.F.F.	065
agricultural-	
county	021
district;	065
assistant	115
aids; visual	062
allocation	115
ambulance;	155
chief	111
appliance	050
appointments (*government*)	021
area; deputy (*government*)	F112
area-	
government	021
local government	022
assessment	115
assistance; national	115
attendance; school	039
authorised (*local government*)	115
bank	115
board;	
docks; national	115
marketing; milk	115
national assistance	115
water	115
borstal	139
briefing	086
budget	115
budget and cost	115
carbonisation (*N.C.B.*)	078
care; child	039
careers	053
cargo	115
catering-	104
shipping	F152
certifying (*Dept. of Transport*)	069
chief-	
fire service	M138
local government-	022
weights and measures dept.	019
prison service	108
railways	095
shipping	087
children's	039
church	115
Church Army	040
claims	005
clerical;	115
higher-	
government	F112
hospital service	F115
local government	022
P.O.	115
coal	115
collecting; authorised	115
colonial	021
commanding-	
armed forces-	
foreign and Commonwealth	M136
U.K.	M135
commercial (*railways*)	013
communications-	F122
Home Office	076
company (*fire service*)	M138
compensation (*N.C.B.*)	115
complaints	115
conciliation	009
conservation;	
assistant (*government*)	115
chief (*government*)	021
senior (*government*)	021
conservation (*government*)	F112
consular	021
consultation (*N.C.B.*)	009
contracts; sales	013
contracts-	013
building and contracting	092
government	016
manufacturing	091

	Code number
Officer; *continued*	
control;	
air traffic	086
budget	115
building	092
development	082
materials (*N.C.B.*)	F333
pest	165
production	115
reservations (*air transport*)	115
rodent	165
roof (*coal mine*)	F314
senior (*Inland Revenue*)	F112
smoke (*local government*)	017
stock (*N.C.B.*)	096
traffic	095
control (*ambulance service*)	111
controlling (*P.O.*)	F123
costing; traffic; railway	115
costs; technical;	004
principal (*P.O.*)	010
senior (*P.O.*)	010
court; county	115
cultivation; assistant	080
customs	019
Customs and Excise	019
cypher (*Foreign Office*)	115
deck-	087
dredging contractors	F330
defence;	
civil-	142
local government	022
passive (*Min. of Defence*)	021
dental	042
design; air traffic control	081
development; cost (*N.C.B.*)	003
discipline (borstal)	139
disinfecting	165
disposal; refuse	336
disposals (*government*)	F112
distribution-	115
gas board	094
N.C.B.	115
district-	
coastguard service	F142
Forestry Commission	111
Min. of A.F.F.	090
river board	019
salvage corps	M138
division (*Ordnance Survey*)	021
divisional-	
fire service	M138
Forestry Commission	111
local government	022
duty (*airport*)	095
economy (*coal mine*)	F333
education	035
electrical (*shipping*)	087
employment;	
senior (*Dept. of Emp.*)	021
youth	053
employment-	009
Dept. of Emp. Job Centre	115
enforcement (*local government*)	088
engineer-	
hovercraft	090
aircraft	085
shipping	087
engineering-	
government	069
shipping	087
enquiry; school	039
enquiry-	115
trade protection society	140
equipment (*local government*)	022
establishment-	009
government	021
estate-	025
forestry	111
local government	115
evaluation; job	010
excise (*Customs and Excise*)	019

(Of)

	Code number
Officer; *continued*	
executive;	
chief-	
government	021
P.O.	099
higher-	
government	021
P.O.	099
senior-	
government	021
P.O.	099
executive- *see also Manager*	
government	F112
insurance	F115
local government	022
P.L.A.	095
P.O.	F115
expenditure (*N.C.B.*)	003
experimental;	080
chief-	
biologist	065
chemist	066
senior-	067
biologist	065
chemist	066
fatstock (*Min. of A.F.F.*)	065
field-	
advisory	065
professional	065
food products mfr.	290
Min. of A.F.F.	090
finance;	
deputy	115
regional-	021
P.O.	099
finance-	115
hospital service	099
local government	022
N.C.B.	099
P.O.	099
financial (*local government*)	022
fingerprint;	137
civilian	115
fire;	
chief	M138
divisional	M138
fire-	M138
coal mine	138
fire brigade	M138
first-	
hovercraft	090
aircraft	085
fire service	M138
shipping	087
fishery-	019
Min. of A.F.F.	090
food (*local government*)	017
forestry	111
freight (*air transport*)	115
fuel	333
government;	
local; n.o.s.	115
n.o.s.	115
grade I—IV (*Dept. of Emp.*)	021
V (*Dept. of Emp.*)	F112
VI (*Dept. of Emp.*)	115
graphics	079
group (*Min. of Defence*)	115
chief (*Min. of Defence*)	021
senior (*Min. of Defence*)	021
health;	
environmental	017
mental	039
public	017
horticultural	065
hospital-	115
prison service	156
house	041
House; Trinity	087
housing	M039
husbandry; stock; live	065
hydrographic	090
hygiene	043

	Code number
Officer; *continued*	
immigration;	019
chief	021
indoor	F112
information; research	026
information-	026
public relations	014
Inland Revenue	115
inspecting (*Dept. of Transport*)	019
inspection (*Dept. of Energy*)	069
instructional	034
insurance	115
intelligence;	
grade II (*Min. of Defence*)	026
trade	011
intelligence-	
government	026
investigating (*Dept. of Transport*)	019
investigation;	
chief (*Customs and Excise*)	019
sales (*P.O.*)	115
veterinary	051
investigation-	
D.H.S.S.	115
local government	039
P.O.	140
J.I.B. (Joint Intelligence Bureau)	026
labour	009
land and minerals (*N.C.B.*)	084
lands	025
legal	001
lettings (*local government*)	115
liaison;	115
customer	101
labour	009
medical	133
press	014
sales	101
technical	090
liaison-	
government	021
manufacturing	090
railways	014
licensing (*local government*)	022
local I (*D.H.S.S.*)	F112
local II (*D.H.S.S.*)	115
local authority	115
magisterial	115
maintenance-	316
local government	F316
P.O.	256
printing	248
management; labour	009
manpower (*N.C.B.*)	009
marketing	013
markets (*Min. of A.F.F.*)	015
measurement; work	010
mechanisation	081
medical-	041
armed forces-	
foreign and Commonwealth	M136
U.K.	M135
membership; district (*motoring association*)	115
merchant navy	087
meteorological	067
methods	010
Milk Marketing Board	115
mining	094
municipal	115
navigating-	
aircraft	085
shipping	087
non-commissioned-	
armed forces-	
foreign and Commonwealth	136
U.K.	135
nursing	M043
o & m-	010
government	M010

	Code number
Officer; *continued*	
o & m- *continued*	
local government	M010
occupational	049
occupations	049
operations;	111
flight	086
organisation (*government*)	M010
outdoor	124
p. & c. (*N.C.B.*)	111
passenger-	
hovercraft	F152
air transport	115
patent(s) (*government*)	090
patrol	140
pensions	115
personnel	009
pest	165
petty-	
armed forces-	
foreign and Commonwealth	136
U.K.	135
planning-	
building and contracting	082
local government	082
manufacturing	075
police-	137
non-statutory	140
port	095
postal (*P.O.*)	115
postal and telegraph	115
power; motive	091
press	054
press and information	054
prevention;	
accident	039
fire-	
fire service	138
hospital service	138
preventive	019
pricing	115
principal-	
government-	021
prison service	F139
printing and binding	F112
prison;	139
chief	108
probation	039
procurement;	
facilities (T.V., etc.)	016
livestock; assistant	016
production;	
milk	065
technical	090
productivity and costs (*N.C.B.*)	074
professional and technological (*government*)-	
grade I, II *see Engineerprof.-*	
grade III, IV	081
progress	115
promotion; sales	013
protection;	
consumer	019
fire	M138
publicity	014
purchasing	016
R.S.P.C.A.	019
radio-	087
aircraft	122
government	111
rates	115
rates and charges (*transport*)	004
rating	005
rating and valuation	005
rebate (*local government*)	022
reception	117
records	099
recruiting (*P.O.*)	009
recruitment	009
reference	115

(Of)

	Code number
Officer; *continued*	
refrigeration (*shipping*)	087
regional-	
public boards	111
government	021
R.S.P.C.A.	019
railways	095
registration	115
rehabilitation	039
relations;	
customer	014
industrial	009
labour	009
public	014
relieving-	M039
shipping	087
rent	005
repeater (*P.O.*)	256
research;	
operational	010
political	026
veterinary	051
research (*government*)	030
reservations (*air transport*)	115
resettlement (*government*)	021
revenue	115
rodent	165
running and maintenance	091
safety; road	039
safety	039
safety and training-	
coal mine-	039
above ground	034
salaries	115
sales	013
salvage;	
fire	M138
marine	087
salvage-	
coal mine	314
manufacturing	L346
salvage corps	M138
salvage corps	M138
Salvation Army	040
sampling; milk	066
sanitary	017
schools	039
scientific; assistant	080
scientific-	067
biological	065
chemical	066
search	115
second-	
hovercraft	090
aircraft	085
banking	115
fire service	M138
shipping	087
section	115
securities-	
banking	115
government	021
security;	140
chief	F140
service;	
colonial	115
fire-	
fire service	M138
government	M138
foreign-	115
grade A1–A8; B1–B4	021
grade B5	F112
health	115
training	034
services; management	028
settlement	115
sheriff	142
shipping (*N.C.B.*)	115
ship's	087
signals (*Min. of Defence*)	081
staff;	
clerical	099

	Code number
Officer; *continued*	
staff; *continued*	
general-	
armed forces-	
foreign and Commonwealth	M136
U.K.	M135
staff-	
gas board	009
government	021
local government	009
railways	009
staffing; domestic	115
stamping	115
standards; trading	019
station-	
airport	115
ambulance service	111
coastguard service	142
fire service	M138
salvage corps	M138
statistical;	
grade D (*Min. of Defence*)	115
statistical-	
electricity board	115
gas board	115
government	011
N.C.B.	011
stock; live	065
store (*Min. of Defence*);	096
naval;	096
assistant	F333
victualling;	096
assistant	F333
stores;	
grade I (*Min. of Defence*)	096
supervising (*Home Office*)	096
stores-	096
Min. of Defence	F333
study;	010
work	010
substitution (*Min. of Defence*);	F112
grade I	021
superannuation	115
supervising (*P.O.*)	F123
supplies;	115
chief	016
supply;	
armament	016
assistant (*Min. of Defence*)	F112
chart (*Min. of Defence*)	F112
commercial	115
fuel	115
supply-	
chemical mfr.	115
engineering	115
Min. of Defence	016
suppression; dust (*coal mine*)	039
survey; social;	
assistant (*government*)	F112
principal (*government*)	021
senior (*government*)	021
survey; social (*government*)	021
survey-	
government	084
P.O.	256
tax;	115
higher grade	F112
taxation (*Inland Revenue*);	115
higher grade	F112
technical;	
assistant (*chemical mfr.*)	080
carbonisation (*N.C.B.*)	078
principal	069
scientific (*N.C.B.*)	090
telecommunications (*Civil Aviation Authority*)	258
technical-	090
work study	010
chemical mfr.	066
civil engineering	089
engineering	081
gas board	081

	Code number
Officer; *continued*	
technical- *continued*	
government-	090
Min. of A.F.F.	065
National Institute of Agricultural Botany	080
P.O.	256
telecommunications	122
telegraph	122
third-	
fire service	M138
shipping	087
tidal (*harbour board*)	115
traffic;	
telecommunications	F121
traffic-	
airline	095
P.O.	F121
port authority	095
road haulage	095
trainee (*coal mine*)	034
training;	
colliery	034
regional (*P.O.*)	M034
sales	M034
training	034
training and education	M034
transport;	
mechanical;	081
chief	069
motor (*P.O.*)	095
transport-	095
Dept. of Transport	081
Trinity House	087
trust	006
vacancy (*Dept. of Emp.*)	115
valuation	005
ventilation (*coal mine*)	039
veterinary	051
visiting (*D.H.S.S.*)	115
wages; assistant	115
wages and control (*N.C.B.*)	F115
warrant-	
armed forces-	
foreign and Commonwealth	136
U.K.	135
county court	142
police service	F137
wayleave	134
welfare; chief	M039
welfare-	039
P.O.	M039
wireless	087
works	068
workshops (*Min. of Defence*)	090
youth	039
Officer-	
hovercraft	090
aircraft	085
armed forces-	
foreign and Commonwealth	M136
U.K.	M135
fire service	M138
insurance	115
shipping	087
W.R.N.S.	M135
Officer's boy	152
Official;	
airline	115
bank	115
brewery	115
claims; marine	005
court	115
government	115
insurance	134
local government	115
N.A.A.F.I.	146
racecourse	063
sports	063
tax (*Inland Revenue*)	115
Official-	
charitable organisation	024
dock board	115

(Of—Op)

	Code number
Official- *continued*	
employers' association	024
N.C.B.	F314
P.O.	115
professional organisation	024
trade union	024
Off-licensee	101
Oil rig worker-	
oil rig construction	262
well drilling	315
Oilman; engine	184
Oilman-	
coal mine	271
shipping	317
Oiler;	
frame (*textile mfr.*)	271
loom	271
machine; printing	271
machine (*textile mfr.*)	271
mould (asbestos)	204
silk	182
skin (leather)	173
tube (*tube mfr.*)	270
wool	199
Oiler-	271
canvas goods mfr.	182
leather dressing	173
varnish mfr.	204
Oiler and banter (*textile mfr.*)	271
Oiler and beltman	271
Oiler and cleaner-	271
textile mfr.	199
Oiler and greaser-	271
motor vehicles	249
Omicer	204
Oncost man (*mine, not coal*)	L346
Onsetter; staple pit (*coal mine*)	331
Onsetter	331
Opener;	
asbestos	176
bale-	L346
textile mfr. (opening dept.)	176
channel	225
fibre	176
hot (*steel mfr.*)	270
mail	115
piece-	
glass mfr.	192
textile mfr.	199
plate (tinplate)	270
silk	178
yarn	178
Opener-	
foundry	L343
textile mfr.-	178
fibre opening	176
tinplate mfr.	270
Operator;	
acidifier	202
addressograph	119
adrema	119
assembly *see* Assembler	
auto	242
autoclave-	
asbestos composition goods mfr.	204
chemical mfr.	184
food products mfr.	202
glass mfr.	204
banbury (*rubber mfr.*)	194
banda	119
barber greene	330
bath; salt (*metal goods*)	237
bay (*garage*)	249
belt (conveyor)	338
bench; draw	234
benzol	184
blending (*custard powder mfr.*)	202
block; bull	234
board; test	259
boiler;	347
sugar	202
boom (*film production*)	062
boot	175

	Code number
Operator; *continued*	
booth; toll	115
borer; hole; pole	330
box; steam	182
brake-	
bakery	200
steelworks	276
bridge; weigh	297
bridge-	338
coal mine	331
building	304
bullard	241
bulldozer	330
burner; kiln (*carbon goods mfr.*)	204
Burrough's	119
burster	119
button	338
cable-	122
cable mfr.	230
calender-	
laundry	162
paper mfr.	188
plastics mfr.	195
rubber mfr.	194
textile mfr.	182
camera-	
photocopying	119
film production	061
printing	061
process engraving	061
television service	061
capstan-	241
railways	338
capsulation	184
car; ingot	338
card;	
cotton	176
punch	119
cash and wrap	116
caster; monotype	205
castings-	
metal mfr.	270
rubber goods mfr.	228
cathedral	192
centrifugal (starch)	202
centrifuge (chemicals)	184
charger (*rolling mill*)	332
check-out	116
chemical	184
cinema	062
cinematograph	062
cipher	122
circuit; printed	283
clipper; veneer	218
coach	325
coal (*power station*)	255
coatings; plastic (*plastics goods mfr.*)	269
coil; steel	270
colorado beetle	165
colorimeter	227
column (*oxygen mfr.*)	184
combine	230
composer; IBM	205
compressor-	
paper, leather board mfr.	203
comptometer	119
computer	119
consol	175
control; pest	165
control-	
railways	255
steelworks	270
control room (*electric*)	255
conveyor	338
cooker-	
canned foods	202
dry batteries	230
cooler; brine (milk)	202
crane	331
crocell	299
cropper	276

	Code number
Operator; *continued*	
crusher;	
lime	198
stone	198
cuber	202
cutter; coal	314
degrease(r)	270
densification (chemicals)	184
depiler (*metal mfr.*)	270
deseaming (steel)	265
detector (*engineering*)	286
dictaphone	118
die cast	235
dip (*metal trades*)	269
disc (*coal mine*)	314
disintegrator (chemicals)	184
display; visual	119
disposal; refuse	348
drawtwist	176
dredger	330
drier (plasterboard)	204
drier's; grain (milk foods)	202
drill;	241
pneumatic	330
drott	330
drum	173
dry cleaner-	
coal mine	198
laundry	162
drying room	204
duplicator	119
dyeline	119
electrical (*rolling mill*)	338
electrolysis	165
elevator	331
Elliot-Fisher	119
embosser (*engineering*)	242
engine	255
evaporator-	
chemical mfr.	184
food products mfr.	202
excavator	330
extruder-	
chemical mfr.	184
metal trades	270
plastics mfr.	195
rubber goods mfr.	194
fan (*coal mine*)	348
film; micro	119
filter; drum; rotary (*chemical mfr.*)	184
filter (*whisky distilling*)	197
flexowriter	119
flotation; froth (*coal mine*)	198
forge	270
frame; spinning	177
freezer (*fruit, vegetable preserving, ice cream making*)	202
froster (*fruit, vegetable preserving, ice cream making*)	202
furnace;	
annealing	237
carburising	237
electric (enamelling)	204
electrical (*metal mfr.*)	231
glass	191
pusher slab	270
treatment; heat	237
furnace-	
ceramic mfr.	191
glass mfr.	191
metal mfr.	231
gammeter	119
garnett	176
gas	184
gauger (cartridges)	286
gearhead	255
Gestetner	119
glass; fibre	223
glazing (explosives)	184
graphotype	118
gravure (printer's)	207
grinder	241

(Op)

Operator; continued
- grinder and roller (*cheese processing*) ... 202
- guide ... 184
- guillotine-
  - *coach trimming* ... 226
  - *coal mine* ... 276
  - *metal trades* ... 276
  - *paper goods mfr.* ... 190
  - *plastics goods mfr.* ... 229
  - *pressed woollen felt mfr.* ... 199
  - *printing* ... 190
- gun; cement ... 316
- hammer ... 270
- heat treatment-
  - carbon goods ... 204
  - metal ... 237
- Heidelberg ... 207
- helio (*Ordnance Survey*) ... 227
- hoist ... 331
- Hollerith ... 119
- homogeniser (ice cream) ... 202
- hot ... 270
- house; power ... 255
- hydrate ... 204
- hydraulic ... 348
- hydro- ... 162
  - *laundry* ... 162
  - *textile finishing* ... 199
- hydro-extractor-
  - *chemical mfr.* ... 184
  - *laundry* ... 162
  - *tannery* ... 173
- IBM ... 119
- ICL ... 119
- incinerator ... 348
- installation (office machinery) ... 119
- intertype ... 205
- J.C.B. ... 330
- jetty ... 334
- jig (*textile mfr.*) ... 199
- jointer ... 224
- kardex ... 119
- keller ... 241
- kettle; sauce and pickle ... 202
- kettle (*chemical mfr.*) ... 184
- keyboard (typesetting) ... 205
- key-to-disc ... 119
- kiln- ... 204
  - *ceramic mfr.* ... 191
  - *wood products mfr.* ... 203
- knife; band (*textile mfr.*) ... 199
- komet (hosiery) ... 181
- lamp (*electric lamp mfr.*) ... 286
- last; seat ... 175
- lathe-
  - *carbon goods mfr.* ... 230
  - *coal mine* ... 239
  - *industrial felt mfr.* ... 199
  - *metal trades* ... 241
  - *wood products mfr.* ... 218
- lift; ... 161
  - fork ... 332
- limelight ... 062
- line;
  - assembly (*vehicle mfr.*) ... 285
  - drag ... 330
  - dye ... 119
  - paint ... 299
  - pickle (*steel mfr.*) ... 270
  - trim (*motor vehicle mfr.*) ... 285
- line-
  - electrical ... 283
  - engineering ... 285
  - process engraving ... 061
- linotype ... 205
- litho; offset ... 227
- loader; power ... 314
- loom ... 179
- ludlow ... 205
- machine see Machinist
- machine tool ... 241
- mangle;
  - bleaching ... 182

Operator; continued
- manifold ... 184
- manipulator (*steel mfr.*) ... 270
- Marconi ... 122
- masseeley ... 227
- mill;
  - ball-
    - *ceramic mfr.* ... 204
    - *chemical mfr.* ... 184
  - boring ... 241
  - foil (aluminium) ... 232
  - hot (*metal trades*) ... 232
  - mortar ... 204
  - plano ... 241
  - pug (chemicals) ... 184
  - rolling ... 232
  - sand (*steelworks*) ... 276
  - saw ... 218
  - sheeting (chemicals) ... 184
  - tube ... 270
- mill-
  - grain milling ... 202
  - plastics goods mfr. ... 195
  - rolling mill ... 232
  - rubber goods mfr. ... 194
  - steel foundry ... 241
- milling-
  - metal trades ... 241
  - soap mfr. ... 184
- mixer-
  - *cast concrete products mfr.* ... 204
  - *sugar confectionery mfr.* ... 202
- mixing ... 184
- mogul ... 202
- monotype ... 205
- moulder (chocolate) ... 202
- multigraph ... 119
- Multilith ... 227
- multi-roller (hats) ... 199
- N.C.R. ... 119
- national ... 119
- night (*telephone service*) ... 121
- offset ... 227
- oil (*metal trades*) ... 344
- oven;
  - coke ... 184
  - vacuum (*food products mfr.*) ... 202
- pan; vacuum-
  - *chemical mfr.* ... 184
  - *food products mfr.* ... 202
- pan (*food products mfr.*) ... 202
- panel-
  - *chemical mfr.* ... 184
  - *steel mfr.* ... 338
- pantograph ... 276
- panzer (*coal mine*) ... 314
- photo (*lithography*) ... 061
- photographic ... 061
- photogravure studio ... 061
- photo-litho ... 061
- photometer ... 286
- photostat ... 119
- pilger ... 270
- pipe; blow (quartz) ... 192
- plant;
  - bakery ... 200
  - benzole ... 184
  - brick ... 191
  - builder's ... 330
  - chemical ... 184
  - chlorination ... 184
  - concrete ... 204
  - constructional ... 330
  - cracker (*oil refining*) ... 184
  - degreasing ... 270
  - dehydration (*fruit, vegetable preserving*) ... 202
  - distillation (chemicals) ... 184
  - drying; grass ... 168
  - drying-
    - *food products mfr.* ... 202
  - electrophoretic painting ... 299
  - flotation ... 198
  - gas ... 184

Operator; continued
- plant; continued
  - mobile (*steel mfr.*) ... 338
  - oxygen ... 184
  - power ... 255
  - sedimentation (*chemical mfr.*) ... 184
  - sinter ... 270
  - spray (*milk processing*) ... 202
  - sterilising (surgical dressings) ... 182
  - sulphur ... 184
  - vacuum (metallisation) ... 269
  - water softener ... 184
  - water treatment ... 184
- plant-
  - bakery ... 200
  - building and contracting ... 330
  - chemical mfr. ... 184
  - coal gas, coke ovens ... 184
  - electricity board ... 255
  - nuclear power station ... 255
  - oil refining ... 184
  - quarry ... 315
  - sewage works ... 310
- plastic(s) ... 229
- plating ... 269
- plough (*coal mine*) ... 314
- point; transfer ... 338
- power samas ... 119
- preserving (fruit pulp) ... 202
- press see Presser
- presser; steam ... 162
- print;
  - blue ... 119
  - photo ... 119
- print room ... 119
- printer's ... 207
- process-
  - *aircraft component mfr.* ... 276
  - *chemical mfr.* ... 184
  - *man-made fibre mfr.* ... 196
  - *oil refining* ... 184
  - *plastics goods mfr.* ... 195
  - *plastics mfr.* ... 184
  - *printing* ... 227
- processor; word ... 118
- producer; gas ... 184
- production see Process worker
- profile ... 241
- progress ... 119
- pullover (*footwear mfr.*) ... 175
- pulpit (*steel mfr.*) ... 232
- pump ... 348
- pumphouse; vacuum (*oil refining*) ... 184
- punch-
  - Hollerith ... 119
  - paper goods mfr. ... 190
- pusher-
  - *coke ovens* ... 338
  - *metal mfr.* ... 270
- radio ... 122
- recorder;
  - film ... 062
  - videotape ... 062
- refinery ... 184
- refrigerator ... 348
- reproduction (*atomic energy establishment*) ... 184
- research (*oil refining*) ... 080
- retort-
  - *coal gas production* ... 184
  - *food products mfr.* ... 202
- Rimoldi ... 181
- ring ... 177
- rodent ... 165
- rolls; calender (*plastics goods mfr.*) ... 195
- Roneo ... 119
- room;
  - closing (*footwear mfr.*) ... 175
  - control-
    - electrical ... 255

(Op—Ov)

Operator; *continued*
  room; *continued*
    control- *continued*
      ambulance service ... 122
      fire service ... 122
    tool ... 241
  ropeway ... 338
  rotaprint ... 119
  rotary (*printing*) ... 207
  router ... 241
  sales; telephone ... 115
  sand blast ... 275
  saw;
    band-
      wood ... 218
      asbestos goods mfr. ... 204
      metal trades ... 276
    circular (meat) ... 186
  saw-
    metal trades ... 276
    sawmilling ... 218
  scoreboard ... 165
  screen; ... 198
    silk ... 208
  screw ... 225
  sensimatic ... 119
  separator; magnetic ... 198
  separator (*food processing*) ... 202
  shear(s); ... 276
    flying ... 270
  shearer; disc (*coal mine*) ... 314
  sheathing (explosives) ... 230
  shoe ... 175
  shop; paint (*vehicle mfr.*) ... 281
  shot blast ... 275
  sieve; rotex ... 201
  sieve (foodstuffs) ... 202
  sifting room ... 202
  silo (*tobacco mfr.*) ... 333
  sinter ... 270
  slitter (*metal mfr.*) ... 276
  slusher (*coal mine*) ... 338
  softener; water ... 184
  spectroscope ... 080
  spray; mechanical ... 281
  stamping ... 225
  steel (*metal mfr.*) ... 270
  stenter ... 182
  sterilizer;
    milk ... 202
    telephone ... 158
  sterilizer (*hospital service*) ... 156
  still ... 184
  stove ... 204
  stretcher (*metal mfr.*) ... 276
  sumlock ... 119
  sunstrand ... 119
  supermarket-
    employee ... 101
       ... 333
  swaging ... 270
  switch (*coal mine*) ... 338
  switchboard-
    telephone ... 121
    power station ... 255
  tabulator ... 119
  take-down (abrasive sheet) ... 203
  tandem (chocolate) ... 202
  tank;
    asphalt ... 316
    glass ... 192
  telecine ... 062
  telecommunications ... 122
  telegraph ... 122
  telephone; ... 121
    radio ... 122
  teleprinter ... 122
  teletype ... 122
  teletypesetting ... 205
  telex ... 122
  till (*retail trade*) ... 116
  tilter (steel) ... 231
  tin house (tinplate) ... 269
  tippler ... 338
  totalisator ... 115

Operator; *continued*
  tow; ski ... 165
  transfer (*metal mfr.*) ... 270
  transport ... 326
  traverser; wagon ... 338
  treater (*petroleum refining*) ... 184
  treatment; heat-
    carbon ... 184
    metal ... 237
  trepanner (*coal mine*) ... 314
  trimming; bullet ... 276
  triples ... 202
  tube-
    lamp, valve mfr. ... 283
    plastics goods mfr. ... 195
  tumbler-
    ceramic mfr. ... 223
    laundry ... 162
  tunnel (gelatine, glue, size) ... 184
  turbine ... 255
  turntable ... 338
  turret ... 241
  twisting ... 177
  type; stringer ... 205
  typographical ... 205
  unit- ... 255
    dry cleaning ... 162
    textile finishing ... 182
  v.d.u. ... 119
  vari-typer ... 205
  vat (*metal mfr.*) ... 269
  vessel; reaction (chemicals) ... 184
  viscoliser (ice cream) ... 202
  votator ... 202
  washery ... 198
  wheelabrator ... 275
  willey (wool) ... 176
  winch ... 331
  winder; fibreglass ... 199
  winder (*paper mfr.*) ... 188
  wireless ... 122
  wireline ... 315
  xerox ... 119
  x-ray ... 045

Operator-
  agricultural machinery ... 169
  construction machinery ... 330
  office machinery- ... 119
    word processor ... 118
  oil refining ... 184
  radio relay service ... 122
  Royal Mint ... 242
Ophthalmologist ... 041
Optical worker ... 192
Optician;
  manufacturing ... 192
Optologist ... 046
Optometrist ... 046
Orchestrator ... 060
Order hand ... 333
Order lad ... 124
Order man ... 333
Order room hand ... 333
Orderly;
  civilian ... 151
  domestic (*hospital service*) ... 151
  hospital ... 156
  kitchen ... 147
  market ... L346
  medical ... 156
  mess ... 146
  nursing ... 156
  road ... 158
  room; dining ... 146
  sanitary ... L346
  street ... 158
  ward ... 156
Orderly-
  office ... 124
  hospital service ... 156
  institution ... 156
Organiser;
  appeals ... 014
  defence; civil ... 022

Organiser; *continued*
  district (*community services*) ... 039
  exhibition ... 106
  help; home ... 039
  meals; school ... 104
  playgroup ... 038
  programme (*broadcasting*) ... 059
  publicity ... 014
  safety; road ... 039
  sales ... 013
  welfare ... 039
  youth ... 039
Organiser-
  further education ... 053
  physical education ... 053
  vocational training ... 034
  political party ... 024
  trade union ... 024
  welfare services ... 039
Organist ... 060
Ornament worker; black ... 266
Ornamenter-
  ceramic mfr. ... 193
  japanned ware mfr. ... 299
Ornithologist ... 065
Orseller (net) ... 199
Orthodontist ... 042
Orthoptist ... 049
Orthotist ... 050
Osseller (net) ... 199
Osteopath ... 049
Ostler ... 172
Otologist ... 041
Otorhinolaryngologist ... 041
Outfitter (*retail trade*) ... 101
Oven hand-
  bakery ... 200
  ceramic mfr. ... 191
  micanite mfr. ... 204
Ovenman;
  biscuit ... 191
  coke ... 184
  glost ... 191
  malleable iron ... 237
Ovenman-
  abrasive coated paper cloth mfr. ... 203
  bakery ... 200
  brake lining mfr. ... 204
  ceramic mfr. ... 191
  food products mfr. ... 202
  japanning, enamelling ... 204
Oven worker; coke ... 184
Ovensman (*bakery*) ... 200
Overman; deputy (*coal mine*) ... F314
Overman (*mining*) ... 094
Over-baster ... 210
Overhauler-
  vehicles ... 249
  rag sorting ... 176
  tramways ... 325
Overlocker ... 212
Overlooker;
  cloth ... 289
  greenhouse ... 299
  loom (maintenance) ... 248
  weaving (maintenance) ... 248
  wire ... 230
Overlooker- see also Foreman
  maintenance (*textile mfr.*) ... 248
  clothing mfr. ... 289
  hat mfr. ... 289
  lace examining ... 289
  warping ... F179
Overseer;
  assistant (*Min. of Defence*) ... 090
  postal ... F115
  radio ... F122
  ship (*Min. of Defence*) ... 076
  telegraph ... F122
Overseer- see also Foreman
  Min. of Defence ... 076
  P.O.- ... F115
    sorting office ... F123

(Ow—Pa)

	Code number		Code number		Code number
Owner-		Oxidiser man	184	Painter; *continued*	
agricultural machinery	169	Oyster bed worker ...	171	spray-	281
amusement	106			*ceramic mfr.* ...	279
art gallery	106			*painting and decorating*	282
assembly rooms ...	104			tin	281
automatic machines ...	106			toy	299
betting shop	164			underglaze	279
billiard room	106	**P**		velvet	227
boarding house ...	102			wagon	281
boat;	317	P.O. n.o.s. (*local government*)	022	Painter-	282
fishing	111	P. and T.O. (*government*)-		*artificial flower mfr.*	299
bowling green ...	106	grade I, II see Engineer- *prof.*-		*ceramic mfr.* ...	279
bus service	325	grade III, IV ...	081	*garage*	281
butchers	186	Packman (*woollen carding*)	L339	*glass etching* ...	299
cab	327	Packer;		*roller engraving* ...	276
café	104	asbestos	316	*tannery*	173
camp; holiday ...	109	cable	287	*textile designing* ...	115
car hire service ...	134	chlorine	287	*vehicle mfr.* ...	281
caravan	109	cop	287	Painter and decorator ...	282
caravan site	109	drum; furnace ...	297	Painter and glazier ...	282
carriage	327	flock (*bedding mfr.*) ...	213	Painter hand	299
chess room	106	gland	271	Painter-decorator ...	282
cinema	106	kiln	191	Pairer-	
circulating library ...	101	oven (*foundry*) ...	270	*corset mfr.*	299
club-	104	potter's	191	*hosiery mfr.* ...	287
sports club ...	106	sagger	204	Palaeographist	036
coach service	325	shoddy	176	Palaeontologist	067
coconut shy	165	wheel	276	Palm and needle hand ...	212
contract cleaning services	111	wool	287	Palmist	165
convalescent home ...	037	Packer-	287	Pan hand; bass	230
dance hall	106	*coal mine*	314	Pan hand (*brush mfr.*) ...	230
detective agency ...	140	*furniture mfr.* ...	287	Pan man;	
drifter	111	*mine, not coal* ...	338	acid	184
drug store	101	*shipbuilding* ...	262	boiling (*foods*) ...	202
dry cleaning service ...	111	*steel mfr.*	287	vacuum (*food products mfr.*)	202
employment agency ...	099	Packer and sorter (*laundry*)	287	Pan man-	
engineering works ...	276	Packer and stacker ...	287	*catering, hotels, etc.* ...	147
fish hatchery	111	Packer-driver	326	*ceramic mfr.* ...	204
fishing vessel	111	Packer-hooper	287	*chemical mfr.* ...	184
fishmongers	187	Packer-labourer	287	*coal mine*	314
flats;		Padder; colour	299	*food products mfr.* ...	202
holiday	109	Padder-		*paper mfr.*	203
service	109	*clothing mfr.*	212	*sugar refining* ...	202
garage	100	*leather dressing* ...	173	Pan worker; revolving (*sugar*	
general store	101	*textile mfr.*	182	*confectionery mfr.*)	202
guest house	102	Paediatrician	041	Panelman (*oil refining*) ...	184
horse	111	Page (*hotel*)	154	Paneller; veneer	224
hotel	102	Page boy	154	Panner-	201
kennels	111	Pager-		*coal mine*	314
launderette	110	*bookbinding*	189	Panner-out	L341
laundry	111	*printing*	227	Pansman (*sugar refining*)	202
loan office	134	*type foundry*	287	Pantographer-	
newspaper	054	Paint boy	L346	*embroidery mfr.* ...	212
nursing home	043	Paint hand	299	*glassware mfr.* ...	192
old people's home ...	037	Paint worker-		*lace mfr.*	226
petrol pump	100	*paint mfr.*	184	*roller engraving* ...	267
petrol station	100	*vehicle mfr.*	281	Pantry boy	147
photographic agency ...	134	Painter;		Pantry man	147
pleasure pier	106	aircraft	281	Paper boy (*newsagents*) ...	124
property	025	biscuit	279	Paper hand (*piano hammers*)	218
public house	103	bottom	299	Paper man (*plasterboard mfr.*)	204
quarry	315	car	281	Paper worker-	
refreshment room ...	104	coach	280	*paper mfr.*	188
restaurant	104	design	079	*printing*	L346
sawmill	218	enamel	279	Paperer;	
school-		engraver's (*textile printing*)	276	chair	299
driving school ...	052	flower	279	sand-	299
educational establishments-	033	freehand	279	*mask mfr.* ...	230
further education estab-		glaze	279	tin (*bakery*) ...	200
lishment	032	heraldic	055	Paperer-	
riding school ...	106	hide (*tannery*) ...	173	*ceramic mfr.* ...	287
shop see Shopkeeper		house	282	*lace mfr.*	287
skating rink	106	landscape	055	*tobacco pipe mfr.* ...	218
skittle alley	106	marine	055	Paperer-on (*whips*) ...	299
stable	111	miniature	055	Paperhanger	282
stall (street, market) ...	130	portrait	055	Paperkeeper	115
taxi	327	pottery	279	Paraflow man (*brewing*) ...	197
taxi and garage ...	100	roller (*textile printing*)	276	Parasitologist	065
tea gardens	104	rough (*glass mfr.*) ...	299	Paratrooper-	
textile mill	199	scenic	282	*armed forces-*	
travel agency	099	skin (*fellmongering*) ...	173	*foreign and Commonwealth*	136
typewriting bureau ...	134	slide; lantern ...	055	*U.K.*	135
Owner-driver; taxi ...	327	slip	279	Parceller	287
Oxidiser (*metal trades*) ...	269			Parchmentiser	203

(Pa—Pi)

	Code number
Parent;	
foster	037
house	037
Parer;	
edge	175
heel	175
sheet (*steelworks*)	276
Parer-	
clothing mfr.	226
footwear mfr.	175
leather dressing	173
rolling mill	276
saw mfr.	276
Parish worker	039
Parkeriser	269
Parlourman	151
Parlourmaid	151
Parochial worker	039
Parter (*clothing mfr.*)	211
Partner; *see also* Owner	
dancing	053
Partsman	333
Passer;	
castings	286
cigar	299
cloth	289
final (*tailoring*)	289
finished (*textile mfr.*)	289
garment	289
glove; finished	289
machine (*clothing mfr.*)	289
piece	289
proof (*lithography*)	227
sample	F231
Passer-	
brush mfr.	299
canned food mfr.	290
cardboard box mfr.	294
clothing mfr.	289
footwear mfr.	299
fur goods mfr.	289
glove mfr.	289
metal trades-	286
rolling mill	270
textile mfr.	289
textile goods mfr.	289
Paster;	
battery	230
biscuit	200
lead	230
sock	299
Paster-	
accumulator mfr.	230
biscuit mfr.	200
footwear mfr.	299
leather dressing	173
leather goods mfr.	299
paper goods mfr.	295
Pasteuriser-	
brewery	197
milk processing	202
Pastor	040
Pastry hand	185
Pastrycook-	
bakery	185
Patcher;	
cupola (*steelworks*)	300
oven	300
transfer	227
vessel	300
wool	226
Patcher (*lithography*)	227
Patent hand	181
Patenter; wire	237
Pathologist;	065
plant	065
veterinary	065
Patissier	F143
Patrolman;	
belt	338
crossing; school	142
road (*motoring organisation*)	327
Patrolman-	140
coal mine	338

	Code number
Patrolman- *continued*	
motor vehicle mfr.	286
motoring organisation	327
railways	306
Pattern girl (*lace mfr.*)	115
,, hand (*lace mfr.*)	115
,, man (*textile mfr.*)	333
,, room hand	333
,, room man	333
,, room worker (*wallpaper mfr.*)	227
Pattison hand (*lead refining*)	231
Pavior;	309
tar	307
tile	300
Pawnbroker	101
Payer (*totalisator*)	115
Pearler	184
Peat worker	172
Pedicurist	165
Pedlar	130
Peeler;	
lemon	202
orange	202
Peeler (*food processing*)	202
Pegger;	
barrel (*textile mfr.*)	199
bobbin	199
card	199
dobby	199
Pegger-	
footwear mfr.	175
textile weaving	199
Penciller-	
clothing mfr.	226
textile mfr.	199
Percher (*textile mfr.*)	289
Perforator;	
card-	
jacquard card cutting	199
stationery mfr.	227
jacquard	199
pattern (*paper dress pattern mfr.*)	227
stamp	227
Perforator-	
bookbinding	227
embroidery mfr.	226
footwear mfr.	175
glove mfr.	226
jacquard card cutting	199
metal trades	242
Perfumer	184
Permanent way man	306
Perryman	197
Pestologist	165
Peter; steeple	316
Petrol man (*road transport*)	333
Pewterer-	261
brewery	260
Pharmaceutical worker	184
Pharmaceutist	044
Pharmacist	044
Pharmacologist	065
Philatelist	101
Philologist	036
Phosphater	269
Photocopier	119
Photographer	061
Photogravure worker	206
Phrenologist	165
Physician	041
Physicist	067
Physiologist	065
Physiotherapist;	047
superintendent	F047
Pianist	060
Picker;	
basket	230
bobbin (*textile mfr.*)	338
bone (*ceramic mfr.*)	204
bowl	298
carpet	183
cloth	183

	Code number
Picker; *continued*	
coal (*railways*)	L346
confectionery	290
cotton	298
cut	183
flint	198
flock	298
flower	172
fruit-	
farming	172
food processing	202
hank	183
hop	172
lime	298
metal (*mine, not coal*)	198
mushroom	172
nut	286
order (*retail trade*)	287
pea-	
farming	172
food processing	298
potato	172
prawn	298
roller	199
silk	176
slate	334
stilt	299
stone-	
coal mine	198
stone dressing	298
thimble	299
web	183
yarn	183
Picker-	
building and contracting	298
ceramic mfr.	204
clothing mfr.	211
coal mine	198
engineering	333
food processing	202
hat mfr.	173
mine, not coal	198
paper mfr.	294
stone dressing	298
textile mfr.-	183
flock mfr.	298
silk throwing	176
wool sorting	298
Picker-out (*galvanized sheet mfr.*)	286
Picker-packer (*vehicle mfr.*)	298
Picker-up-	
galvanized sheet mfr.	338
textile mfr.	199
tobacco mfr.	201
Pickle worker	202
Pickler;	
aluminium	270
beef	202
cloth	182
iron	270
sleeper	203
steel; strip	270
tube	270
underhand	270
wire	270
Pickler-	
fellmongering	173
food products mfr.	202
metal trades	270
tannery	173
textile mfr.	182
Pickman (*coal mine*)	333
Piece boy	297
Piece worker (*coal mine*)	314
Piecener	177
Piecer;	
belt	225
big	177
cotton	177
cross	177
little	177
mule	177
ring	177
side	177

81

(Pi—Pl)

	Code number
Piecer; *continued*	
silk	177
sole	299
twiner	177
waste	176
Piecer-	
leather dressing	173
textile mfr.	177
Piecer-out (*flax mfr.*)	177
Piecer-up (*clothing mfr.*)	212
Pier head man	338
Pierman	338
Pierce worker	266
Piercer;	
saw	266
strap	175
Piercer-	
ceramic mfr.	223
jewellery and plate mfr.	266
pen nib mfr.	242
tube mfr.	270
Pigman	166
Piggeryman	166
Pikeman (*coal mine*)	314
Piler;	338
bobbin	199
hot	338
roving	176
Pilot;	
canal	087
dock	087
helicopter	085
hovercraft	M090
river	087
test	085
Pilot-	
aircraft	085
shipping	087
Pinner; woollen comb	285
Pinner-	
ceramic mfr.	223
lamp, valve mfr.	283
metal trades	285
textile mfr.-	179
textile making-up	199
Pinner-on (*textile mfr.*)	199
Pipe man; brine	260
Pipe man (*coal mine*)	260
Piper; sugar	202
Piper (*sugar confectionery mfr.*)	202
Pisciculturist	171
Pit hand (*tube mfr.*)	231
Pit man; soaking (*steelworks*)	231
Pit man-	
coal mine-	314
above ground	345
mine, not coal	315
steelworks-	270
soaking pit	231
Pit worker; siemens	270
Pit worker (*coal mine*)	345
Pitch man	L346
Pitcher;	
flour	L346
stone	316
Pitcher-	
building and contracting	316
ceramic mfr.	204
meat market	335
Pitcher and malletter	223
Placer;	
biscuit	191
glost	191
kiln	191
litho	279
sanitary	191
tile	191
Placer (*ceramic mfr.*)	191
Plaiter; grass	230
Plaiter-	
cordage	199
textile mfr.	199
Plaiter and finisher (whips)	225
Planeman; engine	306
Planer;	
die	241
edge; plate	276
slate	301
stone	301
Planer-	
metal	241
plastics	229
stereotypes	206
wood	218
coal mine	241
metal trades	241
Planer and slotter; wall	241
Planisher; iron	261
Planisher (*sheet metal goods mfr.*)	261
Planker	199
Planner;	
carpet	226
clothier's	226
die (*footwear mfr.*)	225
footwear	056
gravure	206
group (*N.C.B.*)	075
kitchen	055
line	010
linoleum	316
load	338
materials	090
media	014
mine (*N.C.B.*)	075
production	075
progress	115
sales	013
scheme; pension	011
tool and jig	075
town	082
traffic;	115
air	086
transport	115
work	115
Planner-	
clothing mfr.	226
engineering	075
printing	206
Plant hand;	
acid	184
bakery	200
Plant man;	
benzol	184
dehydration (*food products mfr.*)	202
Plant man (*chemical mfr.*)	184
Plant worker;	
gas	184
hydrating; lime	198
screening	198
sinter	270
Plant worker-	
bakery	200
chemical mfr.	184
coke ovens	184
Planter;	
coffee	107
rubber	107
tea	107
tobacco	107
tree	170
Plasterer; fibrous	302
Plasterer-	302
cast concrete products mfr.	230
coke ovens	L341
plaster cast mfr.	223
Plasterer and decorator	304
Plastics worker	229
Plate hand-	
printing	206
rope mfr.	199
Plate man-	
asphalt spreading	330
hotel, etc.	147
Plate worker;	
iron	262
metal	262
Plate worker; *continued*	
tin-	261
tinplate mfr.-	
female	L344
male	270
zinc	261
Plater;	
barrel	269
boiler	262
brass	269
bridge	262
cadmium	236
chrome	236
chromium	236
constructional	262
copper	236
dip	269
electro	236
engineers; gas	262
framing	262
gold	236
hand	236
heavy	262
hoe	233
hot	182
iron	262
last	261
light	262
lock	269
metal	269
needle	269
nickel	236
roof	262
shell	262
ship('s)	262
shovel	233
silver	236
steel	262
stem	262
structural	262
tank	262
tin-	
tinplate mfr.	269
tinplate printing	207
tool; edge-	233
surgical instrument mfr.	236
white metal	236
wire	269
Plater-	
bookbinding	189
chemical mfr.	262
coal mine	262
construction	262
fertiliser mfr.	184
gas board	262
leather dressing	173
metal trades-	
boiler mfr.	262
boot last mfr.	261
constructional engineering	262
cutlery mfr.	233
edge tool mfr.	233
electroplating	236
iron tank mfr.	262
railway locomotive shop	262
shipbuilding	262
steelworks	262
paper mfr.	188
textile mfr.	182
Plater and gilder	236
Plater-down (*textile making-up*)	199
Plater-welder	262
Platform boy (*steelworks*)	L344
Platform man;	
milk reception	F338
regulating	338
Platform man (*steelworks*)	270
Player-	
musical instruments	060
sports	063
Playwright	054
Pleater;	
accordion	199
cloth	199

(Pl—Po)

	Code number
Pleater-	
clothing mfr.	210
incandescent mantle mfr.	230
textile mfr.	182
Plier; needle (*hosiery and knitwear mfr.*)	181
Plough man-	169
coal mine	314
Plucker; chicken	187
Plucker (*poultry dressing*)	187
Plugger; rod; fishing	299
Plugger (*stoneware pipe mfr.*)	230
Plumber	260
Plumber and decorator	260
Plumber and gasfitter	260
Plumber and jointer	257
Plumber-jointer	257
Plumber-welder	260
Pocket hand	210
Poet	054
Pointer;	
bar	276
brick	300
glove	212
hook; fish	242
machine	212
rod (*wire mfr.*)	276
thermometer	192
Pointer-	
bolt mfr.	276
building and contracting	300
pin, needle mfr.	242
screw mfr.	276
wire mfr.	276
Pointsman-	
L.T.E.	338
road transport	338
Poker-in (*coke ovens*)	L341
Policeman-	
non-statutory	140
airport	137
docks	137
government	137
police force	137
railways	137
Polisher;	
bakelite	229
barrel (gun)	243
bobbin;	243
wood	224
boot	175
bottom	175
brass	243
brush	173
button	230
car; motor (*garage*)	158
celluloid	229
cellulose	299
collar	162
cutlery	243
cycle	243
diamond	266
die	243
dull (*hat mfr.*)	226
edge	192
emery	243
enamel	223
fibre	182
fine (glass)	192
floor-	158
building and contracting	316
frame;	243
spectacle	229
french	282
furniture	282
glass	192
glost	223
gold-	243
ceramic mfr.	223
granite	301
hame	243
hand (*glass mfr.*)	192
hat	226
heald	224

	Code number
Polisher; *continued*	
ivory	230
jewellery	243
key (*piano mfr.*)	222
lathe-	
metal trades	243
stone dressing	301
lens	192
lime	243
marble	301
metal	243
mirror (*cutlery mfr.*)	243
mould (metal)	243
pen; fountain	230
piano	282
pipe (wood)	224
plate (*precious metal mfr.*)	243
plater's	243
racquet; tennis	281
roll (*tinplate mfr.*)	243
roller	243
sand	243
silver-	243
hotels, catering, etc.	147
slab; optical	192
spoon and fork	243
spray	281
steel; stainless	243
stick	299
stone-	301
lithography	276
terrazzo	300
tile-	
asbestos-cement goods mfr.	230
ceramic mfr.	223
tin	243
tube	276
twine	182
wire	276
wood	282
yarn	182
Polisher-	
brass musical instruments mfr.	243
ceramic mfr.	223
clog mfr.	175
footwear mfr.	175
furniture mfr.	282
glass mfr.	192
hat mfr.	226
leather dressing	173
metal trades	243
plastics goods mfr.	229
stone dressing	301
straw hat mfr.	182
terrazzo floor laying	300
textile mfr.	182
Polishing boy	299
Pomologist; research	065
Pontoon man	338
Popper	315
Port worker	334
Porter;	
boy	335
coal	335
despatch	335
dock	334
domestic (*hospital service*)	153
furniture	335
gate	140
general	335
goods-	335
canal	334
railways	160
hall-	154
hospital service	153
head-	
residential buildings	F154
hospital service	F153
hotel	F154
hospital	153
hotel	154
house-	154
L.T.E.	335
kitchen	147

	Code number
Porter; *continued*	
laundry	335
lift	161
lodge	140
lodging	154
mail	160
motor	329
night-	154
market	335
hospital service	153
parcel(s) (*railways*)	160
resident	154
store(s)	335
timber-	334
furniture mfr.	338
timber yard	338
van	329
ward	153
warehouse	335
Porter-	335
food-	335
docks	334
market	335
office	335
residential buildings	154
timber-	334
timber yard	338
auctioneering	335
catering	147
club	154
college	157
entertainment	165
government	335
hospital service	153
hostel	154
hotel	154
institution	153
local government	335
manufacturing	338
retail trade	335
schools	157
transport-	335
railways	160
Porter and liftman	154
Porter-caretaker	157
,, cleaner	158
,, driver	326
,, guard	160
,, handyman	316
,, messenger	338
,, packer	335
,, signalman	160
,, storeman	335
Possession man	142
Post boy-	124
glass mfr.	223
Post girl	124
Postman;	
head	F123
higher grade	123
works	124
Postman-	123
glass mfr.	223
Postman-driver	123
Post office worker	123
Postal worker	123
Poster (*coal mine*)	314
Poster; bill	165
Poster hand	205
Posticheur	230
Potman; asphalt	316
Potman-	
building and contracting	316
cable mfr.	270
catering, hotel, etc.	165
metal mfr.-	231
die casting	235
Potcherman	203
Potter;	
clay	193
furnace; blast	231
shrimp	287
Potter-	
celluloid mfr.	184

(Po—Pr)

	Code number
Potter- *continued*	
ceramic mfr.	193
lead smelting	231
zinc refining	223
Pottery worker	223
Poulterer-	187
farming	166
Poultry boy	166
Poultry hand (*food processing*)	187
Poultry man	166
Poultry worker	166
Pouncer	226
Pounder	225
Pourer (*foundry*)	270
Powder man;	333
bleaching	L340
Powderer	299
Power house man	255
Practitioner;	
Christian Science	040
dental	042
general	041
homeopathic-	050
medically qualified	041
hydropathic	049
medical;	041
registered	041
study; works	010
veterinary	051
Prebendary	040
Pre-boarder (*hosiery mfr.*)	182
Precipitator	184
Pre-former	195
Premixer (chemicals)	184
Pre-packer see *Packer*	
Preparer;	
case	225
colour (*ceramic mfr.*)	204
cylinder	348
dough (artificial teeth)	204
fish	187
food	143
fruit; preserved	202
gelatine	202
glass; safety	223
glaze (*ceramic mfr.*)	204
hair-	176
wig mfr.	230
jute	176
litho (*ceramic mfr.*)	299
lithographic (*printing*)	206
paper	227
plate; lithographic	276
raw ingredient (*flour confectionery mfr.*)	200
starch	182
veneer	224
warp	179
welt	225
yarn	177
for dyeing	199
Preparer-	
ceramic mfr.	223
clothing mfr.	211
embroidery mfr.	226
food preserving	202
footwear mfr.	175
glass mfr.	223
laundry	162
leather goods mfr.	225
lithography	206
metal trades	276
textile mfr.-	176
cotton doubling	182
Preparer and sealer (*cable mfr.*)	276
Preserver; timber	203
Preserver (*food products mfr.*)	202
President (college)	031
Press hand see *Presser-*	
Press man see *Presser-*	
Press operator see *Presser-*	
Press worker see *Presser-*	
Presser;	
barm	202

	Code number
Presser; *continued*	
belt	204
bending	270
blanking	175
block (*plastics goods mfr.*)	195
blouse	162
brick	223
brush; carbon	204
cap	162
carbon	204
clicking	175
clipping	270
cloth	182
clothes	162
cocoa	202
coil	274
coining	242
collar	162
compo	204
component	242
die	193
draw	242
dust (*ceramic mfr.*)	193
electric; edge-setting	162
extruding (*metal trades*)	270
filter-	
coal mine	198
food products mfr.	202
final	162
fitter's	270
flat-	
ceramic mfr.	193
pressed woollen felt mfr.	182
fly-	
cutlery mfr.	242
forging	233
forge	233
fusing	299
garment	162
general	162
glass	192
gramophone record	195
hand-	
metal trades	242
sports goods mfr.	230
tailoring	162
textile finishing	162
heel-	
footwear mfr.	299
rubber goods mfr.	194
Hoffman	162
hollow-ware	193
hop	197
hosiery	182
hot-	
cemented carbide goods mfr.	204
ceramic mfr.	193
metal trades	233
paper mfr.	203
printing	188
rubber goods mfr.	194
textile finishing	182
hydraulic-	
metal trades-	242
forging	233
packing	287
paper merchants	287
plastics goods mfr.	195
textile mfr.	182
jobbing	204
lead (*cable mfr.*)	270
lining; brake	204
lining-	162
footwear mfr.	299
machine-	
clothing mfr.	162
metal trades	242
textile mfr.	182
mantle	162
mica	204
oil (*oil seed crushing*)	202
paper	287
pipe	270
plastics	195

	Code number
Presser; *continued*	
polishing	229
porcelain; electric	193
pottery	193
powder (*chemical mfr.*)	184
power-	
carbon goods mfr.	230
metal trades	242
revolution	175
ring	242
rotary-	
printing	207
textile mfr.	182
rubber	194
sagger	223
scale (*knife handle mfr.*)	230
seam	162
shirt	162
shoe	299
sleeve	162
stamping	242
steam-	
clothing	162
metal	242
rubber	194
steel	233
stock	162
stone; artificial	230
stuff	182
sweetland	202
tailor's	162
terra cotta	193
tile (*ceramic mfr.*)	193
tool	242
top	162
trouser	162
tube	242
underclothing	162
veneer	203
washer	204
yarn	182
yeast	197
Presser-	
asbestos-cement goods mfr.	230
bookbinding	189
cable mfr.	230
cast concrete products mfr.	230
cemented carbide goods mfr.	204
ceramic mfr.	193
chemical mfr.	184
cider mfr.	197
clothing mfr.	162
crayon, pencil mfr.	204
distillery	197
food products mfr.	202
footwear mfr.	299
glass mfr.	192
gramophone record mfr.	195
laundry	162
leather dressing	173
leather goods mfr.	299
metal trades-	242
electric battery mfr.	230
forging	233
rolling mill	233
tube mfr.	270
mica, micanite goods mfr.	204
mine, not coal	198
oil seed crushing	202
paper mfr.	203
patent fuel mfr.	204
plastics goods mfr.	195
plywood mfr.	203
printing	207
rubber goods mfr.	194
textile mfr.-	182
textile packing	137
tobacco mfr.	082
waste merchants	137
wood pulp mfr.	083
Presser and threader	073
Presser-off (*clothing mfr.*)	162
Presser-out (*textile machinery mfr.*)	242

(Pr)

	Code number
Press-pate man	203
Pressureman (*gas board*)	115
Pricer; prescription	115
Pricker (*leather goods mfr.*)	175
Pricker-up	175
Priest	040
Primer; cap	230
Primer-	
brewery	197
cartridge mfr.	230
Principal-	
banking	006
educational establishments-	M033
college of education	M032
further education establishment	M032
primary and secondary schools	M033
teacher training establishment	M032
university	031
government	021
Printer;	
arc light	119
block	208
blue	119
bromide	227
bronze letter	227
calico	227
carbon	206
cloth	227
contact	227
copy	119
dial	227
dyeline	119
embroidery	227
film	227
general	209
glass	208
gold	227
gravure	207
hand	227
hat	227
label (hat labels)	227
letterpress	207
litho; offset	227
lithographic	207
map	207
master	209
mat	281
metal (*process engraving*)	206
Multilith	227
n.o.s.-	209
photocopying	119
ceramic mfr.	227
film processing	227
leather dressing	173
screen printing	208
office; drawing	119
offset	227
optical (cine film)	061
p.o.p.	227
photo	119
photographic	227
photostat	119
phototype	119
plan	119
plate (*ceramic mfr.*)	227
press	207
process	227
rota	119
sack	227
screen	208
silver	227
spray	281
textile	227
ticket;	207
metal leaf	227
title (*film processing*)	227
transfer	227
true to scale	119
wallpaper	227
wax (*textile mfr.*)	182
Printer and stationer	209
Printer-compositor	205
Printer-down	206
Printer's boy	L346
,, devil	L346
,, lad	L346
,, operative	207
Printer-to-metal	206
Prior	040
Prism hand	192
Prism worker	192
Private-	
armed forces-	
foreign and Commonwealth	136
U.K.	135
Probationer (*railways*)	257
Process hand *see* Process worker	
Processman *see* Process worker	
Process worker-	
abrasives mfr.	230
animal foods mfr.	202
asbestos mfr.	176
asbestos-cement goods mfr.	204
Atomic Energy Authority	184
bakery	200
brewery	197
cable mfr.	230
cast concrete products mfr.	230
cellulose film mfr.	184
cement mfr.	184
cemented carbide goods mfr.	230
ceramic mfr.	223
chemical mfr.	184
coal gas, coke ovens	184
dairy	202
distillery	197
dry cleaning	162
electrical engineering	276
fat recovery	204
felt mfr.	199
fibre glass mfr.	223
film processing	227
flour confectionery mfr.	200
food products mfr.	202
glass mfr.	223
jewellery mfr.	276
lamp, valve mfr.	283
leather mfr.	173
leather cloth mfr.	230
linoleum mfr.	230
lubricating oil mfr.	184
meat products mfr.	202
metal trades-	276
steelworks	270
vehicle mfr.	285
mica, micanite mfr.	204
nickel mfr.	231
ordnance factory	184
paint mfr.	184
paper mfr.	203
patent fuel mfr.	184
pharmaceutical mfr.	184
photographic film mfr.	227
plastics goods mfr.-	229
calendering	195
extruding	195
moulding	195
plastics mfr.	184
polish mfr.	184
printing	227
rubber goods mfr.-	228
calendering	194
extruding	194
moulding	194
rubber reclamation	204
starch mfr.	202
tannery	173
textile mfr.-	199
man-made fibre mfr.	196
textile finishing	182
textile printing	227
tobacco mfr.	201
vinery	197
wood products mfr.	203
yeast mfr.	197
Processor;	
data	119
milk	202
pharmaceutical	184
photographic	227
poultry	187
Processor *see* Process worker	
Procurator fiscal	001
Producer;	
egg	107
gas	184
film	M059
Producer (*entertainment*)	M059
Producer hand (gas)	184
Producer man (gas)	184
Production man; press	115
Production worker *see* Process worker	
Products worker; medicinal	184
Professional (*sport*)	063
Professor-	
dentistry	042
medicine	041
surgery	041
educational establishments-	033
college of education	032
further education establishment	032
teacher training establishment	032
university	031
Profiler (metal)	241
Programme boy	125
Programmer	012
Programmetrist	084
Progress hand	115
,, man	115
,, worker	115
Progressor	115
Projectionist	062
Promoter (*sport*)	106
Prompter	059
Pronger (*fork mfr.*)	242
Proofer;	
dry	182
moisture (*transparent paper mfr.*)	203
rot	182
rust	269
water-	
building and contracting	316
clothing mfr.	182
rubber goods mfr.	199
textile mfr.	182
yarn	182
Proofer-	
clothing mfr.	182
lithography	207
rubber goods mfr.	199
textile mfr.	182
Propagator	167
Property man	165
Propman (*coal mine*)	316
Propper; bone brush	230
Propper-	
coal mine-	314
above ground	316
Proprietor *see* Owner	
Prospector (*mining*)	067
Prosthetist	050
Protozoologist	065
Prover;	
colour (*printing*)	227
die	286
file	286
gun	286
meter	286
process (*printing*)	227
stove (*gas board*)	286
Prover-	
lithography	227
Ordnance Survey	227
tube mfr.	286
Prover and tester (*metal trades*)	286

Pr—Ra)

	Code number
Proverman (*bakery*)	185
Provision hand	125
Provost-	
educational establishments-	033
college of education	M032
further education establishment	M032
teacher training establishment	M032
university	031
Pruner; tree-	
forestry	170
fruit growing	167
local government	168
Pruner-	
fruit growing	167
nursery	167
park	168
Psychiatrist	041
Psycho-analyst	041
Psychologist	036
Psychometrist-	036
entertainment	059
Publican	103
Publicist	054
Publisher	101
Pudding worker	202
Puddler (metal)	231
Puffer (*footwear mfr.*)	299
Pug man	204
Pugger	204
Pullboy (*hat mfr.*)	226
Puller;	
base (*clothing mfr.*)	226
baste	226
card; punch	115
conveyor (*coal mine*)	276
fur	173
pallet	230
pea	172
proof	227
rag	176
silk	176
stamp	242
tack	175
waste (*textile mfr.*)	176
wool-	176
fellmongering	173
Puller-	
coal mine	276
fellmongering	173
fur dressing	173
textile mfr.	176
Puller-back (*meat market*)	335
Puller-down	338
Puller-off-	
metal trades	L344
sawmilling	219
tannery	173
Puller-on (*footwear mfr.*)	175
Puller-out (*metal mfr.*)	231
Puller-over (*footwear mfr.*)	175
Puller-up-	L346
coal mine	276
Pulleyman (*coal mine*)	271
Pulpman (*paper mfr.*)	203
Pulper-	
food products mfr.	202
paper mfr.	203
Pulperman (*paper mfr.*)	203
Pulveriser	184
Pumicer-	
horn, etc.	230
precious metal, plate	243
tobacco pipes	224
wood	224
Pump boy	348
Pump hand-	348
footwear mfr.	175
Pumpman; still (*vinegar mfr.*)	348
Pumpman-	348
fishing	317
petrol filling station	127
shale oil refining	184

	Code number
Pumpman- *continued*	
shipping	F317
Pumpman-dipper	348
Pumper; syphon (*gas board*)	348
Pumper-	
lamp, valve mfr.	230
mining	348
Pumpsman	348
Pumpwright	248
Puncher;	
card-	227
jacquard card cutting	199
textile mfr.	199
eye (needles)	242
fancy	175
fishplate	242
jacquard	199
label	227
lamp shade	230
paper	227
pattern (*paper pattern mfr.*)	227
piano (*jacquard card cutting*)	199
rail	242
shoe tip	242
steel bar	242
thumb (gloves)	211
Puncher-	
footwear mfr.	175
glove mfr.	211
metal trades-	242
boiler mfr.	262
shipbuilding	262
zinc smelting	223
paper goods mfr.	227
wool combing	176
Puncher and shearer	242
Puppeteer	059
Purchaser-	
manufacturing	115
retail trade	015
wholesale trade	016
Purification man	184
Purifier; feather	182
Purifier-	184
flock merchants	176
food products mfr.	202
Purifier man-	184
food products mfr.	202
Purler	212
Purser-	102
pier	115
Purserette (hovercraft)	152
Purveyor *see* Shopkeeper	
Pusher;	
tool-	
mine, not coal	094
well drilling	094
truck	338
Pusher (*coal gas, coke ovens*)	338
Pusher-off (*cork products mfr.*)	230
Pusher-out	338
Putter; pony	338
Putter (*coal mine*)	338
Putter-in (*textile mfr.*)	199
Putter-on;	
band	199
tape (*silk spinning*)	199
Putter-on-	
clog mfr.	225
glue mfr.	184
photographic plate mfr.	204
roller engraving	079
textile printing	115
textile spinning	177
Putter-together; scissors	248
Putter-together (*cutlery mfr.*)	248
Putter-up-	
textile mfr.-	287
textile weaving	180
Pyrotechnist	064

Q

	Code number
Q.C.	001
Q.M. (*shipping*)	317
Quarrier	315
Quarry man	315
Quarry worker	315
Quartermaster-	333
shipping	317
Quartermaster-Corporal-	
armed forces-	
foreign and Commonwealth	136
U.K.	135
Quartermaster-General-	
armed forces-	
foreign and Commonwealth	M136
U.K.	M135
Quartermaster-Sergeant-	
armed forces-	
foreign and Commonwealth	136
U.K.	135
Quartz crystal worker	266
Quayman	334
Queen's counsel	001
Quencher man (*coal gas, coke ovens*)	L341
Quiller; comb	229
Quiller (*textile mfr.*)	178
Quilter (*textile goods mfr.*)	212

R

	Code number
Rabbi	040
Rackman (*metal mfr.*)	270
Racker-	333
alcoholic drink mfr.	197
laundry, dry cleaning	298
lithography	207
textile finishing	182
tinplate goods mfr.	338
vinegar mfr.	197
whiting mfr.	338
Radiator man (vehicle)	261
Radiochemist	066
Radiodiagnostician	041
Radiographer; superintendent	F045
Radiographer-	045
industrial	081
Radiologist	041
Radiotherapist	041
Radiotrician	258
Rafter	334
Rag and bone man	131
Rag house worker	203
Rag man	131
Railman-	
coal mine	306
docks	334
railways-	160
shunting	322
Railer (*bedstead mfr.*)	248
Railway employee-	160
shunting	322
Railwayman-	160
shunting	322
Railway worker-	160
shunting	322
Raiser;	
blanket	182
cloth	182
flannelette	182
fund	014
rhubarb	167
steam	347
stock	107
Raiser-	
printing	206
textile finishing	182
Raiser and finisher (*embroidery mfr.*)	226

(Ra—Re)

	Code number
Raker; asphalt	307
Raker-out (*asbestos mfr.*)	L339
Ram man	338
Rammer;	
chair	235
plug	231
Rammer-	
foundry	235
metal mfr.	231
Rammerman	313
Rammer-up	235
Rander (*twine mfr.*)	178
Range worker	L346
Ranger;	
estate	140
forest	170
park	140
wood	170
Ranger-	140
footwear mfr.	175
glass mfr.	299
Ransacker (*fishing net mfr.*)	289
Rasper (*remould tyres*)	228
Rating; engine-room (*shipping*)	317
Rating-	
armed forces-	
foreign and Commonwealth	136
U.K.	135
Ratliner	199
Rayon worker	196
Reacher; drawer's	179
Reacher (*textile mfr.*)	179
Reacher-in (*textile mfr.*)	179
Reader;	
design; textile	115
film (*aircraft mfr.*)	115
instrument	115
lay	040
literary	054
manuscript	115
meter	115
news (*broadcasting*)	059
newspaper	115
press	115
printer's	115
proof	115
publisher's	054
Reader-	
dentistry	042
medicine	041
surgery	041
lace mfr.	199
press cutting agency	115
printing	115
university	031
Reader-compositor	205
Reader-in	179
Reader-off	199
Reamer (*metal*)	241
Reamerer; barrel	241
Reamerer (*metal trades*)	241
Rearer; poultry	107
Re-beamer	179
Recaster	270
Receiver;	
goods	333
grain	333
official	002
of arms	333
Receiver-	
Board of Trade	002
docks	115
laundry	125
leather cloth mfr.	182
rolling mill	270
tobacco mfr.	299
Receptionist;	
beet	333
dental	117
door	165
vehicle (*garage*)	249
Receptionist-	117
television, radio hire	115
cinema, theatre	165

	Code number
Receptionist- *continued*	
garage	249
Reckoner (*tinplate mfr.*)	297
Reclaimer (*rubber*)	204
Reconditioner;	
girder	276
machine	248
Recorder;	
furnace	115
meter	115
milk	115
mould (*steel mfr.*)	115
progress	115
stock	113
temperature	115
time	115
train	115
wagon	115
Recorder-	
laboratory	288
explosive mfr.	115
H.M. dockyard	115
legal services	001
milk marketing board	115
sound recording	062
steelworks	115
Recorder of work	115
Recordist;	
electroencephalographic	050
sound	062
Recoverer;	
acetone	184
solvent	184
zinc	231
Recoverer-	
paper mfr.	203
rubber reclamation	204
Recovery hand *see* Recoverer-	
Recovery man *see* Recoverer-	
Recovery worker *see* Recoverer-	
Rectifier;	
cycle; motor	276
paint (*vehicle mfr.*)	299
tube	270
Rectifier-	184
footwear mfr.	225
metal trades	248
textile mfr.	183
Rectifying man-	184
metal trades	248
Rector-	
church	040
college	031
Red-button	115
Red coat (*holiday camp*)	165
Re-drawer (*silk*)	178
Reducer; data; geophysical	067
Reducer-	
textile printing	182
wool drawing	176
Re-dyer	182
Reeder	179
Reel hand	207
Reelman	188
Reeler;	
bar	270
bobbin	178
cop	178
rope	199
twine	178
twist	178
yarn	178
Reeler-	
paper mfr.	188
photographic film mfr.	227
plastics goods mfr.	229
printing	207
rolling mill	270
textile mfr.-	178
textile bleaching	182
wallpaper mfr.	188
wire rope, cable mfr.	276
Reeler and lacer	178
Reeler boy	299

	Code number
Reelerman-	
paper mfr.	188
rolling mill	270
roofing felt mfr.	199
Referee; official (*legal services*)	001
Referee-	063
medical (*government*)	041
Reference man	140
Referencer	115
Refiner;	
bullion	231
clay; china	198
dripping	202
fat	202
gold	231
lard	202
nickel	231
oil; cotton	202
paint	184
silver	231
Refiner-	
candle mfr.	184
chemical mfr.	184
chocolate mfr.	202
food products mfr.	202
metal mfr.	231
oil refining	184
oil seed refining	202
paper mfr.	188
rubber reclamation	204
sugar refining	202
Refiner hand *see* Refiner-	
Refiner man *see* Refiner-	
Refinery worker; oil	184
Refinisher	281
Refooter (*stockings*)	181
Refractory worker	L342
Refrigerator man (*brewery*)	197
Refueller-	
vehicles	127
airport	338
Regenerator; oil (*coal gas*)	184
Register boy; train	115
Registrar;	
additional	022
cemetery	111
company	030
land	027
probate	001
superintendent	022
of births, deaths and marriages	022
of deeds	022
of marriages	022
of stock	030
of stocks and bonds	030
Registrar-	030
educational services	111
government	021
hospital service	041
legal services	001
local government	022
Post Office	111
Regulating platform man	338
Regulator;	
gas (*coal gas, coke ovens*)	348
steam	347
traffic	F323
Regulator-	
piano, organ mfr.	222
transport	F323
Reheater	231
Re-laster	175
Relayer (*railways*)	306
Reliner;	
bearing	270
brake	299
Reliner (*steelworks*)	300
Remoistener (dextrin)	202
Remoulder-	
glass mfr.	192
rubber goods mfr.	228
Removal hand (*road transport*)	335
Removalman (*road transport*)	335

(Re)

	Code number
Remover;	
belt (*coal mine*)	276
cattle	326
conveyor (*coal mine*)	276
furniture	335
refuse	336
scrap	338
Renderer; lard	202
Renewer; tread	228
Renovator;	
antiques	215
car	261
figure; display	230
Renovator-	
clothing	226
furniture	215
Renter; film	134
Repairman *see* Repairer-	
Repair worker (*coal mine*)-	314
above ground	262
Repairer;	
airway-	
coal mine	314
mine, not coal	315
antiques	215
appliance; domestic	253
bag-	
canvas goods	212
hand bags	225
bank (canal)	316
barge	262
battery	230
beam (*textile mfr.*)	248
belt	225
belting	225
blanket; electric	253
blind	230
boat	214
bobbin	248
body (vehicle)	261
boiler	262
book	189
box;	216
horse	268
brake	248
bridge	316
builder's	304
building	304
cable (electric)	257
canvas goods	212
carpet	183
carriage	248
case-	
watch	266
wood	216
cask	216
chain	233
chair-	215
cane furniture	230
chimney	300
china	223
chronometer	247
clock	247
clockwork	247
coach-	268
railways	248
coil	274
controller	253
conveyor	248
cord (telephones)	256
crate	216
cupola	300
cycle-	248
motor	249
die	245
farm implements	248
film	230
furnace	300
furniture	215
glass	223
hosiery	183
house	304
hydraulic	248

	Code number
Repairer; *continued*	
instrument-	246
dental and surgical instruments	276
musical instruments	222
precision	246
jewellery and plate	266
kiln	300
lamp	248
machine-	248
office machinery	251
magneto	253
mangle	248
meter	246
motor	249
net (fishing nets)	183
oven	300
paint-work (*vehicle mfr.*)	281
pen; fountain	230
pipe (tobacco pipes)	224
propeller	233
property	304
purse	225
radiator (vehicle)	261
rail (*railways*)	306
railway	306
recorder; time	247
reed	230
revolver	248
road-	308
coal mine	314
mine, not coal	306
roof	303
sack	212
saw	276
scale	246
sheet	226
ship	262
shoe	174
spring	233
stove (gas stoves)	248
syphon	248
tarpaulin	212
tent	212
tool	245
toy	230
tractor	248
tub	276
tube-	
boiler mfr.	262
carpet mfr.	248
typewriter	251
tyre	228
umbrella	226
van	261
veneer	224
wagon	248
watch	247
watch and clock	247
wire	257
wireless	258
wringer	248
Repairer-	
clothing	226
dental and surgical instruments	276
domestic appliances-	253
gas appliances	248
electrical machinery	253
footwear	174
instruments	246
jewellery	266
leather goods	225
machinery	248
motor vehicles	249
musical instruments	222
office machinery	251
precious metal, plate	266
radio, television	258
sports goods	230
telephone apparatus	256
watches, clocks	247
ceramic mfr.	223
coal mine	314

	Code number
Repairer- *continued*	
embroidery mfr.	226
L.T.E.	276
Repairer and builder; boat	214
Repairer and jeweller; watch	247
Reporter;	
loading (*L.T.E.*)	115
status (*finance*)	140
train	115
to children's panel	027
Reporter-	
broadcasting	054
newspaper	054
Reporter and signalman; meteorological	122
Representative;	
accounts	115
advertisement	134
advertising	134
agricultural	133
architectural	133
banker's	099
catering	134
circulation	134
claims; insurance	005
commercial	134
company	133
credit	132
default	115
display	134
dock	115
educational	133
freight	134
heating	133
liaison	133
medical	133
newspaper	134
press	054
publicity	134
publisher's	133
sales-	133
property	134
services	134
mail order house	132
P.O.	134
retail trade-	134
door to door sales	132
party plan sales	132
service; railway	134
shipping	134
space (*printing*)	134
technical	133
traffic (*air transport*)	134
Representative-	
services	134
banking	099
electricity board	133
gas board	133
insurance	134
mail order house	132
manufacturing	133
motor factors	125
retail trade-	134
credit trade	132
door to door sales	132
party plan sales	132
trade union	024
transport	134
water board	134
wholesale trade	133
Reproducer;	
design (*textile mfr.*)	115
plan (printer's)	206
Re-roller (*wire mfr.*)	232
Rescue worker	039
Research worker-	067
agricultural	065
biology	065
chemistry	066
economic	011
fire protection	090
fuel	080
medical	080
mining	067

(Re—Ro)

	Code number
Research worker- *continued*	
photographic	080
plastics	080
scientific	067
textile	080
Researcher; market	013
Researcher-	
journalism	030
printing and publishing	030
Reshearer (*metal trades*)	276
Reshearer's boy	L344
Resiner (*brewery*)	L346
Respreader (*silk mfr.*)	176
Restaurant worker	146
Restaurateur	104
Restorer;	
antiques	215
artistic	055
furniture	215
picture	055
tapestry	226
tyre	228
Restorer (*ceramic mfr.*)	223
Retailer-*see also* Shopkeeper-	
market trading	130
Retort hand *see* Retort man-	
Retort man-	
canned foods mfr.	202
charcoal mfr.	184
coal gas, coke ovens	184
Retort worker *see* Retort man-	
Retoucher-	
film processing	227
printing	227
Retreader; tyre	228
Reviser;	
field (*Ordnance Survey*)	079
press	115
proof	115
Reviser (*printing*)	115
Rewinder; motor; electric	274
Rewinder (*textile mfr.*)	178
Rheologist	067
Rheumatologist	041
Ribboner	287
Riddler;	
potato	172
sand-	198
foundry	235
Riddler (*mine, not coal*)	198
Rider;	
dispatch	124
incline bank (*railways*)	338
scramble	063
speedway	063
Rider-	
coal mine	338
entertainment	059
Rifleman-	
armed forces-	
foreign and Commonwealth	136
U.K.	135
Rifler; barrel	241
Rigger;	
aerial	276
factory	272
net	199
salvage	272
scaffolding	264
ship's	272
stage (*shipbuilding*)	264
Rigger-	
gas works	272
rolling mill	248
textile mfr.	199
Rigger and plaiter	199
Rigger and roller	199
Rigger-up (*textile mfr.*)	199
Rincer; bobbin	218
Ringer; bell	060
Rinser;	
bottle	348
file	L344
Ripener; banana	333

	Code number
Ripper;	
back (*coal mine*)	314
face (*coal mine*)	314
muslin	176
rag	176
stone (*coal mine*)	314
Ripper-	
coal mine	314
shoddy mfr.	176
Ripperman (*paper mfr.*)	188
Riser;	
mill	270
steam	347
Riser (*metal rolling*)	270
River (*mine, not coal*)	301
Riverman	316
River worker	316
Riveter-	262
bag frames	285
china	223
corsets	285
curry combs	285
fibre cans	295
footwear	299
glass	223
glove fastenings	299
leather goods	299
plastics goods	296
umbrella ribs	285
Riveter (*soft toy mfr.*)	299
Road man; skip (*mine, not coal*)	306
Road man-	
building and contracting	308
local government	308
mining	306
Road worker	308
Roadsman-	
canal	317
mining	306
Roaster;	
barley	197
malt	197
Roaster-	
food products	202
minerals, etc.	204
Rock hand-	
mine, not coal	315
sugar confectionery mfr.	202
Rockman (*mine, not coal*)	315
Rodder-	
fish curing	202
tube mfr.	276
Rodent operative	165
Rodsman	L340
Roll hand (*steel mfr.*)	270
Roller;	
bacon	186
ball	202
bandage	199
belly	173
bend (*tannery*)	173
butt	173
cogging	232
cold-	232
paper mfr.	188
cross	266
finishing	270
forge	232
head	232
hot-	188
steel mfr.	232
leather	173
mill;	
blooming	232
roughing	270
sheet	232
mill (*iron and steel tube mfr.*)	232
offal	173
pastry	200
piece	176
plate	232
puddled bar	232
rod	232
roughing	270

	Code number
Roller; *continued*	
section	270
side	270
slab	202
spade	232
strip	232
thread (screws)	242
tube-	
metal	270
micanite	204
paper	227
plastics	229
rubber	228
tyre (steel)	232
under	232
wire	232
Roller-	
bookbinding	189
cigar mfr.	201
coal mine	271
flour confectionery mfr.	200
flour milling	202
food products mfr.	202
leather dressing	173
metal trades-	232
fork, hoe mfr.	270
precious metal mfr.	270
oil seed crushing	202
paper mfr.	188
paper tube mfr.	227
rubber goods mfr.	228
sugar confectionery mfr.	202
textile mfr.-	199
flax, hemp mfr.	176
Roller lad (*metal trades*)	L344
Rollerman *see* Roller-	
Roller-up-	
textile mfr.	199
wallpaper mfr.	188
Rolleywayman	306
Rollsman (*copper rolling*)	232
Roofman	L346
Roofer	303
Room hand (*footwear mfr.*)	225
Room worker;	
grey (*textile mfr.*)	333
pattern	333
still	146
stock	333
Ropeman (*mining*)	272
Rope worker (*rope mfr.*)	199
Roper	287
Rope-way man; aerial	338
Rotisseur	F143
Rougher;	
outsole	225
upper (*footwear mfr.*)	225
Rougher-	
foundry	244
glass mfr.	192
rolling mill	270
Rougher and borer (*wood-wind instrument mfr.*)	218
Roughneck	315
Rounder;	
brim	226
machine (felt hat)	226
outsole	175
sole	175
Rounder-	
footwear mfr.	175
hat mfr.	226
tube mfr.	270
Rounder-off	226
Roundsman	128
Rouser	202
Roustabout	L346
Router-	
plastics	229
printing plates	276
wood	218
Router and mounter	276
Rover;	
asbestos	176

(Ro—Sc)

	Code number
Rover; *continued*	
cone	178
dandy (*wool*)	176
Rover (*textile mfr.*)	176
Rubber-	
textile finishing	182
vehicle mfr.	299
Rubber and flatter (*coach building*)	299
Rubber and polisher (*vehicle mfr.*)	299
Rubber goods worker	228
Rubber worker	194
Rubber-down-	299
footwear mfr.	175
jewellery, plate mfr.	244
Rubberer; tyre	194
Rubberiser (*carpets*)	199
Rubber-off-	
footwear mfr.	175
foundry	244
Rucker (*blast furnace*)	L344
Ruler;	
account book	227
machine (*printing*)	227
paper	227
printer's	227
Ruler-	
printing	227
textile printing	267
Ruller (*mine, not coal*)	338
Rullyman	326
Rumbler-	
ceramics	223
metal	243
Runner;	
beer (*brewery*)	287
belt (*coal mine*)	338
bobbin	338
clay	338
deal (*timber merchants*)	335
end	270
metal (white)	270
mould (*ceramic mfr.*)	223
rope	338
wagon-	338
coal mine	338
water	338
wool	338
wort	197
Runner-	
bookmaking	115
ceramic mfr.	338
docks	334
shipping	317
steelworks	331
textile mfr.	338
Runner man (*steelworks*)	331
Runner-off (*hosiery mfr.*)	181
Runner-on (*hosiery mfr.*)	181
Rusher; chair	230
Rustic worker	224

S

	Code number
S.E.A.N.	043
S.O. n.o.s. (*local government*)	022
S.R.N.	043
Sackhand (*sack mfr.*)	226
Sacristan	157
Saddle worker	225
Saddler	225
Safe man (*sugar refining*)	202
Safety man-	
coal mine	276
steel mfr.	039
Safety worker (*U.K.A.E.A.*)	039
Sailor-	
armed forces-	
foreign and Commonwealth	136
U.K.	135

	Code number
Sailor- *continued*	
shipbuilding	276
shipping	317
Sailorman	276
Sale worker	230
Sales; first	125
Salesman;	
advertising	134
bread-	
retail trade-	125
delivery round	128
brush	132
butcher's	125
car	125
cattle	133
cleaner; vacuum	132
commercial	133
commission	133
counter	125
credit	132
delivery	133
drinks; soft	128
export	133
fish-	125
self-employed	187
wholesale trade	133
fish and fruit	125
fish and poultry	125
fishmonger's	125
forecourt (*garage*)	127
ice cream	128
indoor	125
insurance	134
land (*estate agents*)	134
laundry	134
market-	130
wholesale trade	125
meat-	125
wholesale trade	133
milk-	
retail trade	125
delivery round	128
mineral water	133
motor	125
oil	128
outside	133
petrol (*garage*)	127
powder (*mining*)	333
property	134
retail	125
shop-	125
mobile shop	128
showroom	125
space; advertising	134
speciality	133
sundries	133
tea	133
technical	133
telephone	115
travelling-	133
retail trade	132
tyre	133
van	128
warehouse	125
wool (*scrap merchant*)	133
yeast	133
Salesman-	
hawking	130
ice cream	128
self-employed	133
services	134
building and contracting	125
mail order house	132
manufacturers' agents	133
manufacturing	133
retail trade-	125
credit trade	132
door to door sales	132
mobile shop	128
party plan sales	132
wholesale trade	133
Salesman-buyer	015
Salesman-collector	132
Salesman-driver	128

	Code number
Salesman-mechanic	133
Salle worker	294
Saloon boy	144
Salt cake man	184
Salt man	L340
Salt worker	184
Salter;	
dry	202
fish	202
Salter-	
bacon, meat curing	202
tannery	173
Salvage corps man	138
Salvage hand-	L346
coal mine	314
mooring and wreck raising service	317
Salvage man (*coal mine*)	314
Salvage worker-	L346
coal mine	314
Sample hand-	
clothing mfr.	212
footwear mfr.	225
Sample man	333
Sampler;	
grain (*grain milling*)	290
milk	290
tea	290
Sampler-	299
food processing	290
sugar refining	290
Sandman-	L346
abrasive paper, etc. mfr.	203
Sander;	
hand (*furniture mfr.*)	299
wet (*motor body mfr.*)	299
Sander-	
metal trades	244
wood products mfr.	218
Sandwichman	165
Sand worker (*quarry*)	315
Sapper-	
armed forces-	
foreign and Commonwealth	136
U.K.	135
Sanforizer	182
Saucier	F143
Sausage room worker	202
Saw man-	
metal	276
stone	301
Saw worker; hot	276
Sawduster	173
Sawer; *see also Sawyer*	
leg (*bacon and meat curing*)	186
Sawyer;	
back-	218
metal	276
band-	218
metal	276
circular	218
cross cut	218
diamond	266
hot	276
ivory	230
mill	218
rack	218
rail	276
roller	276
slate	301
whip	218
wood pulp	218
Sawyer-	
bone, ivory, etc.	230
meat	186
metal	276
plastics	229
stone	301
wood	218
asbestos-cement goods mfr.	230
coal mine	218
converting mill	218
steel tube mfr.	276
Scabbler (*stone*)	301

(Sc—Se)

	Code number
Scaffolder	264
Scalder (*tripe dressing*)	202
Scaleman-	297
rolling mill	L344
Scaler;	
boiler	276
metal	L344
ship('s)- boiler	L344
boiler	276
Scaler-	
boiler scaling	276
rolling mill	270
shipbuilding	L344
slaughterhouse	297
steel mfr.	270
vehicle mfr.	299
Scalesman	297
Scalloper-	
coal mine	314
textile mfr.	182
Scapler	301
Scappler	301
Scarfer (*steel mfr.*)	265
Scavenger	336
Scene hand	348
Scheduler;	115
materials	090
Scientist;	
agricultural	065
behavioural	036
horticultural	065
research; operational	010
research- biologist	067
biologist	065
chemist	066
social	036
Scientist-	
biologist	065
chemist	066
Scolloper-	
ceramic mfr.	223
lace mfr.	182
Scorer; cricket	115
Scotcher	338
Scourer;	
bottom	175
cloth	199
grease	173
heel	175
piece	199
pin	276
tip	175
wool	199
Scourer-	
ceramic mfr.	223
footwear mfr.	175
foundry	243
leather dressing	173
needle mfr.	276
textile mfr.	199
tinplate mfr.	270
wire mfr.	270
Scout; football	063
Scout-	
college	151
motoring organisation	327
Scragger; spring	286
Scraper;	
boiler	276
gut	204
heel (footwear mfr.)	175
metal	244
ship	L344
Scraper-	
coal mine	314
shipbuilding	L344
Scrap lad	338
,, man	L344
,, shop worker (*celluloid*)	L340
Scrapper-	
metal mfr.	L344
textile mfr.	199
Scratcher-	
linoleum mfr.	204

	Code number
Scratcher- *continued*	
metal trades	243
Screeder	307
Screen hand-	
coal gas, coke ovens	184
coal mine	198
Screen man (*coal mine*)	198
Screener;	
coal	198
coke (coke ovens)	204
paint	184
seed	202
silk	208
Screener-	
chemical mfr.	184
coal mine	198
grain milling	202
iron shot and grit mfr.	204
mine, not coal	198
sewage disposal	310
textile mfr.-	176
linen mfr.	199
Screensman; seed	202
Screensman see Screener-	
Screenworker (*coal mine*)	198
Screwman-	
asphalt spreading	330
metal mfr.	232
Screwer;	
button (bolt, nut mfr.)	276
tube	241
Screwer-	
metal trades-	241
nut, bolt mfr.	276
rolling mill	232
small arms mfr.	241
Screwer-down (*rolling mill*)	232
Scribbler	176
Scriber	245
Scriever	214
Scriever-in	214
Scrivener	115
Scrubber; chair	244
Scrubber (*shop, office cleaning*)	158
Scrubberman (*coke ovens*)	184
Scruff man	231
Scrutineer	115
Scrutinizer; competition	115
Scudder	173
Sculleryman	147
Scullion	147
Sculptor	055
Scurfer;	
boiler	276
retort	L341
Scurfer (*aircraft mfr.*)	L344
Scutcher-	
textile mfr.-	176
textile bleaching, finishing	199
Sealer;	
box	287
car	285
Sealer-	
double glazing	223
lamp, valve mfr.	283
meat market	202
Sealer-in	299
Seaman; landing stage	338
Seaman-	
armed forces- foreign and Commonwealth	136
U.K.	135
fishing	171
shipping	317
Seamer;	
back (hosiery mfr.)	212
can	287
corset	212
cup (knitwear mfr.)	212
german	212
hollow ware	242
hosiery	212
Seamer-	
carpet, rug mfr.	212

	Code number
Seamer- *continued*	
clothing mfr.	212
hosiery mfr.	212
metal trades	242
Seamer-round	212
Seamless hand	181
Seamstress-	212
hospital service	226
institution	226
laundry	226
Searcher; in public records	115
Searcher-	
manufacturing-	142
woollen mfr.	289
Seasonal worker (*agriculture, market gardening*)	172
Seasoner (*paper mfr.*)	203
Seater;	
chair	230
key	241
Seater (*catering*)	144
Second hand; roller's	232
Second hand-	
clothing mfr.	210
fishing	F171
metal rolling	232
steelworks	232
Second man on lorry	329
Secondman (*railways*)	319
Secretary;	
appeals; hospital	024
area (N.C.B.)	023
assistant-	023
charitable organisation	M024
government	020
hospital service	M030
local government	022
professional association	M024
trade association	M024
trade union	M024
association	M024
branch-	
building society	099
insurance	099
trade union	M024
chartered	023
club-	106
burial club	134
youth club	M039
commercial	118
committee	030
company	023
confidential	118
corporation	023
county (youth clubs)	M039
deputy (government)	020
district (insurance)	099
farm	118
financial	023
first	020
fund	024
general-	
charitable organisation	M024
professional association	M024
trade association	M024
trade union	M024
welfare services	M039
group-	
hospital service	M030
trade union	M024
hospital	M030
managing-	
co-operative society	101
welfare services	M039
medical	118
mess	115
national (trade union)	M024
organising-	
charitable organisation	M024
professional association	M024
trade association	M024
trade union	M024
welfare services	M039
parliamentary	020

91

(Se)

	Code number
Secretary; *continued*	
permanent (*government*)	020
political	024
press	054
private;	118
parliamentary	020
principal	021
resident	023
school	115
second	020
sports	106
third	021
under (*government*)	020
Secretary-	118
male-	118
building society	023
charitable organisation	M024
health authority/board	M030
hospital service	M030
hostel	111
insurance	023
manufacturing	023
political association	M024
political club	106
professional association	M024
social club	106
sports	106
trade association	M024
trade union	M024
welfare services	M039
wholesale, retail trade	023
school	115
Secretary and company director	023
Secretary and legal adviser	023
Secretary-accountant	023
Secretary-director	023
Secretary-manager *see* Manager	
Secretary-typist	118
Securer	315
Security man	140
Sediment worker (*whisky distilling*)	197
Seed man	333
Seed worker	167
Seedsman (*wholesale, retail trade*)	101
Seismologist	067
Selector;	
biscuit (*ceramic mfr.*)	298
casing	202
glass	192
gut	204
parts; spare	333
sack	298
skin	298
spares (*vehicle mfr.*)	333
stores	333
timber	333
Selector-	
canvas goods mfr.	298
ceramic mfr.	298
flax mfr.	298
government	333
mine, not coal	298
plastics mfr.	298
Selector and classifier (*mica*)	298
Selector of spares (*vehicle mfr.*)	333
Seller;	
book-	101
H.M.S.O.	125
car	101
fish and chips-	104
employee	125
map	101
newspaper	130
paper	130
programme	125
space (*advertising*)	134
ticket	115
Seller-	
hawking	130
bingo hall	165
totalisator	115
Sempstress	212

	Code number
Sensitiser; film	204
Separator;	
casings; sausage	202
metal and oil	204
milk	202
ore	198
plate (car battery)	283
stitch	175
Separator (*textile mfr.*)	199
Sergeant;	
detective	F137
town	142
Sergeant-	
non-statutory police	F140
airport police	F137
armed forces-	
foreign and Commonwealth	136
U.K.	135
dock police	F137
government police	F137
Min. of Defence	F137
police service	F137
railway police	F137
Royal parks	F137
Sergeant-Major-	
armed forces-	
foreign and Commonwealth	136
U.K.	135
Serger; armhole	212
Serpentine worker	301
Serrator (knives)	276
Servant;	151
agricultural	166
civil; n.o.s.-	115
industrial	L346
college	151
daily	151
domestic	151
farm	166
hunt	172
pier head	338
Server;	
canteen	146
dinner	146
meals	146
process	142
Server-	
confectionery mfr.	202
school meals	146
silk mfr.	338
take-away food shop	125
textile mfr.-	176
hair weaving	199
Servery hand	146
Service hand-	
catering	146
garage	249
Service man;	
carriage	L346
railways	158
ground	250
sales-	
domestic appliances-	253
gas appliances	248
office machinery	251
radio, television	258
Service man-	
automatic vending machines	248
domestic appliances-	253
gas appliances	248
office machinery-	259
electrical	253
mechanical	251
radio, television	258
chemical mfr.	338
chocolate mfr.	202
garage	249
gas board	248
metal trades	248
radio relay service	259
Service room hand	146
Service worker-	
school meals	146
textile mfr.	338

	Code number
Servicer;	
book	189
machinery	271
Servicer-	
motor mfr.	249
textile printing	227
Servitor (*glass mfr.*)	192
Set hand	173
Setter;	
auto (*metal trades*)	238
axle	233
barrel	276
beam	199
block	300
bobbin	199
brick-	300
brick mfr.	191
capstan	238
card-	
textile mfr.	176
textile accessories mfr.	248
carpet	179
chain	199
circle (*textile mfr.*)	276
clamp (*ceramic mfr.*)	191
core	270
crepe (*textile mfr.*)	182
diamond	266
die-	238
wire mfr.	234
door (*vehicle mfr.*)	285
drill	238
driller	238
edge	175
engineer's	238
file	276
film (*textile mfr.*)	227
fire	230
fixture	300
flame	283
forme (*paper box mfr.*)	227
frame	276
fuse; damper	276
gauge	245
gem	266
guide (*steel mfr.*)	270
hand (*tannery*)	173
handle (*textile mfr.*)	248
jewel-	266
watch mfr.	285
jig	238
kerb	309
kiln	191
lathe (*metal trades*)	238
leather	173
lens	223
loom	248
machine;	
automatic	238
board	227
coiling	238
electrode	230
grid	230
heading (bolts, rivets)	238
metalising	230
moulding (rubber)	228
optical	F192
sealing	230
woodcutting	218
machine-	
brush mfr.	230
button mfr.	230
man-made fibre mfr.	248
metal trades	238
paper goods mfr.	227
plastics goods mfr.	229
printing	207
tannery	173
milling	238
mosaic	300
mould (*steelworks*)	270
needle (*textile mfr.*)	276
oven (*ceramic mfr.*)	191
pattern	248

(Se—Sh)

	Code number
Setter; *continued*	
pin	276
pipe	191
press; power	238
press-	
metal trades	238
textile finishing	182
prop (*coal mine*)	314
rate	010
reed	230
retort	300
road	306
roll (*steelworks*)	248
saw	276
spindle	248
spool	179
spring	237
steel (*corset mfr.*)	299
stone (*jewellery*)	266
teasel	182
teazle	182
thermostat	283
tile-	191
building and contracting	300
timber	315
tool;	238
edge	276
machine	238
tube (*textile mfr.*)	199
type	205
van (*railways*)	326
yarn	182
Setter-	
arc welding electrode mfr.	230
brush, broom mfr.	230
carpet mfr.	179
ceramic mfr.	191
glass mfr.	192
metal trades-	238
cutlery mfr.	233
jewellery mfr.	266
typefounding	270
watch, clock mfr.	247
sugar confectionery mfr.	202
tannery	173
textile mfr.	182
Setter and drawer (*ceramic mfr.*)	191
Setter and turner; lathe	239
Setter-in (*ceramic mfr.*)	191
Setter-operator;	
capstan	240
engraving; pantograph	276
lathe;	239
capstan	240
centre	239
turret	240
machine; paper	227
tool	240
turret	240
Setter-operator (*metal trades*)	240
Setter-out;	
lead light	303
mill (*sawmilling*)	276
Setter-out-	
technical drawings	079
metal trades	245
wood products mfr.	F218
Setter-up-	
metal trades-	238
diamond polishing	266
typefounding	270
spectacle mfr.	229
Settlement worker	039
Settler; claims; insurance	005
Settler-	
betting	115
fish hook mfr.	242
hat mfr.	199
Sewage worker	310
Sewer;	
bag	212
ball; tennis	212
belting	175
button	212

	Code number
Sewer; *continued*	
carpet	212
cloth	212
felt	212
fine (*rubber shoe mfr.*)	175
fur	212
glove	212
hand	212
harness (*wool weaving*)	199
hat	212
mantle; gas	212
piece	212
seam	212
skin rug	175
sole	175
spangle	212
tape (*textile spinning*)	271
tent	212
top	212
vellum	189
welt	175
wire	175
Sewer-	
bookbinding	189
canvas goods mfr.	212
carpet, rug mfr.	212
cloth mending	183
clothing mfr.	212
footwear mfr.-	175
rubber footwear mfr.	175
glove mfr.	212
hat mfr.	212
leather goods mfr.	175
powder puff mfr.	226
textile goods mfr.	212
Sewerage man (*local government*)	310
Sewerman	310
Sewer-round	212
Sewing hand	212
Sew-round man	175
Sexer; chick	172
Sexton	157
Shackler	338
Shader-	
artificial flower mfr.	299
ceramic mfr.	204
textile mfr.	199
Shaft boy (*coal mine*)	338
Shaft lad (*coal mine*)	338
Shaftman (*coal mine*)	276
Shaftsman (*coal mine*)	276
Shaker;	
bag	L346
rag	176
waste	176
Shaker (*textile mfr.*)	176
Shaker-out (*laundry*)	162
Shampooer	165
Shanker (*footwear mfr.*)	299
Shaper;	
blades; airscrew-	
metal	241
wood	218
brim	226
chair	224
collar	211
die	241
filament	276
glass	192
tool; machine	240
tool room	240
Shaper-	
clothing mfr.	211
glass mfr.	192
hosiery mfr.	182
incandescent mantle mfr.	230
metal trades-	241
clog iron mfr.	233
steel pen mfr.	276
millinery mfr.	226
wood products mfr.	218
Sharpener;	
gear (*mining*)	233

	Code number
Sharpener; *continued*	
pick	241
pit prop	218
saw	276
tool	241
Sharpener (*edge tool mfr.*)	276
Sherper *see* Sharpener	
Shaver;	
bate	173
gear	241
hood	226
Shaver-	
hat mfr.	226
leather dressing	173
Shearman-	
clothing mfr.	226
metal trades	276
Shearer;	
billet (*rolling mill*)	276
bloom	276
cloth	182
coil (*metal trades*)	276
mat	182
rotary	276
sheep	172
Shearer-	
carpet, rug mfr.	182
coal mine-	276
below ground	314
glove mfr.	226
leather dressing	173
metal trades	276
textile finishing	182
Shearsman; scrap (*metal trades*)	276
Sheather; cable	270
Sheavesman (*coal mine*)	271
Shecheta	186
Shed boy (*railways*)	L346
Shedman-	
docks	334
leather dressing	173
transport	L346
Shed worker-	
railways	L346
tannery	173
Sheerer (metal)	262
Sheet woman	226
Sheet worker (metal)	261
Sheeter;	
asbestos-	
asbestos-cement goods mfr.	230
building and contracting	303
n.o.s.	303
cement; asbestos	303
constructional	303
iron; corrugated	303
roof	303
wagon	160
Sheeter-	
building and contracting	303
chemical mfr.	303
docks	334
paper mfr.	203
plastics goods mfr.	195
railways	160
rubber goods mfr.	194
steel mfr.	262
Shellerman	202
Shepherd	166
Shepherd's boy	166
Sherardizer	231
Sheriff (*Scottish Courts*)	001
Sheriff-substitute (*Scottish Courts*)	001
Shifthand (*coal mine*)	345
Shiftman (*mine, not coal*)	315
Shift worker (*coal mine*)	345
Shifter;	
coal	314
conveyor (*coal mine*)	276
iron	338
scene	348
Shifter-	
coal mine	314

93

(Sh—Sl)

	Code number
Shifter- *continued*	
jute spinning	177
rolling mill	338
Shingler (*iron works*)	270
Ship worker	334
Shipper-	
docks	334
patent fuel mfr.	338
tinplate mfr.	338
wholesale trade	129
Ship's boy	317
Shipsmith	233
Shipwright	262
Shipwright-liner	262
Shiver	230
Shocket	186
Shoddy man	176
Shoe hand	225
Shoe operative	175
Shoeblack	165
Shoer; horse	233
Shoeroom worker	175
Shoot lad (*food, starch mfr.*)	L346
Shooter; trouble	081
Shooter (*gun mfr.*)	286
Shop boy (*printing*)	L346
Shop girl; tailor's	124
Shop worker;	
core (*metal trades*)	235
paint-	L346
vehicle mfr.	281
Shop worker-	
fried fish	125
retail trade	125
take-away food shop	125
Shopkeeper;	
chip potato	104
cook	104
cooked meat	101
eel	104
fish	187
fish and chip	104
fried fish	104
ham and beef	101
ice cream	101
receiving (laundry, etc.)	110
sweet	101
tripe	101
Shopkeeper-	101
butchers	186
fishmongers	187
mobile shop	128
Shopman;	
bottle (*iron, steel tube mfr.*)	270
butcher's	186
meat	186
Shopman (*railway workshops*)	L344
Shopman-cutter (butcher's)	186
Shotman (*mine, not coal*)	315
Shotsman (*coal mine*)	314
Show girl	059
Showman	106
Shredder-	
chemical mfr.	184
food products mfr.	202
Shreinerer	182
Shrimper	171
Shrinker; London	182
Shrinker-	
rubber goods mfr.	228
textile mfr.	182
Shuntman (*mine, not coal*)	338
Shunter-	322
road transport	325
Shutter; door (*coke ovens*)	L341
Shutterer (*building and contracting*)	214
Shuttler	226
Side man (*brewery*)	197
Sider; glass	192
Sider (*glass mfr.*)	192
Sidesman; copper (*brewery*)	197
Siever-	
abrasive paper, etc. mfr.	203

	Code number
Siever- *continued*	
chemical mfr.	184
food products mfr.	202
Sifter;	
dust (*ceramic mfr.*)	204
flour	202
Sifter-	
ceramic mfr.	204
chemical mfr.	184
food products mfr.	202
Sighter; bottle (*brewery*)	287
Signal box lad	321
Signal lad (*railways*)	321
Signalman;	
civilian (*Min. of Defence*)	122
diver's	316
Lloyd's	338
marine	122
port	122
relief	321
Signalman-	
mining	331
railways	321
steelworks	337
yacht club	063
Signaller (*mine, not coal*)	331
Silk worker-	L339
greeting card mfr.	212
Silker (*textile mfr.*)	212
Silksman	202
Siloman (*seed crushing*)	202
Silo worker	333
Silverman	147
Silver worker	266
Silverer-	
electroplating	236
glass mfr.	269
Silviculturist-	170
professionally qualified	065
Singer-	
entertainment	059
textile mfr.	182
Sinker;	
counter	241
die-	
metal trades	245
printing	267
pit	304
seat	175
shaft	304
well	304
Sinker (*mine sinking*)	304
Sinterer-	
metal mfr.	270
mine, not coal	270
Sister-	F043
religion	040
Sister-tutor	F043
Sitter; baby	151
Sizeman-	173
paper mill	203
Sizer;	
bobbin	218
engine (*paper mfr.*)	203
hank	179
slasher	179
tape	179
warp	179
yarn	179
Sizer-	
paper mfr.	203
textile mfr.-	179
rope, twine mfr.	182
Sizer and dryer; back	182
Skater; ice	059
Skeiner (*textile mfr.*)	178
Sketcher; design	115
Skewerer (*textile dyeing*)	199
Skid boy (*rolling mill*)	270
Skilled workman (*P.O.*)	256
Skimmer-	
glass mfr.	204
metal mfr.	231

	Code number
Skinner-	
food products mfr.	186
slaughterhouse	186
tannery	173
Skipman	297
Skipper; yacht	087
Skipper-	
barge, boat	087
building and contracting	F316
fishing	111
shipping	087
Skirt hand	210
Skiver; belt (*abrasive paper, etc. mfr.*)	230
Skiver-	
footwear mfr.	175
leather dressing	173
Slab hand	202
Slab man	301
Slabber;	
tile	300
toffee	202
Slabber-	
builder's merchant	300
fireplace mfr.	300
textile mfr.	199
Slagman (*blast furnace*)	231
Slagger-	
blast furnace	231
steel casting	270
Slaker (*ceramic mfr.*)	204
Slaker man	204
Slasher (*textile mfr.*)	179
Slate worker; enamelled	301
Slater	303
Slater and tiler	303
Slaughterman	186
Slaughterer	186
Sleever-	
cable mfr.	230
clothing mfr.	212
electrical goods mfr.	242
radio valve mfr.	283
Slicer; veneer	218
Slicer-	
bakery	200
celluloid sheet mfr.	229
Slicker (*leather dressing*)	173
Slider (*metal trades*)	239
Slimer (*gut cleaning*)	204
Slingman	192
Slinger-	337
textile mfr.	199
Sliphouse hand	204
Slipper;	
cushion	212
last	225
shoe	225
tie	212
Slipper-	
asbestos-cement mfr.	204
furniture mfr.	212
Slipper operative	175
Slipper worker	175
Slitter;	
fabrics	226
foil; tin	276
metal	276
optical glass	192
paper	190
steel	276
Slitter-	
abrasive paper mfr.	190
paper and printing	190
pen nib mfr.	276
plastics goods mfr.	229
steelworks	276
tobacco mfr.	201
transparent cellulose wrapping mfr.	190
Slitterman (*paper mfr.*)	190
Sliverer	176
Slotter; frame	241

(Sl—Sp)

	Code number
Slotter-	
metal trades	241
needle mfr.	242
paper products mfr.	227
Slubber (*textile mfr.*)	176
Slugger; paste	204
Slugger (*footwear mfr.*)	299
Sluice man	338
Slurryman	184
Slurry worker (*coal mine*)	198
Smallholder-	107
forestry	170
Smash hand	180
Smearer (*waterproof garment mfr.*)	226
Smeller; cask	299
Smelter; steel	231
Smelter-	
glass mfr.	191
metal mfr.	231
Smith;	233
boiler	262
bright	266
chain	270
coach	233
coil-	
spring mfr.	233
tube mfr.	270
cold	276
copper	261
engineering	233
gold	266
gun	248
iron; sheet	261
key	276
lock	248
metal; britannia	266
metal (*gas meter mfr.*)	261
padlock	248
pan;	
copper	261
salt	233
pan-	
salt mfr.	233
plate	262
platinum	266
rope (*coal mine*)	272
saw	276
silver	266
tin	261
tool	233
white	261
Smither	233
Smocker	212
Smoker (*food products mfr.*)	202
Smoother; lining	162
Smoother-	
clothing mfr.	162
lens mfr.	192
Smudger	338
Snagger	261
Sniffer	290
Snipper	176
Soaker;	
lime	173
silk	182
Soaker (*leather dressing*)	173
Soap worker	184
Soaper; rope	199
Soapstoner (*roofing felt mfr.*)	199
Social worker	039
Sociologist	036
Socker	299
Softener;	
lead	231
water	184
Softener-	
flax, hemp mfr.	176
leather dressing	173
Soilman; night	158
Solderer-	265
radio and television mfr.	283
Solderer and jointer; case	265

	Code number
Soldier-	
armed forces-	
foreign and Commonwealth	136
U.K.	135
Solicitor	001
Solutioner-	
footwear mfr.	299
rubber goods mfr.	299
Solutionist (*rubber goods mfr.*)	299
Sorter;	
biscuit	298
bobbin	298
bottle	298
breakage (*food products mfr.*)	298
bulb (*electric lamp mfr.*)	298
card; playing	294
clip	298
cloth	298
coal (*coal mine*)	198
cocoa bean	202
cork	298
coupon	115
diamond	298
dyehouse (*textile mfr.*)	298
egg	298
feather	298
fent	298
fibre	298
flock	298
foil; tin	298
fruit	298
fur	298
gelatine	298
glass	299
glove	289
gum	298
hair	298
head-	
galvanized sheet mfr.	298
P.O.	123
hide	298
hosiery	298
iron (*shipbuilding*)	L344
label	294
last	298
leaf	298
leather	298
letter	123
lime	298
machine (*ceramic mfr.*)	298
mail	123
meat	298
metal; sheet	298
metal-	298
scrap metal dealer	298
mica	298
mohair	298
newspaper	298
order (*mail order*)	115
paper-	
paper mfr.	294
paper products mfr.	294
wallpaper mfr.	294
waste paper merchants	298
parcel-	124
P.O.	123
pipe; ceramic	298
post	123
printer's	294
rag	298
rag and metal	298
refuse	298
rubber	298
sack	298
salvage	298
scrap	298
seed-	298
mustard	202
sheet (*printing*)	294
shuttle	298
skin	298
slag	298
sole	298
spool	298

	Code number
Sorter; *continued*	
stamp	115
stocking	298
stores	298
tape	298
ticket	115
tile; roofing	298
timber	298
tin	298
tube (*textile spinning*)	199
warehouse; biscuit (*ceramic mfr.*)	298
waste-	
textile mfr.	298
weft	199
wood	298
wool-	298
fellmongering	298
woollen	298
yarn	298
Sorter-	
broom, brush mfr.	298
button mfr.	298
ceramic mfr.-	298
roofing tile mfr.	298
cigar mfr.	298
cutlery handle mfr.	298
dyeing and cleaning	298
footwear mfr.	298
fur dressing	298
glass mfr.-	299
glass bottle mfr.	298
incandescent mantle mfr.	298
laundry	298
metal trades-	298
galvanized sheet mfr.	298
mine, not coal	298
P.O.	123
paper mfr.	294
paper goods mfr.	294
printing	294
seed merchants	298
stick mfr.	298
sugar confectionery mfr.	298
tannery	298
textile mfr.-	298
flax, hemp mfr.	298
hair, bass, fibre dressing	298
waste merchants	298
wholesale fish trade	298
Sorter and grader (*canvas goods mfr.*)	298
Sorter and packer	298
Sounder; survey	338
Spare hand-	
fishing	171
rolling mill	270
Specialist;	
beauty	165
ceiling	282
computer (sales)	133
ear, nose and throat	041
flooring	316
organisation and methods	010
reinforced concrete	068
systems	012
taxation	008
woodworm	165
Spectrographer	080
Speeder; braiding machine	199
Speeter (*fish curing*)	202
Spiderman	263
Spiler (*textile mfr.*)	183
Spillager (*coal mine*)	331
Spindle hand	218
Spindler; ribbon	178
Spinner;	
asbestos	177
cap	177
concrete	230
cord	199
crimp	177
doffer; self	177
fibreglass	177

(Sp—St)

Spinner; *continued*
- fly ... 177
- frame ... 177
- fuse; safety ... 199
- gill ... 177
- gimp ... 180
- gut ... 204
- mule ... 177
- nylon ... 196
- paper (*cellulose film mfr.*) ... 177
- pipe-
  - *cast concrete products mfr.* 230
  - *iron, steel tube mfr.* ... 270
- pot (*carborundum mfr.*) ... 204
- rayon ... 196
- ring ... 177
- rope ... 199
- silk; ... 177
  - artificial ... 196
  - glass ... 223
- sugar ... 202
- thread (metal) ... 177
- twine ... 199
- wire ... 276

Spinner-
- metal ... 240
- textiles ... 177
- *electric cable mfr.* ... 276
- *gut processing* ... 204
- *mining, safety fuse mfr.* 199
- *paper twine mfr.* ... 177
- *sugar, glucose mfr.* ... 202
- *textile mfr.-* ... 177
  - *man-made fibre mfr.* ... 196
- *tobacco mfr.* ... 201
- *wire rope mfr.* ... 276

Spiraller; filament ... 276

Splicer;
- film ... 227
- rope- ... 199
  - *coal mine* ... 272
  - *steel mfr.* ... 272
- thread ... 199
- veneer ... 224
- wire ... 272
- yarn ... 199

Splicer-
- rope- ... 199
  - wire ... 272
- textile cords, etc. ... 199
- *coal mine* ... 272
- *textile mfr.* ... 199
- *tyre mfr.* ... 228

Splitter;
- bale (*rubber goods mfr.*) ... L346
- cloth ... 199
- fish ... 187
- fork (*digging, etc. fork mfr.*) 233
- gut ... 204
- hide ... 173
- leather ... 173
- mica ... 204
- skin ... 173
- slate ... 301

Splitter-
- *gut dressing* ... 204
- *leather dressing* ... 173
- *mine, not coal-*
  - *above ground* ... 301
  - *below ground* ... 315
- *rubber reclamation* ... 204
- *textile mfr.* ... 199
- *tobacco mfr.* ... 201

Splitter girl ... 338
Splitter's boy ... L342

Sponger;
- decorative ... 299
- of clayware ... 223

Sponger (*ceramic mfr.*) ... 223
Spool boy (*cinema*) ... 062
Spooler; wire ... 276

Spooler-
- *photographic film mfr.* ... 227

Spooler- *continued*
- *textile mfr.-* ... 178
  - *Axminster carpet mfr.* ... 179
  - *lace mfr.* ... 199

Spoon and fork worker ... 242
Sportsman; professional ... 063
Spotter; photographic ... 227

Spotter-
- *artificial flower mfr.* ... 299
- *dry cleaning* ... 162
- *film processing* ... 227
- *footwear mfr.* ... 175
- *lace mfr.* ... 199
- *laundry* ... 162
- *printing* ... 227
- *textile designing* ... 115
- *textile finishing* ... 289

Spragger (*coal mine*) ... 338

Sprayer;
- agricultural ... 169
- asbestos ... 230
- brush face ... 281
- cellulose- ... 281
  - *ceramic mfr.* ... 279
- colour-
  - *ceramic mfr.* ... 279
  - *glass mfr.* ... 281
- copper ... 270
- crop ... 107
- enamel- ... 281
  - *ceramic mfr.* ... 279
- fruit ... 167
- glaze ... 279
- insulation ... 316
- leather ... 281
- lime (*iron and steel mfr.*) ... 270
- machine ... 281
- metal ... 269
- paint ... 281
- pistol ... 281
- steam ... 182
- tar ... 330

Sprayer- ... 281
- *agricultural contracting* ... 169
- *ceramic mfr.* ... 279
- *insulation contracting* ... 316
- *lamp, valve mfr.* ... 223
- *textile finishing* ... 182
- *wood preservation service* ... 165

Spreader;
- asphalt ... 307
- glue (*abrasive paper, etc. mfr.*) 203
- plaster ... 199
- rubber- ... 228
  - *textile mfr.* ... 199
- tar ... 307

Spreader-
- *building and contracting* ... 316
- *food products mfr.* ... 202
- *laminated plastics mfr.* ... 204
- *laundry* ... 162
- *leathercloth mfr.* ... 199
- *linoleum mfr.* ... 204
- *rubber mfr.* ... 228
- *surgical dressing mfr.* ... 199
- *textile mfr.-* ... 199
  - *flax mfr.* ... 176
- *tobacco mfr.* ... 201

Springer;
- carriage ... 248
- heald ... 179
- umbrella ... 285

Springer-
- *needle mfr.* ... 276
- *textile mfr.* ... 179
- *tube mfr.* ... 270

Springer-in (spectacles) ... 299
Spring worker ... 276
Squarer-up ... 175
Squeezer (*textile dyeing*) ... 182
Squirter; lead (*cartridge mfr.*) 270
Stable boy ... 172
Stable hand ... 172
,, lad ... 172

Stableman ... 172
Stacker ... 338
Stacker and packer ... 333
Stacker-driver ... 332

Stage hand-
- *docks* ... 338
- *entertainment* ... 348

Stageman; landing ... 338
Stager (*shipbuilding*) ... 264

Stainer;
- boot ... 299
- edge (*footwear mfr.*) ... 299
- leather ... 299
- paper ... 203
- shoe ... 299
- wood ... 282

Stainer-
- *furniture mfr.* ... 282
- *glass mfr.* ... 299
- *leather goods mfr.* ... 299
- *tobacco pipe mfr.* ... 282

Staithman ... 334
Staker (*leather dressing*) ... 173
Stallman (*coal mine*) ... 314

Stamper;
- box ... 227
- brass; ... 242
  - hot ... 233
- brush ... 227
- bulb; electric ... 227
- card (*textile mfr.*) ... 199
- cloth ... 227
- cold ... 242
- collar ... 227
- die- ... 242
  - *printing* ... 227
- drop; hot ... 233
- drop-
  - *forging* ... 233
  - *sheet metal goods mfr.* ... 242
- gold-
  - *ceramic mfr.* ... 227
  - *footwear mfr.* ... 227
  - *hat mfr.* ... 227
  - *jewellery mfr.* ... 242
- hammer ... 233
- hollow-ware ... 242
- hot ... 233
- ingot ... 270
- lining ... 227
- metal; hot ... 233
- metal- ... 242
  - *forging* ... 233
- pattern-
  - *ceramic mfr.* ... 227
  - *paper pattern mfr.* ... 227
- printer's ... 227
- relief ... 227
- rubber (*rubber goods mfr.*) 228
- shoe ... 227
- silver ... 242
- size ... 227
- soap ... 227
- sock ... 227
- sole ... 227
- tool; edge ... 233

Stamper-
- *Assay Office* ... 270
- *ceramic mfr.* ... 227
- *footwear mfr.* ... 227
- *Inland Revenue* ... 115
- *metal trades-* ... 242
  - *forging* ... 233
  - *galvanized sheet mfr.* 233
  - *rolling mill* ... 233
  - *tube fittings mfr.* ... 233
- *mine, not coal* ... 198
- *P.O.* ... 123
- *paper goods mfr.* ... 227
- *tannery* ... 227
- *textile mfr.* ... 227

Stapler;
- box (*cardboard box mfr.*) 295
- brush; machine ... 230

(St)

	Code number
Stapler; *continued*	
slipper	299
wool (*textile mfr.*)	179
Stapler-	
bedding mfr.	285
footwear mfr.	299
leather goods mfr.	299
Starch room worker	202
Starcher; clear	162
Starcher-	
laundry	162
textile finishing	182
Starrer	226
Stationman; railway	160
Stationman (*L.T.E.*)	160
Stationer-	101
paper goods mfr.	227
printing warehouse (*Scotland*)	F227
Stationer and printer	209
Stationmaster	095
Statistician	011
Staver (*tube mfr.*)	270
Stayer (*cardboard box mfr.*)	227
Steam hand (*catering*)	146
Steamer;	
hat	226
silk	182
spun pipe	204
Steamer-	
dyeing and cleaning	162
felt hat mfr.	226
straw hat mfr.	182
textile finishing	182
Steel man (*coal mine*)	276
Steelworker-	L344
shipbuilding	262
structural engineering	263
Steephouseman (*starch mfr.*)	202
Steeple jack	316
Steeple peter	316
Steepsman (*starch mfr.*)	202
Steerer (*barge, boat*)	317
Steersman;	317
bridge	338
Stemmer; leaf	201
Stemmer-	
coal mine	314
tobacco mfr.	201
Stemmer and padder	201
Stemmer and waxer (*battery carbon mfr.*)	299
Stencil worker	227
Stenciller;	
aerographing (*ceramic mfr.*)	279
box	299
Stenciller-	299
art needlework mfr.	226
Stenographer	118
Stenter	182
Stenter hand	182
Stenter man	182
Stenterer	182
Stereographer	206
Stereotyper	206
Steriliser; milk	202
Steriliser-	
canned food mfr.	202
hospital service	156
surgical dressing mfr.	182
telephone sterilising service	158
textile mfr.	182
Stevedore;	334
superintendent	097
Steward;	
air	152
bar	145
cabin	152
canteen	144
catering	144
chief-	F144
aircraft, shipping	F152
club	105
railways	F144
club	105

	Code number
Steward; *continued*	
college	111
dining car	144
dwellings	157
estate	107
farm	107
flats	157
flight	152
hostel	111
house;	151
lodging	111
kitchen	F146
laboratory	L346
mess	144
messroom	144
officer's	152
pantry	147
room; billiard	165
saloon (*shipping*)	152
shore	333
wine	144
Steward-	
aircraft	152
canteen	144
club	105
institution	111
naval shore establishment	144
P.O.	144
race course	063
railways	144
service flats	157
shipping-	152
catering	144
university-	L346
catering	144
working men's institute	105
Sticker;	
bill	165
cloth (*needle mfr.*)	287
feather	299
junction (*ceramic mfr.*)	223
label	287
leaf (*artificial flower mfr.*)	299
pattern (*paper pattern mfr.*)	295
poultry	187
punty	223
sole	175
waterproof (*clothing mfr.*)	226
Sticker-	
clothing mfr.	226
footwear mfr.	175
needle mfr.	287
slaughterhouse	186
Sticker-up (*ceramic mfr.*)	299
Stiffener; hat; straw	182
Stiffener (*footwear mfr.*)	299
Still man-	184
hotel, catering, etc.	146
metal smelting	231
Stillhouse man (*distillery*)	184
Stillroom man-	
distillery	184
hotel, catering, etc.	146
Stippler	115
Stitcher;	
bale	L287
box	295
boxing glove	175
collar	175
cricket ball	175
football	175
hem	212
leather	175
lock-	212
slipper mfr.	175
mattress	213
rapid	175
tennis ball	212
veldtschoen	175
wire-	
leather goods mfr.	175
paper and paper goods mfr.	295
Stitcher-	212
bookbinding	189

	Code number
Stitcher- *continued*	
footwear mfr.	175
hosiery mfr.	212
leather goods mfr.	175
paper and paper goods mfr.	295
printing	189
wire goods mfr.	276
Stock hand *see* Stockman	
Stockman-	
farming	166
manufacturing-	333
blast furnace	338
leather dressing	173
rolling mill	338
Stock room hand	333
Stockroom man	333
Stocker;	
coil (*metal mfr.*)	333
lock; plate	224
whip	225
Stocker-	
gun mfr.	224
steel mfr.	L344
tinplate mfr.	333
Stocker-up	338
Stockinger	181
Stocksman-	173
farming	166
Stocktaker; chief (*steelworks*)	F113
Stocktaker-	115
rolling mill	333
steel smelting	F333
Stoker;	
boiler	347
destructor	348
drifter	317
engine-	347
barge, boat	317
railways	319
shipping	317
furnace-	347
ceramic mfr.	191
metal mfr.	231
gas	184
gas plant	184
high pressure	347
kiln;	
brick	191
lime	204
leading	F347
retort (*coal gas*)	184
Stoker-	347
coal gas, coke ovens	184
fishing	317
glass mfr.	191
metal mfr.	231
shipbuilding	231
shipping	317
Stoker-cleaner	347
Stoker-engineer	347
Stoker-mechanic-	
shipping	317
Stoker-porter	347
Stone hand	205
Stoneman-	
coal mine	314
stone dressing	301
Stone worker;	
artificial	230
precious	266
Stone worker-	
cast concrete products mfr.	230
coal mine	314
mine, not coal	315
Stoner (*glass mfr.*)	192
Stopper; glaze	223
Stopper (*ceramic mfr.*)	223
Stopper man (*coal gas, coke ovens*)	L341
Stopperer; glass bottle	192
Storage hand; cold	335
Store boy	335
Storehand	335
Store holder	333

(St—Su)

	Code number
Storeman;	333
chief	F333
head	F333
Storeman-clerk	333
Storeman-driver	333
Storewoman; superintendent (*P.O.*)	F333
Storehouse boy	335
Storehouseman	333
Storer	333
Storeroom man	333
Storesman	333
Stove hand *see Stover-*	
Stoveman *see Stover-*	
Stover; seasoning	204
Stover-	204
bacon, ham curing	202
blast furnace	231
food products mfr.	202
hat mfr.	182
iron foundry	270
leather dressing	173
starch mfr.	202
textile mfr.	182
tobacco mfr.	201
Stower;	
cake	338
cement	338
coal	338
power	314
ship	334
Stower-	
coal mine	314
grain milling	338
railways	160
Straightener;	
axle	233
bar	270
barrel	276
carriage (*textile machinery mfr.*)	248
comb	276
drill	270
hard (*needle mfr.*)	276
iron	270
plate;	270
iron	276
saw	276
prop (*coal mine*)	276
rail	270
rod mills	270
roller	270
section	270
shaft; crank	270
steel-	270
coal mine	276
tube	270
wire	276
yarn	289
at machine	270
Straightener-	
coal mine	276
metal mfr.	270
needle mfr.	276
sheet metal working	261
textile mfr.-	289
flax mfr.	176
hosiery mfr.	182
textile machinery mfr.	248
vehicle mfr.	261
wire mfr.	276
Strainer; toggle	173
Strainer-	
chemical mfr.	184
paint, etc. mfr.	204
tannery	173
textile printing	204
Strainerman (*paper mfr.*)	203
Strander; wire	276
Strander-	
cable mfr.	276
rope mfr.	199
wire rope mfr.	276
Strap man	225

	Code number
Strapper-	
corset mfr.	212
textile mfr.	338
Stratigrapher	067
Straw worker (*hat mfr.*)	226
Stressman	079
Stretcher;	
clip (*textile mfr.*)	182
dry (*textile mfr.*)	182
tube	270
yarn	182
Stretcher-	
metal mfr.	270
tannery	173
textile mfr.	182
Stretcher hand (*aluminium mfr.*)	270
Striker;	
anvil	270
catch (*coal mine*)	338
chain	270
colour	204
forge	270
forger's	270
iron	270
smith's	270
wheel	270
Striker-	
metal trades	270
railways	270
Striker-out	173
Stringer;	
bag; paper	299
bead and bugle	299
pearl	299
racquet	230
Stringer-	
footwear mfr.	175
piano mfr.	222
plastics goods mfr.	229
printing	295
sports goods mfr.	230
Strip worker; copper	270
Striper (*fur dressing*)	173
Stripper;	
biscuit	200
bobbin	199
boiler; locomotive	248
brake	248
cable	299
car	249
card	276
cardboard	227
carriage and wagon	248
carton	227
cloth	176
cop	199
dog	172
engine	248
file	276
film	227
frame	L340
gold	270
gut	186
ingot	270
leaf	201
leather lace	175
liquorice	202
locomotive	248
motor	249
paint; vehicle (*vehicle mfr.*)	299
paper	227
pirn	199
polish	299
rag	176
rubber	228
silver	270
spring	248
tin (*biscuit mfr.*)	200
tyre	228
wool	199
yarn	199
Stripper-	
candle mfr.	L340
cast stone products mfr.	223

	Code number
Stripper- *continued*	
ceramic mfr.	L342
coal mine	314
metal trades-	244
electroplating	269
gold refining	231
wire drawing	234
mine, not coal	315
paper products mfr.	227
process engraving	206
railway workshop	248
textile mfr.	199
tobacco mfr.	201
Stripper and buncher	199
Stripper and grinder	276
Stripper and setter (*soap mfr.*)	184
Stripper-assembler (*cast concrete products mfr.*)	L346
Stripping hand (*hosiery mfr.*)	226
Stubber	276
Studder (*clothing mfr.*)	299
Student *see notes p.4*	
Studhand	172
Stuffer;	
chair	226
cushion	226
soft toy	226
Stuffer-	
mattress, upholstery mfr.	226
textile dyeing	297
toy mfr.	226
Stuff worker; rough (*footwear mfr.*)	175
Stumper	199
Stunner	186
Stunt man	059
Stylist; hair	159
Stylist-	
hairdressing	159
vehicle mfr.	056
Sub-agent (*building and construction*)	092
Sub-contractor *see Contractor*	
Sub-editor	054
Sub-foreman *see Foreman-*	
Sub-ganger *see Ganger-*	
Sub-inspector- *see also Inspector-*	
Min. of Defence	M137
railway-	F318
engineering	306
Sub-Lieutenant-	
armed forces-	
foreign and Commonwealth	M136
U.K.	M135
Sub-officer (*fire service*)	F138
Sub-postmaster-	099
self-employed	101
Sueder	173
Sugar worker	202
Sulphitation man	202
Sulphonator man	184
Sumper	314
Sundriesman	101
Superintendent;	
administrative (*insurance*)	F115
advertisement	014
advertising	014
airport	095
ambulance room	111
assistant;	
overseas telegraph	099
progress	115
radio	099
assistant-*see also Superintendent-*	
cemetery, crematorium	165
P.O.	099
bath(s)-	106
coal mine	F165
branch (*insurance*)	M134
building	157
cargo	097
claims	M005
cleansing (*local government*)	111

(Su)

Superintendent; continued	Code number
club	104
commercial (*transport*)	095
county (*nursing services*)	M043
departmental see Manager-	
depot-	097
transport	095
distribution-	
gas board	094
water works	094
district-	
clothing club	132
gas board	094
insurance	M134
transport	095
divisional (*railways*)	095
dredging	095
drilling	094
dwellings	157
electrical-	091
electricity board	094
Min. of Defence	071
engineering	091
enquiry; hotel	F115
estate (*local government*)	092
factory	091
fire-	M138
insurance	M134
flats	157
flight	095
floor (*department store*)	F125
foundry	091
general (*L.T.E.*)	095
grain-	097
Min. of A.F.F.	021
house;	
boiler	F347
n.o.s.	157
turbine (*electricity board*)	094
ware	097
insurance	M134
kitchen (*hospital service*)	F143
laundry (*hospital service*)	F162
mains	094
maintenance	F316
marine-	095
docks	090
market	111
marketing	013
medical	041
mess	104
meter (*electricity board*)	071
motor (*insurance*)	M134
night-	
hospital service	F043
manufacturing	091
office	099
operating	111
park	106
pilot	087
platform (*coal tar distillers*)	F184
plant (*refinery*)	091
power; motive	091
principal (telegraphs)	099
process	091
production-	091
Min. of Defence	074
progress	F115
radio (*P.O.*)	099
range	165
refinery	091
relations; employee	009
rents (*local government*)	F115
repairs	F316
rescue (*coal mine*)	F142
reservoir	316
sales;	
chief (*P.O.*)	013
senior (*P.O.*)	101
sales-	013
P.O.	M133
sanitary	111
shed (*railways*)	095
shift	091

Superintendent; continued	Code number
shipping	095
shop-	
manufacturing	091
retail trade	F125
staff	009
station;	
assistant	F137
rescue	F142
station-	111
airline	095
store(s)	096
submarine (*P.O.*)	091
supplies (*P.O.*);	F333
chief	096
technical	078
telecommunications	099
telegraph; overseas	099
teleprinter	F122
test	081
town hall	F157
traffic;	095
postal	099
telecommunications	099
transport	095
warehouse	097
welfare	M039
wharf	097
works-	091
building and contracting	092
gas board	094
local government	092
workshop	091
yard	095
of bill distributors	F124
of canvassers	132
of pilots	087
of Stamping-	
1st Class	F112
2nd or 3rd Class	115
of teleprinter operators	F122
of typists	F118
of works	092
Superintendent-	
apprenticeship	034
laboratory	F080
residential buildings	157
sales force	M133
ambulance service	111
bakery	091
banking	099
baths	106
biscuit mfr.	091
building and contracting	092
catering	104
cemetery	111
children's home	M037
clothing club	132
crematorium	111
Customs and Excise	019
D.O.E.	092
docks	095
electricity board	094
engineering-	091
civil engineering	092
structural engineering	092
flour confectionery mfr.	091
garage	091
hospital service	111
infant welfare centre	F043
institution	M037
insurance	M134
Land Registry	021
library	026
local government-	022
highways department	092
metal trades	091
Min. of Defence (Air) designs office	082
motoring association	111
National Physical Laboratory	067
nursing association	M043
old people's home	M037
P.O.	099

Superintendent- continued	Code number
park	106
passenger transport	095
police service	M137
prison service	108
public wash-house	111
R.S.P.C.A.	019
railways	095
retail trade	F125
Royal Mint	091
salvage corps	M138
sewage works	111
storage	097
W.R.N.S.	M135
water board	094
waterguard	019
Supervisor;	
apprenticeship	034
area-	M133
building and contracting	F316
gas board	F260
railway signalling	F321
retail trade	101
banking	F115
building	F316
canteen	F146
cargo; ships	115
catering	F146
centre; service (*electricity board*)	F125
chief (*P.O.*);	F121
senior	111
children's	151
claims	F115
clerical	F115
commercial	F115
communications (*air transport*)	F122
contract(s)-	069
building and contracting	092
control;	F115
budgetry	F115
correspondence	F115
costing	F115
cotton	F183
craft (*oil refining*)	F241
credit	F115
display	058
distribution-	F333
water board	F311
domestic-	F151
hospital service	F156
erection (*building and contracting*)	F316
field; playing	165
field (*market research*)	F115
filing	F115
higher grade (*P.O.*)	F121
hostel	111
loading (aircraft)	F335
mail	123
market	142
meals (schools)	151
meat (*abattoir*)	F186
nursery	F043
office	F115
order	F333
park	F140
payroll	F115
planning; production	F115
playground	151
playgroup	038
pool; swimming	F165
pools; football	F115
postal	F123
pricing	F115
process-	
explosives mfr.	F184
oil refining	F184
processing; data	F119
progress-	F115
L.T.E.	F277
publications	F115
ramp (*air transport*)	FL346

(Su—Ta)

	Code number
Supervisor; *continued*	
research; market	013
reservations (*air transport*)	F115
room;	
dining (*hospital service*)	F146
print	F119
show	F125
rope; trot	338
safety	039
sales-	M133
retail trade-	F125
delivery round	F128
service-	
instruments	F246
electrical engineering	F253
gas board	F248
signalling (*railways*)	F321
staff- *see also* Foreman-	
institution	F151
statistical	F115
steel (*coal mine*)	276
stock	F333
store-	F333
retail trade	F125
technical-	
government	F277
shipbuilding	081
tool	333
trade (*retail trade*)	F125
trainee (*coal mine*)	034
training	034
transport-	
rail	F318
road-	F324
public transport	F323
typing	F118
unit; poultry	F166
wages	F115
warehouse	F333
welfare	039
of sorting assistants (*P.O.*)	F123
Supervisor- *see also* Foreman-	
accountancy	F115
institutions	037
office machines	F119
publicity services	F115
training	034
ambulance service	F155
betting	F115
Department for National Savings	F115
Dept. of Emp.	F112
gas board	F260
insurance	134
local government	F115
mail order house	F113
oil refining	091
P.O.-	F121
sorting office	F123
telegraph service	F122
telephone service	F121
school meals service	151
Stationery Office	F338
Supervisor-instructor (*government*)	034
Supplier;	
leaf	201
timber (*coal mine*)	338
Supply man (*coal mine*)	338
Supply worker (*retail trade*)	333
Supporter (*lamp, valve mfr.*)	276
Suppressor; dust (*coal mine*)	314
Surface hand-	
coal mine	345
mine, not coal	L346
Surface man-	
civil engineering	307
coal mine	345
railways	L346
Surface worker; road	307
Surface worker-	
coal mine	345
mine, not coal	L346

	Code number
Surfacer;	
lens; optical	192
optical	192
road	307
steel shot	230
Surgeon;	041
dental	042
tree	111
veterinary	051
Surgery man	156
Surgical hand (*rubber goods mfr.*)	228
Survey man; retort	115
Surveyor;	
agricultural	025
aircraft	069
boiler and engine (*insurance*)	090
bonus	083
borough	068
building	084
cartographic	084
city	068
colliery	084
control; pest	F165
county	068
design (*Air Registration Board*)	069
district	068
divisional; county	068
electrical	071
fire (*insurance*)	090
group (*N.C.B.*)	084
hydrographical	090
infestation; timber	165
insurance; fire	090
land	084
Lloyd's	019
marine	090
measuring	083
mineral	084
mining	084
nautical	090
naval	090
quantity	083
rating	005
river	090
ship	019
tariff	115
valuation	005
of Customs and Excise	019
Surveyor-	084
Customs and Excise	019
insurance	090
pest control	F165
river authority	090
Surveyor and estimator	084
Surveyor and valuer	005
Surveyor and water engineer	084
Surveyor-engineer	084
Suspender; butt	173
Suspender hand	212
,, man	173
Swabber	226
Swager (*cutlery mfr.*)	276
Swarfer (*tube mfr.*)	276
Sweater-	
hat mfr.	226
metal trades	265
Sweep (chimney)	158
Sweeper;	158
chimney	158
cotton (*textile mfr.*)	L339
loom	199
road;	158
mechanical	327
tube	158
Sweeper lad	158
Sweeper-up	158
Swiftman	270
Swiller-	
bedstead mfr.	L344
enamelling	299
tinplate mfr.	L344
Swingbridge man	338
Swinger	199

	Code number
Switch hand	255
Switchman-	
coal mine	338
electricity board	255
Switchboard hand	255
Synchroniser (*film production*)	227
Syphon man	348
Systematist	065

T

	Code number
T.1 (*P.O.*)	256
T.2A (*P.O.*)	256
T.2B (*P.O.*)	257
T.G. (*government*)	090
T.T.O.-	
Civil Aviation Authority	258
P.O.	F121
Tabber-	
corset mfr.	212
glove mfr.	287
hosiery mfr.	287
laundry	227
Table hand *see* Table man-	
Table man; surface	245
Table man-	
bakery	185
bookbinding	189
box mfr.	227
clothing mfr.	226
food products mfr.	202
footwear mfr.	299
leather dressing	173
printing	227
rubber goods mfr.	228
Table worker-	
cigar mfr.	201
printing	227
Tacker;	
bar (*clothing mfr.*)	210
board	316
staple	175
Tacker-	
corset mfr.	226
footwear mfr.	175
hosiery mfr.	212
tack mfr.	242
tailoring	210
Tacker and turner	210
Tacker-on; insole	175
Tackleman-	
docks	334
steelworks	272
Tackle worker; fishing	299
Tackler;	
bag; paper	227
braid machine	248
dobby	248
jacquard	248
loom	248
Tackler-	
wire weaving	238
paper goods mfr.	227
textile weaving	248
Tagger; label	295
Tagger-	
lace mfr.	299
steel mfr.	270
tube mfr.	270
Tailer (beret)	181
Tailor;	210
merchant	101
Tailor and outfitter	210
Tailoress	210
Taker;	
care-	157
cemetery	157
parks and gardens	140
reservoir	316
woodlands	170

(Ta—Te)

	Code number
Taker; *continued*	
copy (*publishing*)	124
impression (*printing*)	227
money (*entertainment*)	115
number	333
stock; chief (*steelworks*)	F113
stock-	115
rolling mill	333
steel smelting	F333
valuers	115
temperature	231
weight	297
work	FL344
Taker-in; piece (*textile mfr.*)	333
Taker-in-	
textile warehouse	333
glass mfr.	191
textile weaving	179
Taker-off;	
bobbin	199
dipper's	299
machine (*printing*)	207
paper bag	227
Taker-off-	
cast concrete products mfr.	230
ceramic mfr.	299
ceramic transfer mfr.	227
clothing mfr.	226
glass mfr.	223
metal trades	338
plasterboard mfr.	204
quantity surveying	083
textile mfr.-	199
lace finishing	162
wool sorting	298
Taker-out; can (*textile mfr.*)	176
Taker-out-	L346
ceramic mfr.	338
Tallyman; timber	333
Tallyman-	115
self-employed	132
Tallywoman	132
Tallyer (timber)	333
Tambourer (*textile making-up*)	212
Tamer (animal)	059
Tamperman	308
Tankhand (vulcanised fibre)	203
Tankman;	
seed (yeast)	202
storage	348
Tankman-	
glass mfr.	191
non-ferrous metal mfr.	231
Tank worker; wax (*cardboard box mfr.*)	203
Tanker (*galvanized sheet mfr.*)	269
Tankerman (*whisky distilling*)	197
Tanner-	173
net, rope mfr.	182
Tannery worker	173
Taper;	
coil	230
dry	179
Taper-	
cable mfr.	230
cardboard box mfr.	227
electrical goods mfr.	230
footwear mfr.	225
plasterboard mfr.	302
textile mfr.	179
Taper girl	230
Taperer (*metal trades*)	241
Tapestry worker	212
Tapper;	
nut and socket (*tube fittings mfr.*)	242
stay	262
wheel (*railways*)	286
Tapper-	
bolt mfr.	242
carbide mfr.	184
footwear mfr.	175
iron, steelworks	231
railways	286

	Code number
Tapper-out	231
Tar man-	
building and contracting	307
coal gas by-products mfr.	184
Tare man (*textile mfr.*)	287
Targer (*flax mfr.*)	176
Tarmac man (*airport*)	338
Tarmac worker	307
Tarrer;	
bag	182
sack	182
Task worker (*coal mine*)	345
Tassel hand	299
Taster;	
coffee	298
tea	298
wine	298
Taster (*food products mfr.*)	298
Tatter (waste)	L346
Tatooist	055
Taxidermist	165
Taxonomist	065
Tea boy	146
Teacher; *see also notes p.4*	
dancing-	053
primary and secondary education	033
head-	
educational establishments-	M033
further education establishment	M032
music-	053
primary and secondary education	033
sales	034
singing-	053
primary and secondary education	033
swimming	063
Teacher-	
home teacher for the blind	039
educational establishments-	033
college of education	032
further education establishment	032
teacher training establishment	032
Teamer (*tobacco mfr.*)	201
Teamsman (*farming*)	172
Teamster-	338
farming	172
Tearer (*textile printing*)	227
Teaser *see* Teazer	
Teaserman *see* Teazer	
Teazer; shoddy	176
Teazer-	
glass mfr.	191
metal trades	231
textile mfr.	176
Teazerman *see* Teazer	
Teazler	182
Technical class, Grade I, II (*government*)	090
Technical grade (*government*)	090
Technician;	
I, IIA (*P.O.*)	256
IIB (*P.O.*)	257
aids; visual	062
analytical	080
animal (*hospital service*)	053
architectural	088
assistant (*railway signalling*)	259
botanical	080
building	089
camera	246
cardiological	050
cephalographic	050
cine	062
darkroom	227
dental	220
development	090
electrical (*P.O.*)	256
electronic	081

	Code number
Technician; *continued*	
engineering;	081
civil	089
structural	089
factory (*telecommunications*)	252
film	062
histological	080
hospital-	080
audiology	050
cardiography	050
encephalography	050
laboratory	080
pathology	080
hospital theatre	050
insemination; artificial	172
instrument-	246
steelworks	081
laboratory;	080
animal care	053
medical	080
lens; contact	192
maxillo-facial	230
medical	050
mortuary	165
optical	246
orthodontic	230
orthopaedic	230
pharmacy	050
photographic	062
physics (*hospital service*)	080
planning; town	088
quality control	080
radar	259
radio	258
room; control (*gas board*)	184
rubber	080
scientific	080
service (*office machines*)	251
signal (*railways*)	259
sound	062
surgical	050
telecommunications-	259
P.O.	256
television	258
town planning	088
wireless	258
workshop (*education services*)	080
Technician-	090
electrical equipment	253
electronic equipment-	252
maintenance	259
engineering	081
instrument (*steelworks*)	081
laboratory;	080
animal care	053
plastics	090
radio, television equipment	258
surgical, dental appliances	230
telegraph, telephone equipment	256
test; flight	081
textile	080
tunnel; wind	081
armed forces-	
foreign and Commonwealth	136
U.K.	135
civil engineering	089
film studio	062
hospital service	080
P.O.-	256
IIB	257
Techni-colourist; map	079
Technologist;	078
medical	080
medical laboratory	080
scientific (*N.C.B.*)	078
Teemer;	
coal-	334
above ground (coal mine)	338
ladle	270
second	270
Teemer-	
coke ovens	338
steelworks	270

(Te)

	Code number
Teerer (*textile printing*)	227
Tele-ad girl	115
Telegram boy (*P.O.*)	124
Telegraph lad	321
Telegraphist	122
Telephone worker-	
female	121
male	257
Telephonist;	121
shorthand	118
Telephonist-clerk	115
Telephonist-receptionist	120
Telephonist-typist	118
Teller; fortune	165
Teller-	
banking	115
printing	297
Temperer; wire	237
Temperer-	
ceramic mfr.	204
metal trades-	237
blast furnace	204
Templater	245
Tenant; public house	103
Tender;	
back *see* Tenter; back	
bar	145
diver's	316
engine	255
furnace (*metal trades*)	231
lock	338
loom	180
Tenon hand	218
Tension hand	207
Tenter;	
back;	
frame (*textile mfr.*)	176
machine; linen	188
machine (*textile printing*)	227
roving	176
back-	
paper mfr.	188
paper staining	203
textile mfr.-	182
textile printing	227
wallpaper printing	227
boiler	347
box; intermediate	176
box-	176
silk mfr.	199
braid (*silk mfr.*)	199
can	176
card	176
card front	176
card room	176
comb	176
comber	176
conant	248
condenser	176
cotton	176
crane	331
cupola	231
derby	176
devil	176
diver's	316
double	176
draw	176
drawing	176
engine;	
blowing-	
metal mfr.	255
textile mfr.	176
carding	176
engine-	255
textile mfr.	176
engine head	F176
fly	176
frame;	176
cheesing	178
clearing	177
copping	178
doubling	177
draw	176
flyer	177

	Code number
Tenter; *continued*	
frame; *continued*	
jacquard	248
ring	177
twisting	177
front	176
furnace	231
gill	176
hard waste	176
hardener;	
flat	199
roller	199
hoist	331
hosepipe	248
inter	176
jack	176
jig	182
joiner	176
lap	176
machine *see* Machinist	
mule	177
opener	176
padding	182
picker	199
press (*metal trades*)	L344
pump	348
ribbon	176
rover	176
roving	176
scutcher	176
slub	176
slubber	176
slubbing	176
spare	176
speed	176
throstle	177
weaver's	248
weilds	178
Tenter-	
carpet mfr.	248
lace mfr.	248
textile finishing	182
textile weaving	248
Tenterer; woollen	182
Tenterer (*textile mfr.*)	182
Terrazzo hand	300
Terrazzo worker	300
Test hand (*metal trades*)	286
Test man; final (*vehicle mfr.*)	248
Tester;	
acid	288
air conditioning	288
aircraft	286
alkali	288
arc lamp	286
balloon	291
bench (motors, motor cycles)	286
bobbin	299
bobbin slow	299
boiler	286
brake	248
cable	286
can	286
car	249
carbon (*steelworks*)	288
carburettor	286
cask	293
cathode ray tube	286
cell (*dry battery mfr.*)	286
cement	299
chemical	288
cloth (*textile merchants*)	289
coil	286
coke-	288
coal gas, coke ovens	299
cylinder	286
denier	289
drain	316
dye (*textile dyeing*)	289
dynamo	286
egg	290
electrical	286
engine	286

	Code number
Tester; *continued*	
furnace-	231
furnace mfr.	286
gas-	
chemical mfr.	288
gas works	288
gear; chain and suspension	019
gear (*engineering*)	286
glass	288
gramophone	286
hollow-ware	286
installation (electrical)	253
instrument	286
insulation	286
machine	286
matrix (*type founding*)	286
meter	286
milk	290
moisture	299
motor	286
music	348
oil	288
paper	294
pipe; concrete	299
pipe-	
main laying	316
metal mfr.	286
pole (telephone)	293
pump	286
radio	258
record; gramophone	299
road (*vehicle mfr.*)	248
roller-	286
printing roller mfr.	291
rope-	289
metal	286
coal mine	272
section head (*oil refining*)	288
seed	288
shift (*chemical mfr.*)	299
silk (*man-made fibre mfr.*)	289
soil	288
spring	286
stove	286
sub-station (*L.T.E.*)	253
systems (electronic)	286
tank	286
tractor	248
valve	286
vehicle-	248
Dept. of Transport	299
water	288
weight (*balance mfr.*)	246
wire	286
yarn	289
Tester-	
abrasive wheel mfr.	299
asbestos-cement goods mfr.	299
cast concrete products mfr.	299
ceramic mfr.	299
electrical contracting	253
food canning	290
glass mfr.	299
gramophone record mfr.	299
L.T.E.	249
lens mfr.	299
match mfr.	299
metal trades-	286
balance mfr.	246
musical instrument mfr.	222
paint mfr.	288
rubber goods mfr.	291
safety fuse mfr.	299
Tester-fitter	248
Tester-mechanic	248
Tester-rectifier;	
cylinder	276
electrical/electronic equipment	274
engine;	
internal combustion	248
jet	248
instrument;	
musical	222

(Te—Tr)

Term	Code number
Tester-rectifier; *continued*	
instrument; *continued*	
precision	246
Textile operative	L339
Textile worker	L339
Texturer;	
ceiling	282
yarn	177
Thatcher	303
Therapist;	
art	049
beauty	165
dental	050
occupational	049
speech	049
Thinner (*varnish mfr.*)	184
Third hand-	
fishing	F171
foundry	270
rolling mill	270
Threader;	
bobbin	178
brass (*lace mfr.*)	199
draw;	
hose	226
frame	179
heald;	179
wire	276
pearl	299
warp (*hosiery mfr.*)	179
Threader-	
bolt, nut, etc. mfr.	242
carpet mfr.	179
embroidery mfr.	226
lace mfr.	199
lamp, valve mfr.	283
needle mfr.	270
Thrower;	
rayon	177
timber	L346
Thrower-	
brewery	L346
ceramic mfr.	193
distillery	L346
Throwster (*textile mfr.*)	177
Thumber (*glove mfr.*)	212
Tic tac man	165
Ticketer	287
Tier;	
bag	287
bag-blue	287
battery	230
hay	172
hook;	299
cork	287
knot-	
footwear mfr.	225
textile mfr.	183
ream	287
ring	299
sausage	202
smash	180
tackle (fishing tackle)	299
warp	179
Tierer	227
Tier-in (*textile mfr.*)	199
Tier-on; warp	179
Tier-on-	
fishhook mfr.	299
textile mfr.	199
Tier-up (*cloth hat mfr.*)	299
Tile worker-	
cast concrete products mfr.	230
ceramic mfr.	223
plastics goods mfr.	195
Tiler;	303
cork	300
floor	300
glaze	300
range	300
roof	303
wall	300
Tiler and plasterer	300
Tilter	231
Tilterman	231
Timber hand *see* Timber man-	
Timber man-	
building and contracting-	316
tunnelling contracting	315
coal mine-	314
above ground	316
electricity board	316
forestry	170
local government	316
mine, not coal	315
railways	316
timber merchants	338
vehicle mfr.	268
water board	316
Timber worker	338
Timberer (*coal mine*)	314
Timberer-up (*vehicle mfr.*)	268
Timekeeper	115
Timer	247
Tin can operative	242
Tin man-	
sheet metal working	261
tin plate mfr.	269
Tin worker; fancy	242
Tin worker (*sheet metal working*)	261
Tindal; first (*shipping*)	F317
Tinker	261
Tinner;	
coil	269
copper	269
fruit	287
grease	269
wire	269
Tinner-	
food canning	287
metal trades	269
Tinplate worker (*tinplate mfr.*)-	
female	L344
male	270
Tinplater (*tinplate mfr.*)	269
Tinsman; drying (*textile mfr.*)	182
Tinsmith	261
Tinter;	
enamel (*enamel mfr.*)	204
paint	204
Tinter-	
chemical mfr.	204
film processing	227
textile mfr.	182
Tipman; refuse	L346
Tipman (*mine, not coal*)	338
Tipper;	
ballast	334
coal-	
docks	334
patent fuel mfr.	338
steelworks	338
metal	242
ore (steelworks)	338
scrap	338
shale	338
slag	338
umbrella	212
Tipper-	
coal mine	338
docks	334
enamelling	299
mine, not coal	338
Tippler-	
flax mfr.	199
steelworks	338
Tipplerman (*coal mine*)	338
Tipster	165
Tirrer	L346
Tobacco operative	201
Tobacco worker	201
Tobacconist	101
Toffee man	202
Toggler (*leather dressing*)	173
Toner	222
Tonger (*wire*)	270
Tongsman; back	270
Tongsman-	
rolling mill	270
steel hoop mill	270
wrought iron mfr.	270
Tonguer	270
Tool boy	338
Tool man-	338
fustian, velvet mfr.	182
Tool worker; edge	276
Tooler;	
glass	192
stone	301
Tooler (*fustian, velvet mfr.*)	182
Toother (*saw mfr.*)	276
Topman; battery (*coke ovens*)	L341
Topman-	316
bacon curing	202
coal mine	345
coal gas, coke ovens	L341
demolition	316
pile driving	330
Topas	317
Topographer	084
Topper;	
beet (*sugar mfr.*)	202
jam	287
on walk	199
Topper-	
boot polish mfr.	287
clothing mfr.	212
cord mfr.	199
fur dyeing	299
hosiery mfr.	181
Topper and tailer	181
Toucher-up-	
laundry	162
vehicle mfr.	299
Toughener (glass)	191
Tower (*ceramic mfr.*)	223
Towerman-	184
paper mfr.	348
Townsman	134
Toxicologist	065
Tracer; goods (*railways*)	115
Tracer-	114
chocolate mfr.	202
embroidery mfr.	226
footwear mfr.	225
printing	115
Tracer and colourer (*fancy goods mfr.*)	115
Tracker-	
ball bearing mfr.	242
coal mine	314
Trackman-	
mine, not coal	306
railways	306
tramways	306
Trackworker (*vehicle mfr.*)	285
Trader;	
credit	132
market	130
motor	101
street	130
Trader-	101
mobile shop	128
Traffic man (*coal mine*)	338
Trailer-down (*rolling mill*)	270
Trainee *see* notes p.4	
Trainer;	
animal (performing animals)	059
dog	111
hop	166
horse	111
pony	111
Trainer (sports)	063
Trammer	338
Transcriber;	
communications (*government*)	115
music	060
Transferer;	
design (*printing*)	115
hosiery	181

(Tr—Tu)

	Code number
Transferer; *continued*	
lithograph-	
ceramic mfr.	279
printing	206
Transferer-	299
ceramic mfr.	279
glass mfr.	223
japanning	299
linoleum mfr.	115
tinplate mfr.	207
Transformer hand	283
Transit worker (*coal mine*)	338
Translator; tailor's	210
Translator-	054
clothing mfr.	210
footwear mfr.	175
umbrella mfr.	226
Transport man (*docks*)	334
Transport worker-	338
docks	334
waterways	334
Transporter;	
cable (*coal mine*)	338
cattle	326
livestock	326
supplies (*coal mine*)	338
Trapper;	
rabbit	172
wool	176
Trapper-	
forestry	172
textile mfr.	176
Traveller;	
advertisement	134
advertising	134
commercial-	133
drapers; credit	132
services	134
directory	134
drapers; credit	132
grocers	128
insurance	134
van	128
Traveller-	133
retail trade	132
credit trade	132
Traveller-salesman (*credit trade*)	132
Trawler hand	171
Trawler man	171
Treasurer-	
hospital services	006
local government	006
Treater;	
heat	237
timber	203
Treatment worker; heat (*metal trades*)	237
Treer	225
Trenchman	313
Tribologist	076
Trichologist	050
Trimmer;	
asbestos	204
bakelite	229
ballast	334
barge	334
blade (*aircraft mfr.*)	244
block (*rubber goods mfr.*)	228
boat	334
body; car	213
boiler	L346
boot	175
box (*steelworks*)	244
bristle	176
bullet	276
cable	276
cake	200
car	213
card	190
carriage	213
cloth	182
coach	213

	Code number
Trimmer; *continued*	
coal-	L346
coal mine	338
docks	334
shipping	317
coffin	226
disposal; refuse	L346
dog	172
edge	175
face (*coal mine*)	314
fancy (*brush mfr.*)	176
fibre	176
fish	187
floor board (*coach trimming*)	213
heel	175
helmet	226
hosiery (*textile finishing*)	182
house; boiler	L346
ice	L346
inseam	175
lamp-	
railways	L346
shipping	317
leather-	173
vehicle mfr.	213
lime	198
measure	211
meat	186
motor	213
needle	242
pad; heel	228
paper (*printing*)	190
plastic(s)	229
plate (*metal trades*)	276
print; photographic	227
rubber	228
seat; car	213
sheet (*paper goods mfr.*)	190
soap	230
sponge	204
steel	244
tailor's	211
tooth	230
tyre; solid	228
upholsterer's	213
upper	175
vegetable	202
veneer	218
wagon	338
wallpaper	190
window	058
Trimmer-	
artificial teeth mfr.	230
boiler house	L346
bookbinding	189
broom, brush mfr.	230
cement mfr.	230
clothing mfr.	212
coal gas, coke ovens	L341
coal mine	338
docks	334
electricity board	L346
embroidery mfr.	226
fishing	317
footwear mfr.	175
furniture mfr.	213
glass mfr.	223
glove mfr.	226
hat mfr.	212
knitwear mfr.	226
leather dressing	173
leather goods mfr.	175
manure mfr.	L340
metal trades-	244
aircraft mfr.	213
bolt, nut mfr.	242
gold, silver wire mfr.	276
needle mfr.	242
tin box mfr.	242
vehicle mfr.	213
vehicle body building	213
mine, not coal	301
plastics mfr.	229
powder puff mfr.	230

	Code number
Trimmer- *continued*	
power station	L346
railway workshop	213
rubber mfr.	228
shipping	317
textile mfr.-	182
carpet mfr.	199
hosiery finishing	182
Trimmer and finisher (*hosiery mfr.*)	182
Trolley boy-	338
catering	146
road haulage	329
street trading	130
Trolleyman;	338
refreshments	146
Trombonist	060
Trough lad	270
Trouncer-	329
metal trades	276
Trouser hand	210
Trowel hand-	
cement mfr.	184
Trowel worker	300
Trubeniser	182
Truckman-	
blast furnace	338
coal mine	338
road transport	326
Trucker	332
Truer; wheel (*cycle mfr.*)	276
Truer-up; wheel (*cycle mfr.*)	276
Trumpet man	300
Trusser;	
fowl	187
hay	172
Trusser (*farming*)	172
Tryer	286
Tub and bate man	173
Tub hand (*foundry*)	235
Tubber (*leather dressing*)	173
Tube hand	194
Tube worker-	
paper	227
steel	270
Tuber;	
boiler	262
engine (*railways*)	262
mule	177
wire (*wire mfr.*)	237
Tuber-	
boiler mfr.	262
locomotive mfr.	262
rope mfr.	199
textile mfr.	199
wire mfr.	237
Tucker-	
blanket mfr.	182
clothing mfr.	212
textile mfr.	199
Tufnol worker	229
Tufter-	
carpet mfr.	199
mattress mfr.	226
soft furnishings mfr.	226
Tug boy	317
Tug hand	317
Tugman	317
Tugboatman	317
Tumbler (*metal trades*)	243
Tun man	197
Tun room man	197
Tuner; head	F248
Tuner-	
looms	248
musical instruments	222
television	258
vehicles	249
textile mfr.	248
Tuner and regulator (organ)	222
Tunnel man (ice cream)	202
Tunnel oven operative	191
Tunneller-	304
coal mine	314

(Tu—Va)

	Code number
Tupper-	
building and contracting	313
steel mfr.	270
Tupper at stripper and winch	270
Turf worker	168
Turn man; bye (*steelworks*)	L344
Turncock	310
Turner;	
asbestos	230
axle	239
belt (*coal mine*)	276
billiard ball	229
biscuit	200
block; wood	218
bobbin-	218
metal	239
bowl (*tobacco pipe mfr.*)	218
brass	241
bush; axle	239
button	230
capstan	241
centre boss	239
collar	226
commutator	239
conveyor (*coal mine*)	276
copper band	239
core	270
cork	230
counter	218
crank	239
cutter	239
die	239
ebonite	228
engine; rose	266
engine	266
engraver's	239
frame (*shipbuilding*)	276
general	239
glove	226
graphite	230
gun	239
hand-	
clothing mfr.	226
metal trades	239
handle	218
heel (wood heels)	218
insulator	193
ivory	230
lathe;	
capstan	241
centre	239
turret	241
lathe (*metal trades*)	239
locomotive	239
loom	239
machine; pottery	193
maintenance	239
marine	239
mould; fringe	218
mould (*glass mfr.*)	239
optical	241
pan (*coal mine*)	314
patent (*clothing mfr.*)	226
pipe-	260
tobacco pipe mfr.	218
pirn	218
porcelain; electric	193
ring	239
rod (fishing rods)	218
roll	241
roller-	
metal	241
rubber	228
wood	218
textile machinery mfr.	241
rough	239
rubber	228
sheet-	
galvanized sheet mfr.	L344
rolling mill	299
shell	241
shive	218
slipper	225
spiral	218

	Code number
Turner; *continued*	
spool	218
textile	239
tool	239
tube; steel	239
tyre (metal)	239
valve	239
vulcanite	228
wheel-	
abrasive mfr.	230
ceramic mfr.	L342
metal trades	239
wire	276
wood	218
Turner-	
metal	239
plastics	229
rubber	228
stone	301
wood	218
asbestos-cement goods mfr.	230
brewery	197
canvas goods mfr.	226
cemented carbide goods mfr.	230
ceramic mfr.	193
clothing mfr.	226
coal mine	239
footwear mfr.	225
hosiery mfr.	226
leather dressing	173
metal trades-	239
precious metal, plate mfr.	266
plastics goods mfr.	229
process engraving	206
rubber goods mfr.	228
stone dressing	301
vulcanite goods mfr.	228
wood products mfr.	218
wood-wind instrument mfr.	218
Turner and fitter	248
Turner-down (*glove mfr.*)	226
Turner-engineer	239
Turner-fitter	248
Turner-in (*steel mfr.*)	299
Turner-out (*glass mfr.*)	223
Turner-over (*rolling mill*)	299
Turner-up (*rolling mill*)	299
Turnover man (*coal mine*)	276
Turnstile man	140
Turret hand	241
Tutor; private	053
Tutor- *see also notes p.4*	
hospital service	F043
Twinder	178
Twiner (*textile mfr.*)	177
Twiner-joiner-minder	177
Twist hand; plain net	180
Twist hand	180
Twister;	
barley sugar	202
cap (*textile mfr.*)	177
cop	177
cotton	177
doubling	177
false	177
fancy cord	199
fly	177
gut	204
hat wire	242
machine	199
patent-	177
textile warping	179
plain net	177
ring	177
silk	177
single	177
spinning	177
sprig	177
tube	229
twine	199
warp	179
wool	177
worsted	177
yarn	177

	Code number
Twister-	
brush mfr.	230
textile mfr.-	177
rope, twine mfr.	199
Twister and drawer	179
Twister-in (*textile mfr.*)	179
Twister-on (*textile mfr.*)	179
Twister-up (*textile mfr.*)	179
Tyer *see* Tier	
Tyer-on *see* Tier-on	
Tyer-up *see* Tier-up	
Tympanist	060
Typer (*textile mfr.*)	227
Typist;	118
copy	118
shorthand	118
superintendent	F118
vari	205
Typist-clerk	115
Typographer	205
Tyreman (*railways*)	233
Tyre worker; rubber (*perambulator mfr.*)	194

U

	Code number
Umpire (sports)	063
Uncoiler (*tinplate mfr.*)	270
Uncurler (*textile mfr.*)	182
Underbuyer (*retail trade*)	015
Underhand	231
Underbaster	210
Underground worker-	
coal mine	345
mine, not coal	315
Under-manager *see* Manager-	
Underpresser	162
Undersealer (vehicles)	281
Understripper	226
Understudy	059
Undertaker	163
Underwriter	007
Unhairer (*tannery*)	173
Unloader;	
autoclave (ceramics)	338
kiln (ceramics)	338
Unloader-	335
docks	334
Unloader and retort feeder;	
blanching tank (*fruit, vegetable preserving*)	202
Unreeler (*steel mfr.*)	270
Untwister (*hair dressing*)	176
Unwinder	178
Upholsterer	213
Up-twister	177
Urologist	041
Usher;	165
court	165
Usherette	165
Utility man-	L346
coal mine	345

V

	Code number
Vaccinator (poultry)	172
Valet-	151
car (*garage*)	158
Valuer	005
Valve and steam man (*coal gas, coke ovens*)	348
Valveman; hydraulic	248
Valveman-	
cartridge mfr.	276
coal gas, coke ovens	348
steelworks	248
water works	310

(Va—Wa)

Term	Code number
Valver	227
Vamper	175
Van boy	329
Van lad; parcels	329
Van man	128
Varnisher;	
paper	203
spray	281
Varnisher-	299
wallpaper mfr.	203
Vat hand (*electroplating*)	269
Vatman-	
brewery	197
paper mfr.	203
soft drinks mfr.	202
vinegar mfr.	197
wire mfr.	269
Vatter (*brewery*)	197
Veiner	230
Veiner and marker (*artificial flower mfr.*)	230
Velourer	226
Vendor;	
horsemeat	186
ice cream	128
milk	128
news	130
newspaper	130
oil	128
pea and pie	128
pie	128
street	130
Veneer hand	224
Veneerer;	
tyre	228
wood	203
Venereologist	041
Ventriloquist	059
Verderer	170
Verderor	170
Verger-	157
lace machine mfr.	241
Verifier;	
card; punch	119
stock	115
Verifier (*rubber tyre mfr.*)	291
Versteller	266
Vessel man-	
steelworks	231
textile dyeing	182
Vest hand	210
Veterinarian	051
Vicar	040
Vicar-general	040
Vice man;	244
spring	270
Victualler; licensed-	103
off-licence	101
Viewer;	
ammunition	299
ball bearings	286
barrel (gun)	286
cloth	289
component (*metal trades*)	286
cycle	286
garment	289
glass	299
patrol (*metal trades*)	286
plastics	292
of bullets	286
Viewer-	
cartridge mfr.	299
chocolate mfr.	290
clothing mfr.	289
electrical goods mfr.	286
film production	299
food products mfr.	290
hat mfr.	289
metal trades	286
plastics goods mfr.	292
rubber goods mfr.	291
sports goods mfr.	299
textile mfr.	289
wood products mfr.	293

Term	Code number
Violinist	060
Violoncellist	060
Virologist; research	065
Viscose man (*man-made fibre mfr.*)	196
Visitor;	
district	043
health;	043
superintendent	F043
home	043
housing	039
parish	039
school	039
sick	043
tuberculosis	043
under boarded-out order	039
Visitor (Children's Act)	039
Visualiser (*advertising*)	055
Viticulturist	107
Vitrifier (*artificial teeth mfr.*)	191
Vocalist	059
Voicer (organ)	222
Voicer and tuner (organ)	222
Volt boy	276
Vulcanizer	204

W

Term	Code number
Wadder	191
Wageman (*coal mine*)	345
Wagon man	327
Wagoner-	
coal mine-	331
above ground	338
farming	172
mine, not coal	327
Wagoner's boy-	329
farming	172
Wagonwayman	306
Wagonwright	268
Waistcoat hand	210
Waiter;	
commis	144
head	F144
service;	199
silver	144
wine	144
Waiter-	144
stock exchange	124
Waiter-on (*coal mine*)	331
Waitress	144
Walker;	
floor	F125
shop	F125
track (*railways*)	306
Walksman; river	316
Waller; dry	300
Waller-	301
salt mfr.	184
Warden;	
barrack	157
camp	157
castle	157
civil defence	142
club; youth	039
community centre	039
crossing (school)	142
dinner (school)	151
game	172
garage	142
range	165
resident (*L.T.E.*)	157
security	140
station	157
traffic	141
wood	F170
Warden-	
detention centre	108
caravan site	157
day nursery	150

Term	Code number
Warden- *continued*	
forestry	F170
government	157
hostel	111
institution	M037
L.T.E.	142
manufacturing	142
museum, etc.	142
nurse's home	111
old people's home	M037
police service	111
school	142
social settlement	039
youth club	039
Warder;	
chief	F139
river	172
yeoman	142
Warder-	
museum, etc.	142
prison service	139
Wardrobe woman (*theatre*)	165
Ware room worker	338
Warehouse boy-	333
loading, unloading	335
Warehouse hand; lace	338
Warehouse hand-	333
loading, unloading	335
Warehouseman;	
biscuit (*ceramic mfr.*)	F223
black	191
chief	F333
glost (*ceramic mfr.*)	F223
italian	101
stuff	101
Warehouseman-	333
loading, unloading	335
Warehouseman-clerk	333
Warehouseman-packer	333
Warehouse worker-	333
loading, unloading	335
Warehouser-	333
loading, unloading	335
Warmer; rivet	276
Warp hand	181
Warper	179
Warrener	172
Washman (*laundry*)	162
Washer;	
back (*textile mfr.*)	199
barrel	348
basket (*docks*)	L346
benzol	184
blanket (*blanket mfr.*)	199
board	L342
body (*hat mfr.*)	199
boiler	276
bone ash	204
bottle	348
box	348
brush	199
bulb (*lamp mfr.*)	348
cab	158
cake (*man-made fibre mfr.*)	204
car	158
carriage	348
cask	348
churn	348
cloth (*textile mfr.*)	199
coal (*coal mine*)	198
coke	204
cullet	298
dish (*hotels, catering, etc.*)	147
drum	348
feather	199
felt	199
fruit	202
glass-	L342
hotels, catering, etc.	147
grit	198
hair; horse	199
hand (*coal mine*)	198
jar	348
keg	348

(Wa—Wi)

	Code number
Washer; *continued*	
lime	198
lorry	158
meat	202
metal	L342
plate	147
pot	L346
rag (*textile mfr.*)	199
rubber	204
silk	199
skin (*fellmongery*)	173
stencil	L342
sugar beet	202
tin; biscuit	L346
van	158
wool	199
yarn	199
Washer-	
ceramic mfr.	223
chemical mfr.	184
fellmongery	173
fish curing	202
flour confectionery mfr.	L346
grain milling	202
hat mfr.	199
laundry	162
metal trades	270
mine, not coal	198
paper mfr.	188
photographic processing	227
tannery	173
textile mfr.	199
transport	348
Washerman-	
grain milling	202
laundry	162
paper mfr.	188
textile mfr.	199
Washerwoman	162
Washer-off (*textile mfr.*)	199
Washer-up (*hotel, catering, etc.*)	147
Washery hand (*coal mine*)	198
Washhouse hand *see* Washhouseman-	
Washhouseman; wool	199
Washhouseman-	
baths	165
laundry	162
raw silk processing	199
Waste house hand (*textile mfr.*)	L339
Wasteman;	
assistant (*coal mine*)	314
wool	L339
Waste man-	
coal mine	314
textile mfr.	L339
Waste worker (*coal mine*)	314
Watchman-	140
barge	317
Watchman-operator (*petroleum distribution*)	338
Watcher;	
calciner	204
cargo	140
contract	115
customs	115
fire	142
furnace	231
night	140
river	172
ship	140
Watcher-	
Customs and Excise	115
metal mfr.	231
silk finishing	115
Watchmaker and jeweller	247
Watchstander (barge)	317
Water boy (*tinplate mfr.*)	338
Waterman;	
dock	334
furnace; blast	348
Waterman-	
coal gas, coke ovens	L341
coal mine	345

	Code number
Waterman- *continued*	
local government	310
paper mfr.	203
sewage disposal	348
steel mfr.	348
textile mfr.	182
water transport	317
water works	310
Watercress worker	167
Waterguard (*Customs and Excise*)	019
Wax man	173
Waxer;	
block; thread	228
cord	182
stencil paper	203
Waxer-	
battery mfr.	276
leather dressing	173
paper mfr.	203
Weaver;	
asbestos	180
cane	230
carpet	180
cloth; wire	242
contour	180
felt	199
hair (*wig mfr.*)	230
lace	180
loom; pattern	180
netting	180
spare	180
spring	276
thrum	180
time	180
withy	230
Weaver-	
basketry mfr.	230
wig mfr.	230
wire goods mfr.	242
Weaving operative	180
Webber	211
Wedger; clay	223
Weeder	172
Weft boy	338
,, man	333
,, room man	333
Weigh lad	297
Weighman;	297
charge (*foundry*)	338
check	297
wagon (*coal mine*)	297
Weighbridgeman	297
Weigher;	
check-	297
coal mine	297
mine, not coal	297
chemical (*rubber goods mfr.*)	297
coiler	199
colour-	
linoleum mfr.	297
textile dyeing	297
drug (*rubber goods mfr.*)	297
heat	297
ingredient (*flour confectionery mfr.*)	297
powder (*plastics goods mfr.*)	297
pulp	297
tobacco	297
traffic (*coal mine*)	297
weft	297
wool (*woollen mfr.*)	297
Weigher-	
abrasive wheel mfr.	297
carbon goods mfr.	297
cemented carbide goods mfr.	297
coal mine	297
felt hood mfr.	297
flour confectionery mfr.	297
food products mfr.	297
mine, not coal	297
textile finishing	297
wool blending	297

	Code number
Weigher and finisher; coil (*asbestos rope mfr.*)	199
Weigher and mixer; colour	297
Weigher and mixer (*sugar confectionery mfr.*)	202
Weigherman (*card, paste board mfr.*)	333
Weigher-in	297
Weigher-off	297
Weigher-up	297
Weighter (golf club heads)	224
Weightsman	079
Welder;	
chain	265
plastic	296
Welder-	265
footwear mfr.	299
plastics goods mfr.	296
Welder and cutter	265
Welfare worker-	039
school	151
Welter-	
footwear mfr.	175
hosiery, knitwear mfr.	212
Wetter (*footwear mfr.*)	225
Whaler; hosiery	181
Whammeller	171
Wharf man	334
Wharfinger	F334
Wheelabrator	275
Wheelman-	
coal mine	271
copper refining	270
Wheeler;	
ash	338
beam	338
charge (*metal mfr.*)	338
clay (*metal mfr.*)	338
coal	338
coal and ashes	338
coke	338
cullet	338
frit	338
metal (*metal mfr.*)	338
pick (*mine, not coal*)-	
above ground	338
below ground	338
scrap	338
tap (*metal mfr.*)	338
welt	175
wet-	
footwear mfr.	175
leather dressing	173
Wheeler-	338
footwear mfr.	175
leather dressing	173
railway rolling stock mfr.	248
sheet metal working	261
silver and plate mfr.	276
vitreous enamelling	299
wheelwrights	224
Wheeler-in	338
Wheelwright	224
Wherryman	317
Whetter (cutlery)	276
Whimseyer	176
Whip (*hunting*)	172
Whipper;	
blanket	212
sock (*footwear mfr.*)	175
Whipper-in (*hunting*)	172
White room man	287
Whitesmith	261
Whiting worker	184
Whizzerman (*chemical mfr.*)	184
Wholesaler	101
Wicker	299
Willeyer	176
Willier	176
Willow worker	230
Willower-	
paper mfr.	176
textile mfr.	176
Willowyer	176

107

(Wi—Ya)

Term	Code number
Willyer	176
Winchman-	331
shipping	F317
textile mfr.	182
Winder;	
armature	274
ball; golf	228
ball (*textile mfr.*)	178
beam	179
belt; rubber	228
bit (*textile mfr.*)	178
bobbin;	
brass	178
ring	178
bobbin-	
electrical goods mfr.	274
textile mfr.	178
wire mfr.	276
cable	230
cage (*coal mine*)	331
card	178
cheese	178
clear	178
clearer	178
clock	165
cloth (*oil cloth mfr.*)	199
coil	274
coloured	178
cone	178
cop	178
copper (*cable mfr.*)	276
core-	
cable mfr.	276
golf ball mfr.	228
cotton	178
disc; armature	274
double (*textile mfr.*)	178
doubler (*textile mfr.*)	178
doubling	178
drum	178
dynamo	274
electrical	274
element	274
engine-	
mining	331
textile mfr.	178
filament	276
gas	182
hand-	
golf ball mfr.	228
textile mfr.	199
hank	178
incline	331
insulating (*electrical engineering*)	230
jute	178
machine-	
golf ball mfr.	228
surgical dressing mfr.	199
mesh	274
mohair	178
motor; induction	274
pin	178
pirn	178
pit; staple	331
quill	178
rayon	178
reel	178
ribbon	199
ring	178
rope; wire	276
rotor	274
rubber;	178
elastic	199
silk; raw	178
skip (*coal mine*)	331
slip	178
spiral (*paper tube mfr.*)	227
spool-	
electrical goods mfr.	274
textile mfr.	178
stator	274
tape (*electrical engineering*)	199
thread (*textile mfr.*)	178
Winder; *continued*	
towel (*laundry*)	162
transformer	274
tube-	
paper tube mfr.	227
textile mfr.	178
turbo	274
twist	178
universal	178
wallpaper	188
warp	178
weft	178
weight	178
wheel (*lace mfr.*)	178
wire	276
woof	178
wool	178
yankee	178
yarn	178
Winder-	
cable mfr.	276
electrical goods mfr.	274
mining	331
paper mfr.	188
textile mfr.	178
textile smallwares mfr.	199
typewriter ribbon mfr.	199
wallpaper mfr.	188
wire goods mfr.	276
Winderman-	
coal mine	331
paper mfr.	188
Wiper;	
bobbin	199
cutlery (*cutlery mfr.*)	L344
knife; table (*cutlery mfr.*)	L344
scissors	335
Wiper (*glass mfr.*)	L342
Wire boy	223
Wire hand (*cable mfr.*)	276
Wireman;	
electrical	253
electronic	273
indoor	273
instrument	273
overhead	257
radar	273
telegraph	257
telephone	257
Wireman-	
cycle mfr.	285
P.O.	257
railways	257
rediffusion service	257
Wireman-assembler	283
Wire worker; tungsten	270
Wire worker-	276
cable mfr.	230
hop growing	166
silver, plate mfr.	266
Wirer;	
box	242
card (*carpet mfr.*)	199
electrical	253
panel	273
tyre	228
Wirer-	
artificial flower mfr.	230
metal trades-	276
electrical engineering	253
electronic apparatus mfr.	273
telephone, telegraph apparatus mfr.	253
Wirer and paperer	299
Wirer and solderer (*radio and television mfr.*)	283
Wirer-up (*electroplating*)	270
Wiring hand	299
Withdrawer (*coal mine*)	314
Wood hand; show	215
Woodman-	170
mine, not coal	315
Woodworker-	224
aircraft	214
Woodrieve	F170
Woodsman	170
Woodward	F170
Woolleyer	176
Work study man	010
Worker;	
line; *see* Assembler	
assembly *see* Assembler	
production *see* Assembler	
piece *see* Assembler	
production *see* Assembler	
Worker-off (*sugar confectionery mfr.*)	202
Worker-round (*iron, steelworks*)	L344
Worker-up (*quantity surveying*)	083
Worksetter	276
Wrapper;	
bead (*tyre mfr.*)	228
cable	230
tube (*rubber goods mfr.*)	228
Wrapper-	287
cardboard box mfr.	227
inner tube mfr.	228
Wrapper-up	287
Wren (*armed forces-U.K.*)	135
Wrestler	063
Wringman	182
Wringer (*gun cotton mfr.*)	199
Wringer-out (*hat mfr.*)	226
Writer;	
advertisement	054
advertisement drop curtain	282
card	282
chart	115
compiler	012
copy (*advertising*)	054
dial	299
flexo	119
glass	282
law	115
leader	054
letter (*sign writing*)	282
lithographic	115
news	054
poster	282
publicity	054
reports; senior (*broadcasting*)	054
scenario	054
script	054
ship's	115
shorthand	118
sign	282
specialist	054
specifications	090
technical-	054
patents	090
ticket	282
to the Signet	001
to the trade	282
Writer-	
self-employed	054
authorship	054
coach building	282
journalism	054
Min. of Defence	115
newspaper publishing	054
shipping	115
sign writing	282

X

Y

Yachtsman	317
Yard boy (*Min. of Defence*)	124

(Ya—Zo)

	Code number		Code number		Code number
Yard man;		Yardage hand	227	Youth-in-training-	
hotel	L346	Yardsman-		P.O.-	256
metal (*steelworks*)	L344	*blast furnace*	322	motor transport	249
Yard man-	L346	*dairy*	L346	*factories department*	253
coal mine	297	*farming*	166		
farming	166	Yarn man	199		
livery stable	172	Yeast man	202	**Z**	
vulcanised fibre board mfr.	338	Yeast worker	197		
Yard worker;	L346	Yeoman	107		
lime	173	Yoker (*shirt mfr.*)	212	Zinc worker	261
tan	173	Youth worker	039	Zoologist	065

Appendix F

List of Conventional Codings

Occupation	Code number
Agent	101
Assembler	299
Bailiff	142
Baker	185
Banker	006
Barman	145
Bleacher	182
Bookmaker	164
Buffer	243
Builder	305
Cable maker	230
Cap maker	211
Capstan lathe operator	241
Carter	338
Caster	270
Cellarman	197
Chain maker	276
Collector	115
Collier	314
Commission agent	164
Concrete worker	230
Constable	137
Contractor	316
Core maker	235
Dairy hand	202
Dairyman	202
Dairy worker	202
Dealer	131
Designer	056
Driller	241
Drilling machinist	241
Driver	326
Drop stamper	242
Dyer	182
Engraver	267
Fettler	244
Finisher	212
Fireman	138
Fish worker	187
Furnaceman	231
Furnace operator	231
Furrier	101
Ganger	F316
Gas maker	184
Gilder	227
Glass worker	223
Glove machinist	212
Grinder	241
Guillotine operator (female)	190
Guillotine operator (male)	276
Hand press operator	242
Hatter	101
Hewer	314
Houseman	151
House worker	151
Housekeeper	149
Iron worker	L344
Ironer	162
Jeweller	101
Jointer	257
Lathe operator	241
Leather worker	225
Lecturer	033
Lithographer	207
Machine setter	238
Machinist (female)	212
Machinist (male)	241
Matron	M043
Merchant	101
Milkman	128
Miller	241
Milling machinist	241
Miner	345
Model maker	214
Moulder	235
Paper worker	188
Pattern maker	217
Pickler	270
Plant operator	184
Plater	262
Police constable	137
Policeman	137
Police sergeant	F137
Polisher	243
Potman	165
Potter	193
Power presser	242
Press operator	242
Press setter	238
Press worker (female)	162
Presser	242
Process worker	184
Representative	133
Roadman	308
Roofer	303
Salesman	125
Sawyer	218
Seedsman	101
Sewing machinist	212
Shearer	276
Shipper	129
Shop manager	101
Signalman	321
Smelter	231
Spinner	177
Steward	152
Stockman	166
Tile worker	223
Timberman	316
Tin plater	269
Tool maker	245
Tracer	114
Tractor driver	169
Tube drawer	234
Tube maker	270
Turner	239
Waiter	144
Waterman	317
Wirer	273
Writer	054

Appendix G

Relationship between the 1980 operational codes used in the alphabetical index and the 1980 occupation groups

Operational Code	Employment status relationship to 1980 occupation groups			
	Self-employed	Managers	Foremen	Apprentices, etc. Employees n.e.c.
001	001.0	—	—	001.0
002	002.1	—	—	002.1
003	002.2	—	—	002.2
004	002.3	002.3	—	002.3
005	002.4	002.4	—	002.4
006	—	002.5	—	—
007	002.6	002.6	—	—
008	002.7	002.7	—	—
009	003.1	003.1	—	—
010	003.2	003.2	—	003.2
011	004.1	—	—	004.1
012	004.2	004.2	—	004.2
013	005.1	005.1	—	—
014	005.2	005.2	—	—
015	—	005.3	—	—
016	—	005.4	—	—
017	—	—	—	006.1
018	—	—	—	006.2
019	—	—	—	006.3
020	—	007.1	—	—
021	—	007.2	—	—
022	—	008.0	—	—
023	009.1	009.1	—	—
024	—	009.2	—	009.2
025	009.3	009.3	—	—
026	—	009.4	—	009.4
027	009.5	009.5	—	009.5
028	009.6	—	—	009.6
029	—	—	—	009.7
030	009.8	009.8	—	009.8
031	—	—	—	010.1
032	010.2	010.2	—	010.2
033	011.0	011.0	—	011.0
034	012.1	012.1	—	012.1
035	—	—	—	012.2
036	012.3	—	—	012.3
037	013.1	013.1	—	013.1
038	013.2	—	—	013.2
039	—	013.3	—	013.3
040	014.0	—	—	014.0
041	015.1	—	—	015.1
042	015.2	—	—	015.2
043	016.0	016.0	016.0	016.0
044	017.1	—	—	017.1
045	017.2	017.2	017.2	017.2
046	017.3	—	—	017.3
047	017.4	017.4	017.4	017.4
048	017.5	017.5	—	017.5
049	017.6	017.6	017.6	017.6
050	018.1	018.1	018.1	018.1
051	018.2	—	—	018.2
052	018.3	018.3	—	018.3
053	018.4	018.4	—	018.4
054	019.0	019.0	—	019.0
055	020.1	020.1	020.1	020.1
056	020.2	020.2	—	020.2
057	020.3	020.3	—	020.3
058	020.4	020.4	—	020.4
059	021.1	021.1	—	021.1
060	021.2	021.2	—	021.2
061	022.1	022.1	022.1	022.1
062	022.2	022.2	022.2	022.2
063	023.1	023.1	—	023.1
064	023.2	023.2	—	023.2
065	024.1	—	—	024.1
066	024.2	—	—	024.2
067	024.3	—	—	024.3
068	025.0	—	—	025.0
069	026.1	—	—	026.1
070	026.2	—	—	026.2
071	027.1	—	—	027.1
072	027.2	—	—	027.2
073	028.1	—	—	028.1
074	028.2	—	—	028.2

Operational Code	Employment status relationship to 1980 occupation groups			
	Self-employed	Managers	Foremen	Apprentices, etc. Employees n.e.c.
075	028.3	—	—	028.3
076	028.4	—	—	028.4
077	028.5	—	—	028.5
078	028.6	—	—	028.6
079	029.0	029.0	029.0	029.0
080	030.1	030.1	030.1	030.1
081	030.2	030.2	030.2	030.2
082	031.1	—	—	031.1
083	031.2	—	—	031.2
084	031.3	—	—	031.3
085	032.1	032.1	—	032.1
086	—	—	—	032.2
087	032.3	032.3	—	—
088	033.1	—	—	033.1
089	—	—	—	033.2
090	033.3	033.3	033.3	033.3
091	—	034.0	034.0	—
092	—	035.1	—	—
093	—	—	—	035.2
094	—	036.1	—	—
095	—	036.2	—	—
096	—	036.3	—	—
097	—	036.4	—	—
098	—	037.1	—	—
099	037.2	037.2	—	—
100	038.1	—	—	—
101	038.4	038.4	—	—
102	039.1	039.1	—	—
103	039.2	039.2	—	—
104	039.3	039.3	—	—
105	—	039.4	—	—
106	039.5	039.5	—	—
107	040.0	040.0	—	—
108	—	043.1	—	—
109	044.1	044.1	—	—
110	044.2	044.2	—	—
111	044.4	044.4	—	—
112	—	—	045.1	—
113	—	—	045.2	046.1
114	046.2	—	045.3	046.2
115	046.3	—	045.4	046.3
116	—	—	045.5	047.0
117	—	—	—	049.1
118	049.2	—	048.1	049.2
119	050.0	—	048.2	050.0
120	—	—	—	051.1
121	—	—	048.3	051.2
122	—	—	048.4	051.3
123	—	—	052.1	053.1
124	053.2	—	052.2	053.2
125	—	—	054.1	055.1
126	—	—	—	055.2
127	—	—	054.2	055.3
128	056.0	056.0	054.3	056.0
129	057.1	057.1	—	—
130	057.2	057.2	—	057.2
131	057.3	057.3	—	—
132	057.4	057.4	—	057.4
133	057.5	057.5	—	057.5
134	057.6	057.6	—	057.6
135	—	041.0	—	058.0
136	—	042.0	—	059.0
137	—	043.2	060.1	061.1
138	—	043.3	060.2	061.2
139	—	—	060.3	061.3
140	062.1	—	060.4	062.1
141	—	—	060.5	062.2
142	062.3	—	060.6	062.3
143	064.0	064.0	063.1	064.0
144	065.1	—	063.2	065.1
145	065.2	—	063.3	065.2
146	—	—	063.4	066.1
147	—	—	066.2	066.2
148	—	—	067.1	—
149	—	—	—	068.1
150	068.2	—	—	068.2
151	068.3	—	067.2	068.3
152	069.1	—	067.3	069.1
153	—	—	067.4	069.2
154	—	—	067.5	069.3
155	—	—	067.6	070.1
156	—	—	067.7	070.2
157	—	—	071.1	072.1
158	072.2	072.2	071.2	072.2
159	044.3	044.3	073.0	074.0
160	—	—	071.3	075.1
161	—	—	071.4	075.2
162	—	075.3	075.3	075.3
163	075.4	075.4	—	—
164	075.5	075.5	—	—
165	075.6	075.6	075.6	075.6
166	077.0	—	076.1	077.0
167	078.1	—	076.2	078.1
168	078.2	078.2	076.3	078.2

Operational Code	Employment status relationship to 1980 occupation groups			
	Self-employed	Managers	Foremen	Apprentices, etc. Employees n.e.c.
169	079.0	—	076.4	079.0
170	080.0	—	076.5	080.0
171	082.0	082.0	081.0	082.0
172	083.0	—	076.6	083.0
173	085.1	085.1	084.1	085.1
174	085.2	085.2	084.2	085.2
175	085.3	085.3	084.3	085.3
176	087.1	087.1	086.1	087.1
177	087.2	087.2	086.2	087.2
178	087.3	087.3	086.3	087.3
179	087.4	087.4	086.4	087.4
180	087.5	087.5	086.5	087.5
181	087.6	087.6	086.6	087.6
182	087.7	087.7	086.7	087.7
183	087.8	087.8	086.8	087.8
184	089.0	089.0	088.0	089.0
185	091.0	091.0	090.1	091.0
186	038.2	038.2	090.2	092.1
187	038.3	038.3	090.3	092.2
188	094.1	—	093.1	094.1
189	094.2	094.2	093.2	094.2
190	—	—	093.3	094.3
191	—	—	095.1	096.1
192	096.2	096.2	095.2	096.2
193	096.3	096.3	095.3	096.3
194	097.1	097.1	095.4	097.1
195	097.2	097.2	095.5	097.2
196	—	—	095.6	098.1
197	098.2	098.2	090.4	098.2
198	—	—	095.7	098.3
199	098.4	—	086.9	098.4
200	098.5	—	090.5	098.5
201	—	—	098.6	098.6
202	098.7	098.7	090.6	098.7
203	098.8	—	093.4	098.8
204	098.9	—	098.9	098.9
205	100.1	100.1	099.1	100.1
206	100.2	100.2	099.2	100.2
207	100.3	—	099.3	100.3
208	100.4	100.4	099.4	100.4
209	100.5	100.5	099.5	100.5
210	102.1	102.1	101.1	102.1
211	102.2	102.2	101.2	102.2
212	102.3	—	101.3	102.3
213	103.0	103.0	101.4	103.0
214	105.1	105.1	104.1	105.1
215	105.2	105.2	104.2	105.2
216	105.3	105.3	104.3	105.3
217	105.4	105.4	104.4	105.4
218	106.0	106.0	104.5	106.0
219	—	—	—	107.1
220	107.2	107.2	107.2	107.2
221	107.3	—	101.5	107.3
222	107.4	107.4	107.4	107.4
223	107.5	—	095.8	107.5
224	107.6	107.6	104.6	107.6
225	107.7	107.7	084.4	107.7
226	107.8	107.8	101.6	107.8
227	107.9	107.9	093.5	107.9
228	107.10	107.10	095.9	107.10
229	107.11	107.11	095.10	107.11
230	107.12	107.12	107.12	107.12
231	109.1	—	108.1	109.1
232	109.2	109.2	108.2	109.2
233	109.3	109.3	108.3	109.3
234	110.1	—	108.4	110.1
235	110.2	—	108.5	110.2
236	110.3	110.3	108.6	110.3
237	110.4	—	108.7	110.4
238	112.1	112.1	111.1	112.1
239	112.2	112.2	111.2	112.2
240	112.3	112.3	111.3	112.3
241	112.4	—	111.4	112.4
242	113.1	113.1	111.5	113.1
243	113.2	113.2	111.6	113.2
244	113.3	—	111.7	113.3
245	115.0	115.0	114.1	115.0
246	116.1	116.1	114.2	116.1
247	116.2	116.2	114.3	116.2
248	117.0	117.0	114.4	117.0
249	118.1	118.1	114.5	118.1
250	118.2	—	114.6	118.2
251	119.0	119.0	114.7	119.0
252	121.1	121.1	120.1	121.1
253	121.2	121.2	120.2	121.2
254	121.3	121.3	—	121.3
255	—	—	120.3	121.4
256	122.1	—	120.4	122.1
257	122.2	—	120.5	122.2
258	123.1	123.1	120.6	123.1
259	123.2	123.2	120.7	123.2
260	125.0	125.0	124.1	125.0
261	126.1	126.1	124.2	126.1
262	126.2	126.2	124.3	126.2

Operational Code	Employment status relationship to 1980 occupation groups			
	Self-employed	Managers	Foremen	Apprentices, etc. Employees n.e.c.
263	127.1	127.1	124.4	127.1
264	127.2	—	124.5	127.2
265	128.0	128.0	124.6	128.0
266	130.1	130.1	129.1	130.1
267	130.2	—	129.2	130.2
268	131.1	131.1	129.3	131.1
269	131.2	—	108.8	131.2
270	131.3	—	108.9	131.3
271	—	—	129.4	131.4
272	131.5	131.5	124.7	131.5
273	131.6	—	129.5	131.6
274	131.7	131.7	129.6	131.7
275	—	—	111.8	131.8
276	131.9	131.9	131.9	131.9
277	—	—	—.1	—
278	—	—	—	—.2
279	133.1	—	132.1	133.1
280	133.2	133.2	132.2	133.2
281	133.3	133.3	132.3	133.3
282	133.4	133.4	132.4	133.4
283	135.1	—	134.1	135.1
284	135.2	—	134.2	135.2
285	135.3	—	134.3	135.3
286	137.1	—	136.1	137.1
287	137.2	—	136.7	137.2
288	—	—	136.8	138.1
289	—	—	136.2	138.2
290	—	—	136.3	138.3
291	—	—	136.4	138.4
292	—	—	136.5	138.5
293	—	—	136.6	138.6
294	—	—	136.9	138.7
295	138.8	—	134.4	138.8
296	—	—	134.5	138.9
297	—	—	136.10	138.10
298	—	—	136.11	138.11
299	138.12	138.12	138.12	138.12
300	140.1	140.1	139.1	140.1
301	140.2	140.2	139.2	140.2
302	140.3	140.3	139.3	140.3
303	140.4	140.4	139.4	140.4
304	140.5	140.5	139.5	140.5
305	140.6	140.6	—	140.6
306	—	—	139.6	141.1
307	141.2	—	139.7	141.2
308	141.3	—	139.8	141.3
309	141.4	—	139.9	141.4
310	—	—	139.10	142.1
311	142.2	—	139.11	142.2
312	143.1	—	143.1	143.1
313	143.2	—	143.2	143.2
314	145.0	—	144.0	145.0
315	146.1	146.1	146.1	146.1
316	146.2	146.2	139.12	146.2
317	148.0	—	147.0	148.0
318	—	—	149.4	—
319	—	—	—	150.1
320	—	—	149.1	150.2
321	—	—	149.2	150.3
322	—	—	149.3	150.4
323	—	—	151.1	—
324	—	—	151.3	—
325	152.1	152.1	—	152.1
326	152.2	152.2	151.2	152.2
327	152.3	152.3	—	152.3
328	153.1	—	—	153.1
329	—	—	—	153.2
330	155.1	155.1	154.1	155.1
331	—	—	154.2	155.2
332	155.3	—	154.3	155.3
333	157.1	157.1	156.1	157.1
334	157.2	—	156.2	157.2
335	157.3	157.3	156.3	157.3
336	—	—	156.4	157.4
337	—	—	154.4	158.1
338	158.2	—	158.2	158.2
339	—	—	159.1	160.1
340	—	—	159.2	160.2
341	—	—	159.3	160.3
342	—	—	159.4	160.4
343	—	—	159.5	160.5
344	—	—	159.6	160.6
345	—	—	159.7	160.7
346	160.8	—	159.8	160.8
347	—	—	159.9	161.1
348	161.2	—	161.2	161.2
349	—.1	—.1	—.1	—.1
350	—	—	—	—.2